THOMSON
COURSE TECHNOLOGY

PRO TOOLS® LE 6
IGNITE!

By Andrew Hagerman

Pro Tools® LE 6 Ignite!

Copyright © 2004 Muska & Lipman Publishing, a division of Course Technology.

All rights reserved. No part of this book may be reproduced by any means without written permission from the publisher, except for brief passages for review purposes. Address all permission requests to the publisher.

Pro Tools, Mbox, Digi 001, and Digi 002 are trademarks of Digidesign, a division Avid Technology, Inc. All rights reserved. Pro Tools screen displays reprinted with permission of Digidesign.

All copyrights and trademarks used as examples or references in this book are retained by their individual owners.

Senior Vice President, Professional, Trade, Reference Group: Andy Shafran

Publisher: Stacy L. Hiquet

Credits: Senior Marketing Manager, Sarah O'Donnell; Marketing Manager, Heather Hurley; Manager of Editorial Services, Heather Talbot; Acquisitions Editor, Todd Jensen; Senior Editor, Mark Garvey; Associate Marketing Manager, Kristin Eisenzopf; Retail Market Coordinator, Sarah Dubois; Production Editor, Cathleen D. Snyder; Copy Editor, Cathleen D. Snyder; Technical Editor, Ashley Shepherd; Proofreader, Dan J. Foster; Cover Designer, Course Design Team; Interior Design and Layout, Marian Hartsough Associates; Indexer, Katherine Stimson.

Technology and the Internet are constantly changing, and by necessity of the lapse of time between the writing and distribution of this book, some aspects might be out of date. Accordingly, the author and publisher assume no responsibility for actions taken by readers based upon the contents of this book.

Library of Congress Catalog Number: 2003114313

ISBN: 1-59200-150-5

5 4

Educational facilities, companies, and organizations interested in multiple copies or licensing of this book should contact the publisher for quantity discount information. Training manuals, CD-ROMs, and portions of this book are also available individually or can be tailored for specific needs.

MUSKA & LIPMAN
Publishing

Muska & Lipman Publishing,
a Division of Course Technology
25 Thomson Place
Boston, MA 02210
www.muskalipman.com
publisher@muskalipman.com

About the Author

ANDREW HAGERMAN has been a professional musician for the vast majority of his 38 years, beginning with formal musical training as a classical tuba player (yes, I said tuba). During his four years at Northwestern University (resulting in a bachelor's degree), music technology became mainstream in the form of MIDI, and Andrew was immediately hooked. In addition to being a performing musician around the world (including at Disneyland, Walt Disney World, and Tokyo Disney Sea), Andrew has channeled his study of music technology toward compositional pursuits. Active in the planetarium field, Andrew has written original music for clients ranging from the American Museum of Natural History in New York to Caterpillar Tractors. Currently, Andrew is busy as a composer with Singularity Arts, Inc. (http://www.singularityarts.com) as well as the associate course director of the Advanced Workstations course at Full Sail Real World Education, a media technology college in Orlando, Florida.

Dedication

For Junko Yoshida Hagerman,
for her unconditional support and love.
This book would never have been possible without your help!
It's pretty rare when a person meets an angel,
and I'm lucky to call one my wife.

Watashi wa anata o aishite imasu!

Acknowledgments

The creation of a book is a demanding task, and it is impossible to accomplish without the cooperation (and coordination) of people dedicated to excellence in their craft. The team at Muska & Lipman is truly outstanding. From Todd Jensen, who initiated this project and invited me to participate, to Mark Garvey and Cathleen Snyder for their superb editing and coordination of a complex undertaking, and a special thanks to Ashley Shepherd for your technical editing assistance.

Thanks to Dave Oxenreider, Brian Smithers, and Paul McCaskill, three of the best friends a guy could ask for. Each of you had a hand in the creation of this book, and I'm thankful for you all.

Thanks also go out to the great folks at Digidesign, particularly Claudia Curcio, Andy Cook, Mark Altin, and Gil Gowing. I offer the deepest appreciation for your vast technical expertise. Digidesign has provided our industry with a great product, and it's easy to see how when you meet the folks behind the technology.

Last, but certainly not least, thanks to the faculty, staff, and student body of Full Sail Real World Education. I'm fortunate beyond words to teach at a school (and creative environment) that continually inspires and challenges me to strive ever upward.

Contents

	Introduction xii
Chapter 1	**Welcome to Pro Tools LE 6 .... 1**
	What Makes Up a Pro Tools System? 2
	Computer 2
	Pro Tools Audio Interface 3
	Hard Drive(s) 5
	A Word about Installation............................ 7
	Understanding Sessions and Files.......................... 9
	Pro Tools Is a Pointer-Based Application 9
	Regions Versus Files 13
	Non-Destructive Editing 15
	Creating a New Session 16
	Starting the Process 16
	Choosing the Name and Place 17
	Choosing Session Parameters 19
	Closing Your Session 23
	More Basics 24
	Opening a Session When Pro Tools Is Running 24
	Opening a Session When Pro Tools Is Not Yet Launched 27
	Pro Tools' Primary Windows: Edit and Mix 28
	The Transport Window 31
	Quitting Pro Tools 33

CONTENTS

Chapter 2 Getting the Big Picture 35
   Working with the Edit Window. 36
      The Track Area 36
      The Track Show/Hide and Edit Groups Areas 37
      The Audio and MIDI Regions Lists 39
      The Timeline and Tools Areas. 40
      Customizing the Edit Window 41
   Working with the Mix Window 49
      Understanding the Mix Window Layout. 49
      Customizing the Mix Window. 50
   Understanding Other Useful Windows 51

Chapter 3 Getting Started with Audio. 55
   Getting Started 56
   Customizing Your Session: The I/O Setup Dialog Box 57
      Setting Up Inputs 57
      Customizing Your Inputs. 59
      Setting Up Outputs. 64
      Setting Up Inserts 66
      Setting Up Buses. 68
      Managing Your I/O Settings. 70
   Creating Tracks 74
      Making Tracks. 74
      Creating an Aux Input. 76
      Master Faders and MIDI Tracks 77
      Naming Your Tracks 78
      Moving Tracks. 79
   Importing Audio 81
      Importing into the Audio Regions List 81
      Importing Audio to a Track. 86
      Importing Tracks. 88
      New in Version 6: The Workspace Window 91

Making Selections and Playing Audio 96
    How I/O Settings Affect Your Session 96
    Soloing and Muting Tracks 97
    Playing a Selection 99
    Finishing Up: The Save As Function 101

Chapter 4 Basic Editing 103

Understanding the Edit Window. 104
    Using the Tools of the Trade 104
    Navigating. 106
    Zooming 112
Moving Regions on the Timeline: The Edit Modes. 113
    Using Slip Mode 113
    Using Grid Mode. 114
    Using Shuffle Mode. 117
    Using Spot Mode 119
Basic Tool Functions 120
    Understanding the Trim Tool 120
    Understanding the Selector Tool 121
    Understanding the Grabber Tool 122
Basic Editing Operations. 123
    Capturing a Selection 123
    Separating a Region 125
    Trimming a Region 128
    Renaming a Region 130
Assembling a Track 130
    Duplicating Regions 131
    Repeating Regions 133
    Working with Grids. 134
    Cutting, Copying, and Pasting 135
When You're Finished: Cleaning Up and Backing Up. 138
    Deleting Tracks. 138
    Using the Save Session Copy In Feature 140

viii CONTENTS

Chapter 5 **Recording Audio** **143**
    Getting Started: Signal Flow 101 144
        Setting Up the Input 146
        Setting Up the Output 146
        Setting the Output Volume 147
        Setting the Output Pan 148
        Using Tear-Away Strips 148
    Setting Up a Click Track 150
        More Signal Flow: Audio Tracks Versus Aux Tracks 150
        Using the Click Plug-In 151
        Setting Click and Tempo Options 154
    Basic Recording 158
    Understanding Other Recording Options 160
        Punching In and Punching Out 160
        QuickPunch Recording 164
        Loop Recording 166
        For the Brave: Destructive Recording 169
    Tips, Tricks, and Troubleshooting 171
        Naming Tracks and Files 171
        Understanding the Monitor Modes 172
        Low Latency Monitoring—and a Trick! 173

Chapter 6 **Using MIDI** **177**
    Setting Up Your MIDI Studio 178
        Creating a New Configuration 179
        Adding a Synth 181
        Connecting Your Gear 184
    Signal Flow 201: MIDI Versus Audio 185
        Managing the MIDI Signal Path 185
        Setting Up an Aux Track to Monitor Your MIDI Gear 190
    Recording MIDI 191
    Editing MIDI 193
        Editing with Tools 194

  The MIDI Menu 197
  Tempo, Meter, and Bars 204
 More MIDI Tips 206
  The MIDI Input Filter 206
  The Event List 208
  Viewing and Editing Non-Note Data 209
  Panic! 210
  Importing and Exporting MIDI Data 211
 Closing Thoughts on MIDI in Pro Tools 214

Chapter 7   More Editing 217

 Zoom 218
  More Zoom Tools 219
  Zoom Presets 221
 More Ways to Work with Selections 223
  Making Selections Using the Arrow Keys 224
  Making Selections Using the Return Key 224
  Making Selections Using Tab to Transient 226
  A Useful Preference: Timeline Insertion Follows Playback . . . 227
  Navigating and Auditioning a Selection 228
 Beyond the Basics 230
  The TCE Trim Tool 230
  The Separation Grabber Tool 232
  The Smart Tool 234
 Creating and Customizing Fades 236
  Creating a Fade-In 237
  Creating a Fade-Out 240
  Crossfades 242
  Creating Fades Using the Smart Tool 245
 Getting Specific 248
  Constraining Motion 248
  Nudging Regions 249

CONTENTS

Chapter 8 **Basic Mixing** **251**
    More Organization: Memory Locations 252
        Creating a Memory Location 252
        Using Memory Locations 256
    Exploring the Mix Window 257
        Basic Mixer Terminology............................ 258
        More Signal Flow 261
    Fader Groups.. 263
        Creating a Fader Group 264
        Using Fader Groups 266
    Using Effects 267
        AudioSuite....................................... 268
        RTAS 272
        Using Virtual Instruments 277
    Mixing Tips 279
        Using Dynamic-Based Effects........................ 280
        Using Time-Based Effects........................... 281
    Automating Your Mix 284
        The Automation Modes 284
        Plug-In Automation................................ 288

Chapter 9 **Finishing Touches** **291**
    More Fun with Automation 292
        Copying and Pasting Automation..................... 296
    Using Master Faders 297
        Creating a Master Fader............................ 298
        Controlling Your Mix with a Master Fader............... 300
        Basic Mastering Techniques Using a Master Fader 300
    Bouncing to Disk 304
    Backing Up Your Files 313
        Clearing Unused Regions 313
        Compacting Your Session........................... 315

Chapter 10	**Moving to the Next Level: Tips and Tricks** **319**	
	Making the Most of Editing................................320	
	Zoom Toggle...320	
	The Identify Beat Function 321	
	Relative Grid Mode..................................323	
	Tips for the TCE Trim Tool 323	
	Using Strip Silence 327	
	Edit Versus Timeline Selection 330	
	Making the Most of Mixing...............................332	
	Using the Edit Tools 332	
	Toggling Groups.....................................334	
	Advanced Resource Management 335	
	Showing Paths.......................................335	
	Offline Regions and Inactive Elements..................336	
	How to Consolidate (and Why).......................338	
	Refer and Copy Files.................................340	
	Working with Movies....................................342	
	Good Luck 344	
Appendix A	**Review Questions** **345**	
	Questions..346	
	Answers 350	
Appendix B	**Sound, Digital Audio, and MIDI: A Primer**........**351**	
	Sound...352	
	Digital Audio 352	
	MIDI 354	
Appendix C	**Keyboard Shortcuts**...........................**355**	
	Mac OS Keyboard Shortcuts..............................356	
	Windows Keyboard Shortcuts............................365	
	Index **374**	

Introduction

Welcome!

First off, congratulations on becoming a Pro Tools user, and welcome! I realize that such sentiments are on page one of virtually every user's guide and manual, but when Digidesign says that their powerful Digital Audio Workstation (DAW) is the industry standard (and for a reason), you can believe them. Indeed, you can find the full Pro Tools product line, from the Mbox all the way up to HD systems, hard at work in every facet of audio and musical production. It's a serious, professional product, and your decision to buy it (and learn it) is a step in the right direction.

Speaking of steps, remember the old saying, "A journey of a thousand miles begins with a single step?" That's where this book comes in. Gaining a solid fundamental understanding of the basics will ensure that your journey starts off well prepared and heads in the right direction. Here, you'll learn the basic techniques of creating, recording, editing, and mixing MIDI (*Musical Instrument Digital Interface*) and digital audio. You'll learn to harness the power of Pro Tools' impressive array of tools, from software effects, to virtual instruments, to mixes that are automated and edited with some of the best tools in the business.

If you're inspired to create and produce audio, Pro Tools is an obvious choice, and *Pro Tools LE 6 Ignite!* will be your companion during those critical first steps down the road to success and fun!

Who Should Read This Book?

This book is geared toward beginners with little or no experience in working with a DAW. You'll find that the book's highly graphic and plainly worded style makes it easy to follow. It will be a valuable reference later on as well. Nearly every step in the processes discussed is accompanied by clear illustrations, so you won't have to spend your time hunting around the screen for tools and menus. (What fun is *that*?)

Don't worry if you're not a formally trained musician or if you haven't really dealt with digital audio before. The beauty of Pro Tools (and computer music in general) is that even untrained (but creative) musicians can enjoy great success in this kind of environment. Of course, any general music or audio knowledge you bring to the table is an added advantage, but certainly not a requirement for this book.

Pro Tools is a deep program, and even those of us who have been using it for years are still finding new tidbits now and then. For that reason, I don't dedicate the space I have in this book to covering basic computer operations. That means it's up to you to understand the most basic ins and outs of your particular platform (either a Mac running OS X or a PC running Windows XP). Don't worry too much, though—the general computer knowledge required to use Pro Tools is pretty basic, and if you can locate, launch, and close programs already, you're in fine shape.

How to Use This Book

Music in general is a progressive process, and its creation and performance are the results of many small steps taken in order. A solid mastery of Pro Tools works much the same way. This book is organized from the most basic concepts and operations to more complex ones, building skill upon skill. You'll find that most of this book is laid out in a tutorial format; there are even tutorial files you can download and use side by side with the book's examples. Of course, you can also use this book as a point reference source as well, using the clear, illustrated style of this format to your advantage as you locate specific functions.

You'll note that peppered throughout this book are a number of Notes and Tips. Take a look at these to find additional ways to increase your efficiency, additional information on key functions, and even warnings that point out common pitfalls and how to avoid them. Last but not least, you'll find a complete list of shortcuts (key commands for onscreen functions) for both the Mac and PC platforms, straight from the fine folks at Digidesign. Trust me when I tell you that over the years, that section will get pretty well used!

Finally, a Little History . . .

Pro Tools systems can be broken down into two families: TDM and LE. TDM (*Time Division Multiplexing*) systems are based upon a hardware-based architecture, which means that there are dedicated PCI cards with chips dedicated to the tasks of running Pro Tools functions. This means two things: First, it is a reliable, scalable, powerful system—an obvious advantage for professional facilities. Second, it costs more (and it can be a *lot* more).

LE systems aren't hardware-based; they're host-based, which simply means that the host computer (meaning the computer that you're using to run the software) is charged with all the tasks of running Pro Tools, from recording and playback, to effects and automation. This allows an LE system to be a good deal more economical than its TDM counterpart. Of course, since your computer's CPU is doing *everything*, you might not get the same kind of power from an LE system, and there are a few features that are reserved for TDM systems only. The good news—and it's great news, really—is that the software environments in TDM and LE are nearly identical. This means not only can you take advantage of one of the most powerful and well-developed user interfaces on the market, when it's time for you to upgrade to TDM, you'll already know the software.

Pro Tools has recently released its version 6 series (for PC and Mac), which incorporates some real advancements, especially for LE users. Among them are

- A new, cleaner user interface
- Additional editing power, including the popular Time Compress/Expand tool (previously only available in TDM systems)
- New MIDI features, such as options to restore and flatten performance, as well as MIDI time stamping
- A new Workspace window that makes importing audio a breeze
- Up to 32 levels of undo
- Added support for virtual instruments using ReWire

If a lot of this sounds like Greek, don't worry—we'll cover it in the chapters to come. Ready? Let's go!

1

Welcome to Pro Tools LE 6

Congratulations, and welcome to the world of Pro Tools! Over the years, Pro Tools has established itself at the forefront of the DAW (*Digital Audio Workstation*) community, and it can now be found in virtually every level of the audio industry, from music production for CDs to surround sound for theatrical soundtracks. Now, armed with Pro Tools LE's powerful array of functions and features, you'll be able to tap into the world of digital audio for yourself to realize your own creative vision!

In this chapter, we'll discuss the structure, function, and most basic operations of Pro Tools LE 6. In this chapter, you'll learn how to:

- Identify the hardware components of a Pro Tools LE system and their functions
- Organize sessions and data in Pro Tools
- Identify and operate Pro Tools' most basic windows
- Create, open, play, and close a session

What Makes Up a Pro Tools System?

Digidesign's Pro Tools systems fall into one of two families—LE or TDM. The host-based LE systems rely on the processing power of the host computer's CPU for operations such as mixing and effects processing. TDM systems, on the other hand, have dedicated PCI hardware cards, which take care of those kinds of functions. TDM systems, because of their added flexibility and greater processing horsepower, tend to be more commonly found in professional recording studios, whereas LE systems have found their niche in the growing number of home and project studios worldwide.

LE systems, regardless of their specific configurations, all rely on a few key components.

Computer

The host computer is the cornerstone of your Pro Tools LE system. Your computer's CPU will be called upon to do everything from mixing and automation to effects processing, so the more speed your CPU has, the more powerful your Pro Tools software will be. The host computer can be either a PC (running Windows XP) or a Mac (with OS X).

Ideally, your DAW computer should be dedicated solely to music-related tasks. Other applications running on your system can steal from your computer's overall efficiency when running Pro Tools. Also, the task of recording and playing digital audio can be very demanding on your computer's CPU, and other programs can interrupt the steady stream of data to and from your hard drive and cause major problems. Of course, having such a dedicated computer can be impractical for many users; in that case, you should avoid resource-sapping applications (particularly games) and limit the number of programs active during your Pro Tools sessions.

Pro Tools Audio Interface

Your Pro Tools audio interface (which you purchased with your Pro Tools system) is the doorway for audio going to and coming from your computer. Generally speaking, your computer will connect directly to the audio interface, and your various audio devices (mixing boards, keyboards, or microphones) will connect to the interface's available audio inputs. To listen to your session, you should connect the audio outputs of your interface to an amplifier, and from there to monitor speakers. Following is a brief rundown of the audio interfaces available for Pro Tools LE systems and their key features.

Mbox

The core features of the Mbox interface include the following:

- USB connection to the host computer
- Two analog inputs/outputs, plus one stereo S/PDIF input/output
- Two Focusrite microphone preamps
- Headphone outputs
- Supports up to 24-bit/48-kHz digital audio

©2003 Digidesign, a division of Avid Technology, Inc.

CHAPTER 1: WELCOME TO PRO TOOLS LE 6

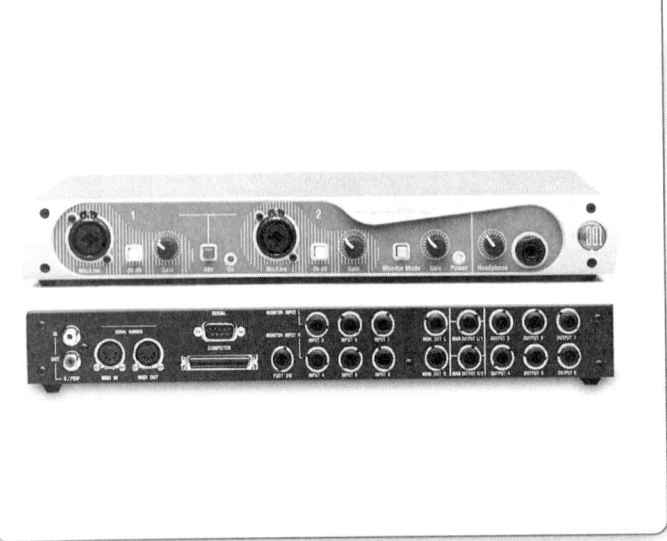

© 2003 Digidesign, a division of Avid Technology, Inc.

© 2003 Digidesign, a division of Avid Technology, Inc.

Digi 001

The core features of the Digi 001 interface include the following:

- Connected to a PCI card in the host computer
- Eight analog inputs/outputs, one stereo S/PDIF input/output, and eight channels of ADAT optical input/output
- MIDI input/output (I/O)
- Two microphone preamps
- Headphone outputs
- Supports up to 24-bit/48-kHz digital audio

Digi 002 R

The core features of the Digi 002 R interface include the following:

- IEEE 1394 (FireWire) connection to the host computer
- Eight analog inputs/outputs, one stereo S/PDIF input/output, and eight channels of ADAT optical input/output
- MIDI I/O
- Four microphone preamps
- Headphone outputs
- Supports up to 24-bit/96-kHz digital audio

WHAT MAKES UP A PRO TOOLS SYSTEM?

> **NOTE**
> The Digi 002 is available in two versions. First, there's the rackmount version, called the Digi 002 Rack, which is a two-rack space module sporting the features listed in this section. There's also the Digi 002, which, in addition to being an audio interface, is also a cool control surface (with faders, knobs, and so on that you can use to control the Pro Tools software).

> **NOTE**
> In Pro Tools LE systems, you can use only one Pro Tools audio interface at a time.

> **TIP**
> If you want to learn more about the specifications of any Pro Tools hardware, the Digidesign Web site (http://www.digidesign.com) is a great place to start. From the Digidesign home page, click on the Products link (located in the upper-left corner) to view a list of the current Pro Tools products.

Hard Drive(s)

Just as traditional tape-based recording studios rely on magnetic tape as a recording and storage medium, Pro Tools relies on hard drives for the recording and playback of its digital audio. The drives can use SCSI, IDE/ATA, or even FireWire connections.

It is important to remember two factors when choosing a hard drive for Pro Tools—size and speed. First, a larger-capacity drive will allow you to store more audio data. This can translate into more minutes of audio that you can store, higher-quality digital audio, or both. A fast drive will allow for more efficient transfer of data (also called *throughput*) when you are recording and/or playing back audio. A faster drive can also translate into higher track counts and more reliability when working with complex sessions.

> **TIP**
> Do you have a question about whether or not a specific computer or hard drive will work with a Pro Tools LE system? Not to worry—Digidesign keeps an up-to-date list of compatible hardware on its Web site. At http://www.digidesign.com/compato, you can find a list of Pro Tools systems along with their supported operating systems. Just click on the link for the operating system that matches your computer. Another way to access the compatibility docs is to visit http://www.digidesign.com and click on the Products link in the upper-left corner. On the Products page, select your audio interface (such as Mbox), and then choose [*your interface*] Compatibility Mac or [*your interface*] Compatibility Windows for a complete list of hardware-related information.

Using a Second Hard Drive

Every computer comes with a hard drive, which provides long-term storage for your operating system, programs, and files. As I mentioned before, Pro Tools also uses hard drives for storing digital audio files and session files. Although it is possible to use your computer's system drive to store your Pro Tools data, it isn't the recommended way to go. Why? Think of it this way: Hard drives are mechanical, motorized devices with read/write heads depositing data to and retrieving data from the surface of a metal platter (the hard disk). Even during normal computer use, the head is busy taking care of data and file requests. If you add to that the demanding tasks of recording and playing digital audio files in real time, a single read head might easily become too busy to keep up with everything, and your session might suffer.

WHAT MAKES UP A PRO TOOLS SYSTEM?

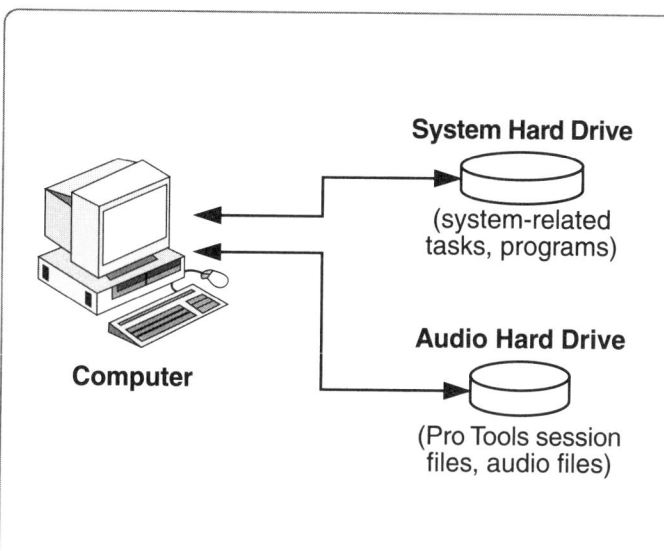

Adding a second drive dedicated to the storage of your Pro Tools sessions will increase your Pro Tools system's performance greatly. You'll still install the Pro Tools application on your computer's system drive, but when you create your sessions, you'll put them on your "audio" drive. That way, you'll have one hard drive occupied with the nominal tasks of your computer and another separate drive dealing only with your Pro Tools session.

NOTE
Partitioning a single hard drive may give the outward appearance of creating a second drive, but in reality there still is only one. Although partitioning can be a convenient way of organizing your data, it doesn't add another physical drive with its own read/write head, so it won't help Pro Tools with the real-time tasks of recording and playing back digital audio.

A Word about Installation

When it comes to installing your Pro Tools software, I've got good news and bad news. First the bad news: Because it can vary, the installation procedure is tough to describe in a book like this. There are many different configurations possible (with different audio interfaces, computers, and so on). Also, because Digidesign is a dynamic company, they are constantly upgrading and tweaking their products. Bottom line: The details of installation are constantly subject to change.

The good news is that Digidesign has got you covered. The documentation you received with your Pro Tools LE software and hardware is the first place to look for information on installation. In the ever-changing world of computers, though, perhaps even that documentation is slightly out of date. Again, the Digidesign Web site is an invaluable resource for the latest software version updates and information on installation and troubleshooting.

From Digidesign's home page (http://www.digidesign.com), click on Support (in the upper menu of options). On the Support page, you will notice several options. Here are a few pages of interest:

- **Tech Support.** This page is a compilation of frequently asked questions, breaking information, and software downloads. From here you can search for an answer to your questions or contact Digidesign's tech support staff.

- **Customer Service.** This is similar to the Tech Support page, although it's a little more general in nature.

- **Answerbase.** On this page, you can type in keywords to see a list of useful links.

- **Compatibility.** This is an up-to-date listing of supported hardware and software.

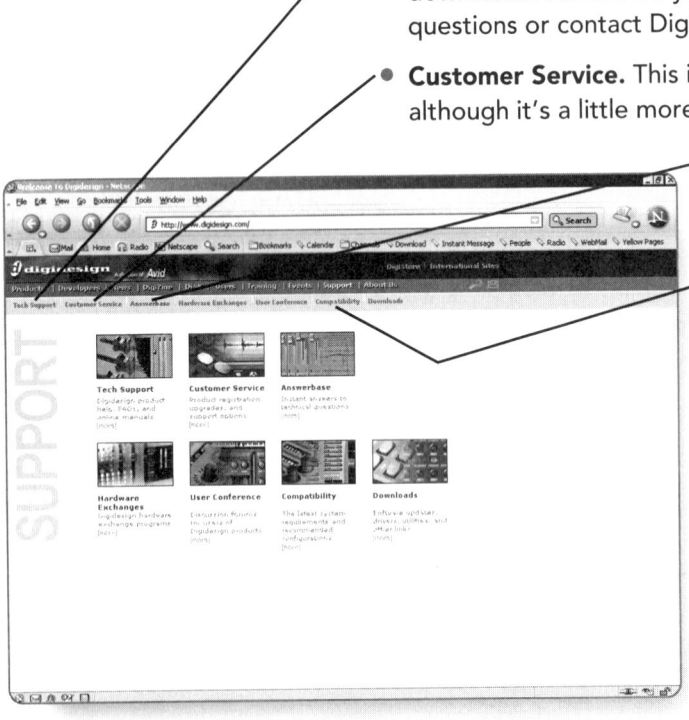

The documentation that came with your Pro Tools hardware combined with a little Net surfing (if needed) should allow you to successfully install and configure your Pro Tools LE system. Once that's done, you're ready to move on.

Understanding Sessions and Files

Before you get any deeper into the world of Pro Tools, you should take a moment to understand the general principals behind this powerful digital audio workstation. An understanding of Pro Tools' functioning and how its different elements work together will serve you well as you continue to grow in this environment.

Pro Tools Is a Pointer-Based Application

It's common to refer to a cursor as a *pointer*, but when you're discussing a pointer-based application like Pro Tools, you're referring to the way the program deals with digital audio data. In Pro Tools' case, this pointer-based structure can be broken down to three interdependent elements—session files, folders, and audio files. In this situation the term "pointer" refers to the way your Pro Tools session file will access (or "point") to other files on your hard drive as your session plays.

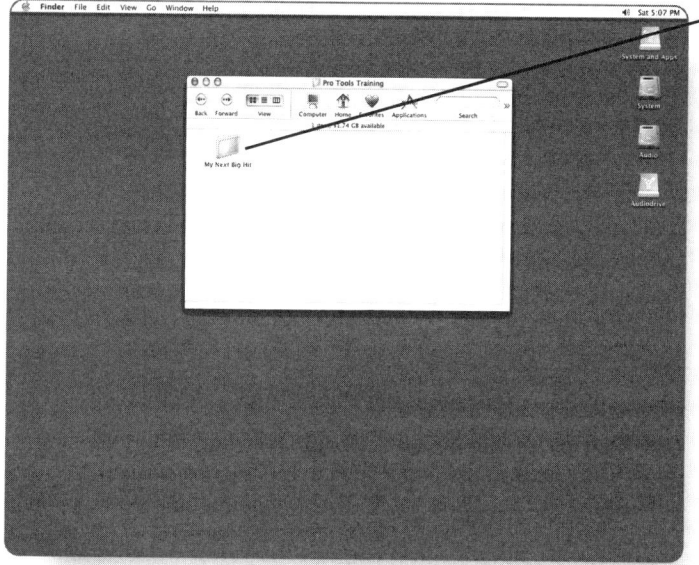

A session folder is created when you create a new session.

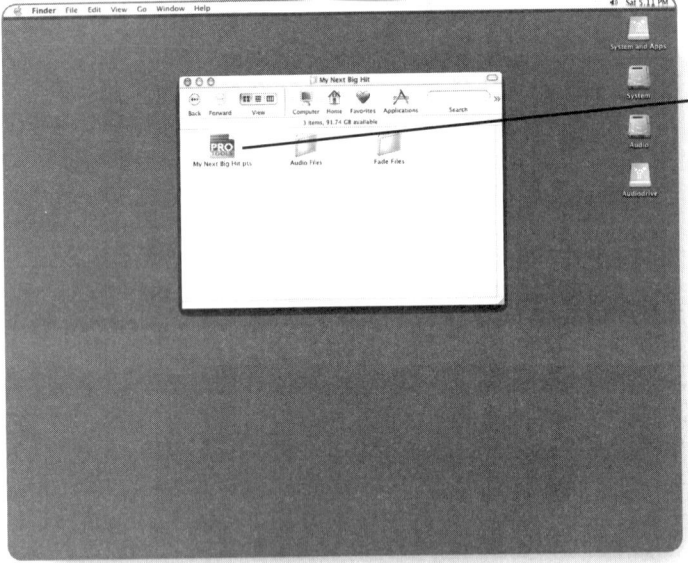

The folder contains the following items (as needed):

- **Session file.** The session file is at the top of the Pro Tools hierarchy. This is the file created by Pro Tools when you create a new session, and it's the file you open to return to a session you already created. Although this file is relatively small, it is the master of all your session elements.

Session files have the .pts suffix and contain the following elements of your session:

- The names, types, and arrangement of all tracks in your session
- All MIDI data
- Essential settings such as inputs and outputs
- All edits and automation data

NOTE
It might sound like all you need is a session file, but that's not quite true. Although the session file contains all the important aspects of a project, it doesn't contain any audio. Instead, the session file points to audio files located elsewhere on your hard drive.

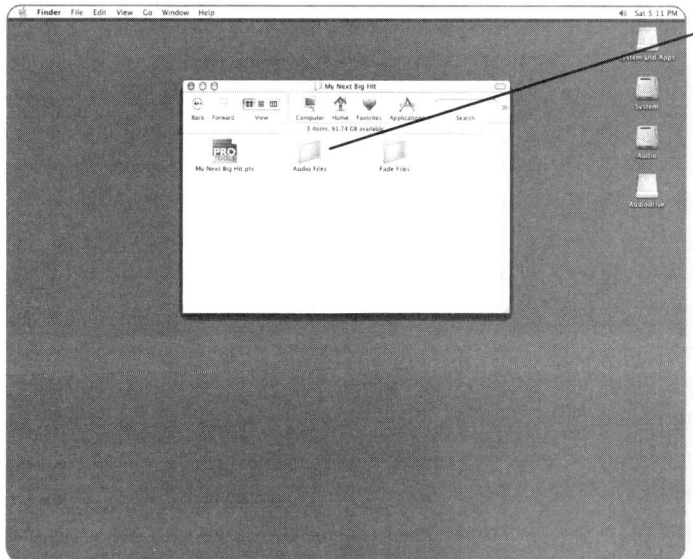

- **Audio Files subfolder.** As soon as audio is recorded, it is stored in an Audio Files subfolder in the session folder. Different takes are stored in this folder as individual audio files. When you play a session, Pro Tools calls upon, or points to, the audio files in this folder.

NOTE

When you record audio in Pro Tools, the name of the file created usually follows the name of the track that it is recorded upon. (This is a common default setting.) For example, if you record onto a mono (one-channel) audio track named Bass, the files created by Pro Tools in the Audio Files folder will be named Bass.01, Bass.02, and so on as you record takes on this track. In the case of stereo audio tracks, two mono files (one for the left side and one for the right) are created. If you record onto a stereo audio track named Stereo Piano, two files named Stereo Piano_01.l and Stereo Piano_01.r will be created.

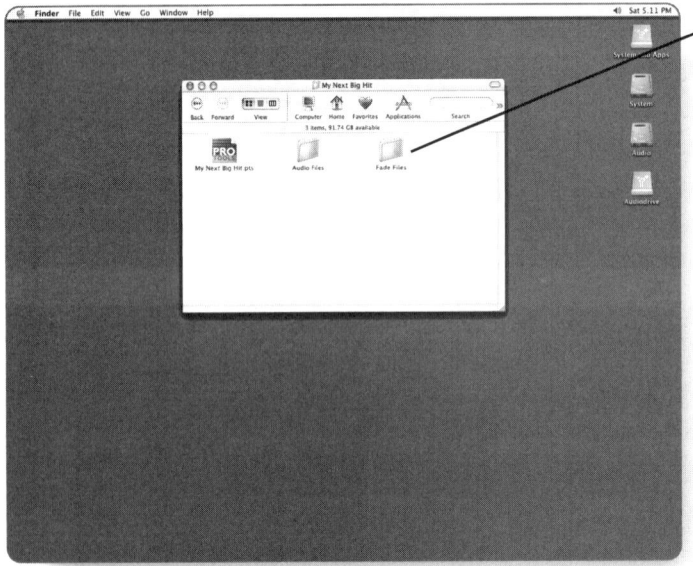

- **Fade Files subfolder.** When you start creating fades (including fade-ins, fade-outs, and crossfades), Pro Tools renders the created fades to files on your hard drive. Audio files are again created, but they're not stored in the Audio Files folder. Instead, they're stored in a folder named Fade Files. It's important to keep in mind that even though fades are audio files, they are significantly different in function from the audio files you record or import into your session (in ways that you'll learn about later); thus they are stored separately.

- **Plug-in Settings subfolder.** In Pro Tools you have the option of using plug-ins, which are programs designed to work within the Pro Tools environment and function as virtual effects. (You'll learn more about plug-ins in Chapter 8, "Basic Mixing.") When you create specific plug-in presets, you can save them in this session subfolder.

- **Video Files subfolder.** When your session calls for a video track, you can save it in this session subfolder.

> ### NOTE
> If you start using video files and/or creating custom plug-in settings, Pro Tools will create additional subfolders as needed. Don't worry about that too much yet—you'll be dealing with those situations later in this book.

> **TIP**
>
> Often people copy or e-mail Pro Tools session files, thinking that they've copied or sent their entire project. However, it's important to remember that the session file alone only refers (or points) to other important elements such as audio files—those audio elements aren't contained in the session file itself. When it's time to save (or move) your work, you'll have to include all the session's dependent files, in addition to the session file itself. For this reason, it's usually a good idea to keep all your project-related files grouped together in the structure shown in this example, so that files aren't accidentally lost.

Regions Versus Files

Given the fact that Pro Tools records audio to individual files on your hard drive, how does the user access these files? When audio is recorded to an audio track (or even MIDI data to a MIDI track), Pro Tools creates an object (or region) in the Edit window. These regions refer (or *point*) to files on your hard drive, triggering them to sound as your session plays.

14 CHAPTER 1: WELCOME TO PRO TOOLS LE 6

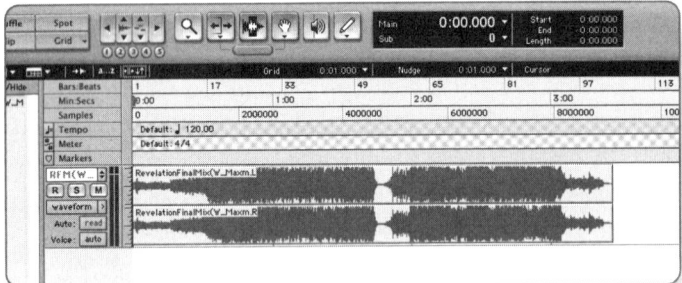

Here's a close-up of Pro Tools' Edit window. There's one audio track in this session, and only one region on that track. That region is referring to a file named RevelationFinalMix (W_Maxm).

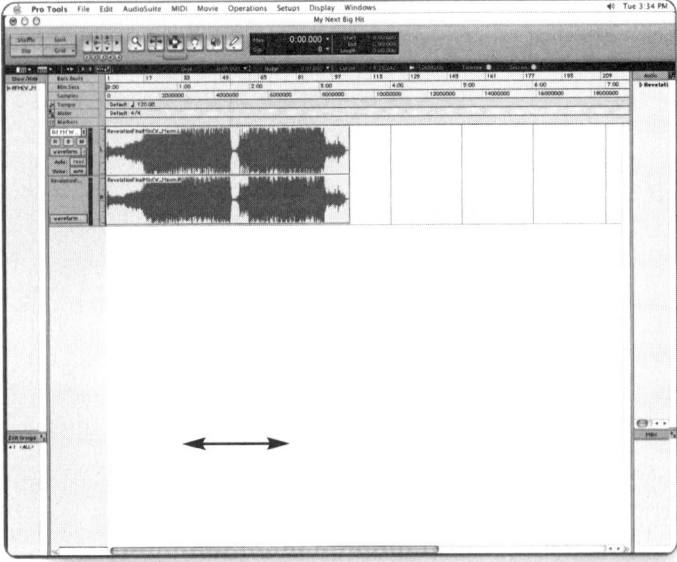

Working with regions has many advantages. One of the first that you'll discover is that you have the ability to move them earlier or later on the session's Timeline, allowing you to precisely position the regions in time. An environment in which you have the ability to manipulate elements independently on the Timeline is commonly known as *non-linear*. In addition to moving regions to different locations in time, you have the option of moving them to other similar tracks. (In other words, you can move a region on a mono audio track to another mono audio track, and so on.)

UNDERSTANDING SESSIONS AND FILES

Non-Destructive Editing

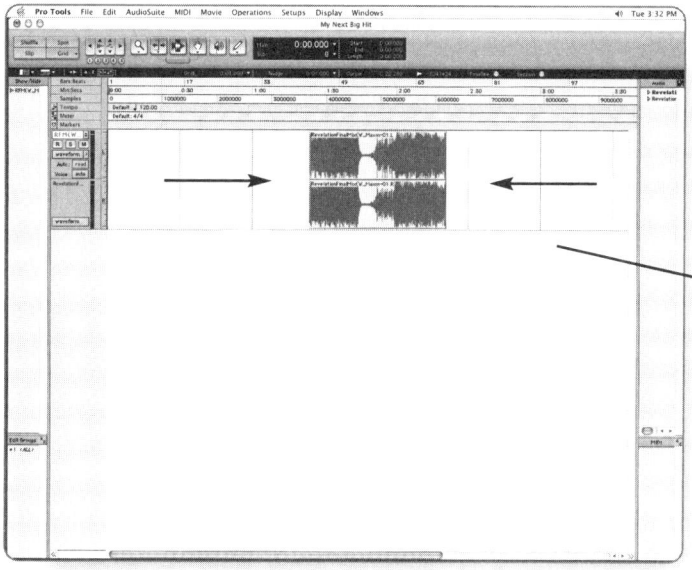

Another great advantage of using regions is that you can non-destructively trim the audio that's being used in your session (meaning that no audio *data* is being lost, so you can always undo what you've done).

In this example, assume that the region named RevelationFinalMix(W_Maxm) is playing an audio file of the same name in the Audio Files subfolder. What if you don't want to use the whole song in your session? No problem—you can just adjust the start or end boundary of that region, effectively taking the unwanted bit of audio out of your session.

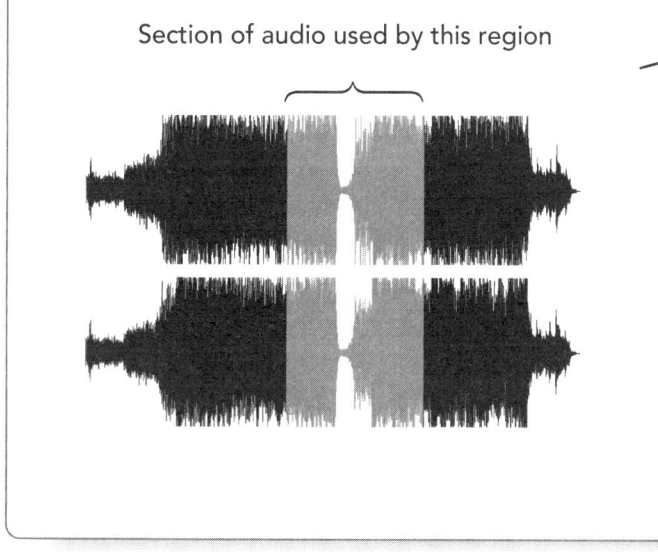

Section of audio used by this region

Does this mean that you've changed the file on your hard drive? No! You've changed only the region that is pointing to that file, so only a portion of that file will be heard in the session. Don't worry; because you haven't changed the audio file (only the region that is pointing to it), you can always drag the region boundaries back out if you change your mind later!

In addition to being able to trim data, there are other situations in which non-destructive editing can aid you in your production work, and you'll discover them as this book proceeds. The bottom line is that a non-linear pointer-based environment coupled with non-destructive recording and editing gives an educated Pro Tools user a huge amount of flexibility and power and the ability to undo changes and operations when needed!

Creating a New Session

Now that you've got your system put together and everything's installed, you can create a new session. Our earlier discussion of how Pro Tools works will come in handy here. In addition to the previous concepts, you'll have to start thinking about how you can best set up your new session and maximize your computer's resources.

Starting the Process

After you've launched Pro Tools, you'll see the program's basic array of drop-down menus. Here's where the important process of creating a session begins!

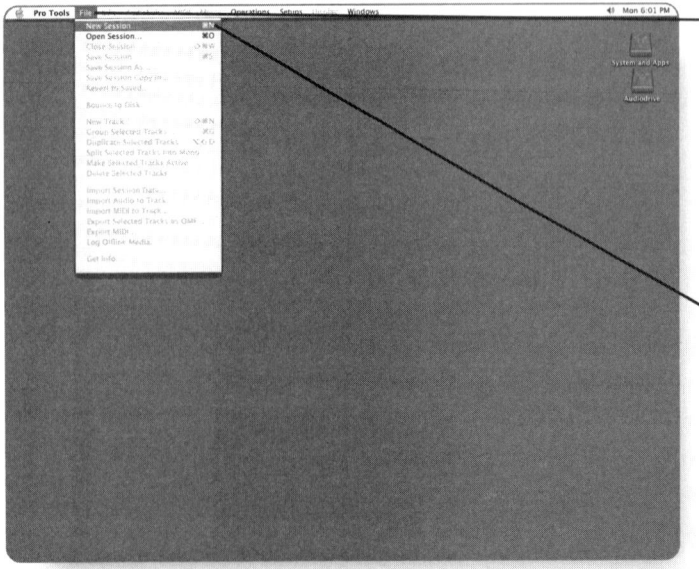

1. Click on **File**. The File menu will appear, containing a list of Pro Tools' basic functions. Because there is no session open at this time, only the New Session and Open Session options will be available; the rest will be grayed out.

2. Click on **New Session**. The new session window will appear.

CREATING A NEW SESSION   17

> **TIP**
>
> As you explore Pro Tools further, you'll notice that there are many functions that have shortcut keys associated with them. These shortcut key combinations are displayed to the right of the command. Although there are far too many shortcuts to learn all at once, learning the combinations for popular functions such as opening or creating a session can help you work more efficiently.

Choosing the Name and Place

Two of the most important skills you can learn as a DAW user are file management and documentation. Knowing where your sessions reside and what kinds of resources they use is critical, especially when you start working on multiple projects at once!

1. The first thing you have to choose is the name of your session. **Type** the **name** in the Save As text box.

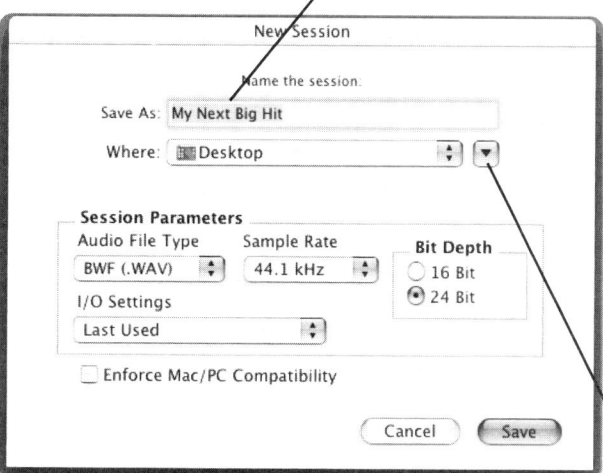

> **NOTE**
>
> According to this screen, this new session will be created on your computer's desktop. This means that the session will be created on your system hard drive. As I mentioned, this is not the best place to keep your session. Choose a location on your audio hard drive instead.

2. Click on the **arrow button** to reveal the navigation window.

CHAPTER 1: WELCOME TO PRO TOOLS LE 6

3. Drag the **scroll bar** at the bottom of the navigation window to the far right to view the hard drives attached to your system.

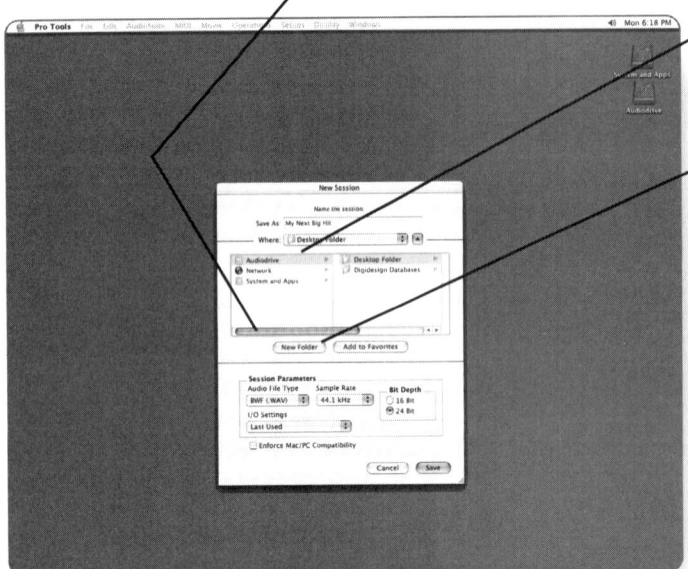

4. Click on your system's **audio hard drive**. The drive will be selected.

5. Next, you might want to create a new folder for your session. **Create** a new **folder** according to the normal conventions of your operating system.

NOTE

In these steps, you'll be navigating between subfolders and files to the drives and folders. This is a bit different in Mac OS X than it was in OS 9, so for the convenience of Mac users who are also learning a new operating system while learning about Pro Tools, I've used OS X for the examples in this chapter. If you're running Pro Tools on a Windows XP system, you'll see a familiar-looking navigation window.

CREATING A NEW SESSION   19

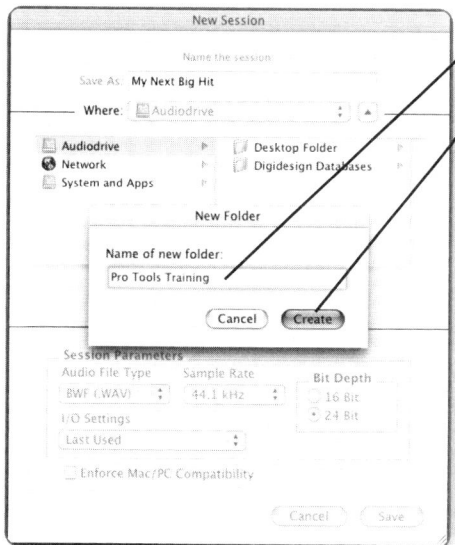

6. Type a **name** for your new folder.

7. Click on the **Create button**. The new folder will be created.

> **NOTE**
>
> If you followed the steps exactly as described, you would create a folder on the Audiodrive hard drive named Pro Tools Training. Inside that folder would be a subfolder named My Next Big Hit. Inside that folder would be a session file (also named My Next Big Hit). In this level, additional subfolders for audio, fades, plug-ins, and so on would be created as needed.

Choosing Session Parameters

You've named your new session and assigned it to a specific location on a hard drive. Though this is a fairly simple and straightforward task, you shouldn't underestimate its importance. The last thing you want is to misplace a session and waste valuable time trying to find it—or worse, inadvertently delete a session because it was in the wrong place! Now that you've done this, your next task will be to choose your session parameters, which will determine other important aspects of your session.

20 CHAPTER 1: WELCOME TO PRO TOOLS LE 6

1. Click on the **Audio File Type button**. A drop-down menu will appear. Choose a file type from the following options:

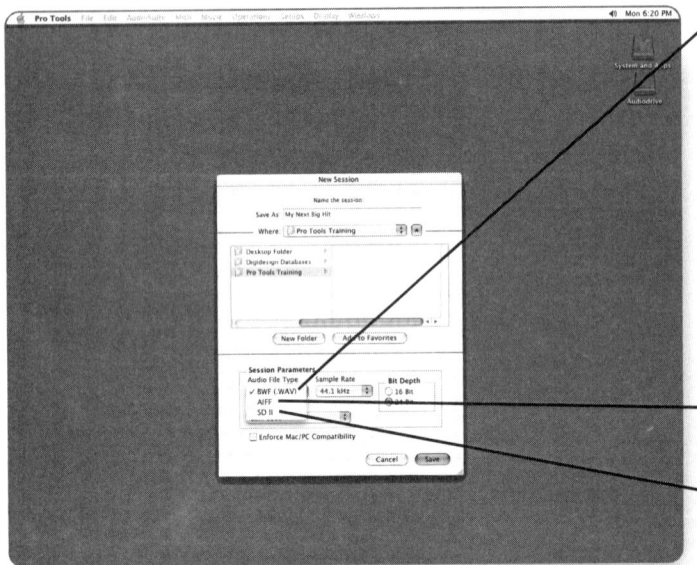

- **BWF (.WAV).** A .WAV file is a Windows standard file. A BWF (*Broadcast Wave File*) contains all the information of a regular .WAV, plus additional information including timestamps (which will be discussed later). This is a good format choice for session files that will be used in Windows XP systems.

- **AIFF.** This is the standard audio file format for Macs.

- **SD II (Sound Designer 2).** This is Digidesign's proprietary file format.

> **TIP**
>
> Pro Tools' default file format is BWF (.WAV) or Broadcast Wave, and this generally works for most applications. If you are planning to share files between Mac and Windows systems, this is the preferred file format.

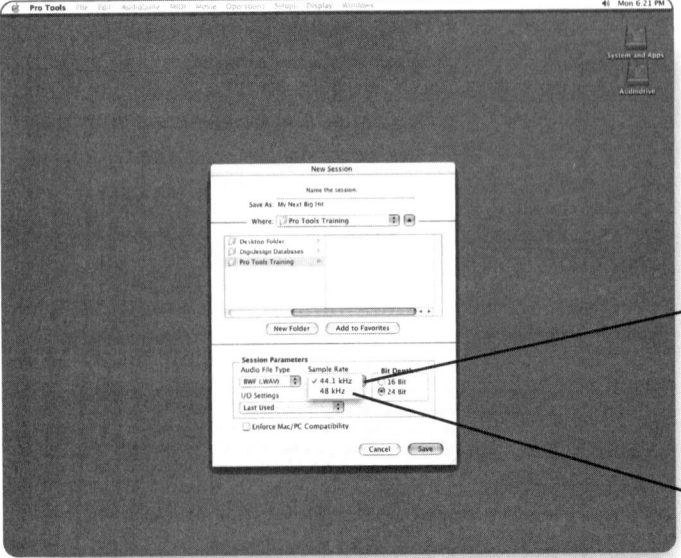

2. Click on the **Sample Rate button**. A list will appear, determined by the sample rates supported by your audio interface.

3. Select a **sample rate** for your session.

CREATING A NEW SESSION

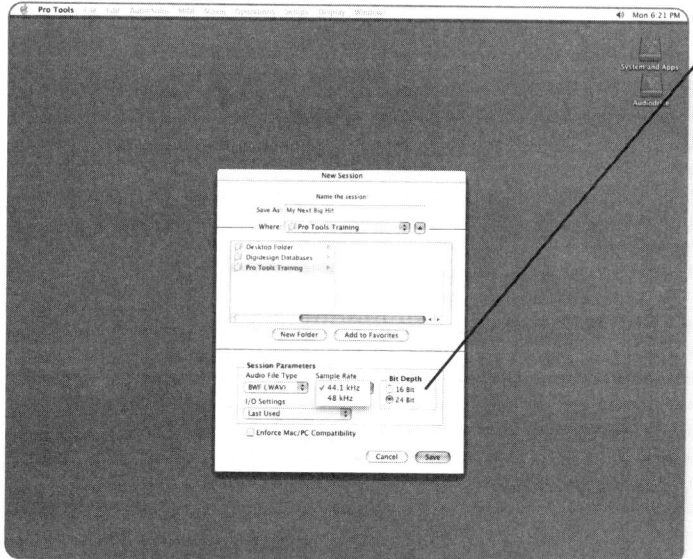

4. Select either **16 bit or 24 bit audio** as the bit depth for your session. The bit depth will be selected.

NOTE

Higher bit depths mean more resolution to your digital audio. A good general rule is to choose the highest bit depth available, even if your final product will eventually be at a lower bit depth. But remember, the higher your sample rate and/or bit depth, the larger your audio file will be, and the more room it will take up on your hard drive!

TIP

A good general rule to follow when selecting a sample rate for your session is that it should match the sample rate of your final product or be a multiple of that sample rate. For example, in a session destined to become an audio CD track, you could choose either 44.1 kHz (the sample rate for an audio CD) or 88.2 kHz (double that sample rate) if that sample rate is supported by your audio interface. If you intend to have your project professionally mastered, you should check with your mastering engineer to learn his or her preference; many prefer the highest sample rates possible.

NOTE

Once selected, the sample rate and bit depth will become the overall sample rate and bit depth for all audio in this session. This means that any audio you import into the session (a process I'll go through in Chapter 3, "Getting Started with Audio") will either have to match these specs or be converted to match the session.

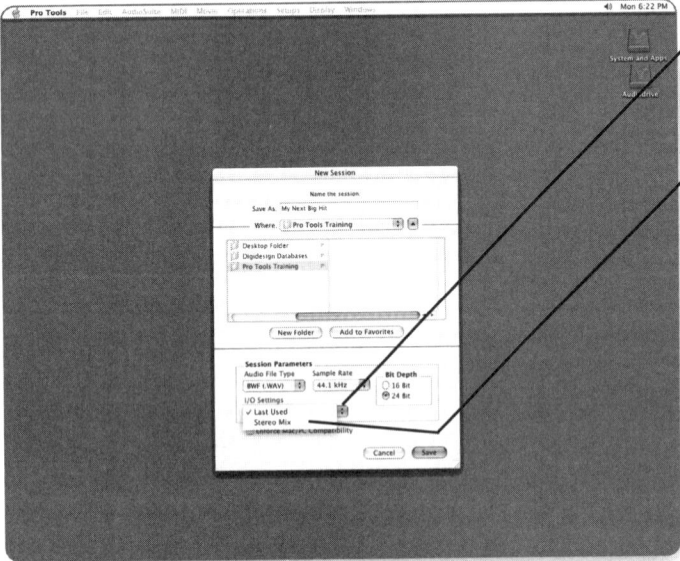

5. Click on the **I/O Settings button**. The I/O Settings drop-down menu will appear.

6. Click on your **I/O (Input/Output) settings** for this session. For now, choose Stereo Mix. The option will be selected.

> **NOTE**
>
> Your I/O settings determine the assignments and names of inputs, outputs, inserts, and buses. Don't worry if this doesn't make a lot of sense now—you'll learn more about how to make the most of your I/O settings later.

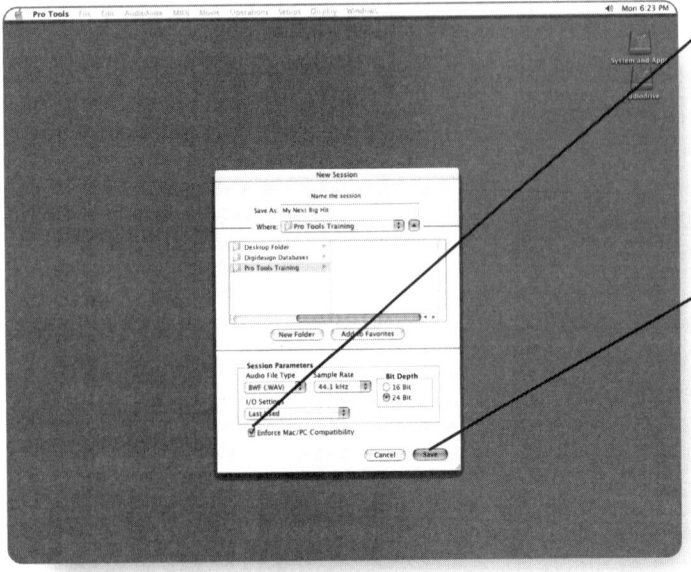

7. Macintosh computers and PCs deal with file names in different ways. If you plan to use this session in both environments, **check** the **Enforce Mac/PC Compatibility check box**.

8. You've made all the choices you need to make to create a new session! **Click** on **Save**. Pro Tools will begin to build your session.

CLOSING YOUR SESSION 23

Closing Your Session

You've just created a new session! The last basic procedure you have to complete is to close down your session.

> **NOTE**
>
> There are many windows in Pro Tools (Mix, Edit, Transport, and so on). The window(s) that will appear when your new session opens will depend on the last window configuration you used in Pro Tools. For this example, it doesn't matter which windows are showing.

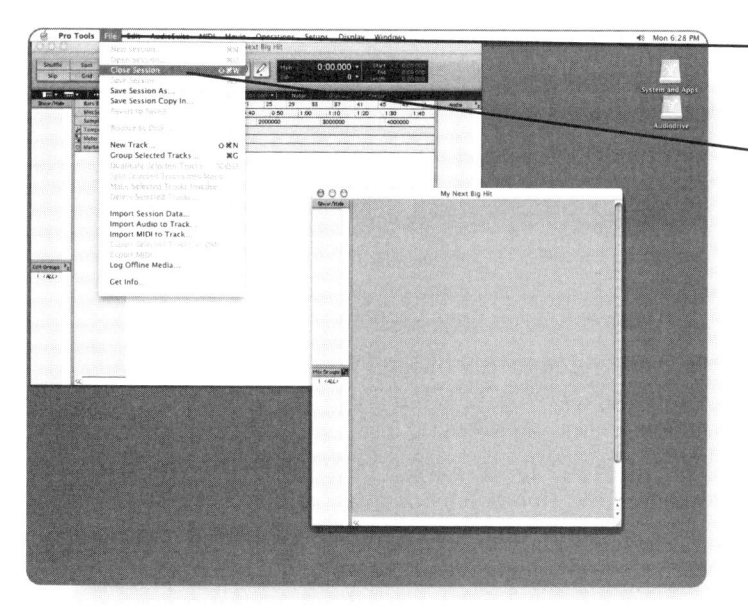

1. Click on **File**. The File menu will appear.

2. Click on **Close Session**. Pro Tools will shut down the current session and make itself ready for the next step.

More Basics

The end of the beginning: You've set up your system efficiently; taken some time to understand the way Pro Tools works; and based upon that understanding, you've created a session. The last step before you dive deeper into Pro Tools is to open a pre-existing session, play it, and close Pro Tools when you're done.

As you learn more about Pro Tools, you'll discover that there's usually more than one way to do any given thing. Different methods usually work better in different situations. Opening a session is no exception—there are two commonly used ways to get up and running!

> **NOTE**
>
> At this stage, you might not have an pre-existing Pro Tools session to work with, but that's not a problem. Go to the Pro Tools LE 6 Ignite! page at http://www.muskalipman.com and download the session named Chapter 1 Session to your hard drive. This session already has some audio tracks with regions, so you'll have to download the session file and the Audio Files subfolder.

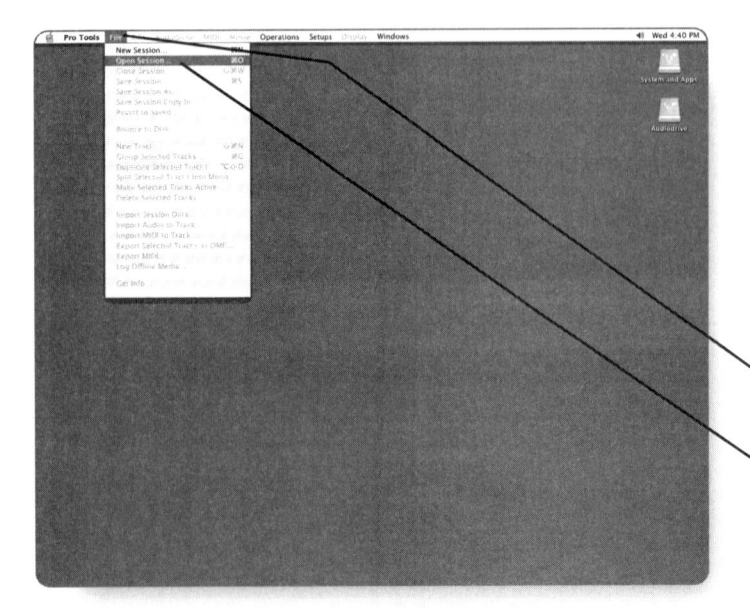

Opening a Session When Pro Tools Is Running

Suppose you've already launched the Pro Tools application. Here's how to open a session:

1. **Click** on **File**. The File menu will appear.

2. **Click** on **Open Session**. The Open dialog box will open.

MORE BASICS

> **TIP**
>
> As I mentioned earlier, Pro Tools includes shortcut keys that can allow you to work more efficiently. The shortcuts for New Session and Open Session (⌘+N and ⌘+O, respectively, on an Mac and Ctrl+N and Ctrl+O, respectively, in Windows) are very useful—and easy to remember as well!

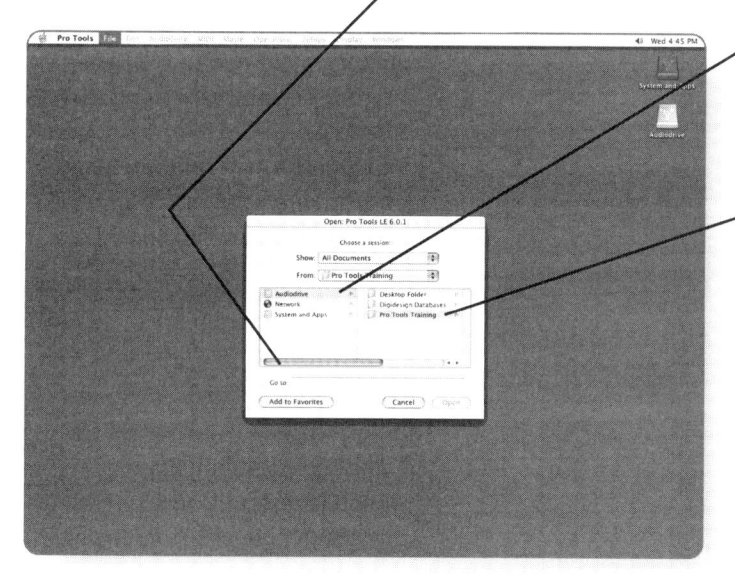

3. Navigate to your **drives**.

4. Select the **drive** that contains the audio session. The drive will be selected and the folders on that drive will appear.

5. Click on the **folder** that contains the session folder. The folder will be selected, and the scroll bar will automatically move to display the contents of that folder.

26 CHAPTER 1: WELCOME TO PRO TOOLS LE 6

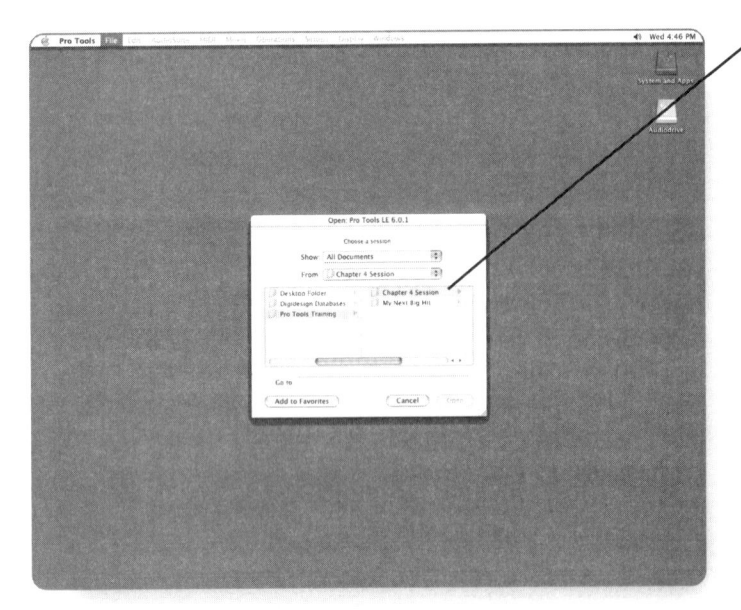

6. **Click** on the **subfolder** that contains the session file. The contents of the subfolder will be displayed.

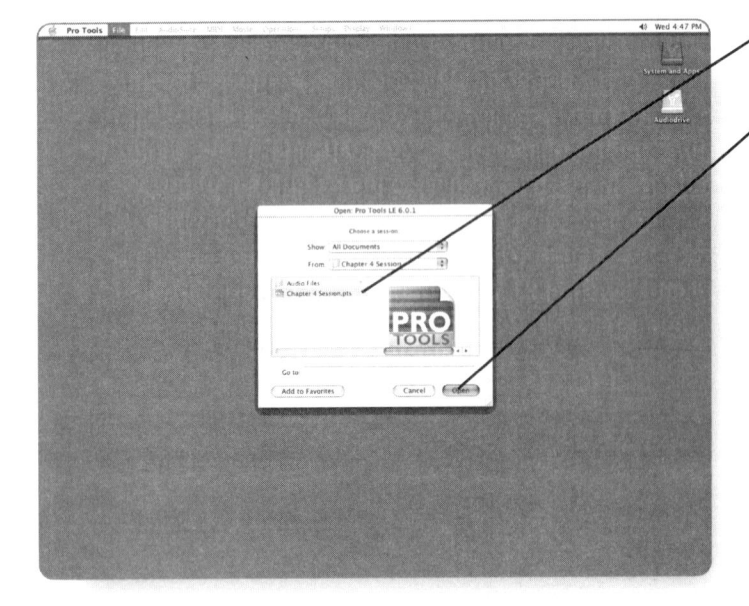

7. **Click** on the **session file**. The file will be selected.

8. **Click** on **Open**. The session will be loaded into Pro Tools.

Opening a Session When Pro Tools Is Not Yet Launched

In this case, suppose Pro Tools is not yet launched. To open a session, follow these steps:

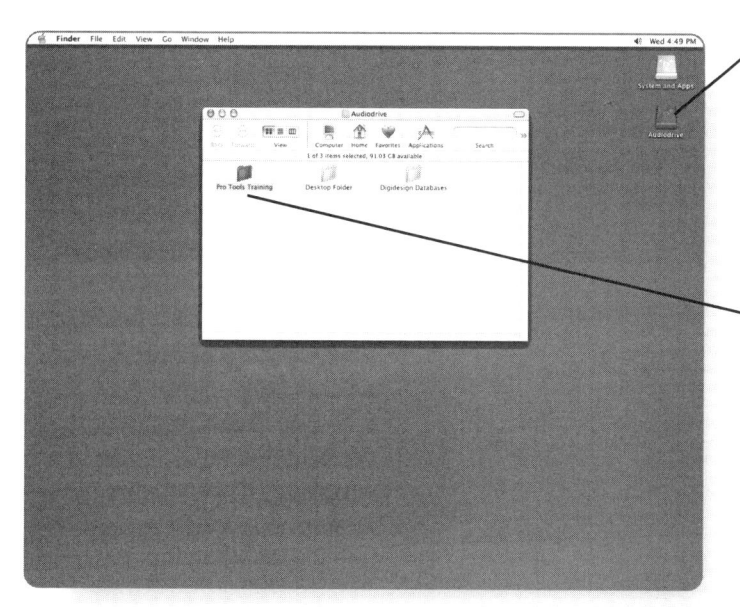

1. Select the **hard drive** that contains your session. On a PC, this will involve using My Computer or Windows Explorer. On a Mac, you can use the Finder or simply click on the hard drive icon on your desktop.

2. Open any **folder** that contains your session folder. The contents of the folder will be displayed.

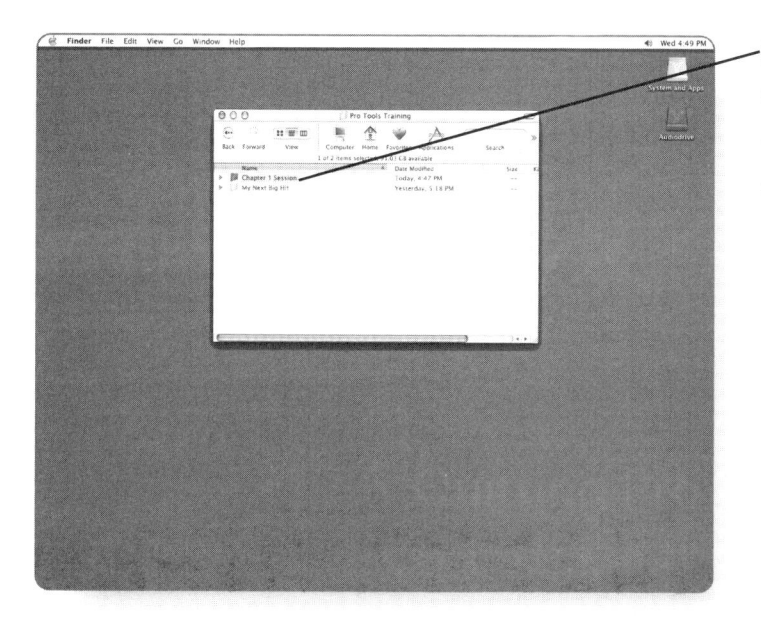

3. Open the **folder** that contains the session file.

The contents of the folder will be displayed.

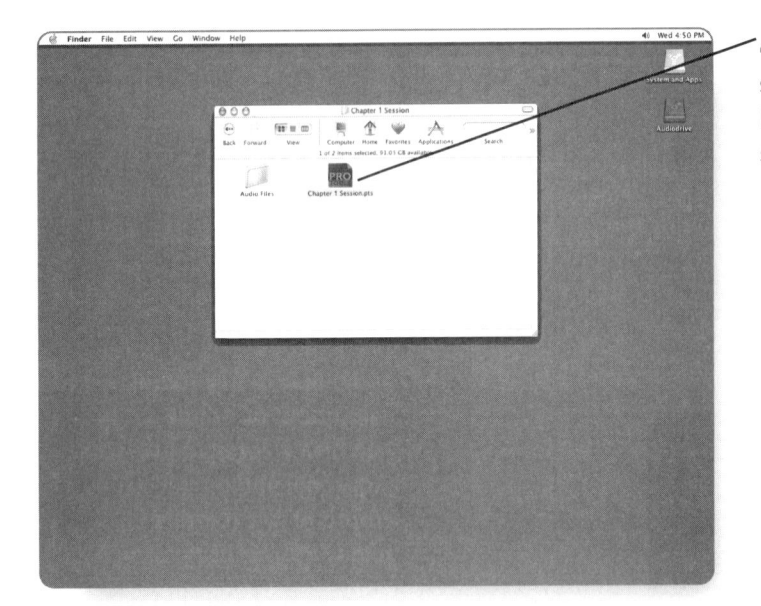

4. Double-click on the **session file**. Pro Tools will be launched automatically, and the session will be loaded.

Pro Tools' Primary Windows: Edit and Mix

When your session has opened, it will display any number of window configurations. These configurations will reflect the windows that were displayed the last time you saved the session. Generally speaking, one of Pro Tools' two main windows, the Edit window or the Mix window, will be shown. It's important to know what each of these two windows does and how to navigate between them.

MORE BASICS 29

You'll use the Edit window not only for editing functions, but also to manage your audio and MIDI regions. I'll go into more detail about the Edit window in Chapter 2, "Getting the Big Picture," but for now you should know that this window can be divided into a few general areas:

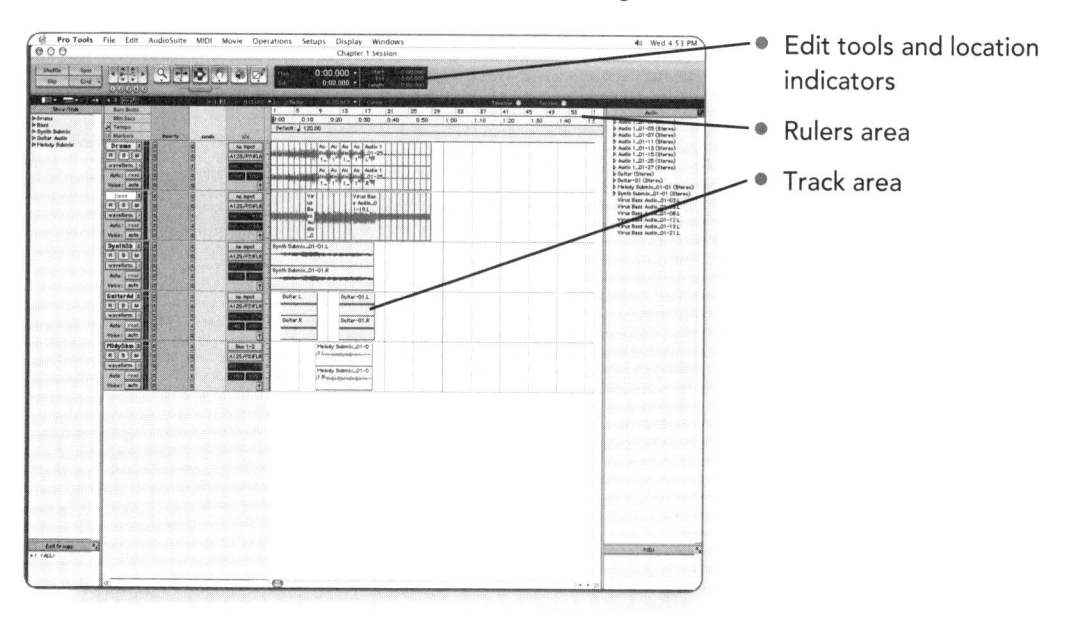

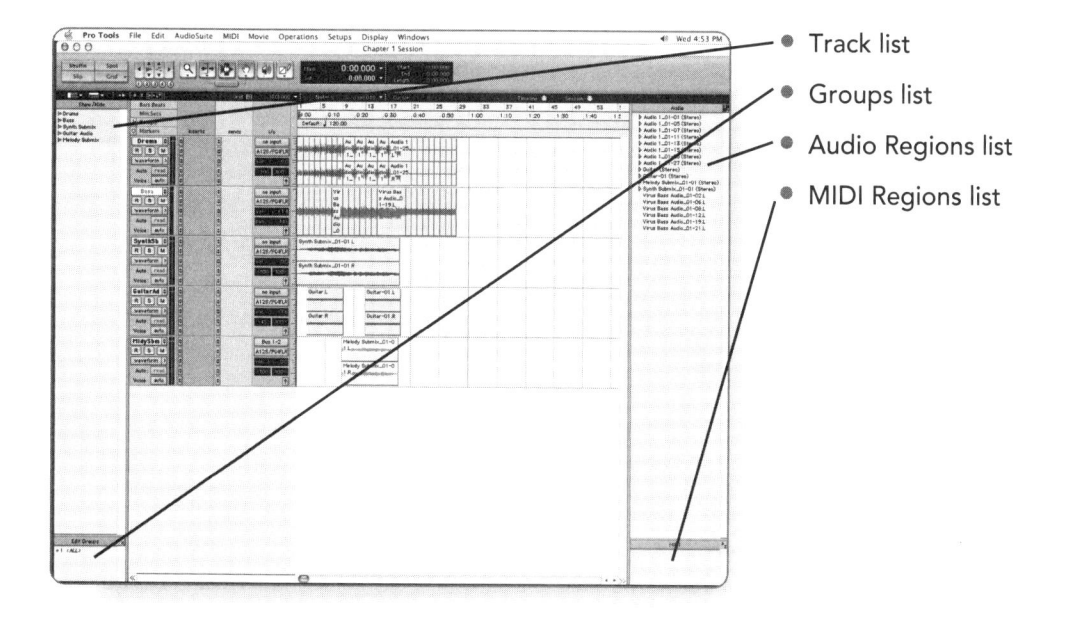

- Edit tools and location indicators
- Rulers area
- Track area

- Track list
- Groups list
- Audio Regions list
- MIDI Regions list

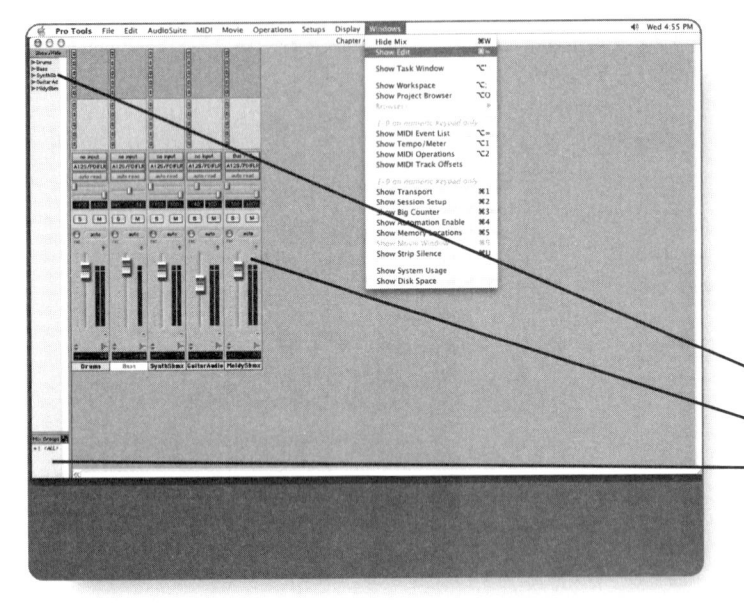

The Mix window also might come up (again, based upon the window that was showing when the session was last saved). As the name suggests, this is where you'll do most (if not all) of your mixing. Here's a very basic overview of what this window shows:

- Track list
- Channel strips
- Groups list

Although you can play your session with either of these two windows showing, for your purposes right now, you'll need to see the Edit window. If you don't see the Edit window, don't worry—changing between the Edit and Mix windows is easy!

1. Click on the **Windows** drop-down menu. The menu will appear.

2. Click on **Show Edit**. The Edit window will be displayed.

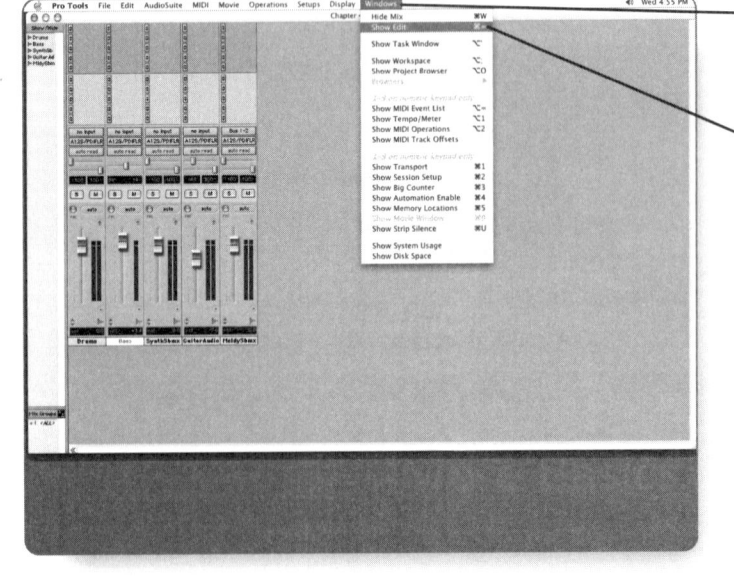

> **TIP**
>
> The shortcut to toggle between the Mix and Edit windows is ⌘+= (equals key) for the Mac and Ctrl+= for Windows. You'll move between these windows a lot, and this shortcut will help you do it quicker!

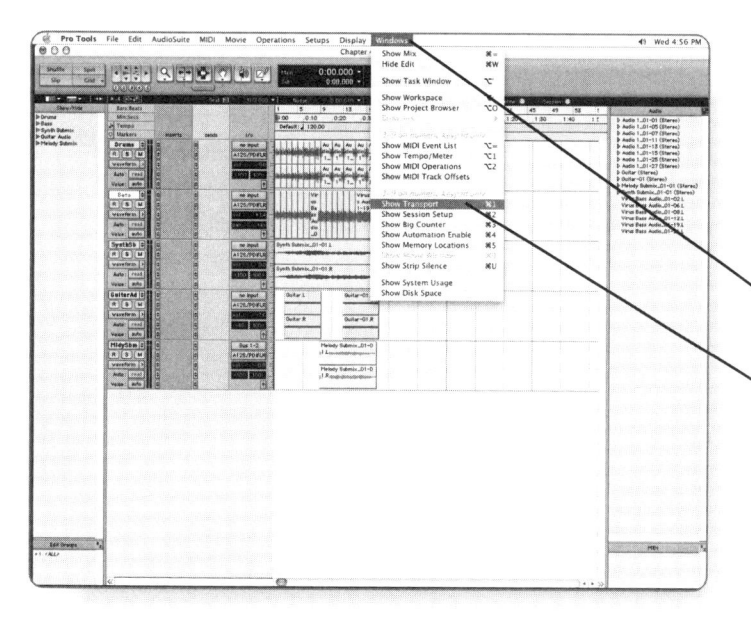

The Transport Window

Yet another window, the Transport window, will be useful in playing your session.

1. Click on **Windows**. The Windows menu will appear.

2. Click on **Show Transport**. The Transport window will appear. Like the Edit and Mix windows, the Transport window has a number of functions, but for now we'll focus on just the basic transport controls:

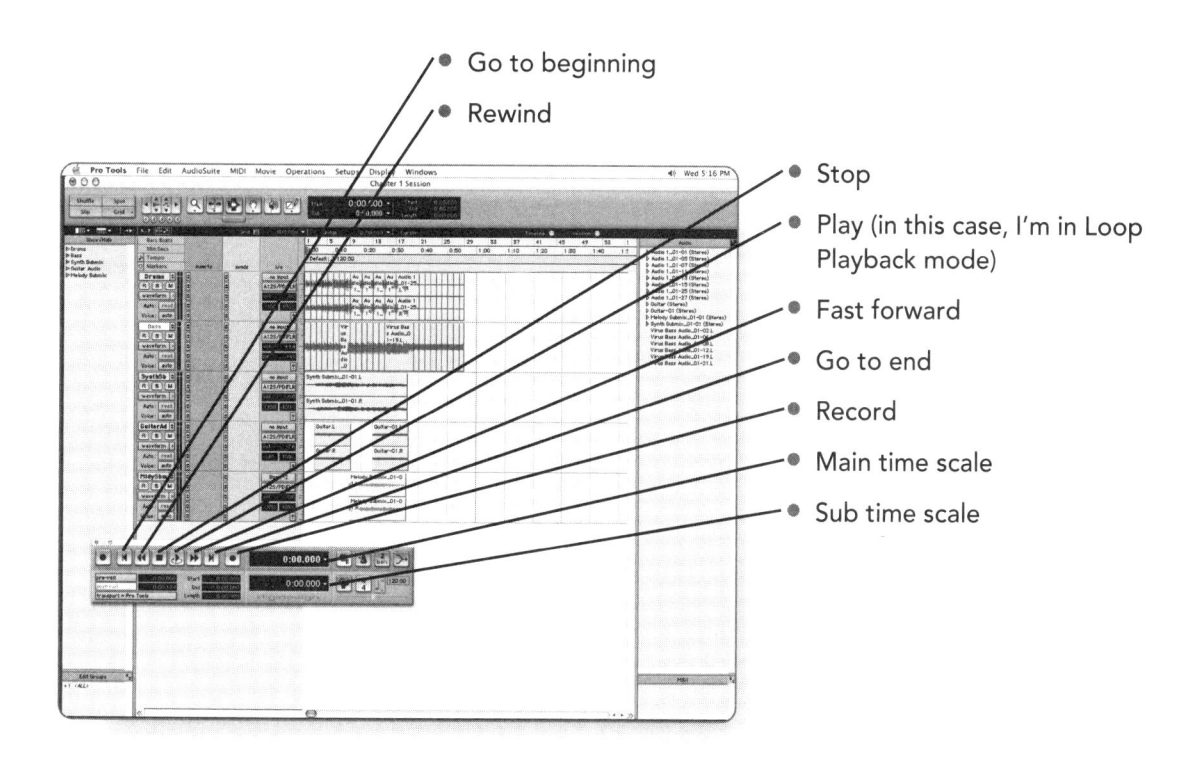

- Go to beginning
- Rewind
- Stop
- Play (in this case, I'm in Loop Playback mode)
- Fast forward
- Go to end
- Record
- Main time scale
- Sub time scale

CHAPTER 1: WELCOME TO PRO TOOLS LE 6

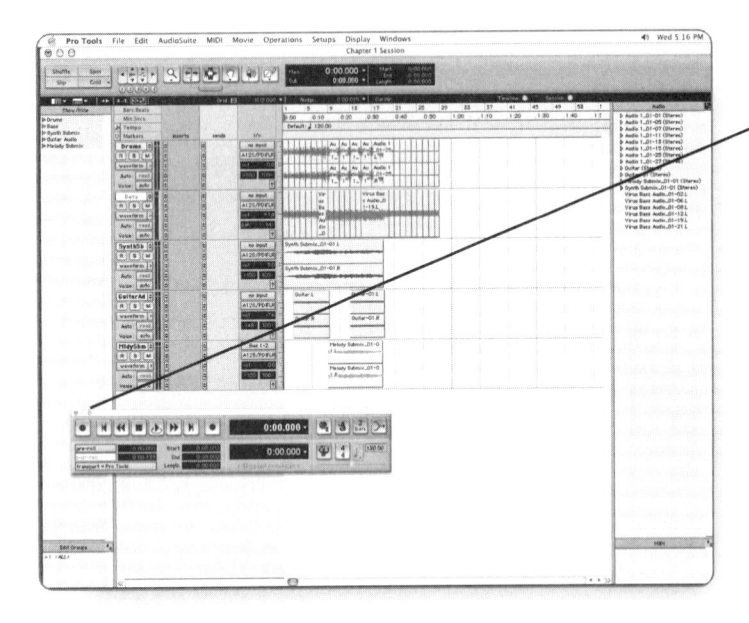

NOTE

If your Transport window doesn't look like it does in this illustration, you can reveal (or hide) the non-tranport-related features (such as the time scales) of the Transport window by clicking on the green button in the upper-left corner of the window.

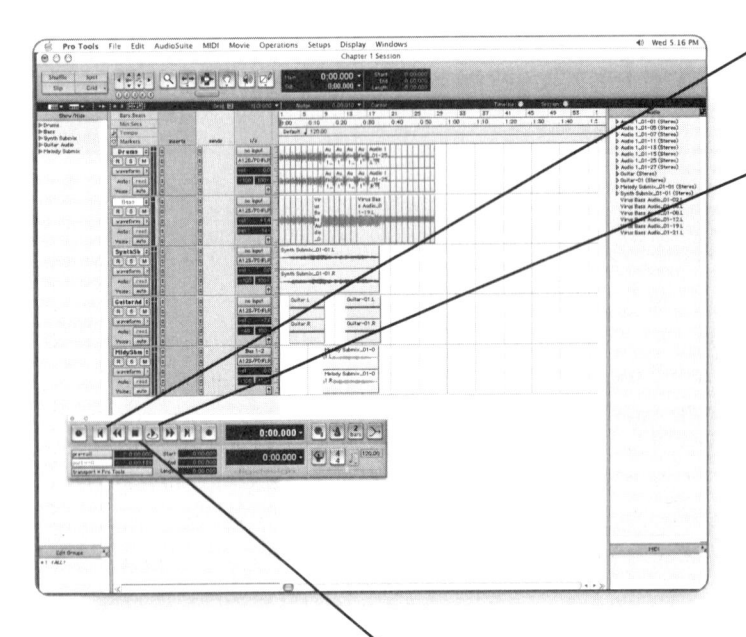

3. Click on the **Go to beginning button** to make sure you're at the beginning of your session.

4. Click on the **Play button**. Your audio will begin playing. You'll notice that a long vertical line travels from left to right in the Track area of the Edit window. This is called the timeline insertion, and you'll notice that as it intersects with different regions, different audio will sound.

5. Click on the **Stop button** when you're finished. The playback will stop.

Quitting Pro Tools

Good job! Now that you're done with the basics, you can close your session and quit Pro Tools entirely.

1. Click on **File**. The File menu will appear.

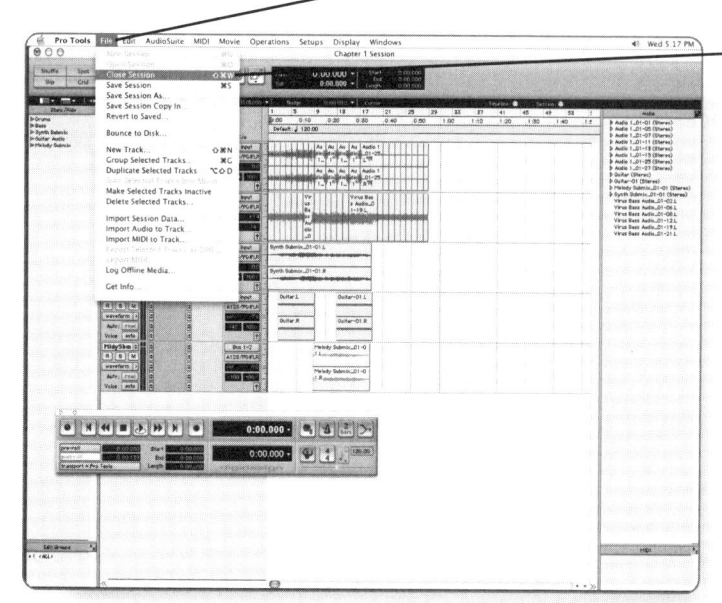

2. Click on **Close Session**. Your session will be unloaded from Pro Tools and all windows will disappear.

NOTE

Before your session closes completely, a window might prompt you to save your changes. This window appears when you make *any* changes to your session and then try to quit Pro Tools before saving those changes. Because you haven't made any significant changes at this point, you can choose Save or Don't Save and move on.

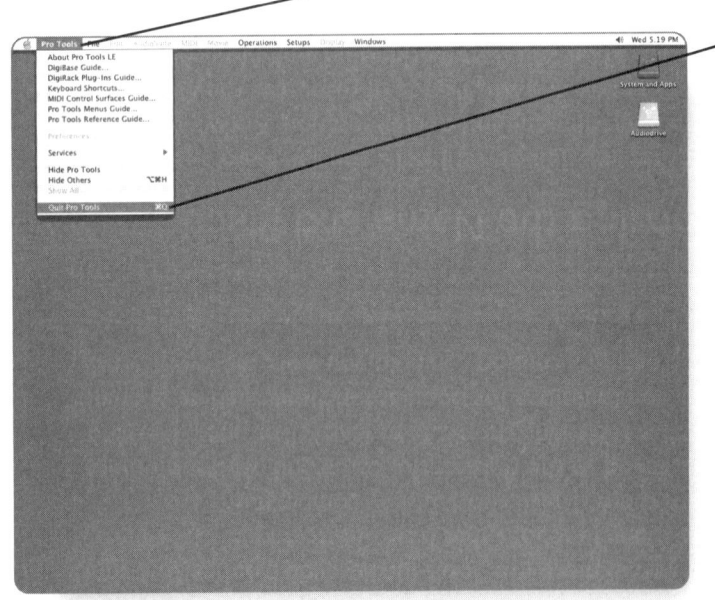

3. Click on **Pro Tools**. The Pro Tools menu will appear.

4. Click on **Quit Pro Tools**. Pro Tools will close. That's it!

> **TIP**
>
> If you're using Pro Tools on a PC, closing the software is exactly the same as the process in virtually every other program you've used in Windows. Simply click on the File menu and select Exit.

2
Getting the Big Picture

You've taken the time to install and set up your Pro Tools system. You've gone the extra mile and learned how Pro Tools thinks about sessions and files. You've even reached the point of creating and opening files. Now it's time to get better acquainted with the layout of the Pro Tools desktop. Although there are a number of windows in Pro Tools, many with specific functions, you will find that getting acquainted with the most common ones will really pay off later. In this chapter, you'll learn how to:

- Recognize the main sections of the Edit window and how to customize them
- Recognize the basic layout and functions of the Mix window
- Access other useful windows such as the Big Counter and System Usage windows

Working with the Edit Window

If there's a primary window in Pro Tools, it's the Edit window. This window is packed with useful tools and information about your Pro Tools session!

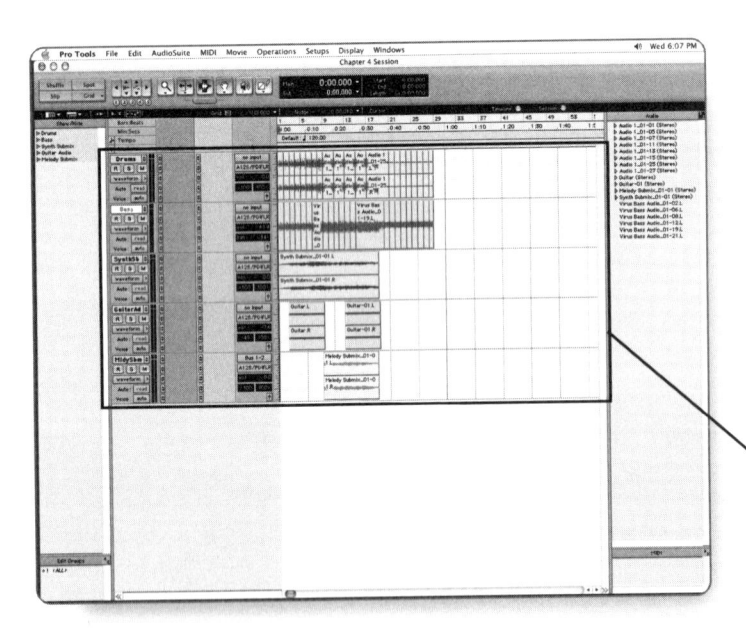

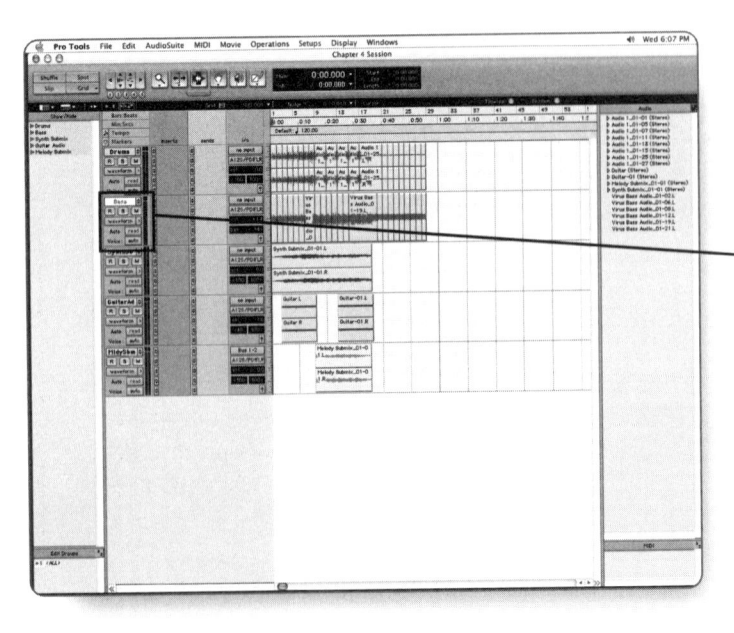

The Track Area

The screens in this section should look familiar—they're from the same session that you opened and played in Chapter 1. As it happens, this is a good representation of a garden-variety Edit window. To follow along, just open the session named Chapter 1 Session.

When you begin a new session from scratch, the Track area will be an empty white field. Any kind of track you create (audio, aux, MIDI, or master fader) will appear in this area as horizontal rows. Here, for example, there are five stereo audio tracks. As discussed in Chapter 1, the colored blocks (the ones other than gray on your screen) are called *regions*.

For each track there is a specific track name. When you need to select a track, you can do so by clicking on the track name button. Each track strip shows a lot of information besides regions and track names; you'll get into that in Chapter 3.

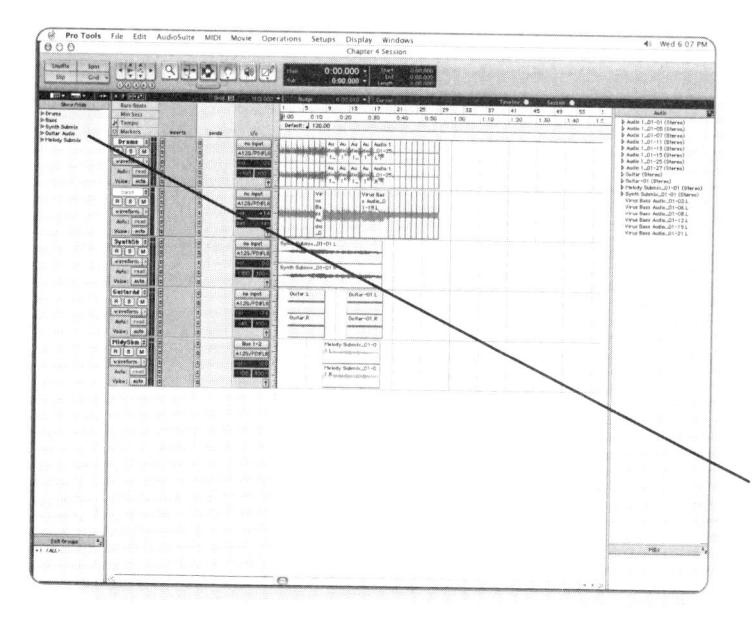

The Track Show/Hide and Edit Groups Areas

Immediately to the right of the Track area, you'll notice two vertical cells—the Show/Hide Tracks area and the Edit Groups area. The Show/Hide Tracks area can be divided into two main parts.

- **Track list.** All the tracks in your session, whether visible or hidden, are listed in this area. Shown tracks are highlighted in this list.

- **Show/Hide menu.** In addition to being a heading for this list, you can click on the Show/Hide button to view a list of options related to displaying and hiding each of the tracks in your session.

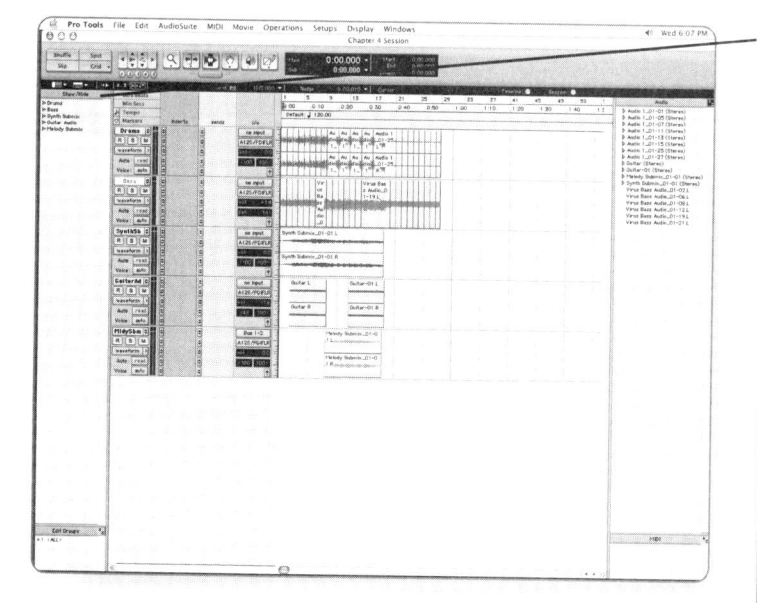

NOTE

All active and unmuted tracks, whether they are shown or hidden, will sound during playback. The ability to hide or show tracks is only a feature to help you manage your editing and mixing desktop. (But it's a feature for which you'll be grateful when your tracks start adding up!)

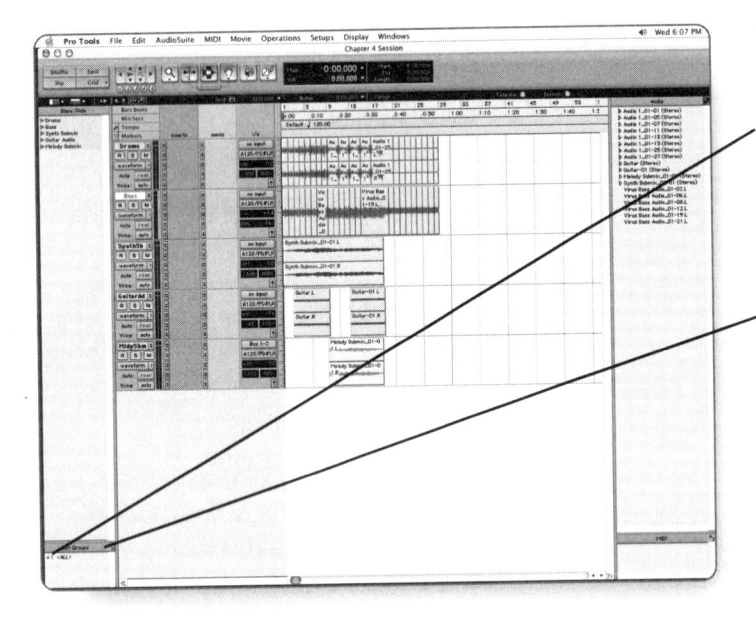

The Edit Groups area can also be divided into two main parts.

- **Edit Groups list.** As you create edit groups, they'll show up here. As with the Track list, active groups will be highlighted.

- **Edit Groups menu.** Like the Show/Hide menu, you'll see a list of group-related functions when you click on the button for this menu.

> **NOTE**
> You'll notice that there's already a group (named All) shown in this list, even though you didn't create it. The All group is created automatically when a session is created. Clicking on the word All will toggle between selecting and deselecting all the tracks in your session. (I'll cover the creation and use of additional groups in Chapter 8, "Basic Mixing.")

WORKING WITH THE EDIT WINDOW

The Audio and MIDI Regions Lists

Just to the right of the Track area, you'll find two more vertical areas. Here's what they do:

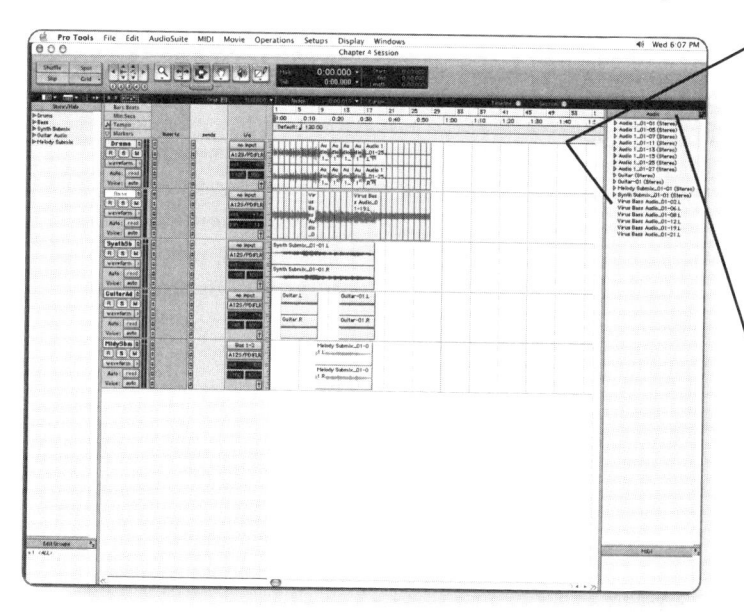

- **Audio Regions list.** This is a complete collection of all the audio regions in your session, whether or not they're being used actively in a track. From here you can drag and drop audio regions onto appropriate audio tracks.

- **Audio button.** At the top of the Audio Regions list, you'll find the Audio button. In addition to serving as a heading for this area, it will display a drop-down menu of audio region-related functions when you click on it.

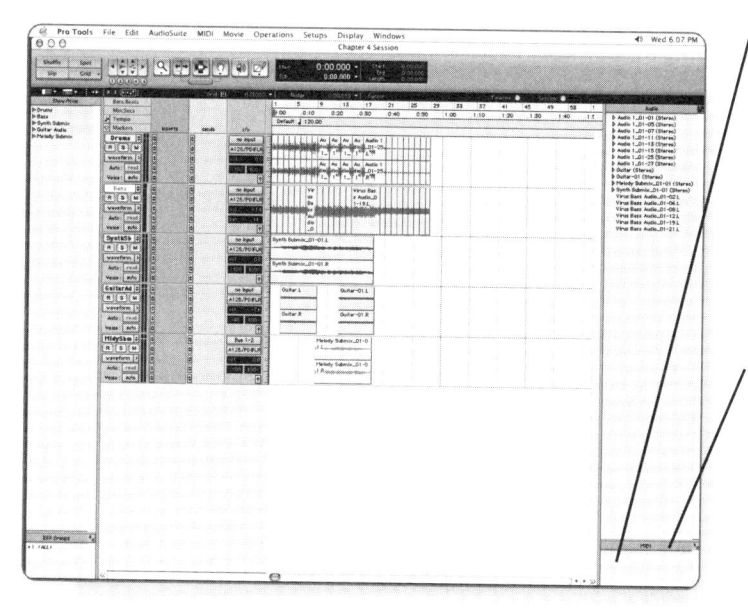

- **MIDI Regions list.** Like the Audio Regions list, the MIDI Regions list organizes regions in your session, but in this case the regions are MIDI (*Musical Instrument Digital Interface*) regions. From this area, you can drag MIDI regions onto a track.

- **MIDI button.** Last but not least, the MIDI button at the top of the MIDI Regions list will display MIDI region-related operations when you click on it.

> **NOTE**
>
> We'll go into MIDI and how to use it in Pro Tools in Chapter 6, "Using MIDI."

The Timeline and Tools Areas

The Timeline area allows you to view the passage of time in your session in a number of different ways. Different scales, such as minutes and seconds or bars and beats, will be useful to you depending upon the kind of work you are doing in Pro Tools. Any combination of the following ruler types can be shown:

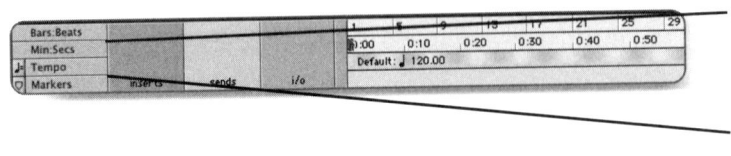

- Timeline ruler types (Bars:Beats, Min:Secs, or Samples)
- Conductor ruler types (Tempo, Meter, or Markers)

> **NOTE**
>
> In this example, you're looking at Bars:Beats, Min:Secs, Tempo, and Markers.

The Timeline itself can be displayed simultaneously in many time scales, with each visible ruler's type displayed to the left of the Timeline.

WORKING WITH THE EDIT WINDOW   41

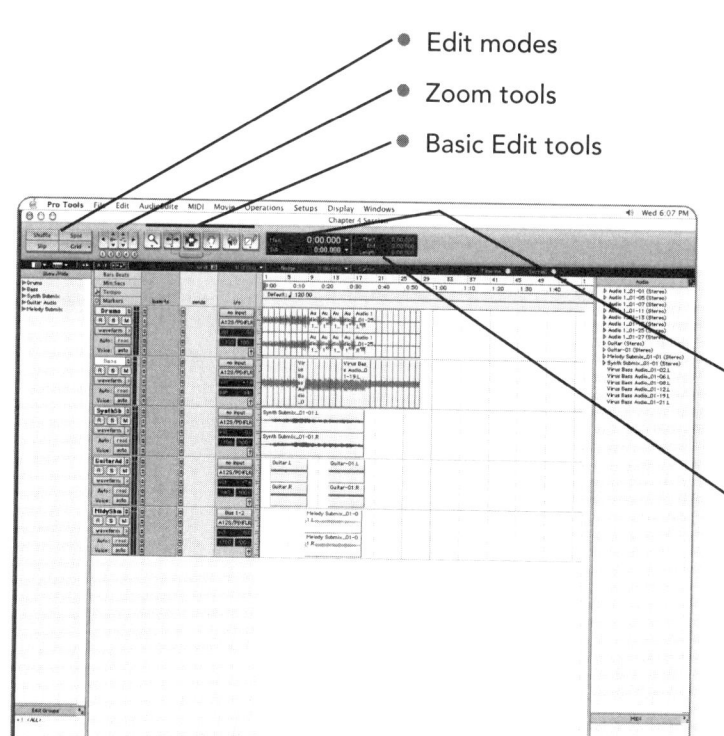

The Edit Tools area can be broken down into a number of functional areas.

- Edit modes
- Zoom tools
- Basic Edit tools

Last but certainly not least, the location and selection displays can give you location information.

- The Main and Sub time scales will tell you exactly where you are in your session.
- The selection area will tell you the beginning, end, and duration of your selection.

Customizing the Edit Window

Now that you've identified the overall layout of the Edit window, you should consider a few options available for organizing your workspace.

Viewing Menus

As you learned earlier, the tops of each of the four Edit window lists serve not only as identifiers, but also as buttons that will reveal drop-down menus of operations specific to that area if you click on them.

42 CHAPTER 2: GETTING THE BIG PICTURE

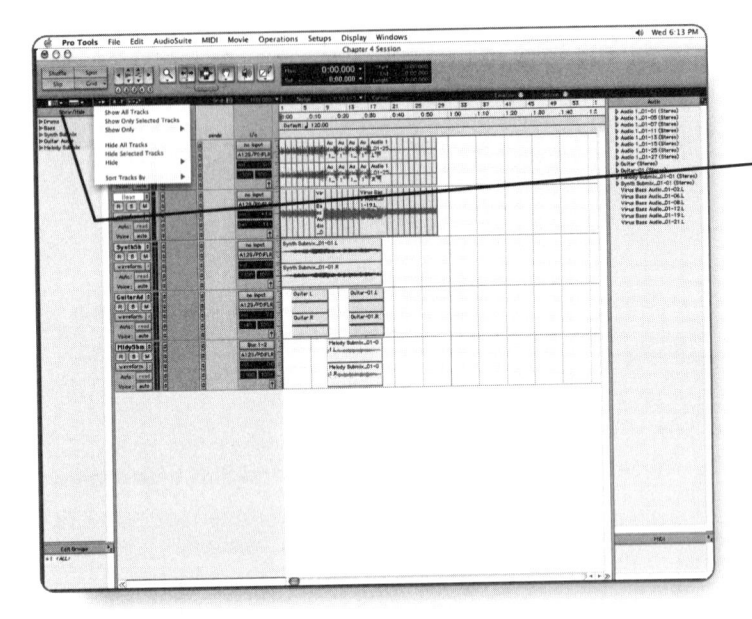

For example, here's how you can show the Track Show/Hide list's drop-down menu:

1. Click on the **Show/Hide button**. The Track Show/Hide drop-down menu will appear. The options in the menu might not mean much now, but don't worry—you'll go into each of these menus one at a time in later chapters.

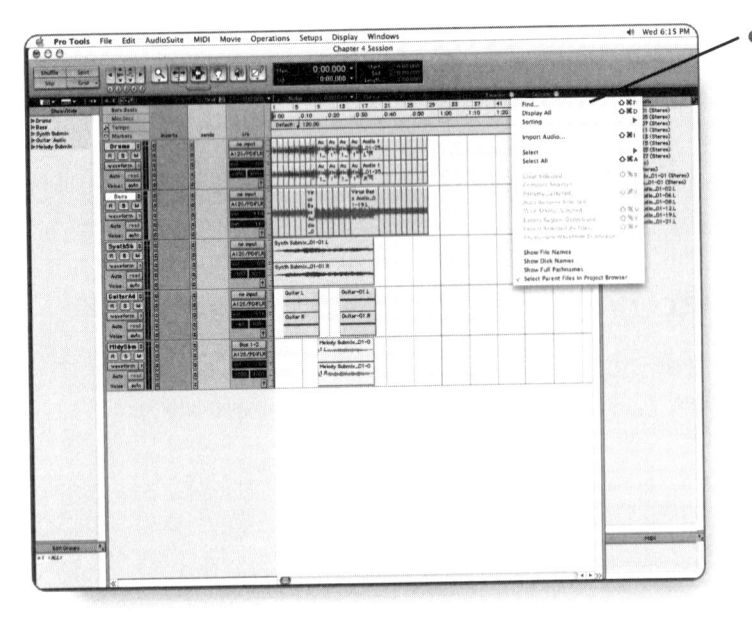

• Here's what you'll get when you click on the Audio Regions button . . .

WORKING WITH THE EDIT WINDOW   43

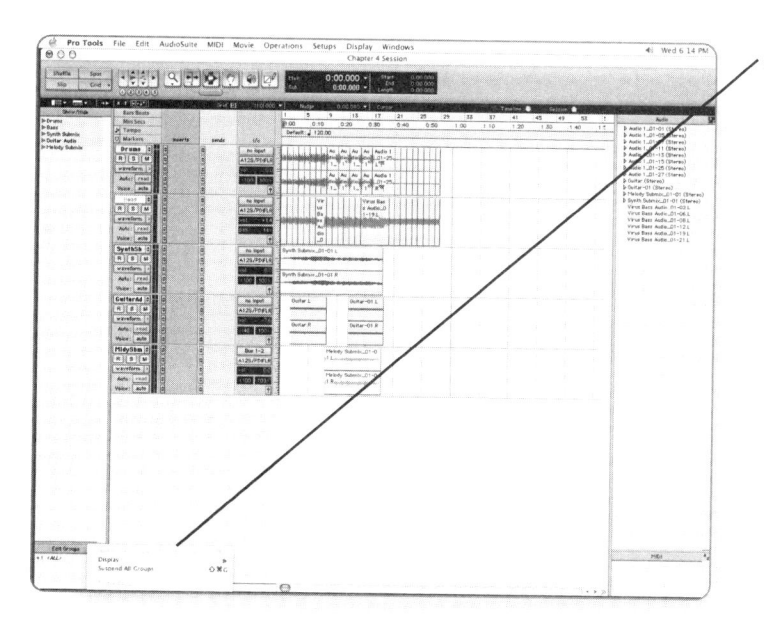

- And the Groups button . . .

- And finally the MIDI button.

Adjusting Region Size

You can customize your desktop in other ways as well. For example, if your session calls for more MIDI regions than audio regions, you might want to give a little more room to the MIDI Regions list on your desktop.

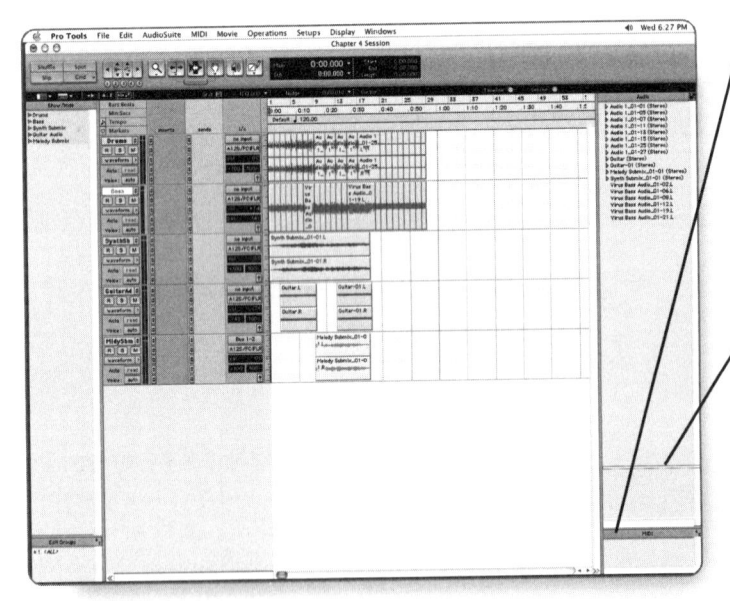

1. **Move** your **cursor** to the boundary between the Audio Regions list and the MIDI Regions list. The cursor will change from the usual arrow into a double arrow to let you know you can adjust the top of the MIDI Regions list.

2. **Click and drag** the **boundary** up or down as needed. As you drag, you'll see a dotted line marking the movement of the boundary.

3. **Release** the **mouse button**. The boundary will be "dropped" and the lists will be reorganized.

> **NOTE**
> You can adjust any of the boundaries (horizontal or vertical) for the Show/Hide, Edit Groups, Audio Regions, and MIDI Regions lists. Adjusting the vertical edges of these areas can affect how much area you have on your screen for tracks.

WORKING WITH THE EDIT WINDOW   45

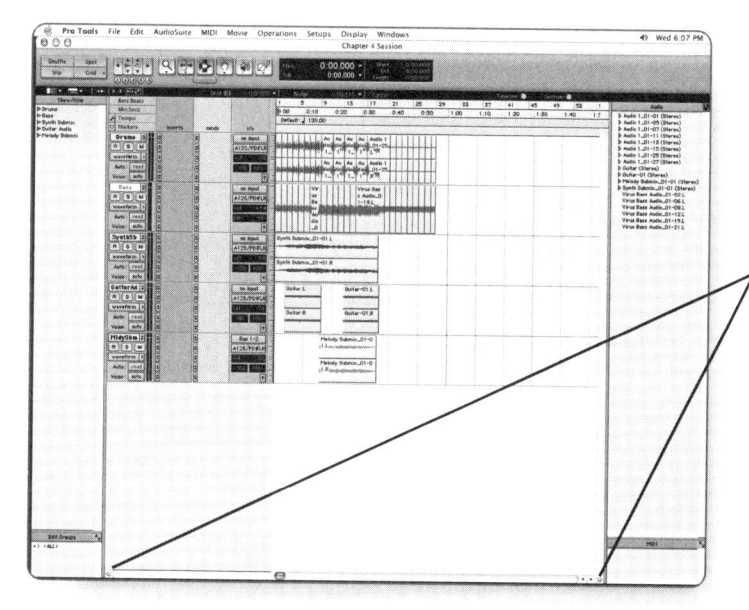

Hiding Regions

In addition to adjusting the sizes of these regions, you can hide them entirely when you're not using them.

1. Click on the **arrows** at the inner bottom corners of either (or both) vertical sections. The columns will be hidden immediately, and more of your Edit window will be usable by your Track area.

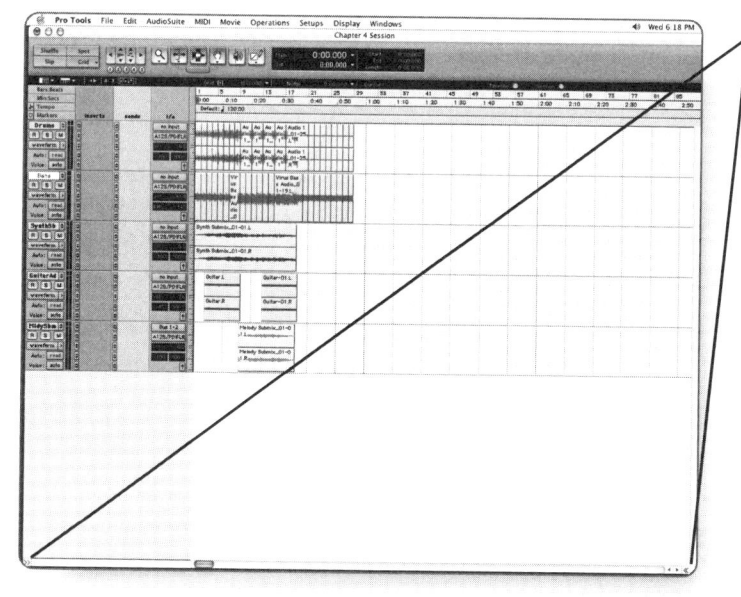

2. Click again on the **arrows** in the lower corner(s) of the Edit window. The sections will reappear immediately.

> **NOTE**
>
> Remember, the window arrangements that appear when you open a session are the same as they were in the session when you last saved it. It can be a bit surprising to open a session and see no region areas in your Edit window. Don't worry, though—you can always follow the aforementioned steps to display the lists.

CHAPTER 2: GETTING THE BIG PICTURE

Displaying Columns

There are a number of columns in the Edit window's Track area that provide track-specific information on things such as inputs, outputs, inserts, sends, and comments.

1. Click on **Display**. The Display menu will appear.

2. Click on **Edit Window Shows**. A submenu of the available columns that can be shown in the Track area will appear. Checked columns are currently displayed.

3. Click on any **column** to check or uncheck it.

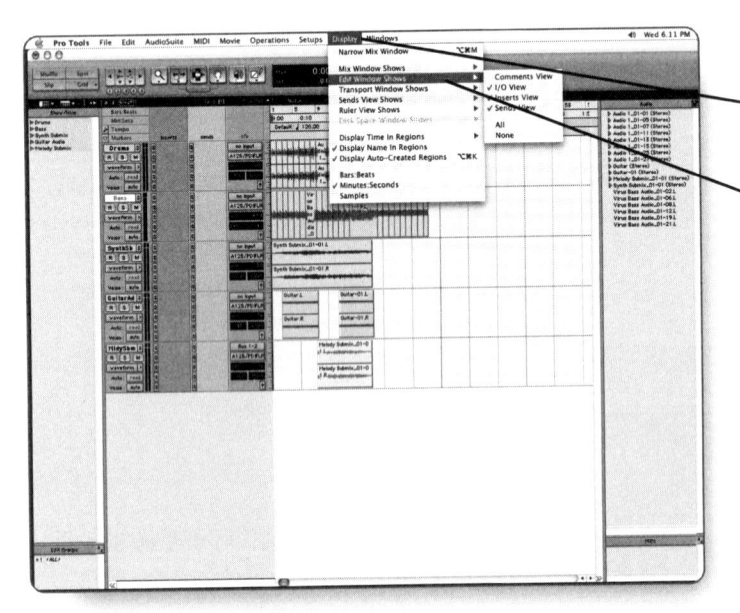

TIP

In addition to selecting columns individually, you can select All or None to show or hide all columns, respectively.

NOTE

Here's an alternative: Click on this icon to show the Edit Window Shows submenu. The menu functions exactly the same, regardless of its location.

WORKING WITH THE EDIT WINDOW   47

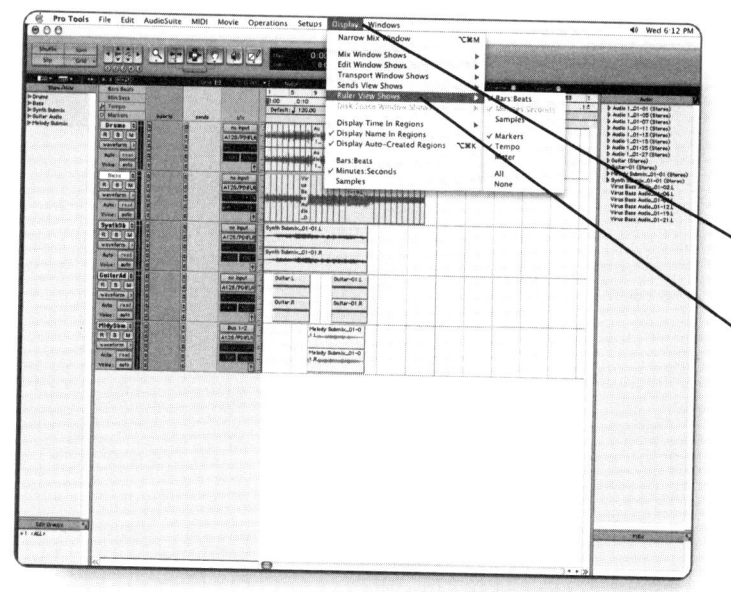

Displaying Time Scales

You can also choose which time scales (rulers) are shown.

1. Click on **Display**. The Display menu will appear.

2. Click on **Ruler View Shows**. A list of the available time scales you can show in the Rulers area will appear. Checked scales are currently displayed.

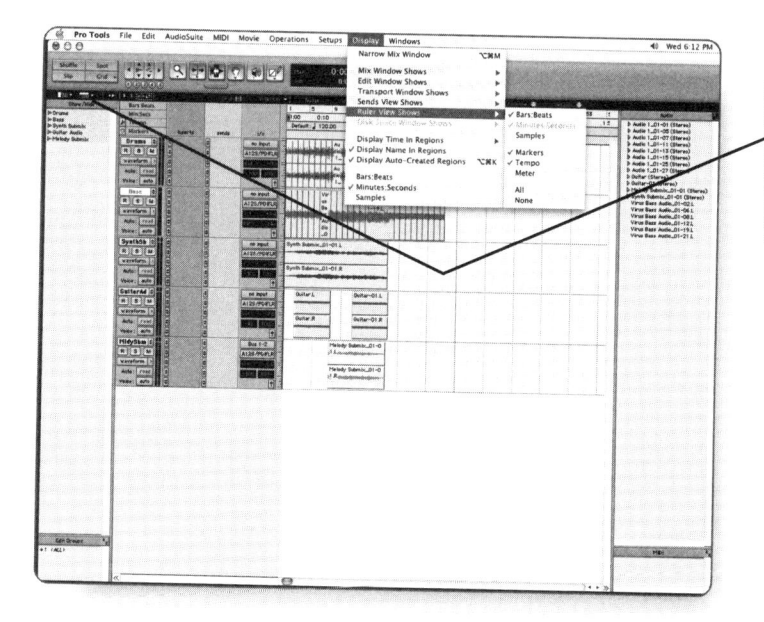

> **NOTE**
> Another alternative: Click here to show the Ruler View Shows submenu.

Adjusting Track Heights

Last, but absolutely not least—track heights. In Pro Tools, you have the ability to change individually the height of each track. This can come in handy, particularly when you have many tracks in your session and you want to see them all, or when you really want to do some microsurgery on one track in particular. Here's how:

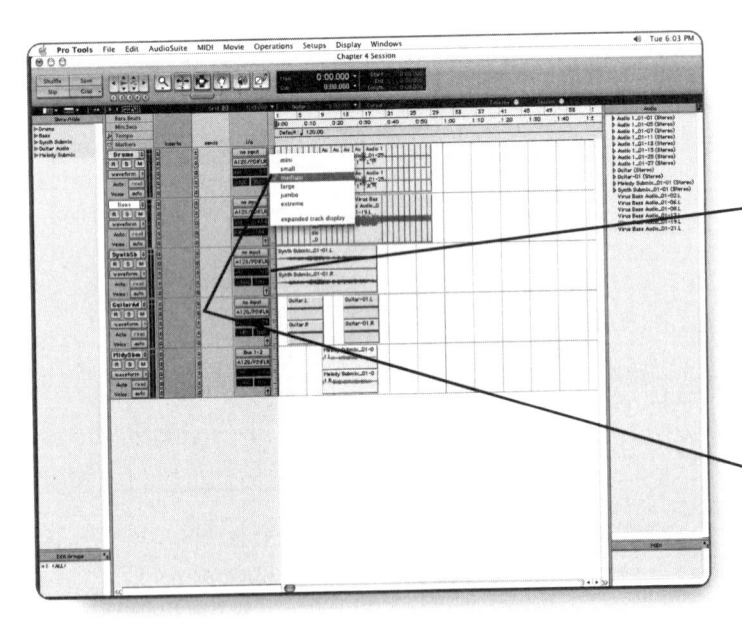

1. Between each track's columns (I/O, Inserts, Sends, Comments) and the region area is a small vertical area showing the amplitude scale. **Click in this area**. The Track Height drop-down menu will appear.

2. Select the desired track **height**. The track will change immediately to match your height choice.

> **NOTE**
> You can change the height of any Pro Tools track (including MIDI and aux tracks, which you'll explore in later chapters). However, the thin vertical area for other types of tracks looks a little different than the amplitude scale of an audio track. MIDI tracks, for example, show a keyboard-like display. In any case, clicking in this area will bring up the same Track Height menu.

> **TIP**
> Here's a useful shortcut: Hold the Option key (Mac) or the Alt key (PC) while you change the height of any one track, and the heights of all shown tracks will change at once.

WORKING WITH THE MIX WINDOW

Working with the Mix Window

After the Edit window, the other primary window you'll be using in Pro Tools is the Mix window. Although there's a good bit of common ground between the Mix and Edit windows, the layout and function of the Mix window is geared toward the mixing and automation phases of your production.

Understanding the Mix Window Layout

Most of the general layout of the Mix window is similar to the Edit window.

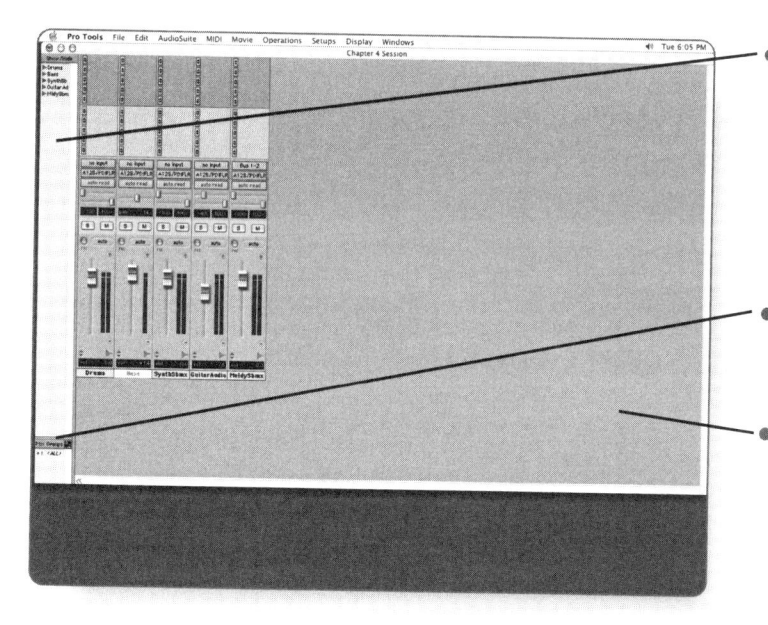

- **Show/Hide area.** This area functions similarly in both the Edit and Mix windows. In the Mix window, as you toggle each track in your session, channel strips to the right will appear and disappear.

- **Mix Groups area.** As you create mix groups, they will show up in this area.

- **Channel Strips area.** When you create any kind of track (audio, aux, master fader, or MIDI), it will appear as a vertical strip.

> **NOTE**
> Tracks that appear at the top of the Edit window will appear on the left side of the Mix window. As tracks descend in the Edit window, they move from left to right in the Mix window's Channel Strips area.

> **NOTE**
>
> There is a one-to-one correspondence between the tracks that are shown (or hidden) in the Edit and Mix windows. Also remember that whether or not a track is shown does not affect that track's audibility.

Customizing the Mix Window

Tailoring your Mix window for maximum ease and efficiency will make mixing much easier. This section presents some of the most common customizations for the Mix window.

> **TIP**
>
> As in the Edit window, clicking on the double arrows in the corner of the Mix Groups area will hide both the Show/Hide and Mix Groups sections. This will give you more space on your desktop for channel strips.

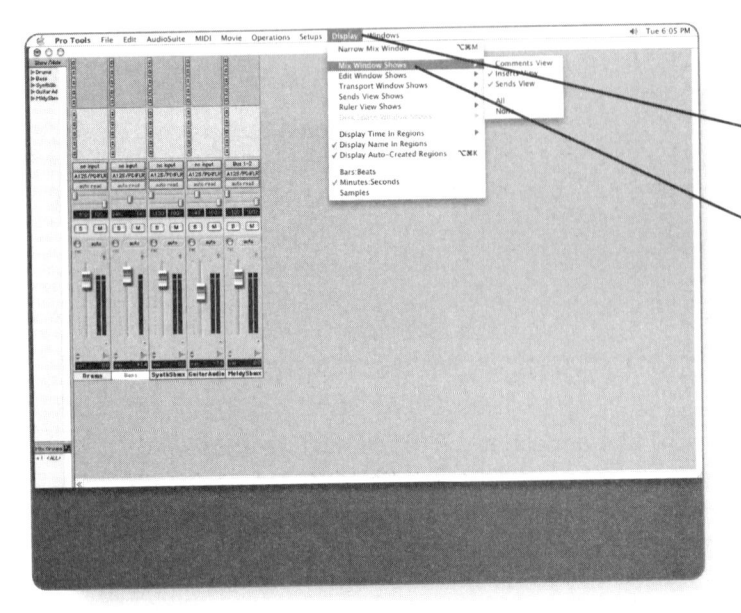

You can also control the aspects of your mixer that are displayed.

1. Click on **Display**. The Display menu will appear.

2. Select Mix Window Shows. A second drop-down menu will appear, showing aspects of your channel strips that you can display or hide. Checked aspects are currently displayed.

3. Click on any **element** (comments, inserts, or sends) to check or uncheck it.

UNDERSTANDING OTHER USEFUL WINDOWS   51

> **TIP**
> In addition to selecting columns individually, you can select All or None to select all the columns or none of them, respectively.

> **NOTE**
> Sends and inserts are particularly useful in the mixing process, and the ability to show and hide them will be helpful as you tweak your mix.

Suppose you have a lot of tracks in your session, and you'd like to see as many of them as possible in the Mix window. Here's how to squeeze more tracks onto your limited desktop.

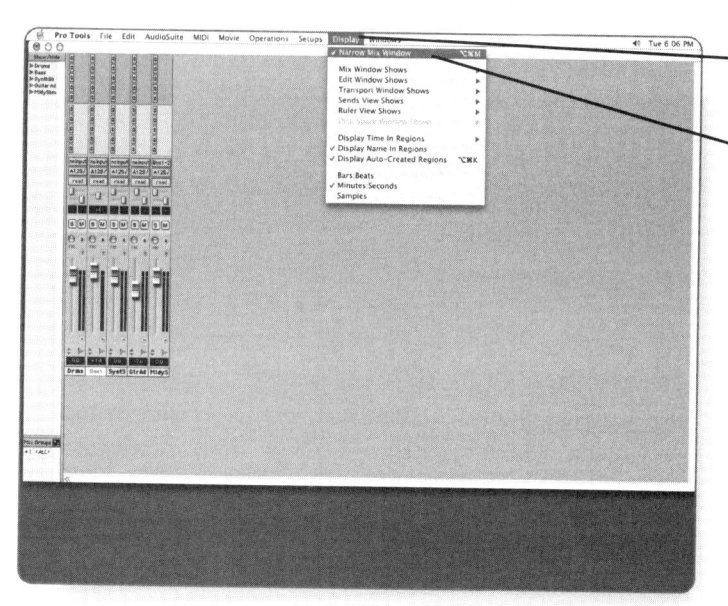

1. Click on **Display**. The Display menu will appear.

2. Select Narrow Mix Window. Technically, the Mix window itself won't narrow, but the individual channel strips will, allowing you to fit more tracks within a given space.

Understanding Other Useful Windows

Even though you'll spend the majority of your Pro Tools life working in the Edit and Mix windows, there are a number of other windows that serve specific purposes. These windows usually operate in conjunction with either the Edit or Mix window (whichever one you're using). You can access these secondary windows through the Windows menu.

CHAPTER 2: GETTING THE BIG PICTURE

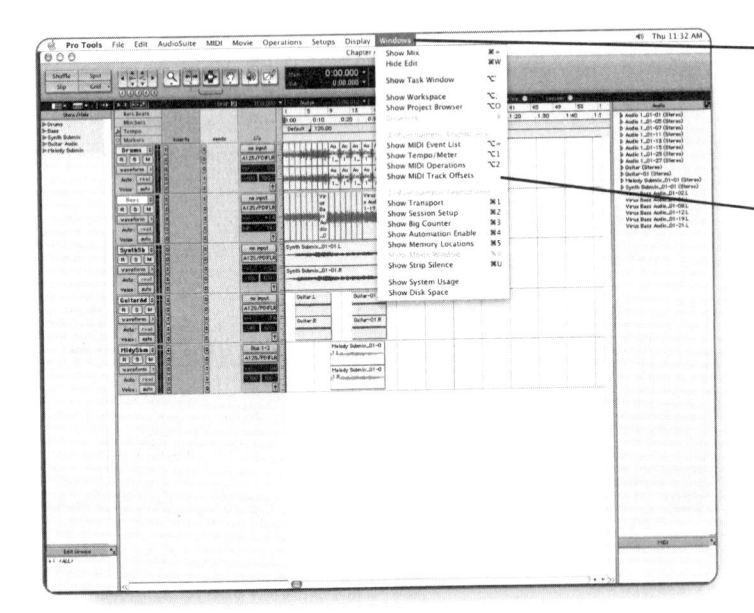

1. Click on **Windows**. The Windows menu will appear, displaying an assortment of window choices.

2. Click on the **window** you want to display. The following list details some of the available windows.

> **NOTE**
>
> You've already worked with the Transport window. (Remember, the shortcut is ⌘+1 on the Mac and Ctrl+1 on the PC.) Like the Transport window, the windows I discuss here will open on top of either the Edit or Mix window.

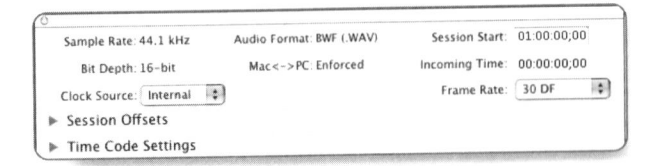

- **Session Setup.** The Session Setup window displays useful information about your session's configurations. The shortcut for the Session Setup window is ⌘+2 on a Mac and Ctrl+2 on a PC.

UNDERSTANDING OTHER USEFUL WINDOWS 53

- **Big Counter.** The Big Counter window is simply a larger display of your main counter, but it really comes in handy when you want to watch your session's progress from across a room! The shortcut for the Big Counter window is ⌘+3 on a Mac and Ctrl+3 on a PC.

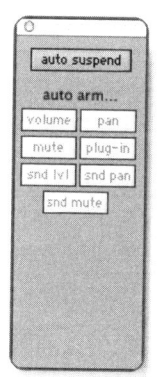

- **Automation Enable.** Automating Pro Tools is a topic you'll work with later in this book. Simply put, it's a way for you to make your mixes and effects more dynamic as your session plays. The Automation Enable window allows you to enable or disable various aspects of your session for automation. The shortcut for the Automation Enable window is ⌘+4 on a Mac and Ctrl+4 on a PC.

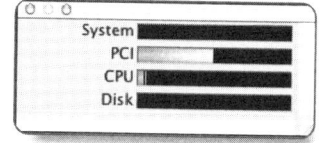

- **System Usage.** As you learn more about how to efficiently use Pro Tools, you'll want to refer to the System Usage window from time to time to check on how your computer is dealing with the tasks associated with Pro Tools. This window gives a simple and efficient view of the workload for your system.

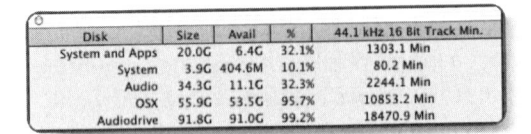

Disk	Size	Avail	%	44.1 kHz 16 Bit Track Min.
System and Apps	20.0G	6.4G	32.1%	1303.1 Min
System	3.9G	404.6M	10.1%	80.2 Min
Audio	34.3G	11.1G	32.3%	2244.1 Min
OSX	55.9G	53.5G	95.7%	10853.2 Min
Audiodrive	91.8G	91.0G	99.2%	18470.9 Min

- **Disk Space.** The size of a hard drive in a DAW is like the amount of tape in an analog recording studio—the more you have, the more you can record. The Disk Space window will let you know how much free space you have for recording audio (at a given sample rate and bit depth) on each of your computer's hard drives.

Congratulations! You now have a fundamental understanding of what Pro Tools is and how it functions, which will help you be a more intelligent user as you delve deeper into this powerful environment. Now you're ready to begin actively using Pro Tools LE and making music!

3
Getting Started with Audio

Now that you have a solid basic understanding of what Pro Tools is and what it can do, it's time to start making things happen. The first step down this road to Pro Tools proficiency is to set up your session and start using audio. In this chapter, you'll learn how to:

- Set up and customize your inputs, outputs, inserts, and buses
- Create audio, aux input, and master fader tracks
- Import audio into your session
- Play your session in different ways

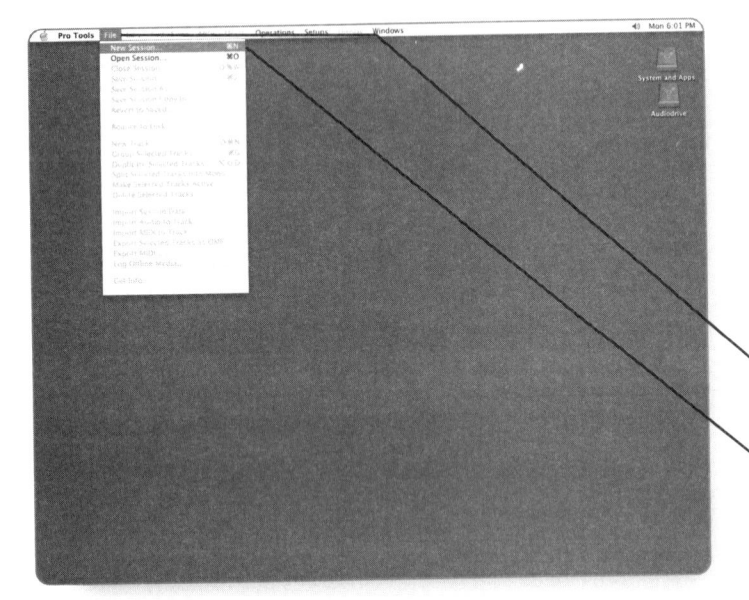

56 CHAPTER 3: GETTING STARTED WITH AUDIO

Getting Started

Before you can move to the next step, you'll have to call upon knowledge that you gained in the first chapter and create a session on which you can work.

1. **Launch Pro Tools**.

2. Click on **File**. The File menu will appear.

3. Click on **New Session**. The New Session dialog box will open.

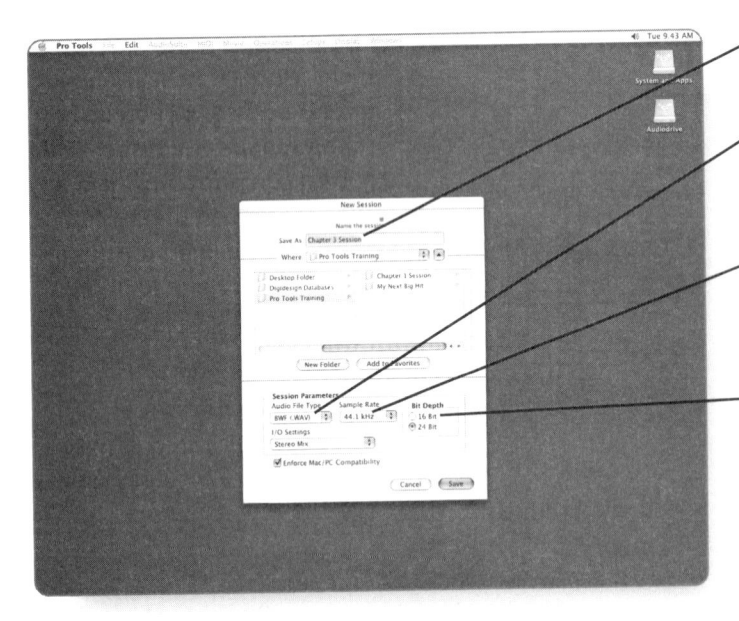

4. Type Chapter 3 Session in the Save As text box.

5. Select BWF (.WAV) from the Audio File Type menu. The option will be selected.

6. Select 44.1 kHz from the Sample Rate menu. The option will be selected.

7. Select the **24 Bit radio button** in the Bit Depth area. The option will be selected.

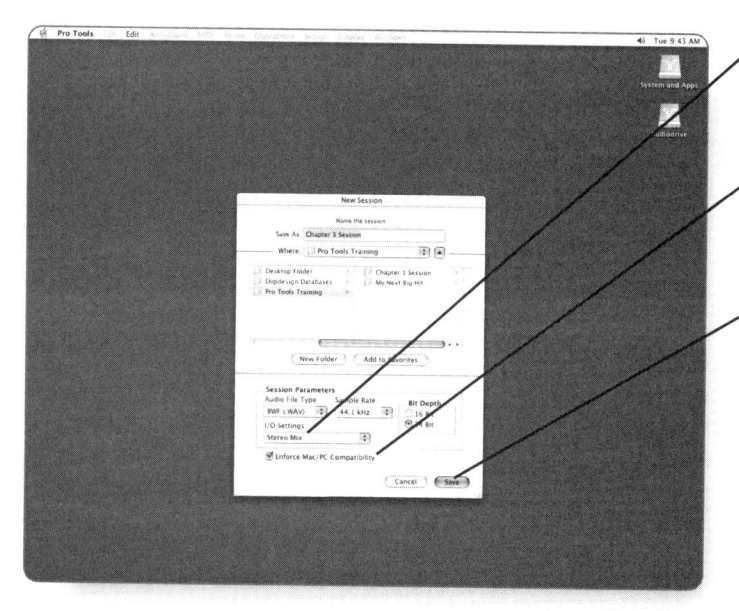

CUSTOMIZING YOUR SESSION: THE I/O SETUP DIALOG BOX   57

8. Select **Stereo Mix** from the I/O Settings menu. The option will be selected.

9. Select the **Enforce Mac/PC Compatibility check box**. The option will be selected.

10. Click on **Save**. Your session will be created and opened automatically.

Customizing Your Session: The I/O Setup Dialog Box

An understanding of Pro Tools' signal flow is critical to using this powerful DAW, and at the heart of signal flow is the I/O Setup dialog box. Take a look.

Setting Up Inputs

When you created this session you chose Stereo Mix as your I/O (Input/Output) setting. This I/O setting is Pro Tools' generic setup for stereo work, and although it works fine as is, you can customize it to match your own studio's setup and boost your productivity right from the start! You can start by taking a closer look at the input setup for your studio—in other words, the connections going into your audio interface, and from there to the Pro Tools software environment.

58 CHAPTER 3: GETTING STARTED WITH AUDIO

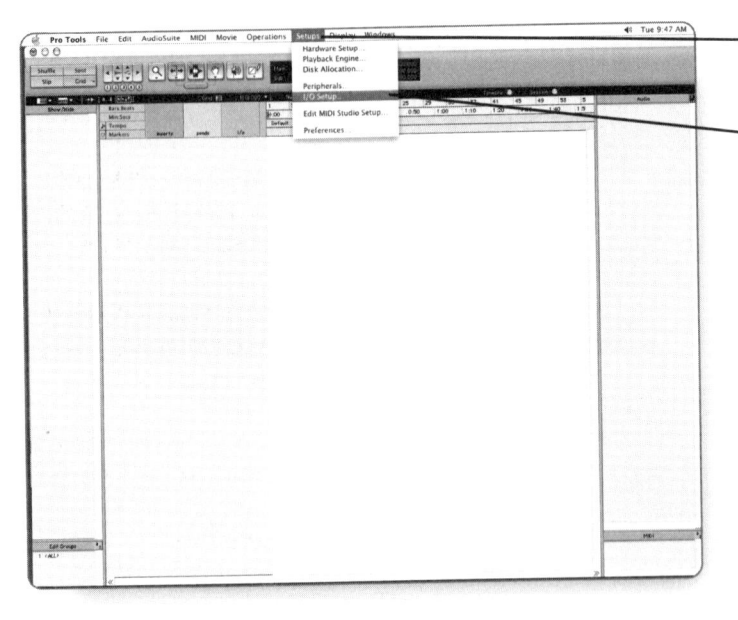

1. Click on **Setups**. The Setups menu will appear.

2. Click on **I/O Setup**. The I/O Setup dialog box will open.

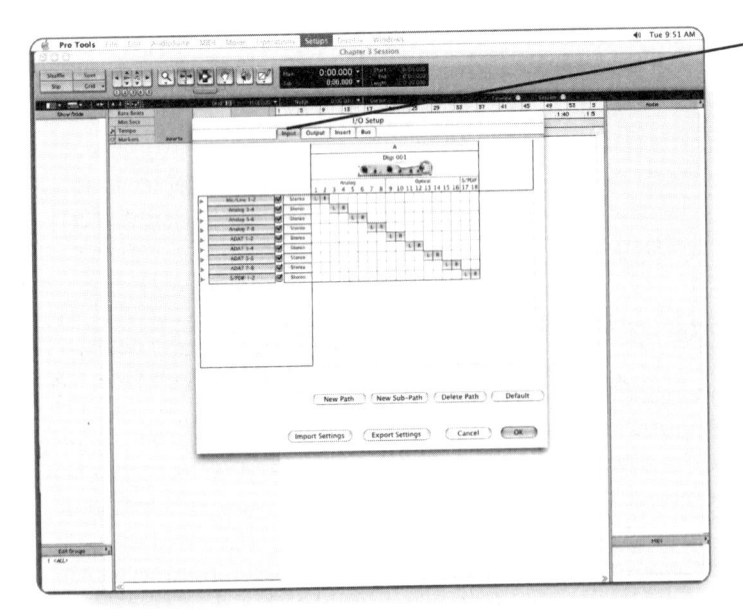

3. Click on the **Input tab**. The tab will move to the front.

NOTE

The examples in this chapter show the windows you'll see if you have a Digi 001 system. If you have any other kind of interface, the window will look a little different (although the function will be the same). At the top of the window, you'll see your audio interface (Mbox, Digi 001, or Digi 002). Directly below the interface, you'll see a listing of all the available inputs for that interface.

Customizing Your Inputs

The grid area and the labels to the left represent paths, which allow you to assign inputs in the Pro Tools software to the physical inputs of your Pro Tools hardware. The window currently displays a default input setup. You'll want to customize your inputs, and the easiest way to do that is to delete these paths and start from scratch. Here's how:

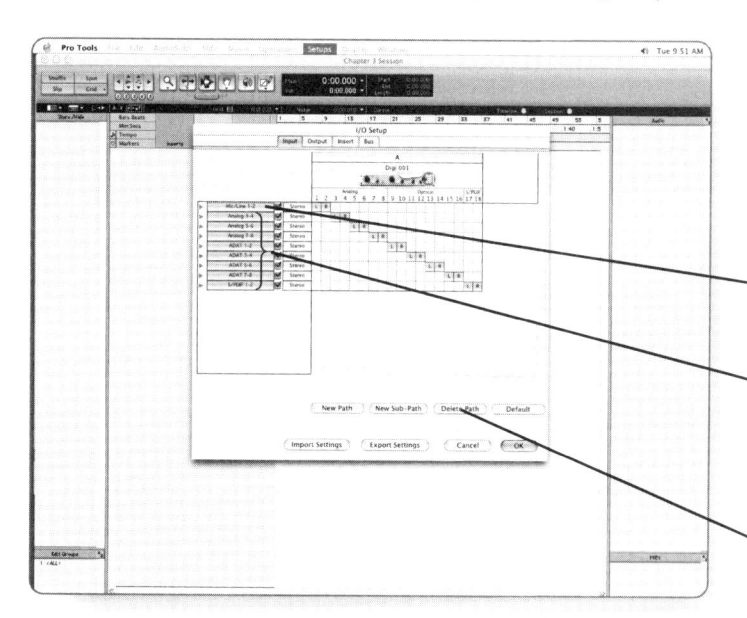

1. Click on the top **path name**. The name will be highlighted.

2. Press the **Shift key** and **click** on the remaining **path names** until all the paths are highlighted.

3. Click on **Delete Path**. All the input paths will disappear.

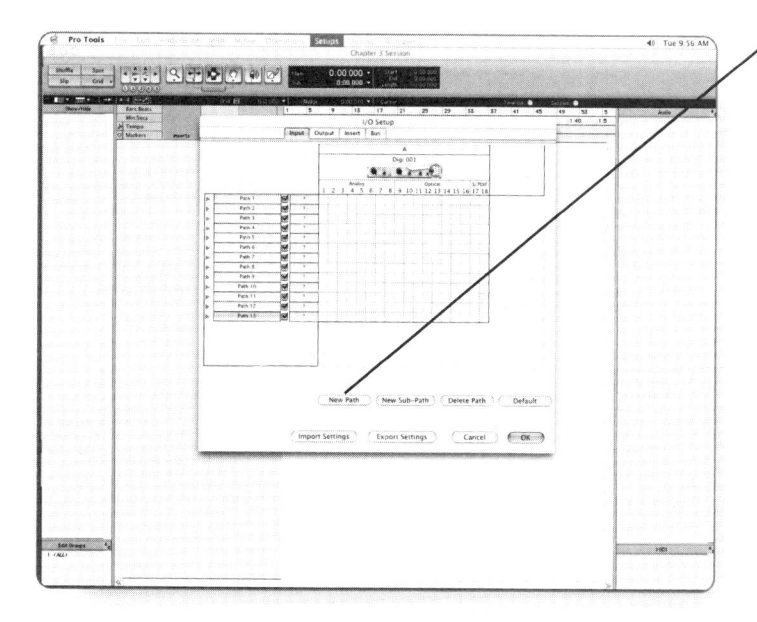

4. Click on **New Path**. A single new path will appear with the default name of "Path 1."

5. Click on **New Path** twelve more times. Additional paths will be created, again with default names.

CHAPTER 3: GETTING STARTED WITH AUDIO

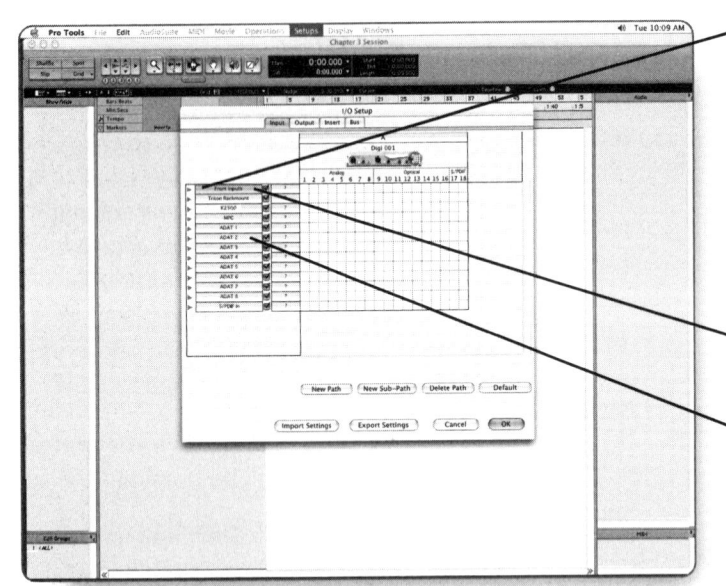

6. Although you've created input paths, they haven't been configured or assigned to physical inputs on your interface yet. That's your next job. **Double-click** on the top **path name**. The path name will be highlighted.

7. Type a descriptive **name** for this path.

8. Repeat steps 6 and 7 for the other applicable default paths, naming each input descriptively.

TIP

A good rule of thumb is to name your inputs for the devices that are connected to your system. As you list these devices, keep track of which inputs are coming from stereo sources and which are from mono sources—it'll come in handy later!

9. Select any unused **paths** and **click** on **Delete Path**. The unused paths will be deleted.

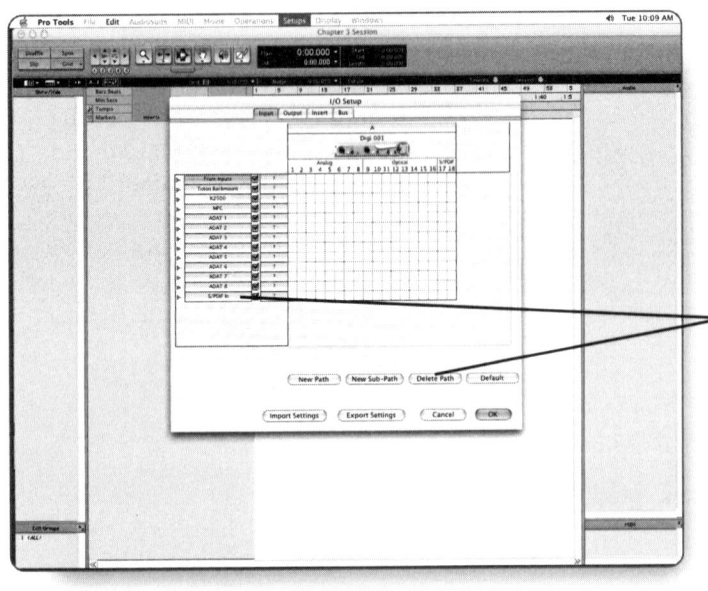

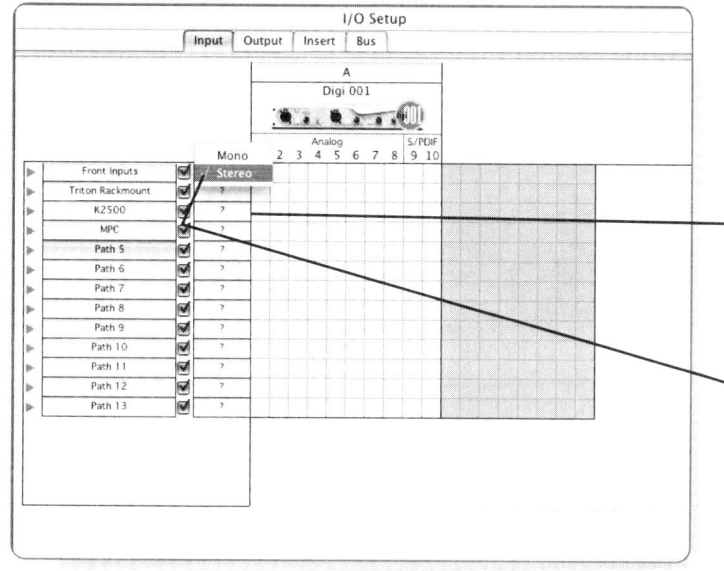

CUSTOMIZING YOUR SESSION: THE I/O SETUP DIALOG BOX

Configuring a Path as Stereo or Mono

Now you need to configure each path as either stereo or mono.

1. Click on the **question mark (?)** to the right of a path name. A path type drop-down menu will appear.

2. Choose a **type** for each path (stereo or mono). The type will be selected.

NOTE

In this case, the first four paths represent connections to stereo devices, the next eight represent the eight individual channels in an ADAT lightpipe connection, and the final path represents a stereo S/PDIF connection. By the way, an ADAT lightpipe connection, included in the Digi 001 and 002 systems (and the 002 Rackmount), is commonly used not only with ADATs, but with any gear that supports a digital ADAT lightpipe connection.

Assigning Your Path

Now it's time to assign your path (in this case, Front Inputs) to specific inputs of your audio interface (in this case, Analog 1 and 2).

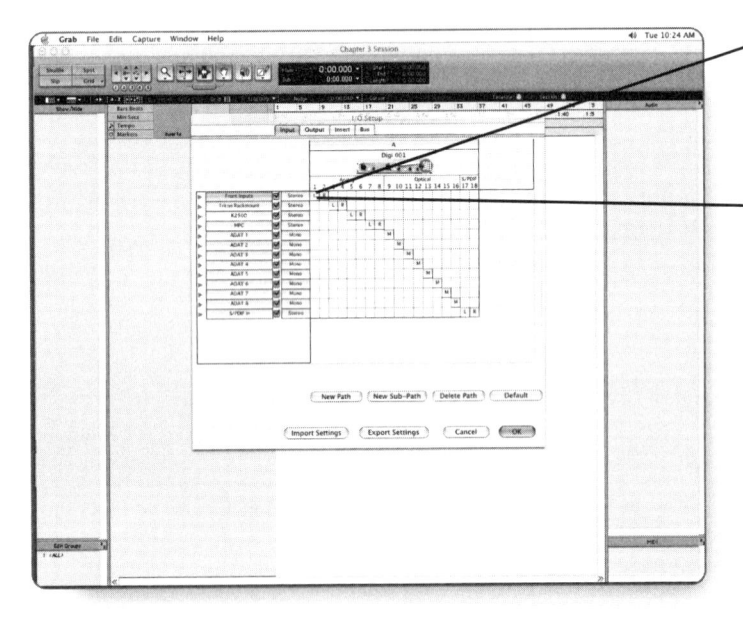

1. Move your **cursor** to the gridded area in the top row. Your cursor will change from an arrow to a pencil.

2. Click in the **square** that matches the output you desire. Because this happens to be a stereo path, two blocks will appear, marked L and R (for left and right).

3. Repeat Step 2 for all your paths.

> **NOTE**
> In the case of a stereo path, click on the square that is assigned to the left channel.

Setting Up Sub-Paths

You've set up your paths, and now it's time to think about sub-paths. *Sub-paths* are individual assignments within a path. For example, take a look at the first path you worked with—Front Inputs. If you have a stereo signal going into those two inputs, you're all set; however, if you want to use each input separately, you should consider setting up a couple of sub-paths within that stereo path.

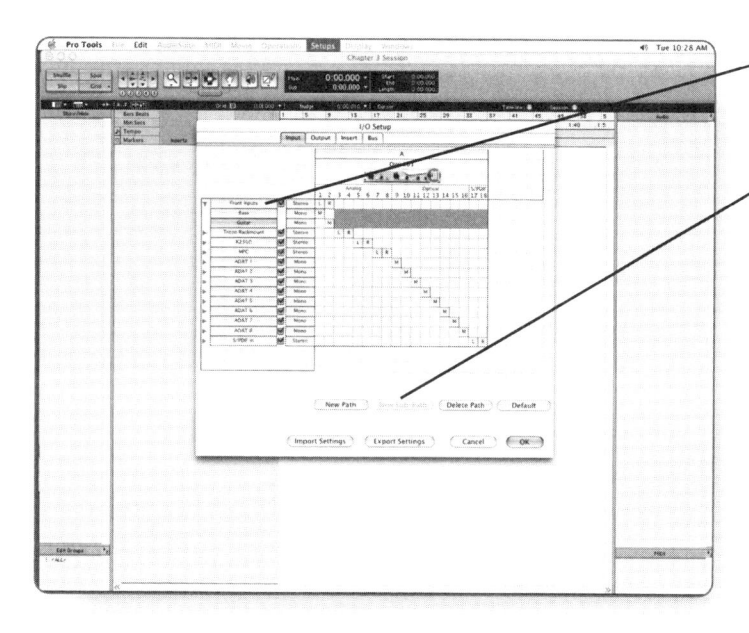

CUSTOMIZING YOUR SESSION: THE I/O SETUP DIALOG BOX 63

1. Click on the first **stereo path name**. The name will be highlighted.

2. Click twice on **New Sub-Path**. Two sub-paths will be created below the first path, with default names (Path 1 and Path 2).

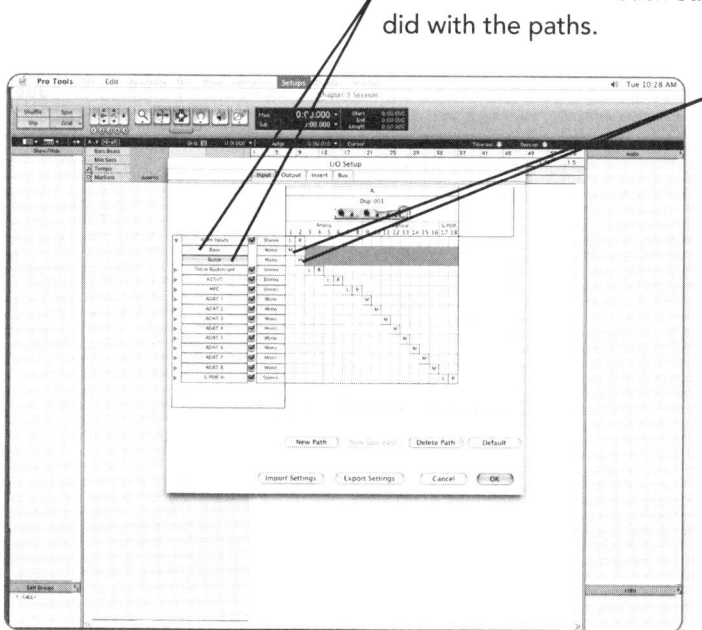

3. Double-click on each **sub-path** and **name it**, just like you did with the paths.

4. As you did with the paths, you need to assign a physical input to each sub-path. **Click** on the desired **grid square**. A block with an M (for mono) will appear.

Changing a Path's Input

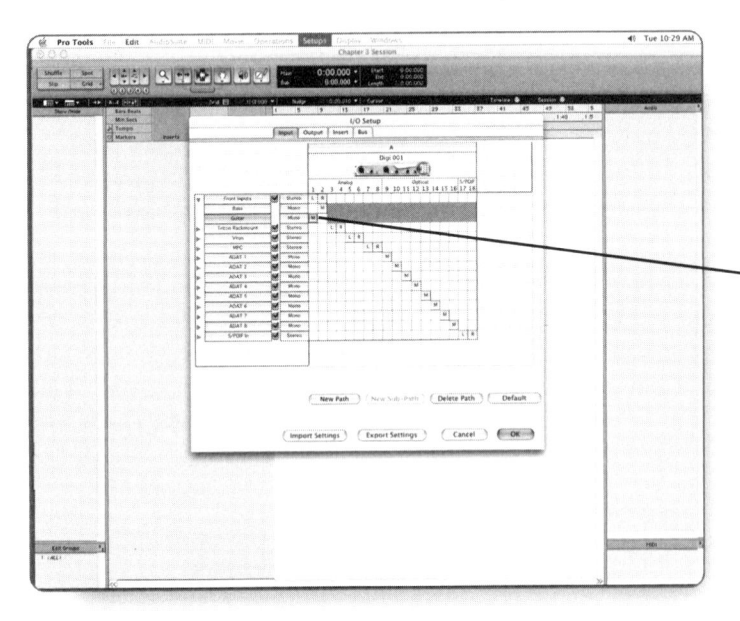

Once you've created a path (or sub-path) and assigned a physical interface input to that path, you're all set. But what if you want to change the input of a specific path? Not a problem.

1. Click and hold the **block** you want to change.

2. Drag the **block** until it is directly beneath the desired input.

3. Release the **mouse button**. The path's input block will be moved to the selected interface input.

Setting Up Outputs

You've set up your system to deal with incoming audio—good job! The next step is to customize how audio exits your audio interface. The good news is that the Output tab of the I/O Setup dialog box is laid out similarly to the Input tab, so this should go a lot quicker!

1. Click on the **Output tab** in the I/O Setup dialog box. The tab will move to the front.

2. Double-click on the first **output path name** and **type Main Output**. (This is the same method you used to name input paths.) The path will be renamed.

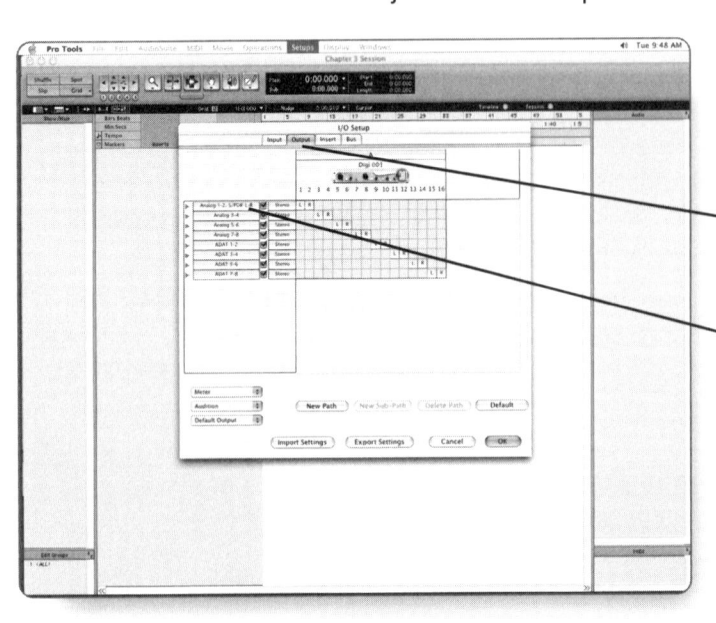

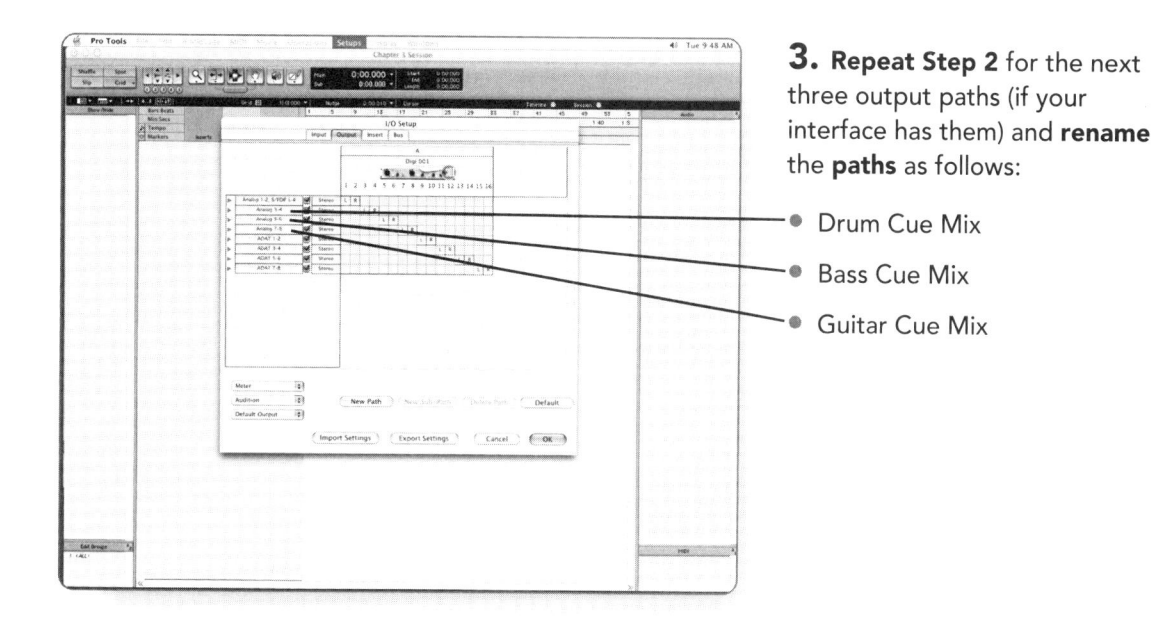

CUSTOMIZING YOUR SESSION: THE I/O SETUP DIALOG BOX

3. Repeat Step 2 for the next three output paths (if your interface has them) and **rename** the **paths** as follows:

- Drum Cue Mix
- Bass Cue Mix
- Guitar Cue Mix

> **NOTE**
>
> This kind of a setup is pretty common for stereo projects. In this case, you would typically use Main Output for your studio monitors. Use the Cue Mix outputs for individual headphone mixes for your recording musicians. Remember, though, that these are all line-level signals and they will need amplification before they go to speakers. Keep in mind also that different interfaces have different numbers (and types) of outputs, and might not have enough free outputs for cue mixes, so it's a good idea to check your interface's documentation for specific information.

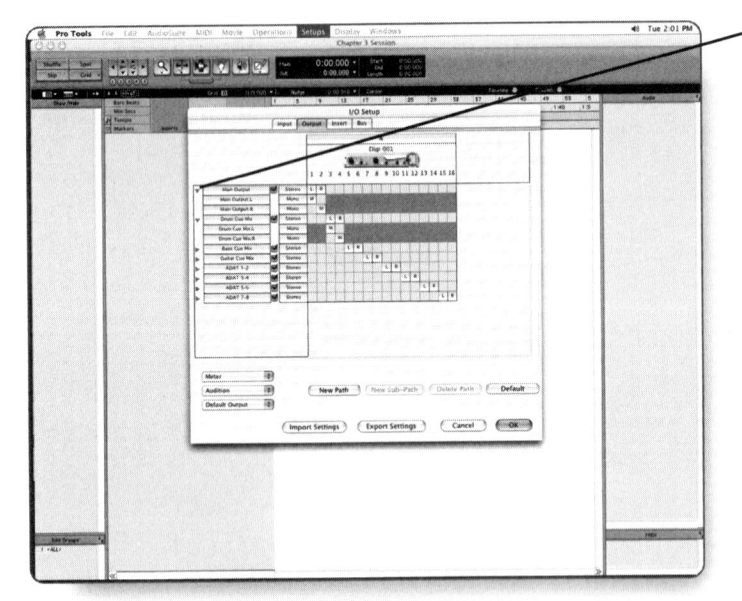

4. Click on the **arrow** to the left of each path to show any existing sub-paths it contains. Because you simply renamed the paths that existed in the first place, each stereo path should have a couple of sub-paths.

> **NOTE**
>
> Here's a rule about paths and sub-paths that is particularly relevant to inputs and outputs: Paths cannot overlap. (In other words, two active paths cannot both use the same physical output.) Sub-paths, on the other hand, *can* overlap.

Setting Up Inserts

In the world of DAWs, you'll be able to use software effects (reverbs, delays, and so on) called *plug-ins*. Does that mean you won't be able to use the rackmount effects you've got in your studio? Nope—you can bring them into the Pro Tools environment through a hardware insert. You'll learn more about inserts and how to use them in Chapter 8, "Basic Mixing," when I talk about mixing.

One thing you need to know about hardware inserts now, though, is how to connect your gear. The rule is simple: Use the same number of inputs for the insert that you used for the outputs. For example, if you have a rackmount stereo reverb unit that you want to use with Pro Tools, you have to use a pair of outputs (for example, #15 and #16) to send a signal to the unit, and you have to use the same numbers (#15 and #16) on the input side to get audio from the reverb back to Pro Tools.

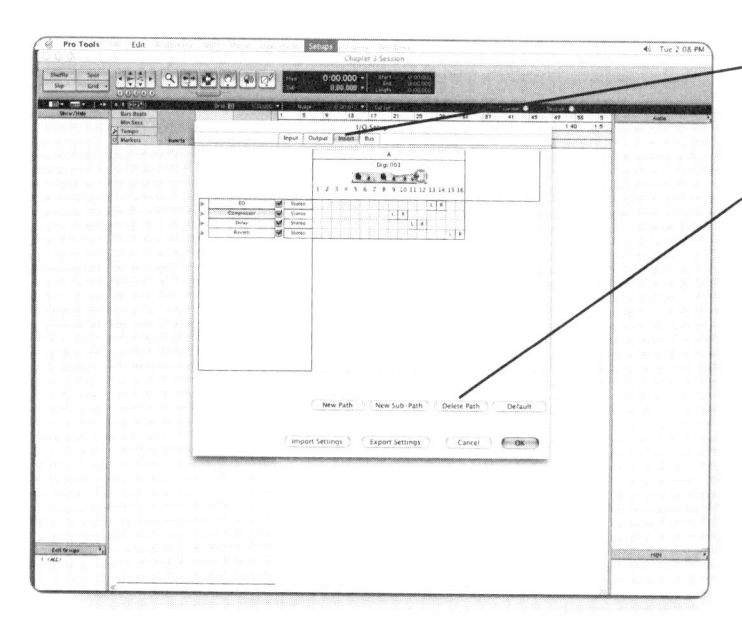

CUSTOMIZING YOUR SESSION: THE I/O SETUP DIALOG BOX 67

1. Click on the **Insert tab** in the I/O Setup dialog box. The tab will move to the front.

2. Click on every **path name** and **click** on **Delete Path**, just like you did with the inputs. The paths will be deleted.

> **TIP**
>
> Here's a shortcut for selecting all paths: Hold down the Option key (for Macs) or the Alt key (for Windows) and select just one path. All paths will be selected instantly!

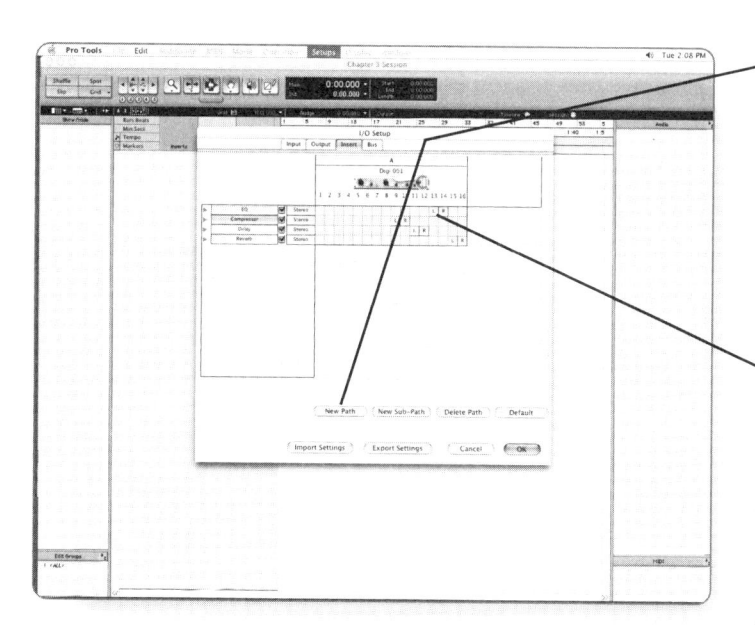

3. Click on **New Path** to create a new path for each of your effects units (if your audio interface has the available physical inputs and outputs to connect an effects unit) and **name** each **path** the same way you did on the Input and Output tabs.

4. Again using the same method you used for setting up your inputs and outputs, **assign** each **path** to the inputs/outputs to which your effect is connected. In this case, my EQ is connected to I/O #13 and #14. As mentioned before, you are setting an input and output pair, with the signal leaving your computer through an interface output and returning to the Pro Tools environment through the same numbered inputs.

> **NOTE**
> You don't have to set up paths sequentially. Although it is often convenient to arrange your paths linearly, you can assign inputs, outputs, inserts, and buses in any order you want.

> **TIP**
> It is possible to create an insert path that uses the same physical inputs and outputs you've already used on the Input and Output tabs. However, you must choose to use either the input and output paths or the insert path—you can't use both in a given session. You can choose to disable a path by removing the check mark from the check box to the right of the path name.

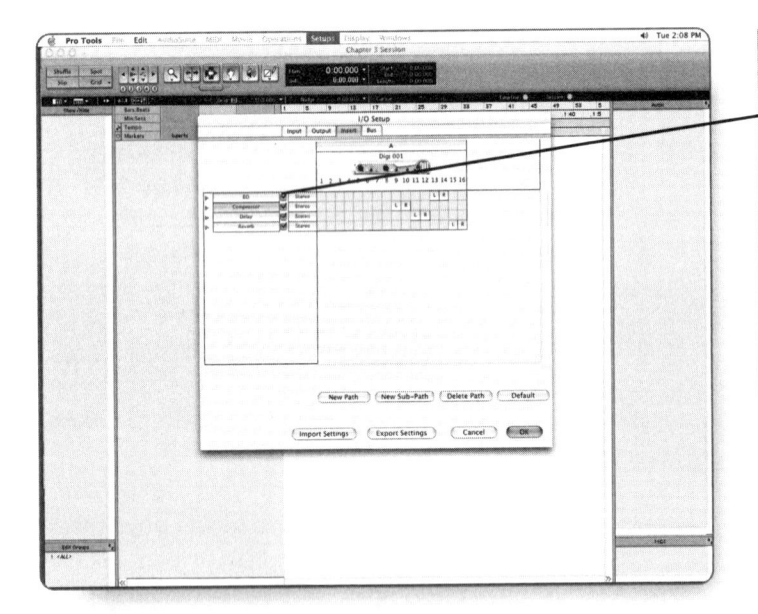

Setting Up Buses

Last but not least is the Bus tab. Buses are like virtual audio cables that you can use within the Pro Tools mixing environment. You'll use them for internal routing in Pro Tools, such as sending "dry" audio from an audio track to a reverb on an aux track. Don't worry if that sounds like Greek—you'll be doing this sort of thing in Chapter 8, using Pro Tools' trusty buses.

Often the default naming of the buses will suffice, and their generic names will suit their multipurpose functions.

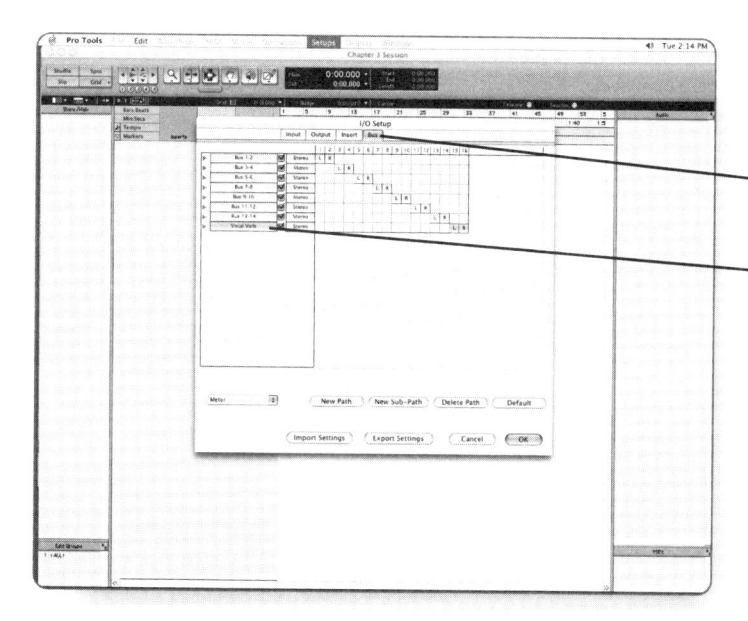

CUSTOMIZING YOUR SESSION: THE I/O SETUP DIALOG BOX

Sometimes, though, you might decide to name your buses more descriptively. Here's how:

1. Click on the **Bus tab**. The tab will move to the front.

2. Because buses are so multifunctional, you really don't need to name them all. In this case, just name the last pair so you know to reserve it to use later for your vocals. **Double-click** on the last **path name** and **type Vocal Verb**. The path will be renamed.

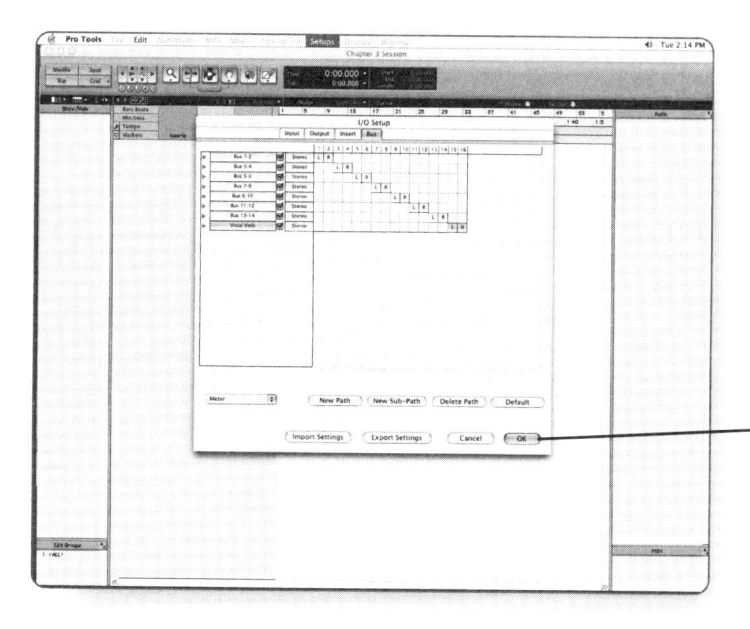

NOTE

Notice how this page is different from the others. There aren't any references to your interface's physical inputs or outputs at the top of the window. That's because your buses are only a part of your Pro Tools software!

3. Click on **OK**. The dialog box will close. You're finished!

CHAPTER 3: GETTING STARTED WITH AUDIO

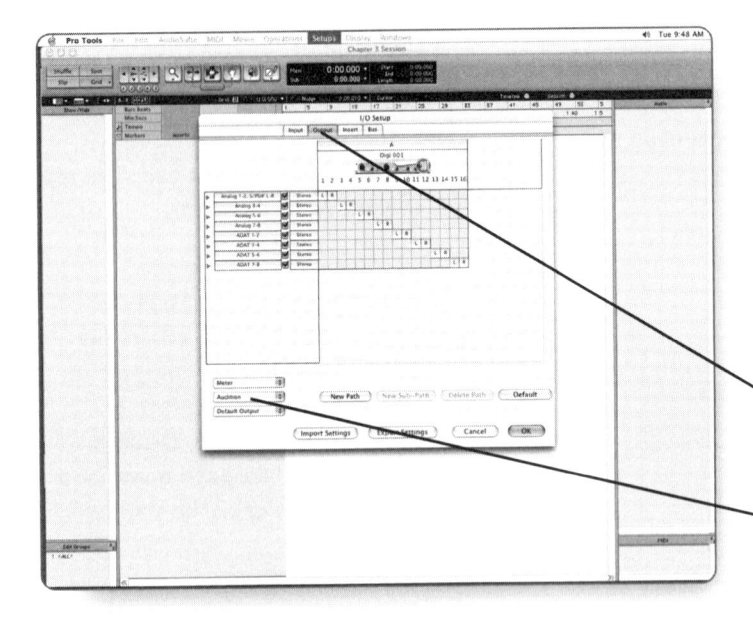

Managing Your I/O Settings

There are a couple useful settings in the lower-left corner of the Output tab. These are global settings that will determine the performance of certain physical outputs.

1. Click on the **Output tab** in the I/O Settings dialog box. The tab will move to the front.

2. Click on the **Audition button**. A drop-down menu of your output's paths will appear.

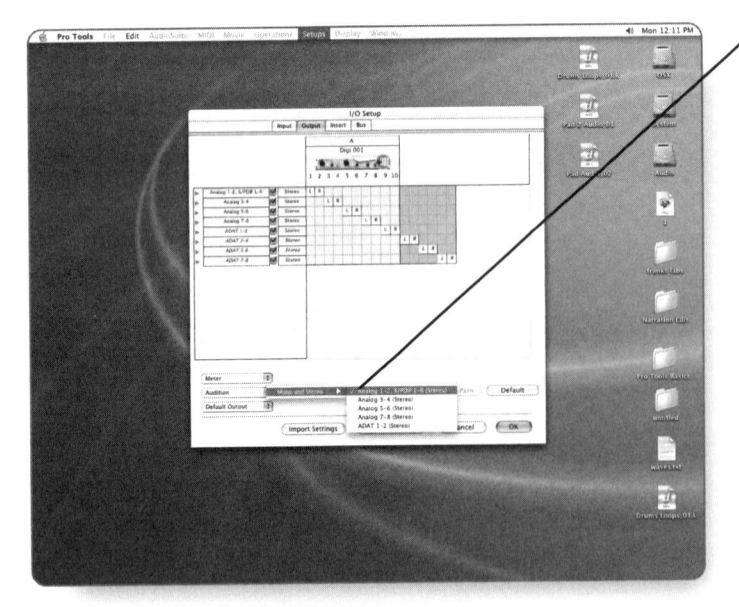

3. Choose the **output** you want to use to listen to audio files *before* you import them into your session. The output will be selected.

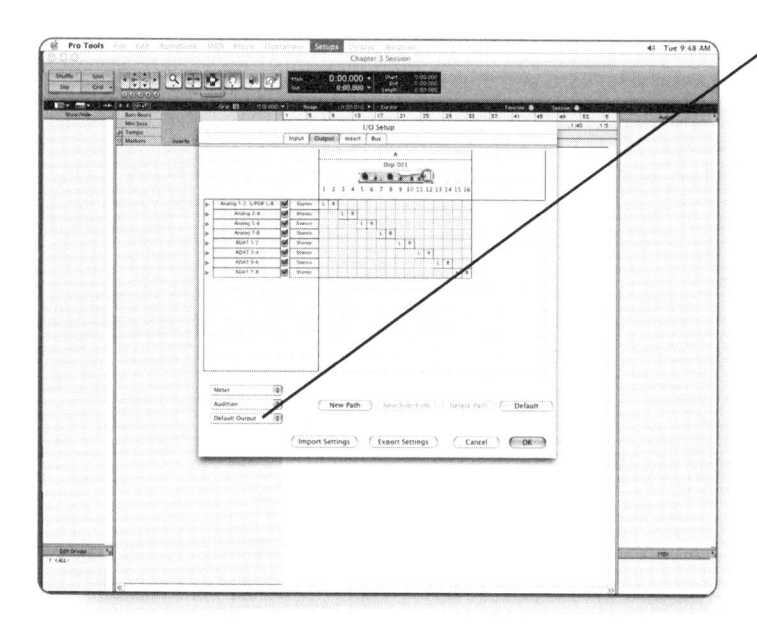

CUSTOMIZING YOUR SESSION: THE I/O SETUP DIALOG BOX   71

4. Click on the **Default Output button**. Another drop-down menu of your output's paths will appear.

5. Choose the **output** you want to be the default output for newly created tracks. The output will be selected.

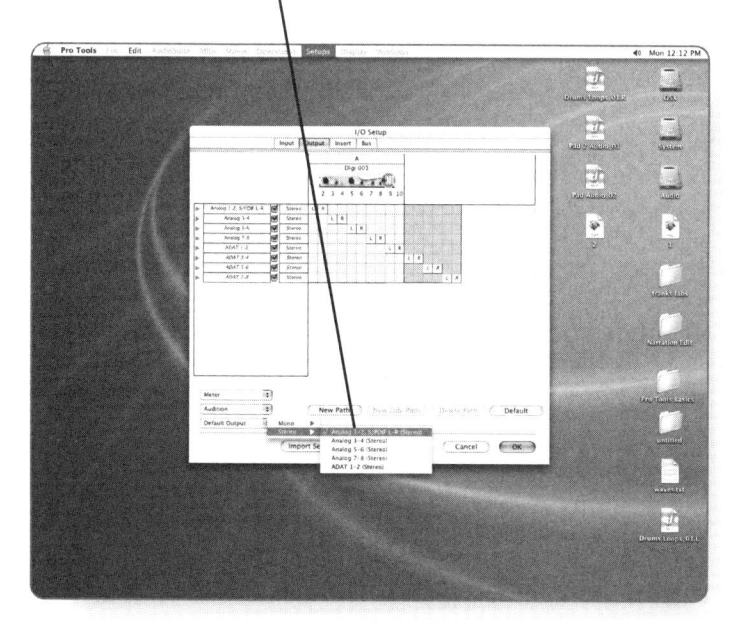

TIP

Usually, you'll choose the output path connected to your studio monitor for the Audition and Default Output features.

NOTE

The Meter setting determines the output path that will be displayed on Digidesign's Pro Control, a high-end control surface for Pro Tools (generally associated with TDM systems).

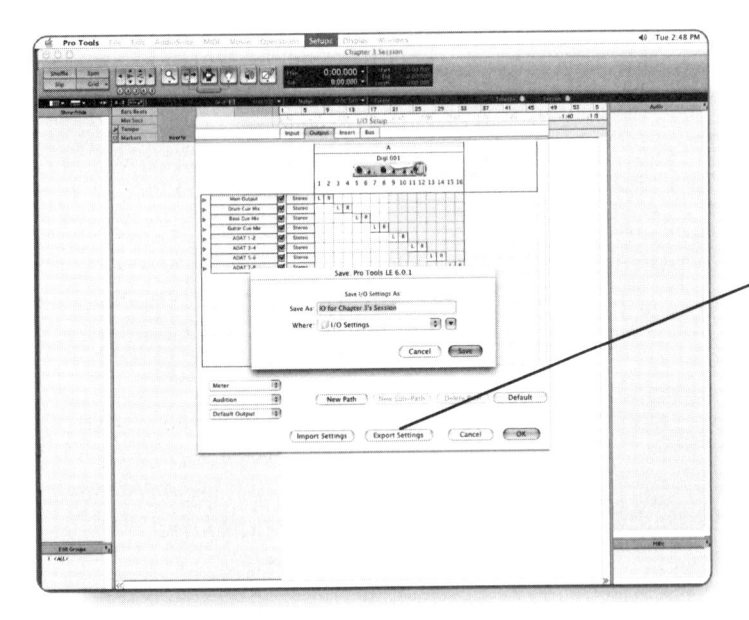

Saving Your I/O Settings

You'll want to save your I/O settings if you plan to use the same ones in another session.

1. Click on **Export Settings**. The Save dialog box will open.

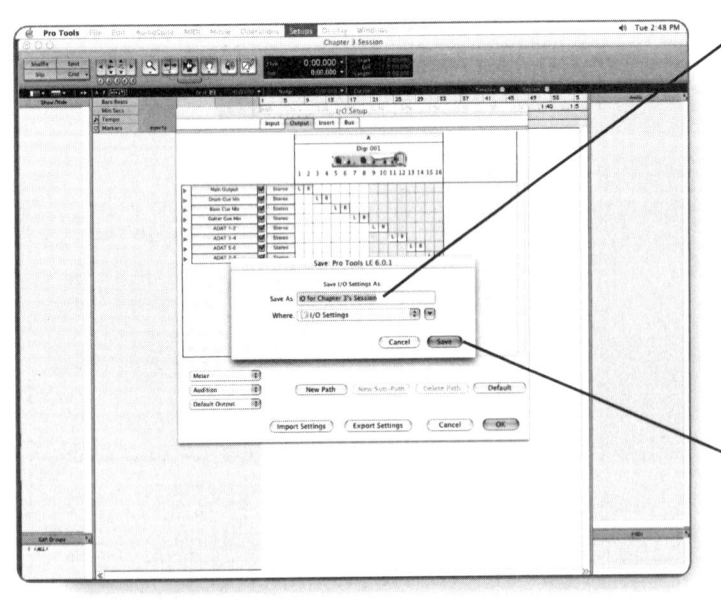

2. Type a **name** for these settings in the Save As text box.

TIP

Choose a descriptive name for your settings so you can recall them easily when you want to use them for another session.

3. Click on **Save**. Your settings will be saved.

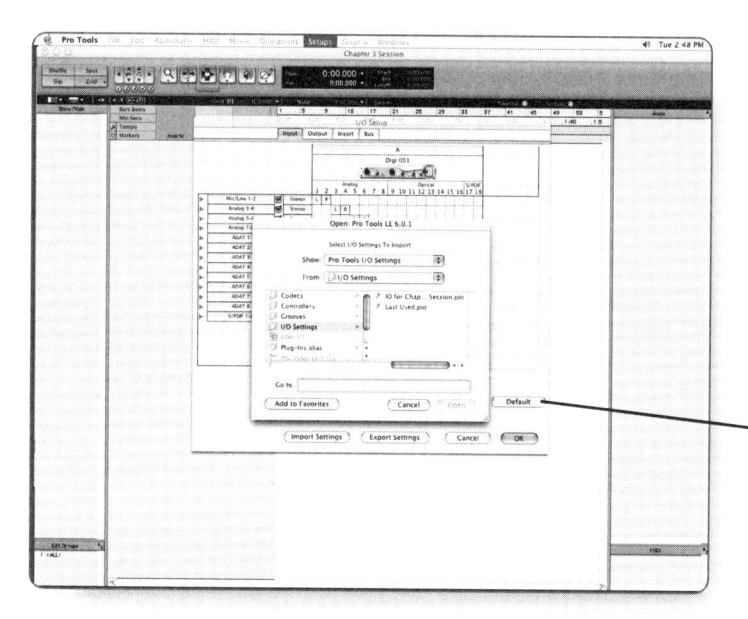

CUSTOMIZING YOUR SESSION: THE I/O SETUP DIALOG BOX

Recovering Your Settings

Once you've customized and exported your I/O settings, you can always recall them. In this exercise, you'll change your paths to their default names and then reload your previously saved settings.

1. Click on the **Default button**. Your paths and labels will be reset to their most basic names and assignments for the displayed page.

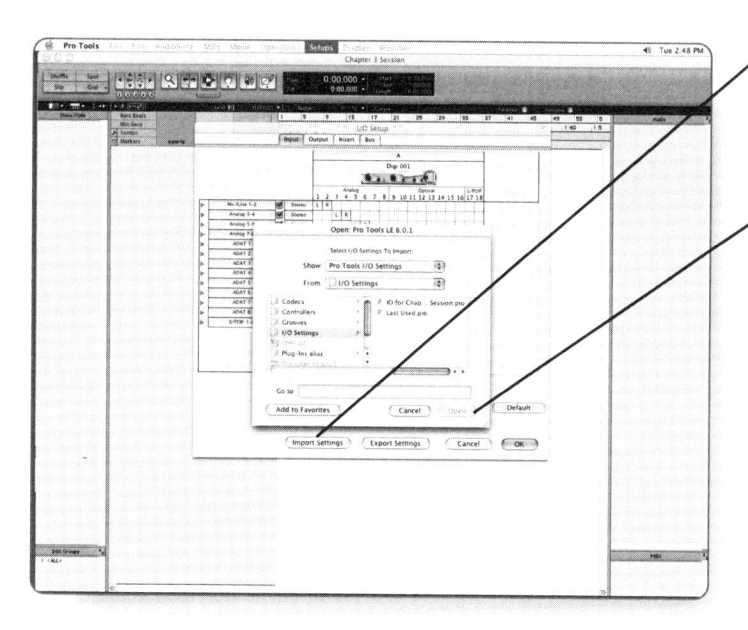

2. To load previously saved I/O settings, **click** on the **Import Settings button**. The Open dialog box will open.

3. Select the desired **I/O settings** and then **click** on **Open**. The I/O settings you selected will be loaded.

> **TIP**
>
> There's another benefit to exporting your tweaked I/O settings: When you create a new session, your new setup will be an option in the I/O Settings drop-down menu when creating new sessions.

CHAPTER 3: GETTING STARTED WITH AUDIO

Creating Tracks

Whether you're looking at the Edit window or the Mix window, you'll notice that your new session opened without any tracks in it. It's up to you to create the tracks you'll need in your session.

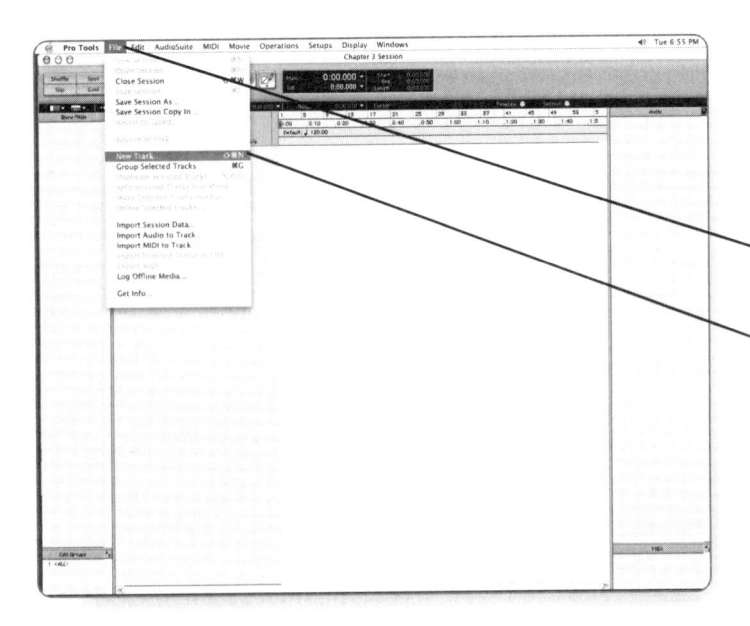

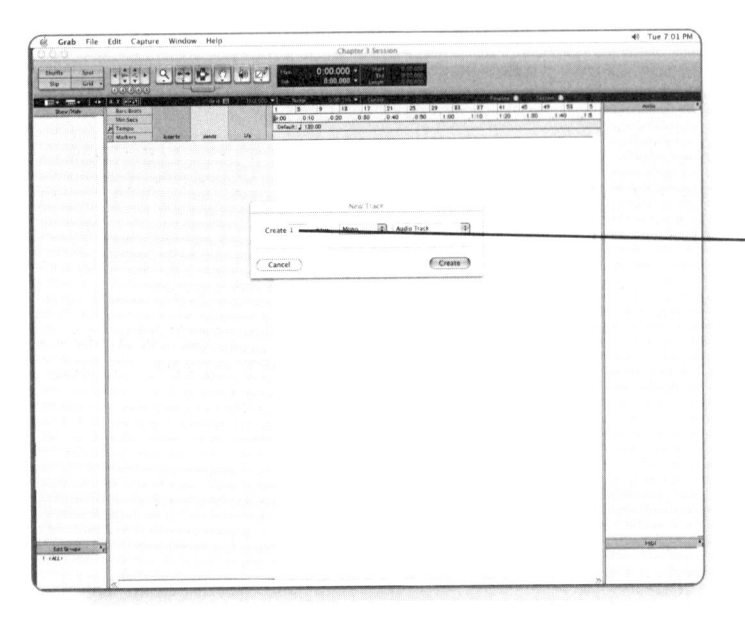

Making Tracks

No matter what kind of track you want to create, you'll start by following the same first few steps.

1. **Click** on **File**. The File menu will appear.

2. **Click** on **New Track**. The New Track dialog box will open.

> **TIP**
>
> Because you'll be making many tracks as you work more and more in Pro Tools, you might want to learn the shortcuts. Shift+⌘+N (Mac) or Shift+Ctrl+N (PC) will call up the New Track dialog box.

3. The dialog box is set up right now to create one mono audio track. For this example, you want to create four tracks instead. **Double-click** in the **Create field** to highlight it (if it isn't already highlighted) and then **type 4** for the number of tracks you want to create.

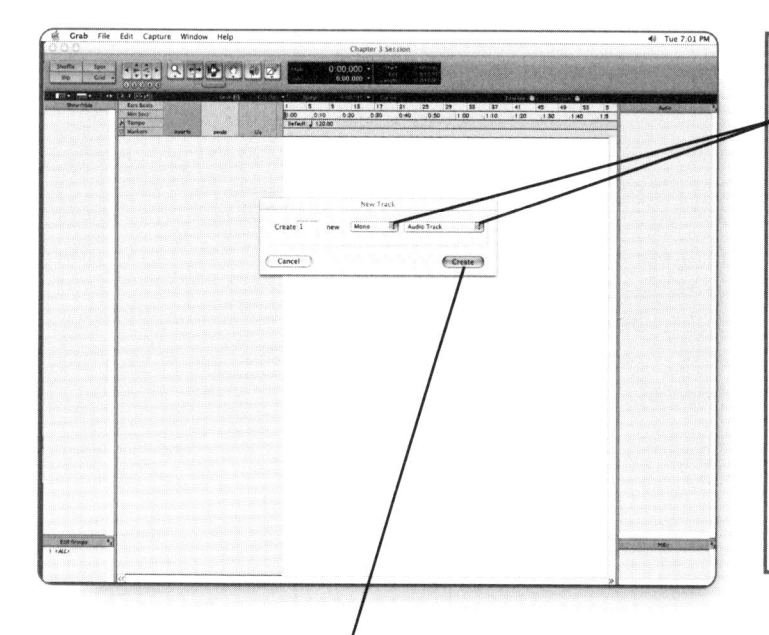

CREATING TRACKS   75

NOTE
The first drop-down menu allows you to specify whether your track will be stereo or mono. The second drop-down menu allows you to select the kind of track you will create. You'll learn more about the different types of tracks available in Pro Tools (such as audio, aux, MIDI, and master fader) and how to use them later.

4. Click on **Create**. The New Track dialog box will close and the tracks will be created in your session.

Now you can create a couple of stereo audio tracks.

1. Open the **New Track dialog box** as you did in the previous section.

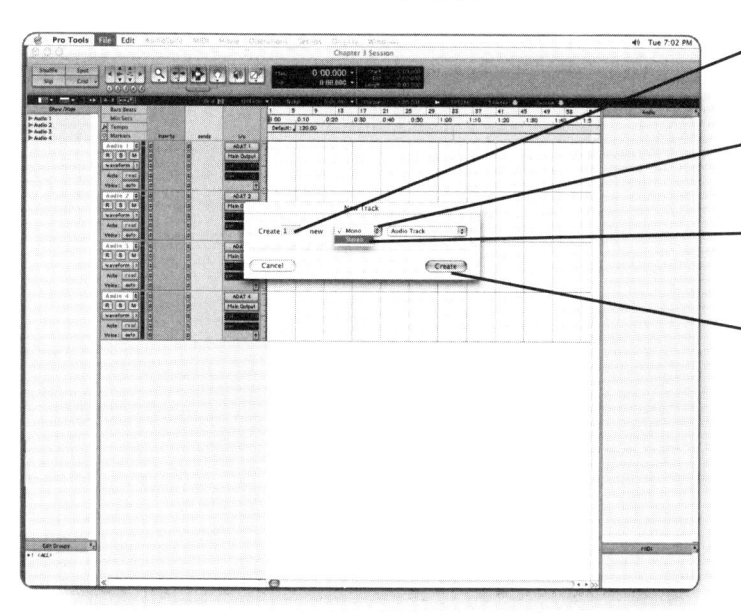

2. Type 2 in the Create field to create two tracks.

3. Click on the first **drop-down menu**. The menu will appear.

4. Click on **Stereo**. The option will be selected.

5. Click on **Create**. Two stereo audio tracks will be created, just as you specified.

Creating an Aux Input

An Aux Input (sometimes called an Aux Track) is similar to an audio track in many respects, except it doesn't use any audio regions. Its main function is to serve as a means of routing audio from a source to a destination or as a place to process one or more audio signals with plug-in effects. You'll learn how to use aux tracks later in this book, and you'll find that knowledge very handy, particularly when you get down to the business of mixing. The process of creating aux tracks is almost identical to creating audio tracks.

1. **Open** the **New Track dialog box** as you did in the previous sections.

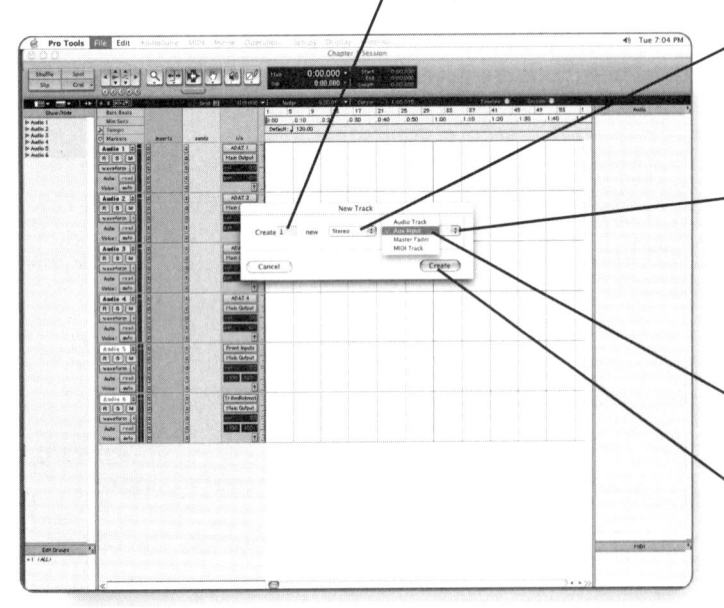

2. **Type 2** in the Create field to create two tracks.

3. **Click** on **Stereo** in the first drop-down menu to make these aux tracks stereo. The option will be selected.

4. **Click** on the **second drop-down menu**. A list of all the different types of tracks that you can create in Pro Tools will appear.

5. **Click** on **Aux Input**. The option will be selected.

6. **Click** on **Create**. Two stereo aux tracks will be created, just as you specified.

Master Faders and MIDI Tracks

As you probably noticed, there are two other types of tracks listed in the track type drop-down menu—master fader and MIDI tracks. Although you might not use these kinds of tracks in every session you create, they will be very useful when you need them.

If you've ever worked with a traditional mixing board, you know what master faders can do. These are the faders that control the overall volume of your entire mix after you have blended all the individual tracks. A master fader in Pro Tools does pretty much the same thing. Simply put, it is a fader that controls the overall volume of a given output path. It will also allow you to add plug-in effects to the entire mix at once.

There's one important thing to remember about MIDI Tracks—MIDI is **not** audio. Rather, it is a digital language that allows different musical devices to communicate, somewhat like a network. You can record (and then edit) MIDI data on a MIDI track in Pro Tools. When combined with Pro Tools' powerful set of audio features, this will open new creative doors!

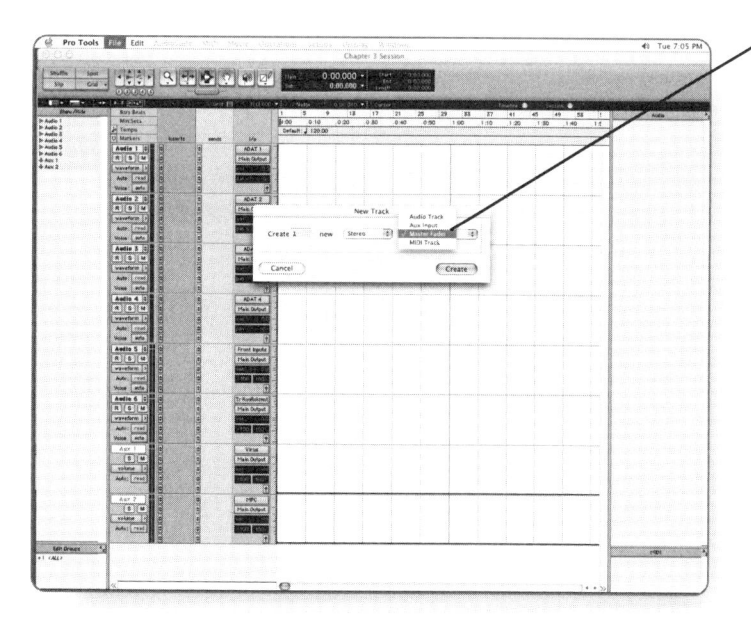

The method of creating a master fader or a MIDI track is almost identical to creating any other kind of track. The only difference is that you'll choose Master Fader or MIDI Track. Just for practice, try creating one new stereo master fader.

> **NOTE**
>
> When you choose to create a MIDI track, you'll notice that there is no stereo or mono option available. Don't worry, it's not a malfunction of Pro Tools—it's because MIDI isn't audio, so the terms *stereo* and *mono* don't really apply in this case.

Naming Your Tracks

One of the most important (maybe *the* most important) aspects of working in a DAW is documentation. Keeping track of your sessions, files, tracks, patches, and so on is absolutely critical, especially as your sessions become more complex.

When Pro Tools creates a new track, it assigns a generic name (such as Audio 1) as a default. Descriptively naming your tracks is a big part of session documentation—and the good news is, it's easy!

1. Double-click on the **name** of the track you want to rename. A dialog box will open.

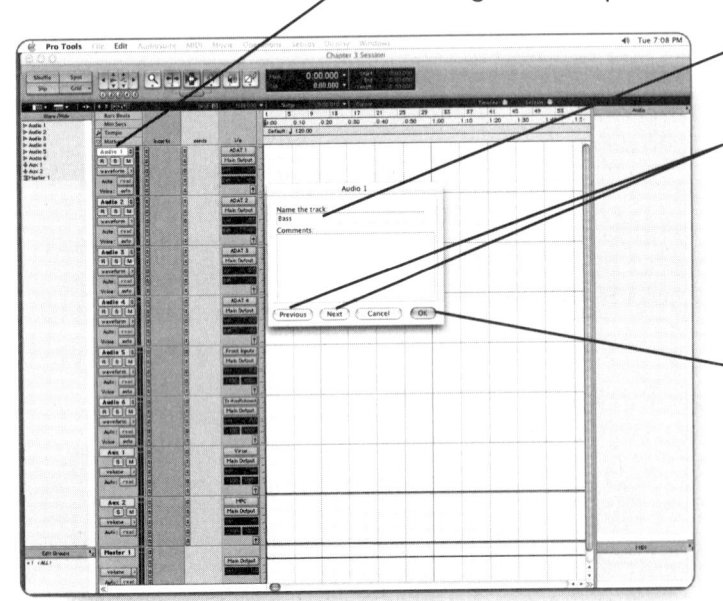

2. Type a **name** for the track in the Name the track field.

3. If you want to continue naming tracks, **click** on **Previous** to name the track above the current track or **click** on **Next** to name the track below the current track.

4. When you're finished naming tracks, **click** on **OK**. The dialog box will close.

NOTE

If you've been following along with this chapter's examples, you should have four mono audio tracks, two stereo audio tracks, two stereo aux tracks, and one stereo master fader. To keep the ball rolling, name each of the tracks as follows: Bass, Guitar, Vocal, Sax, Drums, Synth, Vocal Reverb Aux, Drum Reverb, and Master Volume.

Moving Tracks

After you've assigned names to all your tracks, you'll want to organize them so that related tracks are near each other. Although moving tracks around in the Edit or Mix window won't change how they play back in any way, a logical arrangement of tracks can make the entire production process much easier. There aren't any hard-and-fast rules on how to arrange your tracks—each session is unique, and you have to decide how to arrange your tracks so they make sense to you.

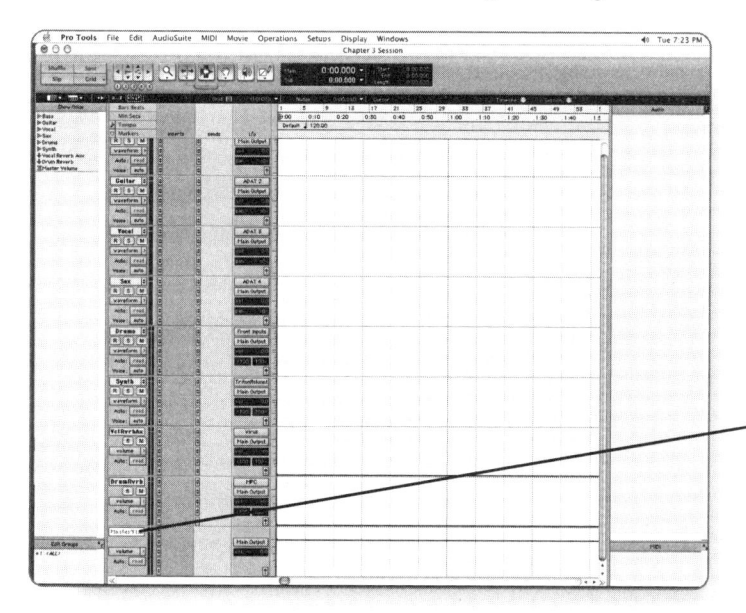

1. Click and hold on a **track name** in the edit area of the Edit window. The track will be selected.

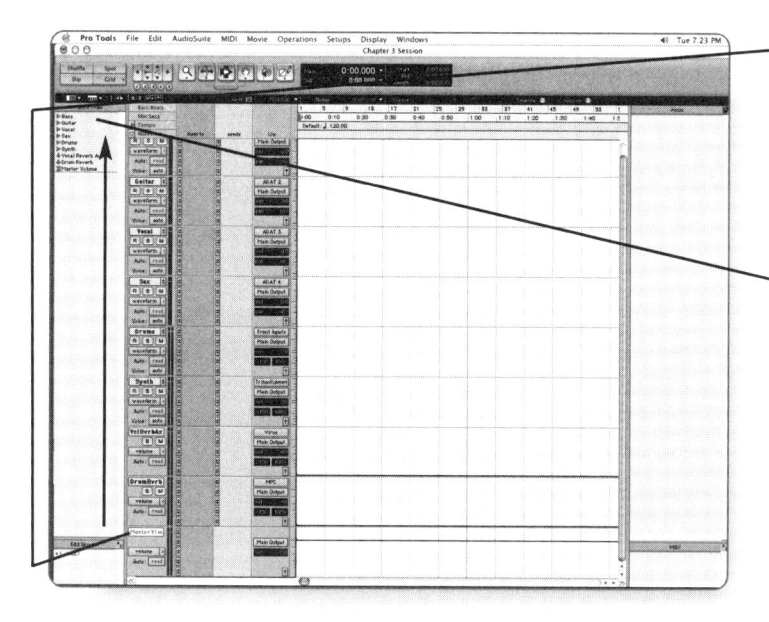

2. Drag the **track** up or down to the desired location. As you drag the track, a thin line will appear, indicating the position the track will assume when it is dropped in its new location.

3. Release the **mouse button** when you have the track at the desired location. The tracks in your session will be reorganized.

CHAPTER 3: GETTING STARTED WITH AUDIO

> **TIP**
>
> Here's another way to do it: Click and hold on the track name in the Track Show/Hide list. A thin line will appear below the track name you have selected, indicating that it's ready to be moved. Drag the track up or down to the desired position. (The thin line will move, indicating where the track will be moved.) When you release the mouse button, your tracks will be reordered.

> **NOTE**
>
> In the Mix window, you click and hold to drag any track to a new location. Of course, instead of dragging up or down, you drag left or right.

> **NOTE**
>
> The Mix window reflects any rearrangement of tracks you make in the Edit window. Tracks are listed in the Edit window from top to bottom; in the Mix window, they're displayed from left to right.

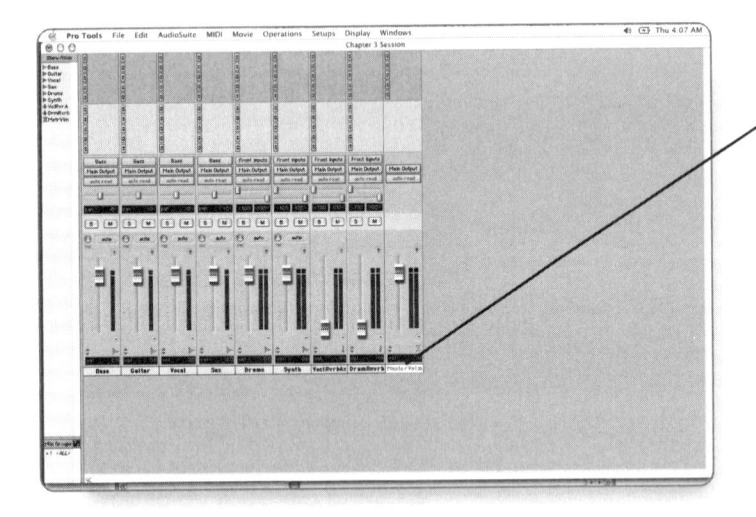

Importing Audio

While you can certainly record live audio in Pro Tools (it wouldn't be much of an audio workstation if you couldn't!), that's not the only way to get sounds into Pro Tools. Indeed, one of the great advantages of a computer-based DAW is that you can import digital audio files into a preexisting project, bypassing the recording process entirely! In Pro Tools LE, there are a number of ways to do this.

Importing into the Audio Regions List

First, try importing an audio file to the Audio Regions list (also commonly called the Audio Regions Bin). Once you've imported to the Audio Regions list, you will be able to use the audio in any suitable audio track.

Choosing Where to Import Audio From

The first thing you need to do is locate the file you want to import into Pro Tools.

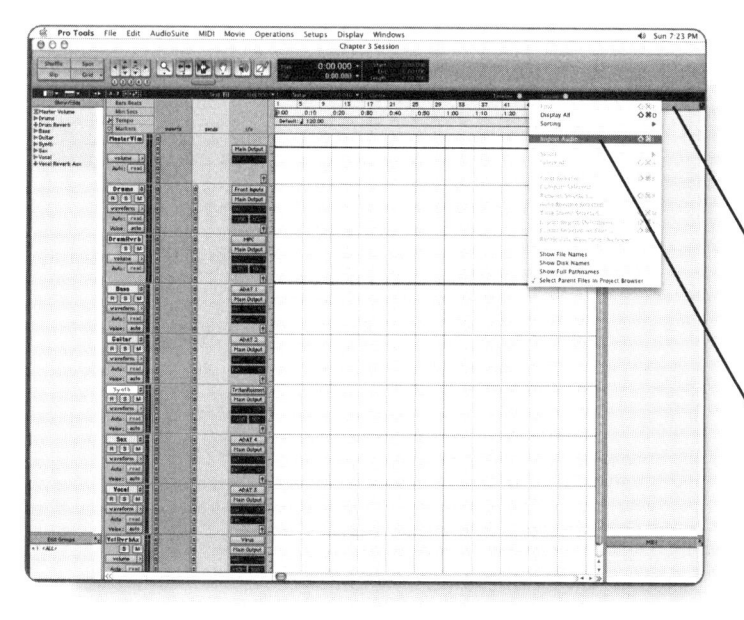

1. Choose Show Edit from the Windows menu to display the Edit window, if it's not already open. The Edit window will be displayed.

2. Click on the **Audio button** at the top of the Audio Regions list. The Audio Regions List drop-down menu will appear.

3. Choose Import Audio. The Import Audio dialog box will open.

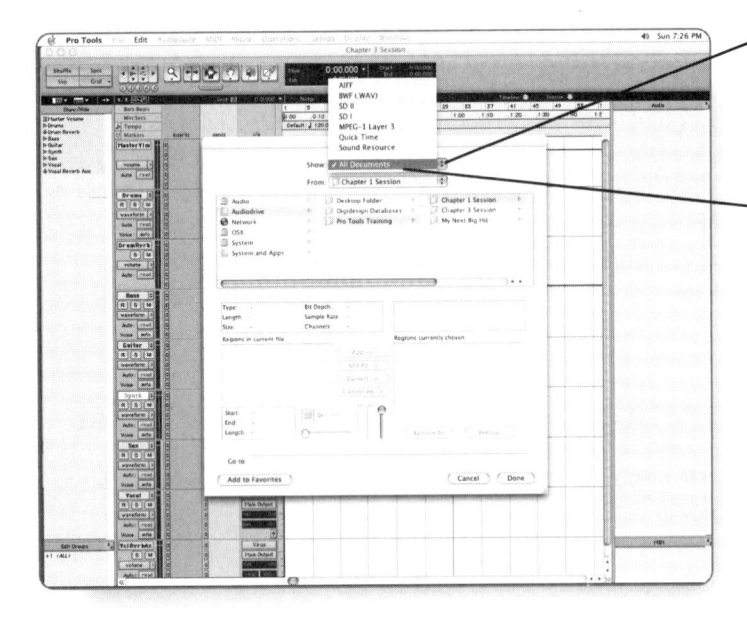

4. Now it's time to choose an audio file to import into your session. **Click** on the **Show button**. A menu will appear.

5. Select All Documents to show all audio files that are compatible with Pro Tools. The option will be selected.

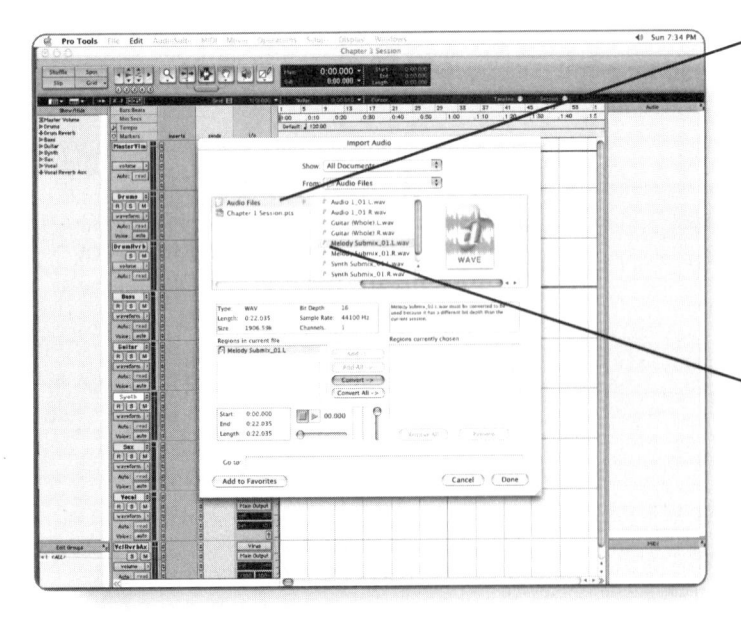

6. Now you're ready to find the audio file you want to use. In this case, you'll be importing some audio from the session you used in Chapter 1. **Navigate** to the **folder** in which you saved the audio you used in Chapter 1. The audio files in that folder will be displayed.

7. Click on the **audio file** you want to import into your Pro Tools session. The file will be selected.

NOTE

The Import Audio dialog box gives you relevant information regarding the file you select.

IMPORTING AUDIO

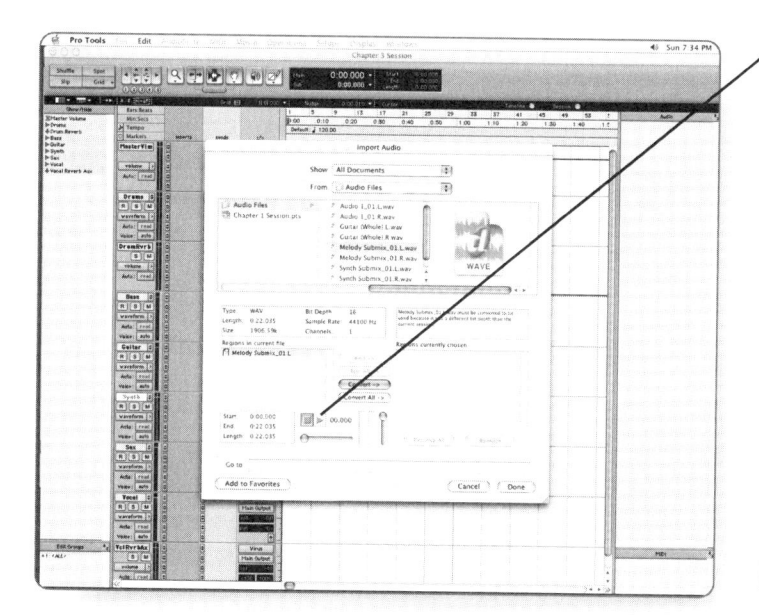

8. Click on the **Play button** to preview your selected file. The file will begin to play.

> **TIP**
>
> If you don't hear your selection, you might want to check the Audition setting in the I/O Setup dialog box. Review the "Managing Your I/O Settings" section earlier in this chapter for more information.

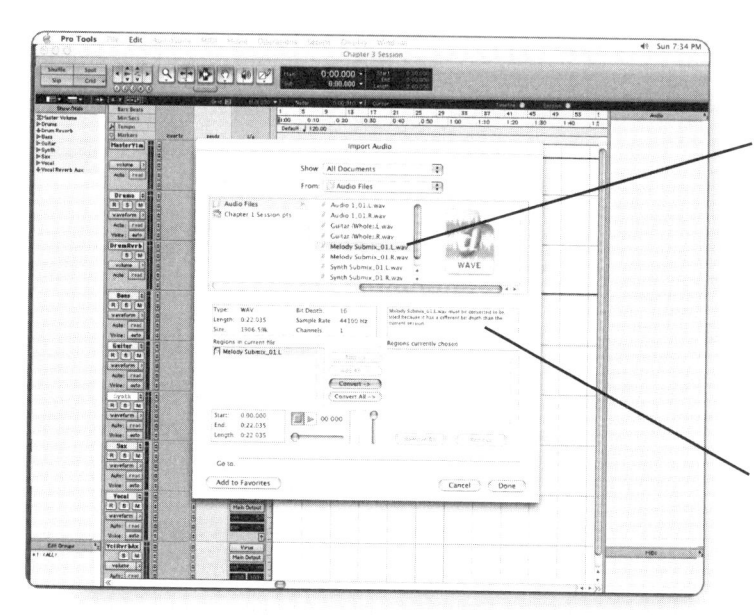

Before you proceed, you should notice a couple things:

- This file has .L listed before the file extension (in this case, it's a .WAV file). This indicates that the file is the left half of a stereo track. The Melody Submix_01.R.wav file is listed right below this file. These two files together are elements of a stereo audio track.

- Pro Tools cannot mix and match sample rates and/or bit depths within a single session. This box indicates that the file does not match the bit depth of the session you're presently working on, and so you will need to convert it to a matching bit depth.

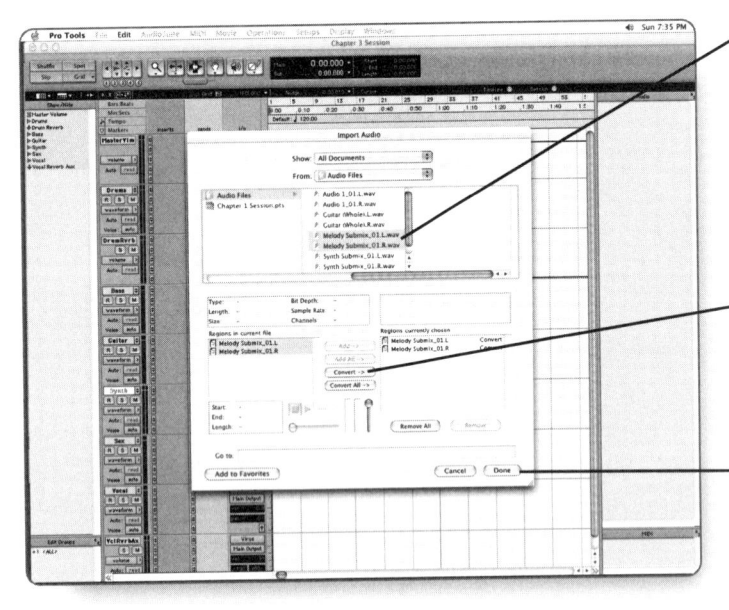

9. Because this file is only half of a stereo track, you'll probably want to import its mate. **Press and hold** the **Shift key** and **click** on the **additional audio file** to select it as well. Both files will be selected.

10. Click on **Convert** to convert both files. Both files will appear in the Regions currently chosen list.

11. Click on **Done** when you're finished. The Choose a Folder dialog box will open, and you're ready to move on to the next step!

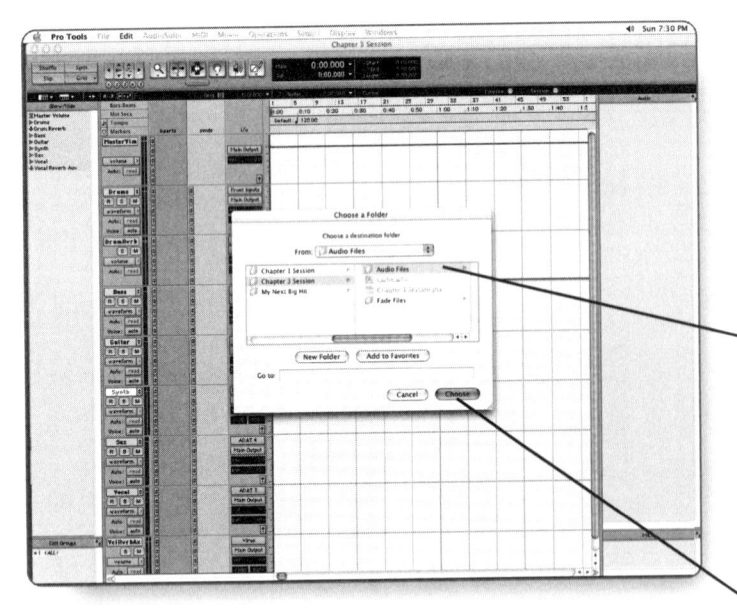

Choosing Where to Import Audio To

Now that you've decided where to import the audio from, it's time to choose the location where the converted files will be stored.

1. In the Choose a Folder dialog box, **select** the **folder** in which you want to save your converted files. In this case, you'll want to store these files in the Audio Files subfolder of the session in which you're working.

2. Click on **Choose**. The audio file will be imported into your session.

IMPORTING AUDIO 85

> **TIP**
>
> Mac users regularly fall into a little trap during this last phase of importing. Often, they are tempted to open the folder, and then try to save the file in it. In this particular case, you just choose the folder itself, simply by highlighting it. The file will automatically be saved inside it.

You'll notice that although the audio file is imported into the Audio Regions list, there is no audio region visible on any of the tracks that you created. Don't worry—that's the way this method of importing is supposed to function. Later, you'll drag this audio file onto an audio track and use it as a sounding element for your session.

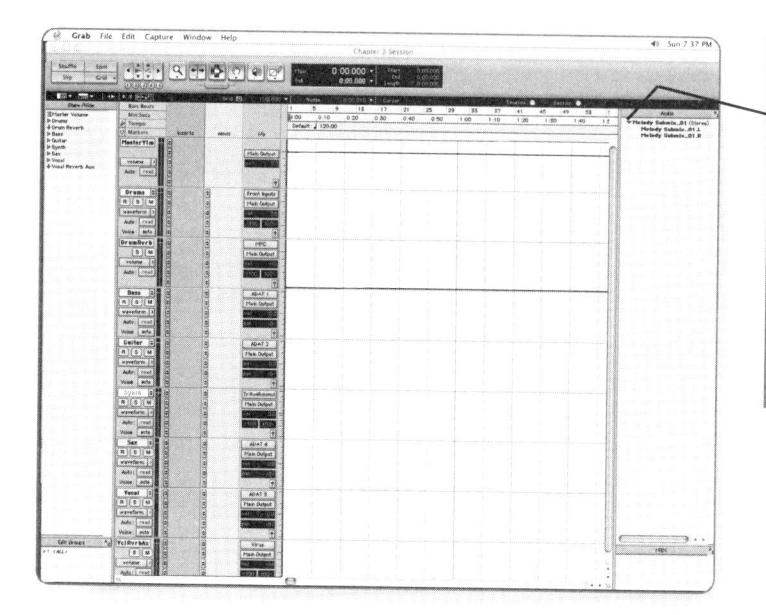

> **TIP**
>
> For every stereo region in your Audio Regions list, you'll see a triangle by the region name. You can click on the triangle to reveal a list of the component mono audio files that make up that stereo audio region.

Importing Audio to a Track

Sometimes, instead of importing an audio file to the Audio Regions list and using it later, you'll want to import audio directly into a track. Pro Tools makes this very convenient by creating a new audio track just for the audio you are importing.

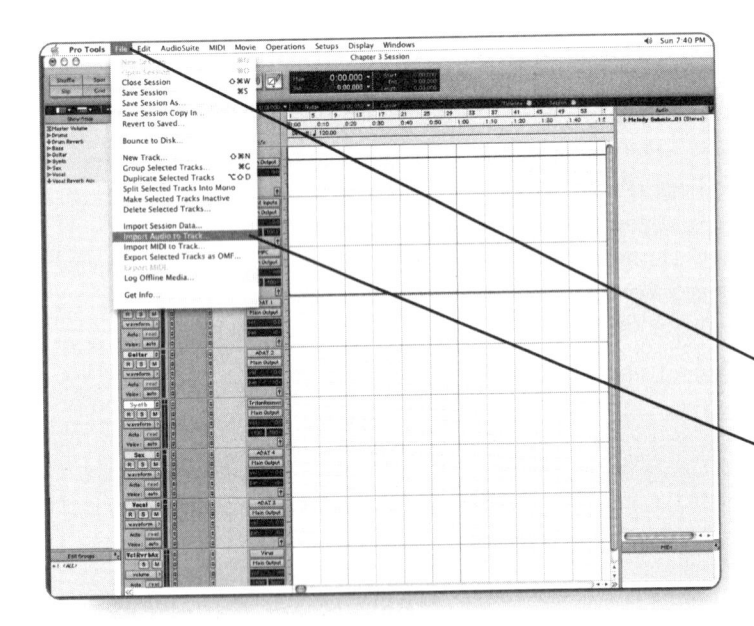

Choosing Where to Import Audio From

Just as you did when you imported audio to the Audio Regions list, the first step here is to locate the audio that you want to bring into your session.

1. Click on **File**. The File menu will appear.

2. Click on **Import Audio to Track**. The Import Audio dialog box will open. This is the same dialog box you saw when you imported audio into the Audio Regions list.

3. Select an **audio file** to import into your session. If you're following the example shown here, you'll want to choose Virus Bass Audio_01.L. The process you use to view the different file types is the same as it was in the previous section.

4. Click on **Done** when you're finished making your choices. Again, the procedure for this exercise is the same as what you did in the previous section.

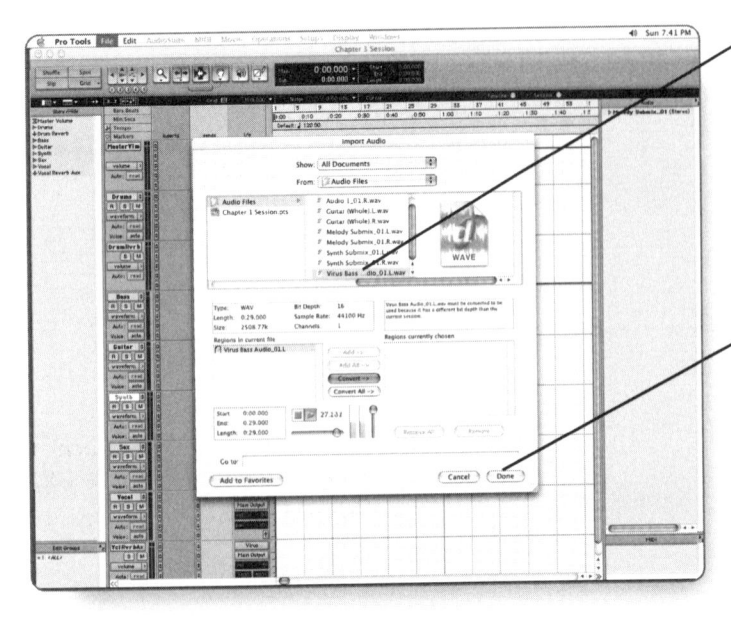

You can still preview the file using the Play button in the lower-left part of the dialog box. The Choose a Folder dialog box will automatically open.

> **TIP**
> You'll notice that you're seeing something a little unorthodox in these examples. In this case, you've taken a file that is obviously half of a stereo track. (Remember, left and right files are identified by .L and .R, respectively.) No problem—Pro Tools is a smart program, and it will create a mono audio track automatically. If you select a right and left file together (as you did when you imported into the Audio Regions list), Pro Tools will create a stereo track automatically for the pair.

Choosing Where to Import Audio To

The process of importing audio files is also the same as what you did when you imported to the Audio Regions list.

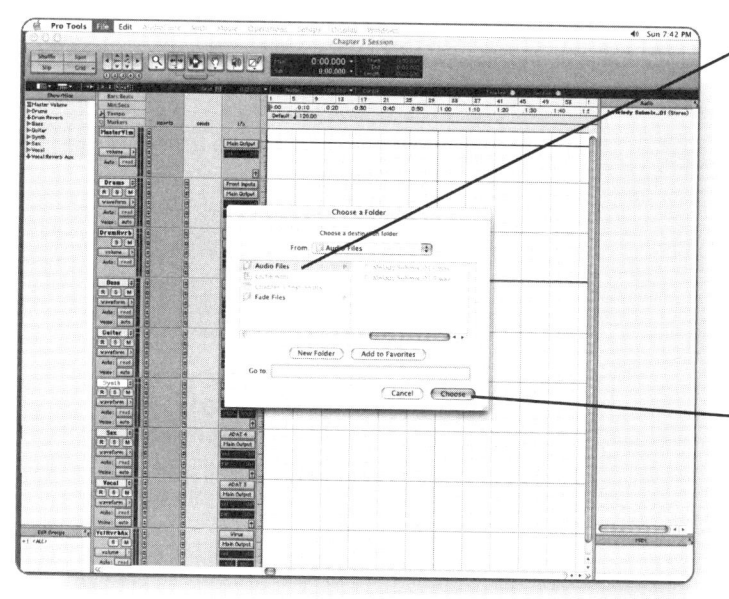

1. In the Choose a Folder dialog box, **select** the **folder** in which you want to save your converted files. In this case, you'll want to store these files in the Audio Files subfolder of the session in which you're working. Notice that the two files you imported earlier are already in this folder.

2. Click on **Choose**. Your session will be shown again, but this time there will be a new audio track (in this case, a mono track). You'll note that the file name will be shown in the region itself.

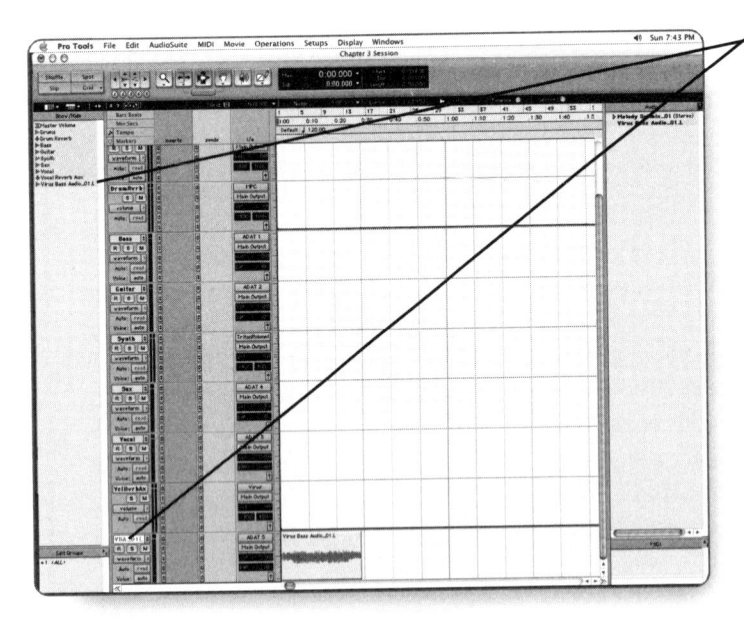

An abbreviation of the region name will be displayed in the track name area, and a full, unabbreviated track name will be shown in the Show/Hide list.

You'll note that, in addition to the creation of a new track, the region has also been imported into the Audio Regions list. In this case, because this newly imported region is mono, there is no triangle before the region name.

Importing Tracks

Importing audio to a track is certainly an easy way to get going with audio, but there is a limitation. The region that you import will be placed at the beginning of your session's Timeline, with no specific editing or mixing. But what if you want to import a tweaked-out track from another session? No problem—Pro Tools can import tracks from a previous session, preserving all edits, volume, pan, and so on, for you to use in your current session!

1. Click on **File**. The File menu will appear.

2. Click on **Import Session Data**. The Open dialog box will open.

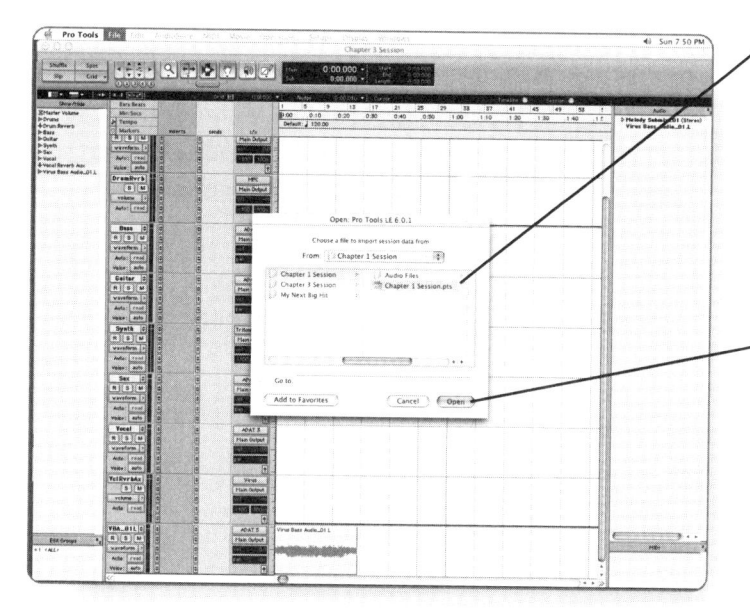

IMPORTING AUDIO

3. Select the **session** from which you want to import a track. Remember, you're not importing just audio anymore, but rather an entire track. That track exists in the session file, which is why you're selecting a session file, not an audio file.

4. Click on **Open**. The Import Session Data dialog box will open.

The Source Properties section of the Import Session Data dialog box provides a wealth of specific information regarding the session from which you'll be importing tracks. Of particular note are the Name, Audio bit depth, Audio sample rate, and Audio file type(s) fields. The bottom of the dialog box contains a list of all tracks in this session.

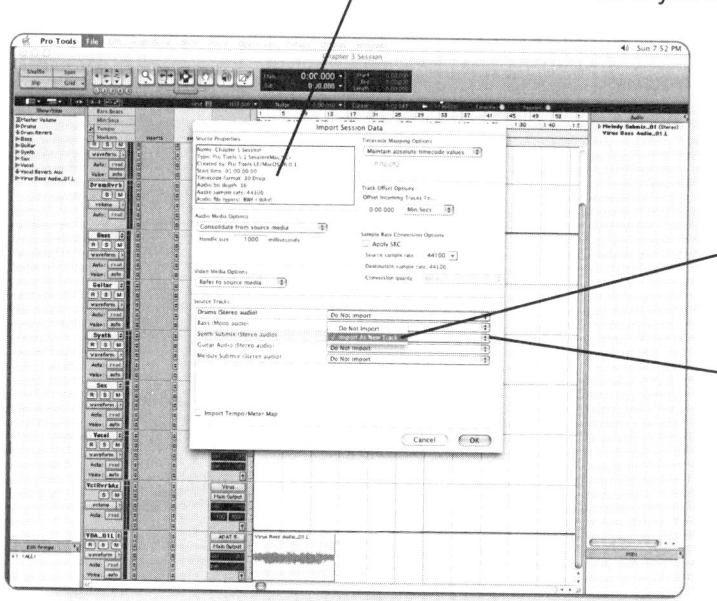

5. Click on the **Synth Submix (Stereo audio) button**. The menu will appear.

6. Choose Import As New Track. The option will be selected.

90 CHAPTER 3: GETTING STARTED WITH AUDIO

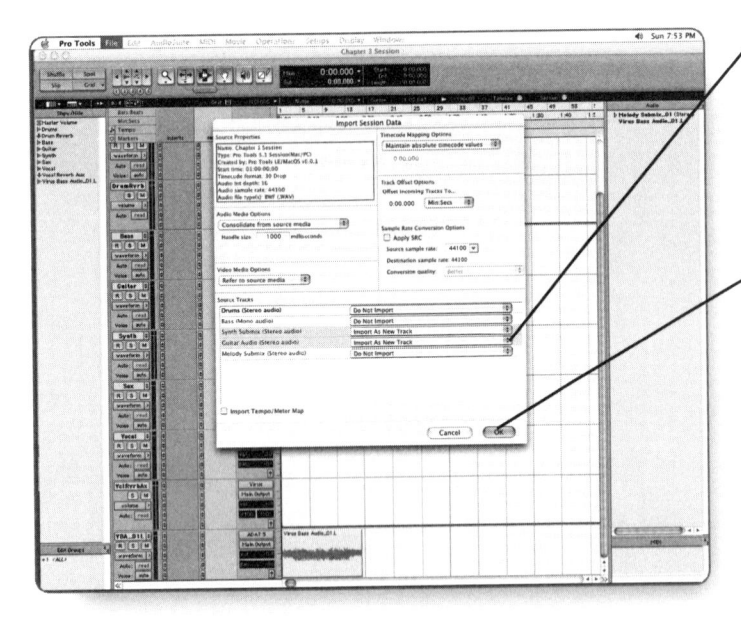

7. It's possible to import more than one track at a time. **Click** on the **Guitar Audio (Stereo audio) button** and **select Import As New Track**. The option will be selected.

8. Click on **OK**. The selected tracks will be imported into your session.

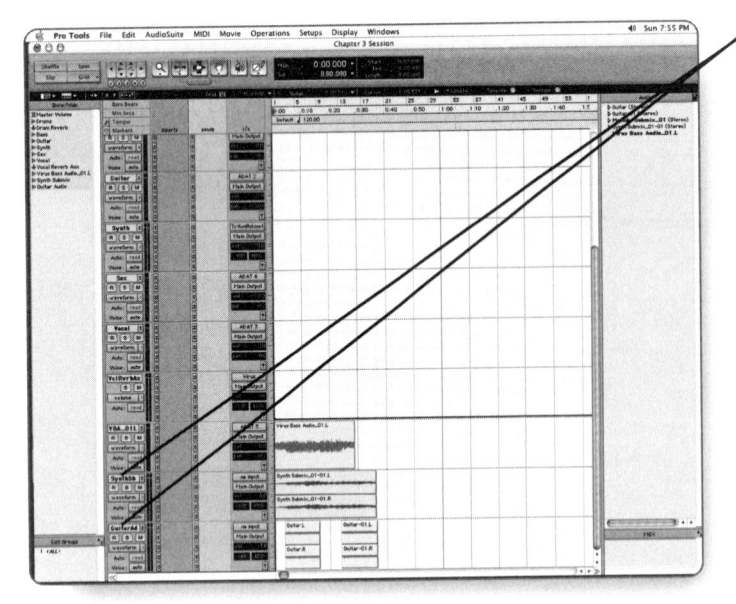

The two new tracks will be created in your session. The interesting thing you'll notice about the guitar track is that you've imported two regions, and they are already arranged at specific times in your session.

IMPORTING AUDIO 91

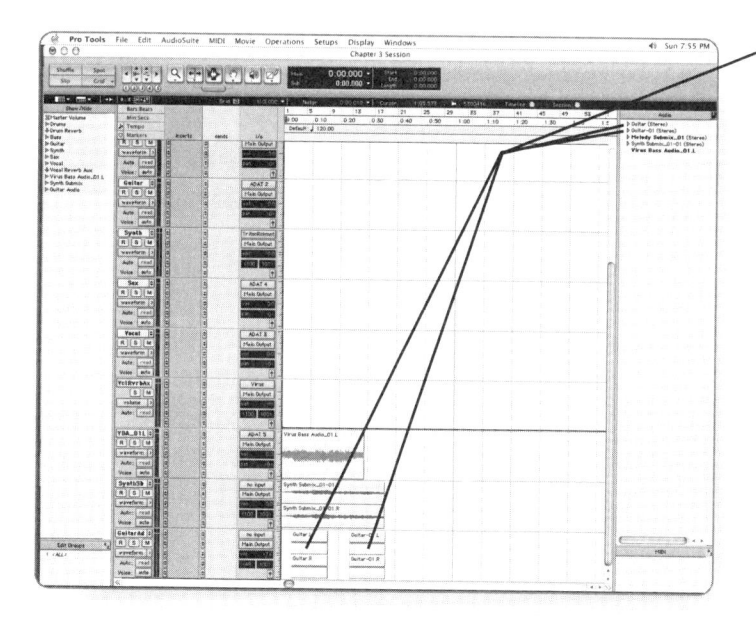

You should also note that each separate region in the guitar track is listed individually in the Audio Regions list.

New in Version 6: The Workspace Window

There's a nifty new feature in version 6.x known as the Workspace window. This window provides you with yet another way to import audio into your session, and it offers a few other useful tools as well.

1. Click on **Windows**. The Windows menu will appear.

2. Click on **Show Workspace**. The Workspace window will appear.

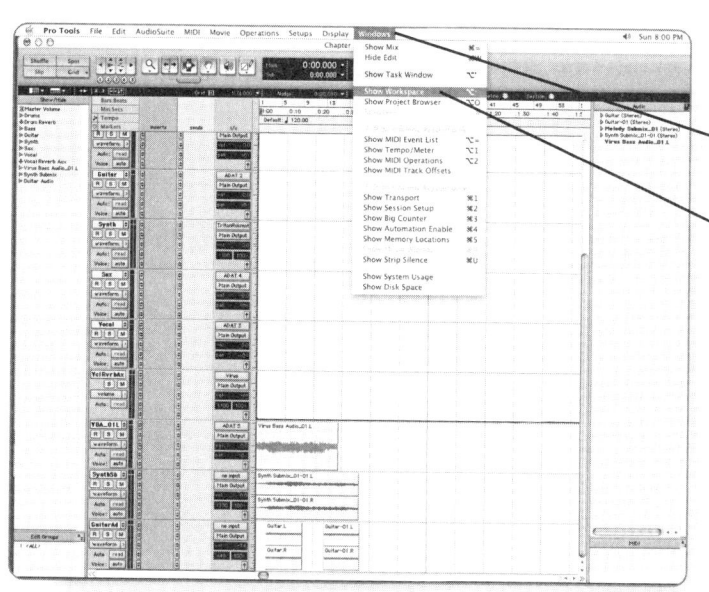

CHAPTER 3: GETTING STARTED WITH AUDIO

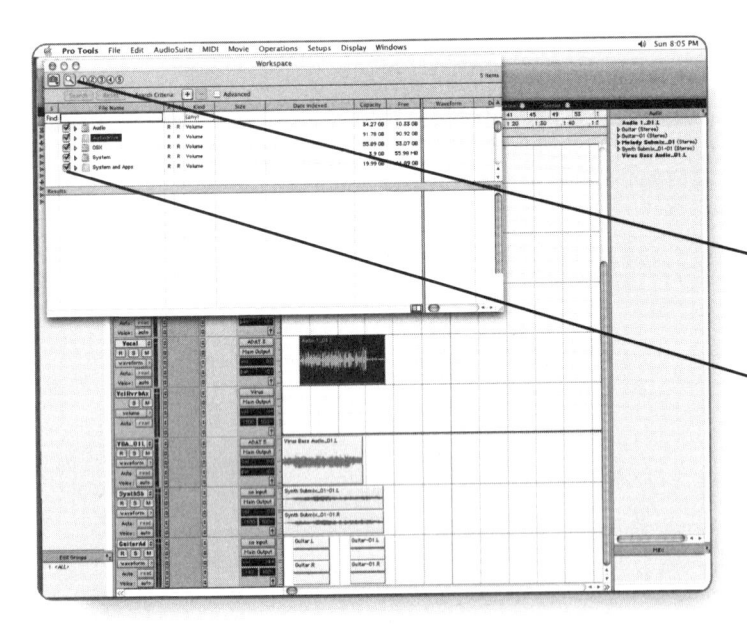

Searching for Audio Using the Workspace

You can easily search for audio using the Workspace window.

1. **Click** on the **magnifying glass button**. The Find section will appear.

2. **Click** on the **check boxes** to select the drives you want to search. The drives will be selected.

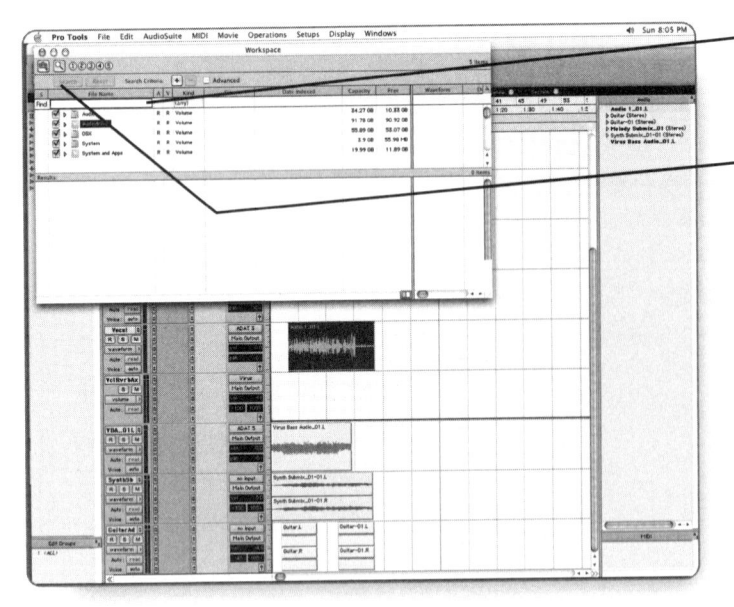

3. **Type** the **name** of the file you want to find in the Find text box.

4. **Click** on **Search**. Matching results will appear in the bottom section of the Workspace window.

IMPORTING AUDIO

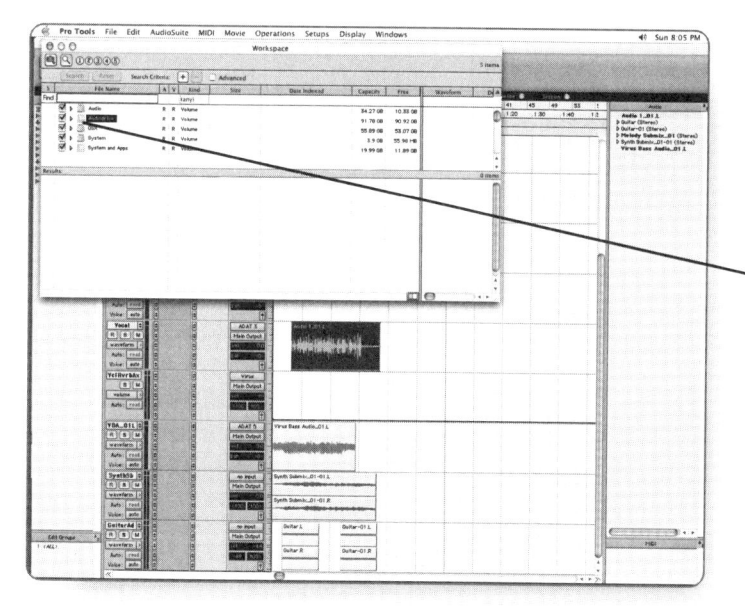

You can also navigate this window in a more traditional way, if you know where to look for a specific file. For this example, import audio yet again from the Chapter 1 session.

1. In the Find section, **double-click** on the **hard drive** where your audio file resides.

2. Navigate through the **folders and sub-folders** of your drive until you find the desired file.

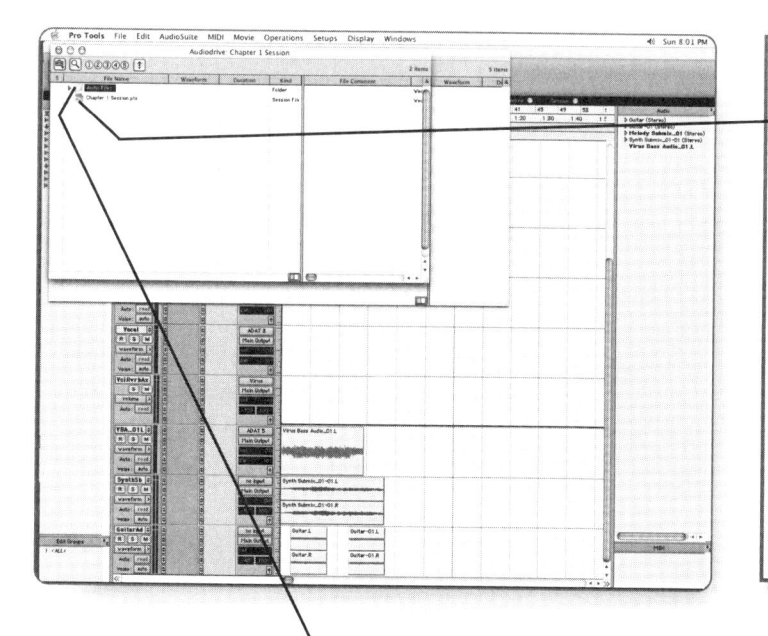

CAUTION

Do *not* click on the session file. You're not importing a track this time; clicking on a session file will only cause Pro Tools to close the present session and open that session file. Don't worry too much, though—Pro Tools will double-check before doing this, and you can always choose to cancel the operation if you clicked on the session by mistake.

3. Double-click on the **Audio Files folder**. The audio files in the folder will appear.

CHAPTER 3: GETTING STARTED WITH AUDIO

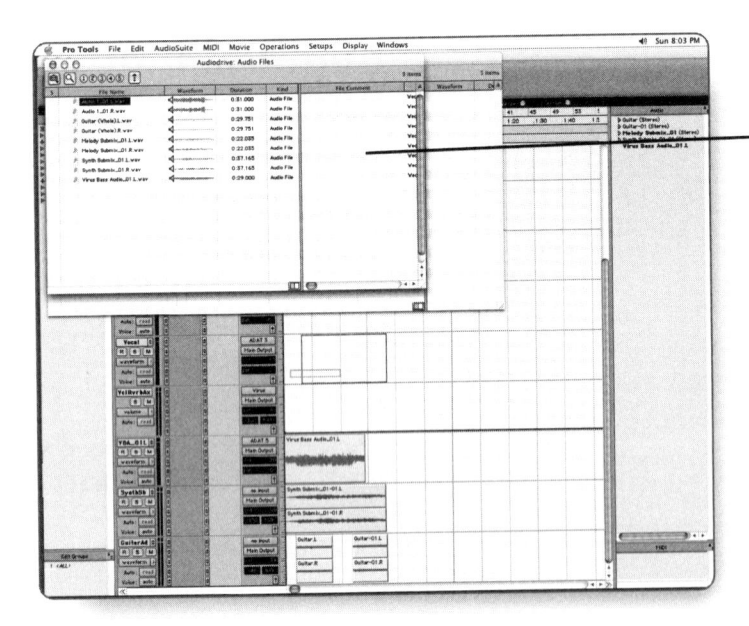

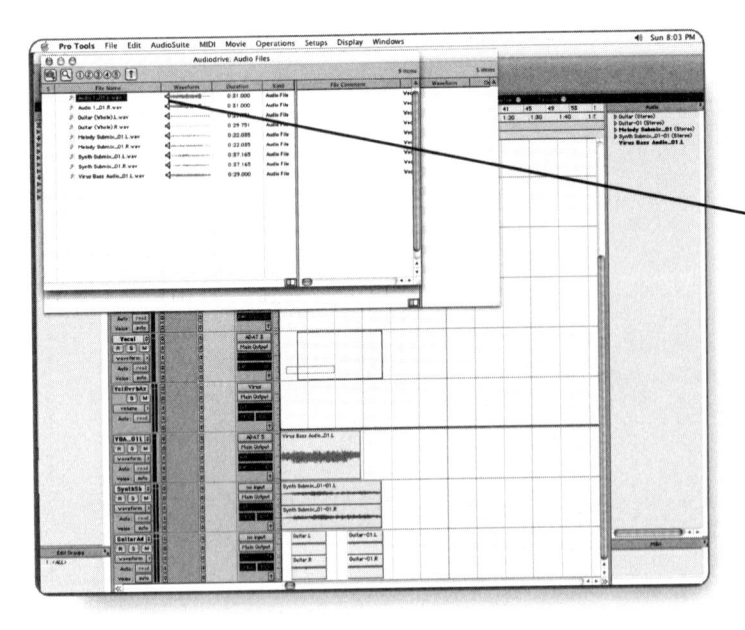

This window provides a few interesting features:

- The secondary window will give you additional information about each of the files (such as sample rate, bit depth, date created, and comments). Use the scroll bar at the bottom of this section to view different aspects of each file.

> **TIP**
>
> You can make this section of the Workspace window a bit more functional by arranging the columns to suit your needs. Just drag and drop each column heading!

- You can audition each audio file by clicking and holding the speaker icon to the right of each file name. The waveform display to the right of the speaker icon will give an indication of the file's characteristics.

IMPORTING AUDIO 95

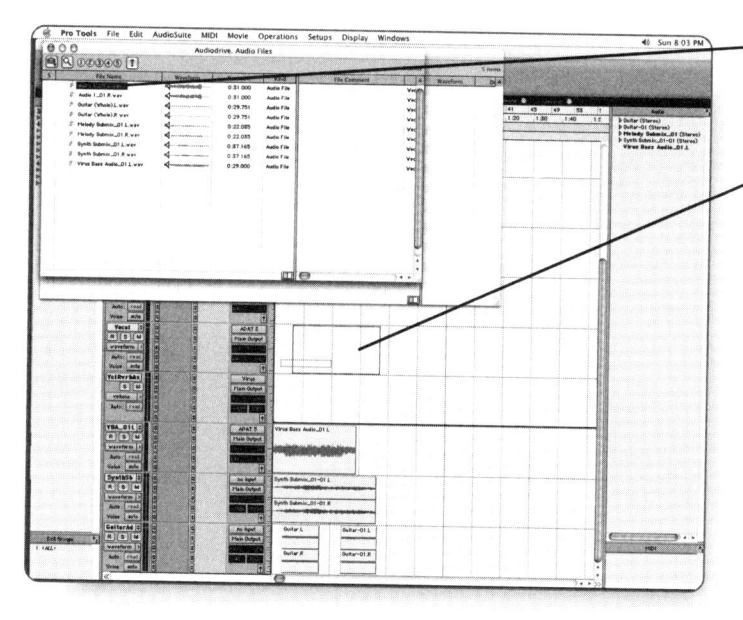

4. Here's the cool part. **Click and hold** the **file** you want to import into your session.

5. Drag the **audio file** onto the Edit window. An outline of the region will appear in the Track area.

6. Release the **mouse button** to drop the file at the desired location.

Again, you'll notice that adding a region to a track will automatically add an audio region to your Audio Regions list. By the way, you can also drag a file directly from the Workspace window to the Audio Regions list instead of to a track.

> **NOTE**
> Did you notice that you didn't have to do any sample rate or bit depth conversion? Pro Tools automatically converts the file if it's necessary! While the conversion process is happening, these buttons will change from green to red, indicating that there is background processing at work.

> **NOTE**
> If you're following along with these sessions, you should delete the region named Audio 1_01.L from your Edit window. Because the region is highlighted when you drag it onto the Edit window, all you have to do is hit the Delete key.

Making Selections and Playing Audio

Now that you've learned how to import audio into your session, you're almost ready to get your hands dirty with some editing. Before you do that, though, you need to move to the next level of playback. Being able to play your session in a few different ways (in addition to being able to play it from the beginning of the session) will allow you to concentrate on specific parts of your project.

How I/O Settings Affect Your Session

It's time for the work you put into your I/O settings to start paying off. You need to make sure your audio tracks are actually going to be output to the correct connections of your audio interface.

There is an output assignment button in the I/O column of each track. By default, each track will be assigned according to the default output setting in the I/O Setup dialog box. In a typical studio setup, this output will be connected to your studio monitors.

MAKING SELECTIONS AND PLAYING AUDIO

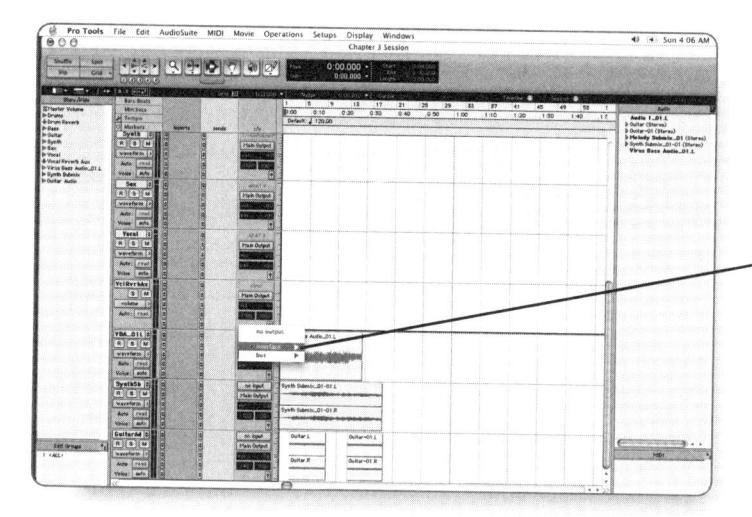

Changing the output is easy; just follow these steps.

1. **Click** on the **output button** for any track. An output drop-down menu will appear.

2. **Click** on **interface**. Another drop-down menu will appear, from which you can select an output path or sub-path you created earlier in your I/O setup.

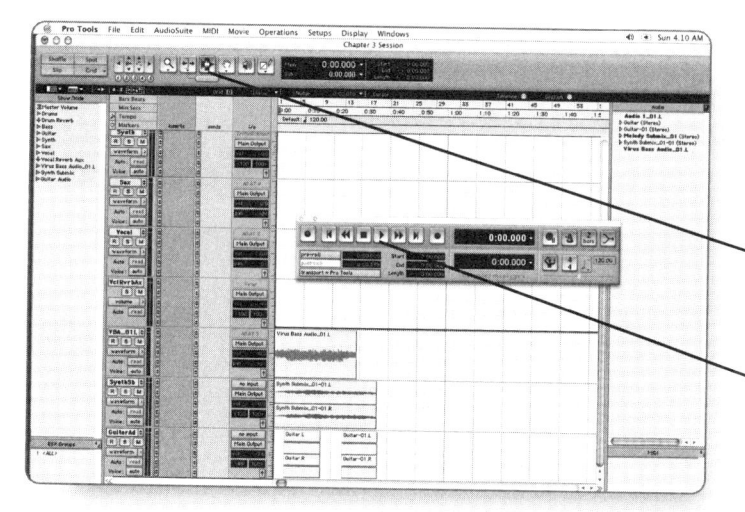

Soloing and Muting Tracks

First, start with a basic playback scenario.

1. **Click** on the **Selector button**. The Selector tool will be selected.

2. If there is a circular arrow in the Play button, **deselect** the **Loop Playback option** in the Operations menu. The arrow in the Play button will disappear.

CHAPTER 3: GETTING STARTED WITH AUDIO

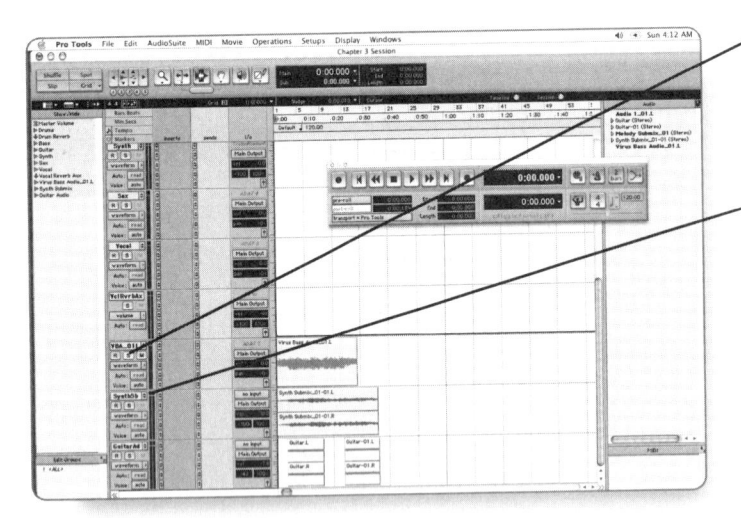

3. Click on the **S button** to listen to a single track in your session. In this case, you will hear a bass part only.

All other tracks will be shown as muted.

> **TIP**
>
> Holding the Shift key while you select the S button on multiple tracks will allow you to solo more than one track at a time.

4. Click on the **M button** to silence a given track. In this case, the bass track will be removed from the mix.

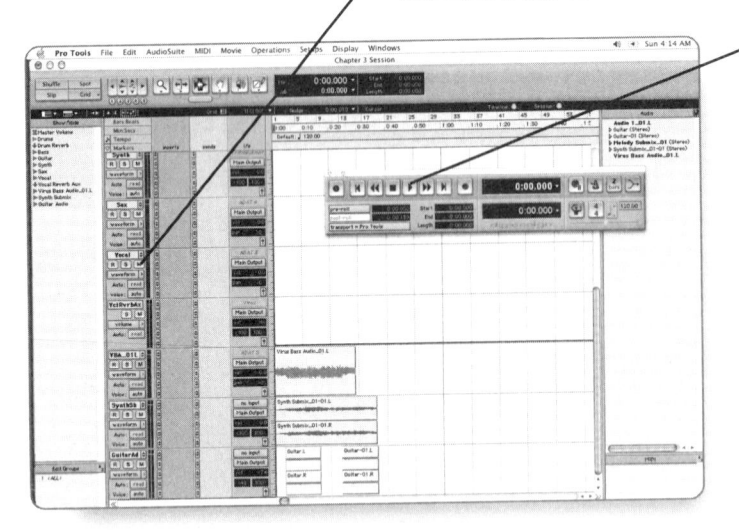

5. Click on the **Play button**. Playback will begin from the beginning of the session. You should hear all un-muted tracks (in this case, a synth track and a guitar track).

> **TIP**
>
> Instead of clicking on the Play button in Step 5, you can also press the spacebar to begin playback from the beginning of the session.

MAKING SELECTIONS AND PLAYING AUDIO

Playing a Selection

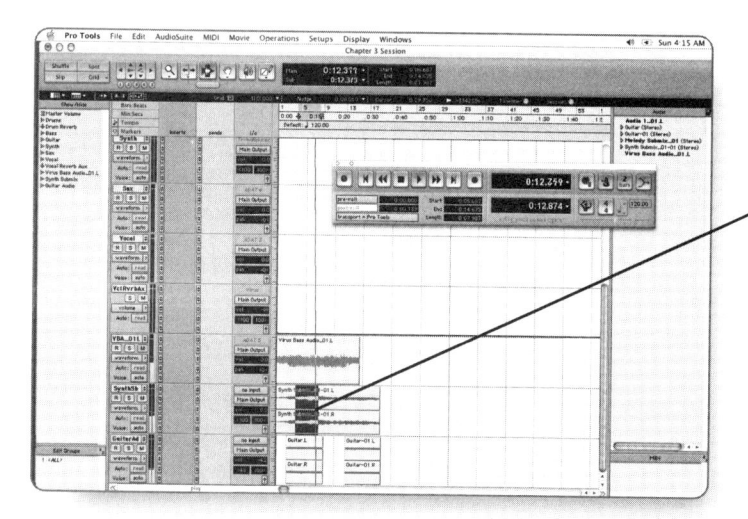

Playing a selection may just be the easiest process of them all!

1. Click and drag over a **section** of any region in your session. The area you select will be appear dark.

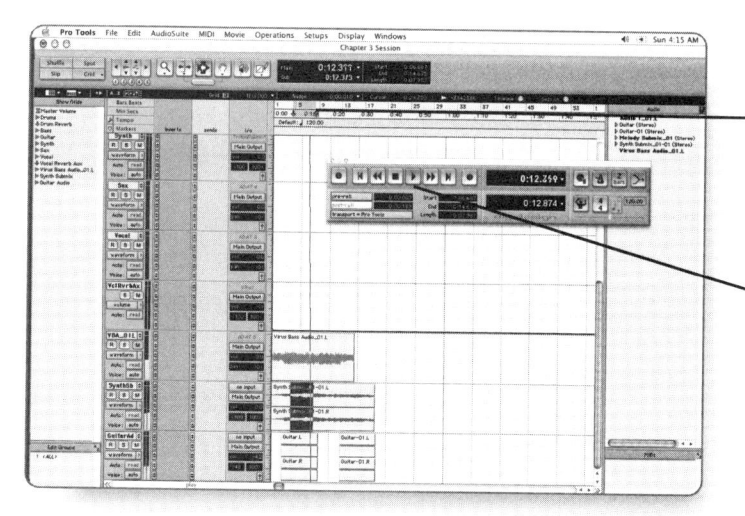

NOTE

Note that the selection that you make is also shown in the Timeline.

2. Click on the **Play button** to play the selection one time.

TIP

Here again, you can press the spacebar instead of clicking on the Play button to play the selection.

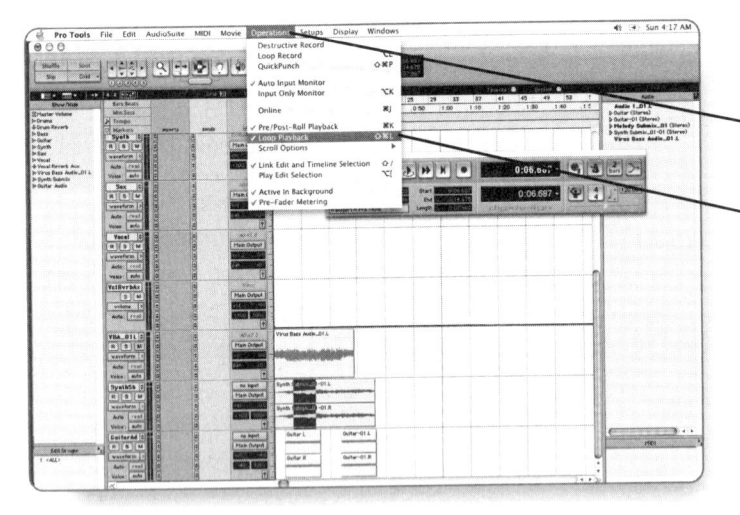

Here's another way to play a selection:

1. Click on **Operations**. The Operations menu will appear.

2. Select Loop Playback. The option will be set.

> **TIP**
>
> Here's a useful shortcut to activate loop playback: In the Transport window, hold the Control key and click on the Play button (Mac) or right-click on the Play button (PC).

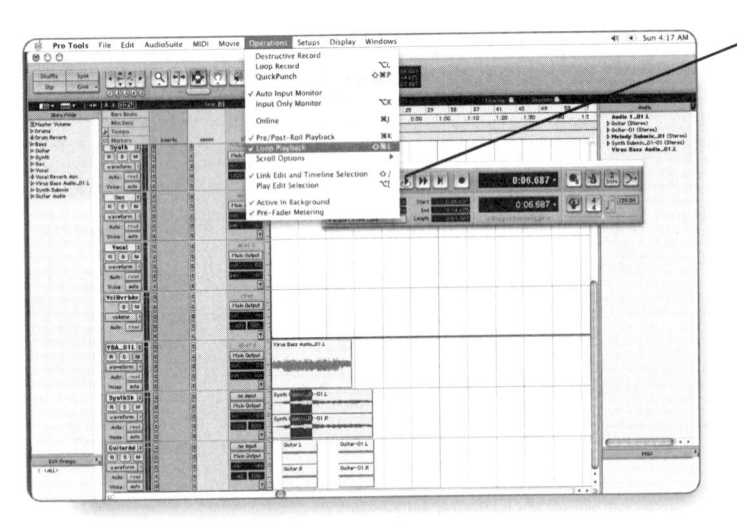

3. Click on the **Play button** to begin loop playback of your selection. The selection will repeat until you press the Stop button (or until you click on the spacebar again).

Finishing Up: The Save As Function

Now you've done some work on your session, so you want to save your work. If you use the Save command, the previous version of the session will be overwritten with the new one. What if you don't want to overwrite the old session? That's where Save As comes into play.

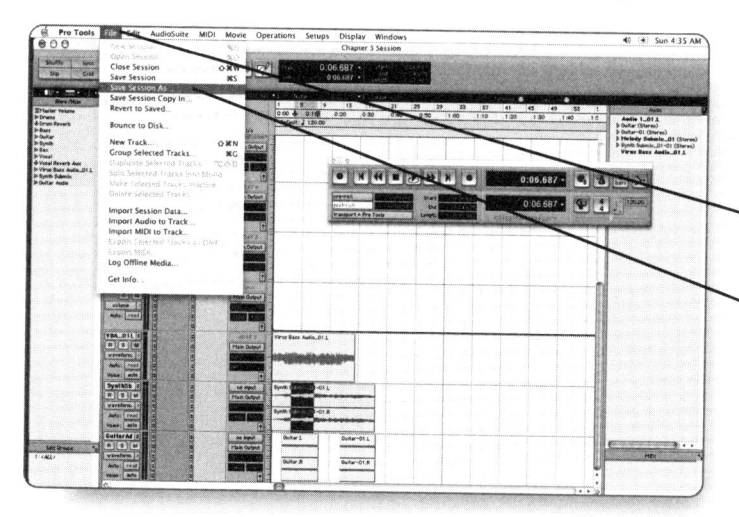

1. Click on **File**. The File menu will appear.

2. Click Save Session As. The Save dialog box will appear.

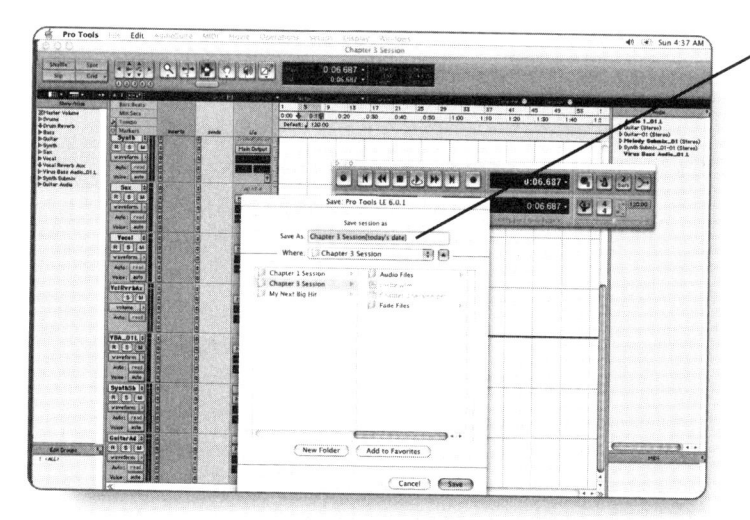

3. Type a **different name** for your session in the Save As text box, to avoid overwriting the original session.

NOTE

It's important to note that both the original session file and the new version of the file can reside in the same session folder and can access the same source audio files.

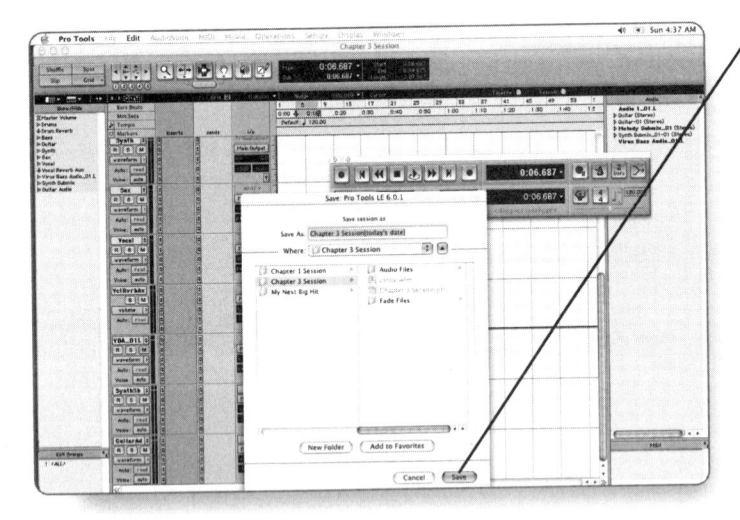

4. Click on **Save**. The new version of the session will be saved with the name you specified in Step 3.

> **NOTE**
>
> There's a maximum of 31 characters allowed for a session file name (including the file extension).

4

Basic Editing

Production can be broken down into a number of phases—tracking (recording), editing, mixing, and mastering. Because it's a computer-based workstation, Pro Tools perhaps shines brightest in the editing phase. In its non-linear environment, you can accomplish in seconds what used to take minutes or hours with a tape-based system. And of course, there is always the Undo function if you make a mistake! In this chapter, you'll learn how to:

- Take full advantage of the functions of the Edit window
- Use Pro Tools' edit modes to their greatest advantage
- Work with Pro Tools' basic editing tools
- Use processes such as cut, copy, and paste to create your own arrangements

Understanding the Edit Window

You took a good first look at the Edit window in Chapters 1 and 2. Now it's time for a closer examination of this powerful window.

> **NOTE**
> You can use the session you created in Chapter 3 as a launching point for the work you'll do in this chapter.

Using the Tools of the Trade

Some of Pro Tools' most useful tools are located in the top row of the Edit window.

In the upper-left corner are the four edit modes—Shuffle, Spot, Slip, and Grid. The mode you choose will determine the manner in which regions can be moved in time in your session. You'll learn more about these modes in the section, "Moving Regions on the Timeline: The Edit Modes," later in this chapter.

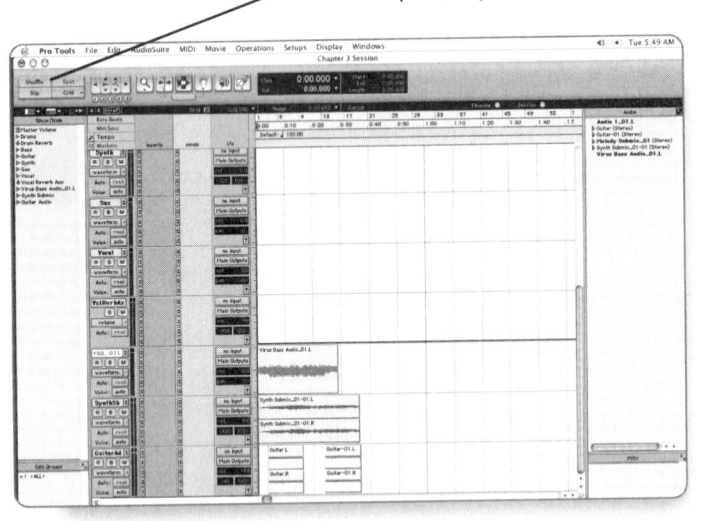

UNDERSTANDING THE EDIT WINDOW   105

Moving to the right, you'll see the zoom tools. These will allow you to zero in on a very brief section of your session (useful for fine editing) or zoom out to view longer sections in your project. You can also zoom in or out using other methods, which will enable you to view your regions in different ways. I'll discuss this more in the next section of this chapter.

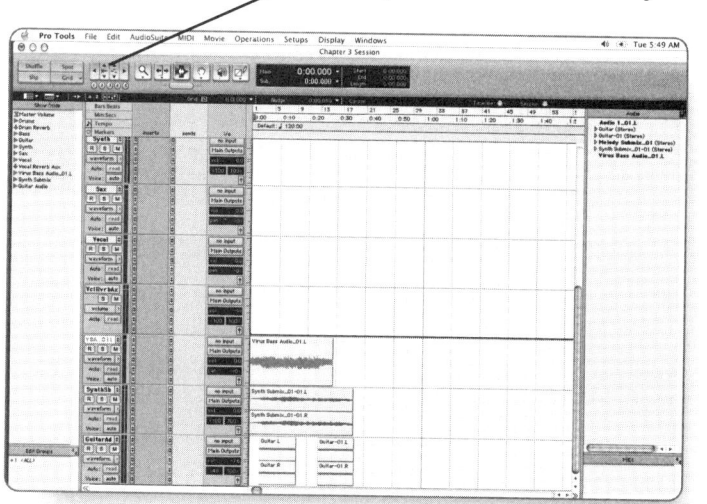

These are the most popular editing tools in the Pro Tools arsenal. From left to right, the tools are Zoom, Trim, Selector, Grabber, Scrub, and Pencil. These tools operate directly on specific regions within your session.

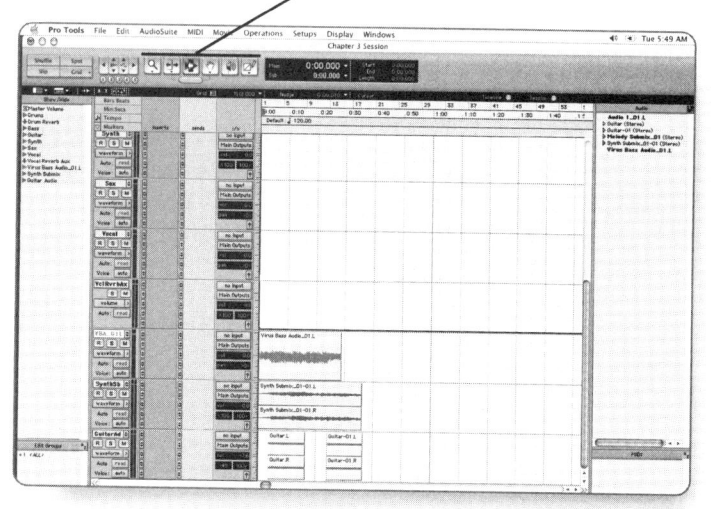

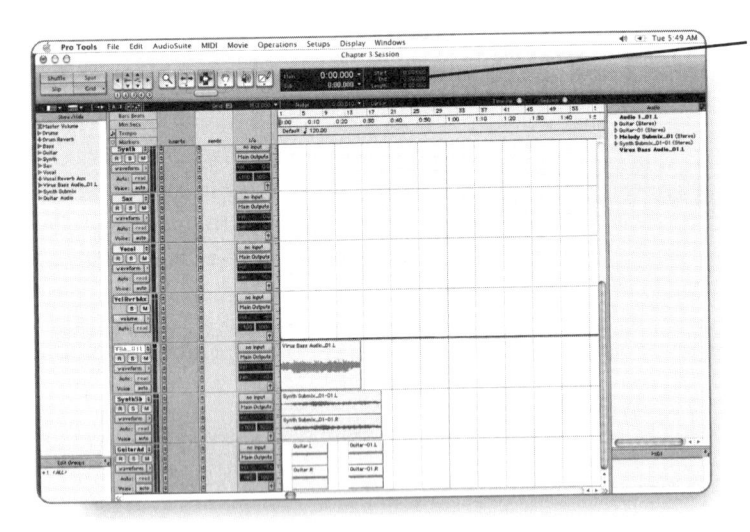

Last but not least are the location displays. To the left you'll see a Main and a Sub display. Both of these displays show you exactly where you are in your session. To the right there are the Start, End, and Length displays, which show you the beginning, end, and duration of your selections.

Navigating

Before you can do anything else, you need to know the basics of how to get around. You'll find that the Selector tool is best suited to this task. Along with this tool, you need to use the location displays so you know where you are.

1. Click on the **Selector tool**. The tool will be selected.

2. Click on the **arrow** to the right of the Main time display. A drop-down menu will appear.

UNDERSTANDING THE EDIT WINDOW

3. Choose Bars:Beats, Min:Secs, or Samples. The time scale of the Main display will change to reflect your selection.

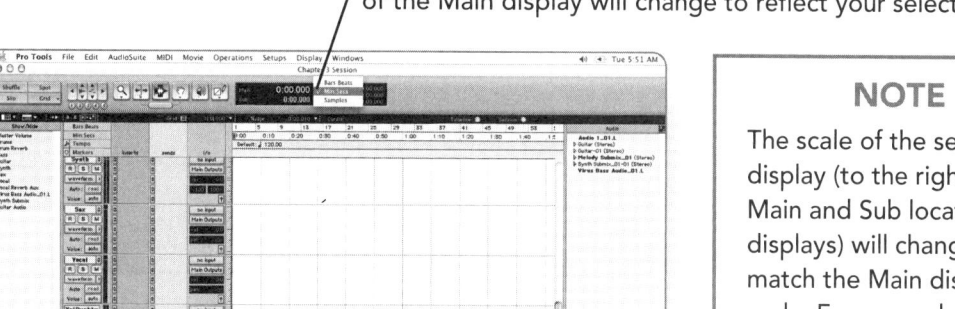

NOTE

The scale of the selection display (to the right of the Main and Sub location displays) will change to match the Main display's scale. For example, if you change the scale to Bars:Beats, the Main time display will count your session as it plays in bars and beats. When you make a selection, that selection will also be shown in bars and beats.

4. Click on the **arrow** to the right of the Sub time display. A drop-down menu will appear.

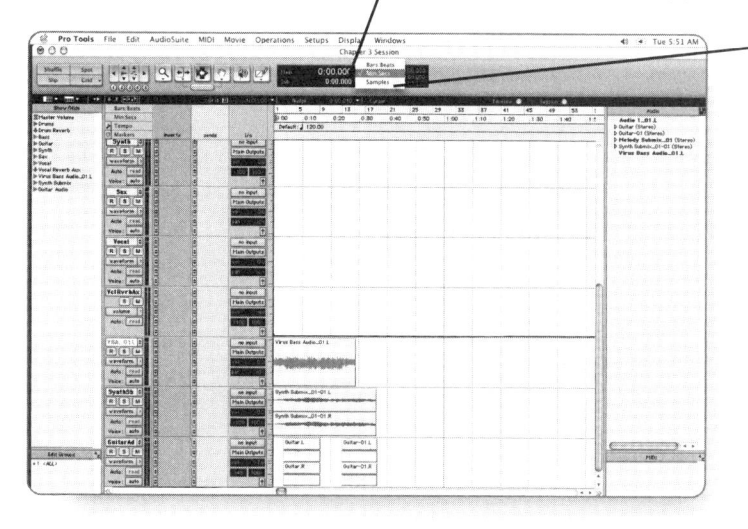

5. Choose any **time scale** for this display. You can choose a different scale than the one in the Main display; that way, you can view your session in two different ways simultaneously.

CHAPTER 4: BASIC EDITING

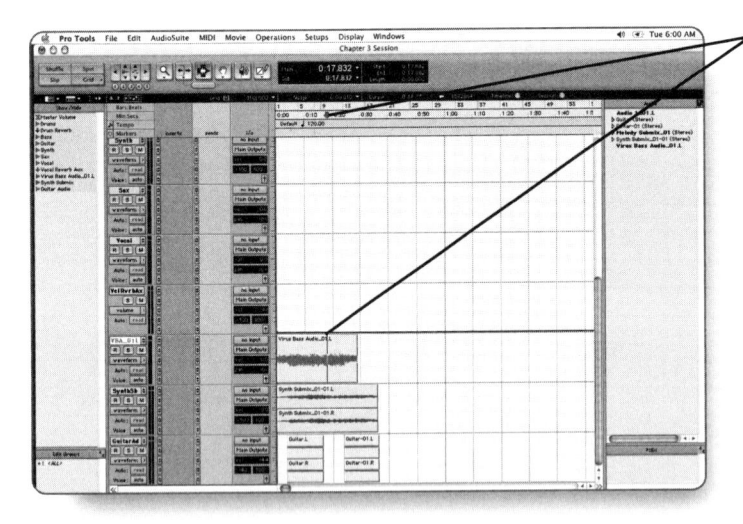

6. Click anywhere in the session's **edit area**. A small line (called a *timeline insertion*) will appear where you clicked. Also, a small blue figure will appear at this location in your Rulers area.

In the Main and Sub time displays, your timeline insertion's location is precisely displayed.

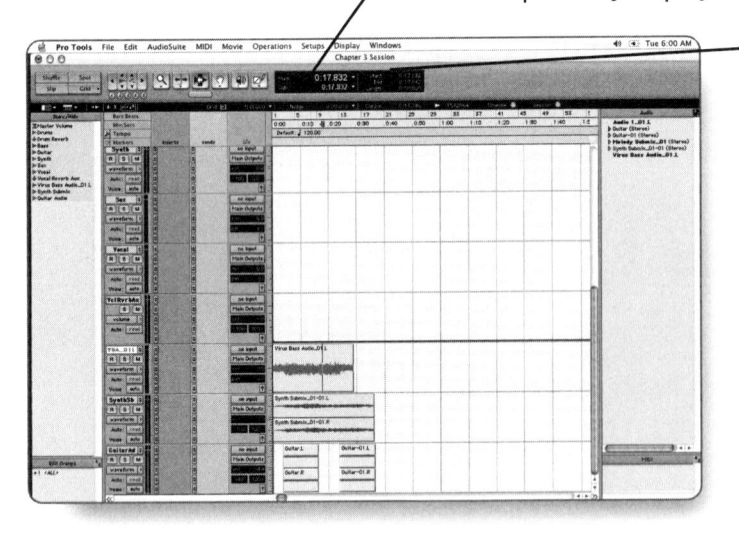

Also, the selection display will show the timeline insertion location. Because you've selected only a single location, the Start and End values are identical and the Length value is zero.

UNDERSTANDING THE EDIT WINDOW 109

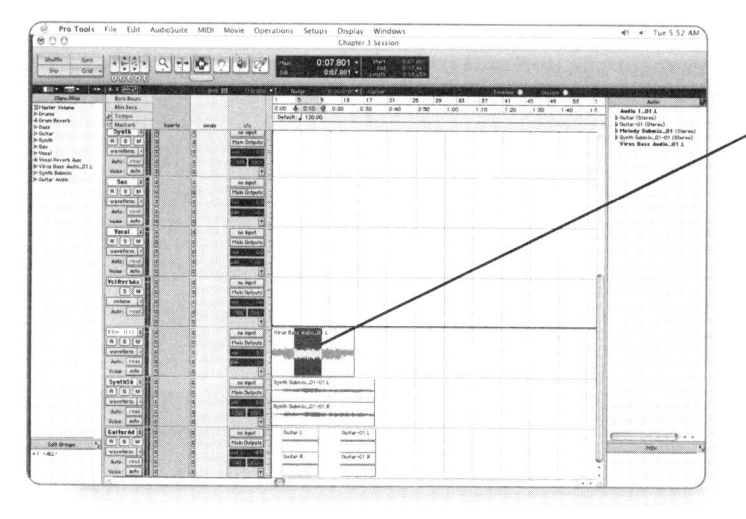

Now, try to make a different kind of selection.

1. Click and drag in the **Track area** to make a selection with a length greater than zero. The wider your selection, the more time you've selected.

In addition to the selection you make in the Track area, a selection is made in the Rulers area. This time, however, the blue figure has split apart into a down arrow (indicating the beginning of the selection) and an up arrow (indicating the end).

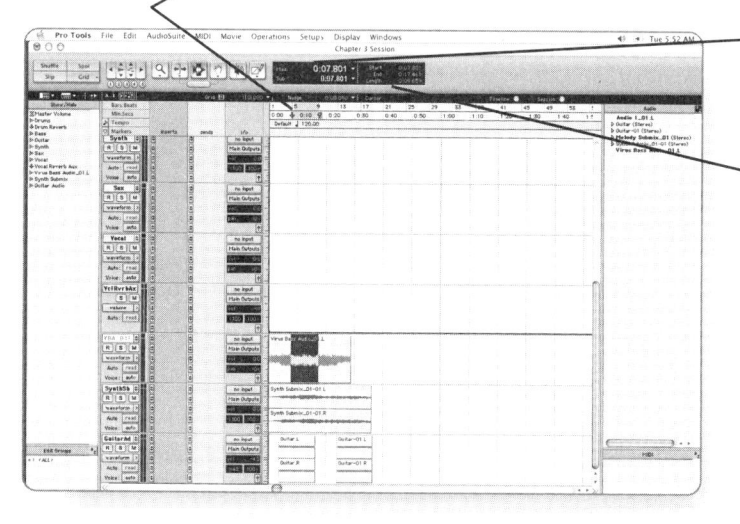

The Main and Sub time displays will show the start of your selection.

The selection display will show the start, end, and length of your selection.

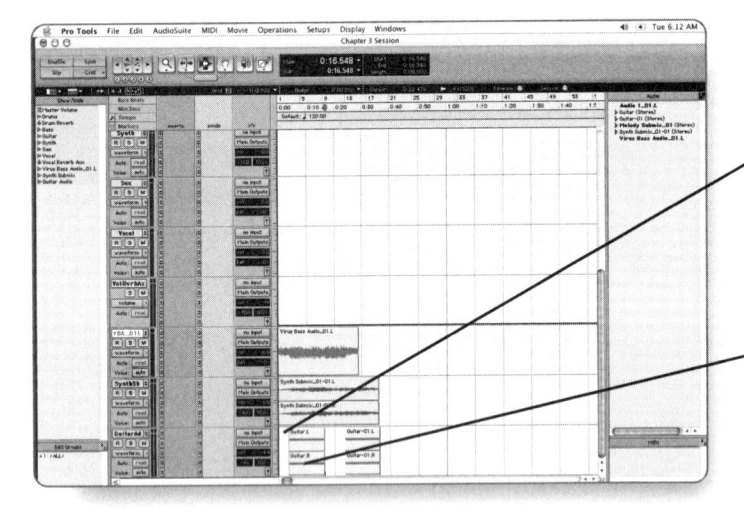

Here's a couple more ways to get around, this time using the Tab key.

1. Still using the Selector tool, **click** on a **track** with a number of regions, before any (or all) regions. A timeline insertion will appear where you click.

2. Press the **Tab key**. The timeline insertion will move to the next region boundary (the start or end of a region).

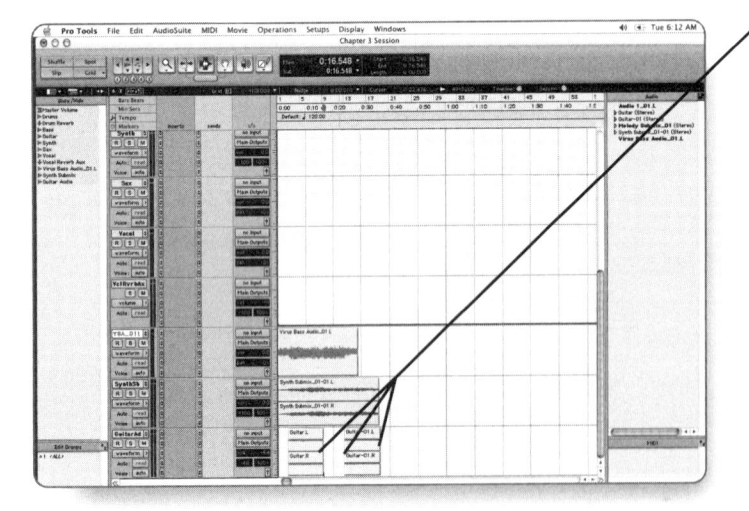

Each time you press the Tab key, the timeline insertion will move to the next region boundary.

> **TIP**
>
> Here's a twist on using the Tab key: Hold the Option key (Mac) or the Alt key (PC) while you press the Tab key to move the timeline insertion to the previous region boundary.

UNDERSTANDING THE EDIT WINDOW 111

Here's another way to use the Tab key.

1. Click on the **Tab to Transient button**. The option will be selected.

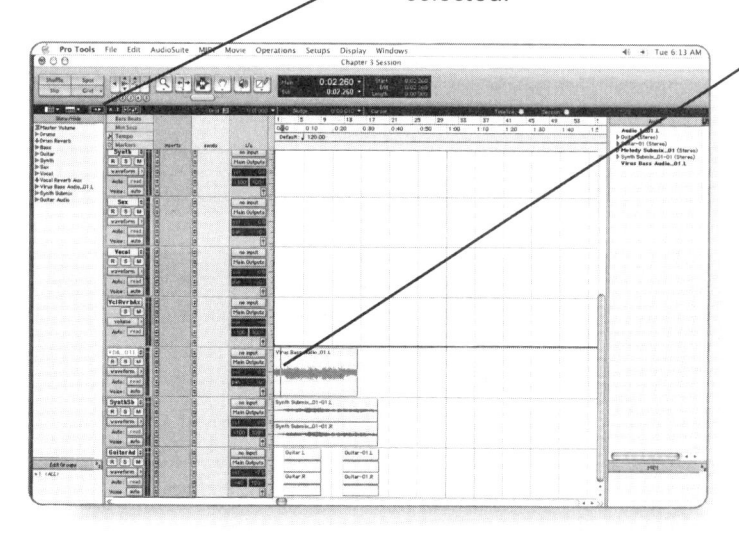

2. Click once on a **region with audio** to move the timeline insertion. The timeline insertion will be moved.

3. Press the **Tab key**. This time, instead of moving to region boundaries, the timeline insertion will jump from transient to transient.

> **TIP**
> Again, the Option key (Mac) or the Alt key (PC) will move the timeline insertion backward in time.

> **NOTE**
> So what the heck *is* a transient anyway? Simply put, a transient is the initial high-energy peak at the beginning of a waveform, such as one caused by the percussive action of a pick or hammer hitting a string. Different types of instruments have different kinds of transients, but they tend to be good visual cues when editing, indicating the beginnings of notes (or words, in the case of a spoken track).

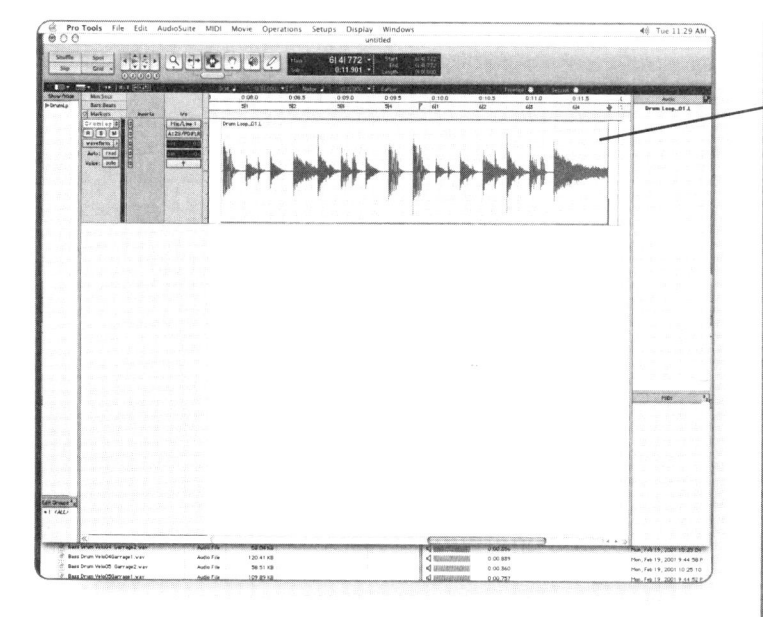

When you're using the Tab to Transient button, you might want to get a closer look at the audio. That's where zooming comes in!

Zooming

Sometimes when you're editing, you'll want to get a close look at your audio. When you're finished, you might want to then get an overview of your entire session. To do this, you need to know how to use the zoom tools.

1. Click on the **left zoom arrow** to zoom out. Each time you click on this button, your view will encompass a greater span of time.

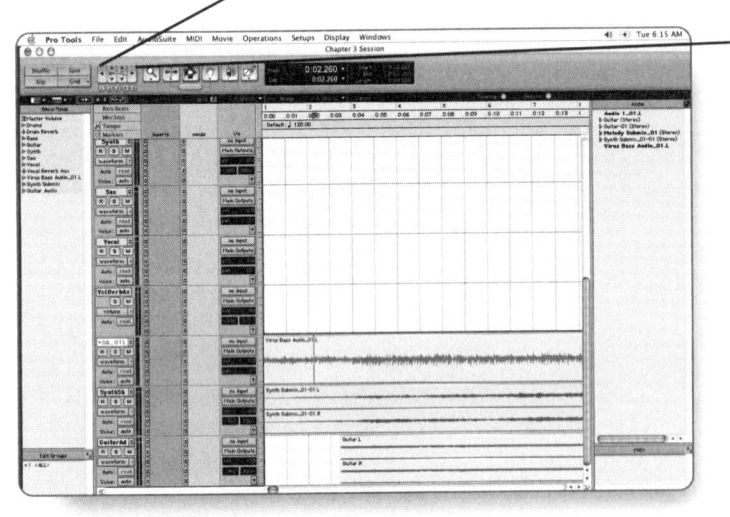

2. Click on the **right zoom arrow** to zoom in. Each time you click on this button, you will gain a finer view of your session.

> **NOTE**
> You will notice that your zooming centers on your timeline insertion's location.

> **TIP**
> You might use these shortcuts more than any others covered in this book: On Macs, ⌘+] (right bracket) will zoom in and ⌘+[(left bracket) will zoom out. On PCs, it's Ctrl+] to zoom in and Ctrl+[to zoom out.

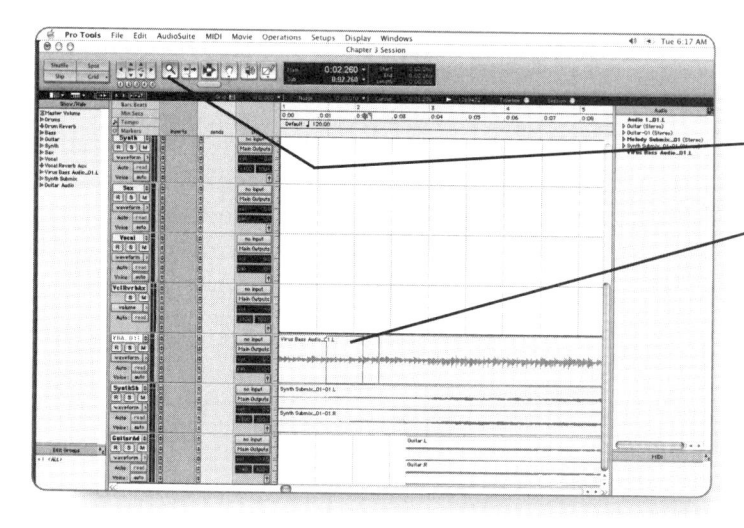

MOVING REGIONS ON THE TIMELINE: THE EDIT MODES   113

Here's another way to zoom in on a specific section.

1. Click on the **Zoom tool**. The tool will be selected.

2. Click and drag on a **track** to select an area. The area will be selected.

3. Release the **mouse button**. The view will zoom in on the selected area.

Moving Regions on the Timeline: The Edit Modes

Pro Tools has four edit modes that determine how regions behave in your session. Each mode is unique, and soon you will get a feeling for which mode is best suited to a given task.

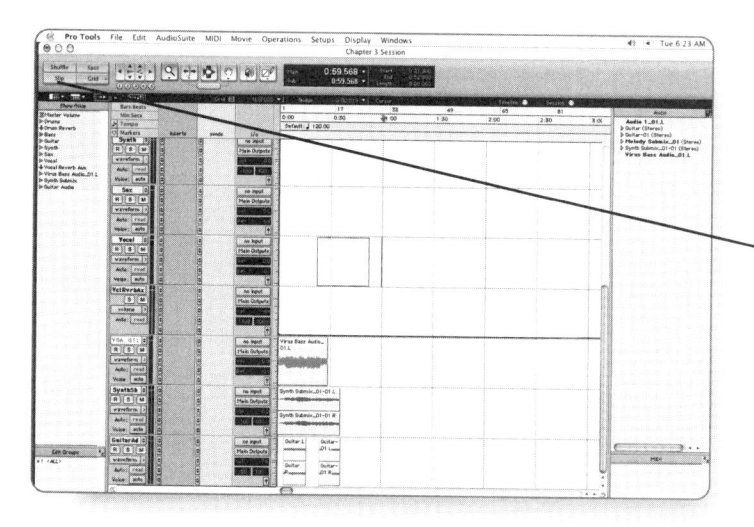

Using Slip Mode

When you need it, Slip mode gives you the most freedom of motion with your regions.

1. Click on the **Slip mode button**. The mode will be selected.

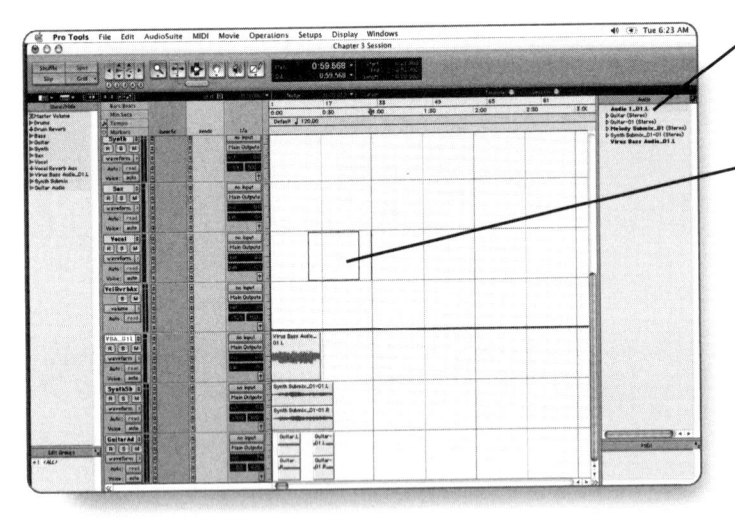

2. Click and hold a **region** in the Audio Regions list. The region will be selected.

3. Drag the **region** onto a track. You will see an outline of the region, indicating where it will be placed when you release the mouse button.

> **NOTE**
>
> It is important to remember that when you're working with mono regions, you can only drop them onto mono tracks. On the other hand, when you drag stereo regions onto the Timeline, they can occupy a single stereo track or two mono tracks.

Using Grid Mode

Sometimes it is convenient to have your regions snap to predetermined increments or grids. This can be particularly useful when you're working on a music-based project, when it's convenient to have your regions align themselves to bars and beats.

MOVING REGIONS ON THE TIMELINE: THE EDIT MODES 115

First you should set up your Main location display and grid value so you can maximize the effectiveness of this mode.

1. Click on the **Main down arrow** and **change** the **Main location display** to Bars:Beats. The scale will be shown in Bars|Beats|Ticks. Note that the selection display will also change scale.

2. Click on the **Grid arrow.** The Grid menu will appear.

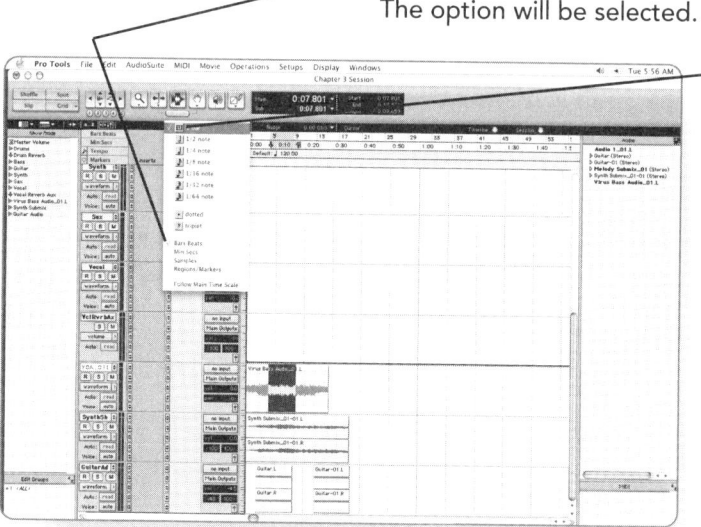

3. Select the **Bars:Beats** as the grid scale you want to use. The option will be selected.

4. Choose 1 bar for the grid resolution. The option will be selected.

NOTE
Because this scale is musical, you will see grid resolutions such as bars, half notes, quarter notes, and so on.

116 CHAPTER 4: BASIC EDITING

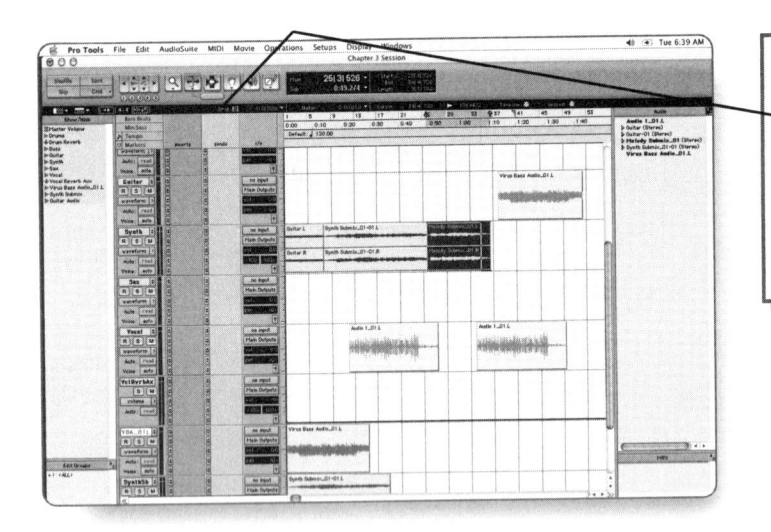

> **NOTE**
> Notice that the grid indicator to the left of the drop-down menu will change to match your choice.

5. Click on **Grid**. The mode will be selected.

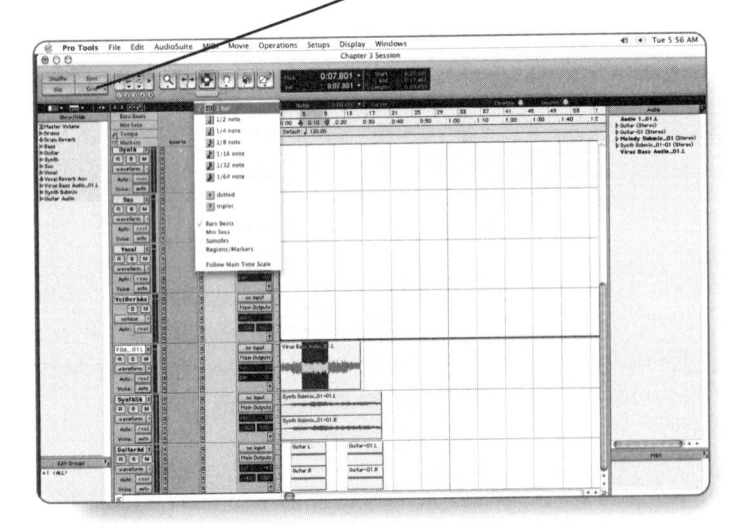

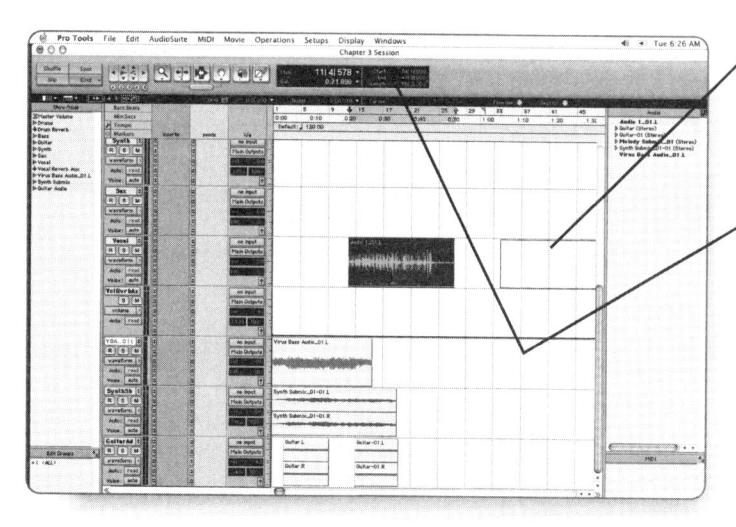

MOVING REGIONS ON THE TIMELINE: THE EDIT MODES

6. Drag a **region** from the Audio Regions list onto the Track area. The region will snap from bar to bar as you drag it.

As you drag the region, you'll notice that the selection display will reflect the beginning, end, and duration of the region. Because you're in Grid mode and your grid resolution is 1 bar, the start value will always change in one-measure increments.

Using Shuffle Mode

Shuffle mode operates in a much different way than either Slip or Grid mode. In this mode, regions move end to end with each other. When you see how this mode works, you'll see how it can be useful for stitching together verses, choruses, and so on into a seamless final product!

1. Click on **Shuffle**. The mode will be selected.

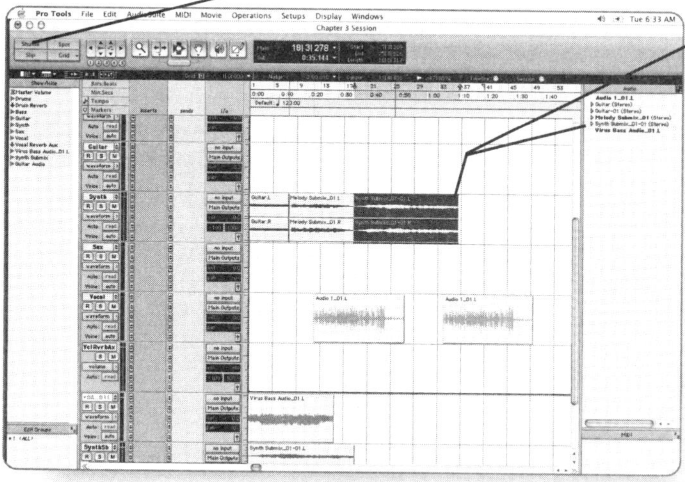

2. One by one, **drag and drop** various **regions** from the Audio Regions list onto a single track. Wherever you drop these regions, they will snap end to end with the previous region, starting with the first region, which automatically snaps to the beginning of your track.

3. Now you can actually shuffle the regions a bit. **Click** on the **Grabber tool**. The tool will be selected.

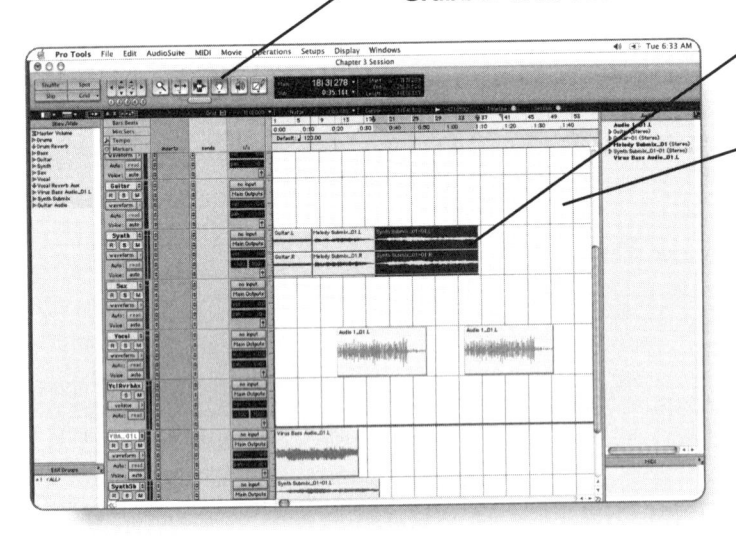

4. Click and hold on a **region**. The region will be selected.

5. Drag the **region** over another region on the track.

6. When a dark line appears at the beginning of the preceding region, **release** the **mouse button** to drop the region. The regions will be reorganized.

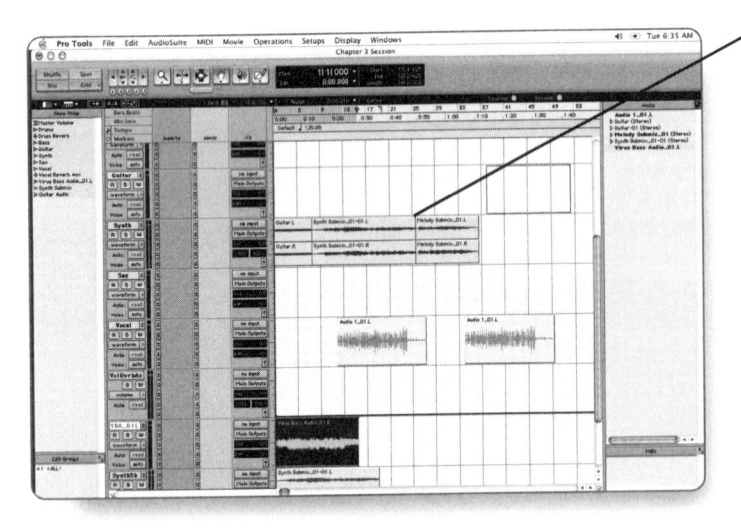

Note that all regions remain end to end, despite the fact that they have been moved. Of course, you can move more than one region at a time. In fact, you can shuffle regions forward and backward at will and create new arrangements of these regions, while keeping all the regions snugly end to end.

MOVING REGIONS ON THE TIMELINE: THE EDIT MODES

Using Spot Mode

You can use Spot mode when you want to assign a region to a specific numeric value. This is of particular use when you're assigning audio to sync with video (also known as *spotting*). Although this mode lacks the freedom of motion of the other modes (by design), it is a quick way to place a region at a specific location.

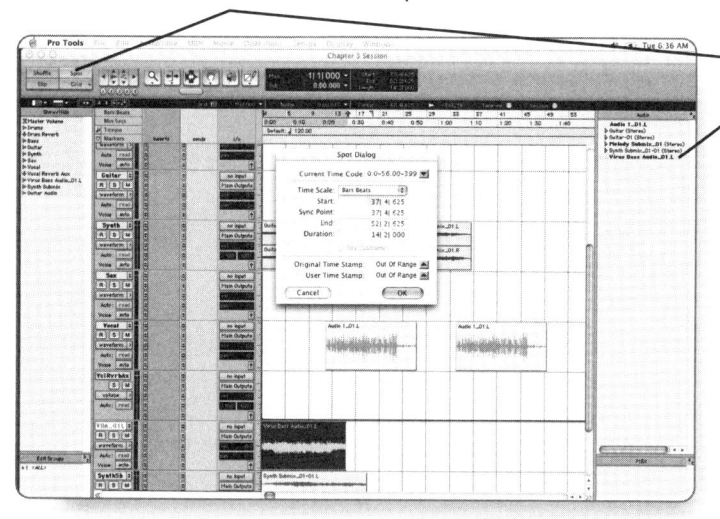

1. Click on the **Spot button**.

2. Select a **region** and **drag it** onto an appropriate track.

3. Release the **mouse button** to drop the region on the track. The Spot Dialog box will open.

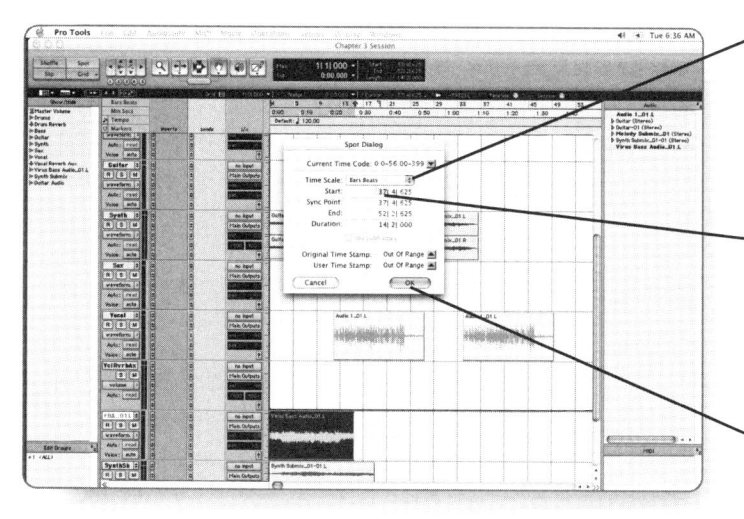

4. Click on the **Time Scale button** and **select** the **time scale** you want to use to position your region. The time scale will be selected.

5. For now, you should only worry about the start of the region. **Type** exactly **where you want your region to start** in the Start field.

6. Click on **OK**. The region will be placed on the track at the specified location.

Basic Tool Functions

The three major edit tools you'll use are the Trim, Selector, and Grabber tools. I touched on some of these functions earlier, but I want to go just a little deeper before you start putting them into action. I'll take them one at a time, from left to right.

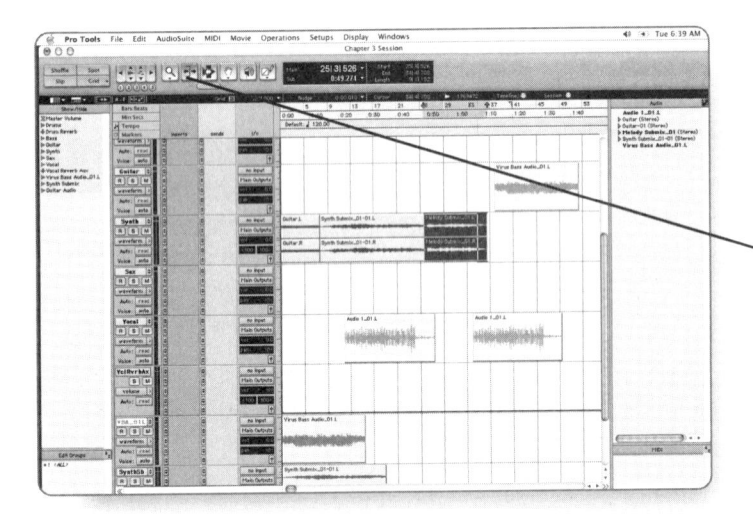

Understanding the Trim Tool

The first tool in line is the Trim tool.

1. Click on the **Trim tool**. The tool will be selected.

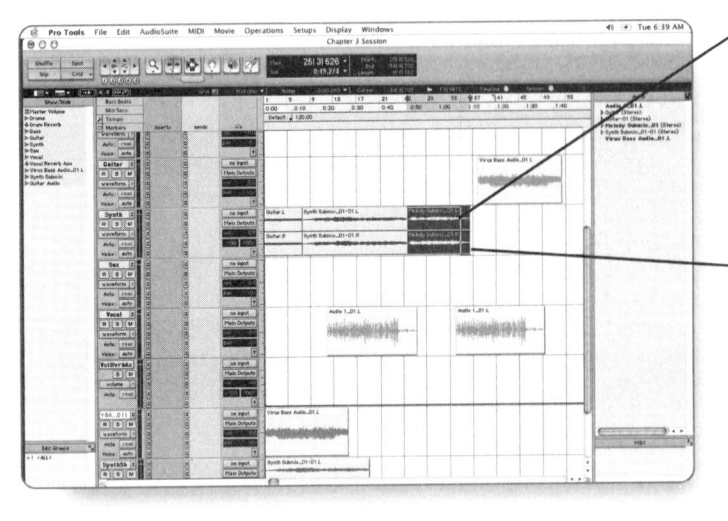

2. Position your **cursor** at the beginning or end of a region. The cursor will take on the appearance of a bracket, indicating that you're using the Trim tool.

3. Click and drag the region's **edge**. The region boundary will change.

BASIC TOOL FUNCTIONS

> **NOTE**
>
> There are a few things to keep in mind when you're using the Trim tool.
>
> - Trimming a region is non-destructive. The fact that you're trimming the region only changes the part of the audio file you are choosing to use in your session.
> - Every time you use the Trim tool, a new region is created in the Audio Regions list.
> - When you're in Grid mode, your trimming will snap to the current grid values.

Understanding the Selector Tool

You already used the Selector tool to select a segment of your session to play. Now you're going to use it to clean up your session over a number of tracks.

1. Click on the **Selector tool**. The tool will be selected.

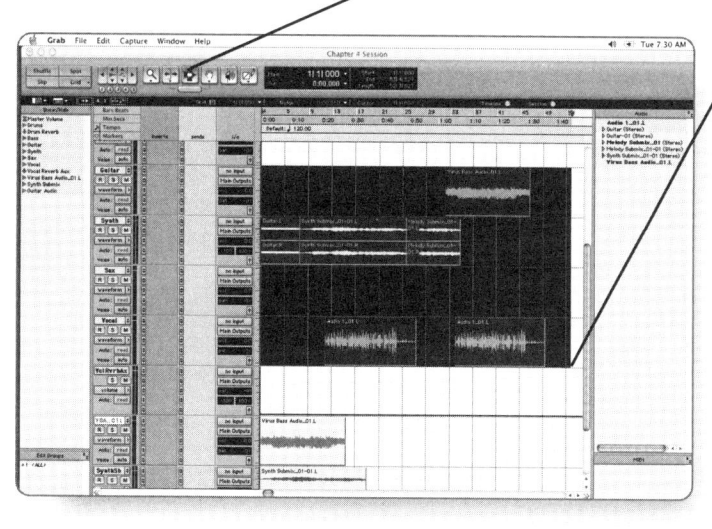

2. Starting in one corner, **click and drag** a **square area** that includes regions you want to remove from your session. The regions will be selected.

3. Press the **Delete key**. The regions will be removed from your tracks.

> **NOTE**
>
> Remember that you're working in a non-destructive environment. The regions you clear from your tracks won't be removed from the Audio Regions list or your hard drive.

Understanding the Grabber Tool

Finally you get to the Grabber tool. You've used it before, but this section will show you how to move more than one region at a time.

1. Click on the **Grabber tool**. The tool will be selected.

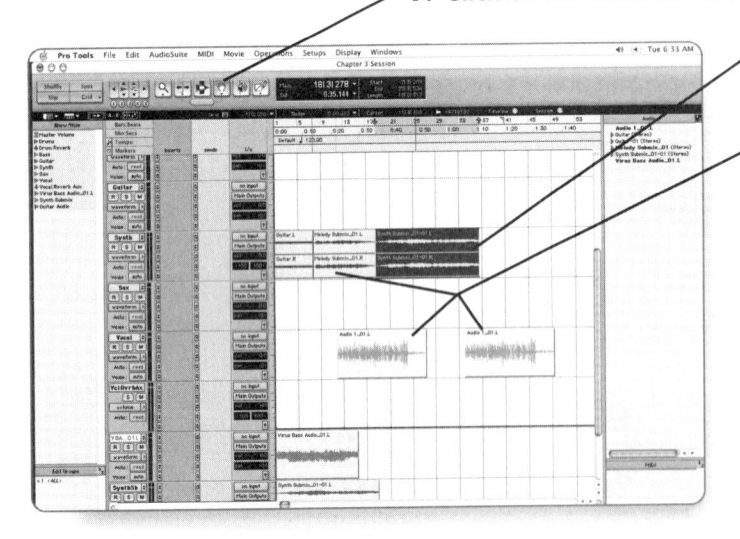

2. Click on a single **region**. The region will be highlighted.

3. Press and hold the **Shift key** and **click** on **additional regions**. The regions will be highlighted.

> **NOTE**
>
> As you grab additional regions using the Grabber tool, a shaded area will appear. This area will include not only all the regions you directly selected, but also all regions that fall within that area.

4. Drag and drop the **regions** you selected. Take care, though—all regions that fall within your selection area will be moved as a group!

Basic Editing Operations

Now you're going to combine a number of tools you've already learned to use with a few new tricks to recreate the bassline from the Chapter 1 session. In addition to tools from this chapter, you'll be drawing on some knowledge you picked up in earlier chapters. Put it all together, and you'll have a good idea of how to put together tracks of your own!

> **NOTE**
>
> If you're working with your Chapter 3 session, you'll want to clear all regions from every track except Virus Bass Audio, Synth Submix, and Guitar Audio. Next, you might want to import the Bass track from the Chapter 1 session. If you don't recall how to do this, review Chapter 3. Because there's already a track named Bass in this session, the new track will be named Bass.1.

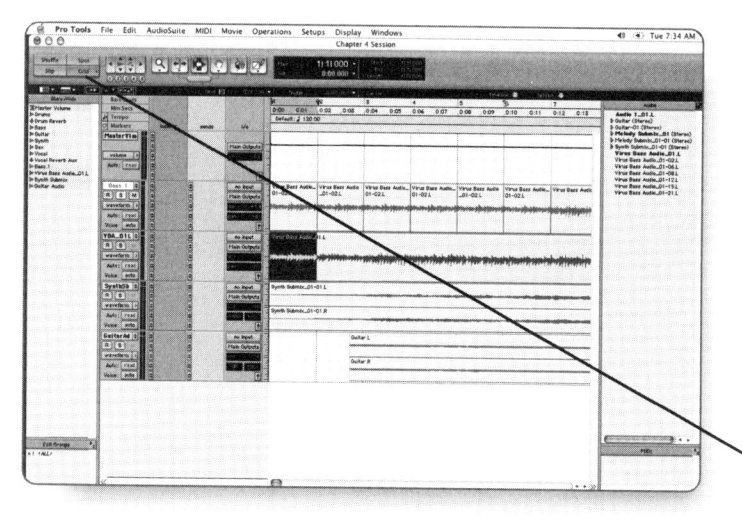

Capturing a Selection

Here's the situation: In this example, you have a reference track named Bass.1. Below it, you will see a track named Virus Bass Audio_01.L, which simply contains a single region. Your task is to reconstruct the bass track from this single region.

1. Click on **Grid**. The Grid mode will be selected.

124 CHAPTER 4: BASIC EDITING

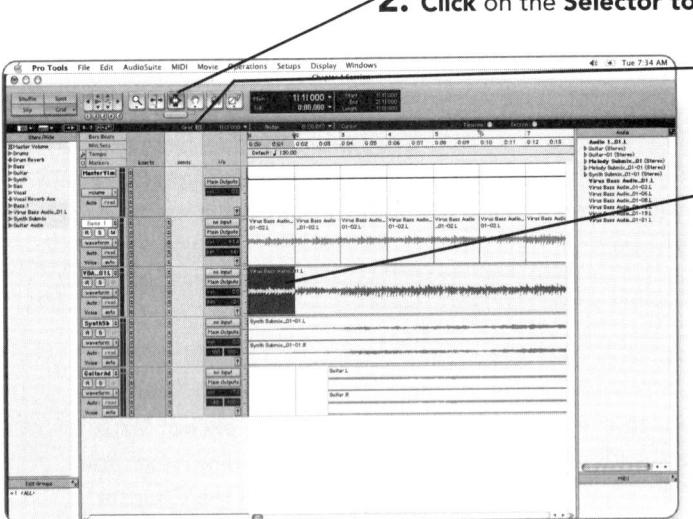

2. Click on the **Selector tool**. The tool will be selected.

3. Double-check the **grid resolution** to make sure it is 1 bar.

4. Select the **first measure** on the Virus Bass Audio track. The measure will be selected.

> **NOTE**
>
> Notice that this segment of audio is identical to the first region of the Bass.1 track.

5. Click on **Edit**. The Edit menu will appear.

6. Click on **Capture Region**. The Name dialog box will open.

BASIC EDITING OPERATIONS

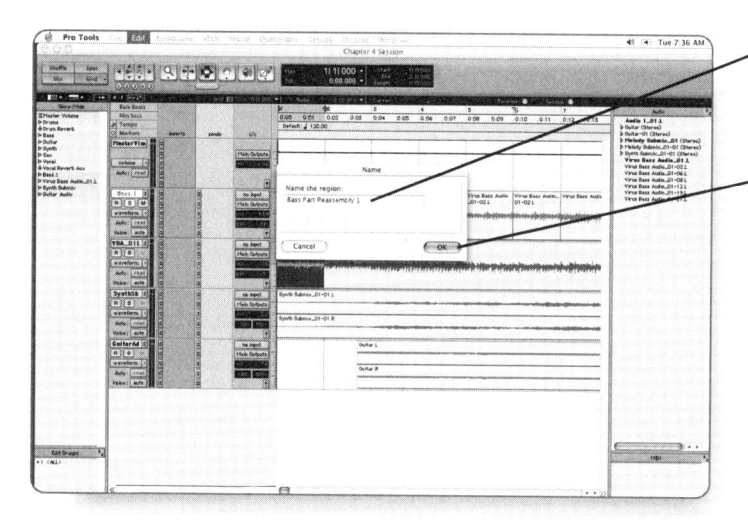

7. Type a descriptive **name** for the region you want to capture in the Name the region text box.

8. Click on **OK**. The Name dialog box will close and the new region and file that is a copy (or capture) of the area you selected will be created. You can see your newly created region in the Audio Regions list.

Separating a Region

Here's another way to create a region. This time, instead of capturing a selection, you're simply going to start chopping up your big region into smaller, more manageable regions. Visually, these two methods might appear quite similar, but by separating a region, you won't be creating any new files on your hard drive. (When you capture a selection, Pro Tools renders a new audio file in your Audio Files subfolder.)

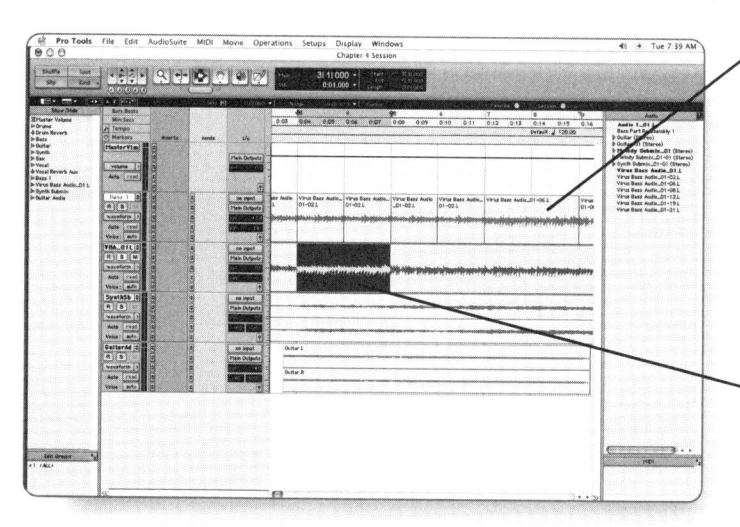

1. If you're working with the Chapter 3 session, **double-click** on the **region** named Virus Bass Audio_01-06.L to highlight it. Listen to the region alone to get an idea of how it sounds. You'll want to solo the track to hear it by itself. (See Chapter 3 for a refresher on how to solo a track.)

2. Select measures 3 through 5 on the Virus Bass Audio track. It's easy when you're in Grid mode!

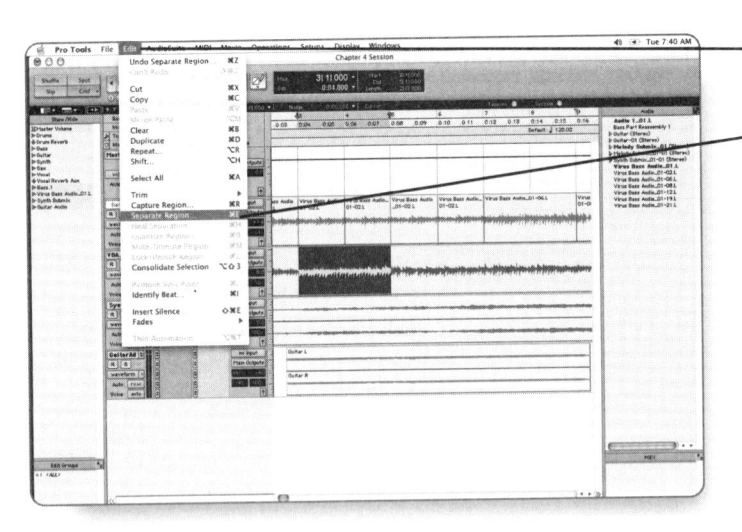

3. Click on **Edit**. The Edit menu will appear.

4. Click on **Separate Region**. The Name dialog box will open.

5. Type a descriptive **name** for the region you want to create in the Name the region text box.

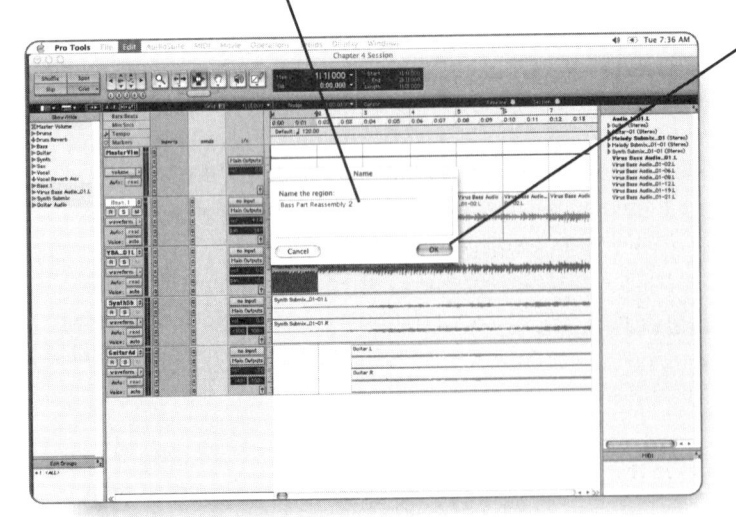

6. Click on **OK**. The window will close and your region will be separated.

TIP

What if Pro Tools is not asking you to name your new regions? What if it's creating new names on its own? No problem! You can disable or enable the Auto-Name feature by selecting the Setups menu, choosing Preferences, and then clicking on the Editing tab. You can select or deselect the Auto-Name Separated Regions field to enable or disable this feature, respectively.

BASIC EDITING OPERATIONS

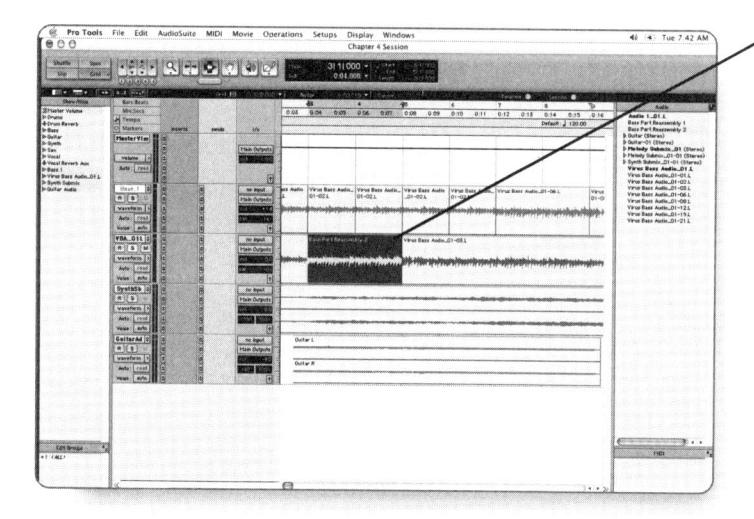

Your original region will be cut into three smaller regions. The region that matches your selection will be in the middle.

> **NOTE**
>
> If you're working with the Chapter 3 session you created earlier and you're following the steps in this chapter, then you're well on your way to rebuilding the bass part from scratch. Good for you! Now you're ready to do some work on your own.
>
> To get to the next step, you need to use either the Capture Region or Separate Region function to create the next three regions. To do so, follow these steps:
>
> 1. Listen to the region beginning at measure 9 on the reference track (bass.1). Find the section on the Virus Bass track that matches it, and then capture or separate a region. Name this region Bass Part Reassembly 3.
>
> 2. Repeat the same steps to create a new region that sounds like the one beginning at measure 12 of the reference track, and name it Bass Part Reassembly 4.
>
> 3. Finally, create a region that matches the region on the reference track that starts at measure 15 and ends at measure 20. (Keep in mind that this section is five measures long.) Name this region Bass Part Reassembly 5.
>
> One last thing to keep in mind: Although capturing or separating will do the job as far as the session goes, there are differences in the way each function works. Capture will leave the original region intact on the Timeline and will create a new file in your Audio Files folder. Separating a region will alter the region in your track, and it won't create any new files in your session's Audio Files folder.

There are two different ways you can create the final region you need to build the bass track—trim or crop.

Trimming a Region

There are two ways to trim a region. Because you're in Grid mode, trimming with the Trim tool is easy to do.

1. **Click** on the **Trim tool**. The tool will be selected.

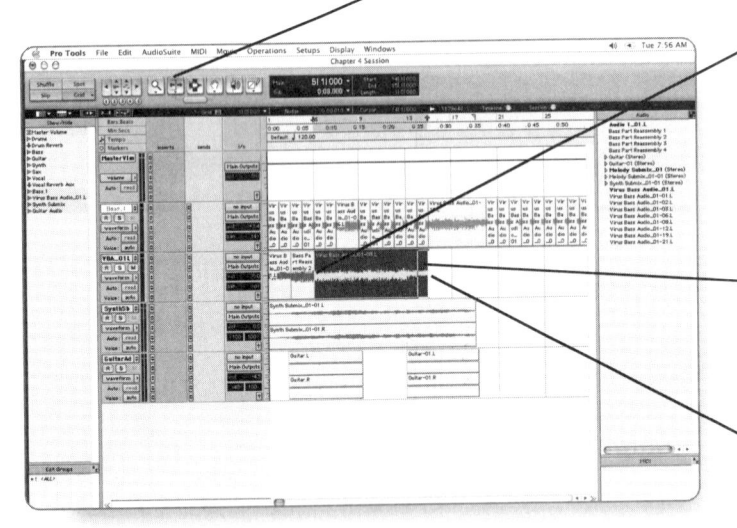

2. **Click and hold** on the **region border** you want to change and **drag** the **boundary** to the desired location. As you drag, Pro Tools will indicate where the boundary is moving.

3. **Release** the **mouse button**. A new region will be created (but not a new audio file) with the new region boundary.

4. If necessary, **repeat steps 1–3** for the other end of the region.

NOTE

Before you can re-edit this region to get the same results, you need to undo the trimming you just did. You can access the Undo function from the Edit menu, or you can use the shortcut keys (⌘+Z on a Mac and Ctrl+Z on a PC). Pro Tools provides up to 16 levels of undo.

BASIC EDITING OPERATIONS 129

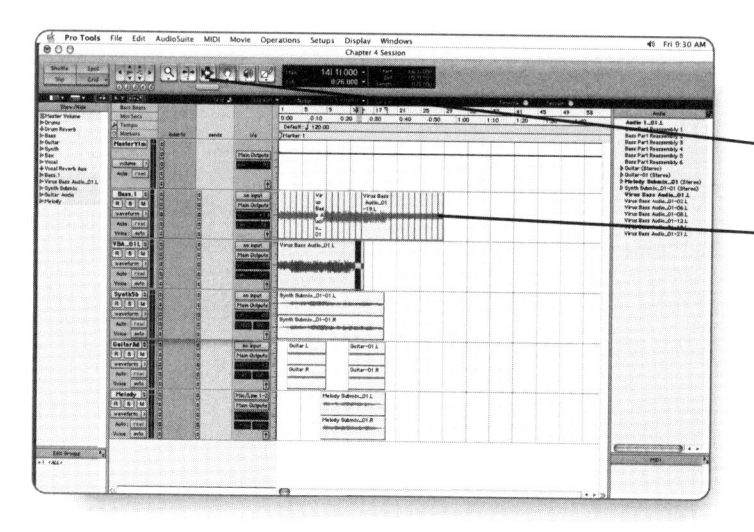

Here's another way to get the job done:

1. Click on the **Selector tool**. The tool will be selected.

2. Select the **area** of the audio region that you want to retain.

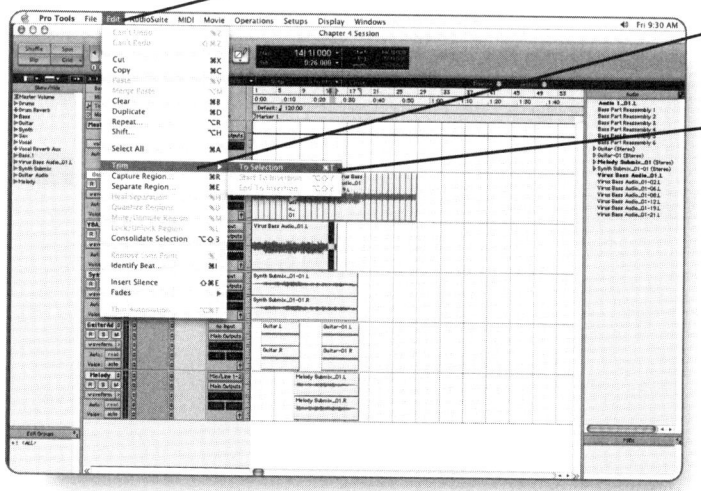

3. Click on **Edit**. The Edit menu will appear.

4. Click on **Trim**. The Trim submenu will appear.

5. Because you've made a selection (as opposed to setting a timeline insertion point), the only option you can use is To Selection. **Click** on **To Selection**. The region will be trimmed to your selection.

Renaming a Region

When you're finished (with any of the edit processes we've discussed), you might want to rename the regions you have created. Here's how to rename any region:

1. **Click** on the **Grabber tool**. The tool will be selected.

2. **Double-click** on the **region** you want to rename. The Name dialog box will open.

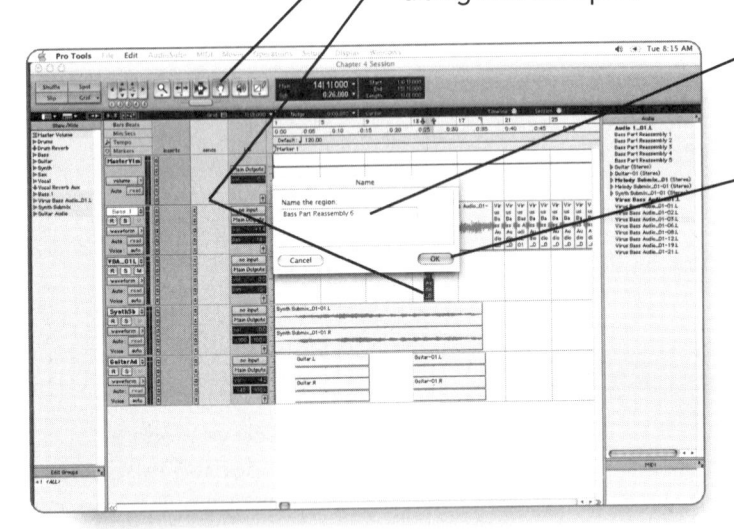

3. **Type** the **name** you want for the region in the Name the region text box.

4. **Click** on **OK**. The Name dialog box will close and the region will be renamed.

Assembling a Track

After you've created regions, the next step in the process is to organize them on the track. Of course, what you've already learned about the edit modes will aid you greatly in this process, but there are a couple additional tricks that can make the process even easier!

> **NOTE**
>
> If you're following the examples shown here, you will want to select all remaining regions on the Virus Bass Audio track and remove them from the track, leaving a blank track on which to assemble your newly created regions.

ASSEMBLING A TRACK 131

Working in Shuffle mode makes the job easy!

1. Click on **Shuffle** if you're not already in Shuffle mode.

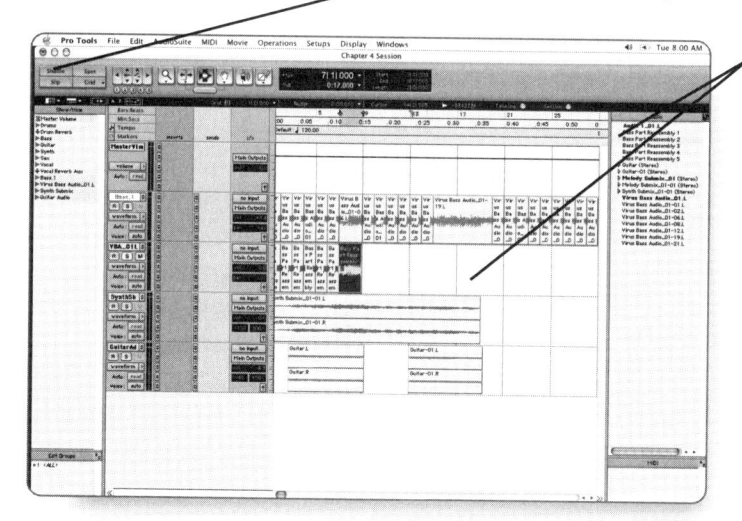

2. One by one, **drag regions** onto the desired track in the order that you want them to be played back.

> **NOTE**
>
> If you're following the example, drag Bass Part Reassembly 1 onto the track five times, and then drag Bass Part Reassembly 2 onto the track once. Remember from earlier in this chapter that in Shuffle mode, it doesn't matter where you drop your regions—they'll automatically move to the edge of the preceding region.

Duplicating Regions

Of course, you *could* just drag the same region onto a track over and over and have a repeating loop, but that can get really boring very quickly. Here's another way to make a copy of a region or selection and place it after the original:

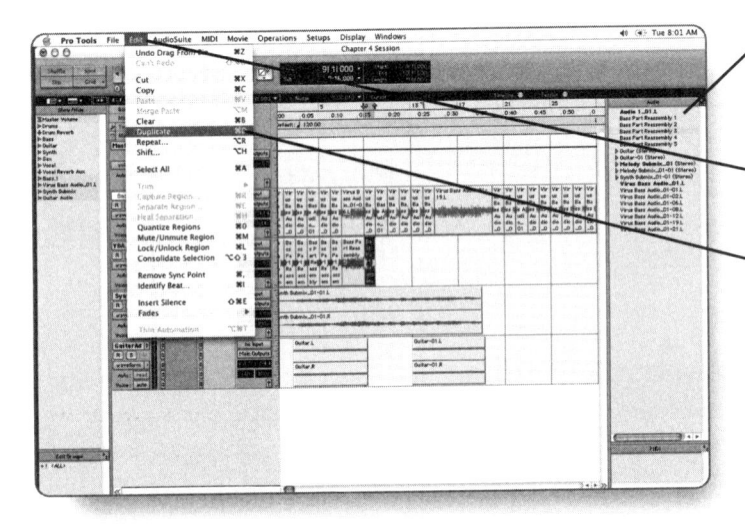

1. Drag and drop a single **region** onto a track or otherwise **select** a **region**.

2. Click on **Edit**. The Edit menu will appear.

3. Click on **Duplicate**. The region will be copied immediately after the preceding selection.

> **TIP**
>
> The shortcut for the Duplicate function is ⌘+D on a Mac and Ctrl+D on a PC.

> **NOTE**
>
> If you're following the example shown, you'll want to duplicate Bass Part Reassembly 3 two times, and then add Bass Part Reassembly 4 at bar 12. Finally, you'll add Bass Part Reassembly 3 another two times, and then Bass Part Reassembly 5. Then you'll be ready to continue.

Repeating Regions

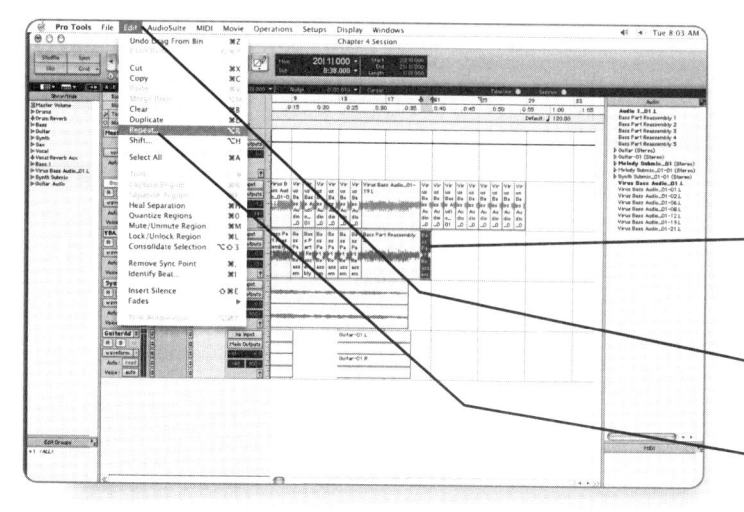

Repeating regions is similar to duplicating regions, but with a twist.

1. Drag and drop a single **region** onto a track or otherwise **select** a **region**.

2. Click on **Edit**. The Edit menu will appear.

3. Click on **Repeat**. The Repeat dialog box will open.

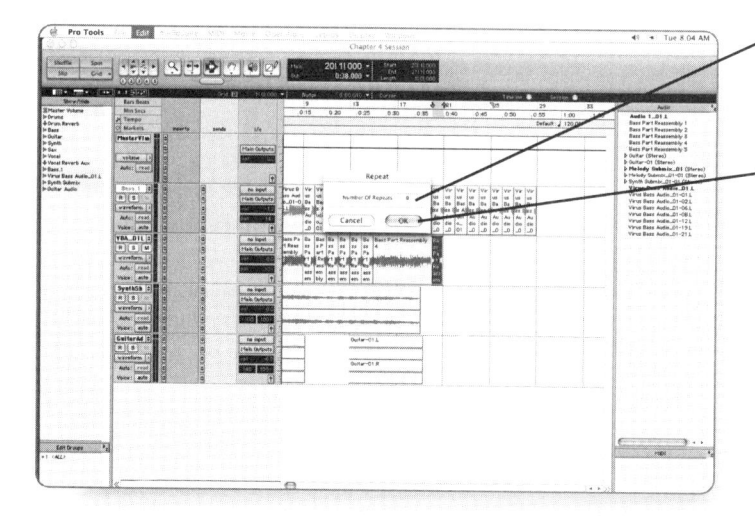

4. Type the **number of times** you want the region to repeat in the Number of Repeats text box.

5. Click on **OK**. The selected region will be repeated the specified number of times, just as if you had used the Duplicate command a number of times.

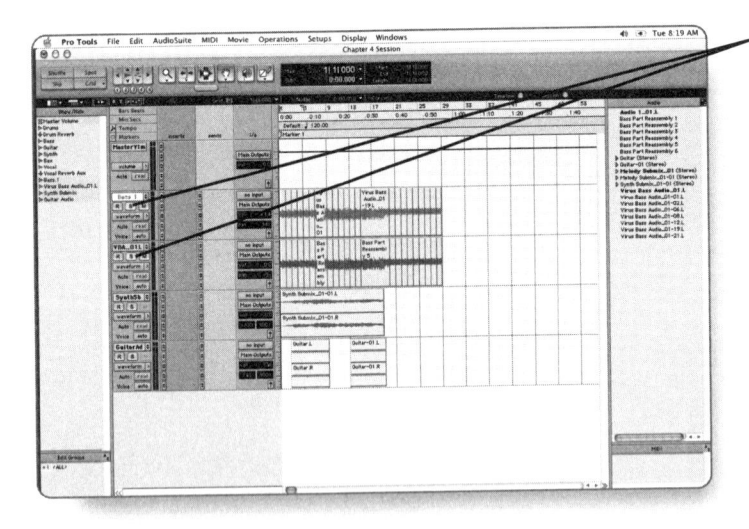

6. Solo both **bass tracks** and **play them** together. The tracks should sound identical. If they do, then you're done! (If they don't, then it's time to take a close look at the reference track and the track you just created and find where they disagree, and then redo the necessary steps in this section.)

Working with Grids

Hopefully by now you're getting a good idea of the usefulness of working in Grid mode. However, using a grid as wide as a whole measure might not work for you in all situations. You can change the grid and see the possibilities.

> **NOTE**
>
> If you're following the examples in this chapter, you'll want to create a new track named Melody. If you don't remember how to create a new track, take a look back at Chapter 3.

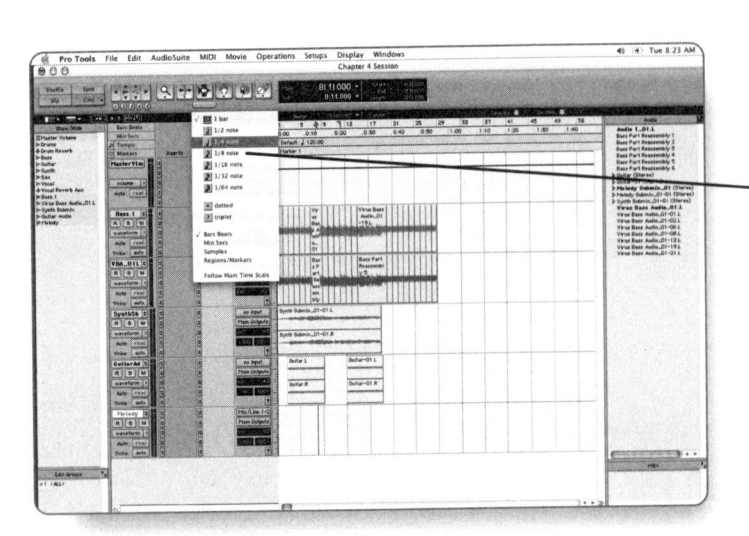

1. Click on the **arrow** next to the Grid value. The Grid menu will appear.

2. Select the **scale** (for example, Bars:Beats or Min:Secs) if you want to change the scale of your grid. If you want to continue in the same scale, **click** on the **grid value** you want. The grid will immediately change in the Edit window.

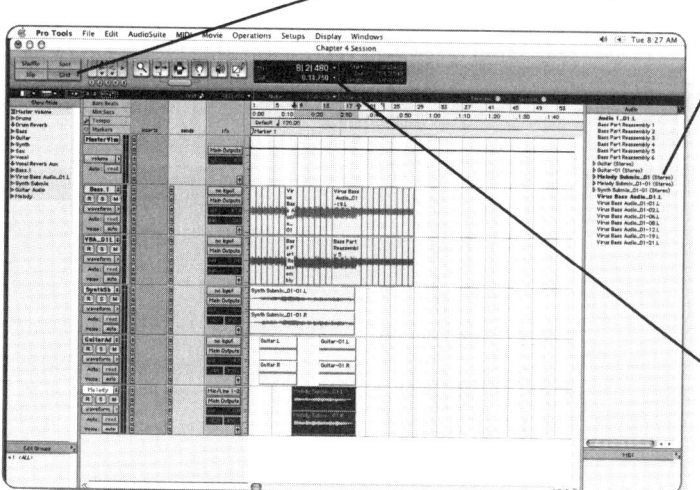

3. Click on **Grid** if you're not already in Grid mode.

4. Drag a **region** onto a track. As you drag the region in the track, the region will move in different increments and allow you to drop your region at different locations.

5. Drop the **region** at the desired location.

The location, as well as the start, end, and length of the selected region, will be shown in your location displays.

Cutting, Copying, and Pasting

Cut, copy, and paste are pretty tried-and-true staples of most audio software, and Pro Tools is certainly no exception. These processes are very straightforward and easy to use.

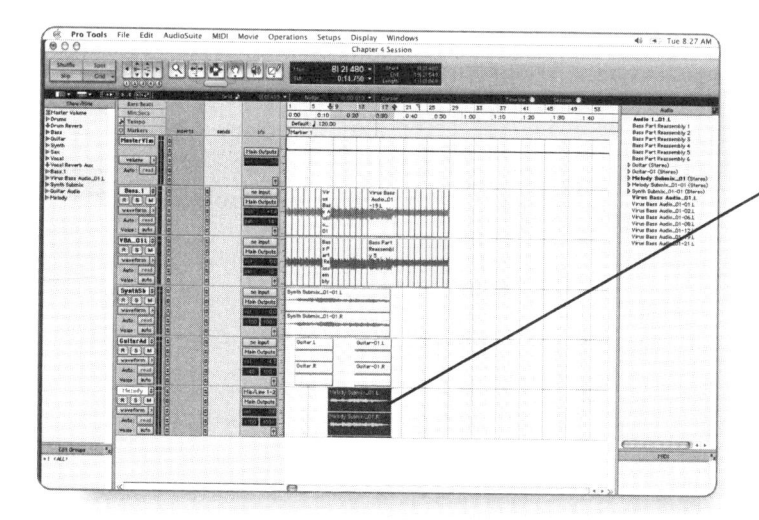

Copying a Region

Copying a region can be quite useful—and easy!

1. Select the **region** you want to copy.

> **TIP**
>
> One of the easiest ways to select a region is to double-click on it if you are using the Selector tool. You can also click on the region if you're using the Grabber tool.

CHAPTER 4: BASIC EDITING

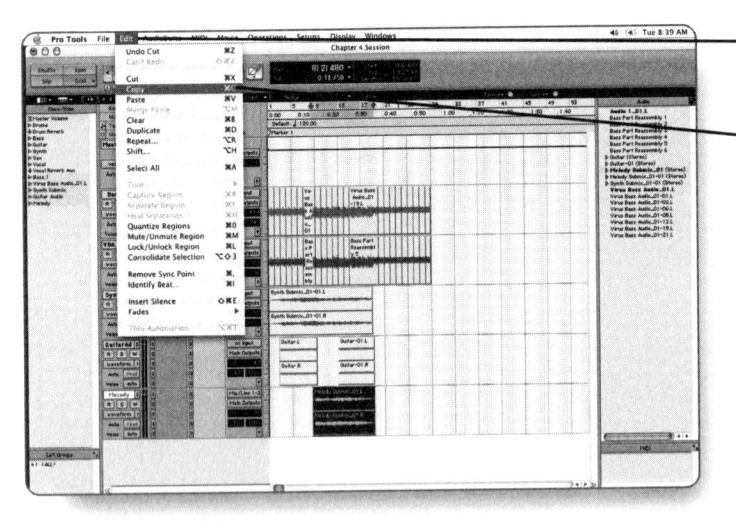

2. Click on **Edit**. The Edit menu will appear.

3. Click on **Copy**. The region will be copied to the clipboard.

> **TIP**
> The shortcut for the Copy command is ⌘+C on a Mac and Ctrl+C on a PC.

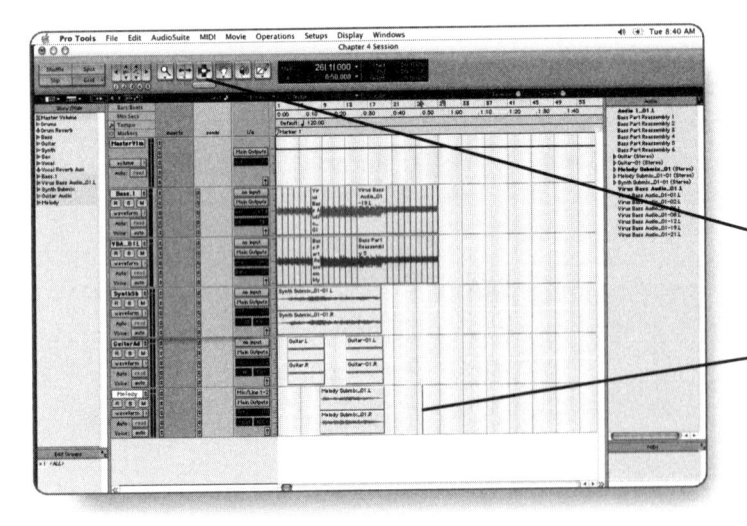

Pasting a Region

A copied region means nothing until it's pasted to a new location. Here's how to do this:

1. Click on the **Selector tool** if it's not already selected. The tool will be selected.

2. Click in a **track** at the location where you want to paste the region you copied.

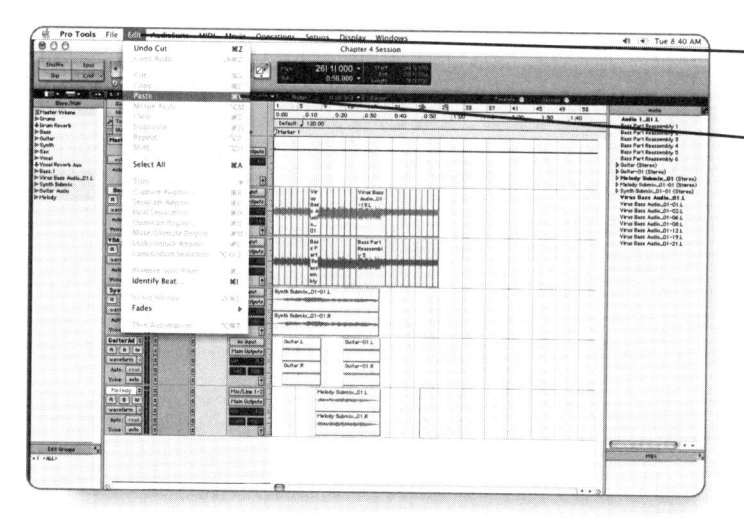

ASSEMBLING A TRACK   137

3. Click on **Edit**. The Edit menu will appear.

4. Click on **Paste**. The region will be pasted at the location you selected.

> **TIP**
>
> The shortcut for the Paste command is ⌘+V on a Mac and Ctrl+V on a PC.

Cutting a Region

Because you're not going to use that region, go ahead and cut it.

1. Select the **region** you want to cut. The region will be selected.

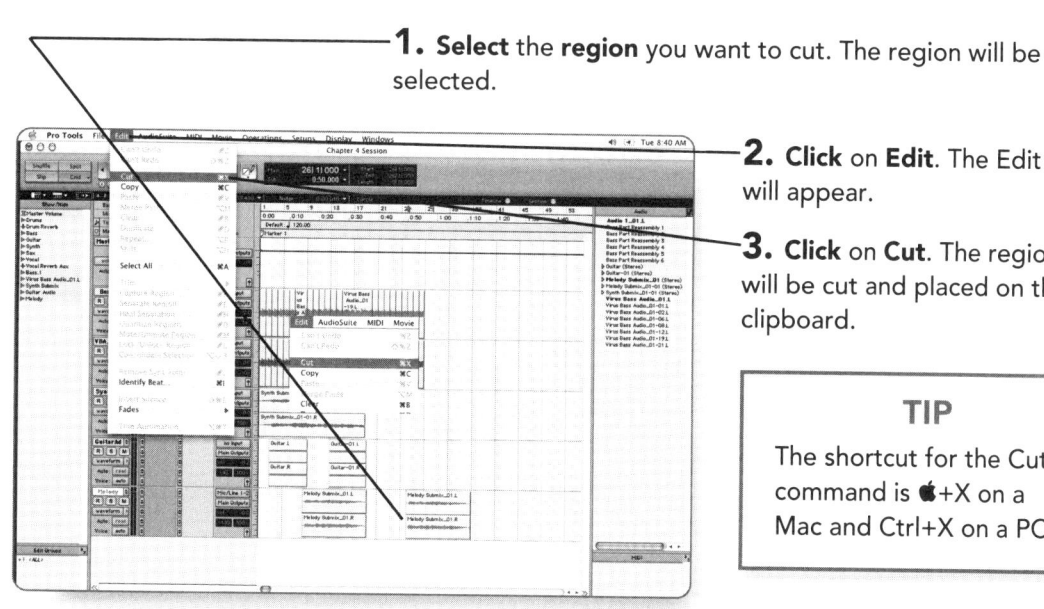

2. Click on **Edit**. The Edit menu will appear.

3. Click on **Cut**. The region will be cut and placed on the clipboard.

> **TIP**
>
> The shortcut for the Cut command is ⌘+X on a Mac and Ctrl+X on a PC.

When You're Finished: Cleaning Up and Backing Up

Now that you've done a significant amount of work, it's time to tidy your session a little. Also, if you've been following the examples, then you've been working on the Chapter 3 session and you might want to save your work under another name. In this section, I'll talk about a powerful new way to save and back up your sessions and files.

Deleting Tracks

Deleting unused tracks will make your session more manageable and will also free up valuable resources for other tracks to use.

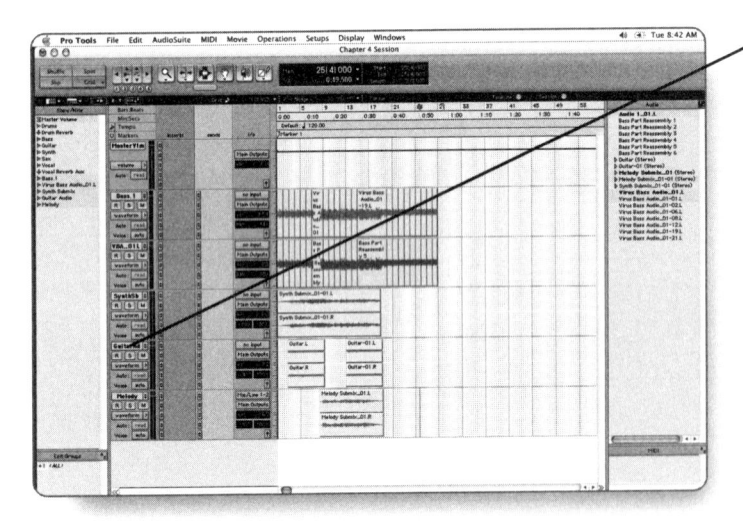

1. Select the **track** you want to delete by clicking on its name. The track will be selected.

> **TIP**
>
> If you want to delete multiple tracks, you can do so by holding down the Shift key while you select tracks. Then follow steps 2–4, just as if you were deleting a single track.

WHEN YOU'RE FINISHED: CLEANING UP AND BACKING UP

NOTE
If you're working on the Chapter 3 session, choose the track named Bass.1.

2. Click on **File**. The File menu will appear.

3. Click on **Delete Selected Tracks**.

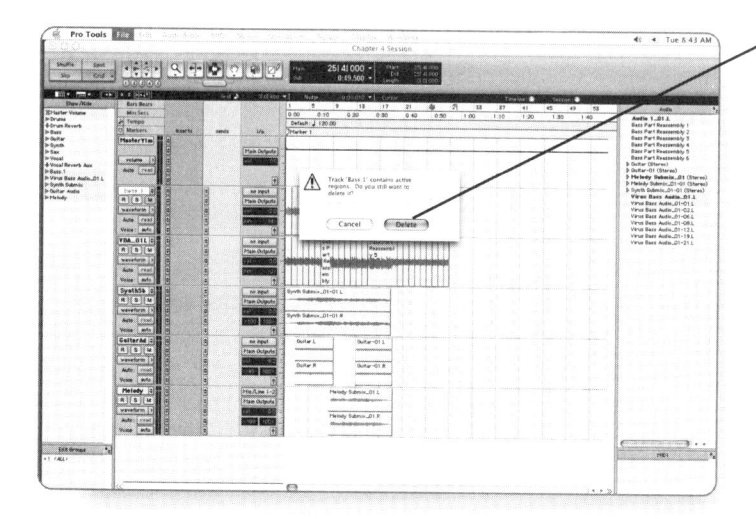

4. When a track contains active regions, a message box will appear. **Click** on the **Delete button** to confirm your decision to delete the track.

Using the Save Session Copy In Feature

By now you know that you can use the Save Session As command and save your session as Chapter 4 Session (or whatever you want to name it). The session, however, would be saved in the Chapter 3 folder. If you want to save your session with a different name *and* create a new folder, complete with all the dependent audio files, the Save Session Copy In feature is for you!

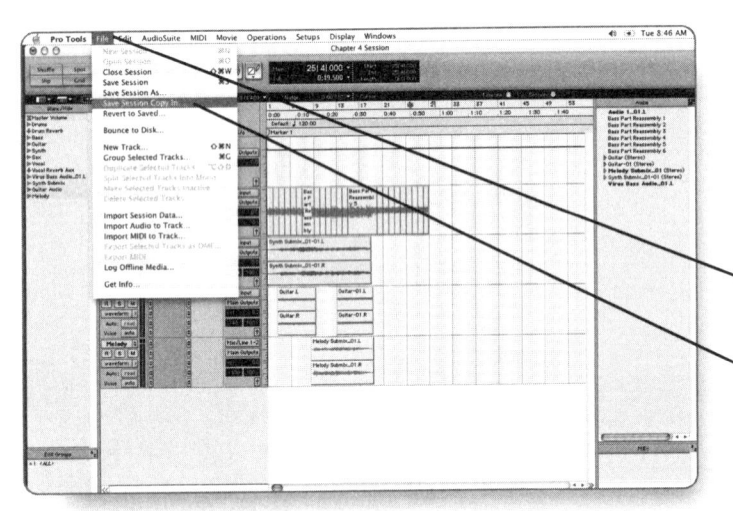

1. Click on **File**. The File menu will appear.

2. Click on **Save Session Copy In**. The Save dialog box will open.

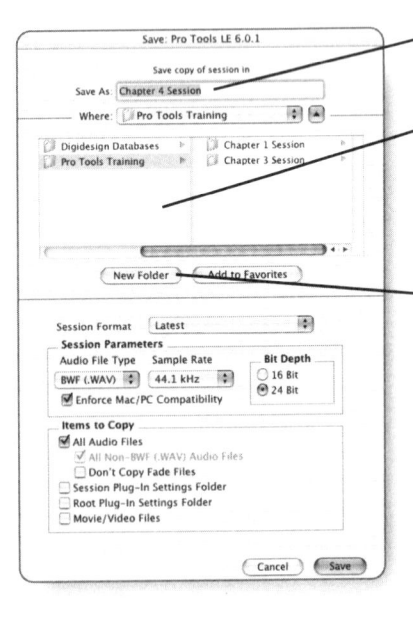

3. In the Save As text box, **type** a descriptive **session name** that is different from the original session name.

4. Select a **location** for your session. This section is identical to the related sections in the dialog boxes when you choose Save or Save As. This time a new folder will be created for your new session, though.

5. If you want to create your session folder *within* another folder, **click** on the **New Folder button**. The New Folder window will open.

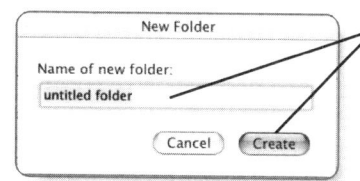

WHEN YOU'RE FINISHED: CLEANING UP AND BACKING UP   141

6. Type a **name** for your new folder in the Name of new folder text box, and then **click** on **Create**. The new session folder will be saved within this new folder.

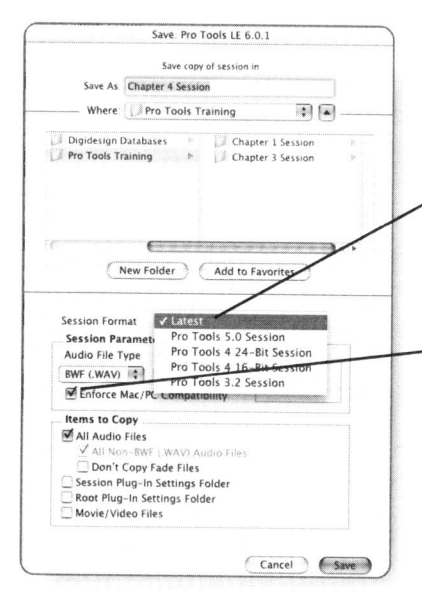

Save Session Copy In also gives you the option to resave all of the elements of your session (audio files, fade files, and so on), which gives you a whole new dimension of flexibility. Here are some things to consider:

- **Session Format menu.** This drop-down menu contains options for previous versions of Pro Tools. You might select one of these other formats if you intend to open this session in an older version of Pro Tools.

- **Session Parameters section.** These are the same options you saw when you initially created your session. You can select different file types, sample rates, and/or bit depths for your session. Pro Tools will automatically convert audio files as needed in your new session's Audio Files folder.

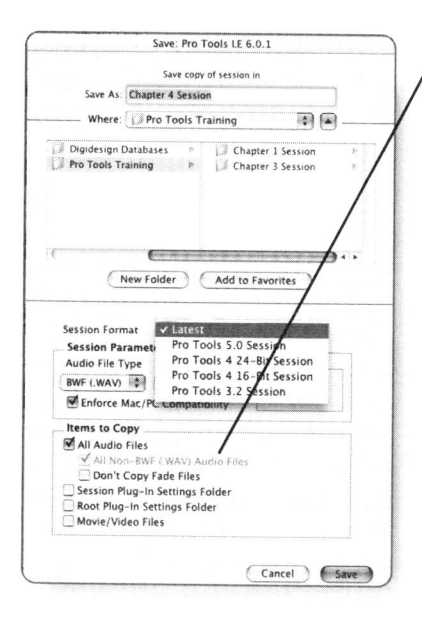

- **Items to Copy section.** You can choose the elements of your original session that you want to copy over to your new session folder. Click to select the boxes that represent aspects of your old session that you want to create in your new session folder.

> **TIP**
>
> Backing up (or *archiving*) your work is a tremendously important part of production. It might not be terribly exciting, but you'll be glad you established good file-saving habits if something unexpected happens!
>
> Save Session Copy In is particularly suited to archiving because it makes copies of your original session in a separate (and hopefully safe) place. Additionally, this process intelligently gathers all the elements your session needs (assuming you selected them in the Items to Copy section) and saves them in one central location. Bottom line: When you're backing up your session (for example, making a CD-ROM of your work for long-term storage), Save Session Copy In is a very smart way to go!

5
Recording Audio

Everything we've talked about up to this point is crucial to being an informed Pro Tools user. Sooner or later, though, you'll want to actually *record* some audio as opposed to importing files, right? No problem—this is another area where Pro Tools shines, and the flexibility this software affords has helped it earn its place as a leader in the field. In this chapter, you'll learn how to:

- Set up a click track
- Make your first recording
- Use punch-in/punch-out recording and other recording options
- Make the most of your monitoring options

144 CHAPTER 5: RECORDING AUDIO

Getting Started: Signal Flow 101

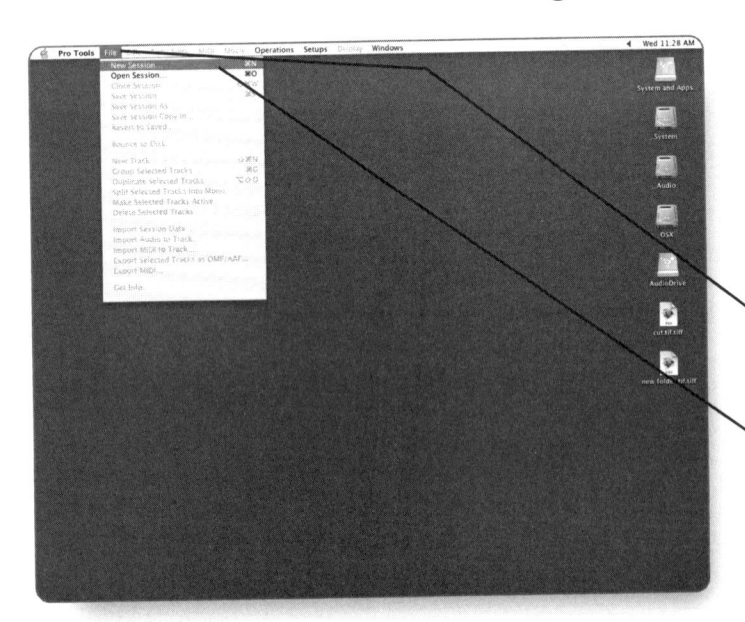

You took a good first look at the Edit window in Chapters 1 and 2. Now it's time to take a closer look! First, though, you'll need to create a new session. (See Chapter 1 for a complete rundown of this process.)

1. After you launch the Pro Tools application, **click** on **File**. The File menu will appear.

2. Click on **New Session**. The New Session dialog box will open.

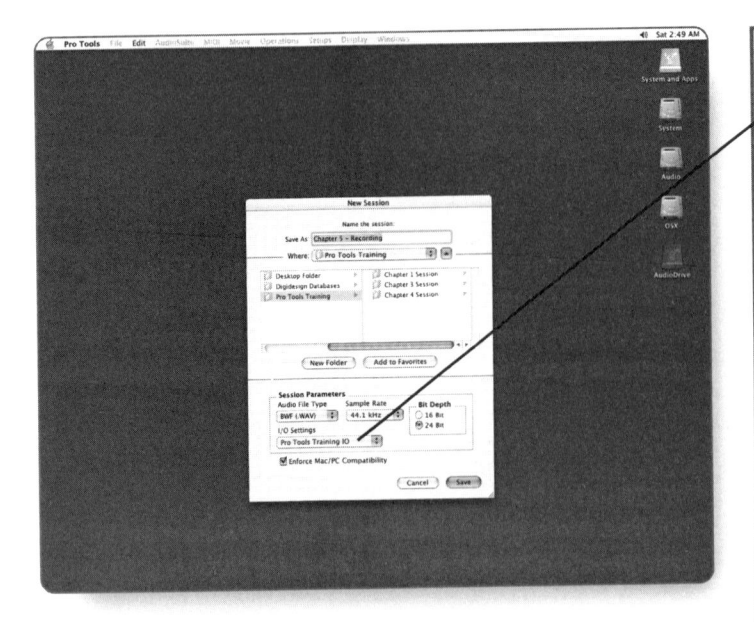

NOTE

Make special note of the I/O settings. By default, Pro Tools' New Session dialog box opens with Last Used as a default I/O setting. These are the settings last used in Pro Tools. Of course, you might not know what settings you'll get, especially in a multi-user facility. Generally speaking, you'll want to specify an I/O setting of your own (like the I/O settings you created in Chapter 3).

GETTING STARTED: SIGNAL FLOW 101　　145

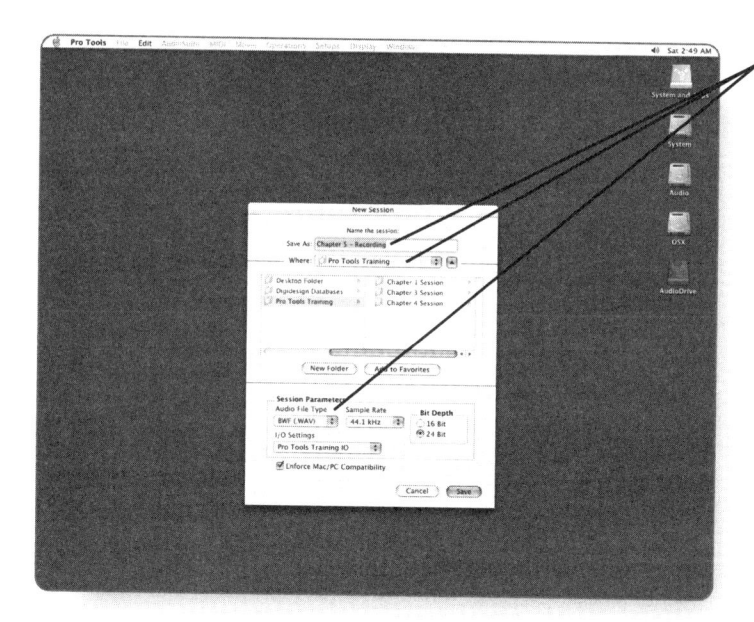

3. Choose your new session's **name, location, and settings** and then **click** on **Save**. Your new session will be created by Pro Tools.

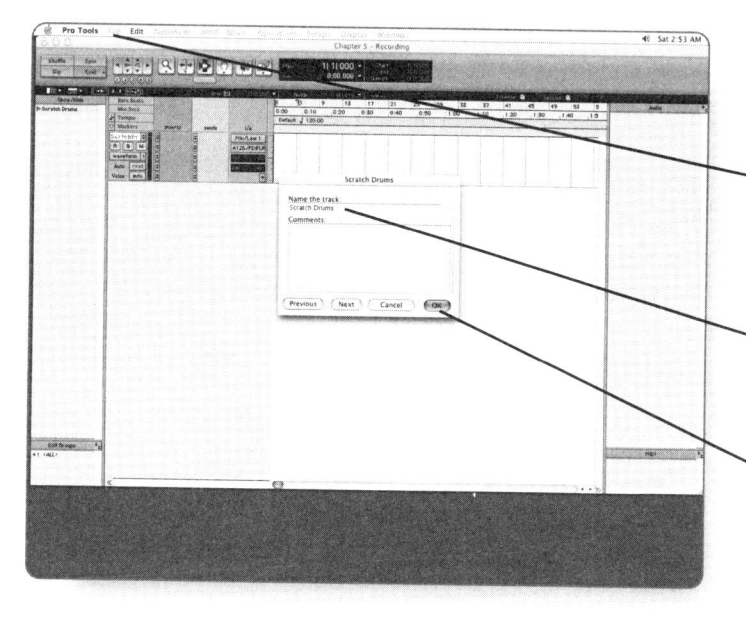

If you're going to record audio, you need to create an audio track on which to record.

1. Click on **File** and **select New Track**. A dialog box will open. Create a mono audio track, as you learned to do in Chapter 3.

2. Type a descriptive **name** for the track in the Name the track text box.

3. Click on **OK**. Your track will be created.

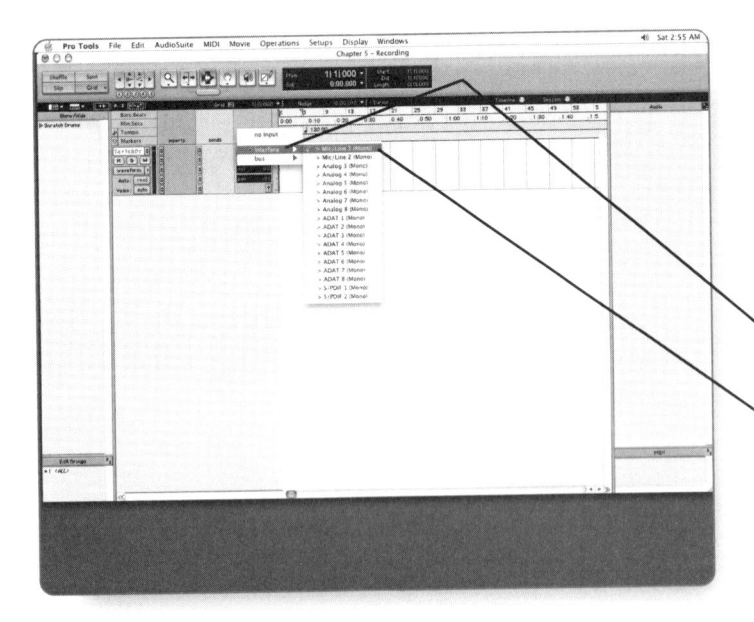

Setting Up the Input

The top button in the I/O column of each track shows the input of the track. You can click on the button to select an input.

1. **Click** on the **Input button**. A drop-down menu will appear.

2. **Click** on the **physical input or bus** that your audio will be coming from (as specified in your I/O settings). The input will be selected.

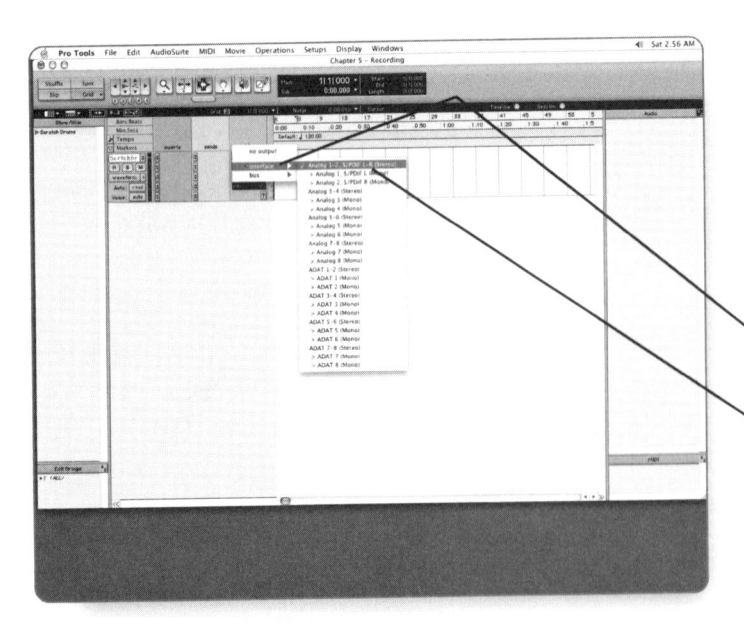

Setting Up the Output

The next button down shows the output of the track. You can click on the button to select an output.

1. **Click** on the **Output button**. A drop-down menu will appear.

2. **Click** on the **physical output or bus** to which you will output your audio (as specified in your I/O settings). The output will be selected.

GETTING STARTED: SIGNAL FLOW 101

> **NOTE**
> You'll notice that in addition to selecting physical inputs or outputs (aka interface connectors), you can also select something called a bus. A *bus* is like a virtual audio cable that can route audio within the Pro Tools software. You'll learn the basics of how to use buses in Chapter 8, "Basic Mixing."

Setting the Output Volume

The third field shows the volume of the track's output. You can adjust the volume by clicking in this field.

1. Click in the **Volume field**. A volume fader will appear.

2. Click and drag the **fader** to the volume level you desire, and then **release** the **mouse button**. The volume will be adjusted.

CHAPTER 5: RECORDING AUDIO

Setting the Output Pan

The fourth field shows the pan of the track's output. You can adjust this setting by clicking in the field.

1. Click in the **Pan field**. A small slider will appear.

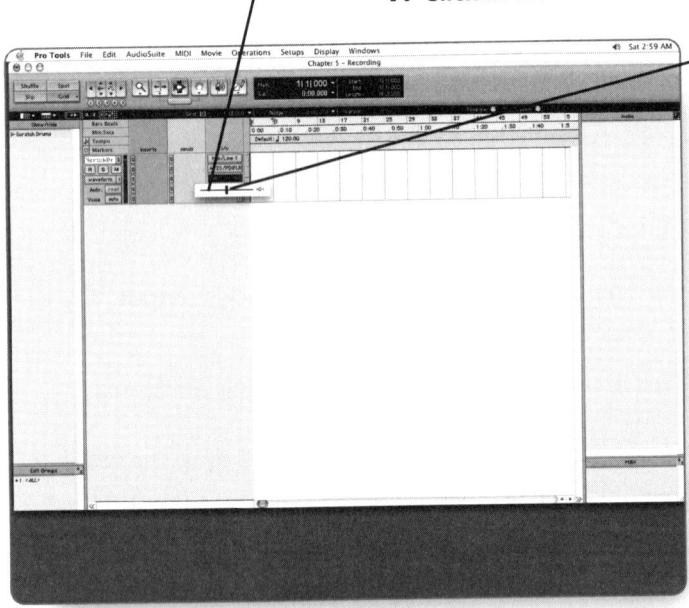

2. Click and drag the **slider bar** to the pan you desire, and then **release** the **mouse button**. The output pan will be set.

> **NOTE**
>
> The output volume and output pan control the track's output only, not the input level. This means that to avoid clipping when recording, you'll want to bring down the level of your sound source (instrument, microphone, and so on) rather than the volume fader on the track.

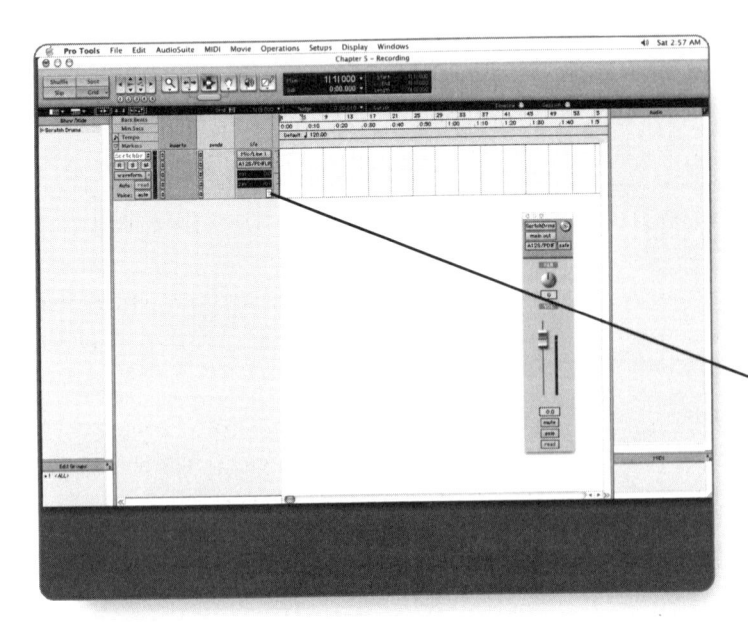

Using Tear-Away Strips

There's another way to view and manipulate this essential track-related data.

1. Click on the **icon** beneath the output pan display. (The icon looks like a tiny fader.)

GETTING STARTED: SIGNAL FLOW 101   149

A track tear-away strip will appear. Note that much of the track-related data you've set up on the track is shown here as well:

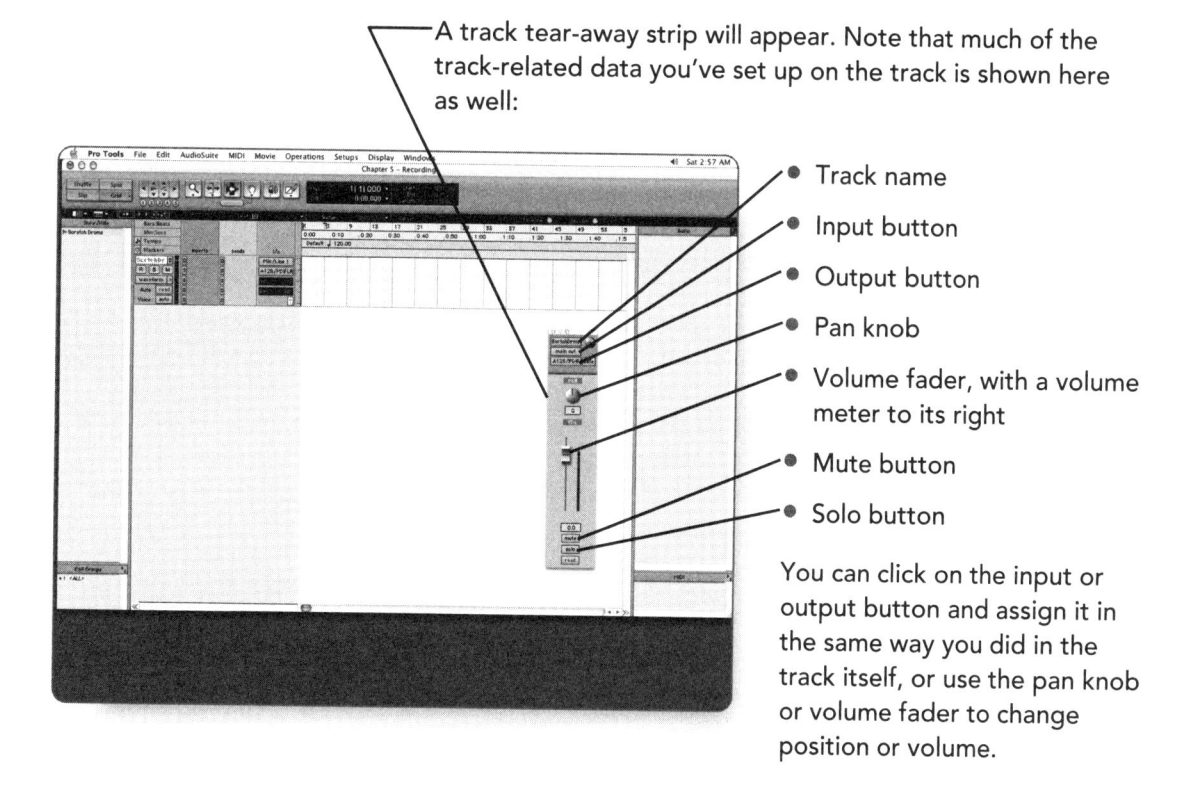

- Track name
- Input button
- Output button
- Pan knob
- Volume fader, with a volume meter to its right
- Mute button
- Solo button

You can click on the input or output button and assign it in the same way you did in the track itself, or use the pan knob or volume fader to change position or volume.

> **NOTE**
>
> Tear-away strips can look a little different depending upon the type of track being shown. For example, if you are looking at a track with a mono output, no pan knob will be displayed. If you're working with a stereo track's tear-away strip, you'll see two volume meters (one for each mono audio file that comprises the track).

> **TIP**
>
> You can quickly reset your volume to unity (0.0) or your pan to center (0) by holding the Option key (Mac) or the Alt key (PC) while you click on the volume or pan controls in either the track or the tear-away strip.

Setting Up a Click Track

You might be wondering just what a click track is. Fair question—even though it's a fairly common term, it's surprising how many musicians don't know what a click track is or what it's used for. The answer: A click track is an audible track in a multi-track environment that indicates the tempo of a song through a series of short tones (usually click sounds). This is much the same way that a metronome helps a musician keep tempo in the practice room. This feature is not specific to Pro Tools—indeed, click tracks have been used for decades, dating back to the earliest analog recording studios, when multiple musicians would all listen to the same click track on their headphones as they played, in order to stay in time with each other.

Although you certainly won't need a click track every time you work with Pro Tools, you'll find that click tracks are a convenient way to keep everything in sync as you add track upon track to a complex session. Especially suited to music-oriented work, click tracks are very common in studios worldwide, and the ability to work with them is considered an essential skill.

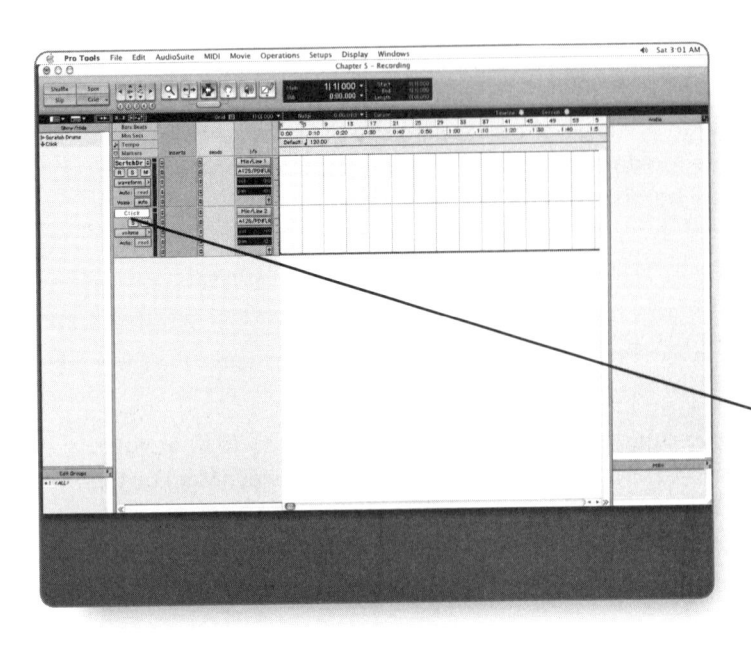

More Signal Flow: Audio Tracks Versus Aux Tracks

Your click track will be an aux track. Why? Go ahead and create an aux track, and you'll see what makes it different from an audio track.

1. Create a **mono aux track** named Click. (See Chapter 3 if you need a quick review of how to create a mono aux track.)

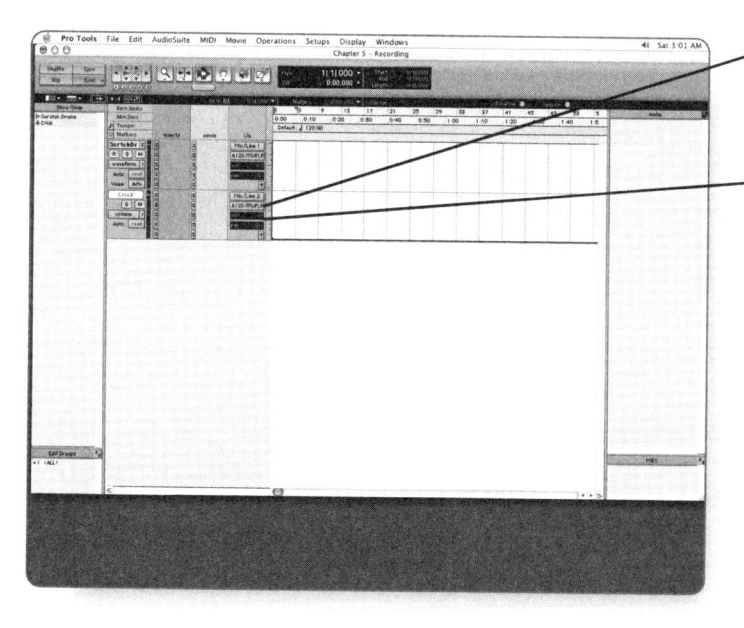

2. Assign the **outputs** so you can hear the track through your monitor speakers.

3. Set the **output volume** to unity (0.0).

Notice that the aux track is virtually identical to the audio track above it. That's because audio tracks and aux tracks are closely related. However, even though an aux track is an audible track, it certainly isn't an audio track. The main difference between the two is that an audio track can play back regions in your session (as you've already seen). To do this, an audio track uses voices. (A *voice* is defined as a channel of audio going to or coming from your hard drive.) Mono audio tracks use one voice and stereo audio tracks use two, up to a maximum of 32 active voices in a Pro Tools LE system. The most significant difference between an audio track and an aux track is that an aux track doesn't use a voice, which means you can't use audio regions on an aux track. However, because an aux track doesn't eat up one of your session's 32 voices, using an aux track whenever possible (like, for example, for a click track) will conserve resources so you can get the maximum performance out of your system.

You can start by using your newly created aux track for a click track.

Using the Click Plug-In

Plug-ins are programs that run within your Pro Tools system. They can be anything from virtual effects such as reverbs and equalization to virtual instruments such as the click plug-in, which plays click sounds. In this case, the plug-in will create a click for your session. You'll learn more about plug-ins in Chapter 8.

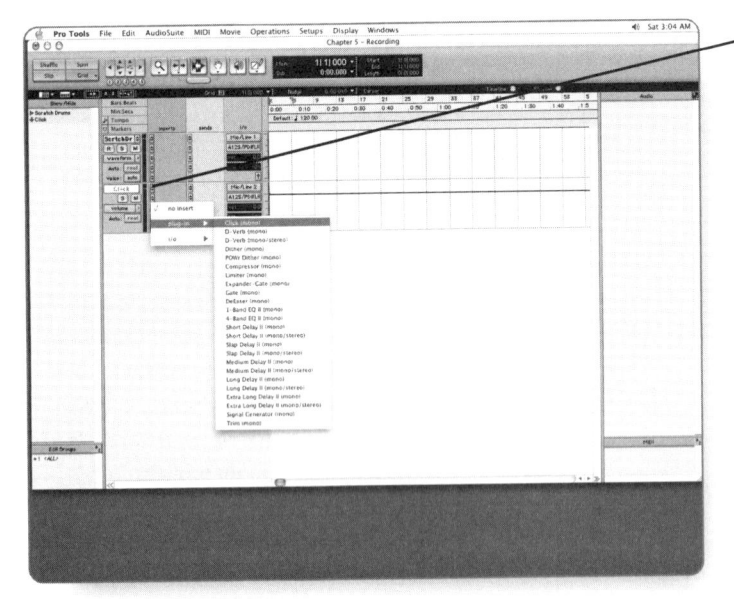

1. You will need to use an insert to launch your plug-in. **Click** on one of the five available **insert selector buttons** on your aux track. An insert menu will appear.

> **NOTE**
>
> Any effects that you put on inserts will be processed in order, from the top insert down to the bottom. When mixing, it's important to understand the order of your signal through effects, so the placement of effects on your inserts is crucial. In the case of this click track, the click plug-in is the only effect you'll be using on the track, so it doesn't matter which of the five inserts you use.

2. Choose plug-in. A submenu will appear.

3. Click on **Click (mono)**. The Click plug-in window will appear.

SETTING UP A CLICK TRACK

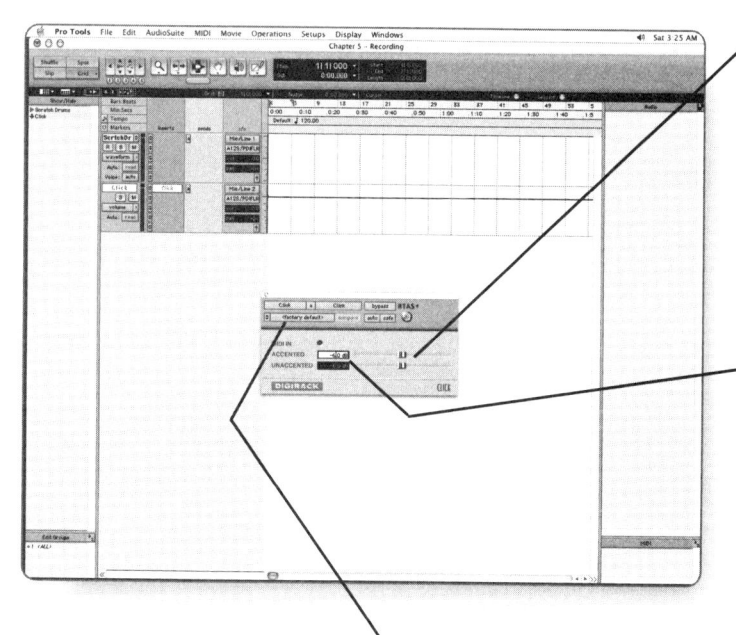

4a. Adjust the **Accented** (for each measure's beat 1) **and Unaccented** (for the other beats) **sliders** to get the best overall volume. You can change these values at any time in your session.

OR

4b. Type a **value** in the Accented or Unaccented field to adjust the values manually. **Press** the **Enter key** when you're finished to confirm your entry.

5. Click on the **plug-in preset name**. A preset drop-down menu will appear, from which you can choose a tone for your click.

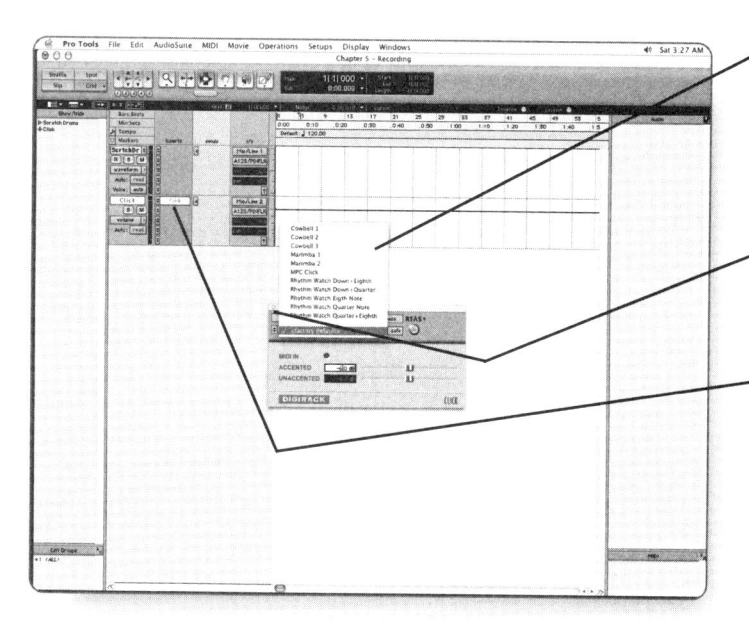

6. Choose a **tone** for your click track. The tone will be selected. Again, you can change this choice at any time in your session.

7. When you're finished, **click** on the **close button**. The Click plug-in window will close.

8. If you want to change your settings as you work, **click** on the **insert button** to reopen the Click plug-in window.

Setting Click and Tempo Options

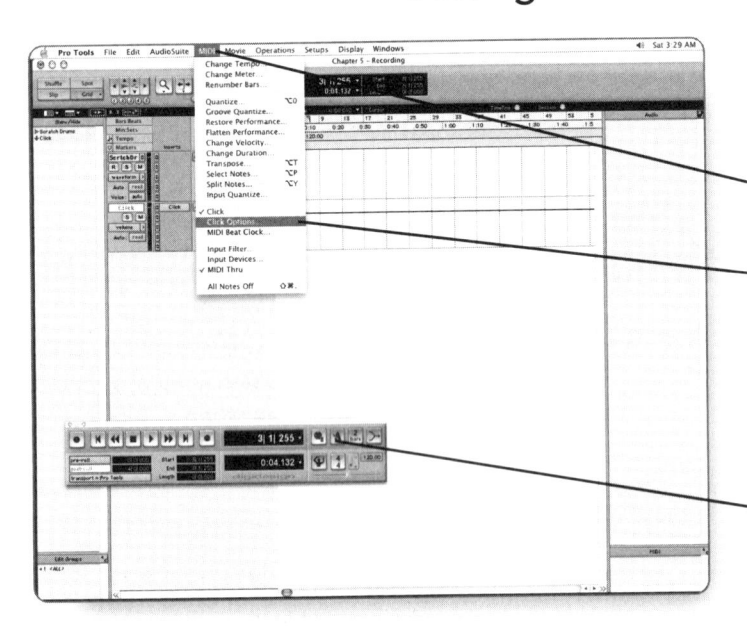

The last thing you need to do is set up how your click track will behave.

1. Click on **MIDI**. The MIDI menu will appear.

2. Choose Click Options. The Click/Countoff Options dialog box will open. This dialog box controls when the click will play.

> **TIP**
> Another way to access the Click/Countoff Options dialog box is to double-click on the Metronome icon in the Transport window.

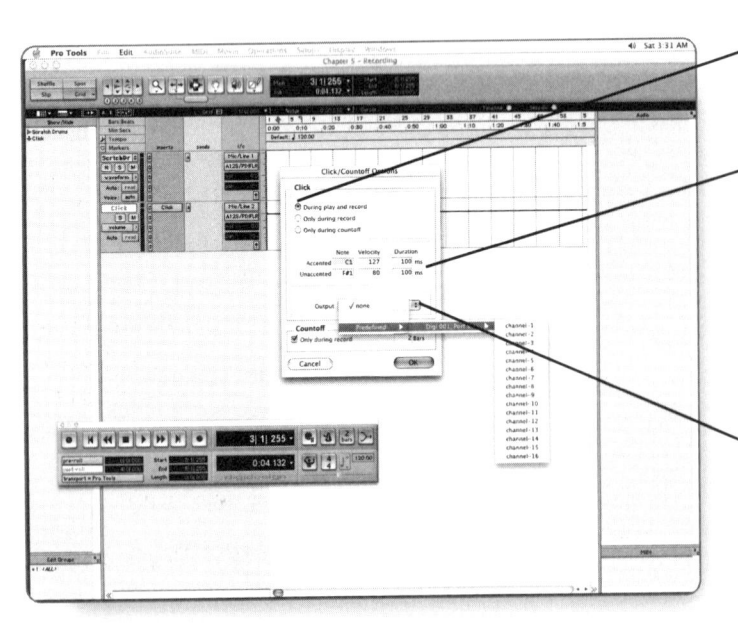

3. Click on the **During play and record radio button**. The option will be selected.

4. You have the option of sending click information to a MIDI synthesizer (which I'll discuss more in Chapter 6, "Using MIDI"). **Enter notes, velocities, and durations** for the Accented and Unaccented fields.

5. Click on the **Output menu** and **select** a **MIDI output port** for your click information. The option will be selected.

SETTING UP A CLICK TRACK   155

> **TIP**
> If you're using the click plug-in, you don't need to worry about assigning a MIDI output.

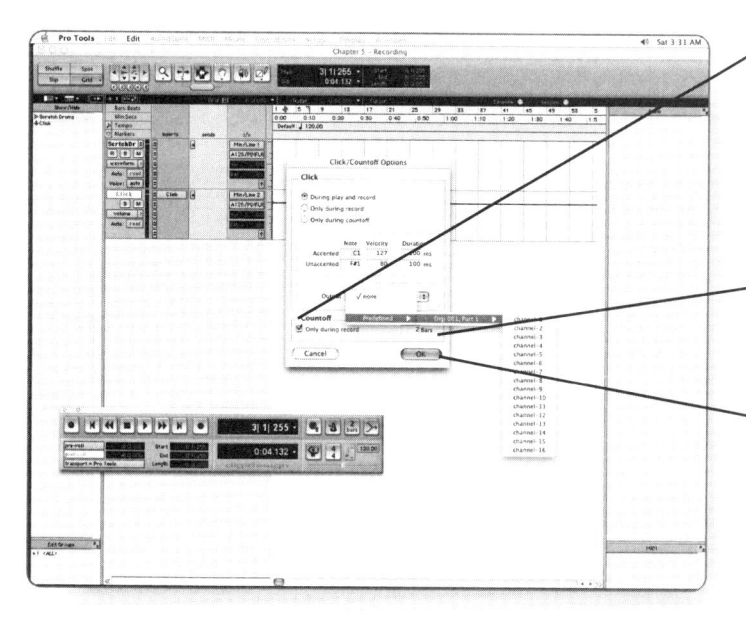

6. Select the **Only during record check box** to ensure that your click will only count off before recording; otherwise, it will count off whenever you play. The option will be selected.

7. Enter the **number of bars** you want for your countoff in the Bars field.

8. Click on **OK**. The Click/Countoff Options dialog box will close.

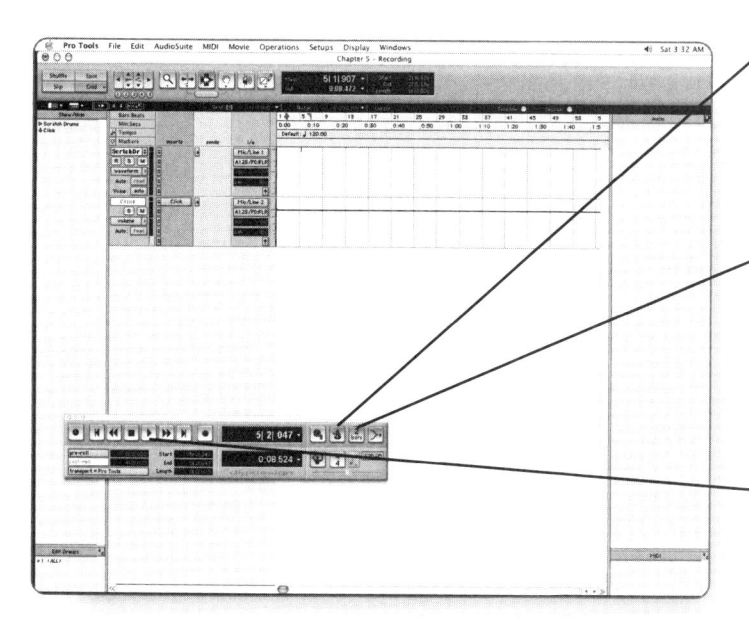

9. Click on the **Metronome icon** in the Transport window to activate the click, if it isn't already selected. The icon will be highlighted.

10. Click on the **Countoff icon** in the Transport window, if it isn't already selected. The icon will be highlighted. (Remember, you can disable the countoff at any time by deselecting this icon.)

11. Click on the **Play button** to play your session from the beginning. You will hear a countoff and your click.

CHAPTER 5: RECORDING AUDIO

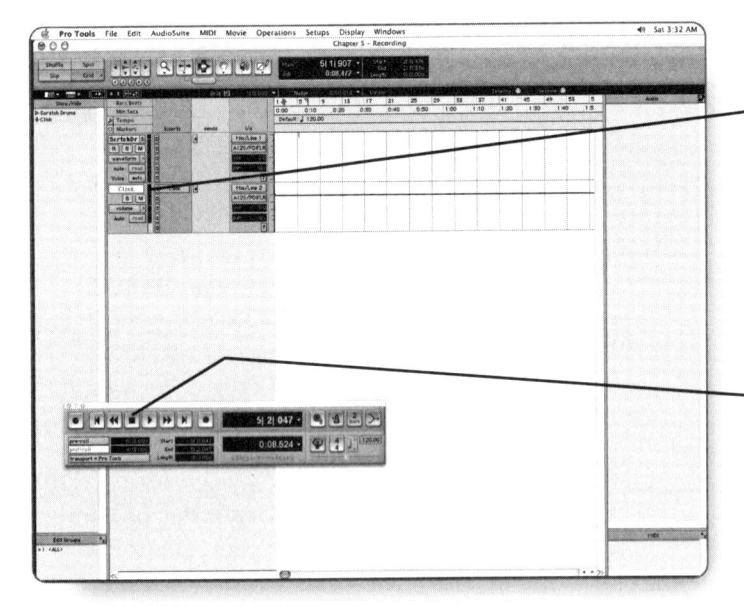

NOTE

Take a look at the volume meter of the click aux track. The volume of your click will be shown in the meter display to the right of the track name.

12. When you've confirmed that your click is working, **click** on the **Stop button**. Your session will stop and you will return to the beginning of the session.

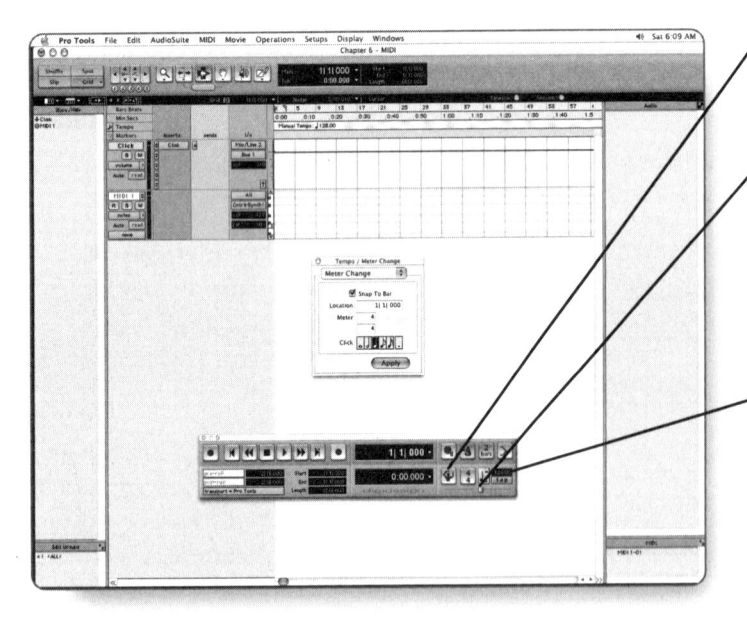

13. Deselect the **Conductor icon**. The tempo slider will appear solid now.

14a. Use the **tempo slider** to set the desired tempo. The tempo value will change in the field above the word "tap."

OR

14b. Type a **tempo** in the numeric field above the word "tap."

SETTING UP A CLICK TRACK   157

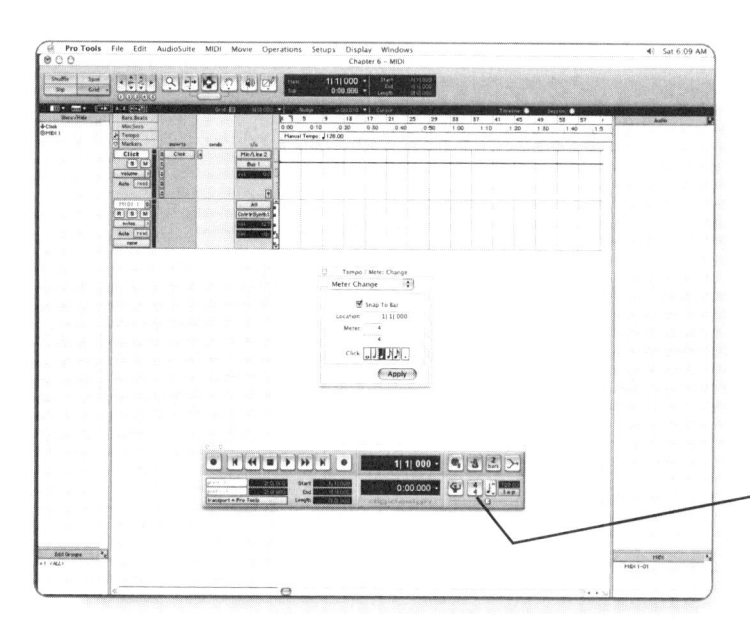

TIP

Here's another way to enter a tempo: You can click on the tap button beneath the tempo numeric display, and then click your mouse in tempo. The numeric display will change to reflect the tempo of your clicks. You can cycle through the beats as many times as you want until you settle upon the tempo you want to use.

15. **Click** on the **Meter Controls button** to change the meter. The Tempo/Meter Change dialog box will open.

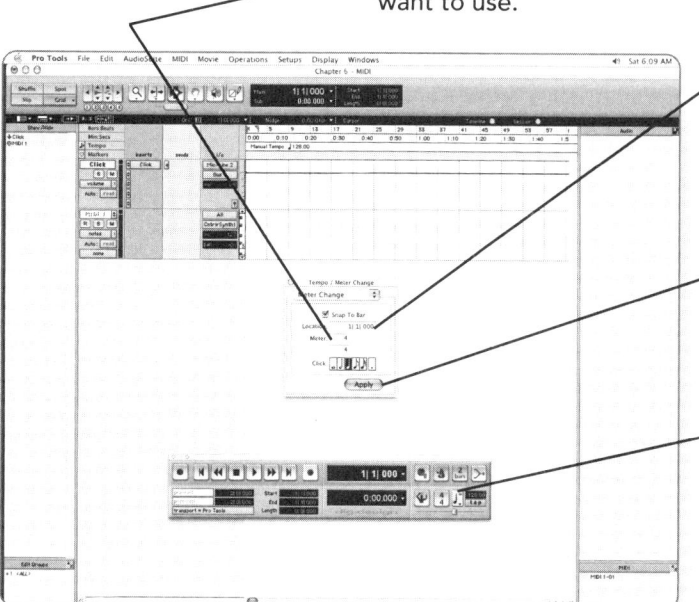

16. **Type** a **value** in the Meter field to select the meter you want to use.

17. **Type** a **location value** in the Location field to change meters throughout your music. The value in this field is displayed in bars | beats | ticks.

18. **Click** on **Apply**. Your meter change will be applied, and the Tempo/Meter Change dialog box will close.

19. Now let's determine which kind of note will be the resolution of your click track. **Click** on the **Note icon**. The Note menu will appear.

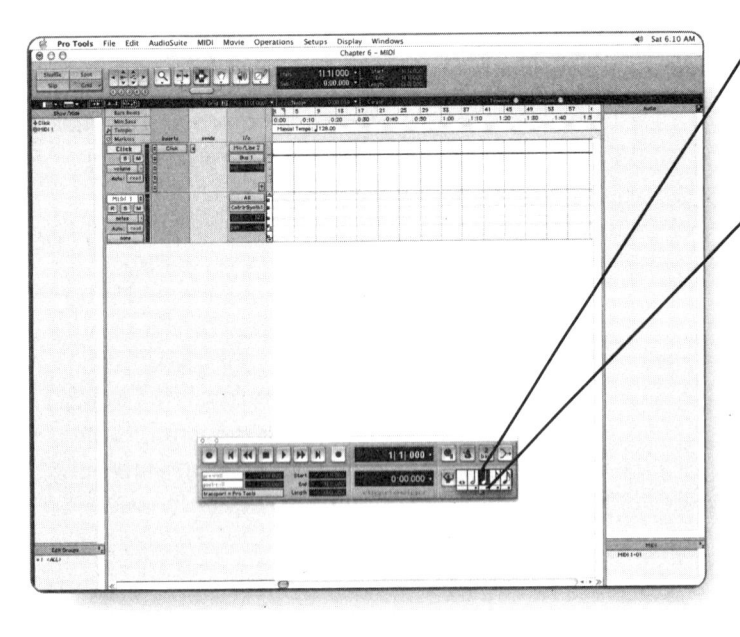

20. **Click** on the **note value** that matches the desired value of your click. The value will be selected.

21. **Click** on the **dot** to use a dotted-note value for your click. The option will be selected.

Basic Recording

You're all set—let's go! Now you're ready to record some audio from the outside world into the Pro Tools environment.

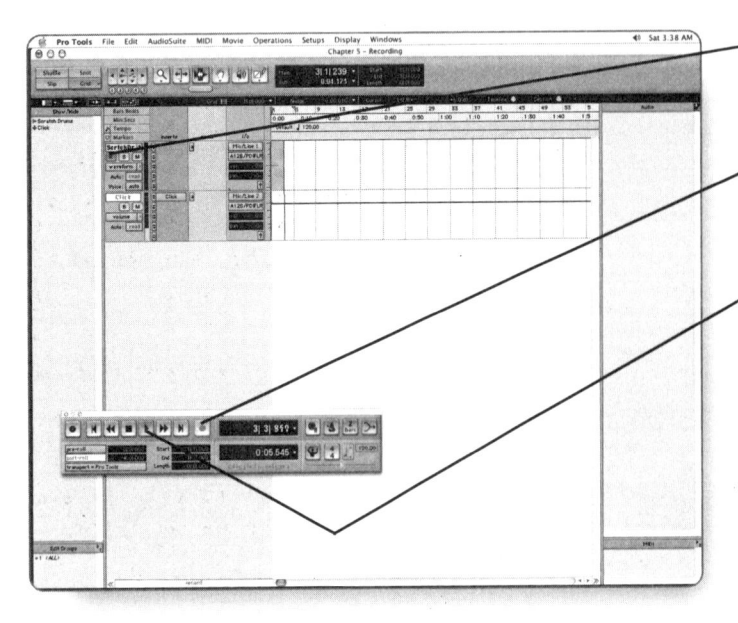

1. **Click** on the **R button** to arm the track for recording. The track will be armed.

2. **Click** on the **Record button** in the Transport window. The Record button will begin to flash.

3. **Click** on the **Play button**. Recording will begin. As you record, Pro Tools will display the incoming waveform.

BASIC RECORDING 159

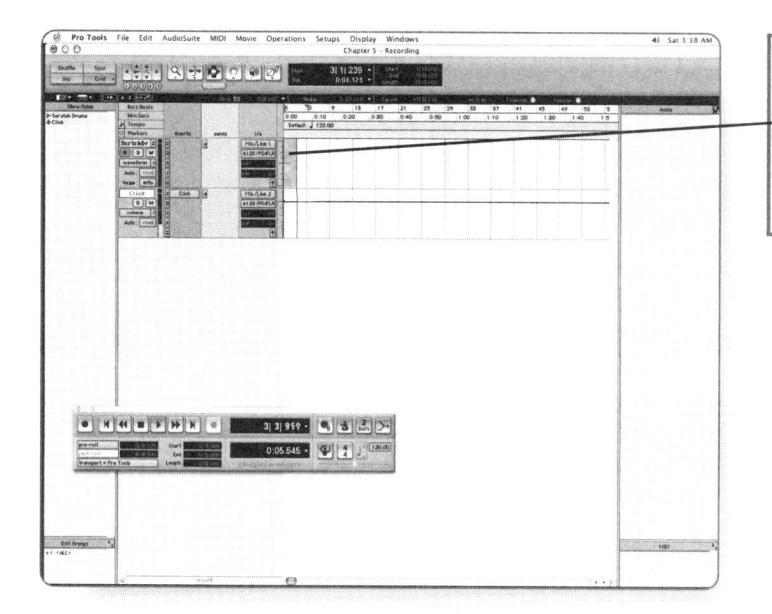

TIP
The shortcut for record/play is ⌘+spacebar (Mac) or Ctrl+spacebar (PC).

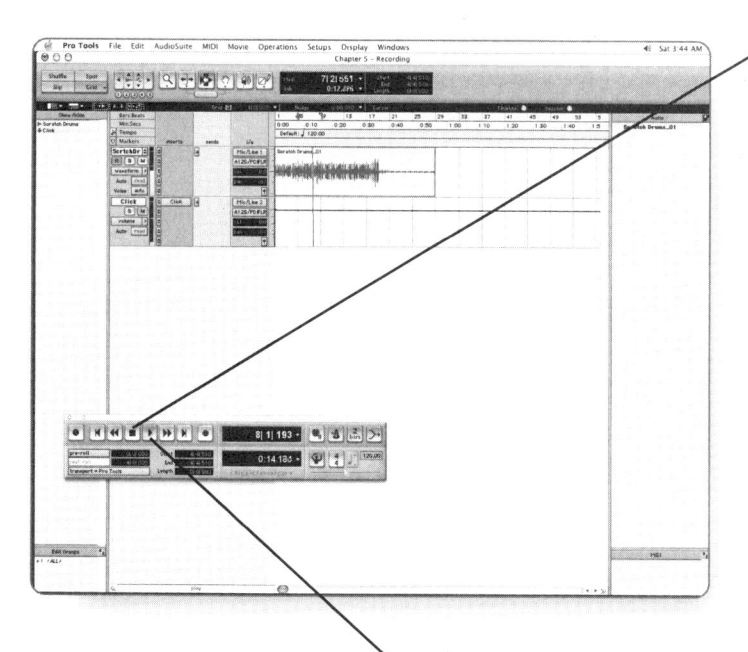

4. Click on the **Stop button** when you want to stop your recording. An audio region will be created in your track. The region will also be listed in the Audio Regions list.

NOTE
Before you listen to your track, make sure the Record button is not highlighted and the track is not armed.

5. Click on the **Play button**. You will hear your newly created track. If you don't want to hear the click track, simply mute it.

Understanding Other Recording Options

Congratulations! You've taken another important step down the road of Pro Tools use. Now I want to explore some different ways to record audio that can come in useful when you need to accomplish specific goals.

Punching In and Punching Out

Suppose you recorded a perfect tape, except that one measure! Not a problem when you're working with Pro Tools; you can specify a segment of your audio and replace it. Remember, too, that Pro Tools operates non-destructively, so you don't have to worry about losing your original take!

1. Click on the **Selector tool**. The tool will be highlighted.

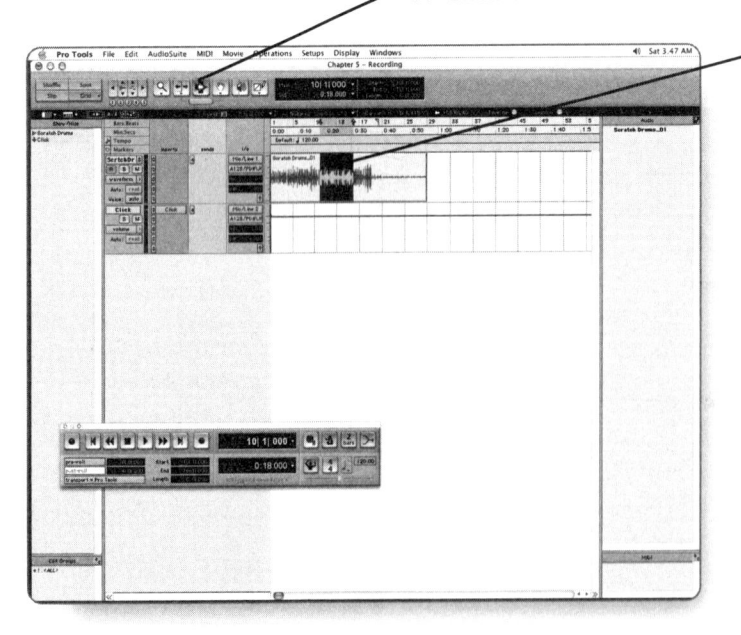

2. Mark the **area of audio** upon which you want to re-record.

> **NOTE**
>
> Use Grid mode if you want to punch in right on bars or beats (remember to make sure your grid is set to the correct value) or Slip mode to select in a more flexible way. For more information on the edit modes, refer to Chapter 4.

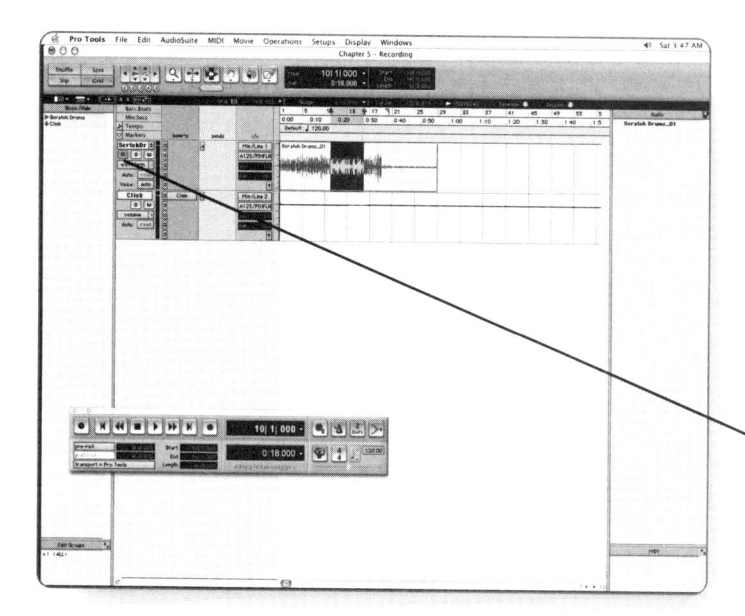

UNDERSTANDING OTHER RECORDING OPTIONS 161

> **TIP**
> There is another way to make your selection. While you're playing back your track, press the down arrow key to begin your selection and the up arrow key to end your selection.

3. Click on the **R button** on the audio track you want to re-record. The track will be armed for recording. You'll note that the selection in the Rulers area, which is usually bordered by blue arrows, is now bordered by red arrows.

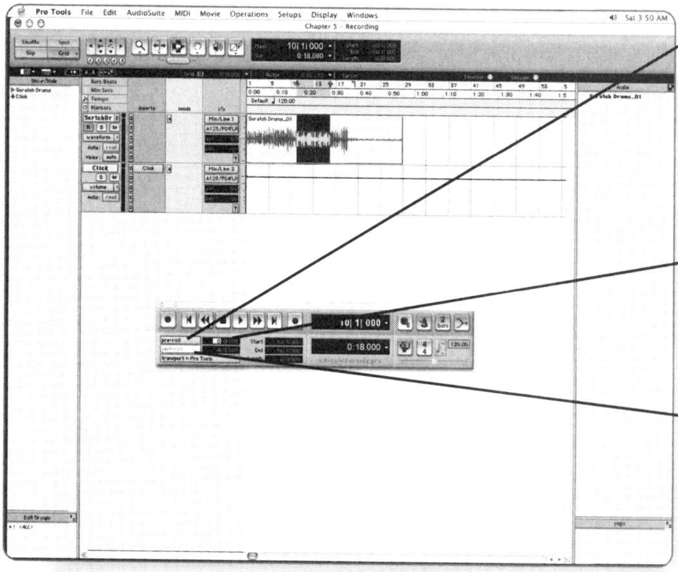

4. If you want to hear a little bit of your original track before or after your punch in/out, you'll want to set up a pre-roll and/or a post-roll. **Click** on **pre-roll**. The option will be enabled.

5. Click inside the **text box** to the right of the pre-roll button and **type** the **length** of your pre-roll value.

6. Click on **post-roll**. The option will be enabled.

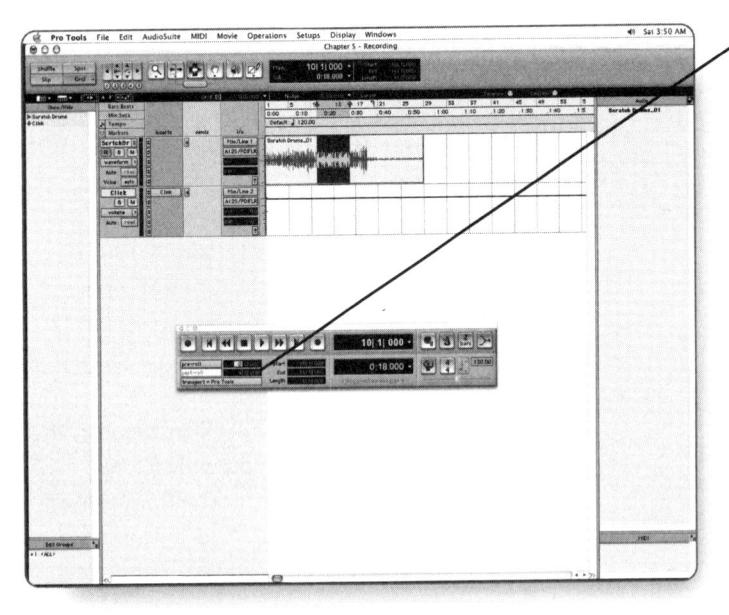

7. Click inside the **text box** to the right of the post-roll button and **type** the **length** of your post-roll value.

8. Press Enter to confirm your entry. Bear in mind that the scale of this value follows the Main location display. A small green flag in the Rulers area will represent your enabled post-roll.

> **TIP**
> You can drag and drop the arrows and flags on the Ruler timeline to change your selection, pre-roll time, or post-roll time. You can also hold the Option (Mac) or Alt (PC) key and click before or after a selection to instantly move your pre- or post-roll to that location.

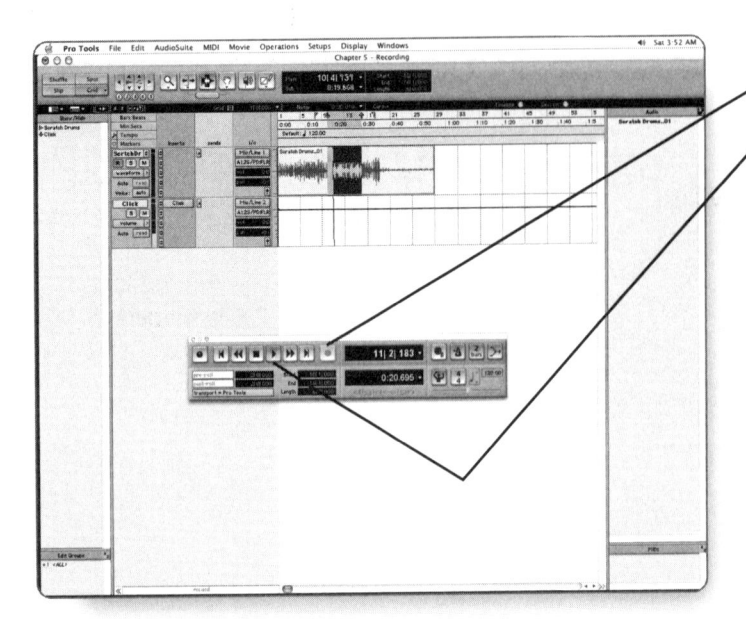

8. Click on the **Record button**.

9. Click on the **Play button**. Play will begin at the pre-roll location because you selected a pre-roll. When the timeline insertion reaches the selected area, Pro Tools will begin recording and will continue recording until the end of the selection. Pro Tools will then exit recording mode and continue playing for the post-roll duration. When it reaches the end of the post-roll duration, it will stop playing.

UNDERSTANDING OTHER RECORDING OPTIONS 163

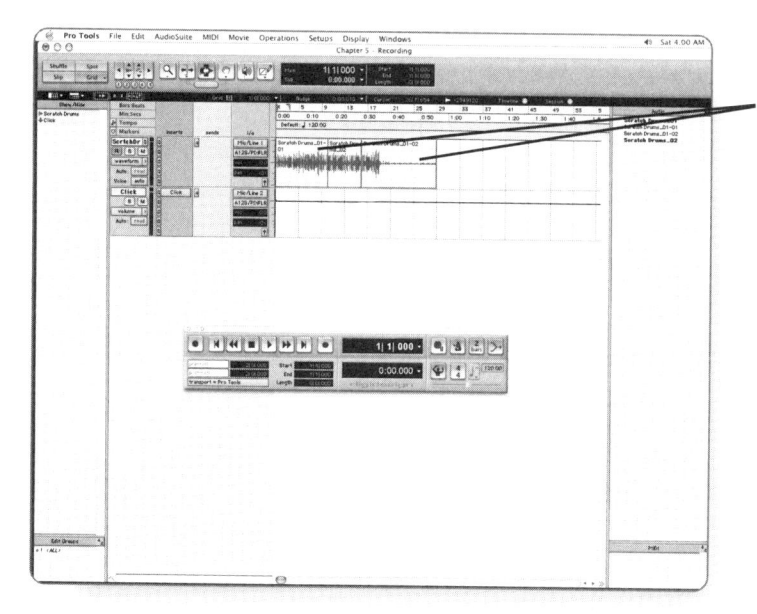

Here's what you'll end up with:

- Your original region has been split into two other regions.

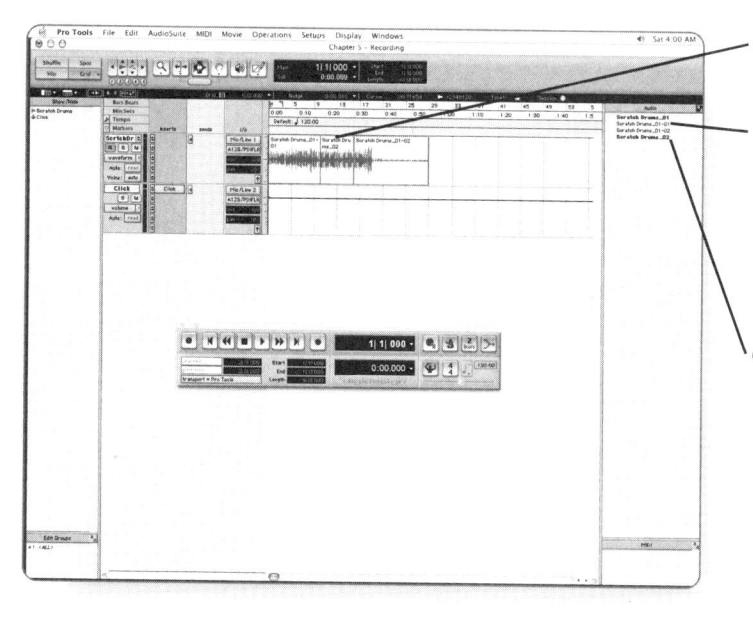

- Your punch-in has been recorded as a new region.

- Both regions now appear in the Audio Regions list. However, these regions are not shown in bold text because they are only incomplete parts of a whole file.

- Your punch appears in bold text because it is a whole file region, which means that it represents an entire file in your Audio Files folder.

QuickPunch Recording

The main limitation of basic punch-in and punch-out is that it's a one-shot thing. So what if you want to make a single pass, but you want to punch in and out more than once? QuickPunch is for you! There are a couple ways to get into QuickPunch mode.

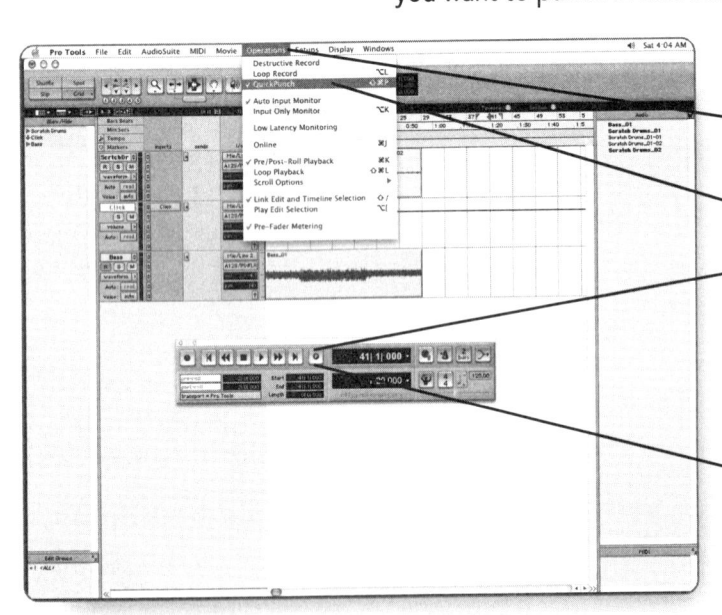

1. **Click** on **Operations**. The Operations menu will appear.

2. Click on **QuickPunch**.

The QuickPunch feature will be enabled, indicated by a letter "P" displayed on the Record button.

TIP

Here's another way to access QuickPunch mode: Hold the Control key while clicking on the Record button (Mac) or right-click on the Record button (PC) to scroll through various recording modes. QuickPunch mode is indicated by a "P" on the red Record button.

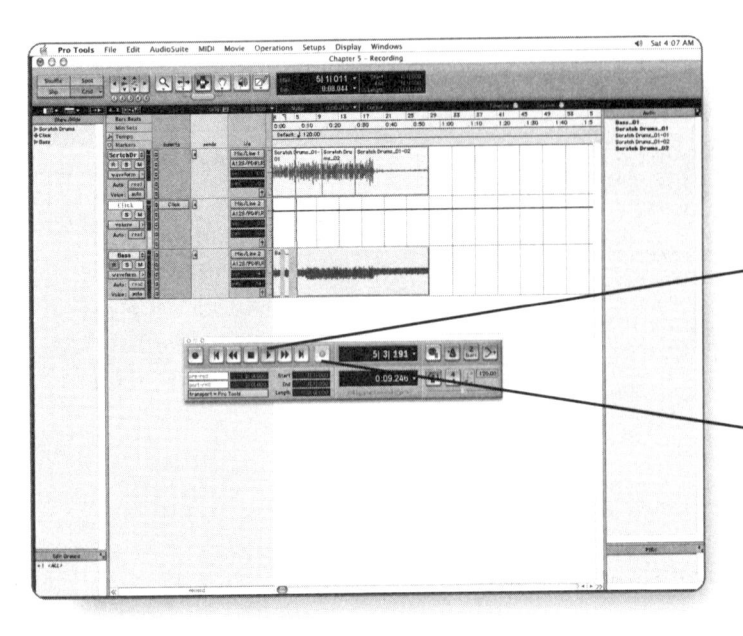

3. Click on the **Play button** at a point prior to when you want to record new audio. Your session will play as normal.

4. Click on the **Record button** when you want to begin recording. Recording will start.

UNDERSTANDING OTHER RECORDING OPTIONS

5. Click on the **Record button** again when you want to stop recording. Recording will stop.

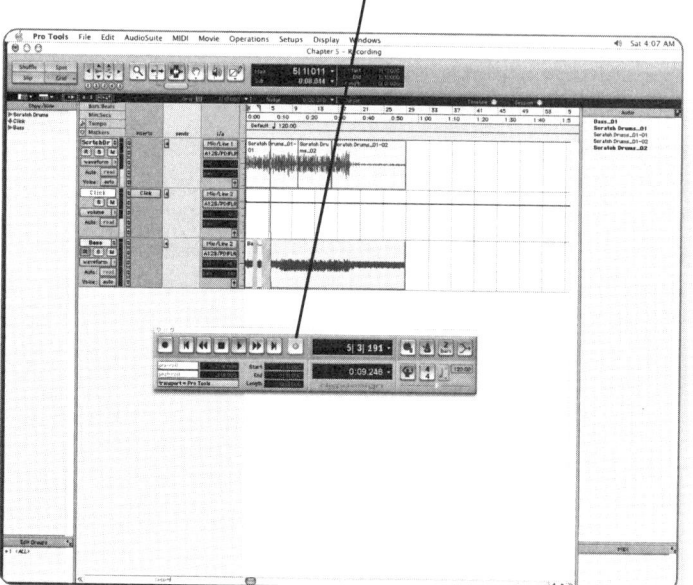

NOTE

You can go into and out of record mode a number of times (up to 100 per running take) by clicking on the Record button.

TIP

Here's another way to punch in and punch out in QuickPunch mode: During playback, press ⌘+spacebar (Mac) or Alt+spacebar (PC).

Here's what you'll end up with:

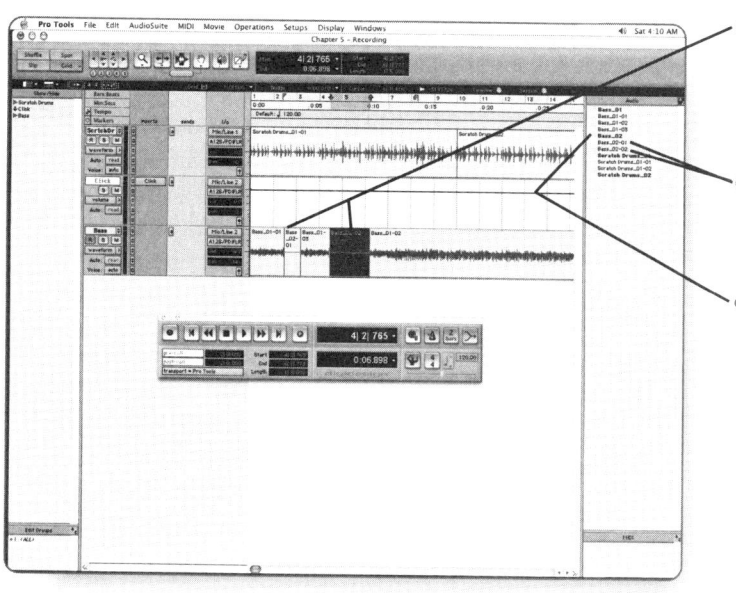

- New regions will be created in your track to reflect each time you engaged and disengaged recording.

- As you might expect, new regions will also be added to the Audio Regions list.

- The regions created in the track are not whole file regions. They are regions of a larger file.

> **TIP**
> This whole file region is created because when you start playback in QuickPunch mode, Pro Tools is already recording. The simple act of toggling the Record button merely creates regions on your track. This has a hidden benefit: What if your timing was a little off when you engaged or disengaged recording? No problem—just use the Trim tool to adjust the region boundaries as needed. Additionally, holding the ⌘ key (Mac) or the Ctrl key (PC) will adjust both adjacent boundaries at the same time, ensuring that there is no gap created as you trim.

Loop Recording

Okay, suppose you want to record several passes at a certain section (a guitar solo, for example), and then pick the best one. You'll want to use Pro Tools' Loop Record function.

1. Click on **Operations**. The Operations menu will appear.

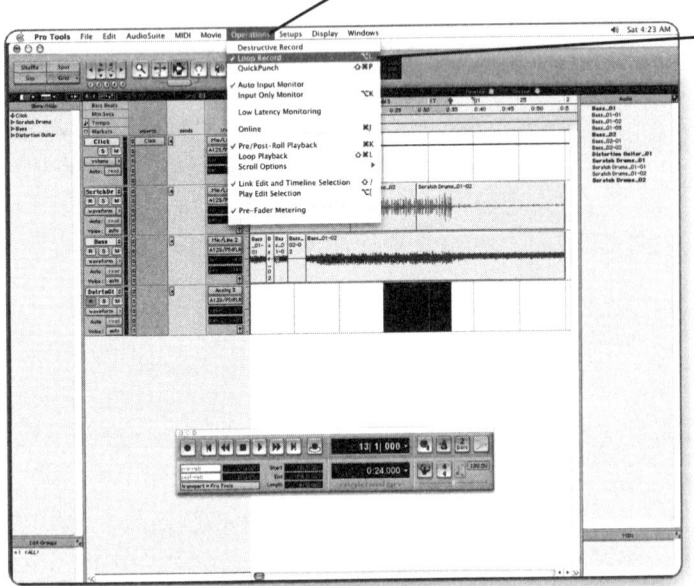

2. Click on **Loop Record**. The Loop Record feature will be enabled.

> **TIP**
> Here's an alternative way to access Loop Record mode: Hold the Control key while clicking on the Record button (Mac) or right-click on the Record button (PC) to scroll through various recording modes. Loop Record mode is indicated by a looping arrow around the red Record button.

UNDERSTANDING OTHER RECORDING OPTIONS 167

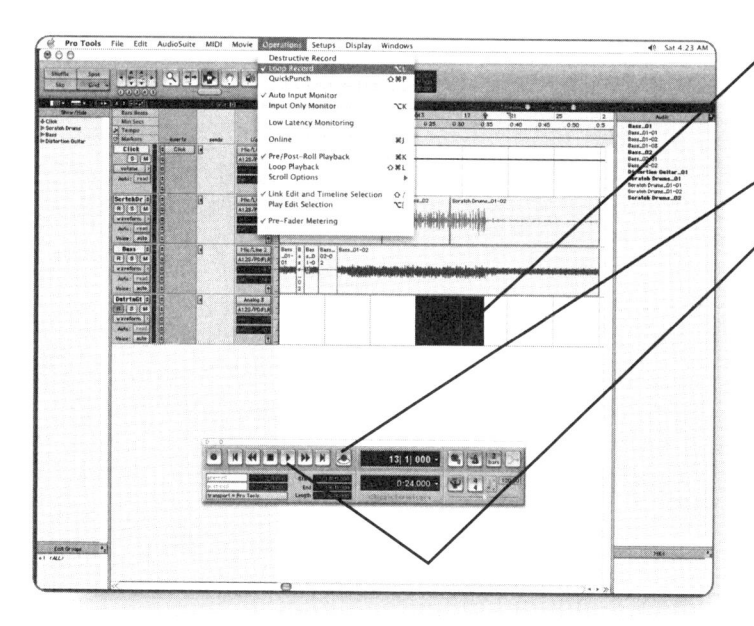

3. **Use** the **Selector tool** to select the section you want to loop. The area will be selected.

4. **Click** on the **Record button**.

5. **Click** on the **Play button**.

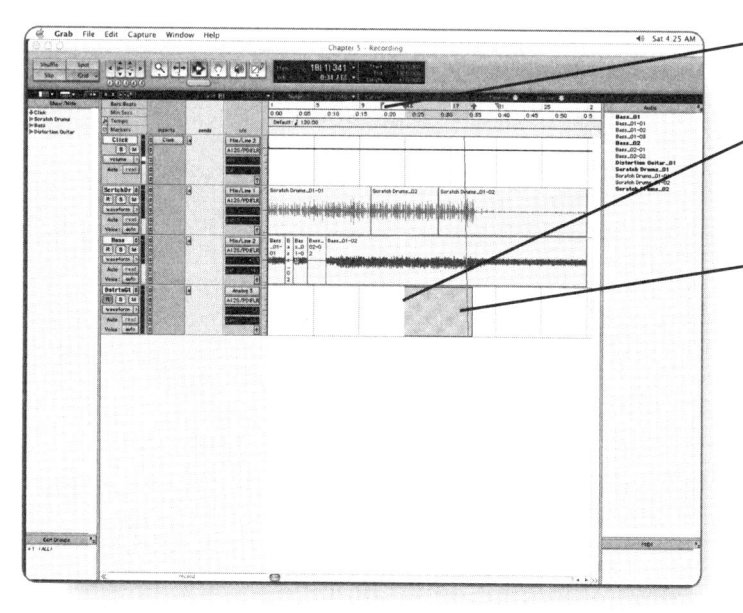

Playback will begin at the pre-roll position (if pre-roll is enabled).

When the selection is reached, Pro Tools will begin recording audio.

At the end of the selection, recording will begin again from the beginning of the selection (even if pre-roll is enabled).

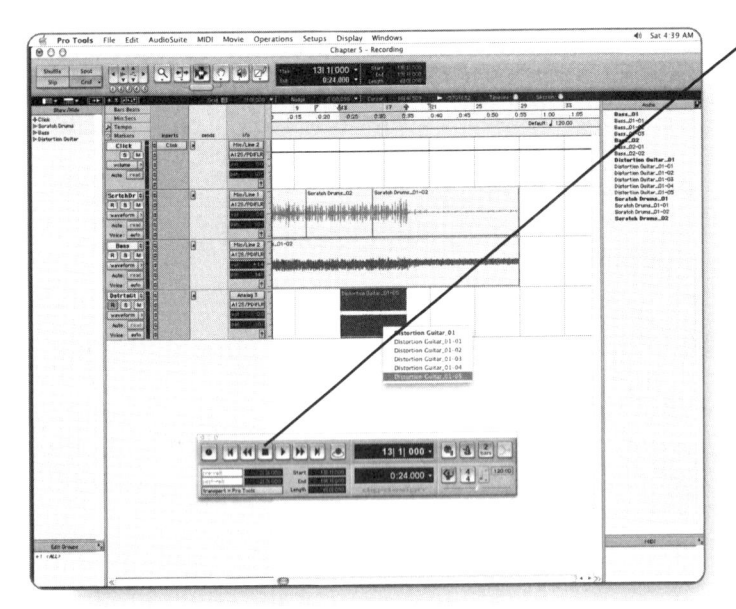

6. When you've got enough takes, **click** on the **Stop button**. The latest take will appear in the selected area.

> **NOTE**
>
> In the Audio Regions list, notice that there is a whole file region (in bold text) that contains all the takes in sequence. Although it is not specifically used in the track, it represents the parent file in which all the individual takes reside. Below the whole file region are individual "takes" numbered sequentially in the order in which they were recorded.

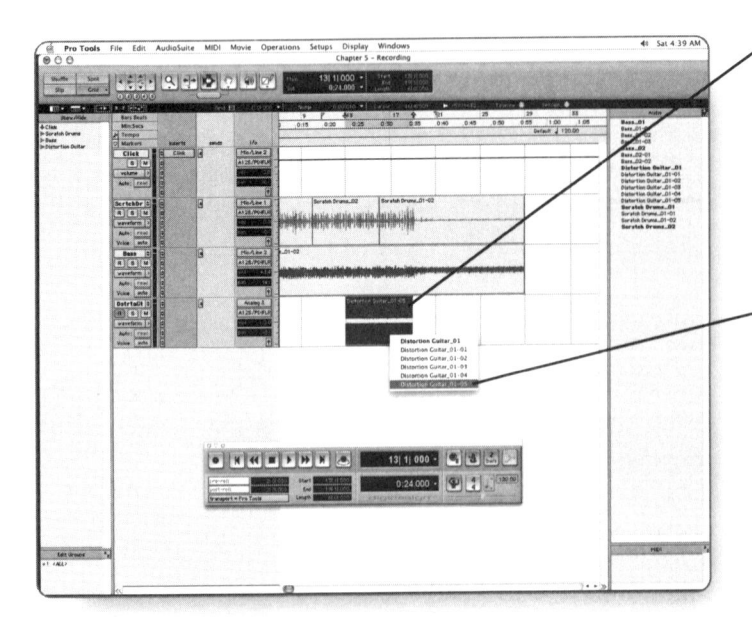

7. **⌘-click** (Mac) or **Ctrl-click** (PC) inside the **region** to reveal a drop-down menu that displays all the regions that match the same start time as the current region—in this case, all of your takes.

8. **Click** on the **take** you want to use. The take will be selected.

UNDERSTANDING OTHER RECORDING OPTIONS 169

For the Brave: Destructive Recording

Thus far, you've only seen non-destructive recording, meaning that you never erase any audio in the process of punching in, punching out, or looping. You can, however, record directly into an audio file that you created earlier. Be careful, though; there's no way to undo what you've done if you make a mistake!

1. Click on **Operations**. The Operations menu will appear.

2. Click on **Destructive Record**. The Destructive Record feature will be enabled.

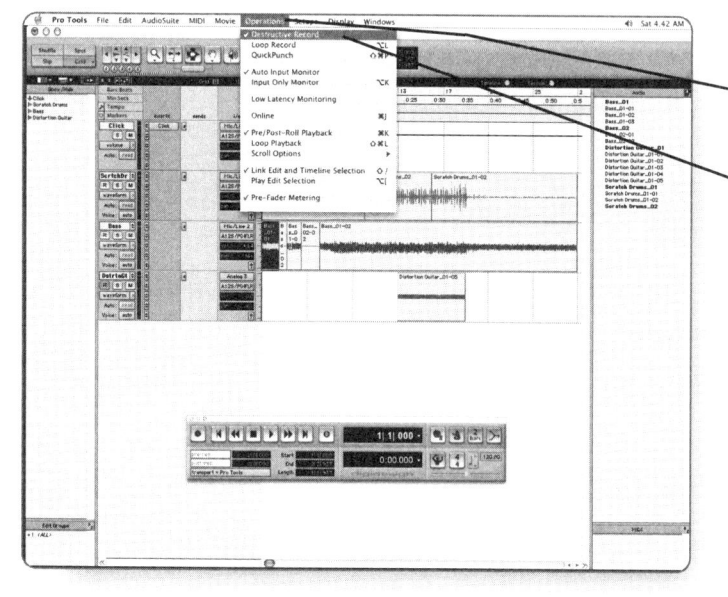

NOTE

Here's another way to access Destructive Record mode: Hold the Control key while clicking on the Record button (Mac) or right-click on the Record button (PC) to scroll through various recording modes. Destructive Record mode is indicated by a D on the red Record button.

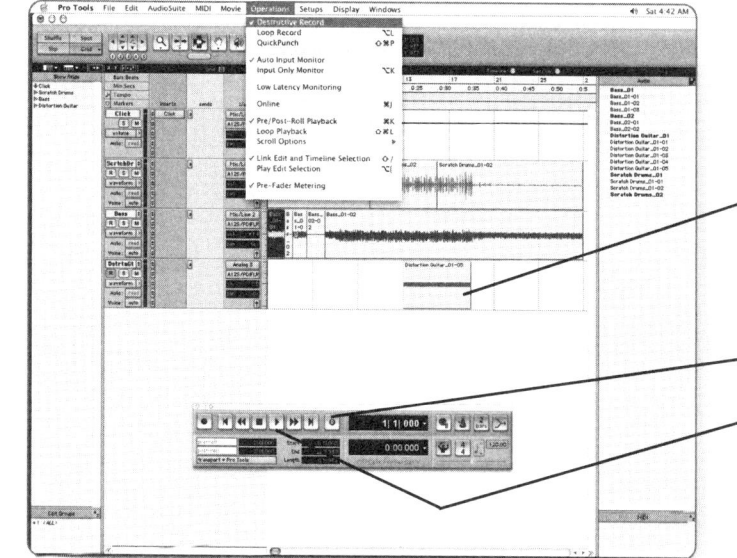

3. Use the **Selector tool** to select a section of the audio track that you want to overwrite. The area will be selected.

4. Click on the **Record button**.

5. Click on the **Play button**.

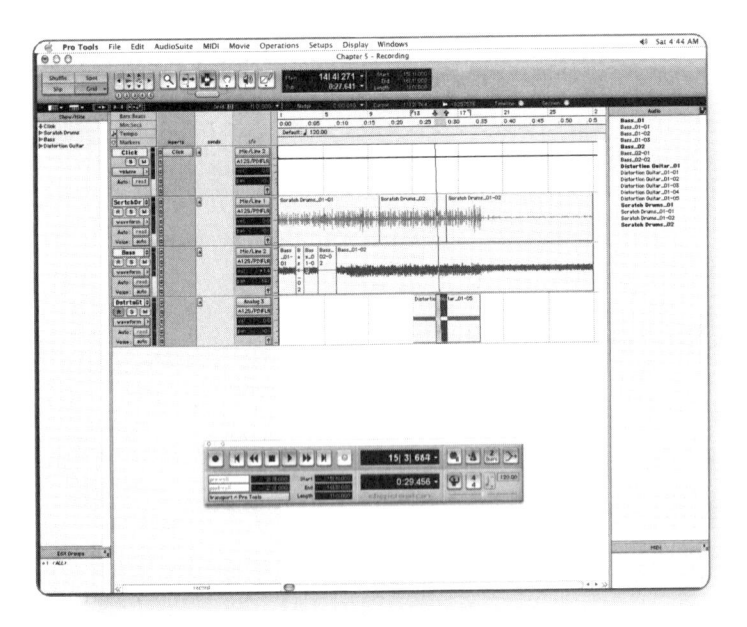

At this point, the process works exactly the same as basic punching in and punching out. Your session will begin playing at the pre-roll position (if you've enabled pre-roll), and then it will automatically begin recording at your selected area. It will stop recording at the end of your selection and play for the post-roll amount (if enabled). The real difference between destructive recording and the other modes becomes apparent when the dust has settled.

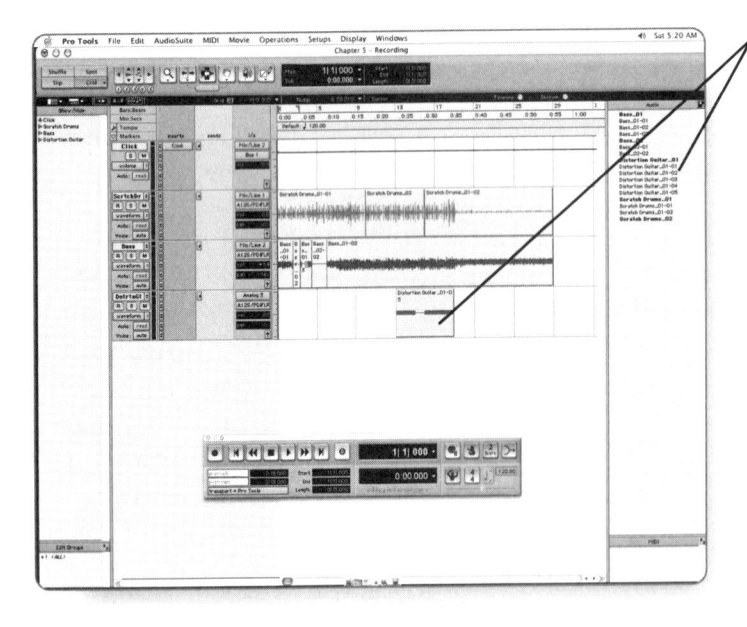

The important distinction between destructive recording and other modes is that no new regions have been created—in the track itself or in the Audio Regions list. What you've done is permanently change the file you originally recorded!

Tips, Tricks, and Troubleshooting

Fantastic! You're on your way to running a great tracking session! This section includes a few final thoughts to call on when you need them.

Naming Tracks and Files

One very important thing to remember when it comes to good file management practices: The names of the regions that you record will follow the names of the tracks on which you're recording them. That means a track named Scratch Drums, for example, would yield recording passes named Scratch Drums_01, Scratch Drums_02, and so on.

That being said, the rule of thumb is to name your tracks *before* you record audio to them. However, if you ever forget to do this or if you ever want to change the name of a region after that region has been created, it's easy to do.

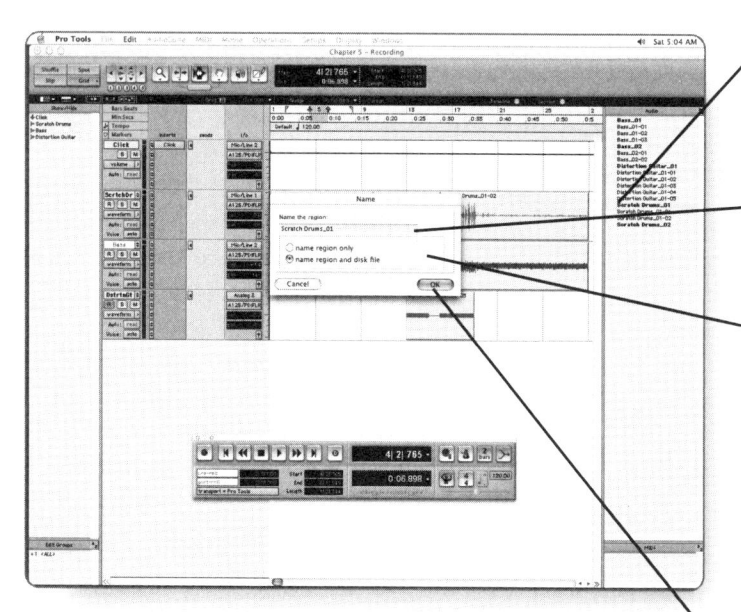

1. Double-click on the **region** you want to rename in the Audio Regions list. The Name dialog box will open.

2. Type the new **name** for the region in the Name the region text box.

3. If the region is a whole file region, you have the option of naming the region in the session only or changing the name of the region *and* the file name as it appears on your hard drive. **Click** on the **name region only** or **name region and disk file radio button** to select an option, if appropriate.

4. Click on **OK**. The Name dialog box will close and the region will be renamed.

Understanding the Monitor Modes

In addition to all the different modes of recording that you've learned about, there are two monitor modes that affect how you hear your audio during the recording process.

1. Click on **Operations**. The Operations menu will appear.

2a. Select Auto Input Monitor if you want to hear what you previously recorded right up to your punch-in point. Pro Tools will behave as if it is in playback mode during pre-roll and post-roll periods, and will automatically switch over to monitoring your input only during the selected overdub area.

OR

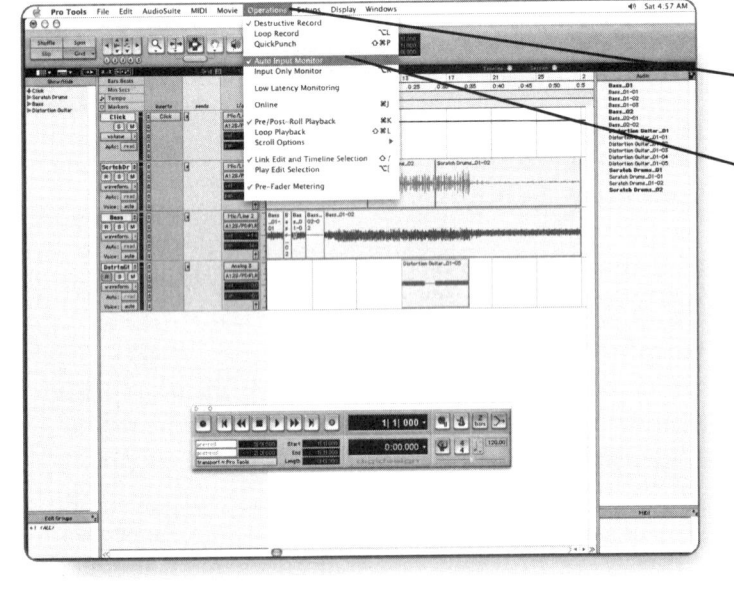

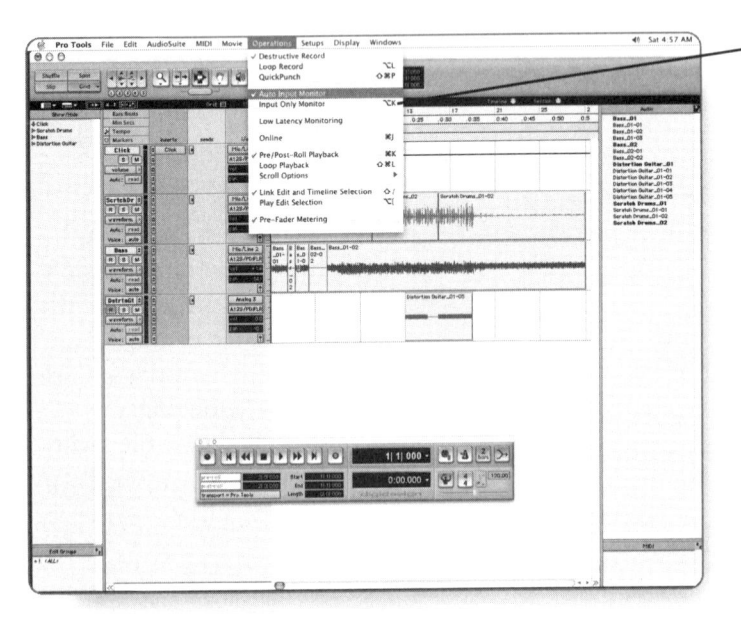

2b. Select Input Only Monitor if you don't want to hear what you've already recorded during a punch-in/punch-out situation. Pro Tools will still only record during the selected area, but for the pre-roll and post-roll durations, you'll hear the live input rather than the previously recorded audio on the track.

Low Latency Monitoring—and a Trick!

When you are recording, you might have noticed a bit of delay (called *latency*) between the time a note was played and the time it was heard through the monitors. The bad news is that this is the normal functioning of host-based DAWs. The good news is that there's a solution to this problem in Pro Tools, called *low latency monitoring*. This monitoring mode bypasses the step of running audio through the host computer's processor, causing the delay you hear. Bypassing this processing (where plug-ins are processed) allows you to hear your input without any delay.

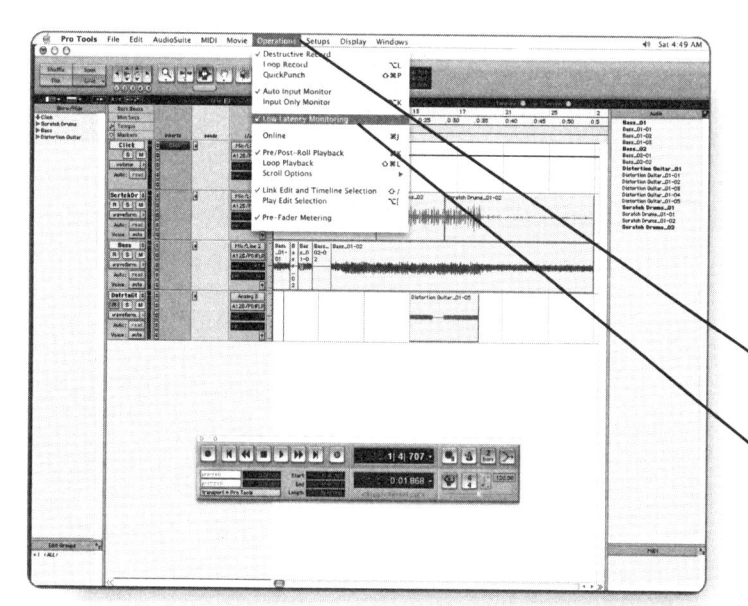

1. Click on **Operations**. The Operations menu will appear.

2. Click on **Low Latency Monitoring**.

The good news is that your latency problem just got a lot better. The bad news (you knew there'd be some, right?) is that the click plug-in has turned dark, indicating that the plug-in has become inactive. This is the price of low latency monitoring—plug-ins become inactive. Does that mean you have lost the use of your click? Yes and no—read on!

Because the click plug-in won't work in this mode, you need to figure out another way to hear it. The solution to this problem is to bounce—in other words, record—from one track to another. Because this bounce is internal (entirely within the Pro Tools environment), you can use a bus to make this transfer. I'll go deeper into the application of such concepts in Chapter 8, but for now let's solve the problem!

CHAPTER 5: RECORDING AUDIO

1. First, **make sure** that you're **not** in **Low Latency Monitoring mode**.

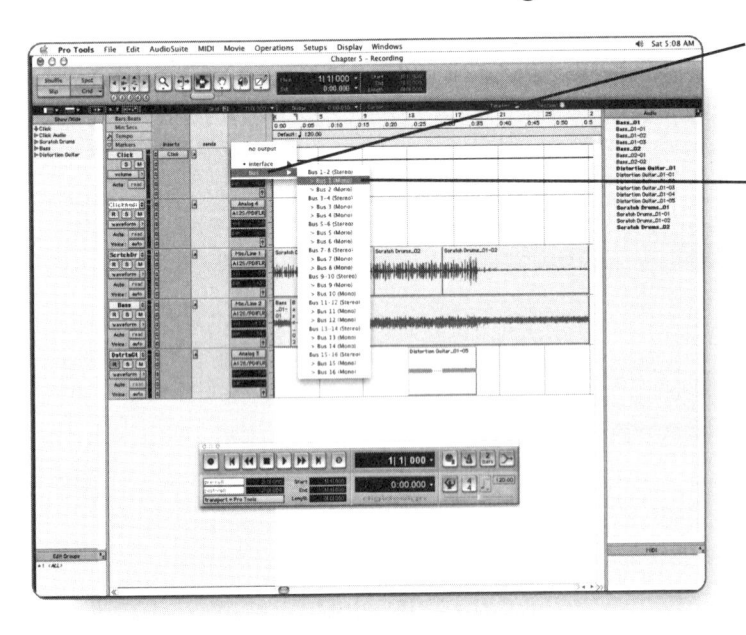

2. Click on the **click track's output**. A drop-down menu will appear.

3. Choose an unused mono **bus**. In a session, already used buses appear in bold text.

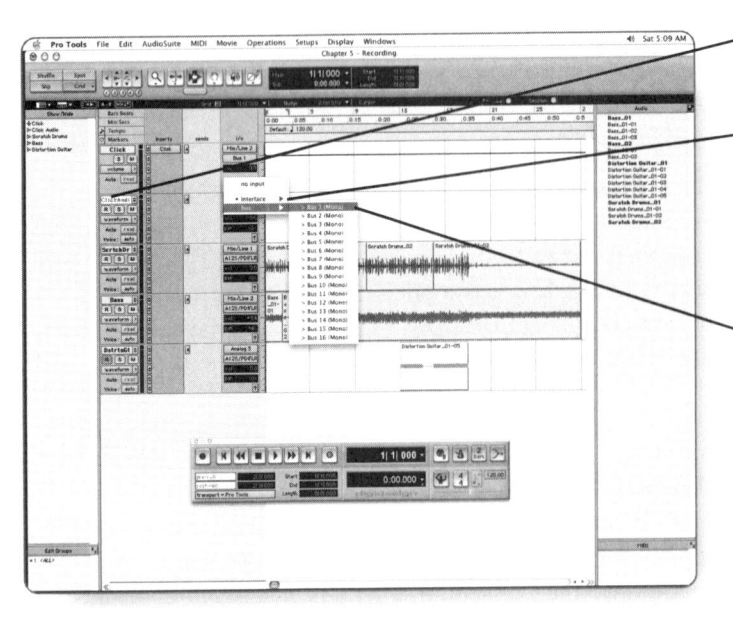

4. Create a **mono audio track** and **name it** descriptively.

5. Now you need to set the input so you can record from the click track. **Click** on the track's **Input button**. A drop-down menu will appear.

6. Choose the same **bus** you selected for the click track's output. The bus will be selected.

TIPS, TRICKS, AND TROUBLESHOOTING 175

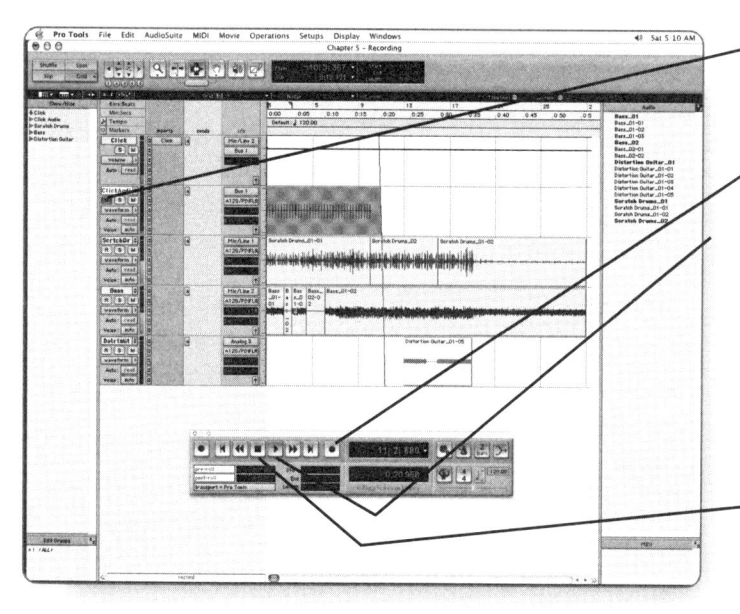

7. **Click** on the **R button**. The track will be armed for recording.

8. **Click** on the **Record button**.

9. **Click** on the **Play button**. Recording will begin on the audio track. Whereas the click plug-in creates the click in real time, the click track will be recorded as audio on the audio track.

10. **Click** on the **Stop button** when you've recorded enough of the click. The recording will stop.

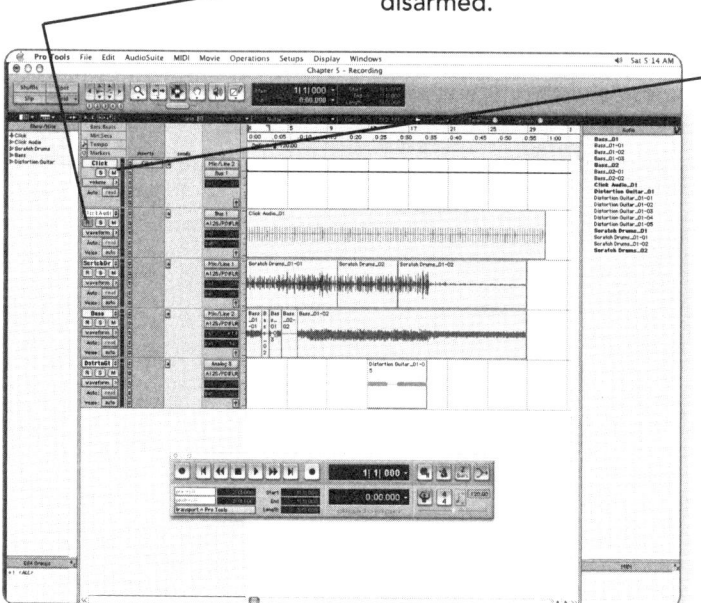

11. **Click** on the **R button** again. The click audio track will be disarmed.

12. **Mute** the **click aux track**. The track will be muted.

> **NOTE**
>
> Alternatively, you can delete the click aux track entirely. You don't need it anymore!

You will now hear your click track even when you're in low latency mode!

> **NOTE**
>
> If you're working with an Mbox audio interface, you'll notice that Pro Tools doesn't give you a low latency monitoring option. Does that mean you're out of luck? No way! The solution lies in the Mbox's Mix knob, which is second from the bottom on the front of your Mbox. When the knob is all the way to the input side, you'll monitor signal coming directly into the interface only, and you won't hear the Pro Tools software at all. When the Mix knob is set all the way to playback, you'll only hear audio coming from Pro Tools. Here's how to eliminate the latency problem using the Mbox's Mix knob:
>
> 1. Set the Mix knob to twelve o'clock, giving you an even balance between input and playback.
>
> 2. Record arm the audio track on which you want to record. Now if you play, you should hear a doubled signal. (The earlier signal is from the input side of the mix; the latent (delayed) signal is coming from the Pro Tools software, routed through the playback side of the mix.)
>
> 3. Mute the track on which you want to record. You can still record onto the track, but you won't hear that annoying delayed signal.
>
> 4. Adjust the Mix knob to get the desired balance between your live input and the Pro Tools software playback.
>
> 5. Record as normal.
>
> 6. When you're finished recording, you can change your mix to playback so you won't be distracted by any audio going into your Mbox.

6
Using MIDI

MIDI is a language that allows keyboards, synthesizers, and other components to communicate with one another. Since its inception in the early 1980s, MIDI has proved to be an invaluable creative tool to musicians of all kinds, and it has changed the face of the music industry.

Not too long ago, music software did either audio or MIDI, but certainly not both. Thankfully, those days have changed, and there are a number of products such as Pro Tools that incorporate the creative power of MIDI and all the advantages of digital audio. In this chapter, you'll learn how to:

- Set up your MIDI studio
- Route MIDI and audio signals so you can work with synthesizers in Pro Tools
- Record and edit MIDI data.

> **NOTE**
>
> A mastery of MIDI is a study in itself, for which volumes of information have been written. It's virtually impossible to become MIDI-savvy after reading one chapter in a single book. Therefore, for the purposes of this book, I will assume you have a fundamental understanding of MIDI, and I'll focus on how to use MIDI in the Pro Tools environment. For a good book on the subject of MIDI, check out *MIDI Power!* (Muska & Lipman, 2002).

Setting Up Your MIDI Studio

Before you can do anything with MIDI, you need to configure your setup and identify your devices. Don't worry; it's easy!

1. Click on **Setups**. The Setups menu will appear.

2. Click on **Edit MIDI Studio Setup**. The Audio MIDI Setup dialog box will open.

SETTING UP YOUR MIDI STUDIO

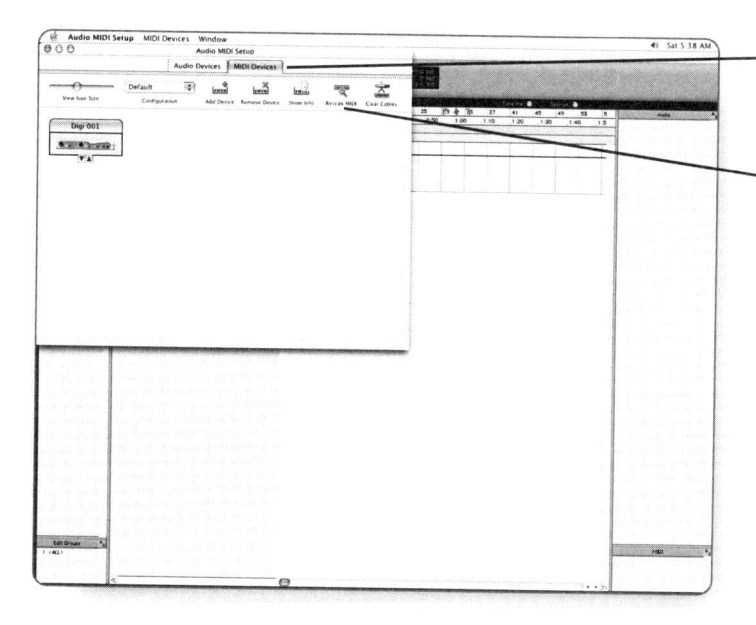

3. Click on the **MIDI Devices tab**. The tab will move to the front.

4. Click on **Rescan MIDI** to make sure your MIDI setup has the best starting point. All MIDI interfaces attached to your computer will appear.

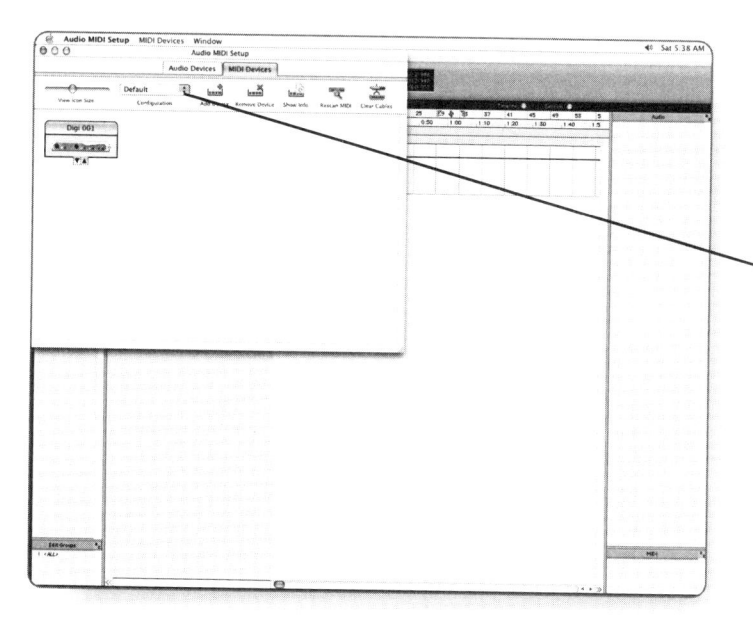

Creating a New Configuration

Now it's time to create a new configuration.

1. Click on the **Configurations menu**. The menu will appear.

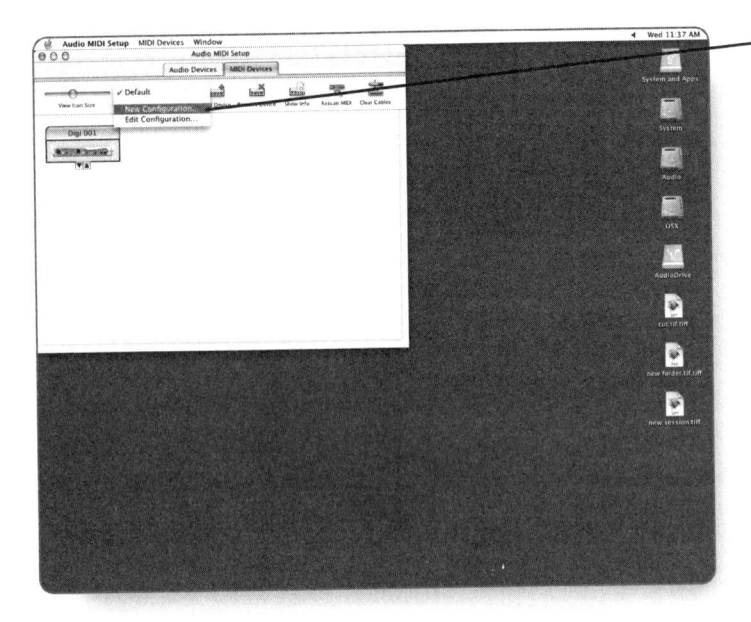

2. Click on **New Configuration**. A naming dialog box will open.

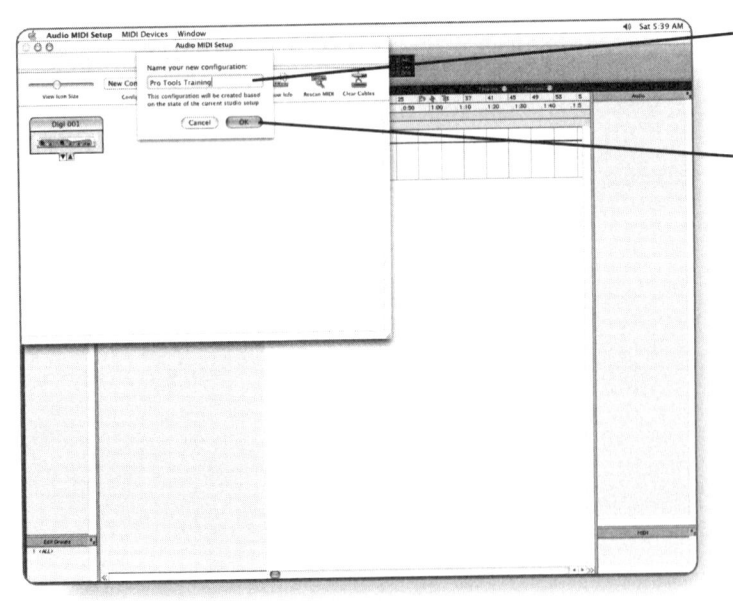

3. Type the **name** of your new configuration in the Name your new configuration text box.

4. Click on **OK**. The dialog box will close and your new configuration name will appear in the configuration field (which previously read "default").

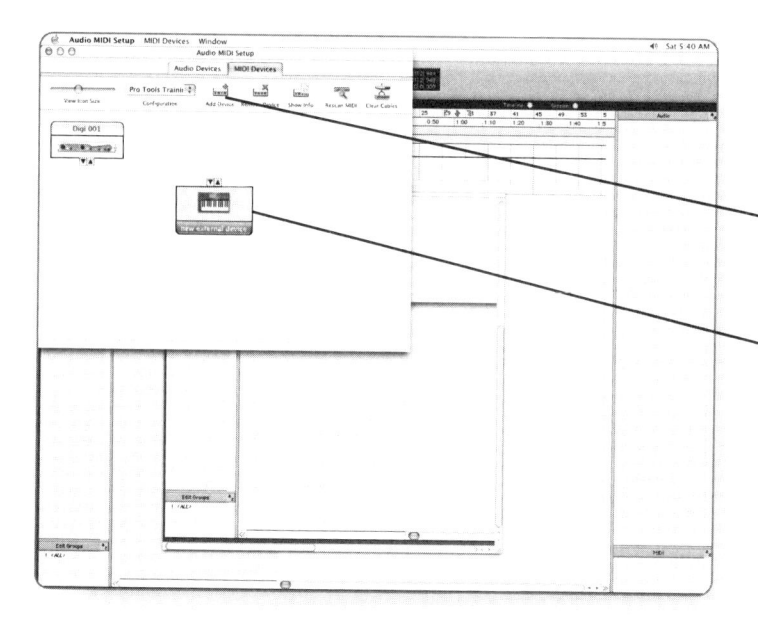

Adding a Synth

Now you can add a synth to your setup.

1. Click on the **Add Device icon**. A new external device icon will appear.

2. If this new device icon is overlapping your MIDI interface, **drag and drop it** out of the way.

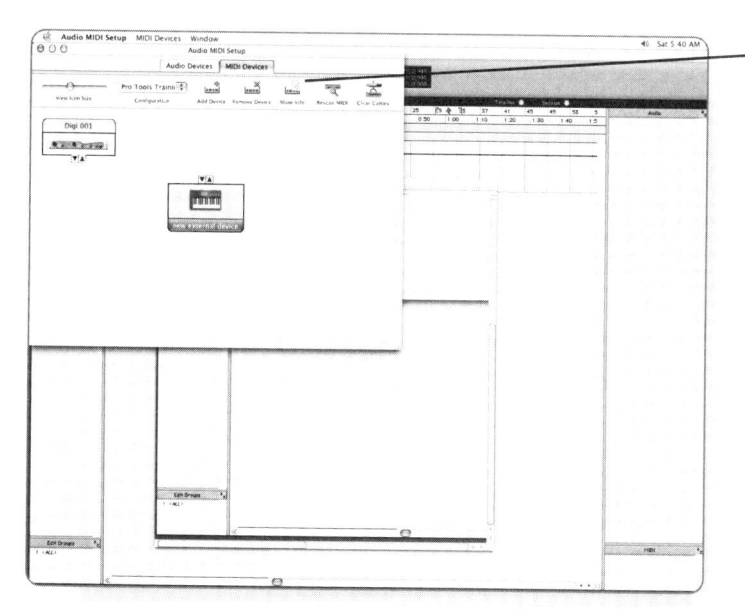

3. Now you can set up this new device. **Click** on the **Show Info icon**. A dialog box will open.

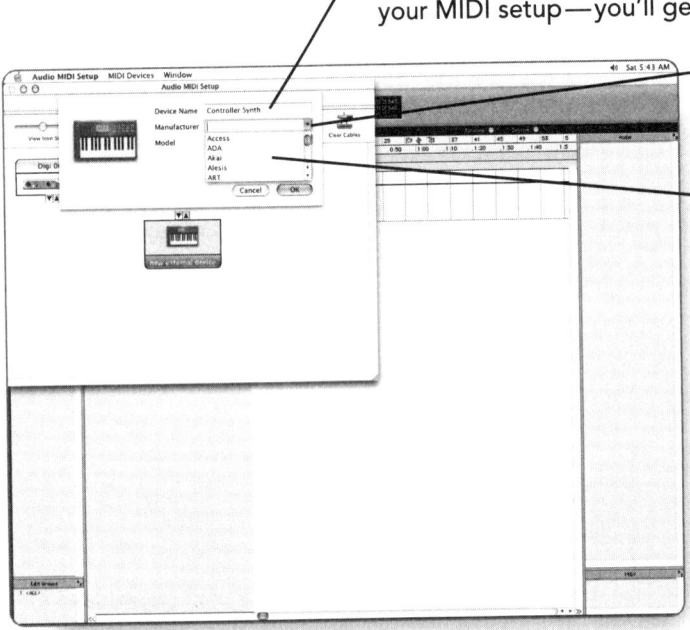

4. Type a descriptive **name** for the new device in the Device Name text box. At this point the device can be any device in your MIDI setup—you'll get more specific about it later.

5. Click on the **Manufacturer down arrow**. The Manufacturer drop-down menu will appear.

6. Click on the **name** of the manufacturer of your MIDI device. The name will be selected. (Now you're getting more specific!)

> **NOTE**
>
> If you don't see your manufacturer listed in the Manufacturer menu, just type the name in the Manufacturer field.

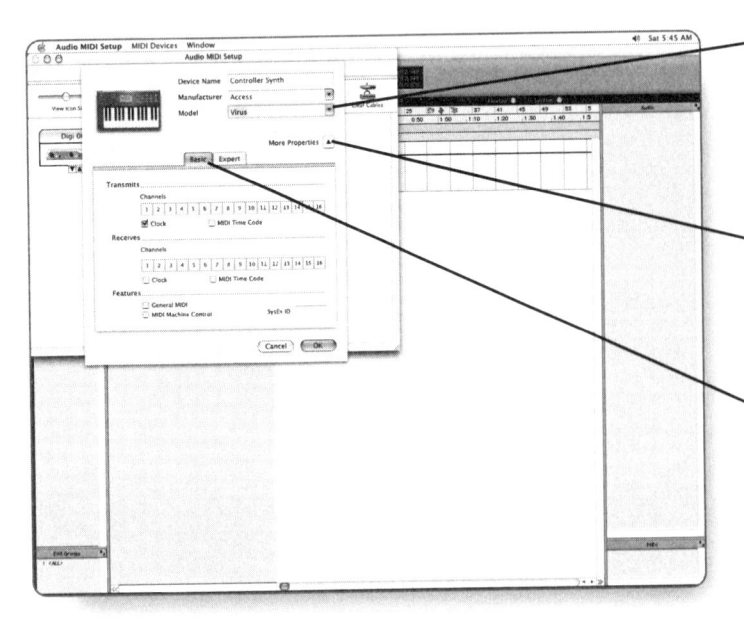

7. Click on the **Model menu** to choose the model of your new device the same way you chose the manufacturer. The model will be selected.

8. Click on the **More Properties** button. The dialog box will expand to show you more options.

9. Click on the **Basic tab**. The tab will move to the front.

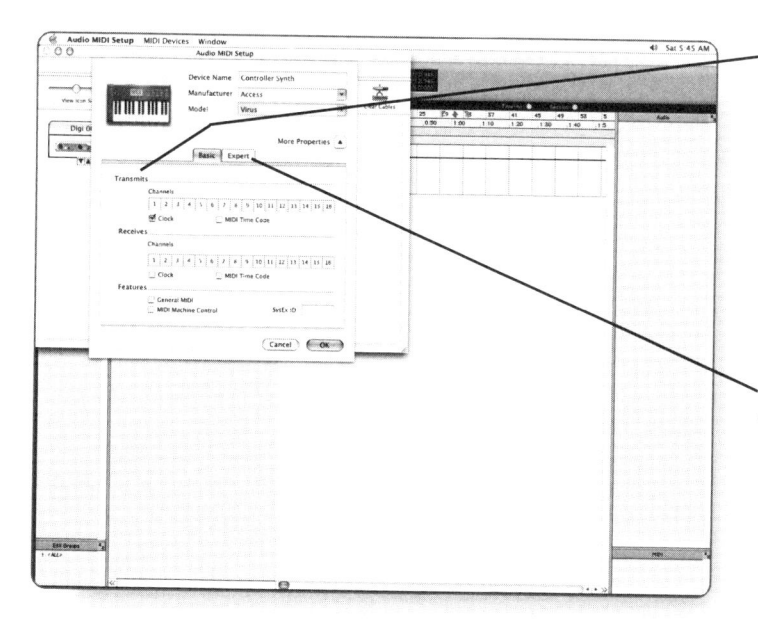

SETTING UP YOUR MIDI STUDIO   183

This section will allow you to choose the channels your device will transmit or receive. You can also choose to enable options such as the MIDI clock, MIDI time code, or MIDI machine control. Selected items (including MIDI channels) will appear highlighted in blue.

10. Click on the **Expert tab**. The tab will move to the front.

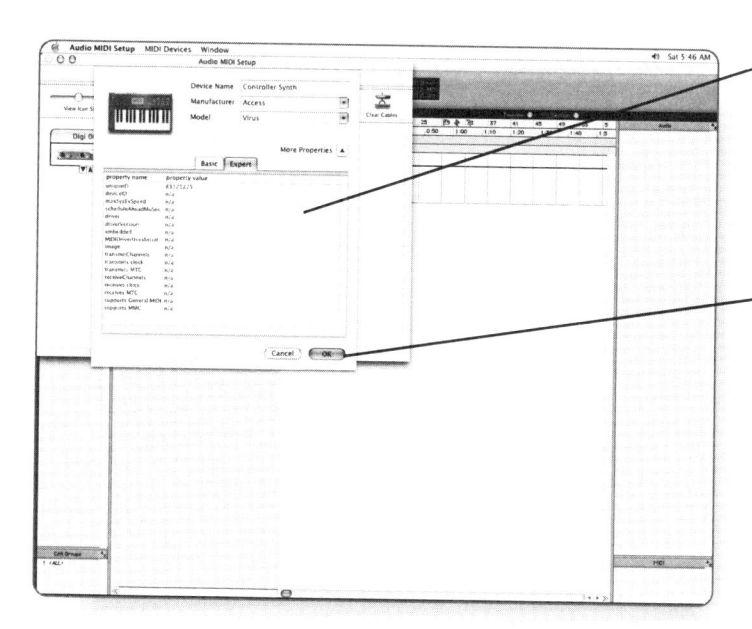

This page will display some of the finer points of this device's setup. Though fairly low-level, this information may come in handy during configuration/troubleshooting.

11. Click on **OK**. The dialog box will close.

Connecting Your Gear

Now you can connect your gear in a traditional configuration—in other words, connect the output of your MIDI interface to the MIDI input of your device, and connect the MIDI output (*not* the thru) of your device into an input on your MIDI interface. After you physically connect your MIDI cables to and from your MIDI interface and device, follow these steps.

1. Click and hold the MIDI interface's appropriate **MIDI out port**, which is indicated by a down arrow.

2. Drag your the **MIDI out port** to the MIDI device's MIDI in port, which is also indicated by a down arrow.

3. Release the **mouse button**. The two devices will be connected.

4. To complete the traditional setup, **drag and drop** the **connection** from your device's MIDI out port to the appropriate MIDI in port for your MIDI interface.

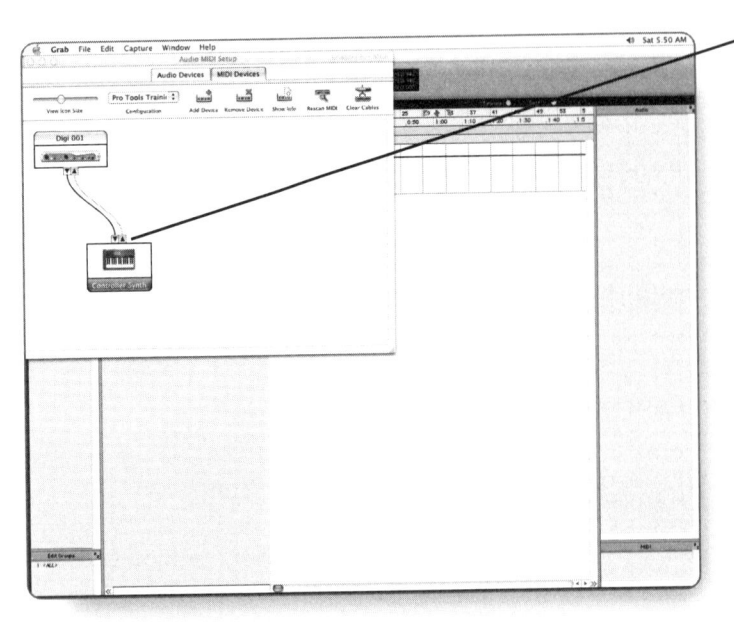

> **NOTE**
>
> If you want to remove an individual connection, click on the "cable" between the MIDI interface and device. The cable will turn blue. Press the Delete key to delete the connection.

> **TIP**
> There's another way to access the basic functions of the MIDI setup. You can click on the MIDI Devices menu to display all MIDI setup operations, including a couple that you haven't used yet. (These new operations are self-explanatory, though.)

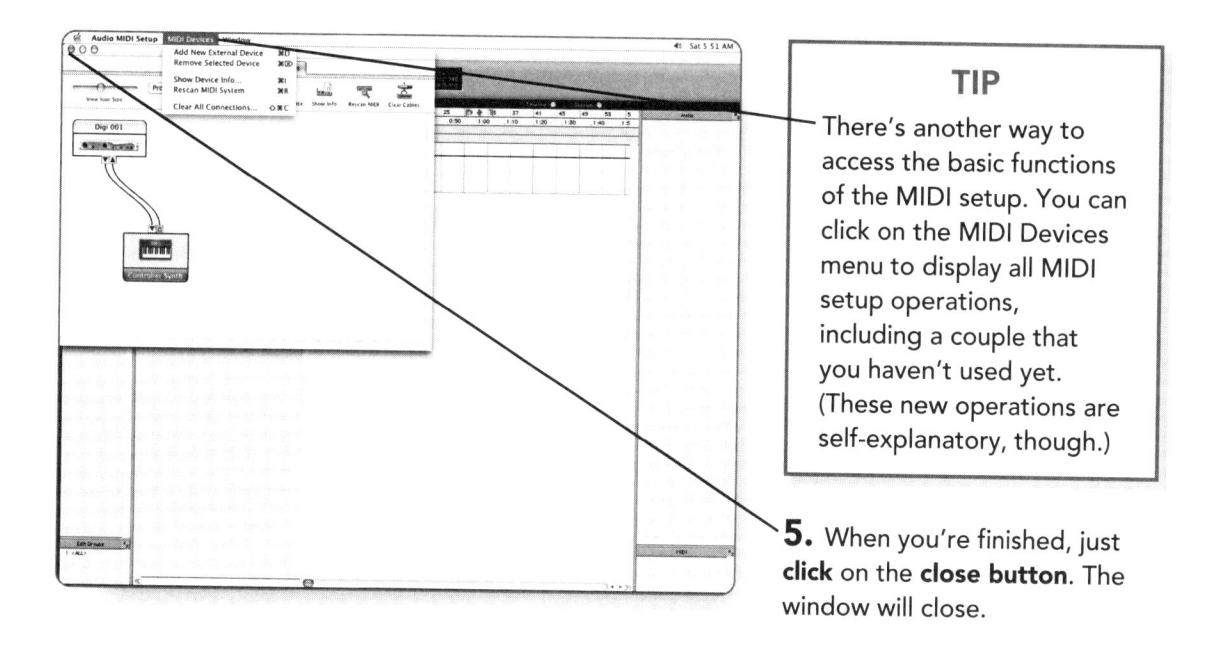

5. When you're finished, just **click** on the **close button**. The window will close.

Signal Flow 201: MIDI Versus Audio

Here's the important thing to remember about MIDI as opposed to audio: MIDI is *not* audio. MIDI isn't even audible—it's a digital language that allows musical hardware components to communicate with and control each other on a fundamental level. The common misconception that MIDI and audio are somehow related comes from the fact that the use of MIDI allows musical gear with MIDI connections to make sound.

Given that MIDI and digital audio are fundamentally different (although interdependent), it comes as no surprise that MIDI must have its own rules of signal flow. The good news about this is that you can manage both the MIDI signal path and the audio signal path simultaneously in one session.

Managing the MIDI Signal Path

The good news about MIDI data routing is that the look and feel of a MIDI track is similar to an audio or aux track.

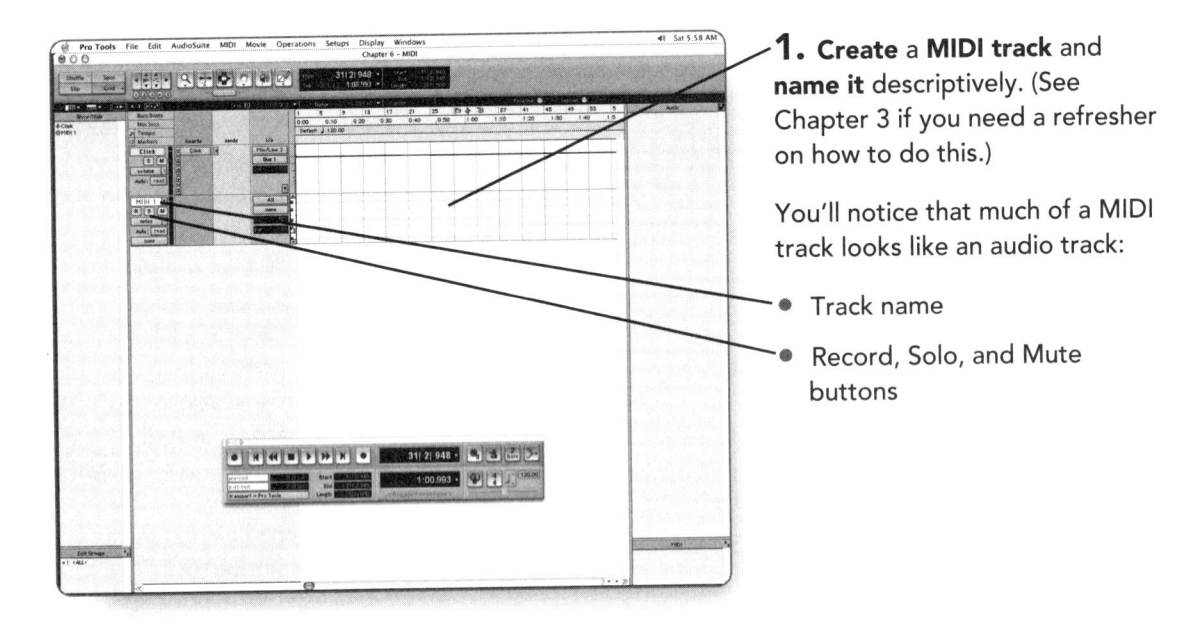

1. Create a **MIDI track** and **name it** descriptively. (See Chapter 3 if you need a refresher on how to do this.)

You'll notice that much of a MIDI track looks like an audio track:

- Track name
- Record, Solo, and Mute buttons

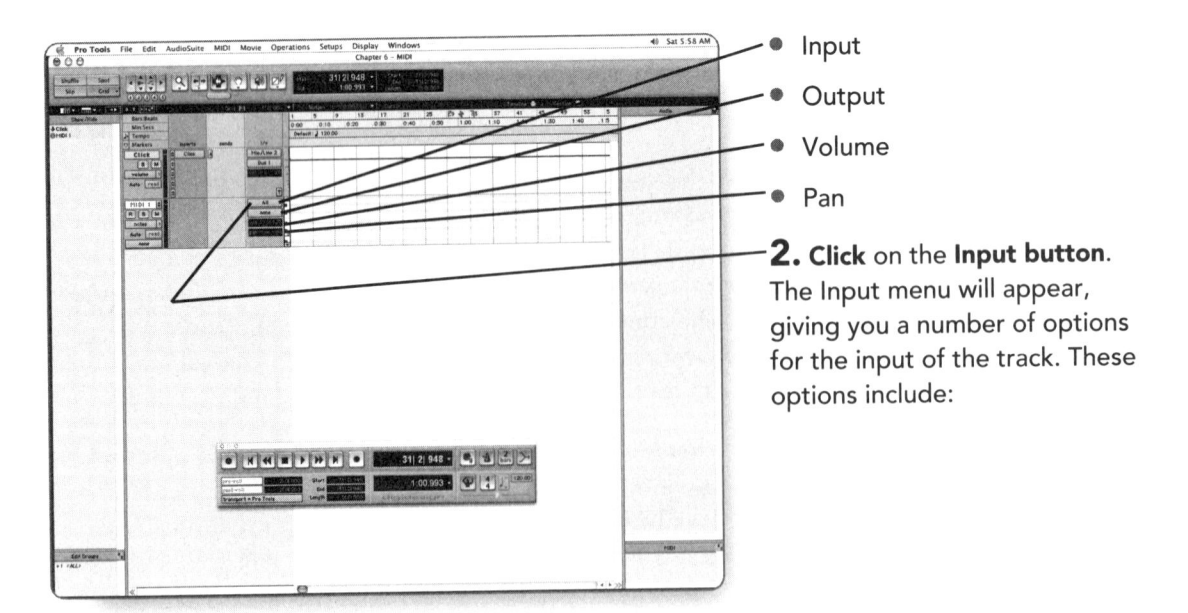

- Input
- Output
- Volume
- Pan

2. Click on the **Input button**. The Input menu will appear, giving you a number of options for the input of the track. These options include:

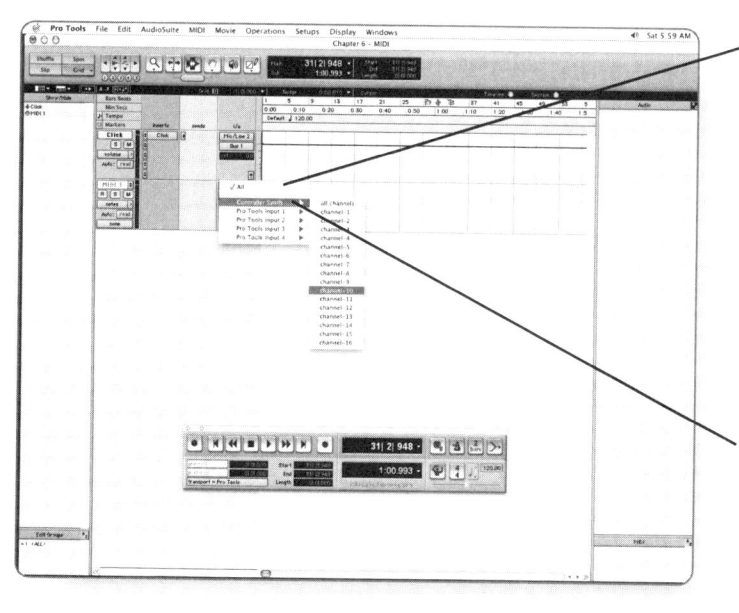

- Selecting All as an input will allow the track to accept MIDI data on any channel from any port. This is a particularly efficient way to work if you're a single user in a multi-keyboard studio. With All selected, you can move from MIDI instrument to MIDI instrument without having to change your input selection.

- Each input device you create in your MIDI setup will appear as an input option. You can specify a single device or even a specific MIDI channel as an input for your track. This is useful in multi-keyboard setups in which you have multiple musicians at one time. You can assign multiple tracks to accept input from only one MIDI port for each track; this way, you can isolate each musician's performance to a separate track even if all the musicians are playing simultaneously.

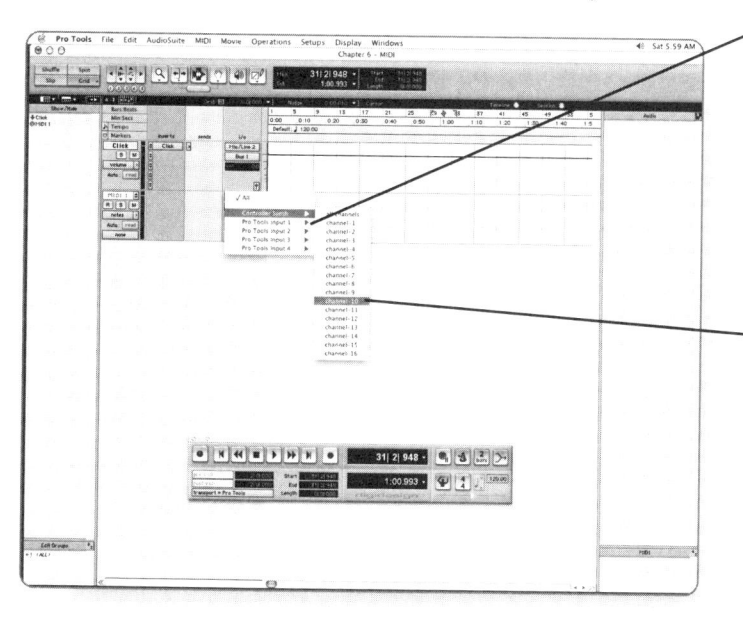

- Pro Tools has four virtual MIDI inputs, which can communicate with other MIDI software applications within your computer. These internal MIDI connections include synchronization via MIDI time code (MTC) or MIDI clock.

3. Select the **input** that matches the MIDI device you want to play. The input will be selected.

188 CHAPTER 6: USING MIDI

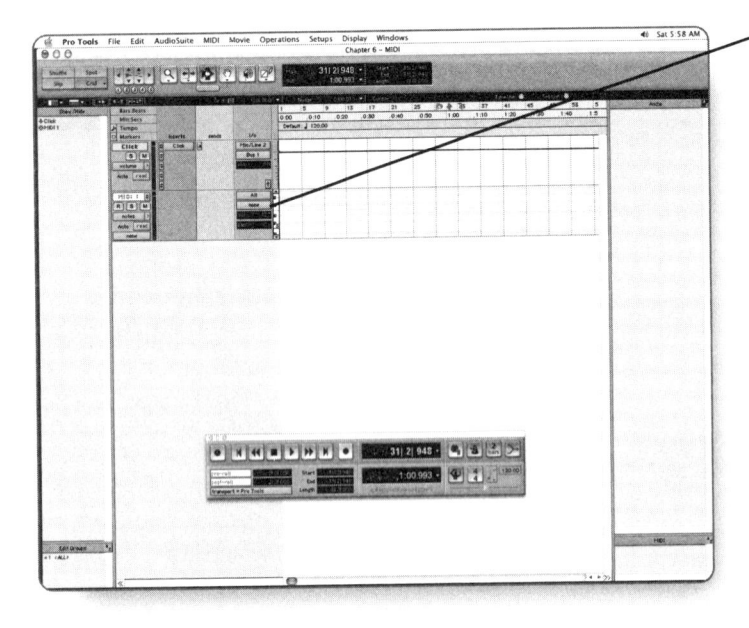

4. Click on the **Output button**. The Output menu will appear.

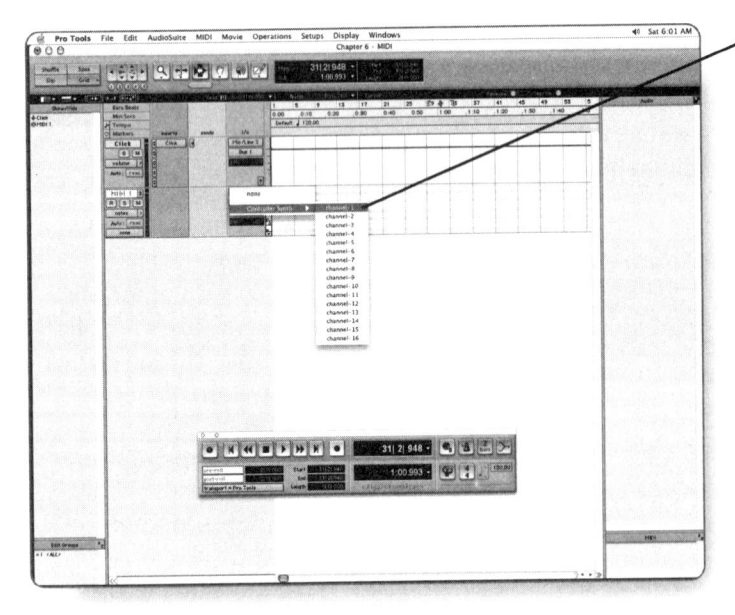

5. Click on the **device and MIDI channel** you want to sound when you play. The device and MIDI channel will be selected.

> **NOTE**
>
> The MIDI device that you physically play does *not* have to be the MIDI device that makes a sound. In this situation, the device you actually play is commonly called a *MIDI controller*. Do not confuse this with *controller data* such as a modulation wheel or pitch bend.

SIGNAL FLOW 201: MIDI VERSUS AUDIO   189

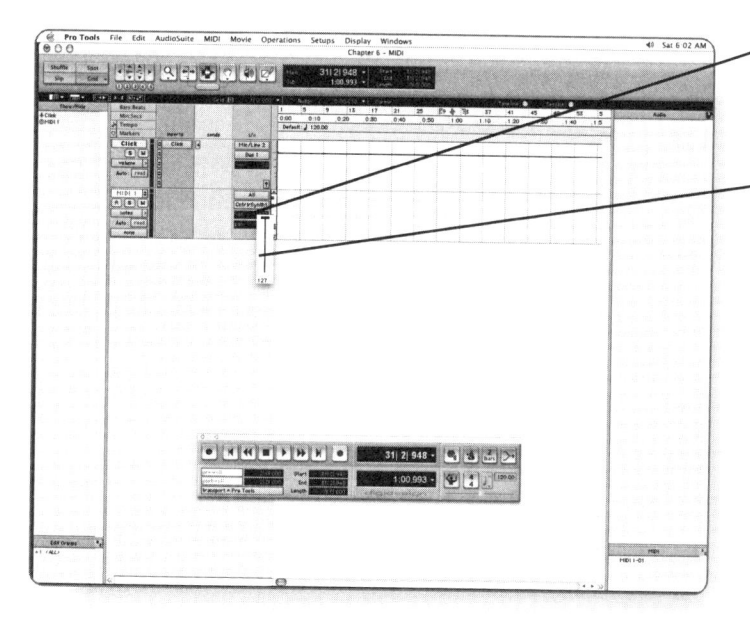

6. Click on the **Volume display area**. A small fader box will appear.

7. Click and drag the **slider** on the fader box to adjust the volume to suit your mix. The MIDI volume will be adjusted.

> **NOTE**
>
> Note that this fader controls MIDI volume, which is why it has a maximum of 127. MIDI volume has a range of 128 steps, from 0–127.

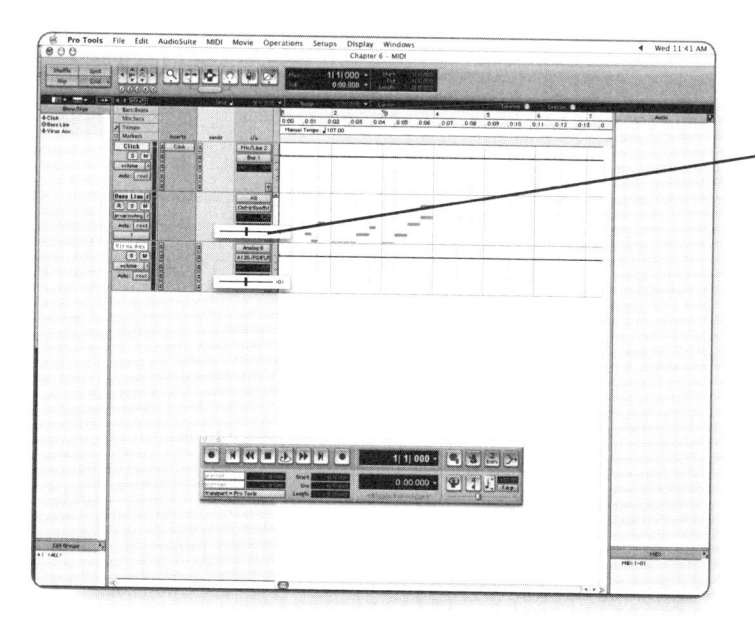

8. Click in the **Pan display area**. A small slider box will appear.

9. Click and drag the **slider** on the box to adjust the pan value to your taste. The value will be adjusted.

Now your MIDI track is set up to route MIDI data from the master device to the slave device. When you play your controlling instrument, you should see an indication on the slave device that it is receiving MIDI data. At this point, your slave device should respond to the MIDI data by making sound.

Setting Up an Aux Track to Monitor Your MIDI Gear

So how can you hear your slave device through Pro Tools? First, connect the audio outputs of the slave device to the audio inputs of your Pro Tools interface, and then follow these steps.

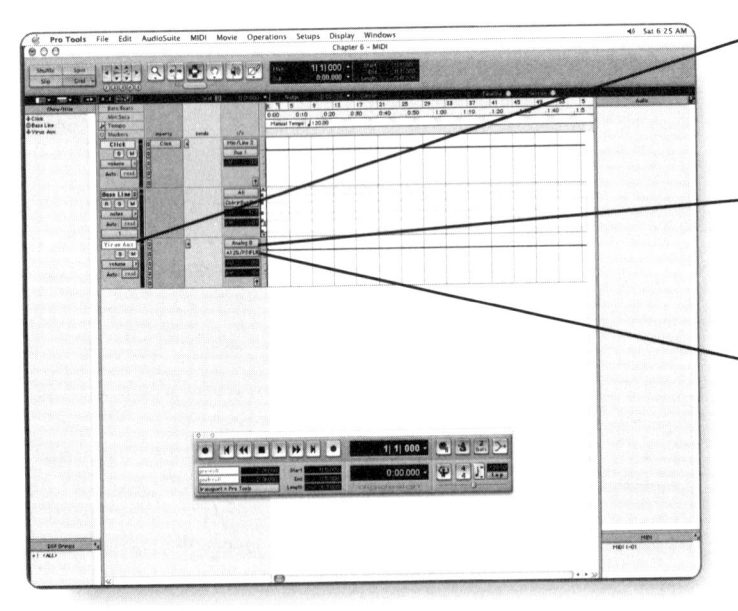

1. **Create** a new **aux track** and **name it** descriptively. This track will allow you to hear your MIDI device.

2. **Assign** the **input** of this aux track to match the inputs to which your MIDI slave device is attached.

3. **Assign** the **output** of this aux track to the outputs attached to your monitor speakers.

At this point, you've completely configured your MIDI signal flow, as well as an audio signal routing that will allow you to listen to your gear. Now when you play your controller device, you should trigger your slave device and listen to the output through an aux track!

Recording MIDI

Recording MIDI is very similar to recording audio in many respects, but with some extra flexibility. The first step is to pick a sound that you want to use.

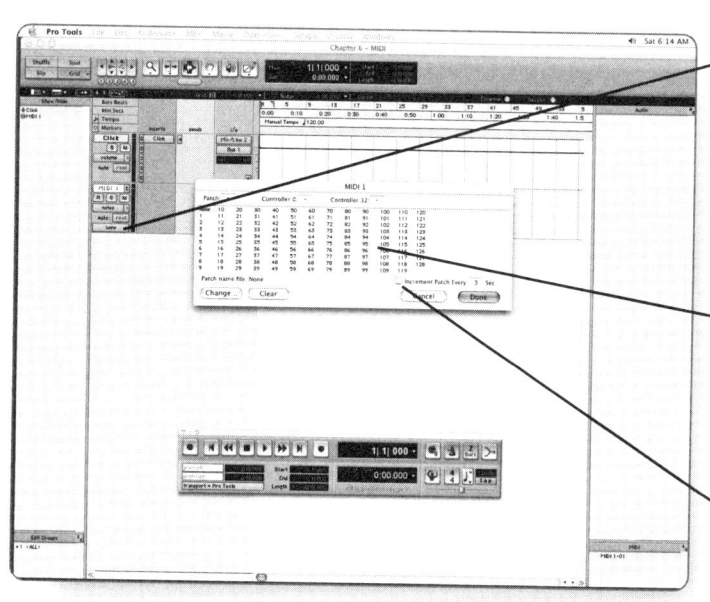

1. Click on the **Program Change button**. A dialog box containing a patch list for the MIDI device will be displayed. Depending on the device, the patch list displayed will consist of numeric or text names.

2. Click on the **number of the patch** you want to use. The patch will be selected.

> **TIP**
>
> Here's a useful feature: If you're searching for just the right sound, select the Increment Patch Every *n* Sec check box to cycle through all the sounds in this bank. You can specify the speed at which patches are changed (in seconds) by entering the value in the appropriate field.

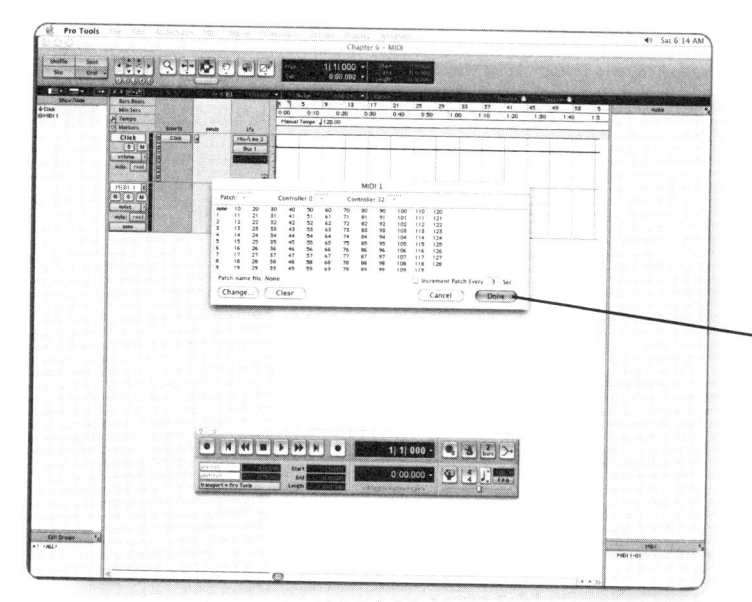

3. Click on **Done**. The dialog box will close. The program number or name will appear on the Program Change button.

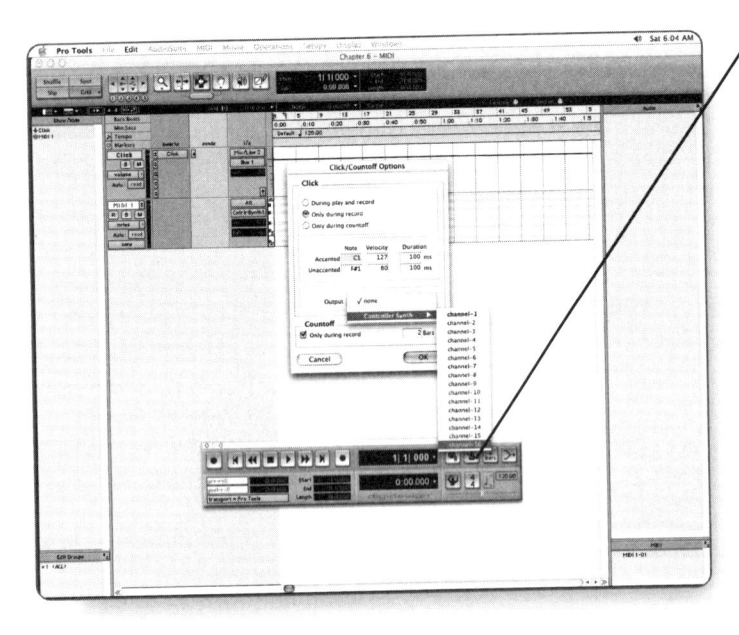

4. Before you start recording, you might want to assign your click track to a MIDI device (if you're not using the click plug-in). **Double-click** on the **Metronome icon**. The Click/Countoff Options dialog box will open.

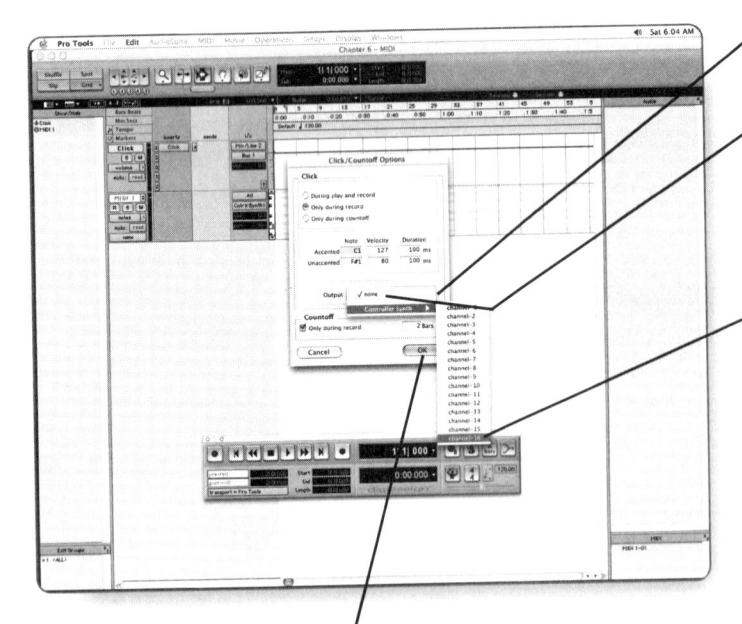

5. Click on the **Output button**. The Output menu will appear.

6a. If you're using the click plug-in, **click** on **none**. The option will be selected.

OR

6b. If you want to use a piece of MIDI gear for the click, **select** the **device and the MIDI channel** you want to use for the click sound. The device and channel will be selected.

7. Click on **OK**. The Click/Countoff Options dialog box will close.

Now it's time to actually record the MIDI. The process of recording MIDI is nearly identical to recording audio.

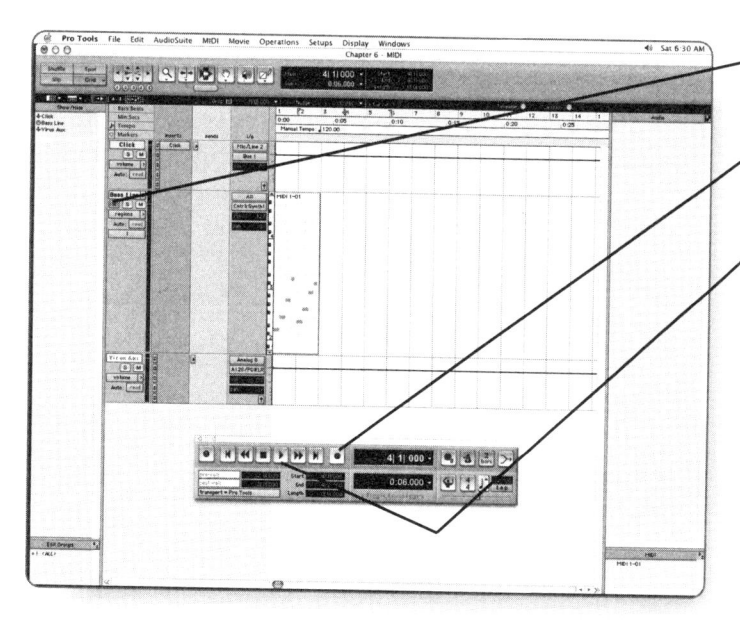

8. **Click** on the track's **R button** to arm the recording.

9. **Click** on the **Record button** in the Transport window.

10. **Click** on the **Play button**. The recording process will begin. It operates the same as when you record audio, with pre-rolls, post-rolls, and so on.

> **TIP**
>
> There's a nifty MIDI feature called Merge that allows you to record over a pre-recorded MIDI track and add to the data that's already there instead of erasing notes that you already played. It's an especially useful feature when you're working in Loop Record mode.

When you're finished, you'll have a region, as you did when you recorded audio. This time, however, you'll see MIDI note data within the region, rather than audio waveforms!

Editing MIDI

There's a whole world of flexibility open to you when you work with MIDI. Operations that are extremely difficult with digital audio, such as fixing one note in a chord, are easy with MIDI!

194 CHAPTER 6: USING MIDI

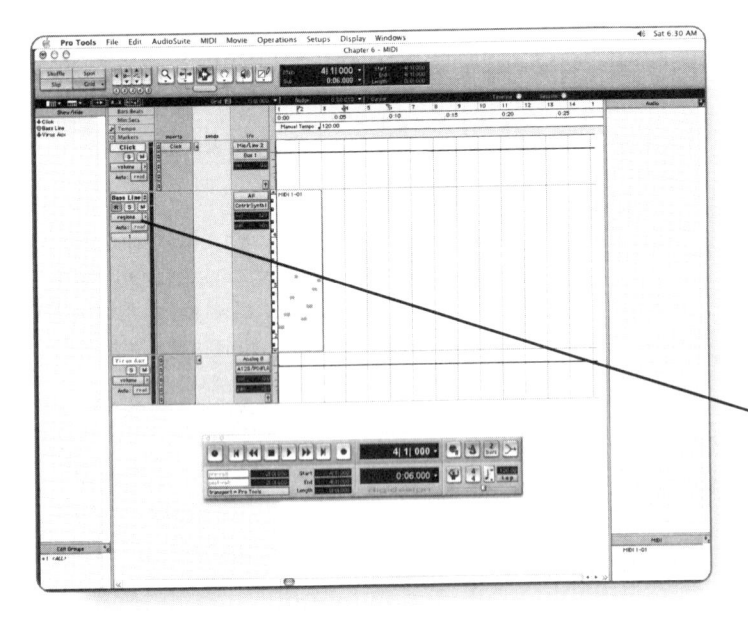

Editing with Tools

There are many ways to edit MIDI data. You can start by using tools that are already familiar to you. So far you've been working with regions, but that won't give you the kind of flexibility you want with MIDI. You need to look at the track in another way.

1. **Click** on the **regions button**. The regions menu will appear.

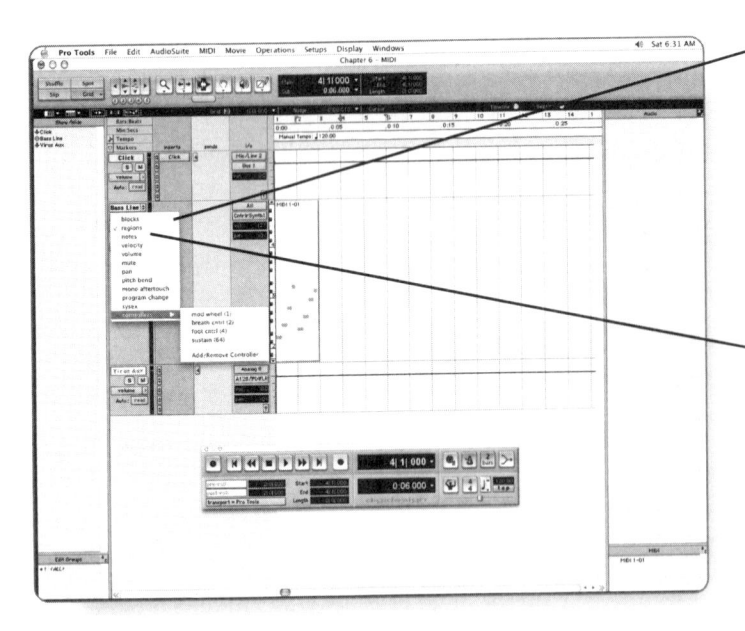

The menu includes options so you can control the kind of data you will view and manipulate. Because this is a MIDI track, the menu will display all editable aspects of MIDI in Pro Tools, including controllers and system exclusive data.

2. You'll be working on note data first, so **click** on **notes**.

EDITING MIDI

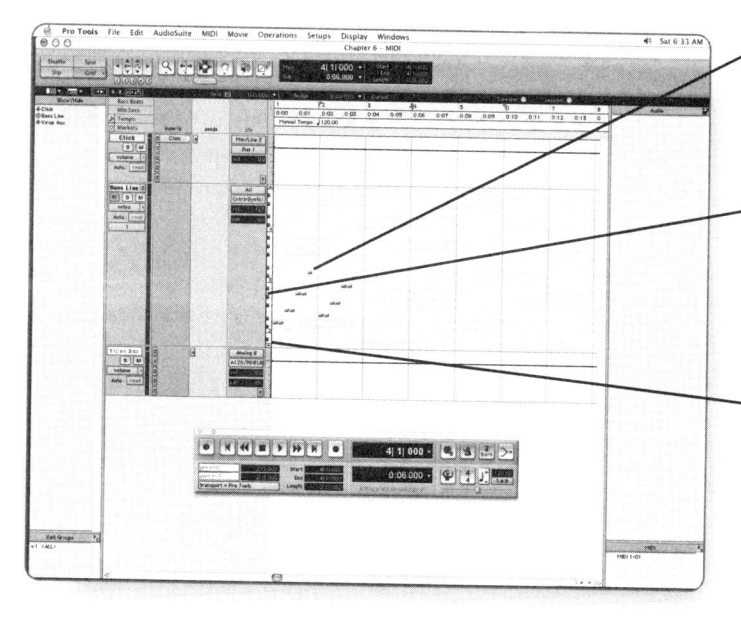

The familiar regions will disappear, leaving only a series of small blocks. Each of these blocks represents a MIDI note.

On the left edge of each MIDI track's Timeline, you will notice a keyboard graphic. This graphic identifies the pitches of the MIDI notes in the track.

3. Click on the **arrow** at either end of the keyboard graphic to scroll up and down the register of the track.

The Grabber Tool

One of the nicest things about Pro Tools is that the basic editing tools are easy to get to, and they're named well. The Grabber tool does just what it says it does—it allows the user to grab objects in the Edit window and move them.

1. Click on the **Grabber tool**. The tool will be selected.

2. Click on a single **note** in your track. The note will be highlighted, indicating that it is selected.

3. Drag and drop the **note** to a different pitch or timing as desired.

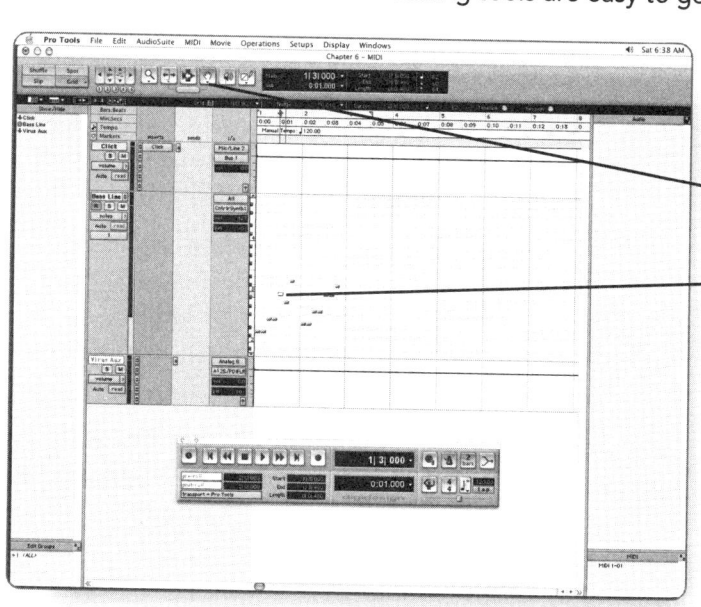

196 CHAPTER 6: USING MIDI

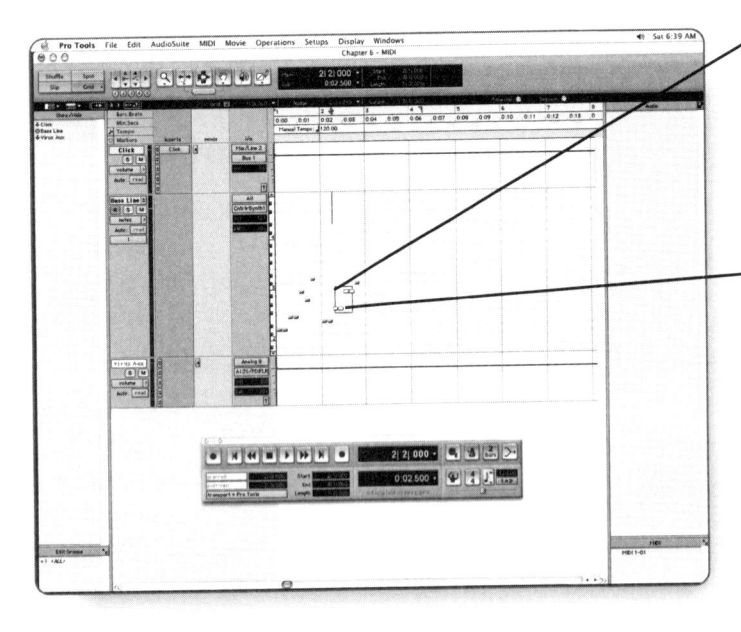

4. If you want to move more than one note at a time, **drag** a **box** around the notes you want to change. The group of notes will be highlighted, indicating that they are selected.

5. Drag and drop the **group of notes** in the same manner that you moved a single note.

The Trim Tool

The Trim tool, the next of the primary edit tools, allows you to adjust the beginning and/or end of MIDI notes in much the same way you've changed region boundaries when working with audio.

1. Click on the **Trim tool**. The tool will be selected.

2. Click on either **end** of a single note in your track. The note will be highlighted, indicating that it is selected.

3. Drag and drop the **end** of the note as desired. The duration of the note will be lengthened or shortened as appropriate.

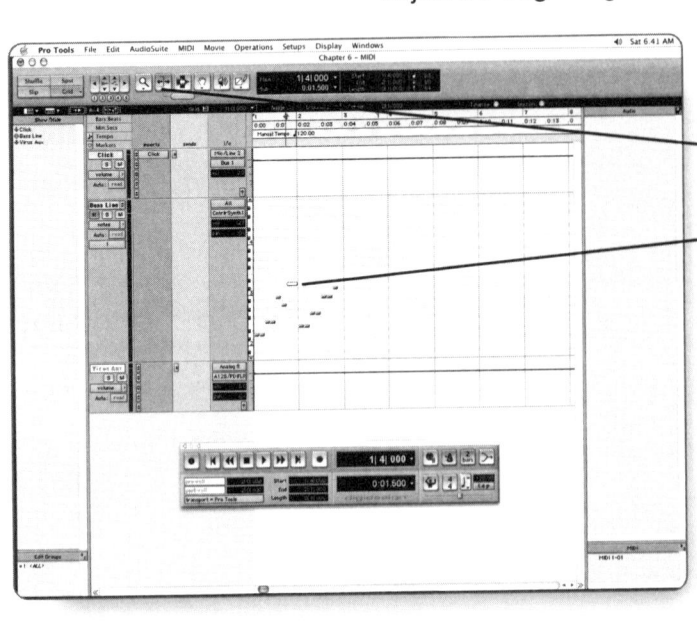

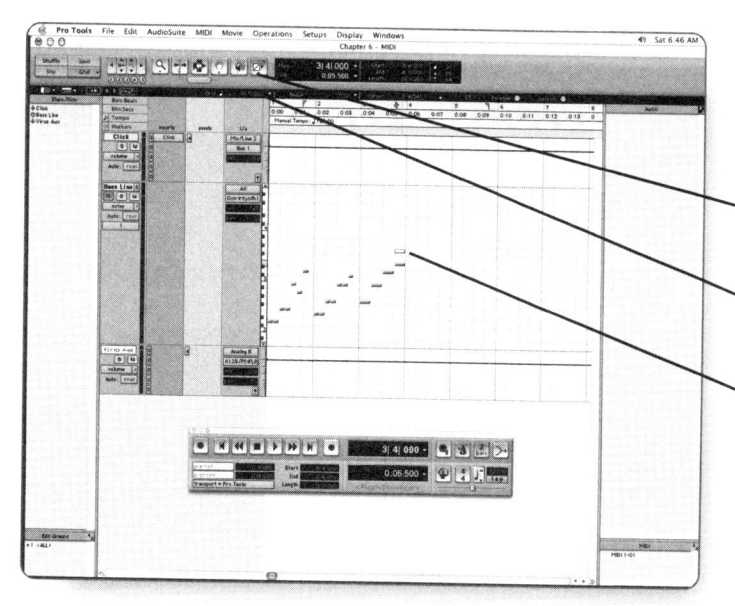

The Pencil Tool

Using the Pencil tool, you can create a MIDI note.

1. Click on the **Pencil tool**. The tool will be selected.

2. Select Grid mode and **set** the **grid** to ¼ note.

3. Click on any **open area** of your track. Wherever you click, a MIDI quarter note will be created.

NOTE
In addition to creating MIDI notes, the pencil is a multi-functional editing tool, as well. If you click in the body of a pre-existing note, the Pencil tool will take on the function of a grabber. If you move the Pencil tool to either end of the note, it will become a trim tool.

The MIDI Menu

In addition to editing with tools, you can also powerfully transform your MIDI with functions from the MIDI menu. Most of these features are commonly found in most MIDI sequencers, but it is helpful to know where to find them and the specific layouts of such windows.

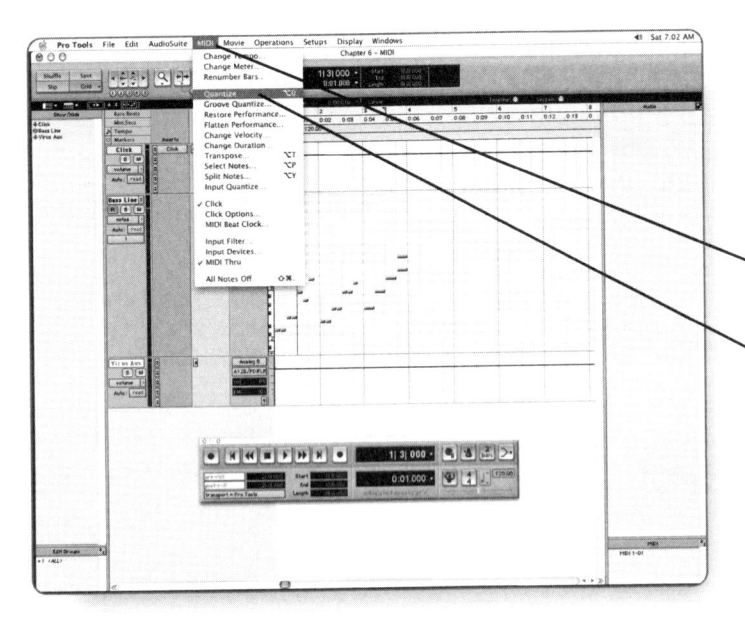

Here's how you start the process:

1. Select the **group of notes** you want to process. The notes will be selected.

2. Click on **MIDI**. The MIDI menu will appear.

3. Choose the **process** you want to apply to the selection. There are a number of processes you can apply; the next few sections will explain these processes in more detail.

Quantize

Quantize is a MIDI function that aligns the timing of MIDI notes to a grid. It is commonly used to fix timing errors or create a mechanically timed track when the style of music calls for it. Pro Tools' Quantize dialog box includes all the basic parameters, in addition to Include within and Exclude within options, which allow you to set thresholds of notes to be quantized based upon the distance of given notes from the grid.

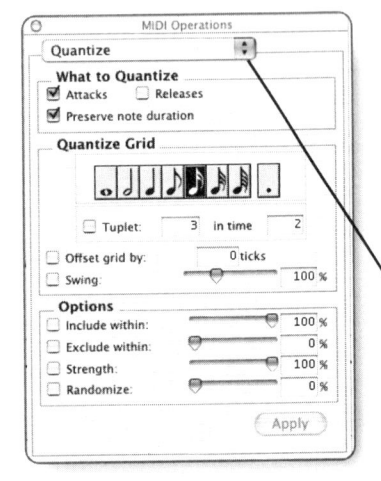

TIP

You can change MIDI processes without going back to the MIDI menu. Simply click on the menu at the top of the dialog box to reveal a menu of MIDI functions.

> **TIP**
> Users often apply the Randomize feature to a MIDI drum track, in the hopes that it will "humanize" the track. This usually has a negative effect upon the groove. However, used sparingly, the Randomize feature works well when you are dealing with a section of musical sounds (strings, brass, and so on)—it takes the edge off the mechanical accuracy sometimes associated with MIDI.

Groove Quantize

The Groove Quantize feature operates similarly to the Quantize feature, but in this case a pre-defined set of parameters is applied to the data to create a specific musical feel.

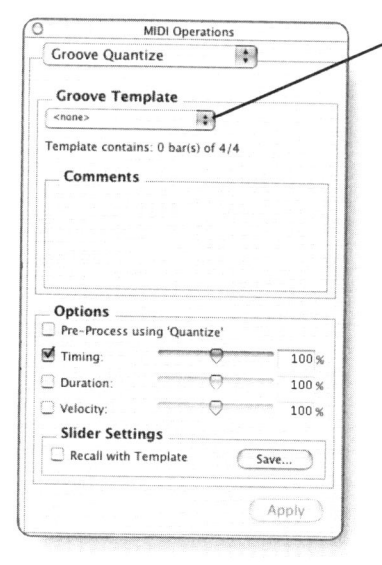

1. Click on the **Groove Template button**. A drop-down menu will appear.

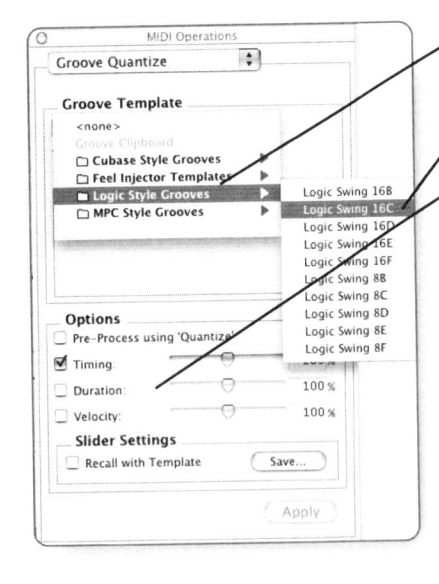

2. Choose any **groove folder** shown. A set of specific groove templates you can use will be displayed.

3. Click on a **template**. The template will be selected.

4. Set any **options** you desire in the Options section of the dialog box. These parameters allow you to determine the degree to which the selected template will be applied to your MIDI data.

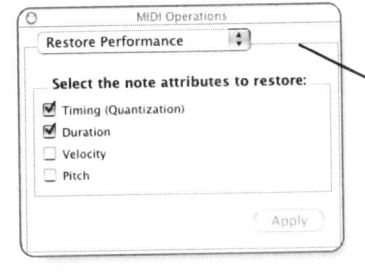

Restore/Flatten Performance

Think of the Restore Performance option as an improved version of the Undo feature. What makes this function so special is that it extends beyond the last time you saved your session and the 16 levels of undo that Pro Tools already has. Furthermore, you can selectively restore specific aspects of your MIDI data (timing, duration, velocity, and pitch), so you're not locked into an all or nothing situation. When you restore your performance, it will revert to the last time the performance was flattened.

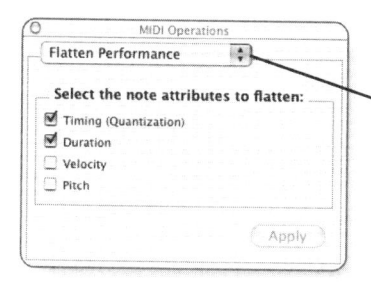

When you choose the Flatten Performance option, you "print" your MIDI data to your session and remove the option to undo any edits that you've performed. When you restore a performance in the future, it will revert to this new flattened state.

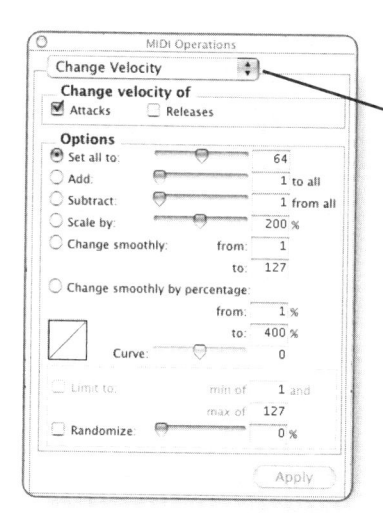

Change Velocity

The Change Velocity feature sports options with which you can manipulate MIDI velocity (how fast a key is pressed). In addition to Set all to (which assigns a single velocity value to all notes), you can proportionally change the velocity of a set of notes. Additionally, you can use the Change smoothly option to gradually change the velocity from the beginning of the selection to the end, resulting in an increase or decrease in intensity.

Change Duration

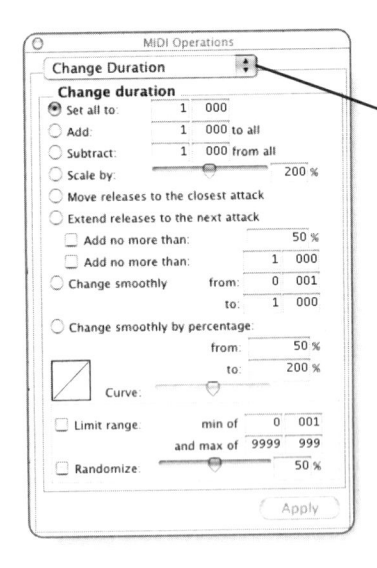

The Change Duration option has similar features to the Change Velocity option, but the options affect the length of the selected notes.

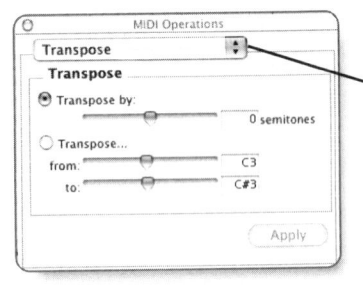

Transpose

Transpose is a MIDI function that changes the note number of MIDI data, effectively changing the pitch of your MIDI music. The options for Pro Tools' Transpose function are very simple and straightforward: You can adjust your music by semitones (or half steps) or you can transpose from one reference note to a target note.

> **TIP**
>
> When you transpose a section of a song, you might want to exclude your drum tracks from that transposition. Transposing drum kit patches tends to radically change the instrument assignments!

Select Notes/Split Notes

After you've selected notes using the Selector or Grabber tools, you can further logically select notes by setting certain criteria for them. Once you've selected those notes, you can then transform them with another process.

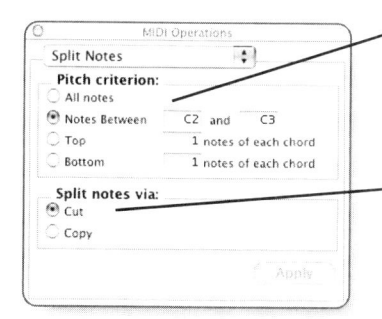

- For both the Select Notes and Split Notes options you will select notes based on some sort of pitch value. You can set a range (using the Notes Between function) or you can pick out notes starting from the top or bottom of a chord.

- The only difference between the Select and Split functions is the Split notes via option. All the pitch criteria are the same in the Split Notes feature as they are in the Select Notes feature, but in the Split Notes feature you can cut or copy the selected notes from the original track to be pasted elsewhere.

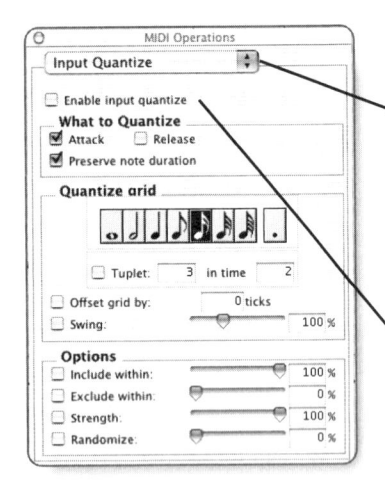

Input Quantize

The Input Quantize feature works exactly like the basic Quantize function except for one thing. Whereas Quantize is applied to MIDI data *after* it has been recorded, Input Quantize processes the audio as it is being played in the session. This feature is particularly nifty for technically challenged people like me because it fixes my timing as I play!

Select the Enable input quantize check box to enable the Input Quantize feature. One thing to remember, though—Input Quantize will stay enabled until you turn it off!

Tempo, Meter, and Bars

Your session's bars and beats time scale is actually a MIDI tempo map. You can set it up from the MIDI menu.

1. Click on **MIDI**. The MIDI menu will appear.

2. Click on **Change Tempo**. The Tempo/Meter Change dialog box will open. This dialog box should look familiar—it's the same dialog box you worked with in Chapter 5 (although you accessed it from the Transport window in that chapter). You can choose the location (in bars and beats) at which you want to change your tempo and the value to which you want to set your tempo.

EDITING MIDI

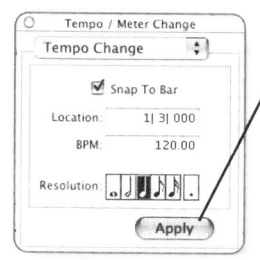

3. When you're done, **click** on the **Apply button**. (This will *not* close the dialog box.)

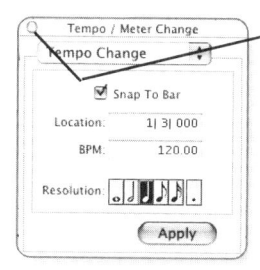

4. Click on the **close button** to close the dialog box.

Changing the meter is just as easy as changing the tempo.

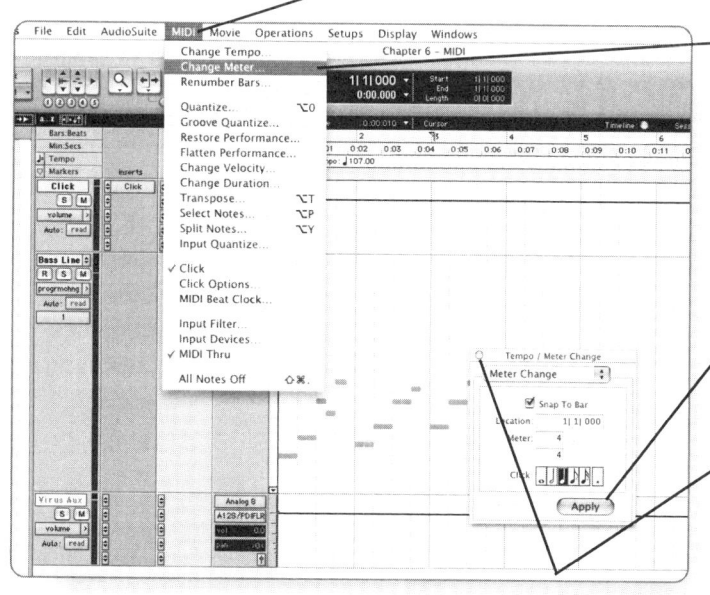

1. Click on **MIDI**. The MIDI menu will appear.

2. Click on **Change Meter**. The Tempo/Meter Change dialog box will appear. Again, you explored this dialog box in Chapter 5.

3. When you're done, **click** on the **Apply button**. (This will not close the dialog box.)

4. Click on the **close button**. The dialog box will close.

And renumbering the bars is even easier.

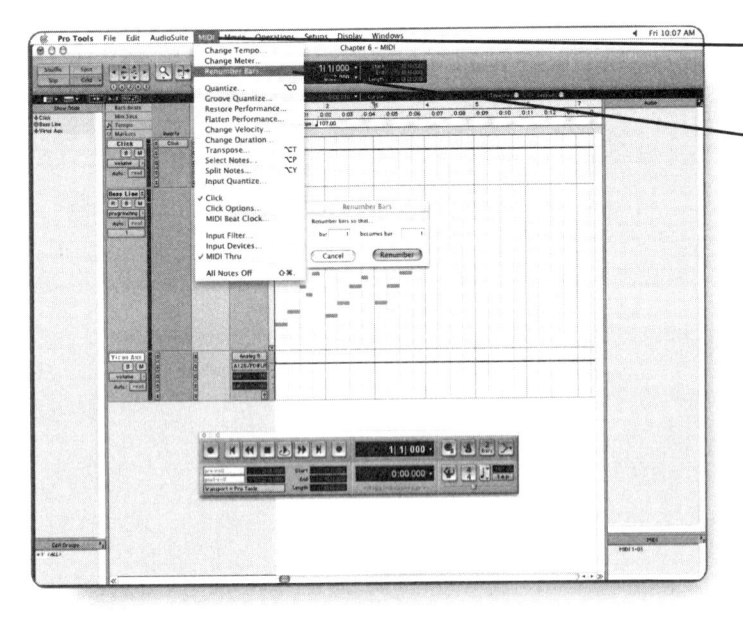

1. Click on **MIDI**. The MIDI menu will appear.

2. Click on **Renumber Bars**. The Renumber Bars dialog box will open. In this dialog box you can transpose the number of the measures in your session. This doesn't change the way the session plays, but it does change the numbering of its bars and beats.

More MIDI Tips

You will be using MIDI tracks side by side with audio and aux tracks in Pro Tools from this point on, but before you finish your focus on the wonderful world of MIDI, there are a few more things I want to discuss.

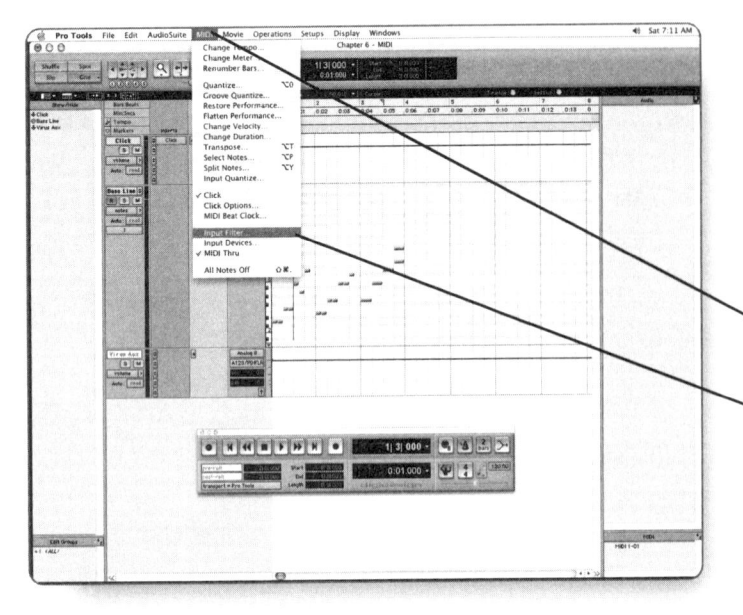

The MIDI Input Filter

Sometimes you don't want to record *everything* that comes through your MIDI cable. Not a problem—just filter out the unwanted bits (literally!).

1. Click on **MIDI**. The MIDI menu will appear.

2. Click on **Input Filter**. The MIDI Input Filter dialog box will open.

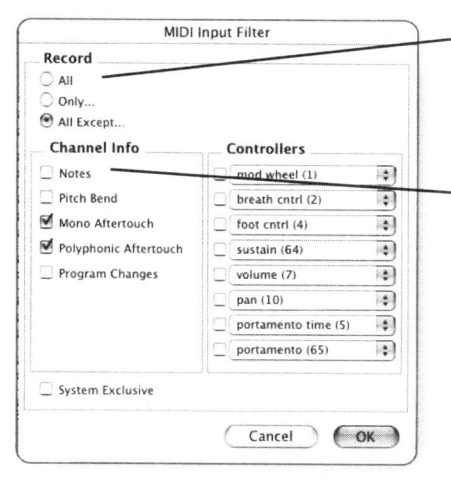

3. Choose an **option** for how you're going to filter your data. Select All to record everything, Only to record only selected data, or All Except to record everything *but* the selected data.

4. Select the **MIDI channel messages** in the Channel Info area that you want to include or not (depending on your record setting). The options will be selected.

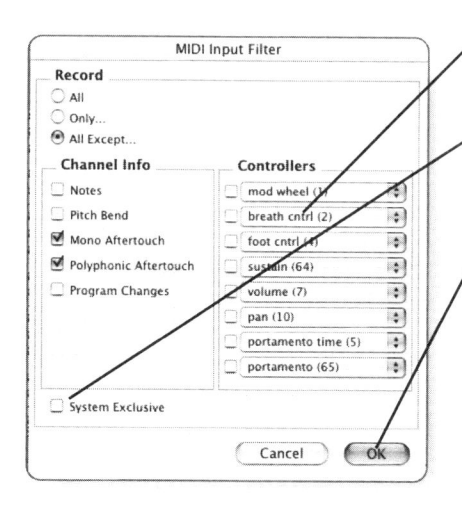

5. Select your **controller data** by clicking on the menus in the Controllers area.

6. Select the **System Exclusive check box** to record (or not, again depending on your record setting) this unique aspect of MIDI data.

7. Click on **OK**. Your settings will be saved and the MIDI Input Filter dialog box will close.

> **NOTE**
> System exclusive data is a very different form of MIDI data. Rather than being relevant to any sort of musical information, this data contains device-specific settings. You can use system exclusive data (aka *sysex*) to change global settings, load patches, and more. Although the study of MIDI at this level falls well outside the scope of a Pro Tools book, gaining a mastery of sysex will serve you well.

The Event List

MIDI tweakers rejoice! In addition to tools and drop-down menu processes, you can use the MIDI Event List window, a simple yet powerful window in which you can type the exact values you want! If you've used a MIDI sequencer before, you have probably seen this kind of window. Here's how to use it in Pro Tools:

1. Click on **Windows**. The Windows menu will appear.

2. Click on **Show MIDI Event List**. The MIDI Event List window will appear. The following list presents some highlights of the MIDI Event List window.

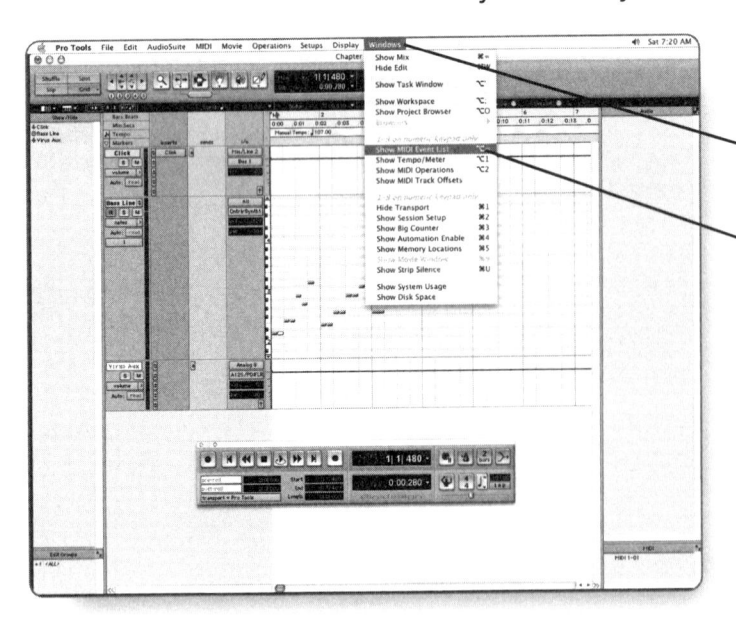

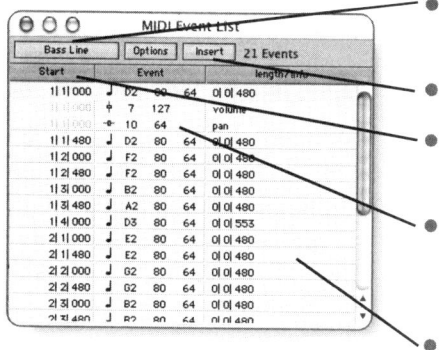

- This button shows the track name of the selected MIDI track.

- You can click on Insert to create a new MIDI event.

- The Start column shows the beginning time for each event, listed sequentially.

- The Event column shows the type of data (note, pan, and so on) displayed by a small icon to the left of the column, as well as the value of that event.

- The length/info column shows more specific information about each event.

So how do you tweak this data? Easy—just click on the value you want to change, type the new value, and press the Enter key!

Viewing and Editing Non-Note Data

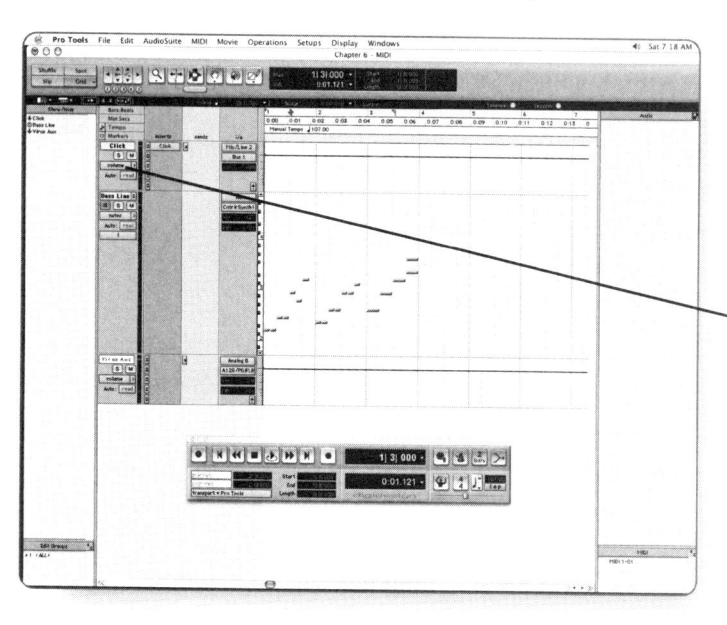

Of course you can edit non-note data in the MIDI Event List, but can't you edit non-note data (such as volume, velocity, or pan) on the track itself? Sure, but you've got to know how to view it before you can edit it.

1. On this track, you're looking at (and thus able to edit) note data, as indicated by the label on the Track Display Format button. **Click** on the **button**. A menu of other MIDI data you can view will appear.

210 CHAPTER 6: USING MIDI

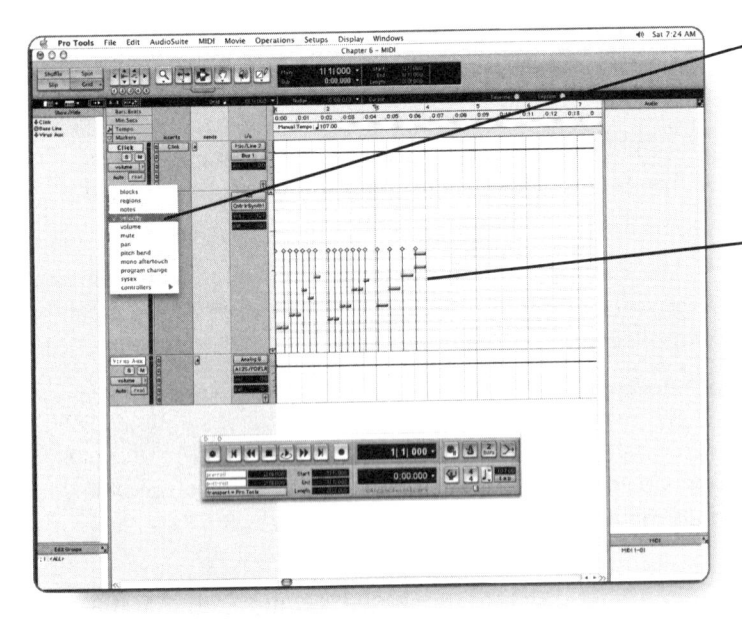

2. Select the kind of **MIDI data** with which you want to work. The track to the right will change to show the kind of data you selected.

In this case, velocity data is shown. Although you can still see the notes in the background, you see velocity stems for each note event, and that's the only kind of data you can manipulate. It's easy from there because you can use the same tools you used for the note data (such as the Grabber tool, the Trim tool, the Selector tool, and so on) to change these values.

Panic!

Reality check: Sometimes things go wrong. Worse yet, sometimes the things that go wrong can be audible. When that happens, the most important thing to do is stop the data! Whatever you do, don't forget this tip!

1. Click on **MIDI**. The MIDI menu will appear.

2. Click on **All Notes Off** (quickly!). A MIDI note-off command will be sent on all channels and on all ports of your MIDI interface, and through the four virtual MIDI connections.

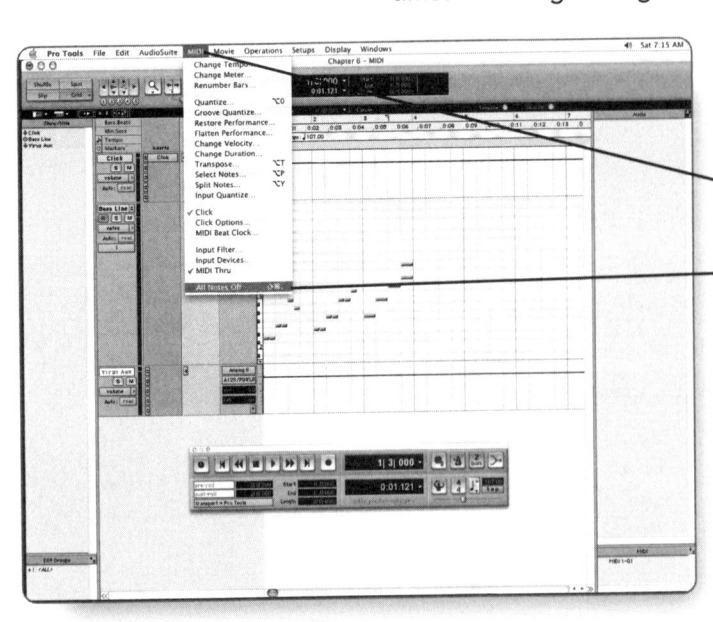

MORE MIDI TIPS   211

> **TIP**
> The fastest way to trigger the All Notes Off function is to use the shortcut keys. Shift+⌘+. (period key) will do it on the Mac, and Shift+Ctrl+. (period key) will do it on the PC.

Importing and Exporting MIDI Data

One of MIDI's greatest advantages lies in its broad compatibility. Regardless of any proprietary file format, nearly every MIDI application can utilize the industry's SMF (*Standard MIDI File*) format. Pro Tools, although a relative newcomer to the world of MIDI, is no exception.

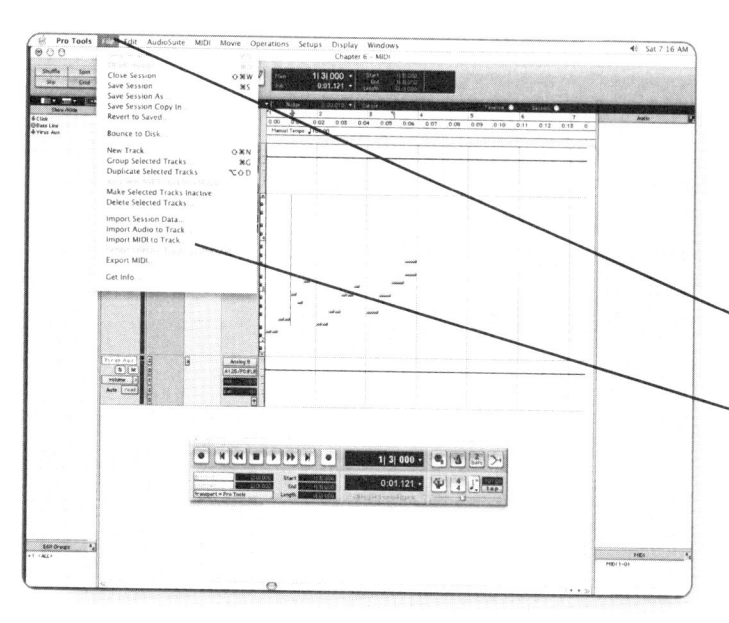

Importing MIDI Data

Just as you can import an audio file to an audio track, you can import a standard MIDI file to one or more MIDI tracks in your session.

1. Click on **File**. The File menu will appear.

2. Select Import MIDI to Track. The Open dialog box will open.

CHAPTER 6: USING MIDI

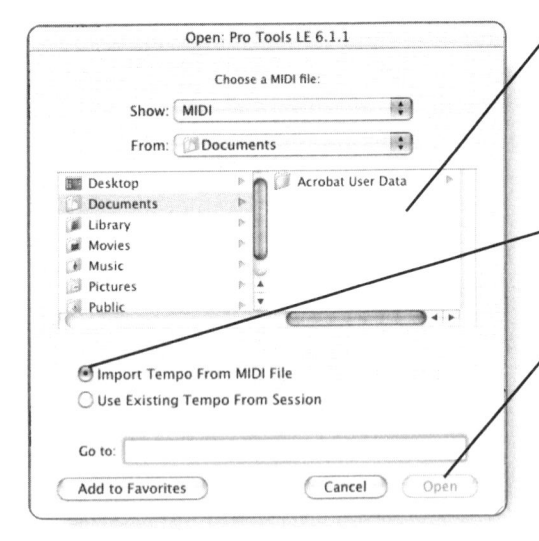

This dialog box functions much like any other open file dialog box you've worked with up to this point. Of course, in this case you'll be looking for a standard MIDI file to open (or more to the point, to import).

3. Click on **Import Tempo From MIDI File** or **Use Existing Tempo From Session**, depending on your preference. The option will be selected.

4. Navigate to the **file** you want to import and **click** on **Open**. Pro Tools will automatically create MIDI tracks and place the MIDI data on them. Also notice that the MIDI regions will appear in the MIDI Regions list in the lower-right corner of the Edit window.

> **NOTE**
>
> Keep in mind that even after you import your MIDI data, you have to set your MIDI output and an aux track before you can play and hear your MIDI data through the Pro Tools mixer.

TIP

Although importing MIDI directly to a track is probably the quickest way to get up and running, you can also import MIDI to the MIDI Regions list. Just click on the MIDI button at the top of the MIDI Regions list and choose Import MIDI. You will see the same dialog box you saw when you imported to a track. You can open a standard MIDI file in the same manner. In this case, however, the MIDI data will be imported to your session's MIDI Regions list—not to any track. (You'll have to create a MIDI track and drag the region manually to use it.)

Exporting MIDI Data

When you save your session, your MIDI data will be saved in the session file. However, you can also save the MIDI data by itself as a standard MIDI file, so you can open it in any MIDI sequencer.

1. Click on **File**. The File menu will appear.

2. Select Export MIDI. The Save dialog box will open. This dialog box looks very similar to the session save window, and you will select your destination file and location in the same manner, but there is one notable difference.

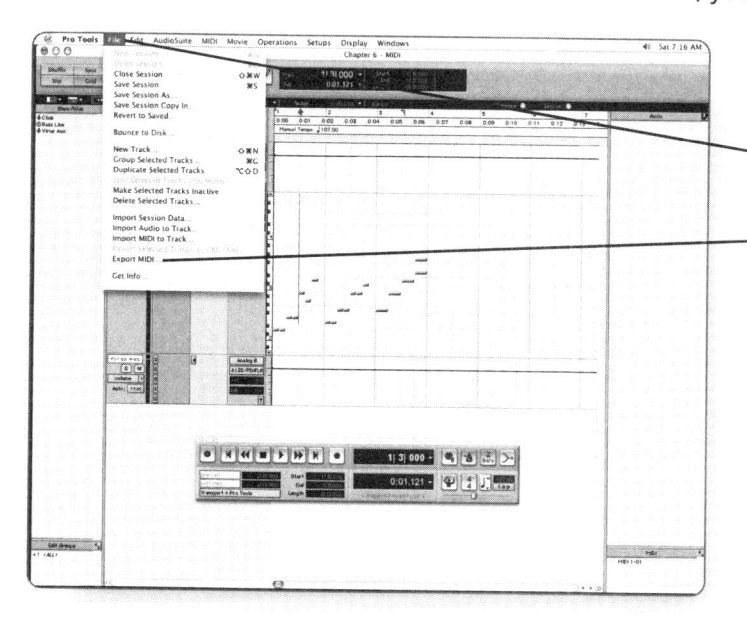

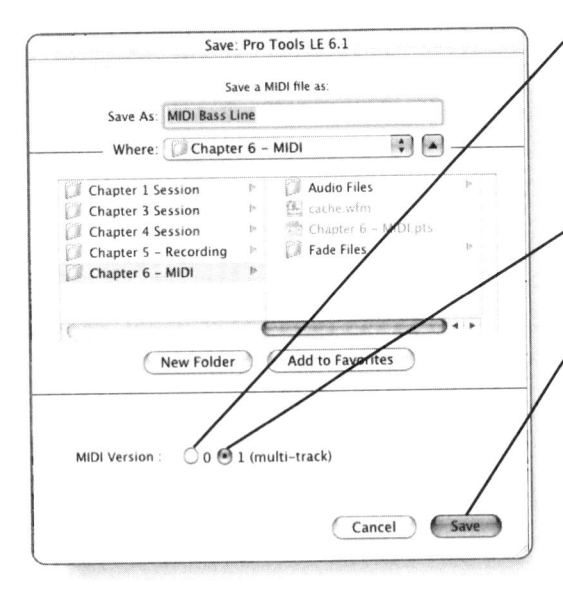

3a. Select the **0 radio button**. All the MIDI data will be saved as one MIDI track, regardless of how many tracks you have in your session.

OR

3b. Select the **1 (multi-track) radio button**. The multi-track environment of your MIDI data will be preserved.

4. **Click** on **Save**. The MIDI data from your session will be saved to a standard MIDI file.

Closing Thoughts on MIDI in Pro Tools

When MIDI came out in the early 1980s, it turned the musical world on its ear. I even took advantage of its power and used it as a composer, to compensate for my shortcomings on the keyboard! Even in its primitive state, the ability to play a MIDI keyboard slowly and play the recording back quickly was a huge help!

Of course, time marched on and the next thing we knew, hard disk recording had begun. In addition to the growing crop of MIDI applications, you had the ability to record to your computer rather than to analog tape; from there you could accomplish in moments the kinds of editing that took hours using a razor blade and cutting block. At this point, there was still a division between MIDI applications and hard disk audio applications, so you had to jump from application to application, using the right tool for the right job despite the inconvenience.

CLOSING THOUGHTS ON MIDI IN PRO TOOLS

Recently, MIDI and digital audio applications have been merging into one-stop production workstations, incorporating MIDI *and* digital audio functionality. Pro Tools, already the leading DAW on the market, has consistently added more powerful and intuitive MIDI functionality with each successive version, and the outlook is bright because future versions hold the promise of even greater power.

As we move into the future, production environments will become more comprehensive. The distinction between MIDI and digital audio will continue to blur in integrated applications. Although with this greater power will come greater responsibility to understand the distinctions between the MIDI language and audio (and how to use them together), the potential to do great work will continue to expand and aid musical people in their creative pursuits.

> **NOTE**
> Pro Tools version 6 now supports MIDI Time Stamping, which means that when you are using a MIDI Time Stamping-compatible MIDI interface, you can achieve up to sub-millisecond accuracy with the timing of your notes, effectively eliminating MIDI latency.

7

More Editing

Although the editing power of a DAW ranks high in the production world, the editing process itself can sometimes be lacking in the way of glamour. A good editor knows that the prospect of editing essentially boils down to simple functions done many, many times. Patience is a virtue in this phase of production, and it is put to the test when you cut and paste, drag and drop, and perform like functions repeatedly. Indeed, it's not uncommon for a professional editing session to involve hundreds of individual editing operations! The good news is that you already learned the basics of editing in Chapter 4 (cleverly named "Basic Editing"). Now you're going to learn more efficient and flexible ways to work and expand upon the basic editing tools you've already begun to use. The idea behind these techniques is that the time you save with each editing function will add up. By mastering these new processes, you'll not only save time, but you'll also become a better and more creative editor! In this chapter, you'll learn how to:

- Use and customize the zoom tools
- Use the variations of the Trim and Grabber tools
- Boost your editing efficiency by using the Smart tool

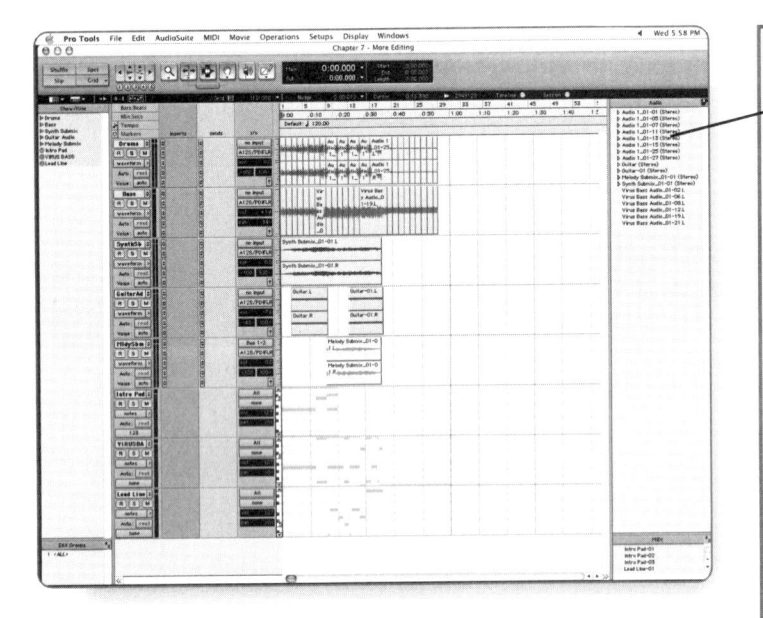

CHAPTER 7: MORE EDITING

> **NOTE**
> The examples used in this chapter are based upon the session you used in Chapter 1. I've taken the liberty of adding some MIDI parts to illustrate some of the zoom tool functions. If you want to follow along with the specific examples in the book, just open the session from Chapter 1, add some MIDI tracks, record some MIDI data (or just write it in using the Pencil tool), and save the session as Chapter 7–More Editing. Your session should end up looking something like this.
>
> Don't worry too much about routing signal in the MIDI tracks (unless you want to create some cool tracks to go along with the session) because you'll only be looking at the MIDI data in the context of using the zoom tools with it.

Zoom

Zooming is not only one of the most basic things you'll do in any given editing session, it's also one of the most frequent things you'll do. Of course, the first step down the road of efficient zooming is to learn the shortcuts associated with basic zooming (see Chapter 4). The following sections will discuss other ways to zoom and how to use them.

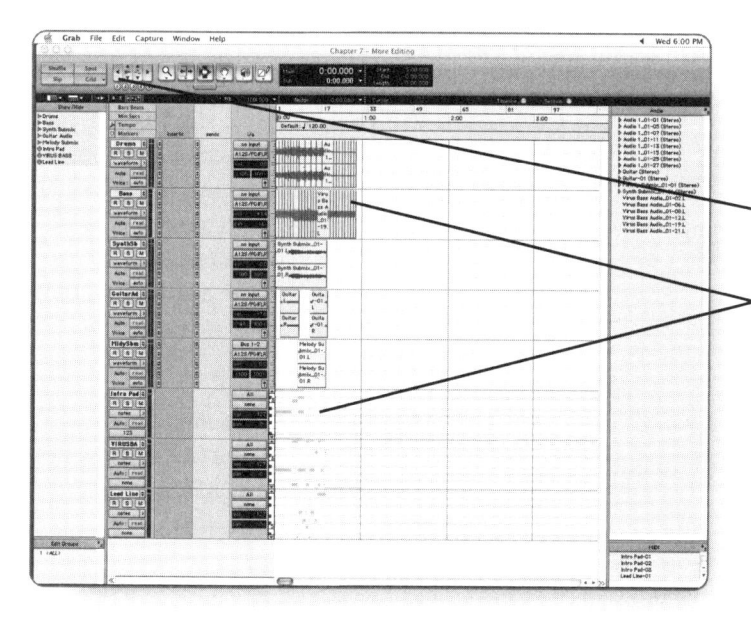

More Zoom Tools

Let's start from what you already know and work from there.

1. Click on the **Zoom Out button**.

As you've seen before, your view of your session's Timeline will expand, and a longer duration will be shown in your Edit window. Note that all tracks, audio and MIDI, are zoomed together.

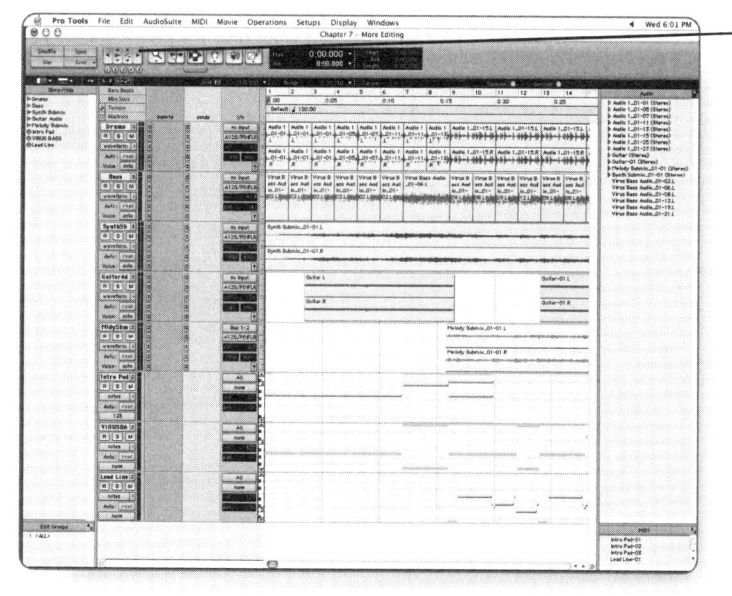

2. Click on the **Zoom In button**. Again, as you've seen before, your view will narrow in on a smaller slice of time with each successive click of the button. Again, you'll see that audio and MIDI tracks are zoomed at the same rate. The Zoom In and Zoom Out buttons will allow you to zoom in on the time scale, and although they won't affect the speed at which your session will play back, they will allow you to view your regions and data differently to suit different kinds of editing.

3. Click on the **Audio Zoom Up button**.

With each click of this button your audio data zooms up, allowing you to more clearly see low-level signals. Also, notice that all of your audio tracks have zoomed up at the same time, but your MIDI data has remained unchanged.

4. Click on the **Audio Zoom Down button**. The height of your audio waveforms will be reduced with each click of this button.

> **TIP**
>
> Although this kind of zooming is not quite as common as zooming in on the horizontal time scale, the shortcut keys are still useful to know. On the Mac, the shortcut is ⌘+Option+] (right bracket) to zoom up and ⌘+Option+[(left bracket) to zoom down. On the PC, it's Ctrl+Alt+] (right bracket) to zoom up and Ctrl+Alt+[(left bracket) to zoom down.

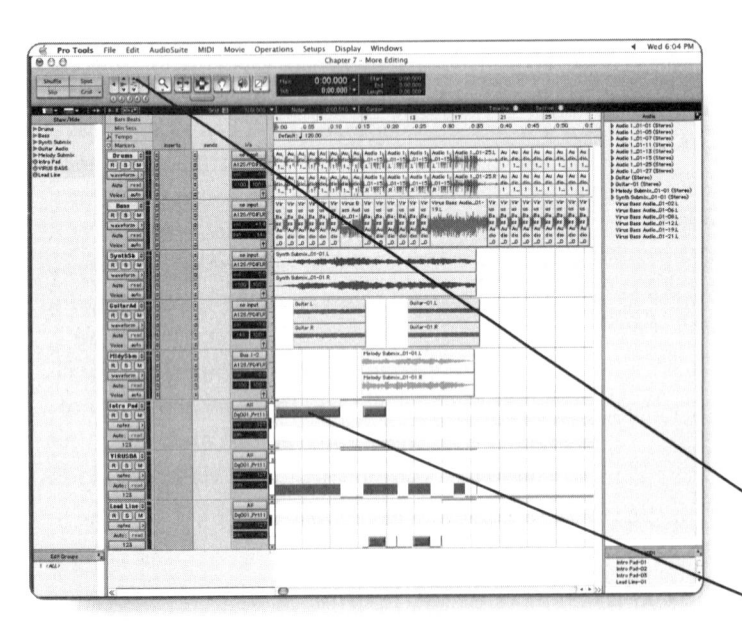

5. Click on the **MIDI Zoom Up button**.

With each click of this button, your MIDI data will zoom up, allowing you to more clearly see individual notes. Note that all your MIDI tracks have zoomed up at the same time, but your audio tracks are unchanged when you click on this button.

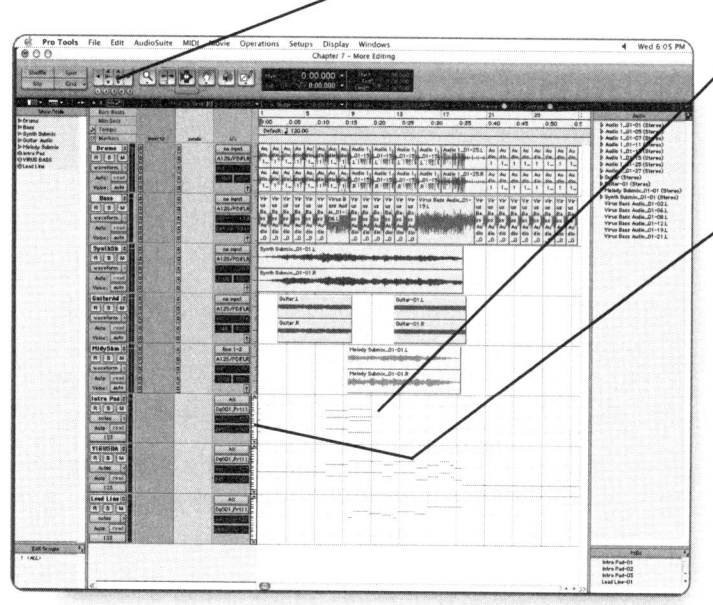

6. Click on the **MIDI Zoom Down button**.

Your MIDI data will zoom down, allowing you to see a greater range of notes at one time in the Edit window.

As you zoom up or down, you will see less or more of the keyboard graphic on the left edge of each MIDI track. You can use this display as a reference point to see how broad (or narrow) of a tonal range you're viewing. Low pitches are displayed toward the bottom of each MIDI track, and high notes are toward the top. You can scroll up and down the MIDI note range by clicking on the up and down arrows at each end of the keyboard graphic.

> **TIP**
> On the Mac, the shortcut for MIDI height zooming is ⌘+Shift+] (right bracket) to zoom up and ⌘+Shift+[(left bracket) to zoom down. On the PC, it's Ctrl+Shift+] (right bracket) to zoom up and Ctrl+Shift+[(left bracket) to zoom down.

Zoom Presets

I'm going out on a limb with this comparison, but go with me on this: Take the average car radio. If you're a music lover, you probably use it quite a bit. On most car radios, there are a number of buttons (usually below the main display) that you can use to set the stations you listen to most often. Once you set them up, you can simply press an individual button and immediately jump to your favorite channel.

CHAPTER 7: MORE EDITING

Many Pro Tools users find that, although they use all the zoom tools *a lot*, they tend to use certain zoom amounts more frequently than others. Like on a car radio, you can set up your most common zoom presets and jump between them at the click of a single button. In fact, setting these presets is pretty similar to setting the presets on your car radio!

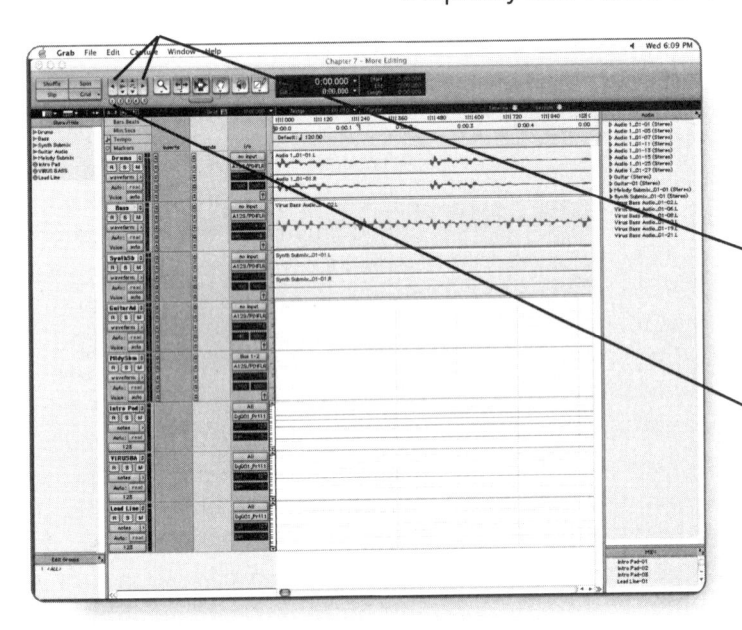

1. Click on either of the **time** (the vertical axis) **zoom tools** until you settle upon your most commonly used zoom setting.

2. Hold down the **key** (Mac) or the **Ctrl key** (PC) and **click** on the first **Zoom Preset button**. The button will flash briefly to let you know that the preset has been stored.

3. Repeat Steps 1 and 2 to set a preset for the second Zoom Preset button.

4. If you want to go back to your first zoom preset, **click** on the **first Zoom Preset button**. Your previously stored zoom preset will be immediately recalled.

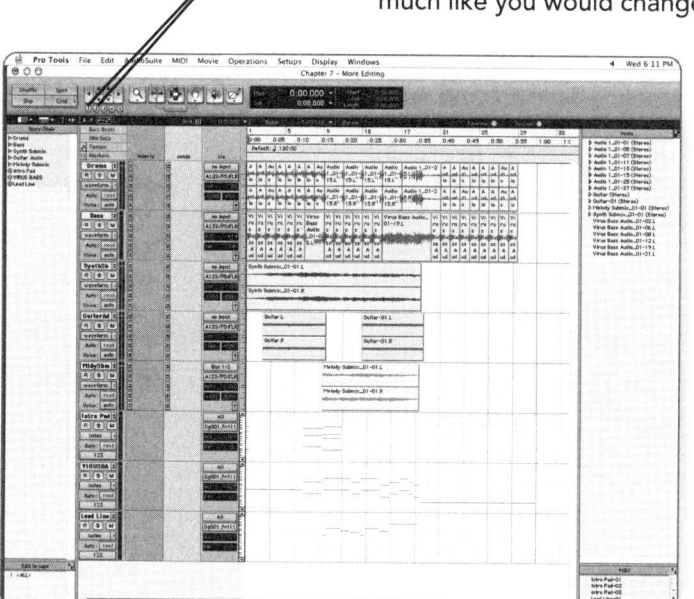

From this point on, it's easy. Simply set the five presets for the five zoom settings you use the most. At that point, you can click on the Zoom Preset buttons to switch zoom settings, much like you would change favorite stations on your car radio.

> **NOTE**
> The Zoom Preset buttons will recall only the horizontal (time) zoom amount, not the vertical zoom levels for audio and MIDI tracks.

> **TIP**
> The shortcuts to switch between your presets are pretty straightforward. Just hold the Control button (Mac) or the ⌘ button (PC) and press 1, 2, 3, 4, or 5 on your keyboard (above the alphabet section).

More Ways to Work with Selections

After you get comfortable with these more flexible ways of zooming, you'll want to take a look at some different ways of making selections.

Making Selections Using the Arrow Keys

In Chapter 4, you saw that the boundaries of your selection were represented in the Rulers area (above the tracks) by a down arrow and an up arrow, representing punch-in and punch-out points, respectively. Using the arrow keys is an easy way to make a selection as your session plays.

1. Choose a **starting point** (before the point where you want your selection to start) with the Selector tool or the Transport window. The starting point will be selected.

2. Start playback. (Remember, you can use the Start button on the Transport window or you can press the spacebar.)

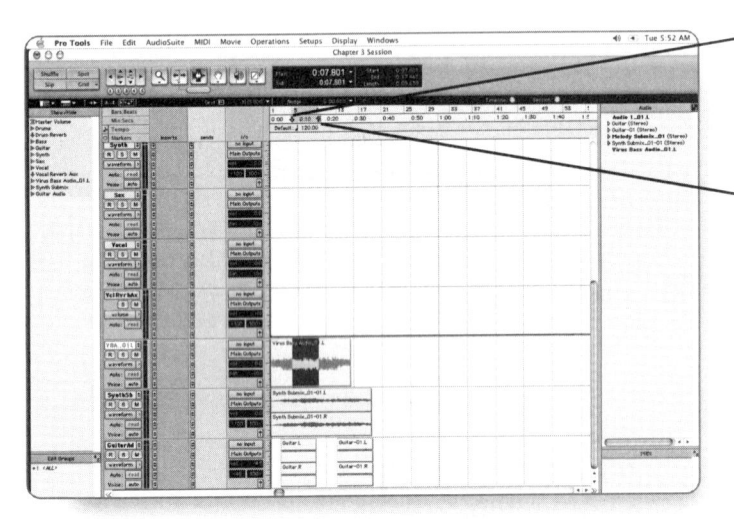

3. As your session plays, **press** the **down arrow key** on your keyboard at the point where you want to begin your selection.

4. While your session is still playing, **press** the **up arrow key** on your keyboard when you want your selection to end.

> **TIP**
>
> If you're a little late or early on a punch-in or punch-out, don't worry. You can adjust your selection by holding the Shift key while you drag either end with your mouse.

Making Selections Using the Return Key

You've already learned that pressing the Return key (Mac) or the Enter key (PC) will send you back to the beginning of the session. Here's how to use this function a little differently. This method will allow you to make a selection from the beginning of your session to a specified point.

MORE WAYS TO WORK WITH SELECTIONS

1. Click on the **Selector tool**. The tool will be selected.

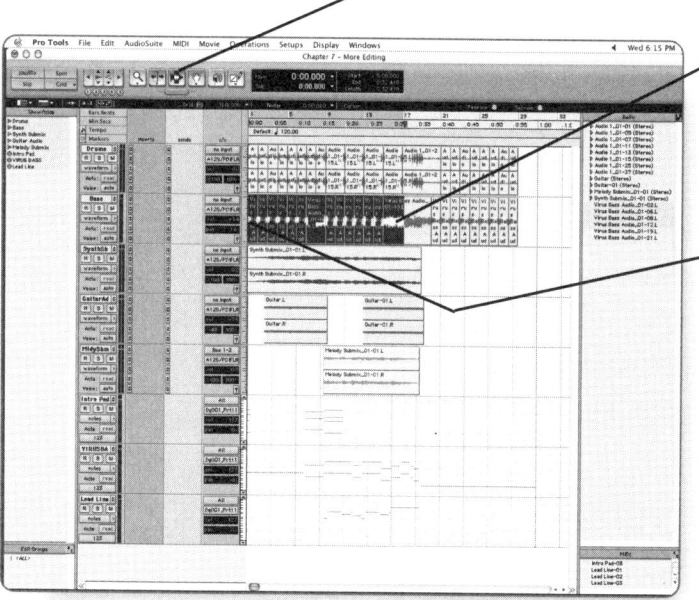

2. Click on the **point** on a desired track at which you want your selection to end. A flashing timeline insertion will appear at the location you click.

3. Press and hold the **Shift key** and **press** the **Return key**. A selection will be made from the beginning of the session to the timeline insertion that you created with the Selector tool.

Here's a variation of that process that will allow you to make a selection from a specified point to the end of your session.

1. Click on the **Selector tool** if it's not already highlighted. The tool will be selected.

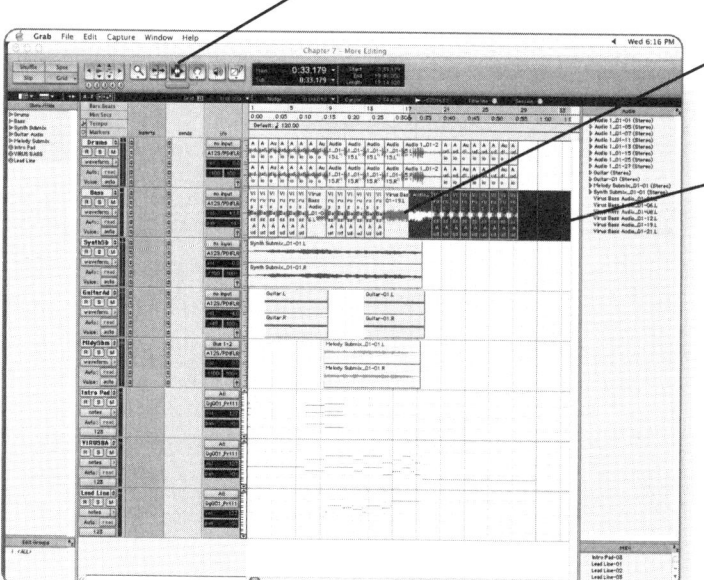

2. Click on the **point** on a desired track at which you want your selection to start.

3. Press and hold the **Option and Shift keys** and **press** the **Return button**. A selection will be made from the timeline insertion that you created with the Selector tool to the end of your session.

> **NOTE**
> You'll notice that in this example, the selection went off the right edge of the Edit window. You might think that it's pretty troublesome to work with selections that go beyond your visible range, and you'd be right. Don't worry, though; I'll talk about how to quickly navigate and audition a selection in just a little bit. Read on. . . .

Making Selections Using Tab to Transient

The Tab to Transient function is cool for two reasons. First, it's a great concept, although by no means a unique one these days. Second, *it works*, a fact which certainly does distinguish it from similar features in competing software. That being said, the Tab to Transient feature is a great way to make certain kinds of selections, particularly for those of you who enjoy chopping up beats into loopable segments.

1. Click on the **Tab to Transient tool**. The tool will be selected.

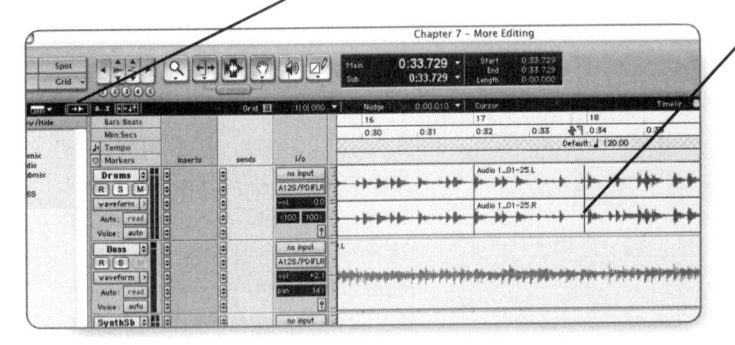

2. Use the **Selector tool** to set a timeline insertion a little before the transient you want to start with. The timeline insertion will be set.

3. Press the **Tab key**. As you've seen before, the timeline insertion line will jump from transient to transient each time you hit the Tab key. Stop tabbing when you get to the transient that marks the desired beginning of your selection.

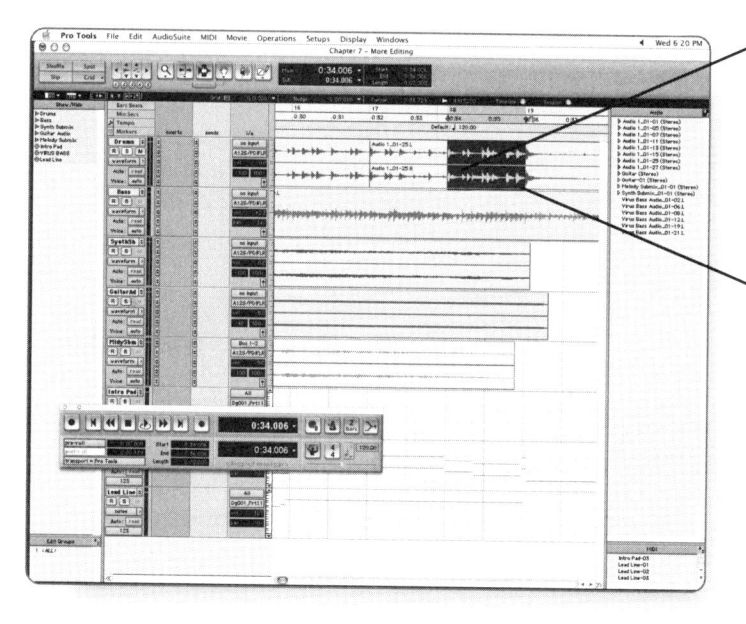

4. Press and hold the **Shift key** and **press** the **Tab key**. Again, the timeline insertion will jump from transient to transient, but this time a selection will be made in the process.

5. When you reach the end of your desired selection, **stop pressing** the **Tab key**.

A Useful Preference: Timeline Insertion Follows Playback

Suppose you've selected a nice loopable selection. You'll want to go into Loop Playback mode and hear your work. Sounds great, doesn't it? Then you hit Stop, and the selection goes away! Is this a bug within Pro Tools? Nope—it's the effect of a preference named Timeline Insertion Follows Playback, which you can set in the software. You can either enable or disable this preference. Either mode has its uses, but it's important to understand this preference's functioning so you can know when to use it and when not to!

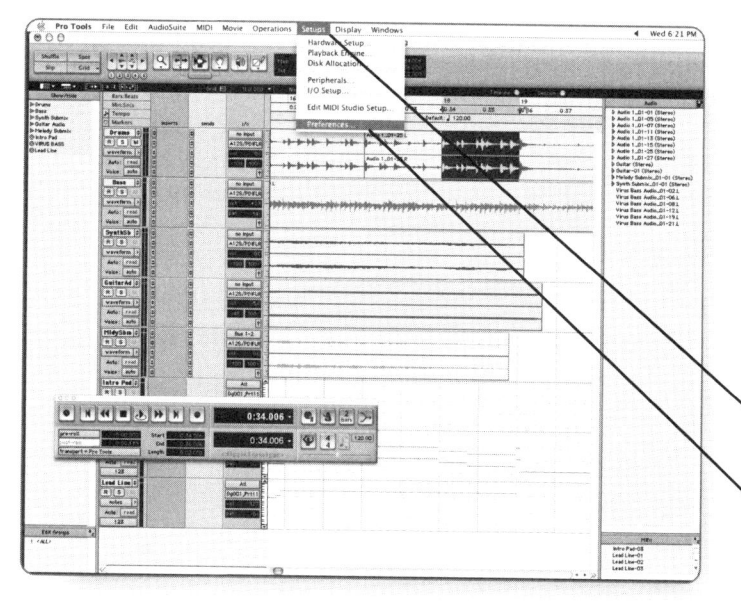

1. **Click** on **Setups**. The Setups menu will appear.

2. **Click** on **Preferences**. The Pro Tools LE Preferences dialog box will open.

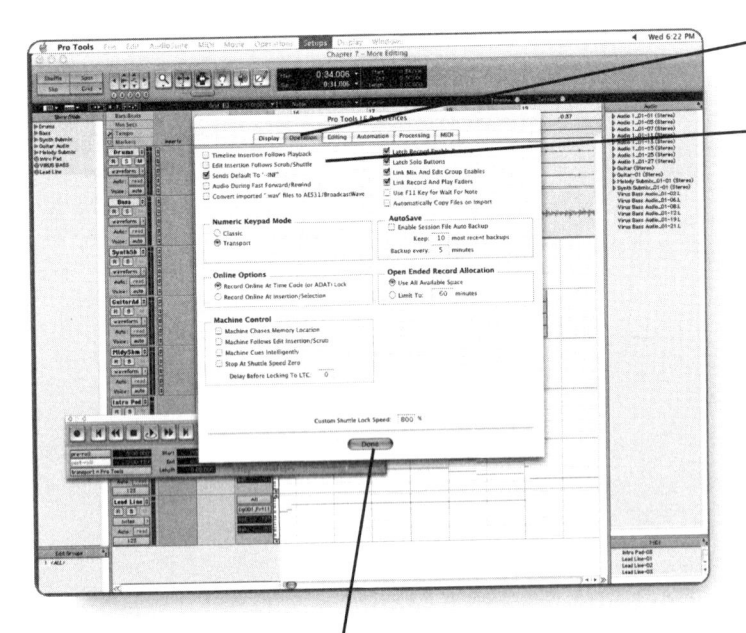

3. Click on the **Operation tab**. The tab will move to the front.

4. Select or deselect the **Timeline Insertion Follows Playback check box**. Here's what the options mean:

- **Checked.** Playback will begin wherever the timeline insertion is set. When playback stops, the timeline insertion will jump to the point where you stopped. When you start playback again, it will pick up where you left off. If you have made a selection, that selection will be lost when you hit Stop.

- **Unchecked.** Playback will begin wherever the timeline insertion is set. When playback stops in this mode, the timeline insertion will stay where it was originally set. When you start playback again, it will start from the original position. If you have made a selection, that selection will be maintained when you hit Stop, making this the ideal mode for editing loopable selections.

5. Click on **Done** when you've selected the desired preferences. Your preferences will be set and the dialog box will close.

Navigating and Auditioning a Selection

When you make a selection, the most important parts are the beginning and the end. You'll be listening to the boundaries of your selection many times, just to make sure you've got everything you want and nothing you don't.

MORE WAYS TO WORK WITH SELECTIONS

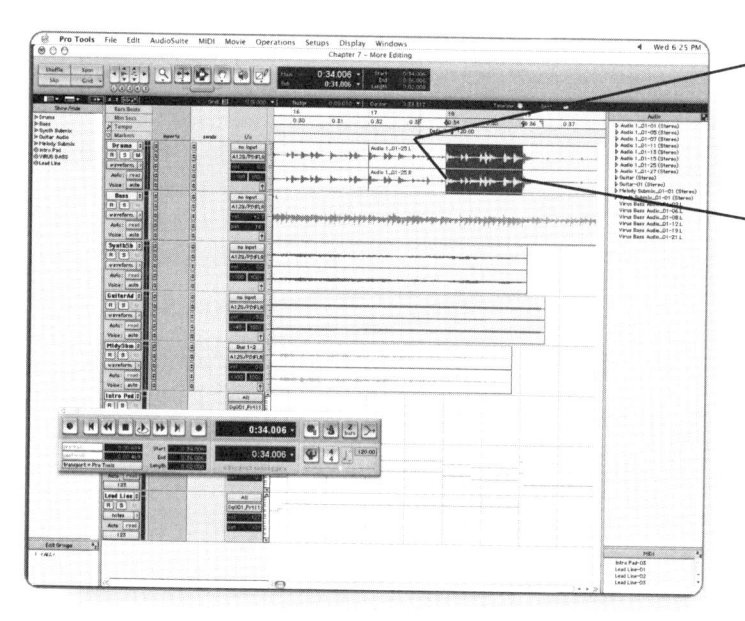

1. **Press** the **left arrow key**. The timeline insertion (and the Edit window's focus) will move to the beginning of the selection.

2. **Press** the **right arrow key**. The timeline insertion will move to the end of the selection.

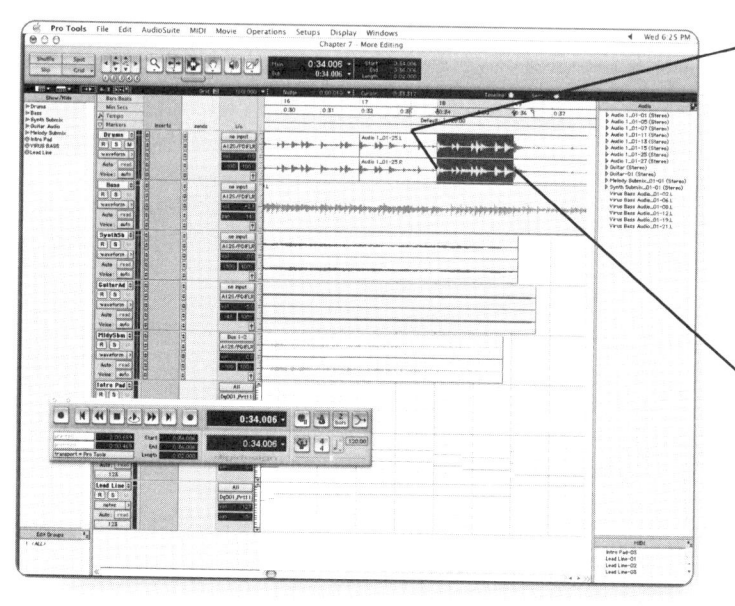

3. Now it's time to audition the boundaries of your selection. **Press and hold** the **Option key** (Mac) or the **Alt key** (PC) and **press** the **left arrow key**. Your audio will play up to the beginning of your selection by the pre-roll amount (even if pre-roll isn't highlighted).

4. **Press and hold** the **Option key** (Mac) or the **Alt key** (PC) and **press the right arrow key**. Your audio will play up to the end of your selection by the pre-roll amount.

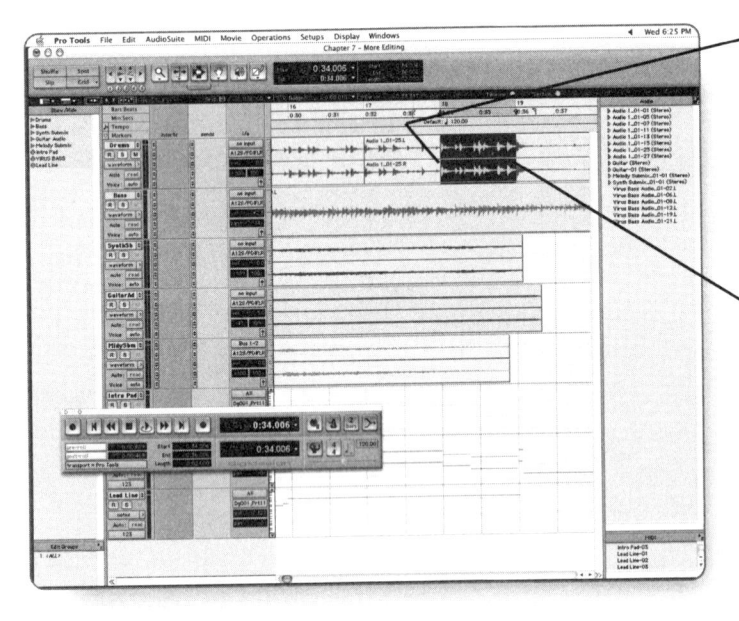

5. Press and hold the ⌘ **key** (Mac) or the **Ctrl key** (PC) and **press** the **left arrow key**. Your audio will play from the beginning of your selection by the post-roll amount (even if post-roll isn't highlighted).

6. Press and hold the ⌘ **key** (Mac) or the **Ctrl key** (PC) and **press** the **right arrow key**. Your audio will play from the end of your selection by the post-roll amount.

Beyond the Basics

You've already worked with the basic editing tools, and things like trimming, selecting, and grabbing are starting to become familiar by now. Some of these tools have secondary layers to them, giving them added functionality. And then there's the Smart tool. . . .

The TCE Trim Tool

First on the list is the TCE (*Time Compress/Expand*) Trim tool. This dandy little tool will allow you to stretch or compress the duration of an audio region without changing the pitch!

BEYOND THE BASICS   231

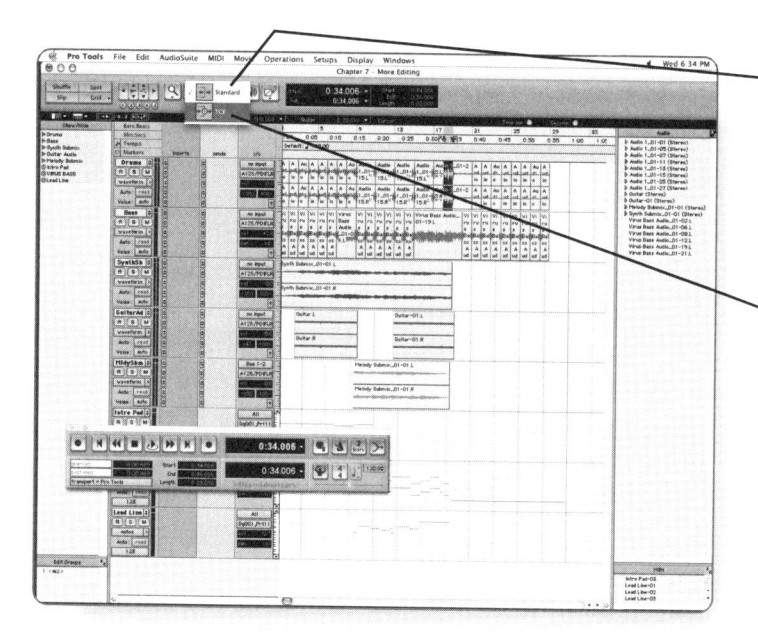

1. Click and hold the small **arrow** in the lower-right corner of the Trim tool button until the menu appears. The currently selected version of the Trim tool will be checked.

2. Click on **TCE** to change to the TCE Trim tool.

The icon for the Trim tool will change to reflect this different function. Make sure that it is highlighted. (If it isn't, just click on the icon.)

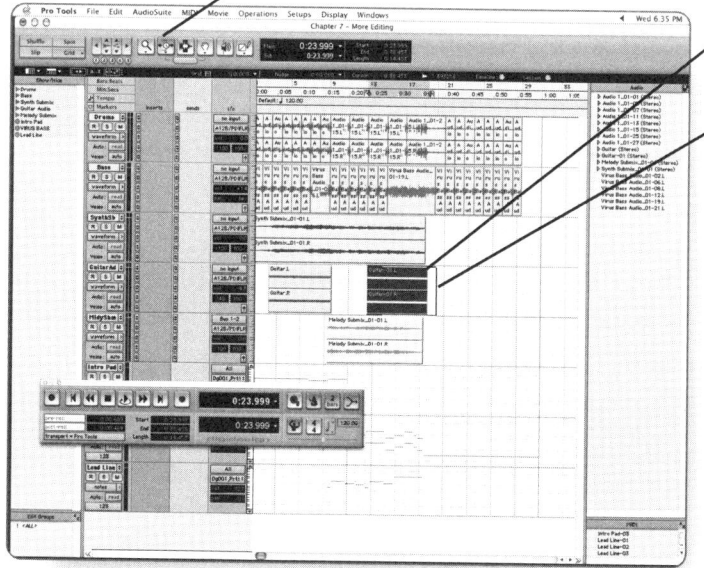

3. Click and hold either **boundary** of a region.

4. Drag the **boundary** in or out, as if you were using the regular Trim tool. When you release the mouse button, a new audio file will be created with a different duration than the original region, but without a different pitch.

TIP
The TCE Trim tool is really useful in Grid mode. Suppose you've imported a drum loop that doesn't match the tempo of the rest of your session. Just make sure your grids are a musical unit (like quarter notes, for example) and use the TCE Trim tool. The edges of the region will snap to the nearest grid point when released, and you'll be perfectly in tempo!

The Separation Grabber Tool

The regular Grabber tool will allow you to move regions around in your session. The Separation Grabber tool will let you take a selection from within a single region and move just that selection. This is a cool trick, but you have to go through a few steps first.

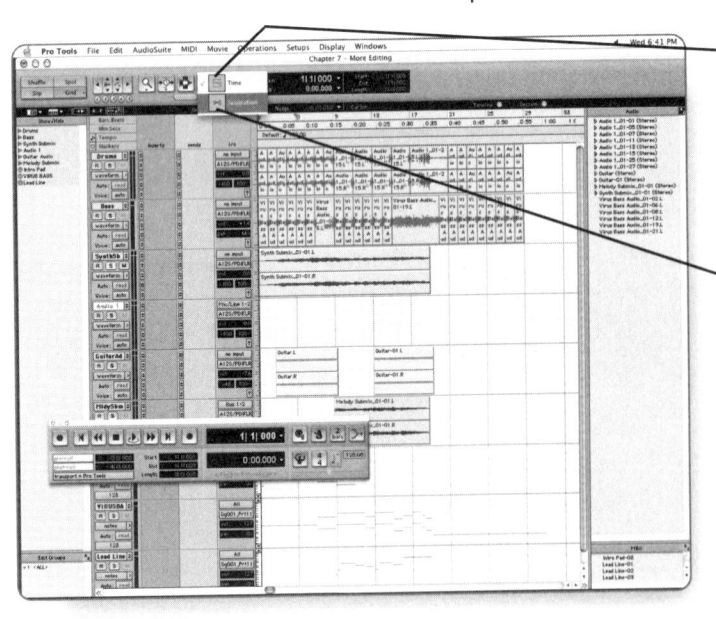

1. Click and hold the small **arrow** in the lower-right corner of the Grabber button. A menu will appear. The currently selected version of the Grabber tool will be checked.

2. Click on **Separation** to change to the Separation Grabber tool.

BEYOND THE BASICS 233

3. Click on the **Selector tool**. The tool will be selected. (Have faith; we're going somewhere with this.)

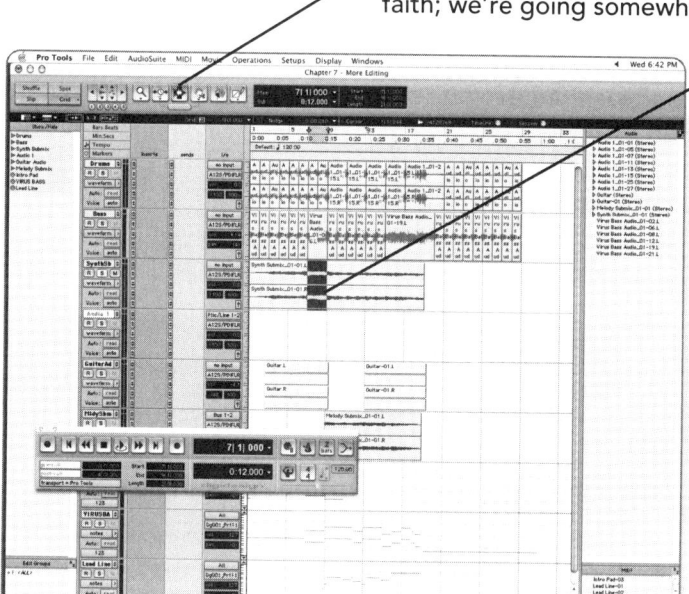

4. Select the **section** of a region that you want to separate. The section will be selected.

5. Click on the **Separation Grabber tool**. The tool will be selected.

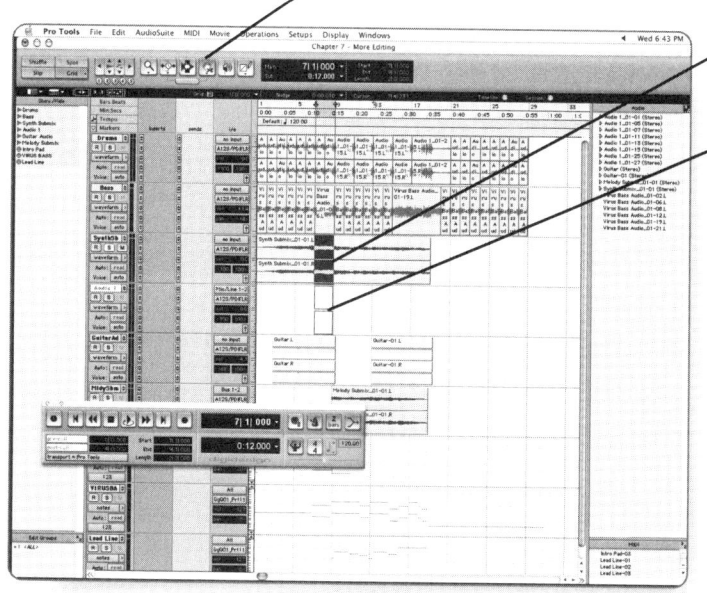

6. Click and hold on your **selection**.

7. Drag and drop the **selection** to the desired destination.

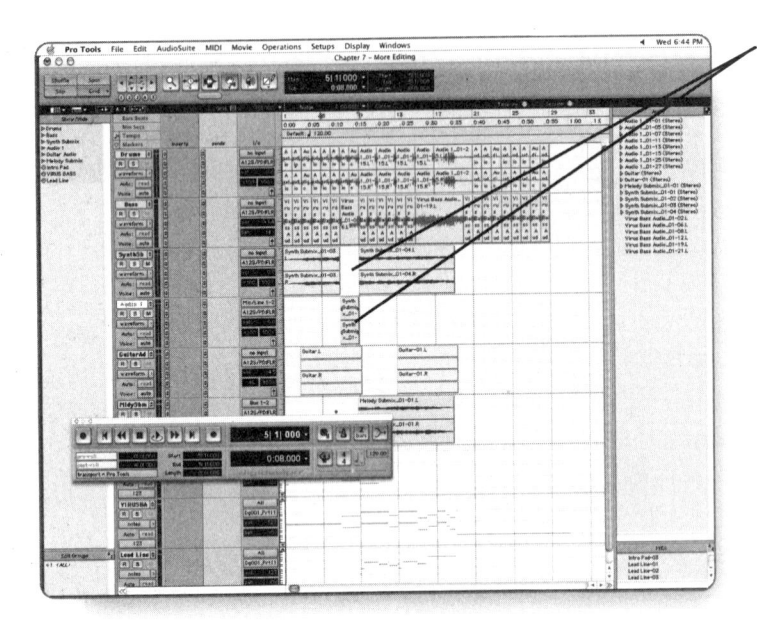

The selection will be removed from the source track and will become its own region, shown in the Audio Regions list.

> **TIP**
>
> If you want to drag out a selection of a region but leave your source region unchanged, hold down the Option key (Mac) or the Alt key (PC) as you drag.

The Smart Tool

The Smart tool is a real timesaver, combining the use of many editing tools at once and adding some additional functionality for good measure. It might take you a while to get used to using the Smart tool, but once you've got it under your belt, you'll really start saving time.

The idea behind the function of the Smart tool is that when your cursor is in different places on a track, it will take on different tool behaviors.

1. Click on the **Smart bar** below the three primary edit tools to activate the Smart tool. The button will be highlighted, and so will the three tools above it (Trim, Selector, and Grabber), which should give you a hint as to the Smart tool's function.

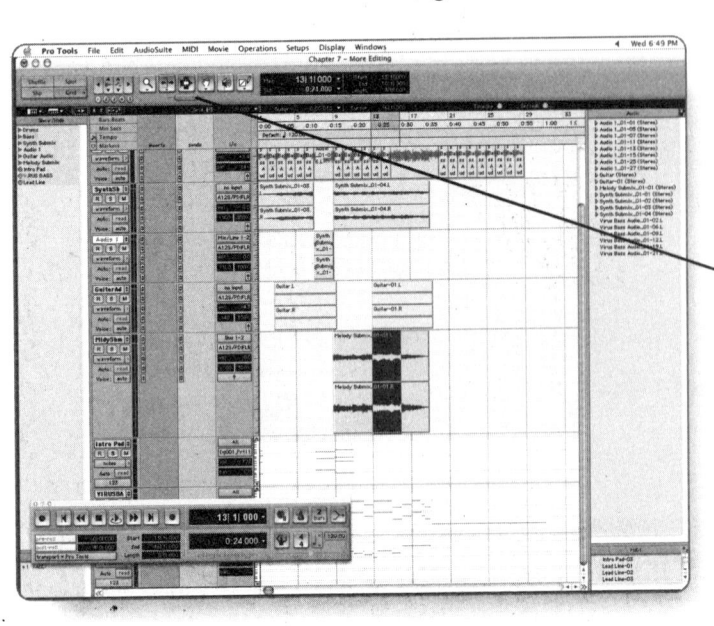

BEYOND THE BASICS   235

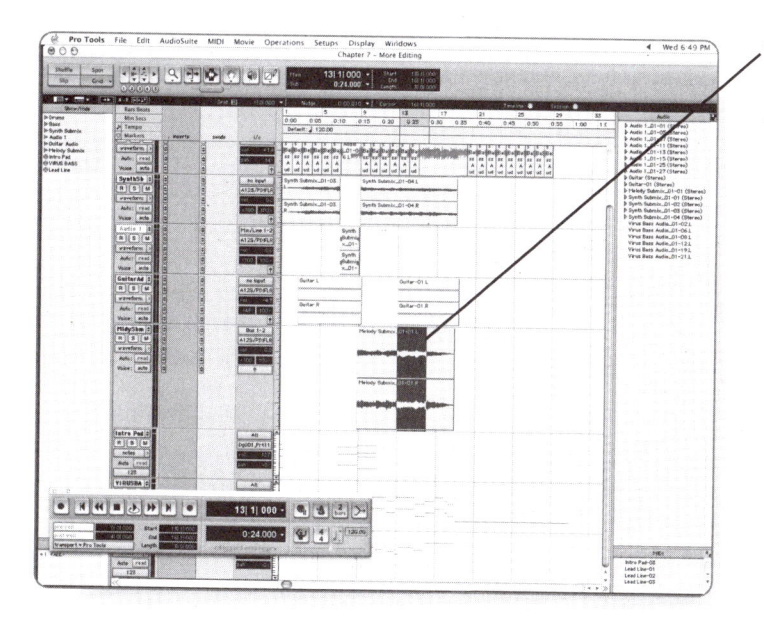

When your cursor is in the upper half of a track, it will take on the function of the Selector tool.

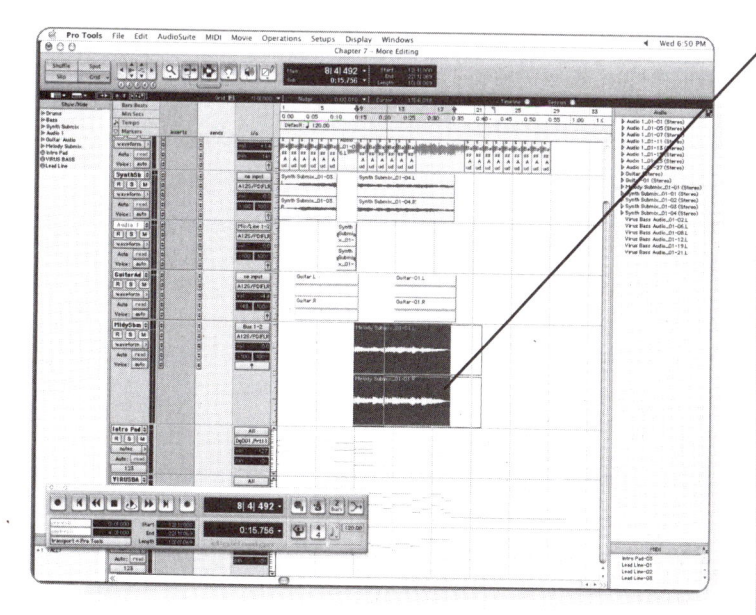

When you move your cursor to the lower half of a track, the cursor will take on the behavior of the currently selected version of the Grabber tool.

> **TIP**
>
> The Smart tool works particularly well when you have the Separation Grabber tool selected. Just move your cursor to the top half of a track to make your selection, and then move your cursor to the bottom half of the track and drag the selection out!

236   CHAPTER 7:   MORE EDITING

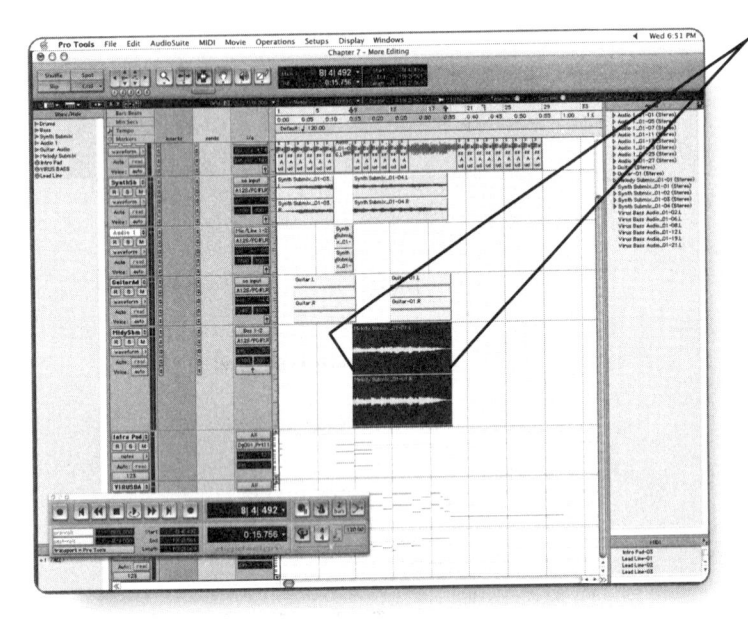

When you move your cursor to either end of a region, the cursor will change its function to that of the currently selected version of the Trim tool.

> **NOTE**
>
> If you move your cursor to the corners, you'll notice that it will take on a different function, beyond that of the Trim, Selector, or Grabber tool. Be patient—you'll get to the answer in a couple of pages!

> **TIP**
>
> Because the position of the cursor within a track is so critical when you are working with the Smart tool, you should take special care with smaller track heights. (Mini height is particularly tricky.)

Creating and Customizing Fades

You can use fade-ins and fade-outs to soften the edges of a region. Additionally, you can create crossfades between regions to make a smooth transition from one region to another. Of course, this is nothing new in the world of DAWs, but Pro Tools makes fades easy to create and tweak. You can even use the Smart tool to create them!

CREATING AND CUSTOMIZING FADES

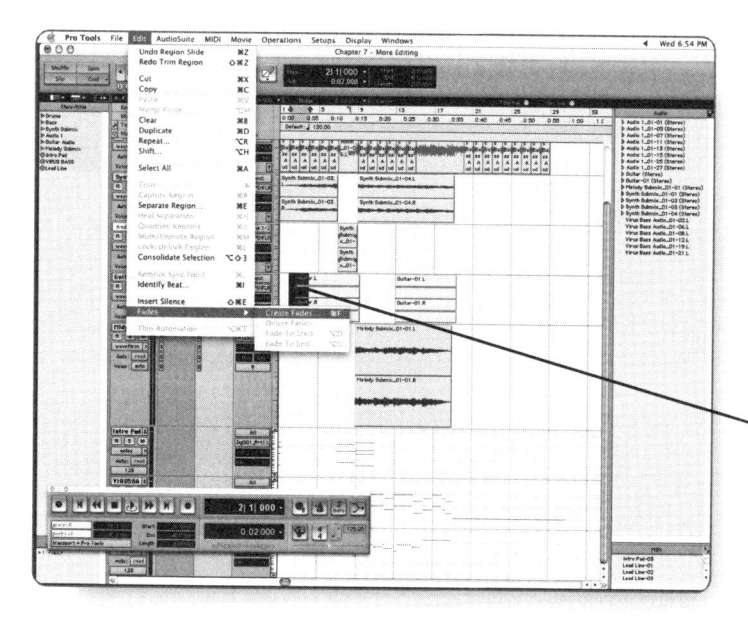

Creating a Fade-In

Everybody has heard fade-ins in a mix, when a song starts from a silent beginning and gradually gets louder until it reaches its running volume. In Pro Tools, however, you can create a fade-in for an individual region *within* a mix. Here's how:

1. Using the Selector tool (or the Selector mode of the Smart tool), **select** the **area** of a region that you want to become a fade-in. The area will be selected.

> **NOTE**
>
> It's important to make sure that your selection starts at or before the region boundary and ends where you want the fade-in to end.

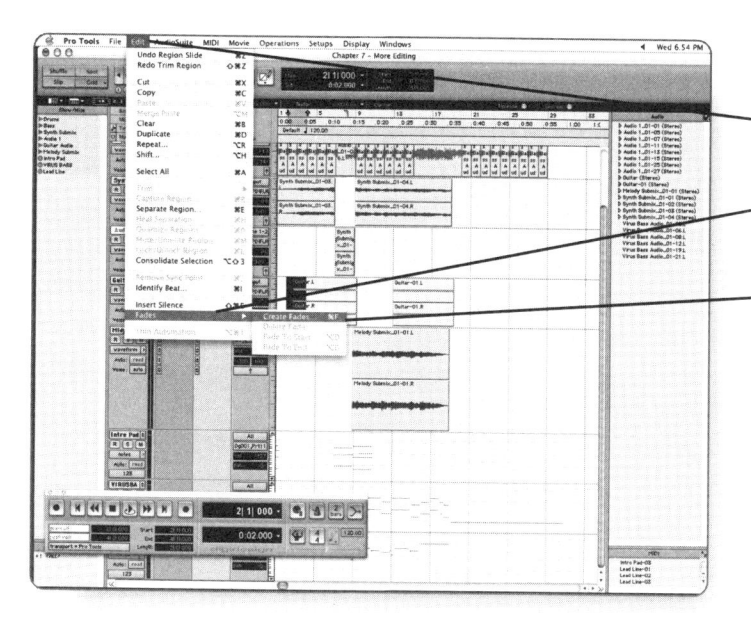

2. Click on **Edit**. The Edit menu will appear.

3. Click on **Fades**. The Fades submenu will appear.

4. Click on **Create Fades**. The Fades dialog box will open.

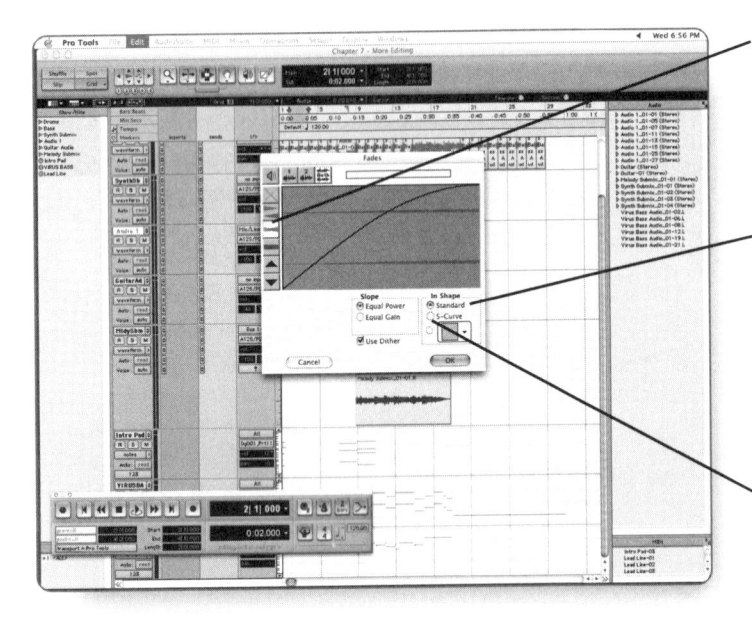

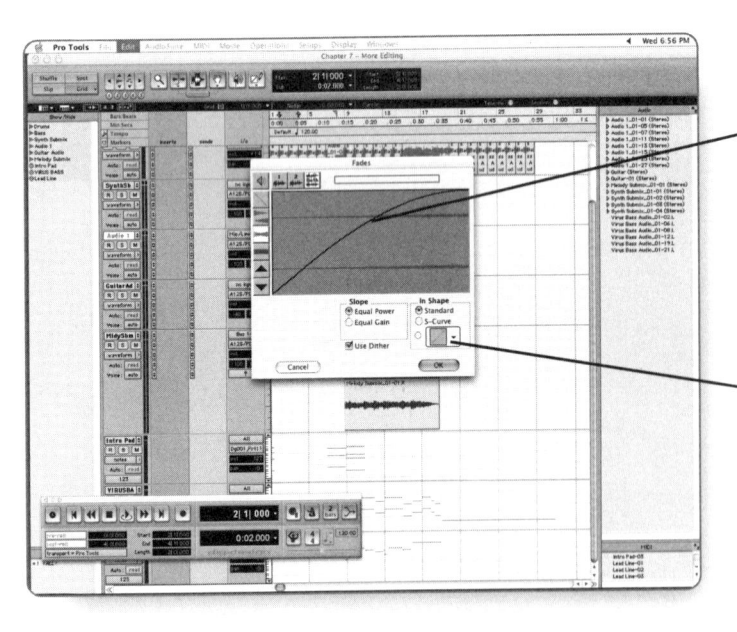

5. Click on the **Waveform Display button** to show a graphical view of the audio you will be fading in. The waveform will be displayed.

6a. Click on the **Standard radio button** in the In Shape section to select a standard curve. The option will be selected.

OR

6b. Click on the **S-Curve radio button** in the In Shape section to select an S curve, which rises quickly, evens out, and then rises again to full volume. The option will be selected.

OR

6c. Click and drag the **fade curve** to change its shape. The contour of your fade-in will change along with the shape of the fade curve.

OR

6d. Click on the **Preset Curve Selection down arrow**. A drop-down menu of additional fade-in curve presets will appear.

CREATING AND CUSTOMIZING FADES 239

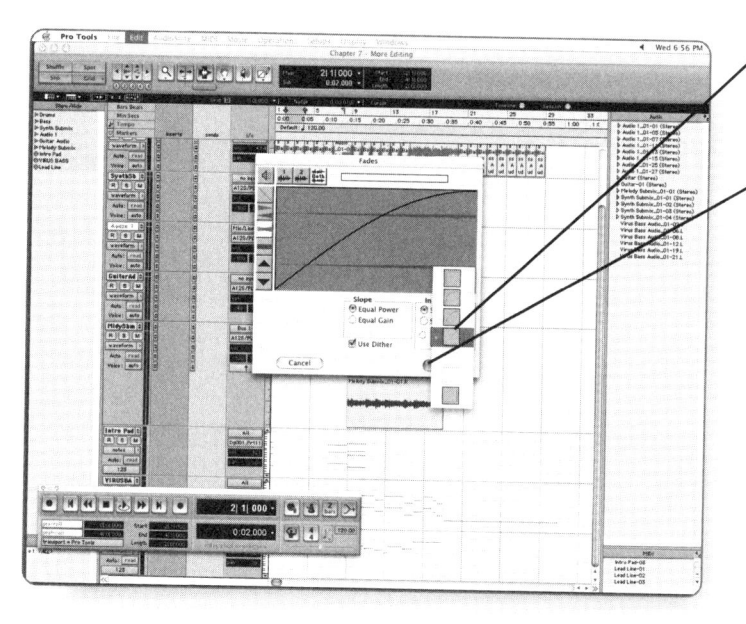

7. Click on the desired **fade-in curve preset**. The option will be selected.

8. Click on **OK**. The Fades dialog box will close.

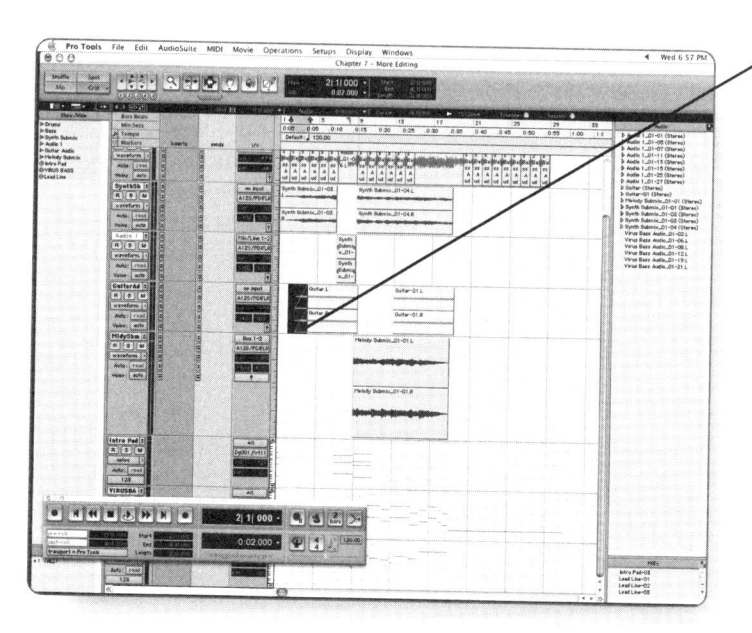

At the beginning of the region, you'll now see a fade region. This section is marked by a vertical line, indicating that it is a fade-in. This fade region represents a fade file located in the Fade Files subfolder. Although this is certainly a region (attached to another audio region) and an audio file, it will not be displayed in the Audio Regions list.

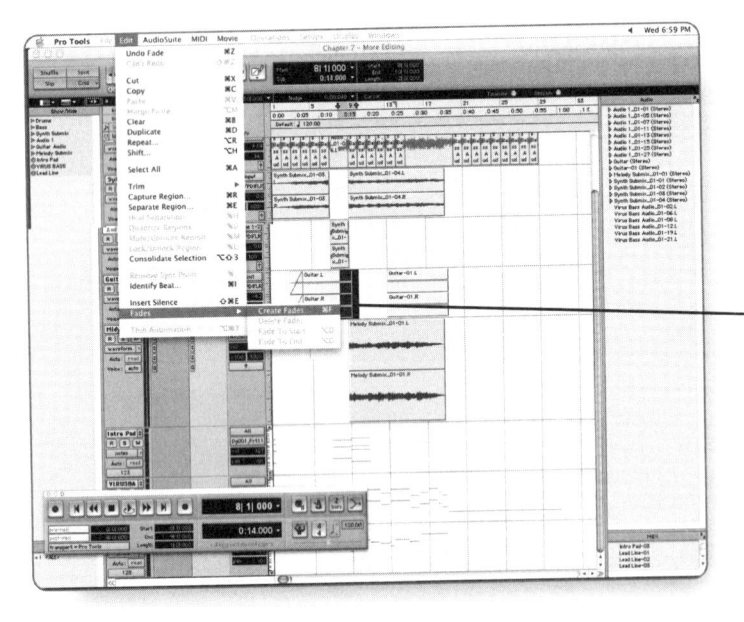

Creating a Fade-Out

After you've created a fade-in, creating a fade-out will be easy. It really is just a mirror image of the fade-in process.

1. Select the **area** of a region that you want to become a fade-out. Make sure your selection starts at the point that you want your fade out to begin and ends at or after the region boundary.

2. Click on **Edit**. The Edit menu will appear.

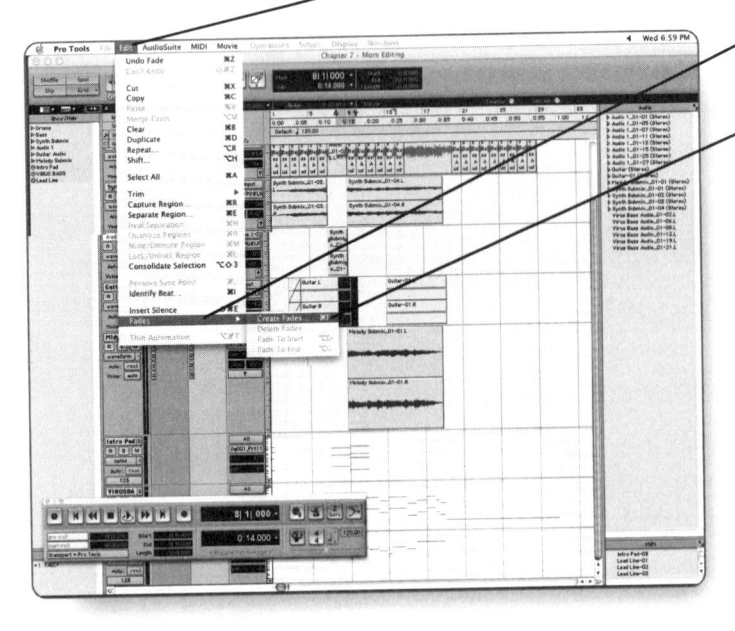

3. Click on **Fades**. The Fades submenu will appear.

4. Click on **Create Fades**. The Fades dialog box will open.

CREATING AND CUSTOMIZING FADES   241

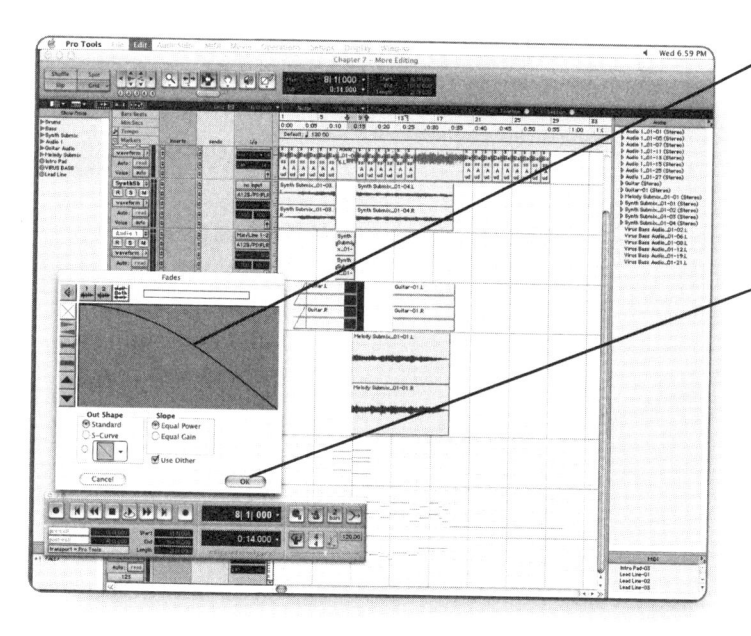

5. **Use** the **options** in the Fades dialog box to customize your fade-out, just as you did your fade-in. It still operates the same, just in the opposite direction!

6. **Click** on **OK**. The Fades dialog box will close.

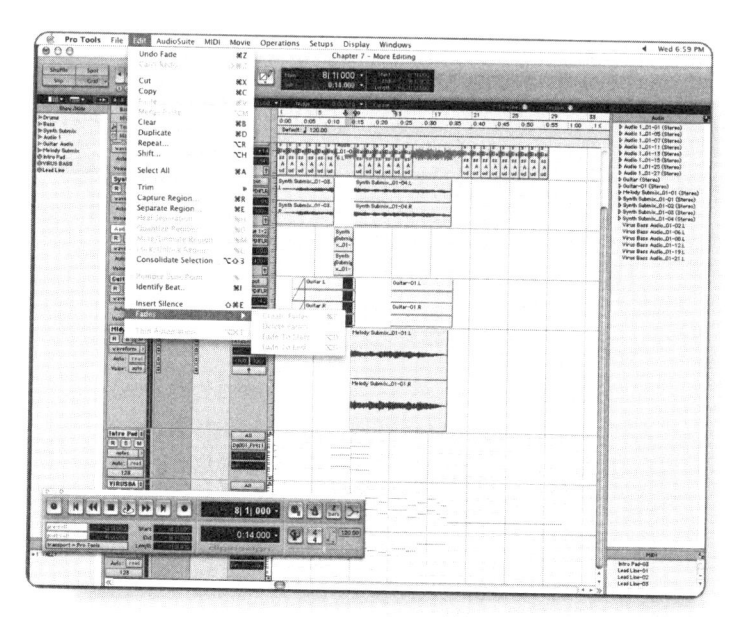

CAUTION

You've probably noticed that when you use these methods for creating fade-ins and fade-outs, Pro Tools automatically knows whether you want to create a fade-in or a fade-out. Here's something to be careful about when you create a fade-in or fade-out: If you don't select to the end (or beginning) of a region, Pro Tools will get confused about what you want to do. Even if you go to the Edit menu and select Fades, the Create Fades option will be grayed out and unavailable.

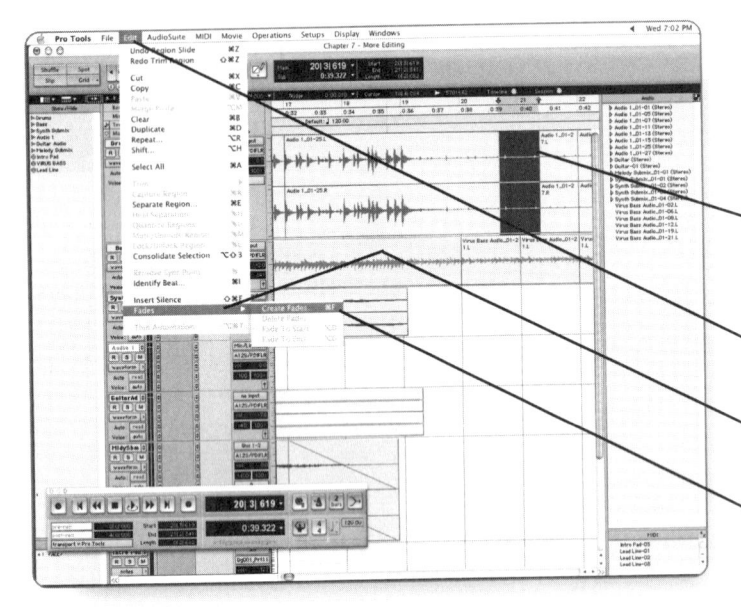

Crossfades

Here's how to crossfade between two overlapping regions.

1. Select an **area** of two overlapping regions that you want to become a crossfade.

2. Click on **Edit**. The Edit menu will appear.

3. Click on **Fades**. The Fades submenu will appear.

4. Click on **Create Fades**. The Fades dialog box will open.

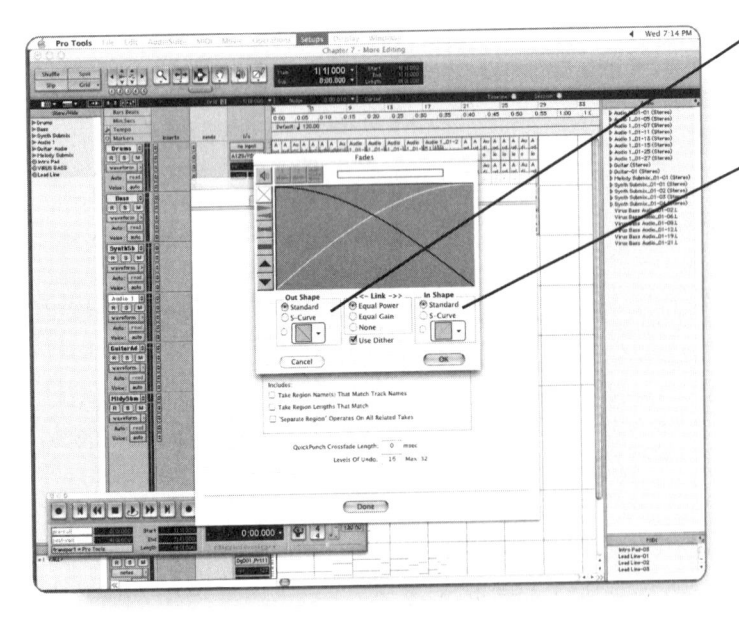

5. Set up the **fade-in portion** of your crossfade the same way you would a standalone fade-in.

6. Set up the **fade-out portion** of the crossfade in the same way.

CREATING AND CUSTOMIZING FADES 243

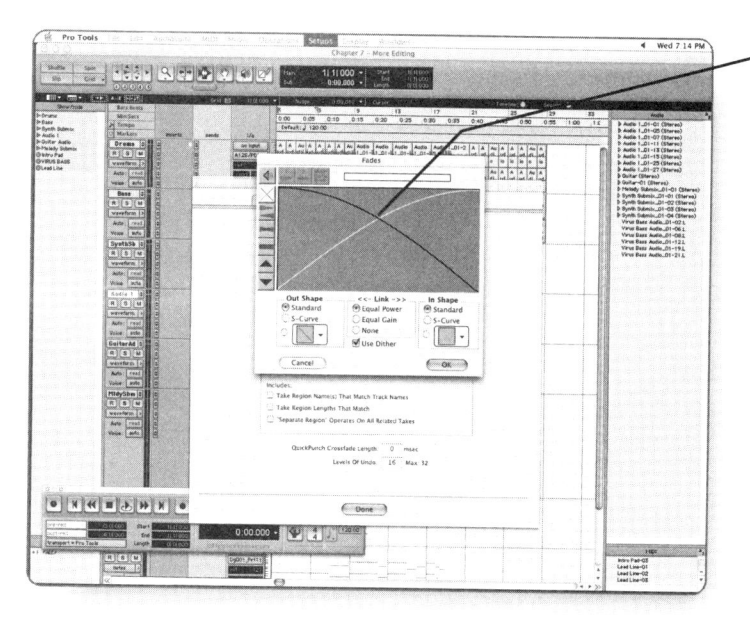

7. Drag the **crossing point** of your crossfade earlier or later, depending on your preference for this particular crossfade.

You'll notice that the fade-in and fade-out components of this crossfade are joined, and changes to either aspect will affect the other. Take a look at this linking.

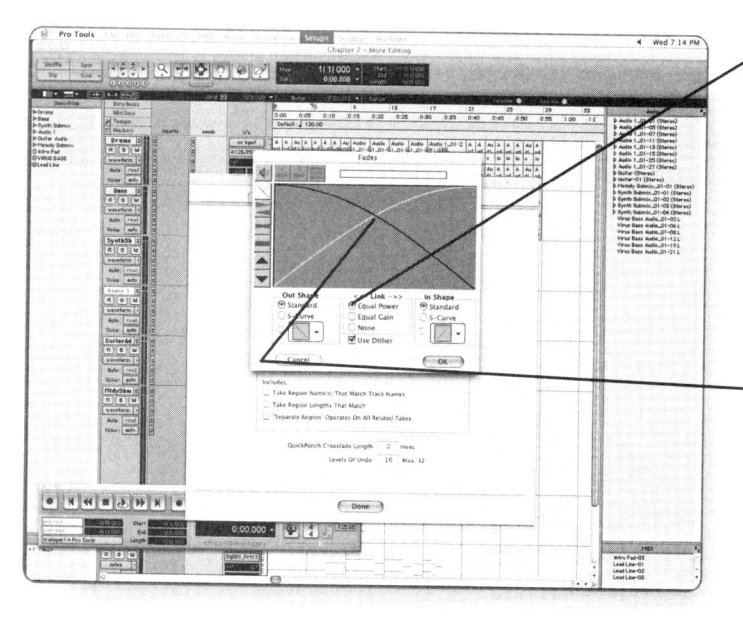

1. Click on the **Equal Power radio button**. The option will be selected. Use this option when you're crossfading audio that is not identical. These curves will prevent the volume drop that can sometimes occur and is commonly perceived as a smooth transition between regions.

2. Move the **crossover point** from left to right. Notice that it remains at the same position, slightly above the middle of the dialog box.

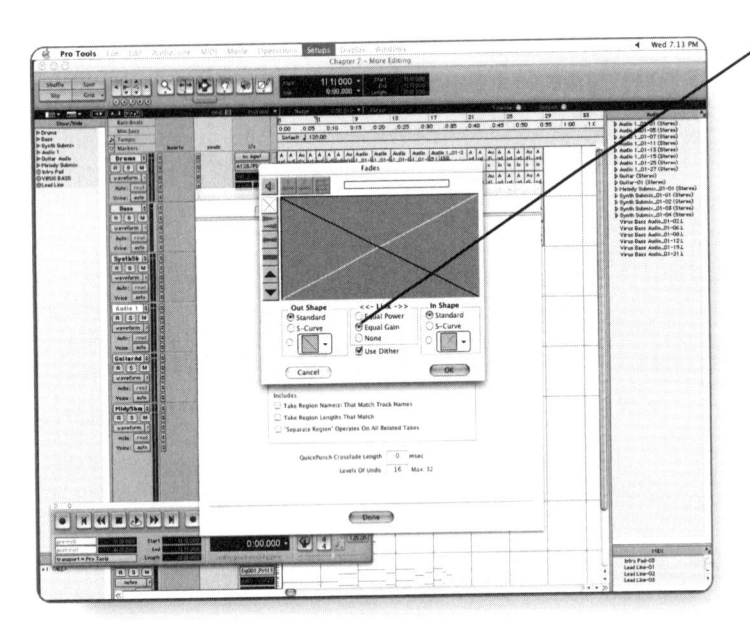

3. Click on the **Equal Gain radio button**. When you select this as a linking option, your crossover point will not be boosted in any way, although you can still move the crossover point from left to right (earlier to later). When you are crossfading identical or similar audio, this linking will give you the desired smooth transition from region to region.

4. Click on the **None radio button**. This will change one half of a crossfade without changing the other half.

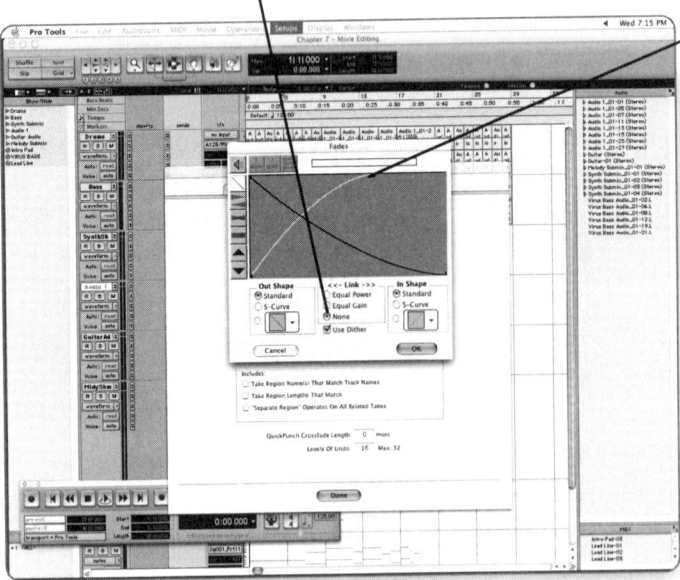

5. Click on the **small black handle** at the beginning or end of a fade curve. They're tricky to click on with your mouse, but once you do get them, you will be able to drag and drop them anywhere you want, and all other aspects of the crossfade will remain unchanged.

> **NOTE**
>
> Although the None link mode might not be the most commonly used mode of crossfading, it is often the mode of choice if you need a specific non-linear transition.

Creating Fades Using the Smart Tool

In addition to the triple benefit of trim, select, and grab that you get with the Smart tool, you can also quickly create fade-ins, fade-outs, and even crossfades!

1. Click on the **Smart bar** to activate the Smart tool. The Smart tool will be selected.

2. Move your **cursor** to the upper-right corner of a region. The cursor will change to a small square with a diagonal line through it, which looks a bit like a fade-out region.

3. Click and drag your **mouse pointer** to the left and **release** the **mouse button** when you want your fade-out to start to create a fade-out region.

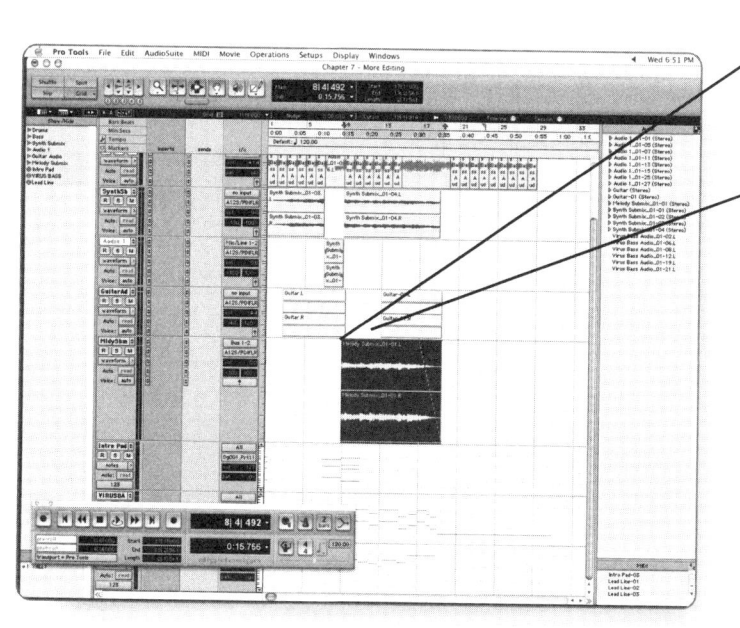

4. Move your **cursor** to the upper-left corner of a region to create a fade-in.

5. Click and drag your **mouse pointer** to create your fade-in the same way you created your fade-out (only in the opposite direction).

CHAPTER 7: MORE EDITING

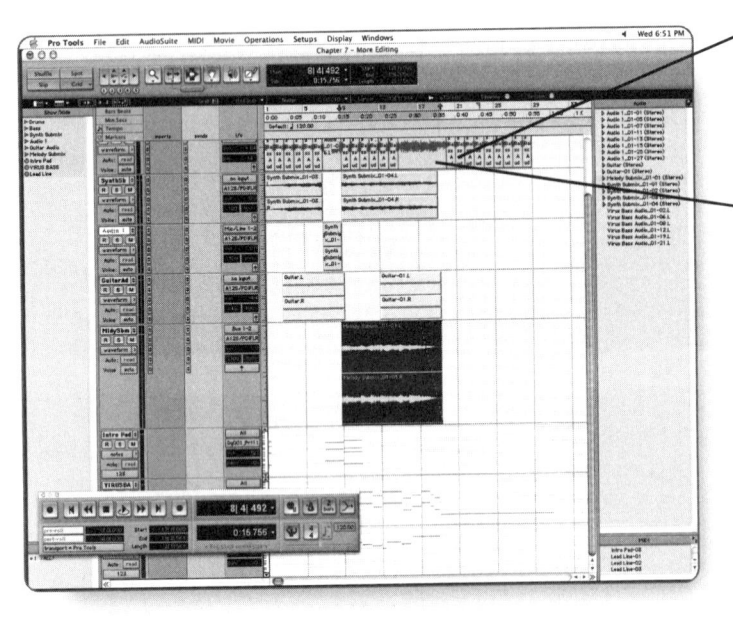

6. Move your **cursor** to the bottom corners of two adjacent regions. Now your cursor will be able to create a crossfade!

7. Click and drag your **mouse** left or right to create a crossfade centered on the regions' boundaries.

So how can you control the contours of your fades when you use the Smart tool to create them?

1. Click on **Setups**. The Setups menu will appear.

2. Click on **Preferences**. The Pro Tools LE Preferences dialog box will open.

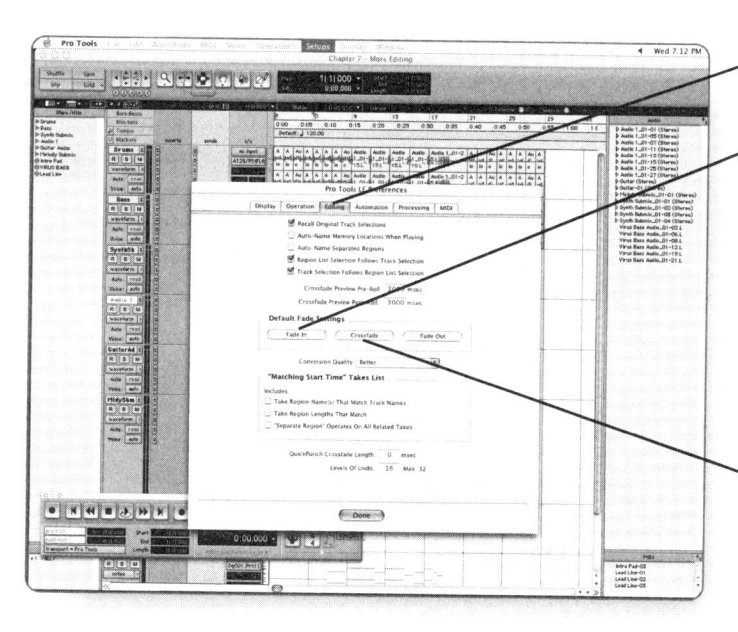

CREATING AND CUSTOMIZING FADES 247

3. Click on the **Editing tab**. The tab will move to the front.

4. Click on the **Fade In button**. The familiar fade-in setup window will appear.

5. Configure the **fade-in curve** as your default fade-in. (See "Creating and Customizing Fades" earlier in this chapter for details.)

6. Click on the **Crossfade button**. The Crossfade setup window will appear.

7. Configure the **crossfade curve** as your default crossfade.

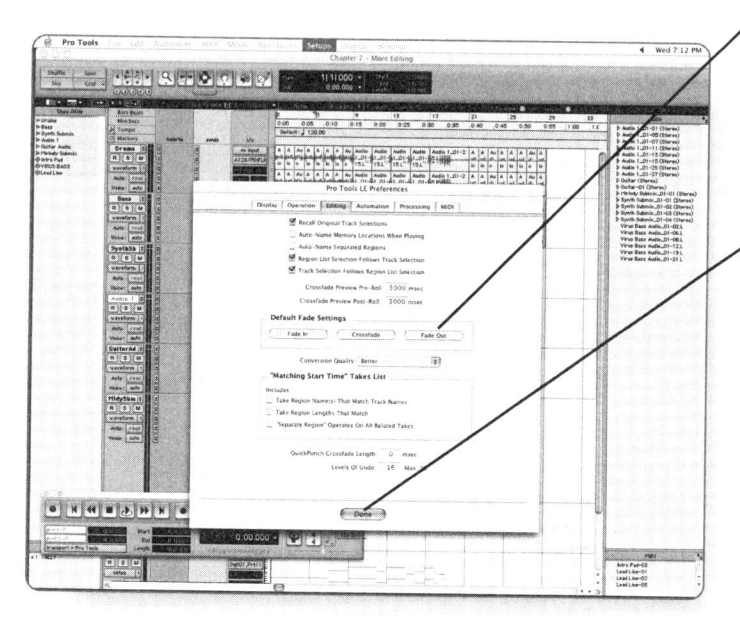

8. Click on the **Fade Out button**. The fade-out setup window will appear.

9. Configure the **fade-out curve** as your default fade-out.

10. Click on the **Done button**. Your settings will be saved and the Preferences dialog box will close.

TIP

It's a good idea to set up your most commonly used fade-in, fade-out, and crossfade settings in the Preferences dialog box. Each time you create a fade using the Smart tool, the fade curve will be based upon these preferences.

> **NOTE**
> Regardless of whether you used the Smart tool, if you create a fade and you later want to change its contour, double-click on the fade region with the Grabber tool. The Fades dialog box will open again so you can make your changes. Note that any changes you make in this dialog box will not affect your preferences.

Getting Specific

Before you move on to the task of mixing, I want to get a little tweaky (if that's really a word) with the timing of regions.

Constraining Motion

Here's how to move a region from track to track without changing its timing by even one sample!

1. Using the Grabber tool, **press and hold** the **Control key** while clicking (Mac) on the region you want to move or **right-click** (PC) on the **region** you want to move. When you drag your region to another track, it will remain aligned to its original position, regardless of horizontal mouse movements.

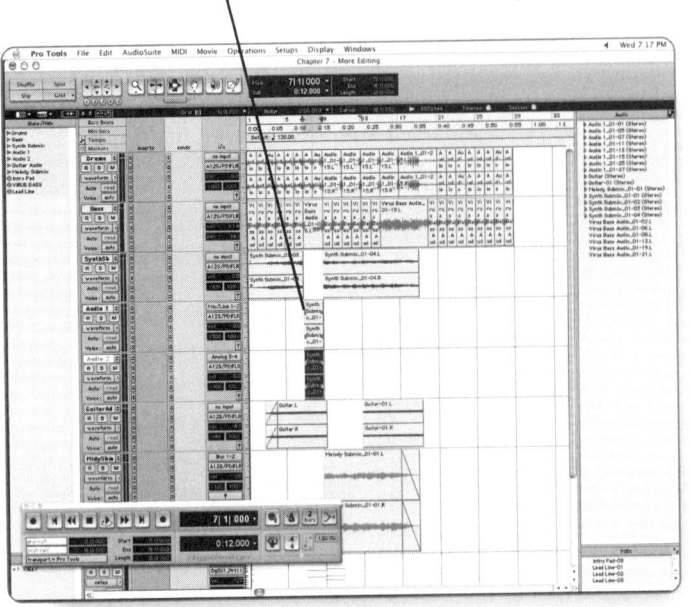

> **TIP**
> You can make a copy while remaining in sample-accurate sync with the original by holding down the Option key (Mac) or the Alt key (PC) while you perform this action.

GETTING SPECIFIC 249

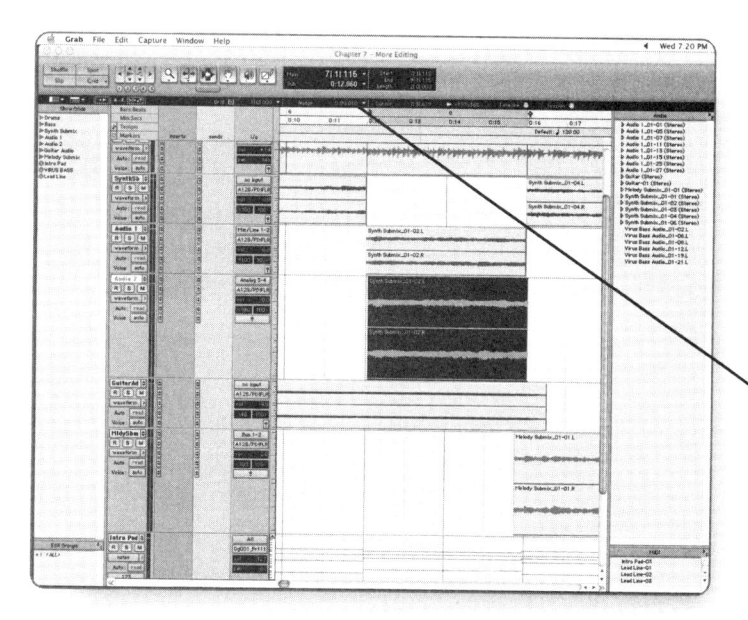

Nudging Regions

Using the Nudge function, you can move regions (or region boundaries) by small incremental amounts, and you can get very specific with your locations. First, though, you'll have to set up your nudge amount.

1. Click on the **Nudge options arrow**. The Nudge menu will appear.

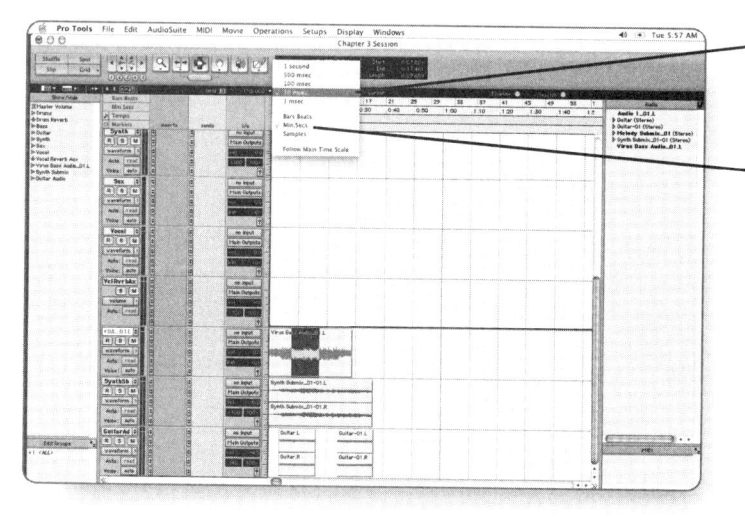

2. Select the **scale** by which you want to nudge your region. The scale will be selected.

3. Select the **increment** by which you want to nudge. The increment will be selected.

CHAPTER 7: MORE EDITING

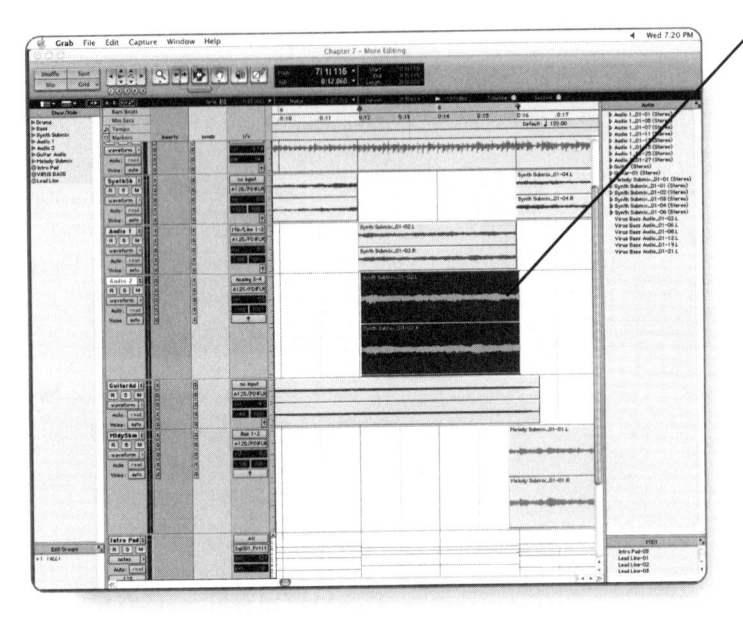

4. Select the **region** you want to move. The region will be selected.

5a. Press the **+ (plus key).** Your region will be moved to later (to the right) by the nudge amount.

OR

5b. Press the **− (minus key).** Your region will be moved earlier (to the left) by the nudge amount. The change in location might be visually imperceptible, so you'll want to keep an eye on your location display.

> **TIP**
>
> Holding Option+Shift (Mac) or Alt+Shift while pressing the plus or minus keys will nudge only the left boundary of the region. Holding ⌘+Shift (Mac) or Ctrl+Shift (PC) while pressing the plus or minus keys will nudge only the right boundary. Neither of these variations on the Nudge feature will move your audio in time; they will only change the boundary.

That's all for now! Next—mixing!

8
Basic Mixing

There are two schools of thought when it comes to Pro Tools mixing—mixing inside the box or outside the box. Mixing inside the box occurs when you use virtual mixer and virtual effects *within* the Pro Tools environment. At any given time, you will only need to listen to the stereo output of your mix from your Pro Tools interface because all the required processing is performed by your computer (the "box"). Mixing outside the box refers to the practice of assigning individual tracks to individual outputs of your Pro Tools interface, and from there to the individual channels of a physical mixing board. The mixing and automation is performed by this external mixer, and Pro Tools is reduced to a recording, editing, and playback capacity only. For the purposes of this book, you'll explore mixing inside the box (which, incidentally, is a method that has been used on countless professional projects). In this chapter, you'll learn how to:

- Work with the specific layout and function of the Mix window
- Use fader groups
- Use file-based and real-time effects
- Work with traditional mix routing
- Use basic automation techniques

More Organization: Memory Locations

Once you go into the Mix window, it will be a little more difficult to navigate through your session Timeline. You won't have the convenience of clicking on a specific time on a track and moving your timeline insertion there (although you will still have the Transport window if you want it). However, you can make navigation a little easier by setting up a few memory locations.

Memory locations are presets you can recall at the touch of a button, similar to the zoom presets you created in the last chapter. In this case, though, you can recall specific selections, locations, zoom settings, and more!

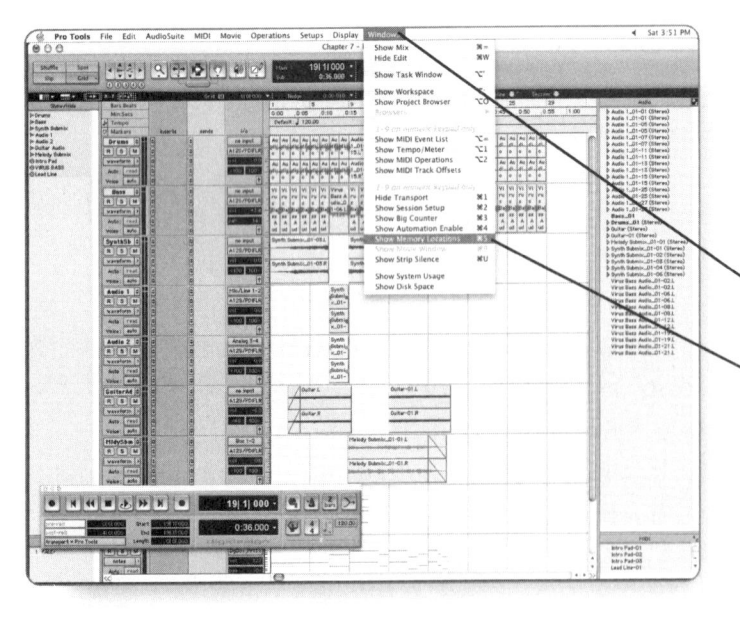

Creating a Memory Location

Of course, before you can use memory locations, you have to create them!

1. Click on **Windows**. The Windows menu will appear.

2. Click on **Show Memory Locations**. The Memory Locations window will appear.

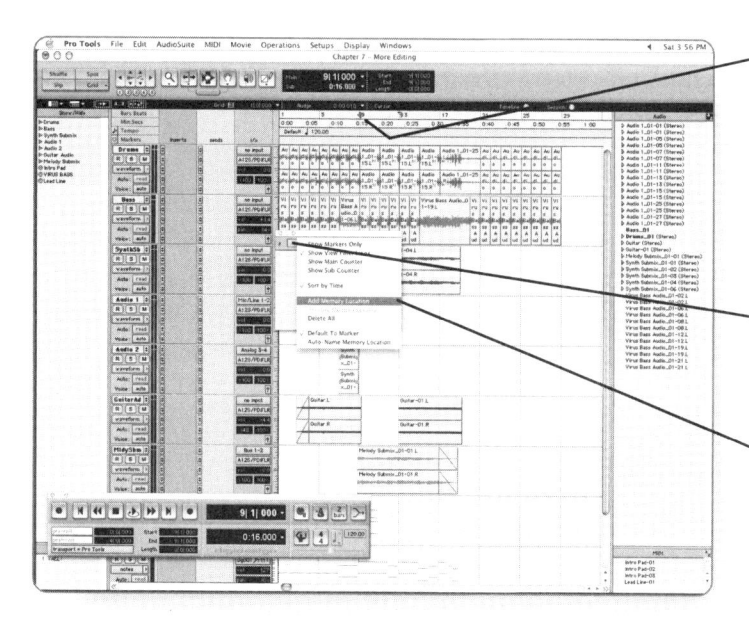

MORE ORGANIZATION: MEMORY LOCATIONS 253

3. Using the Selector tool, **place** your **timeline insertion point** at a significant point in your session. In this case, I've placed it at the beginning of measure 9, where the melody starts.

4. Click on the **Name button** in the Memory Locations window. The Name menu will appear.

5. Click on **Add Memory Location**. The Memory Location 1 dialog box will open, allowing you to set up your memory location.

6. Select the **time property** that you want this memory location to recall. The choices are:

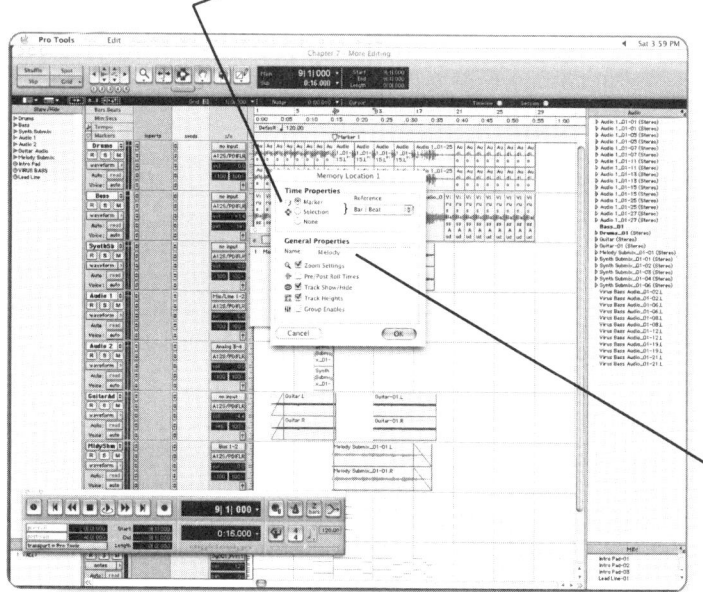

- **Marker.** The timeline insertion will jump to a specific location when the memory location is chosen.

- **Selection.** A selected area will be recalled when the memory location is chosen.

- **None.** The timeline insertion/selection will not change when the memory location is chosen.

7. Type a descriptive **name** for this memory location in the Name text box.

8. Check the **General Properties check boxes** that match the settings you want to be recalled with this memory location. The settings will be selected. In this case, when this memory location is recalled, the current zoom settings, track show/hide, and track heights will be recalled. Other characteristics, such as pre-/post-roll and group enables, will not change when you recall this memory location.

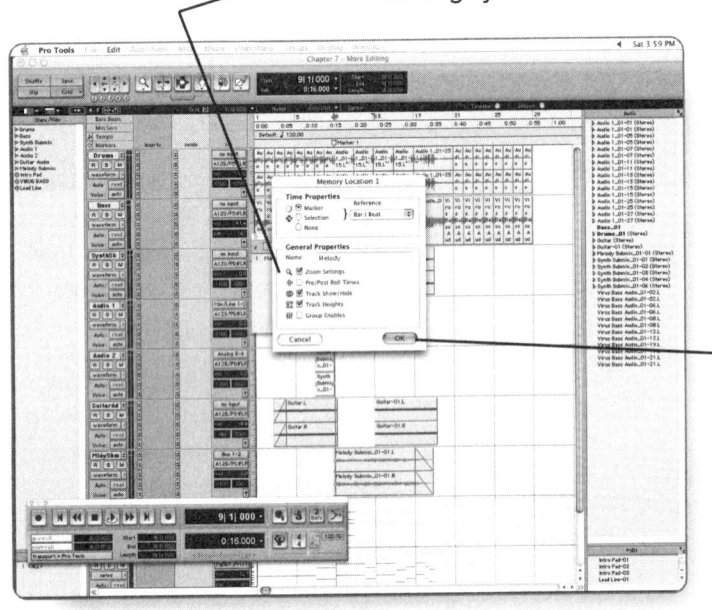

9. Click on **OK**. Your memory location will be saved, and the Memory Location 1 dialog box will close.

10. Now try setting up another, different memory location. **Select** a **different location** (in this case I selected the beginning of the outro) **and a different zoom setting**.

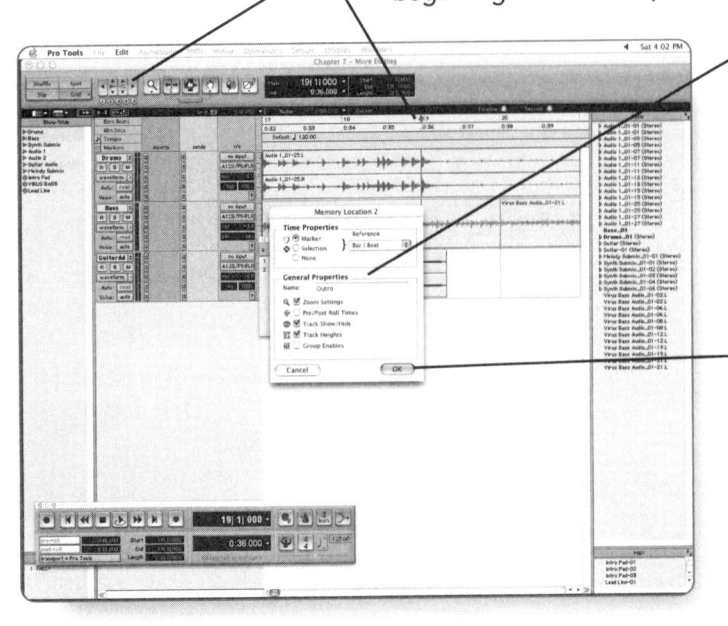

11. Create and set up a new **memory location** in the same way that you set up the first one (by clicking on the Name button, selecting Add Memory Location, and setting up the desired parameters of this new memory location).

12. Click on **OK** when you're finished. The second memory location will be created and the Memory Location 2 dialog box will close.

MORE ORGANIZATION: MEMORY LOCATIONS 255

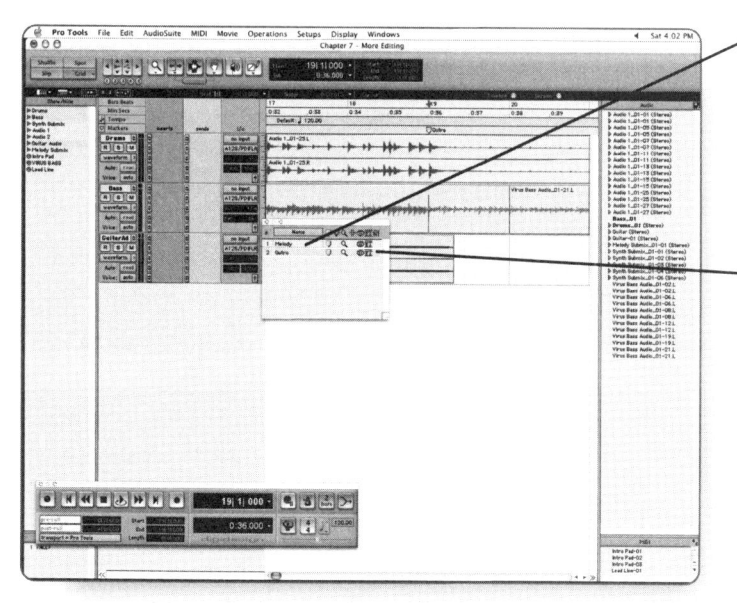

By clicking on either memory location name, you will instantly recall its location on the time scale, as well as all included parameters, such as zoom settings and track show/hide.

If you forgot what parameters are enabled, just look to see what icons are included for each memory location. From left to right, the icons are Marker, Selection, Zoom, Pre-/Post-Roll, Track Show/Hide, Track Height, and Group Enable.

TIP
You can recall any created memory location from your keyboard easily. On the Mac or PC, press the period key, and then the number of the memory location you want to recall, and then the period key again.

TIP
You can also create memory locations as your session plays by pressing the Enter key.

Using Memory Locations

Beyond this, there's no big mystery to creating and using memory locations, but before you jump into the Mix window, take a quick look at some of the other options open to you.

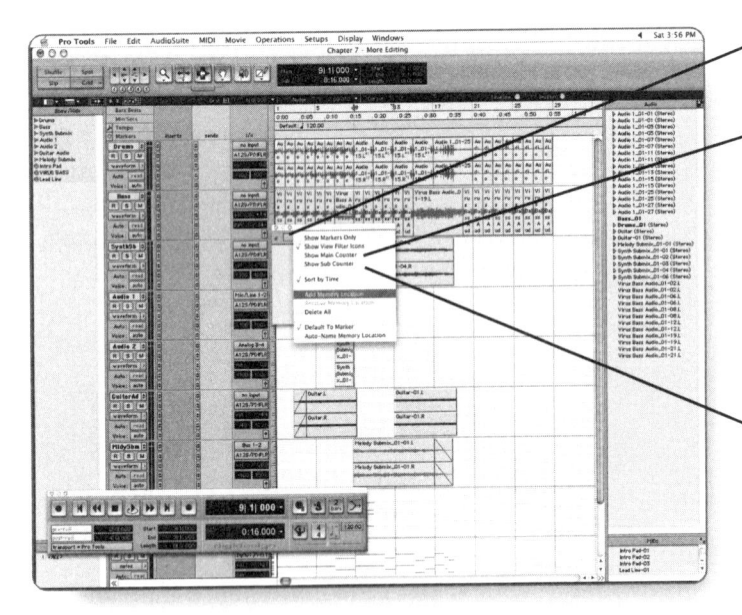

1. Click on the **Name button**. The Name menu will appear.

2a. Select the **Show Main Counter option**. The location of each memory location in relation to the main counter scale will be displayed (as shown at the top of the Edit window).

OR

2b. Select the **Show Sub Counter option**. The location of each memory location in relation to the sub counter scale will be displayed (as shown at the top of the Edit window).

OR

2c. Select the **Sort By Time option**. Your memory locations will be sorted depending on how early or late they are in your session, rather than by the order in which they were created.

OR

2d. Select the **Default To Marker option**. The Memory Location dialog box will be set to start off with the Marker option chosen.

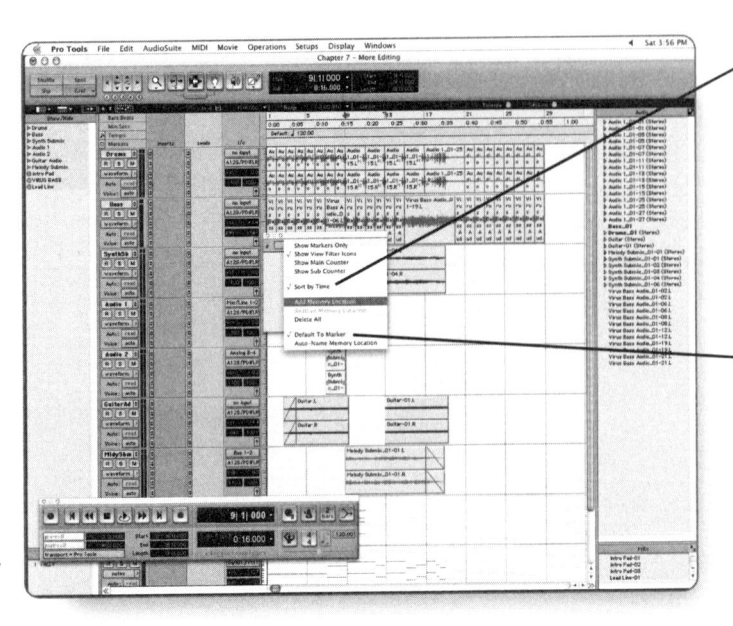

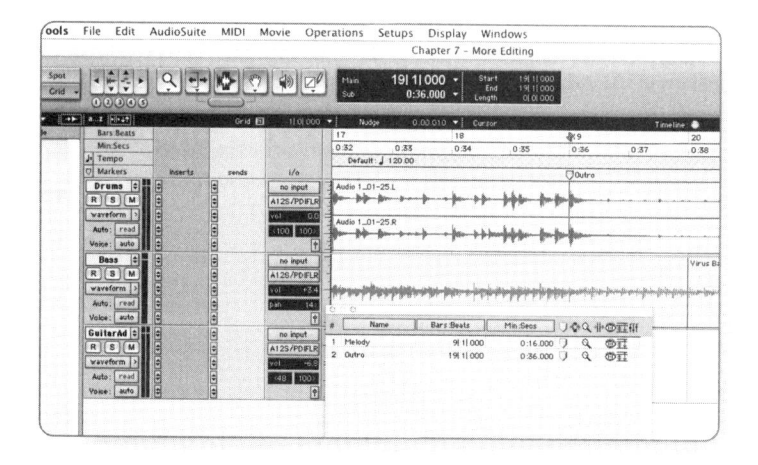

Here's what the window will look like when the two memory location options are selected. Note the two new columns created, and that their time scales reflect the currently selected main and sub counter scales. Each memory location's specific position is shown in these columns. Either or both of these two options can come in mighty handy, particularly when you're working in the Mix window, where it's harder to visualize your time position in your session.

Now that you're set, on to the Mix window!

Exploring the Mix Window

You looked at the Mix window before (way back in Chapter 2). Now it's time to dig deeper.... The first thing to do is to switch over to the Mix window (which you learned how to do in Chapter 2). Depending on how you left the Mix window last time, you might see the channel strips appearing rather narrow. If you do, just follow these steps to view them normally.

1. Click on **Display**. The Display menu will appear, showing the Narrow Mix Window option checked.

2. Click on **Narrow Mix Window** to uncheck it. The channels will be shown in their normal mode.

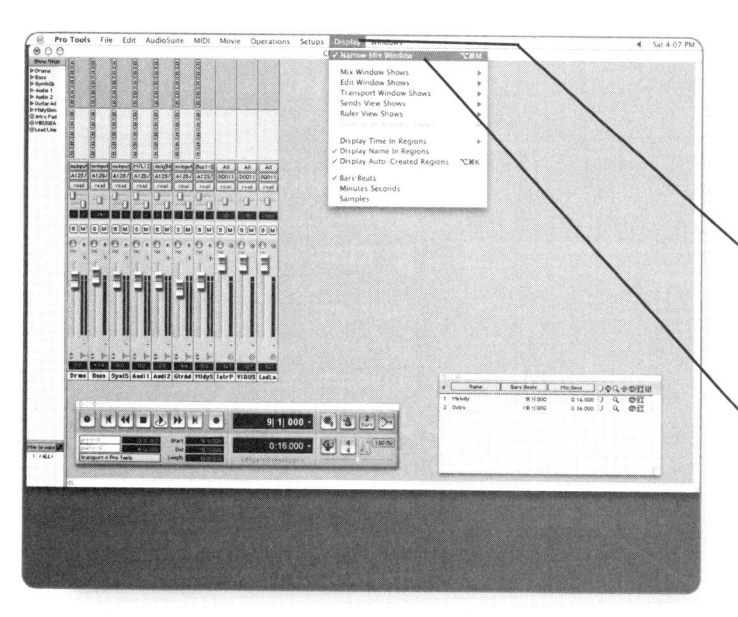

> **TIP**
> There are certainly times when the Narrow Mix Window mode is desirable. For example, when your session contains too many tracks to be normally displayed at once in the Mix window, switching to Narrow Mix Window mode will allow you to view more of your mix at once.

Basic Mixer Terminology

Just for a little reminder, this section reviews the basic layout of the Mix window.

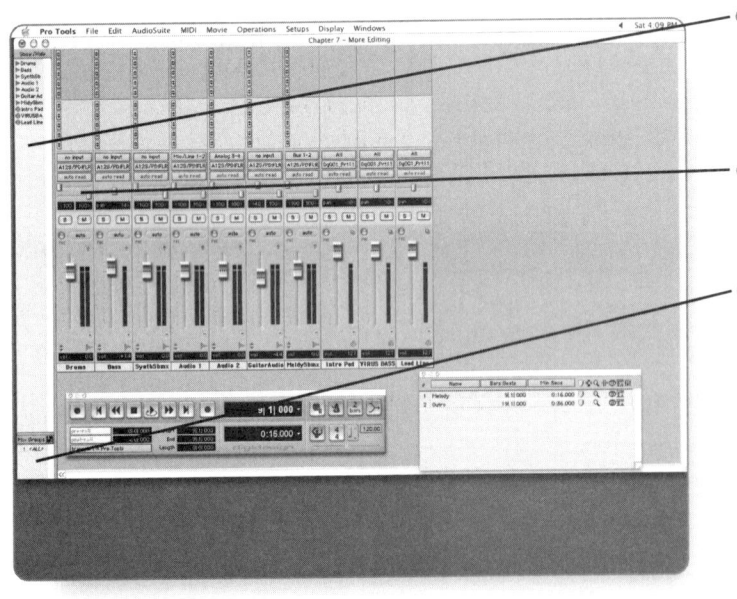

- **The Track Show/Hide List.** As in the Edit window, highlighted tracks are displayed as channel strips.

- **Channel Strips.** There is a separate channel strip for each shown track.

- **The Groups List.** You'll learn more about this in just a few pages.

EXPLORING THE MIX WINDOW 259

Now take a look at the different sections of each channel strip.

- At the top of the channel strip is the Insert section. The important thing to remember is that any audio passing through that channel strip will be routed through the inserts first. You've got five inserts to use, and it is here that you will launch *plug-ins*, which can be virtual effect units or even virtual instruments.

- Next are the sends. You'll use one or more of the five available sends to route a portion of your track's processed audio to another destination. Sends are commonly used in conjunction with other tracks to create more complex effect situations.

> **NOTE**
> You'll see that the three tracks on the right side have no inserts or sends. That's because these are MIDI tracks, and inserts and sends can route only audio data.

CHAPTER 8: BASIC MIXING

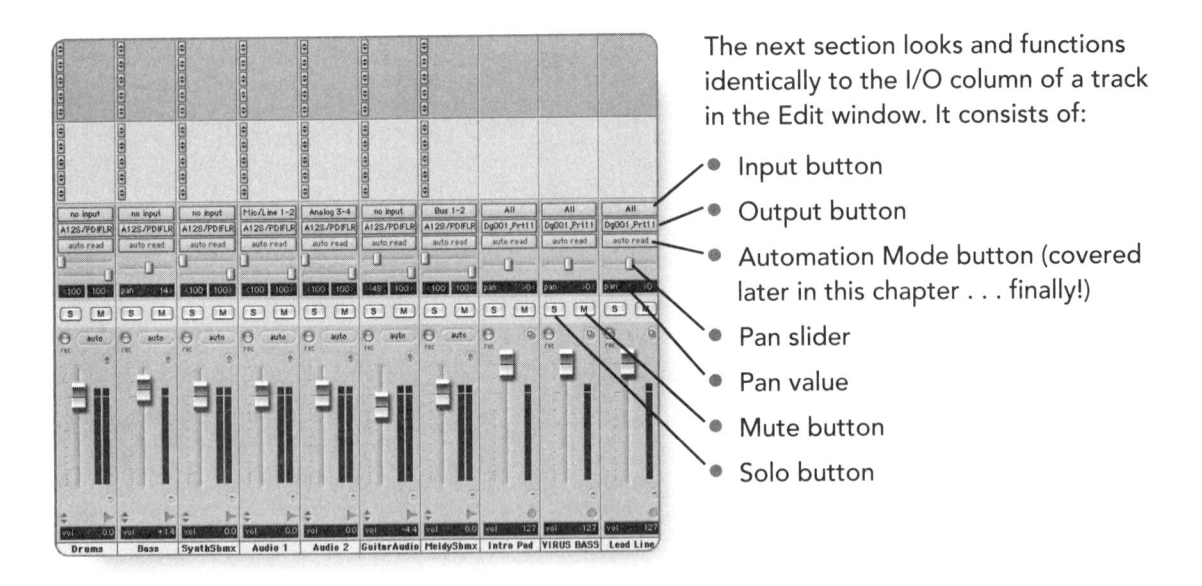

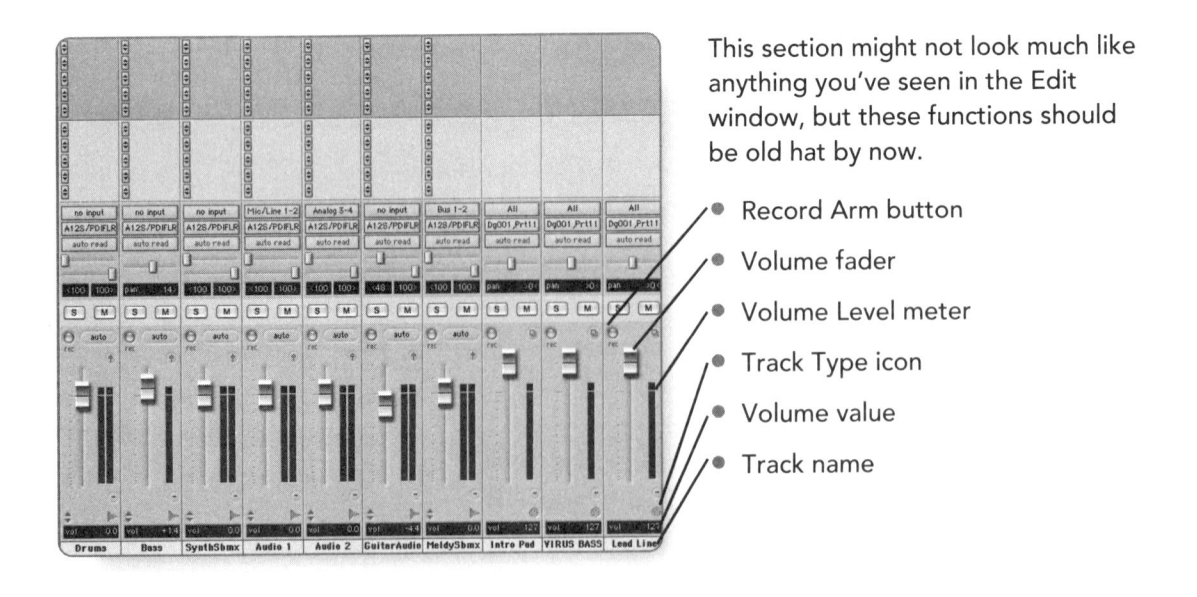

The next section looks and functions identically to the I/O column of a track in the Edit window. It consists of:

- Input button
- Output button
- Automation Mode button (covered later in this chapter . . . finally!)
- Pan slider
- Pan value
- Mute button
- Solo button

This section might not look much like anything you've seen in the Edit window, but these functions should be old hat by now.

- Record Arm button
- Volume fader
- Volume Level meter
- Track Type icon
- Volume value
- Track name

> **NOTE**
> The icon at the bottom-right corner of each channel strip will let you know what type of track it is. A pink waveform indicates an audio track; a green MIDI plug indicates a MIDI track. A green arrow signifies an aux track, and a yellow sigma marks a master fader. The same icons can be found to the left of each track in the Track Show/Hide list.

> **NOTE**
> You can easily tell whether the track is stereo or mono by taking a look at the volume meters and pan sliders. One meter and pan signifies a mono track, and a stereo track will have two meters and pans. (The top pan is for the left side of the track, and the bottom pan is for the right side of the track.)

More Signal Flow

Whenever you talk about mixing, you're really talking about signal flow. The more complex your mix gets, the more complex the routing of that signal will be.

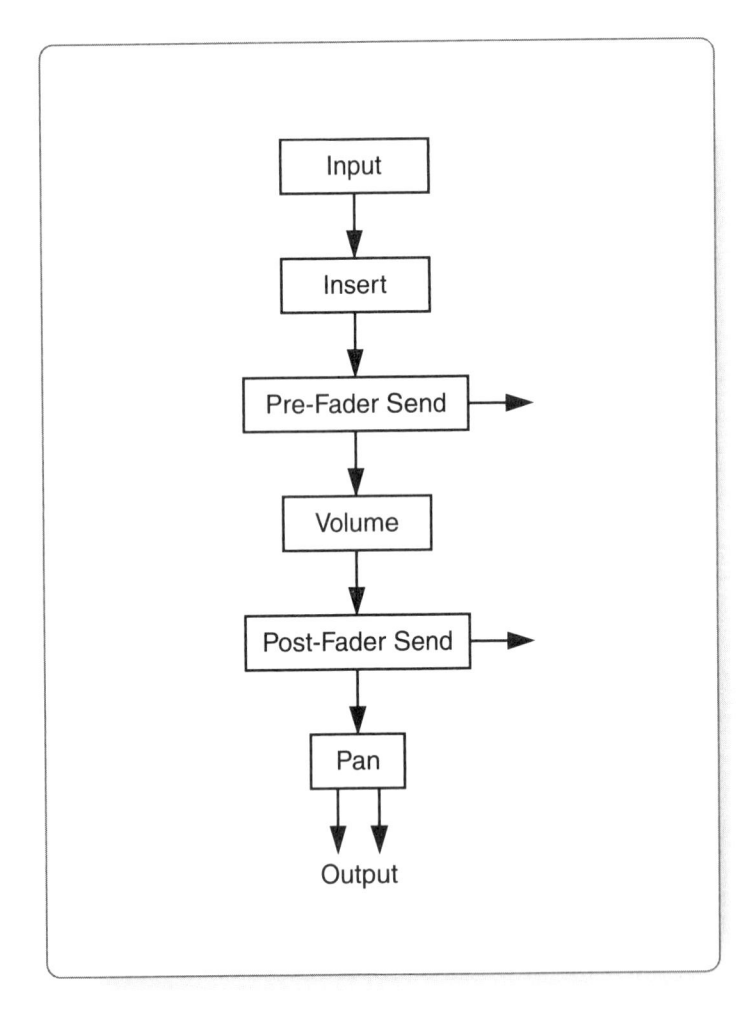

The following list will go through the order of audio signal flow within a track.

1. Input. On an audio track, input can be from an interface input (if you're recording), from a bus or from your hard drive. With aux tracks, the input can only be from an interface input (although you can't record) or a bus.

2. Insert. After the input, 100 percent of your signal passes through the insert.

3. Pre-Fader Send. This makes a copy before the signal hits your volume fader. The destination of this send can be an interface output or a bus.

4. Volume Fader. This is where you control the output volume of the track.

5. Post-Fader Send. This makes a copy after the signal has been altered by the volume fader. As with a pre-fader send, the destination can be an interface output or a bus.

6. Pan Slider. Panning comes next and allows the signal to be varied between a pair of outputs, usually left and right. This is how you will create a stereo mix of several mono or stereo tracks. If you route your track to a singular output, no pan slider will be needed and you won't see one in the channel strip.

7. Output. After all these stages are passed, the signal goes to the Pro Tools mix engine and out of an interface output pair.

Fader Groups

One of the neat things about mixing in Pro Tools is that you can link faders together, so that moving one fader will move a number of faders. This is particularly useful when you have a good relative blend between a number of tracks (for example, a nice balance between all the drums). By making a fader group of these tracks, you can adjust the volume within your entire mix, while maintaining the group's relative levels.

First, though, you should get a feel for what a fader group can do. As luck would have it, Pro Tools automatically creates a group (named All) when a new session is created. Take a look at what it does.

1. **Click** on the **All group name**. The group name will be highlighted and the group, which includes all the tracks in your session, will be active.

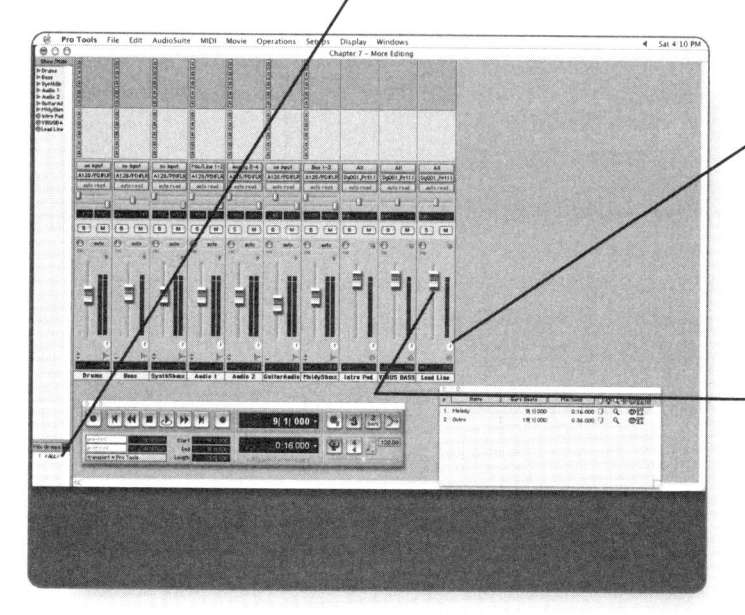

> **NOTE**
> At the bottom right of each channel strip is a small group icon. When a group is activated, the group's members will display a lit group icon.

2. **Click** on any **volume fader** and **drag it** to change the volume of the track. Because you're using the All group, all the tracks will move proportionally.

CHAPTER 8: BASIC MIXING

> **NOTE**
>
> In a session that uses more than one group, you can highlight more than one group at a time, making multiple groups simultaneously active within your session. Simply click on any group you want to enable, and it will become active.

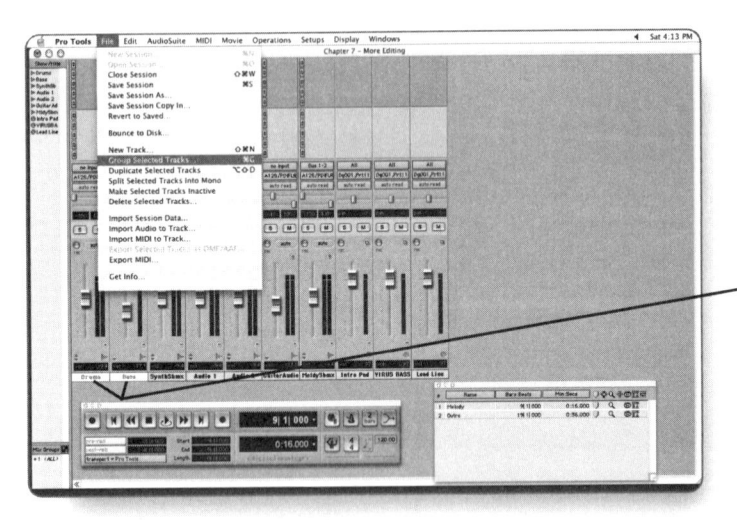

Creating a Fader Group

You can also set up a new group of your own. Simply follow these steps.

1. Press and hold the **Shift key** and **select** any number of **tracks** that you want to group together. The tracks will be selected.

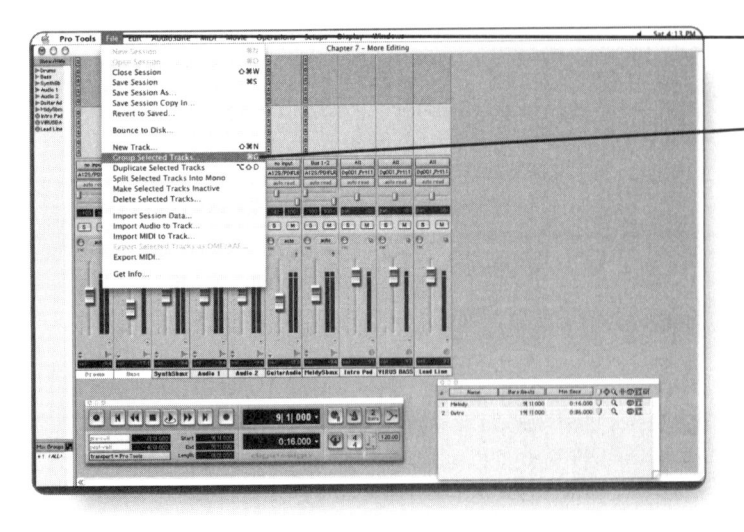

2. Click on **File**. The File menu will appear.

3. Click on **Group Selected Tracks**. The New Group dialog box will open.

FADER GROUPS 265

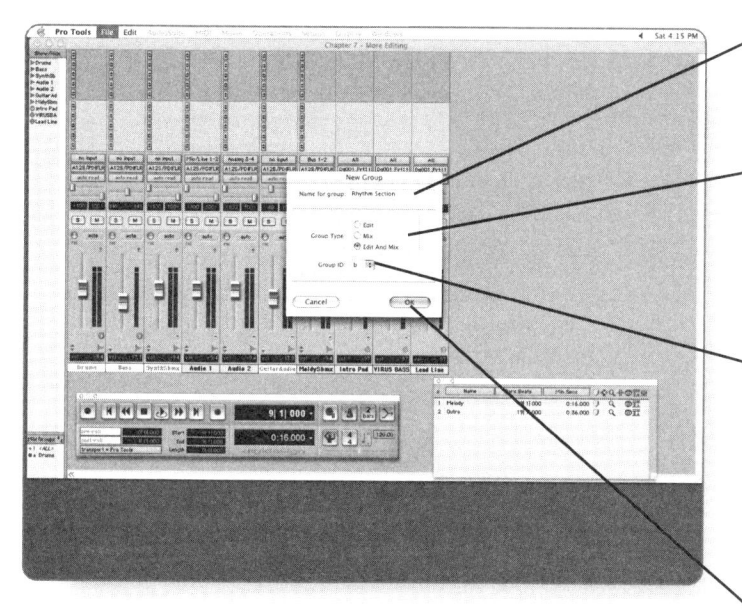

4. Type a **name** for your new group in the Name for group text box.

5. Click on a **Group Type radio button** to choose whether the group will exist in the Edit window, the Mix window, or both. The option will be selected.

6. Pro Tools will automatically assign a letter to your group for labeling purposes. **Click** on the **Group ID button** if you want to select a different letter for the group.

7. Click on **OK**. Your settings will be saved and the New Group dialog box will close.

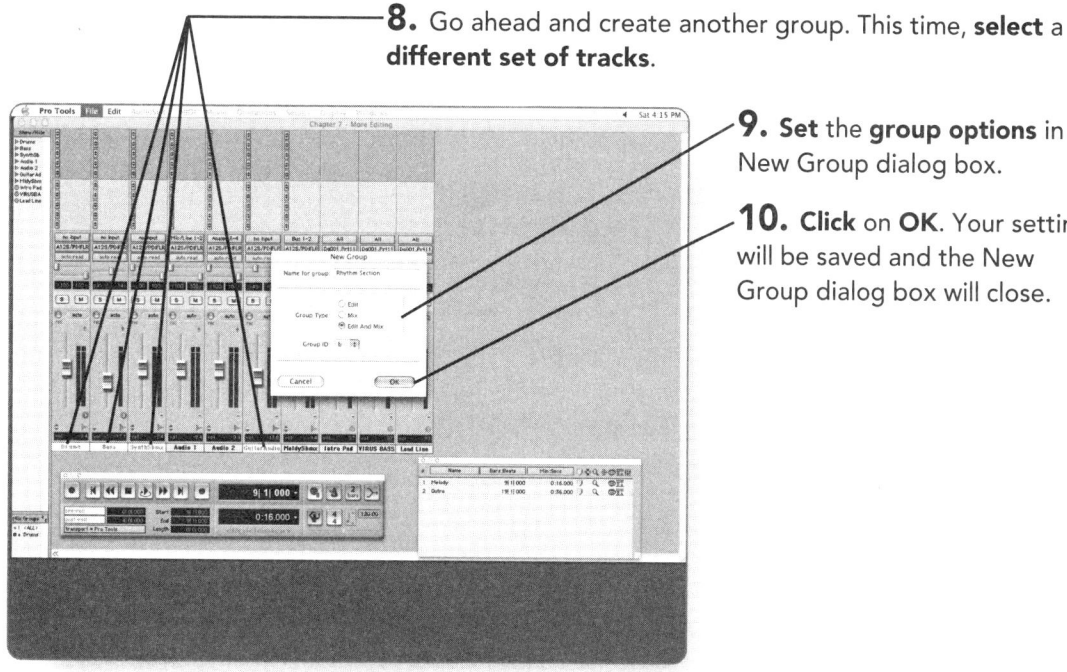

8. Go ahead and create another group. This time, **select** a **different set of tracks**.

9. Set the **group options** in the New Group dialog box.

10. Click on **OK**. Your settings will be saved and the New Group dialog box will close.

> **NOTE**
> You'll notice that this group includes the two tracks that were previously selected for the first group. Pro Tools allows tracks to be members of two groups at the same time. This can be very helpful, for instance, if you want to group your tom-tom tracks together and then group those tracks together with the rest of the drum kit. These are called "nested" groups.

> **TIP**
> What if you want to add or remove tracks from a group you've already created? It's easier than you might think. After you choose all the member tracks that you want to be members of a given group, select Group Selected Tracks, just as you would when creating any group. This time, though, choose the letter of the group you want to change from the Group ID drop-down menu. Click on OK, and you're done!

Using Fader Groups

There's just a little more to learn about fader groups before you continue.

- An empty circle to the left of a group signifies that some, but not all, members of that group are selected. In this case, some members of the All group are selected, but not all of them.

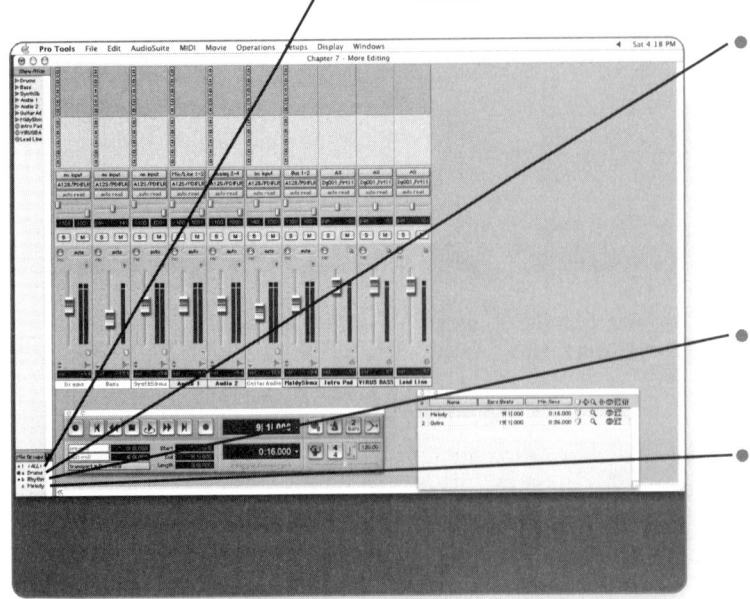

- A circle with a dot means that all members of the group are selected, plus other tracks. Here all members of the Drums and Bass group (the drums and bass tracks) are selected, plus some other tracks.

- A solid dot means that all members of that group are selected, and no others are.

- No dot or circle by a group signifies that no members of that group are selected.

> **TIP**
> A quick way to select all the members of a group is to click to the left of the group name in the group list.

Since it's possible to have a fader group within another fader group (called a *nested* fader group), how do you know if a given track is a member of more than one active group?

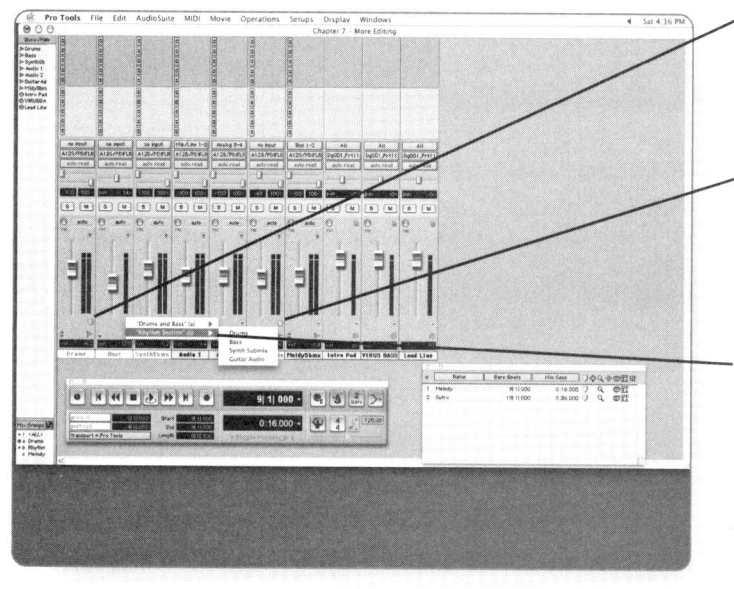

- An uppercase letter means that the track is a member of more than one currently active group.

- A lowercase letter in a group icon (at the bottom right of the channel strip) shows that the track is a member of only one active (highlighted) group.

- You can click on the group icon to reveal a menu of all the active groups in which the track is a member. In this example, the bass track is a member of two groups. If you move your mouse to either group, a list of all members in that group will be displayed.

Using Effects

Many software applications use plug-ins—programs that run within programs. In word processors, plug-ins can be editing tools or macros; graphics applications have visual effect plug-ins; and so on. Pro Tools is no slouch when it comes to plug-ins. Pro Tools plug-ins include all manner of effects processors and even virtual instruments. Because they're software, they have all the benefits and flexibility of software, and they save you money and rack space in your project studio!

CHAPTER 8: BASIC MIXING

In a Pro Tools LE system, plug-ins fall into two families—file-based plug-ins (called AudioSuite) and real-time plug-ins (called RTAS, or Real-Time AudioSuite). First you will tackle AudioSuite.

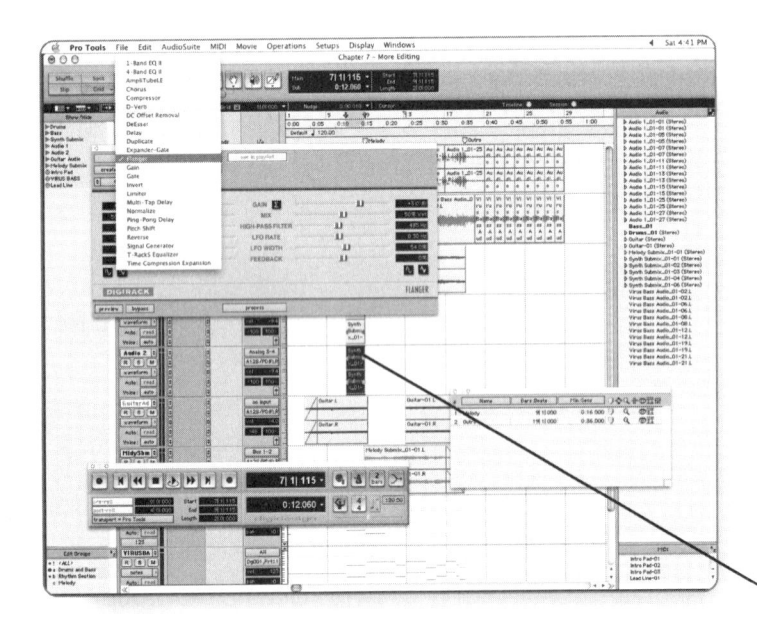

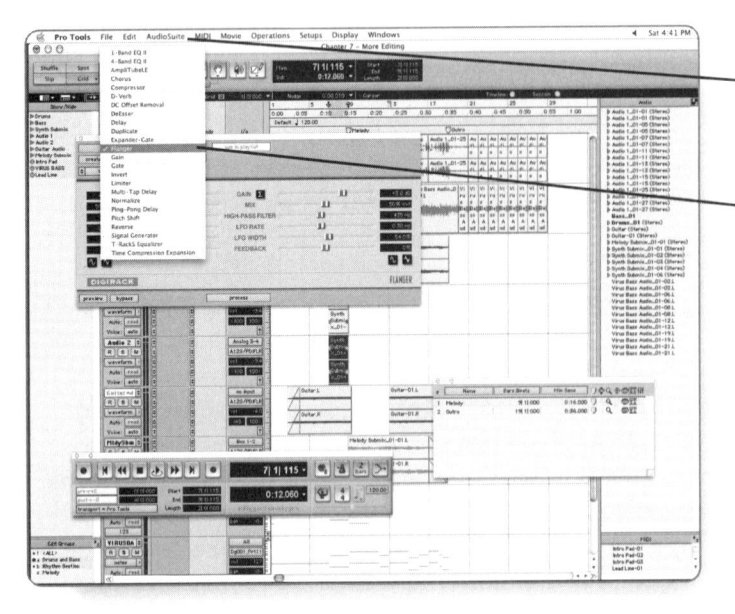

AudioSuite

AudioSuite plug-ins are, generally speaking, the most basic of the Pro Tools arsenal of effects. They operate on files (hence the name file-based), and this is not done in real-time as your session plays. This means that these plug-ins cannot be automated in your Pro Tools session. Still, there are some pretty powerful tools to work with here, and it's a good idea to get familiar with them. Here's how they work:

1. Select the **region or selection** you want to process. The region or selection will be selected.

2. Click on **AudioSuite**. A menu of available AudioSuite plug-ins will appear.

3. Click on the desired **effect**. The plug-in's window will appear.

Although different effects have different appearances and parameters, they share some common elements.

USING EFFECTS

4. Click on the **Plug-in Selector button**. A list of available AudioSuite plug-ins will appear, from which you can change to another plug-in.

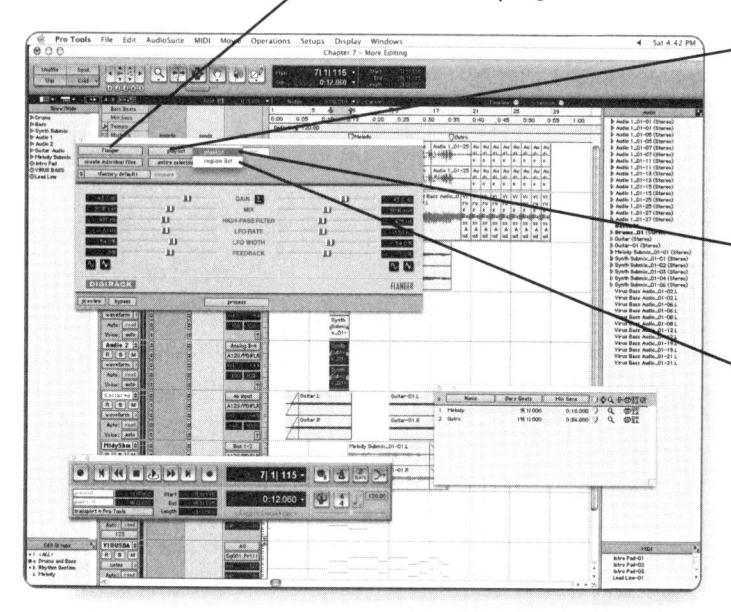

5. Click on the **Selection Reference button** to determine which selection will be processed. A menu with two options will appear.

- **Playlist.** The playlist option will process the single selection in your track.

- **Region list.** The region list option will process the currently selected regions in the Audio Regions list and change all corresponding regions being used in your session.

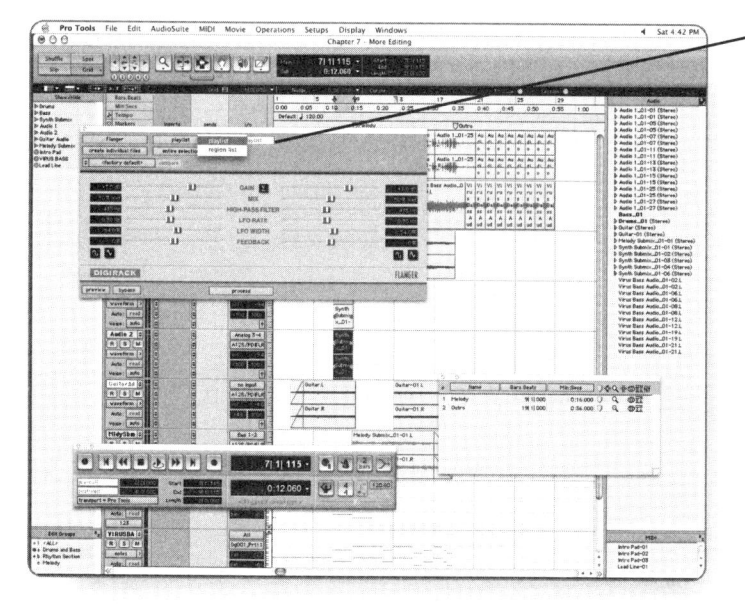

6. Select use in playlist if you want the processed audio to appear in your tracks and also in the Audio Regions list. The button will be highlighted.

> **NOTE**
>
> When the use in playlist button is not selected, the processed audio will only appear in the Audio Regions list.

CHAPTER 8: BASIC MIXING

7. Click on the **File Mode button** to determine how the audio will be processed. A menu will appear, showing three different processing options.

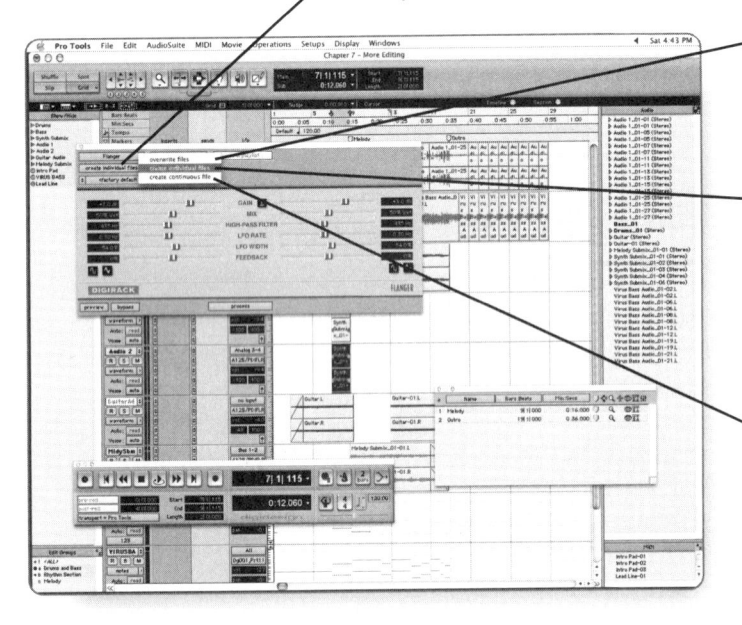

- **Overwrite files.** This option processes the audio file directly and *destructively*. It *cannot* be undone.

- **Create individual files.** This option is non-destructive and creates separate audio files for each processed region if your selection includes more than one region.

- **Create continuous file.** This option will process a selection that includes more than one region non-destructively and create a consolidated single file.

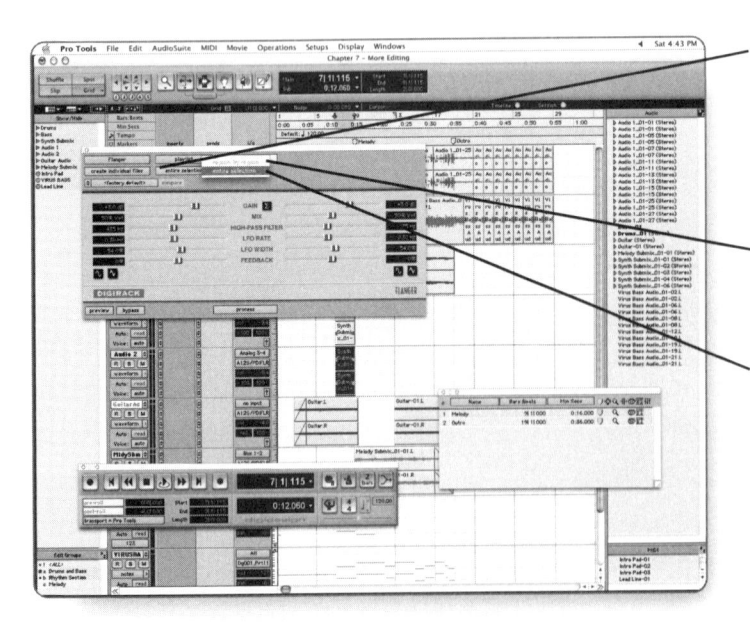

8. Click on the **Process Mode button** to determine how your regions will be analyzed prior to processing. A menu will appear, showing two options.

- **Region by region.** This option will analyze individually each region within a selection.

- **Entire selection.** This option will analyze multiple regions as a whole.

USING EFFECTS 271

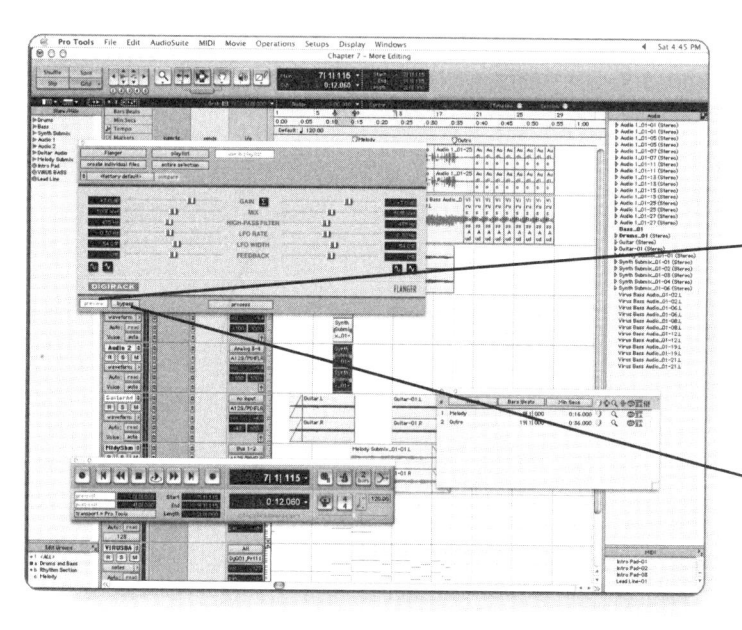

> **NOTE**
> The entire selection option is commonly used when you are normalizing multiple regions of different volumes. With this mode enabled, each individual region within a larger selection will be analyzed and processed individually.

9. Click on the **preview button** to audition the effect before processing the file. The selection will play with the effect temporarily applied for your evaluation.

10. Select the **bypass option** to allow the signal to pass through the effect unprocessed. The button will be highlighted.

11. When you change a parameter, the compare button will appear solid. **Click** on the **compare button** to allow A/B comparisons while editing.

12. Click on the **Plug-in Librarian button** to choose the selected preset for the plug-in. A menu of available presets will appear.

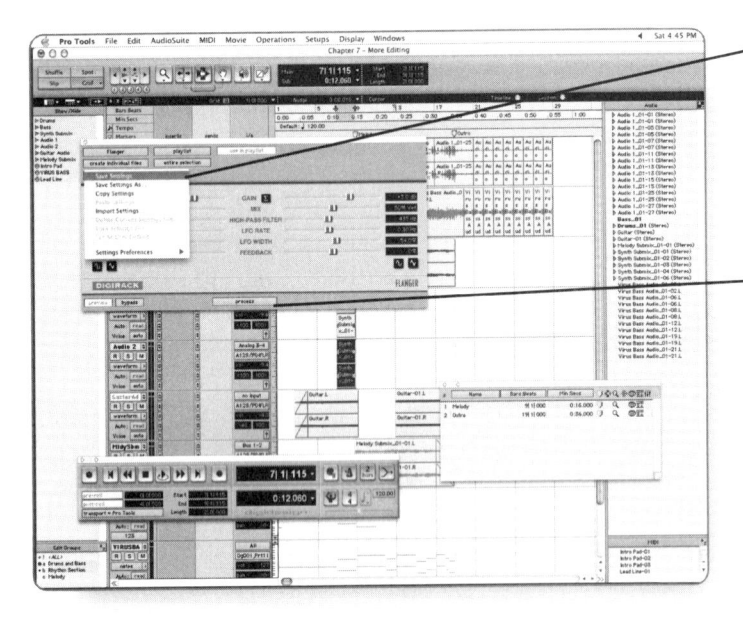

13. **Click** on the **Settings button** (the arrowed button to the immediate left of the Plug-in Librarian button) and **select** a preset-related **function**. The function will be selected.

14. **Click** on **process** to finally apply your effect. The effect will be rendered to a new audio file (or will overwrite your original file destructively if you have chosen the overwrite files option in Step 7).

RTAS

The next evolutionary step in Pro Tools' plug-in effects is the RTAS line. A number of RTAS plug-ins have AudioSuite counterparts (the EQs, for example), but the distinction between the two types is an important one. In the case of an RTAS plug-in, instead of processing audio on a file-by-file basis, the plug-in resides on a track's insert and processes the incoming signal as the session is played (in real time).

There are two huge benefits that come with using RTAS plug-ins. First, because the audio is being processed in real time, the audio files on your hard drive won't be changed as the audio plays, which allows you to experiment freely with different plug-ins and settings without worrying about filling your hard drive with tons of edited files. Also, as a result of RTAS's real-time qualities, you can automate the parameters of your plug-in, meaning that your effects can change dynamically over time.

Using RTAS Plug-Ins

The following steps detail how to start using RTAS plug-ins in your session.

1. On an unused insert on the track you want to affect, **click** on the arrowed **insert button**. A drop-down menu will appear.

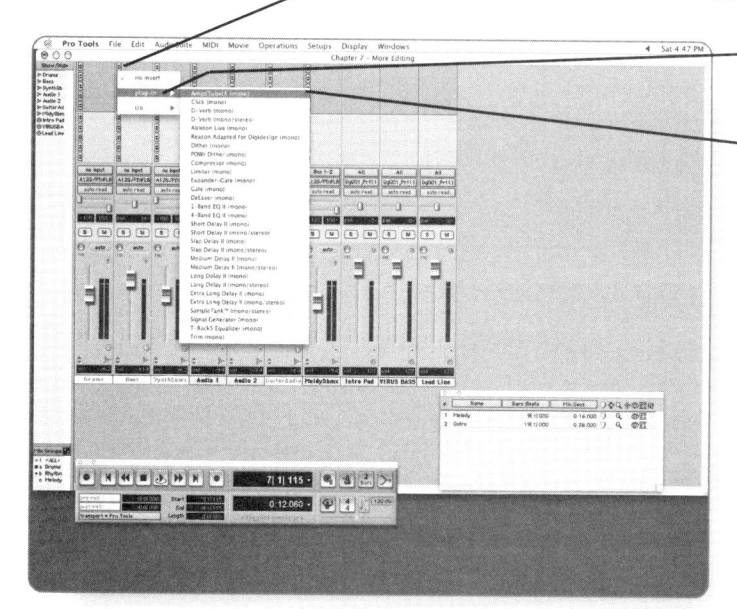

2. Click on **plug-in**. The plug-in menu will appear.

3. Click on the **plug-in** you want to launch. An effects window will open. This window will appear differently depending on the effect, but there are some common buttons that you should know.

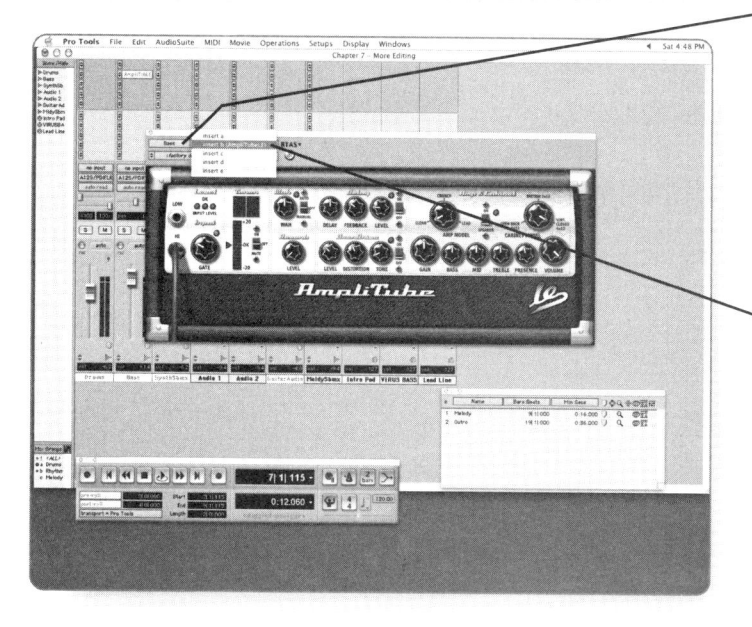

4. The Track Selector button tells you what track the effect is on. **Click** on the **Track Selector button**. A list of available tracks will appear. From this list you can select another track and immediately open the Insert window for that track.

5. The Insert Selector button to the right of the Track Selector button tells you what insert the effect is on. **Click** on the **Insert Selector button**. A list of all the inserts on the track will appear. From this list you can select any of the inserts for your track and jump to that insert immediately.

> **TIP**
>
> Because inserts are processed in a series, from top to bottom, the order in which effects are placed in your tracks is indeed significant. For example, a virtual amplifier placed before a reverb will sound a good deal different than an amplifier placed after a reverb. The good news about this is that it's easy to change the order (or even the track assignment) of an RTAS plug-in simply by dragging and dropping the insert icon to a new location in your mixer.

Digging Deeper into RTAS

Okay, so far it's pretty straightforward, but things will get a little more complicated as you continue. For example, when you open a plug-in on a stereo track, you have a few more options.

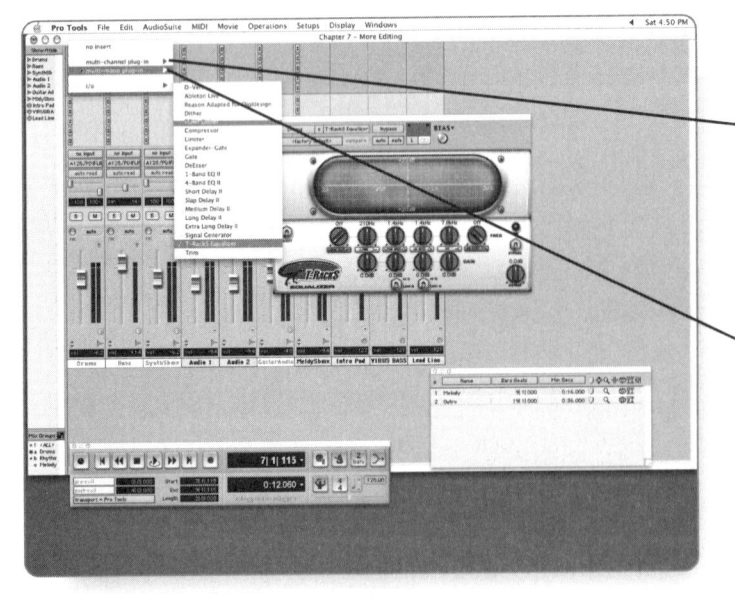

1. On a stereo track, **click** on an **insert button**.

2a. Click on **multi-channel plug-in**. In the case of a stereo track, a list of stereo plug-ins will appear.

OR

2b. Click on **multi-mono plug-in**. This option is available if you have tracks with more than one channel (such as stereo tracks). A list of mono plug-ins will appear. When you select a plug-in, it will be opened twice, although only one plug-in window will be shown. A multi-mono plug-in window has several important features.

USING EFFECTS

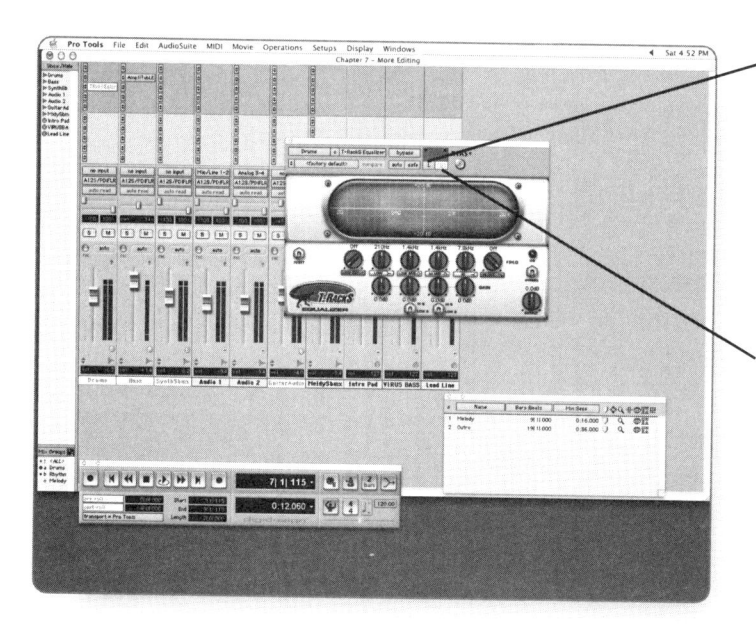

- The Channel Selector button will display either an L or an R to signify the side of the multi-mono plug-in you're presently viewing. When the Link button is highlighted, both the left and right sides will appear identical.

- The Link button is unique to multi-mono plug-ins. When the button is highlighted, both instances (left and right) of the mono plug-in will share the same parameter settings. When the Link button is not highlighted, both sides are independently configurable.

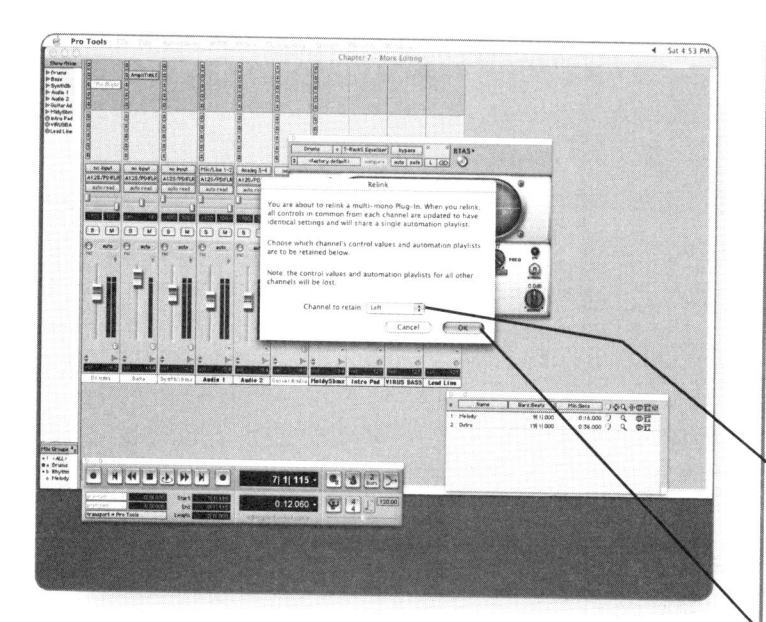

> **NOTE**
>
> If you unlink the two halves of a multi-mono effect and then choose to re-link them, the Relink dialog box will appear. This dialog box is pretty self-explanatory. To relink the two multi-mono plug-ins, you have to choose one side's parameters to be applied to the other side.
>
> Click on the Channel to retain button to reveal a drop-down menu that contains both left and right sides.
>
> Once you've chosen which side's settings you want to keep, you can click on OK.

1. Each plug-in you launch (or instantiate, as Digidesign likes to say) will appear as a rectangular button next to its corresponding insert. **Click** on the desired **button** to reveal the effect window.

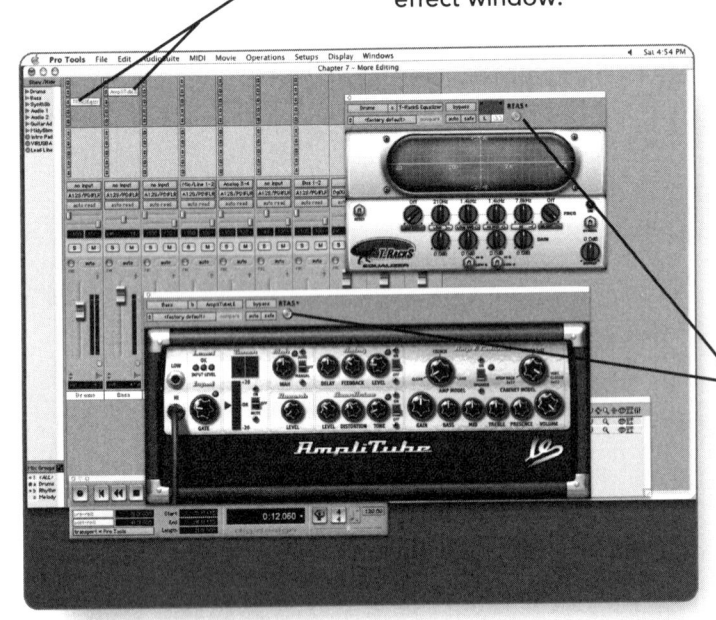

You'll notice that by default, only one effect window can be open at a time. (Clicking on a new plug-in will replace the previous plug-in window with the new one.) So what if you want to view more than one plug-in window at a time? That's when the Target button comes into play.

2. The rule for the Target button is that there can only be one active target at a time. **Click** on the **target** to deselect it. You'll be able to open two (or more) effect windows at a time.

> **NOTE**
> If you're using a control surface (a Digi 002, for instance), only the effect with the active Target button will be accessible from the surface's knobs and faders. Your mouse, however, will still manipulate all the open effect windows, regardless of the Target buttons' statuses.

> **TIP**
> You can also open more than one plug-in window at a time by holding down the Shift key while you click on a plug-in button on an insert. However, there can still be only one targeted effect at a time. (The first plug-in you opened will retain the active target.)

Using Virtual Instruments

Still further down the path of plug-in evolution are the virtual instruments. In a Pro Tools system, these plug-ins are RTAS, just like the plug-ins you've seen thus far, but with an interesting twist: Virtual instruments don't process audio; they *make* audio! Think of them as the marriage between software plug-ins and MIDI synthesizers, taking advantage of both worlds. With virtual instruments, you not only have the power of a MIDI synth without the bulk of hardware; you also have the ability to automate its parameters just like any RTAS plug-in. (Don't worry; we'll talk about that next.)

The secret to using virtual instruments is in the setup, which really is just a variation of a typical MIDI setup.

As with a typical MIDI setup, you need two tracks to get MIDI data and audio data to work within Pro Tools—a MIDI track (for MIDI data) and an aux track. In a traditional setup, the aux track would be used to route audio from an outside source into Pro Tools, and back out through an interface output. In this case, you still need the aux track, even though there is no outside source involved.

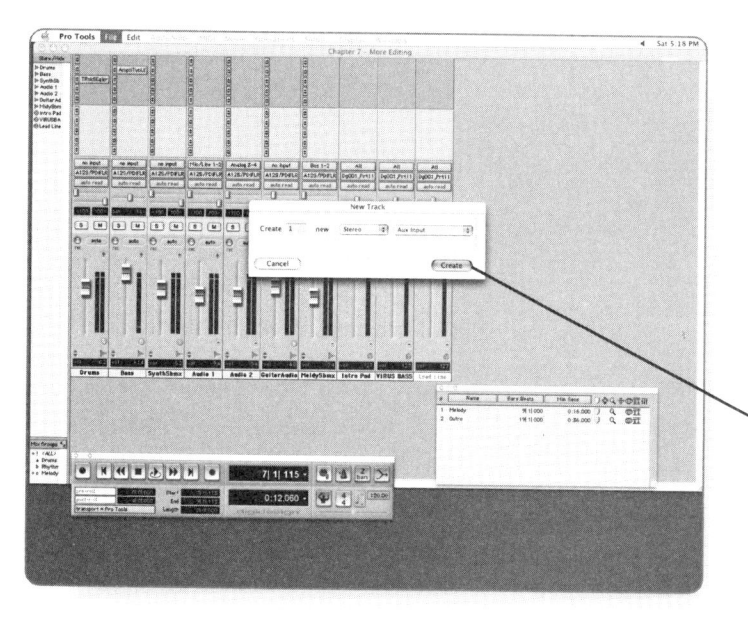

In this session, you've probably noticed that there's already a track with MIDI data. (If you don't have one in your session, you should take a moment to create one). You'll also need an aux track, so your next job is to create one. (If you can't remember how to create an aux track, you can refer to Chapter 3.)

1. After you've set the parameters for a stereo aux input track, **click** on **Create**. A new stereo aux input track will be created.

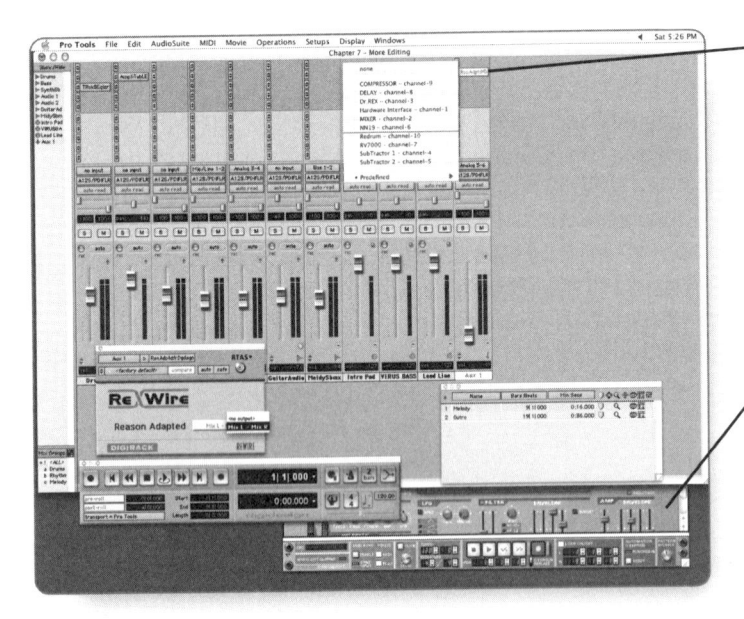

2. Click on an **insert button** on the aux track and **open** a **virtual instrument plug-in**. In this case, I've opened Reason Adapted, a virtual instrument that is included with many versions of Pro Tools LE (although it is technically a separate application).

The virtual instrument will be launched in its own window. In the case of Reason Adapted, a complete virtual synth environment will be instantiated. The Reason Adapted software communicates with Pro Tools through a bit of software called ReWire, which serves as virtual MIDI and audio communication between the two applications.

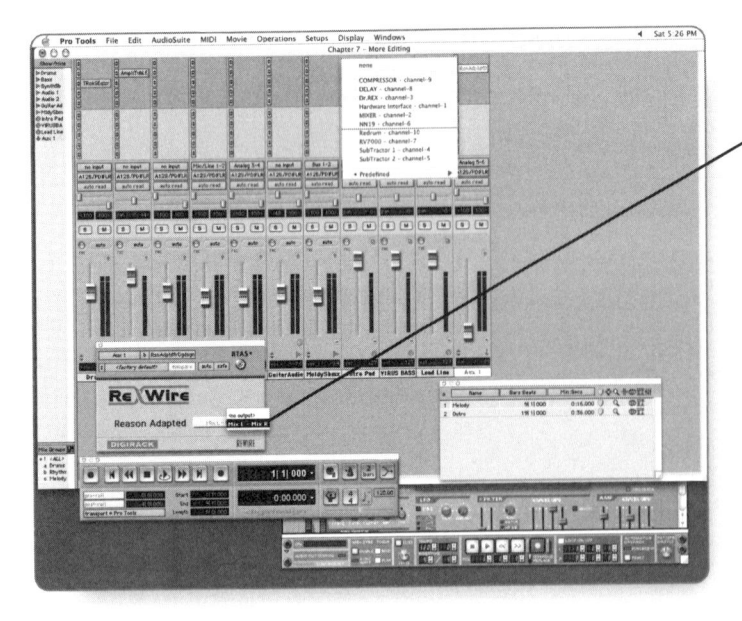

3. Click on the **output button** in ReWire and **select** an **output** for your software synth.

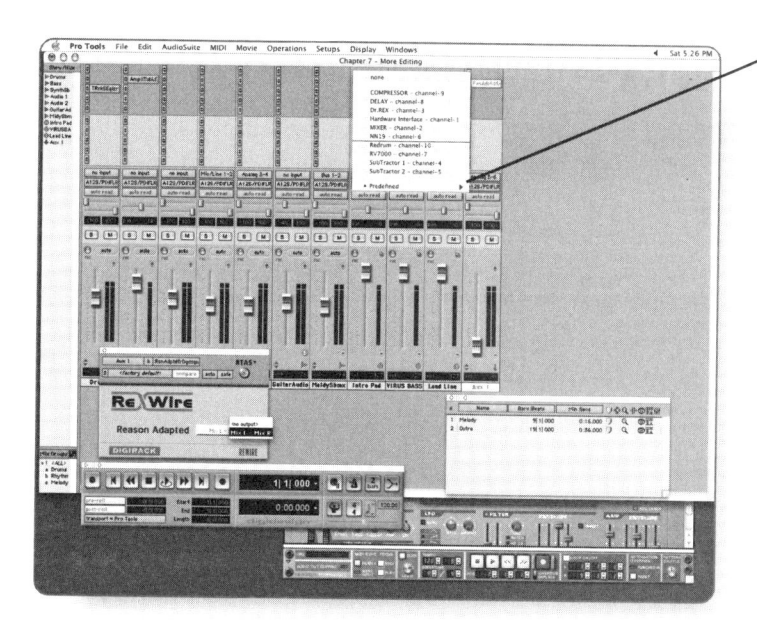

4. Now all you need to do is set up the output of your MIDI track. Pro Tools will automatically add the virtual instrument(s) to the list of outputs once the plug-in is instantiated. **Click** on the **output button** of the MIDI track and **select** the **instrument** you want to control from the drop-down menu.

> **NOTE**
>
> When you play your session, you will see MIDI data being played in your MIDI track's level meters. Remember that what you're seeing is not audio, but rather control data being sent to the virtual instrument on your aux input track. The levels you see on the aux track are the audible signal being routed to your monitor speakers.

Mixing Tips

Of course, the point of the mixing process is to achieve just the right blend of audio elements in your session. Over the years, certain conventions have arisen to help mixing engineers work more efficiently, and these conventions have become something of a tradition. You should start out by learning some traditional effects routing.

Using Dynamic-Based Effects

Traditional effects tend to fall into one of two categories—dynamic-based effects or time-based effects. I want to start with dynamic effects. Dynamic-based effects change the volume level without changing duration in any way. Some of the most common examples of dynamic effects are equalizers, compressors, and limiters. Traditionally, these types of effects will process all of the track's audio, with little thought of creating a wet/dry kind of mix with these processes. Here's the traditional routing for dynamic effects:

1. Click on an **insert** on the track you want to affect and **select** a **dynamic-based effect** (such as the EQ shown here). The plug-in window will appear.

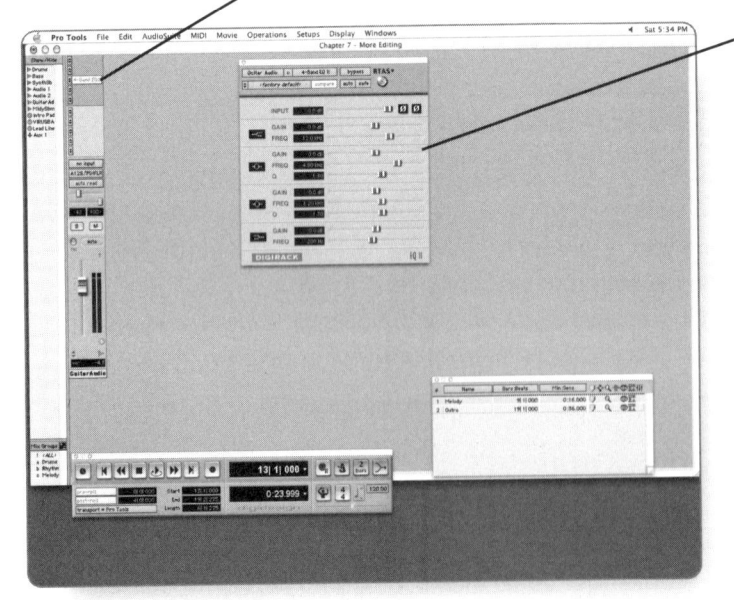

2. Adjust the **parameters** of the effect to suit your mix's needs.

When you're finished tweaking the effect, you're finished with the routing. Although it is simple enough, this sort of routing works well with dynamic effects because 100 percent of the signal to the track first passes through the insert. This example shows a classic model—the entirety of a guitar track's signal passing through an equalizer.

Now that you've got your guitar nice and EQed, you can add a bit of reverb.

Using Time-Based Effects

Time-based effects *do* affect the duration of the sound beyond that of its original waveform. This family includes effects such as reverb, delay, and echo. In these cases, you generally will want to have some sort of a wet/dry mixing situation (*wet* meaning an affected signal and *dry* referring to an unaffected signal). What better way is there to mix the two than with two separate faders in your Mix window?

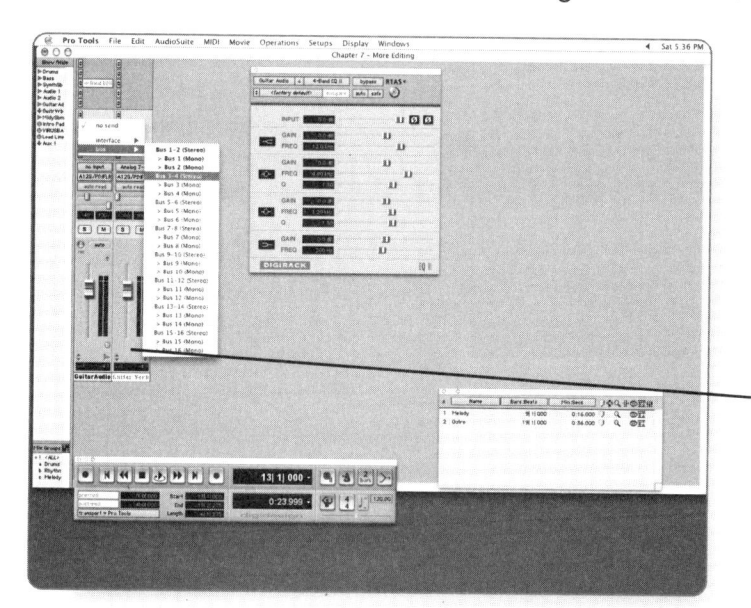

1. Create a **stereo aux track**.

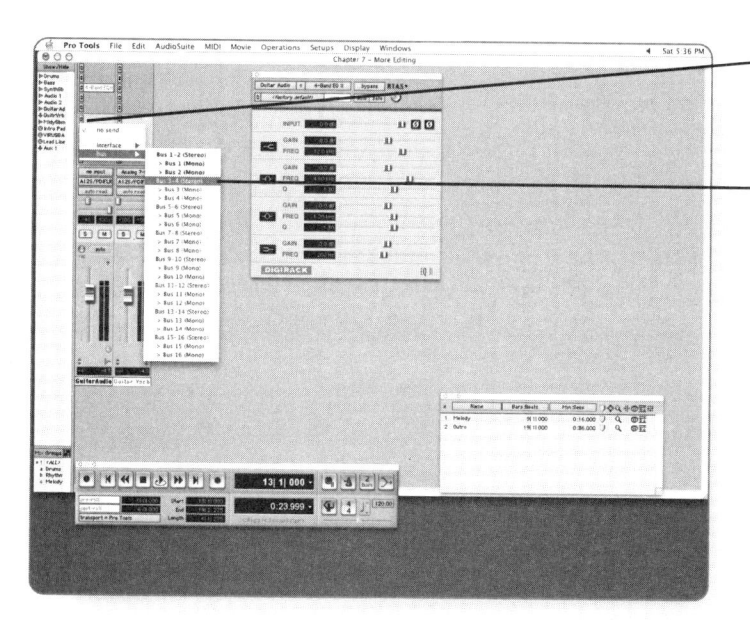

2. Click on an **arrowed send button**. A drop-down menu will appear.

3. Because you'll be routing audio from one track to another within Pro Tools, you'll use a bus. **Click** on **bus** and then **select** an **unused bus**. (Buses used in the session will be shown in bold.)

CHAPTER 8: BASIC MIXING

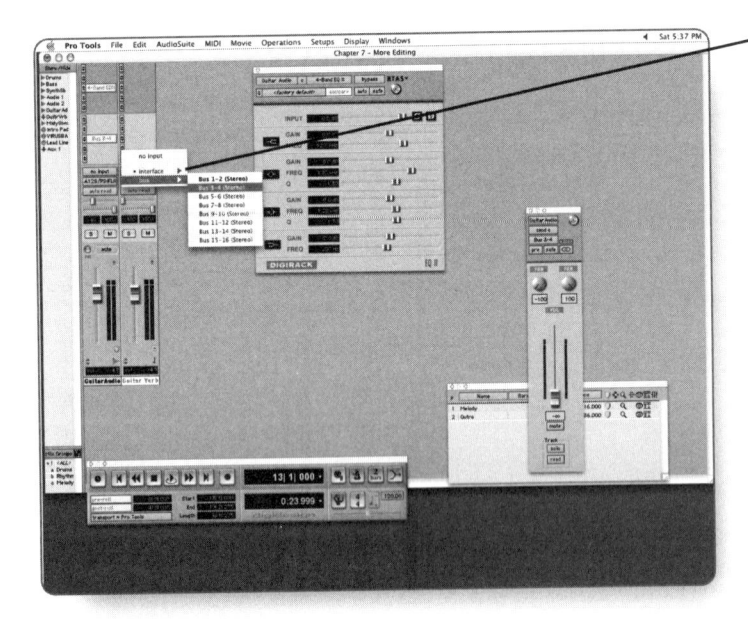

4. After you've sent a copy of your audio track through a bus, you need to set the input of the aux track. **Set** the **input** to match the same bus you chose for your audio track's send. The input will be set.

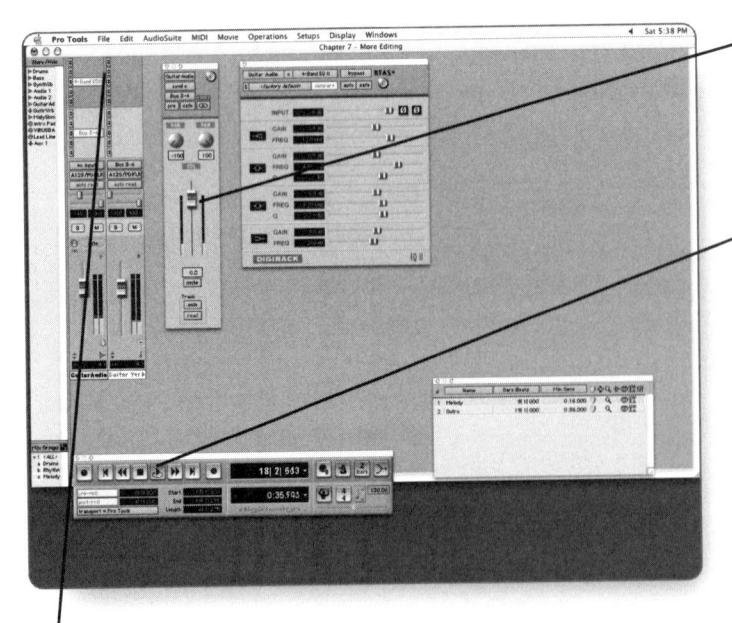

5. Drag the **bar** on the volume fader on the send's tear-away strip to increase the volume. The volume will be adjusted accordingly.

6. Play your **session** to test your connection. If you've routed the audio signal correctly so far, signal that is shown in the audio track's meter will also be shown in the send's tear-away strip and the aux track's meter.

7. Click on an **insert arrow** button on the aux track. A drop-down menu will appear.

MIXING TIPS 283

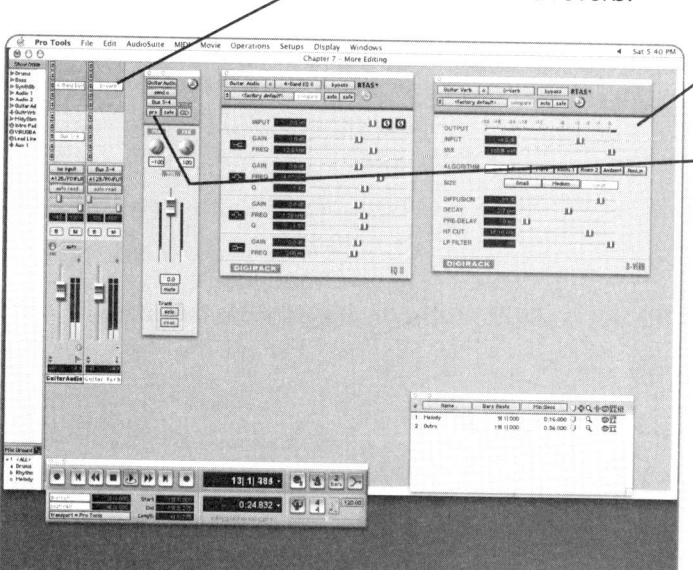

8. Select a **time-based effect** from the menu. In this case, I have chosen a reverb.

9. Adjust the **settings** for the plug-in.

10. Only one more thing: When the pre button is highlighted, the send will be a pre-fader send, meaning that the output of the send will not be affected by the audio track's volume fader. When the pre button is not highlighted (the Pro Tools default mode), the send is a post-fader send, and the volume fader of the audio track will affect the volume going out of the send, and from there to the aux track.

> **NOTE**
>
> Although a post-fader send is generally more common (hence it is the default in Pro Tools), both pre- and post-fader sends have their uses. It all depends on the results you want. Choose post-fader if you want to have your dry track (the audio track) and your wet track (the aux input) blend and then have the dry track's level affect the wet track's output. This way, when you raise and lower the volume fader on the dry track, you'll raise and lower the signal being routed to the aux. If, however, you want the wet and dry tracks to be completely independent, use a pre-fader send. Because signal will be routed to the aux track *before* the dry track's fader, a full signal will be sent to *both* faders. Experiment!

> **NOTE**
> Most plug-in effects have a mix parameter that allows you to blend a dry and wet signal. Often this setting defaults to 100 percent wet, but not always. Be sure to check your plug-in's mix parameter; in a mixing situation like this, you'll want the mix to be 100 percent wet.

That's it! Now you have a dry fader (the audio track) and a wet track (the aux track), and you can adjust the balance as you want.

Automating Your Mix

Automation is truly one of the coolest things about mixing in Pro Tools. It basically refers to the ability to record parameter changes over time, to be recalled when you play your mix again. Not only can you automate faders and pans (features traditionally reserved for expensive mixing consoles), but you can even automate plug-in parameters!

Before you start dealing with mix automation, you should get some terminology straight. Audio and MIDI data are *recorded*, and automation is *written*. This might seem like a matter of semantics, but you'll see the differences as you read on.

The Automation Modes

There are five automation modes, which determine the way your fader, pan, and other motions will be written into the session. Understanding the distinction between the modes is the best way to start working with automation.

AUTOMATING YOUR MIX

1. Click on the **Automation Mode button** on a track. A drop-down menu of the five automation modes will appear. The modes are

- **Auto off.** In this mode, automation cannot be written or played back, even if automation has been previously written.

- **Auto read.** Automation cannot be written in this mode, but previously written automation will be played back.

- **Auto touch.** Only the parameter that is "touched" (by clicking with your mouse or using a control surface) will write automation. When the parameter is released, it will return to any previously written automation.

- **Auto latch.** This mode is similar to auto touch—only the parameter that is "touched" will write automation. When the parameter is released in this mode, however, it will remain at the last value and continue to write automation at that position until you stop the transport.

- **Auto write.** In this mode, automation will be written on all enabled parameters, regardless of whether the parameter is being touched.

NOTE
With all of these modes, automation can only be written during playback, and writing will stop when playback is stopped or, in the case of auto touch, when you let go of the parameter you are automating.

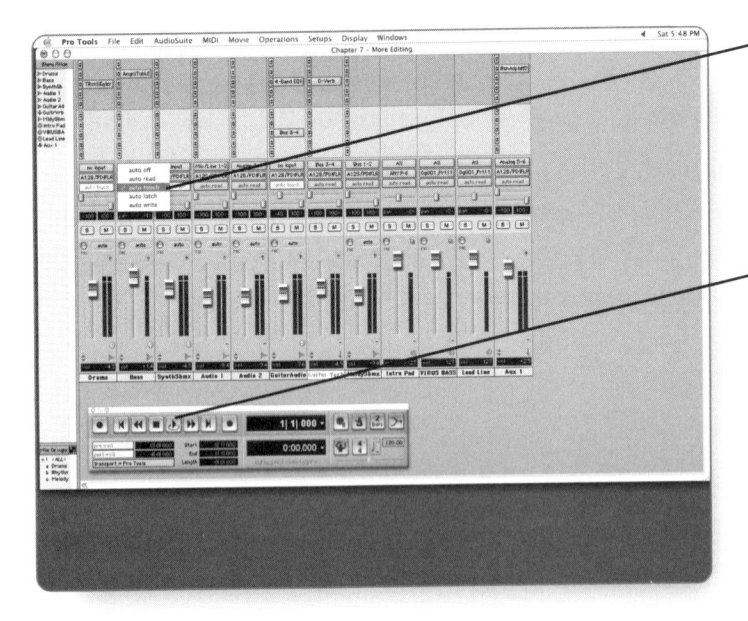

2. Click on the **Automation Mode button** for each track to select an automation mode for that track. You can choose a different automation mode for each track.

3. Click on the **Play button** in the Transport window. Your session will begin playing.

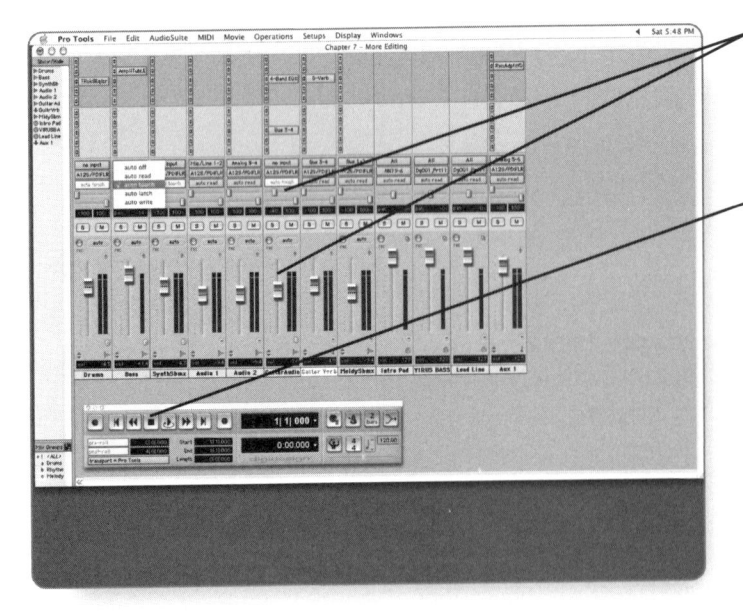

4. Click on a **mix parameter** (such as volume or pan) and move it to create automation data.

5. Click on the **Stop button**. Your session will stop playing.

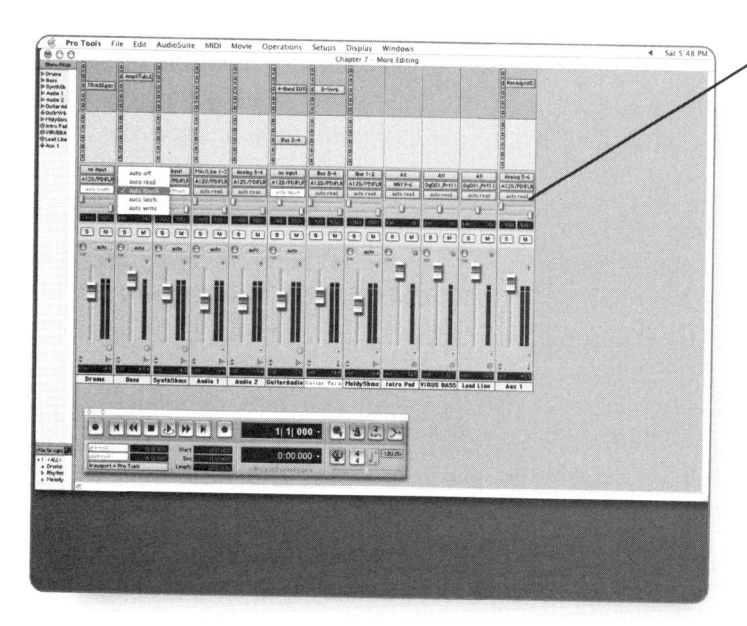

6. Click on the **Automation Mode button** and **select auto read mode** when you're finished writing automation. This will ensure that you don't inadvertently write automation. The motion of the mix parameters you previously wrote will be shown as your session plays back.

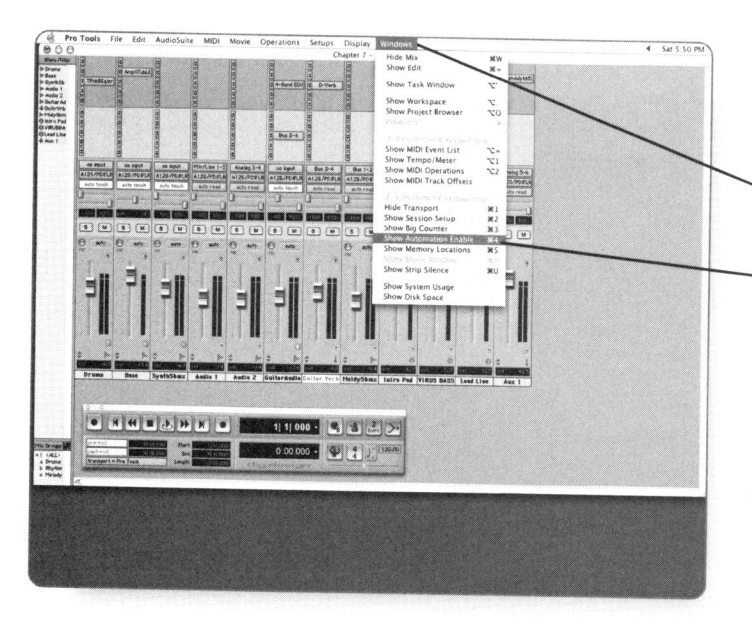

So how can you find out which mix parameters can be automated?

1. Click on **Windows**. The Windows menu will appear.

2. Click on **Automation Enable**. The automation window will appear. The seven highlighted icons (volume, pan, mute, plug-in, snd lvl, snd pan, and snd mute) represent automatable mix parameters.

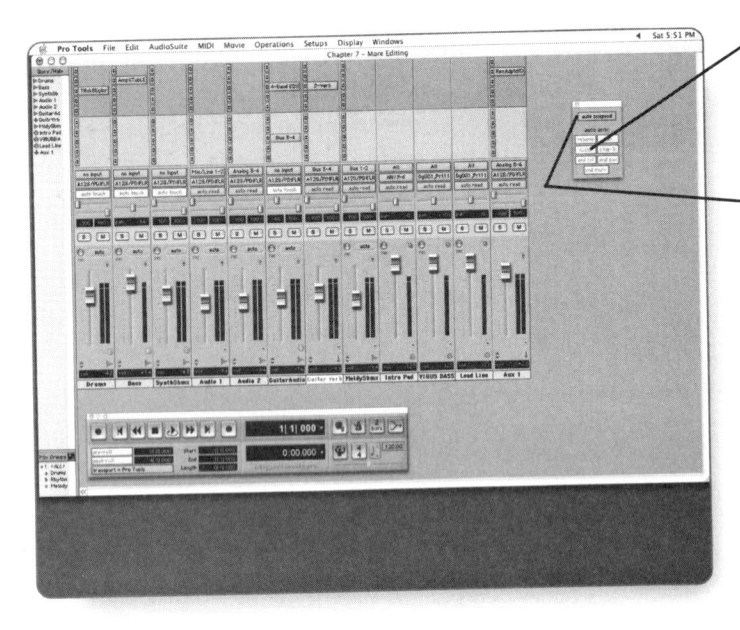

3. Click on an **Auto Arm** button to remove the highlighting. The parameter will be rendered unwritable.

4. Click on the **auto suspend button**. Automation (writing and playback) will be disabled.

Plug-In Automation

Virtually every knob or button of a plug-in can be automated. There are two methods by which you can do this.

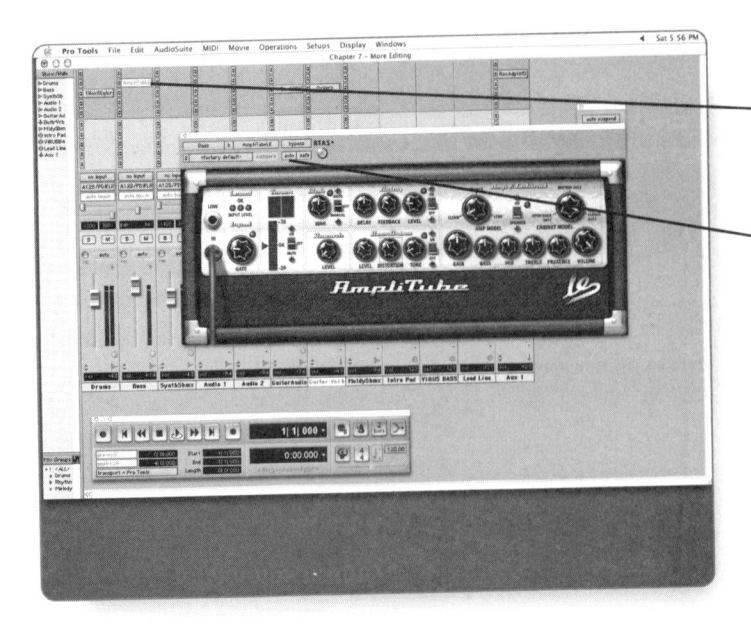

Method One

1. Click on the **plug-in** you want to automate. The plug-in window will appear.

2. Click on the **auto button**. The Plug-In Automation dialog box will open.

3. Highlight the **effects parameters** you wish to automate.

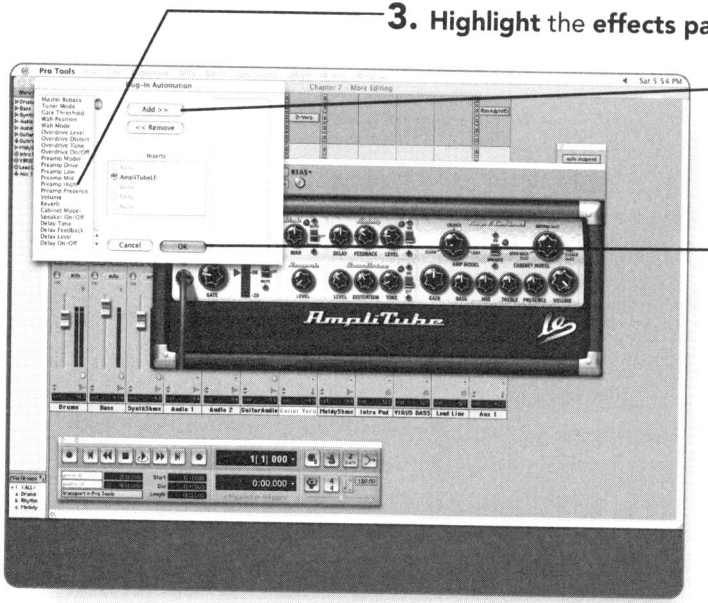

4. Click on the **Add button**. The selected parameters will be shown in the list to the right of the button.

5. When you're finished, **click** on **OK**. Your settings will be saved and the Plug-In Automation dialog box will close.

Method Two

1. Press and hold the **Control+Option+⌘** (Mac) or **Ctrl+Start** (PC) **keys** and **click** on the **parameter** you want to automate. A menu will appear.

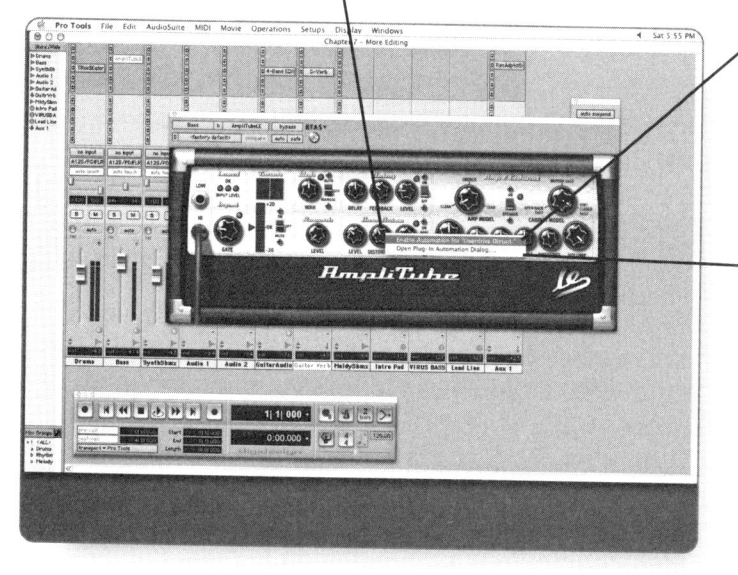

2a. Click on **Enable Automation for "parameter name."** The parameter will be ready to be automated.

OR

2b. Click on **Open Plug-in Automation Dialog**. The Plug-In Automation dialog box you saw in method one will open. At this point you can follow steps 3 through 5 from the "Method One" section.

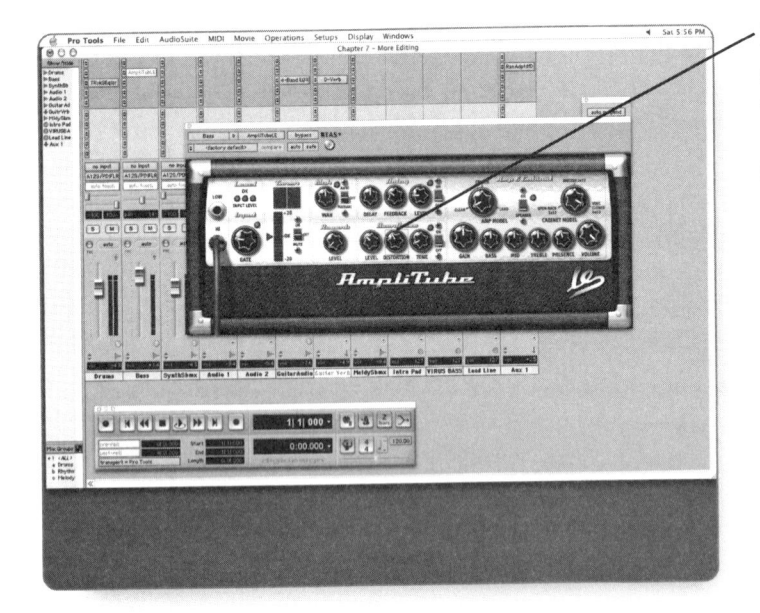

Parameters enabled for automation will be displayed with a colored box around them. In auto read mode, the box will be green; in any of the write modes, the box will be red.

Next stop . . . the mixdown!

9

Finishing Touches

Almost done! Now that you're at the threshold of finishing your first project, it's interesting to look back at all you've accomplished to get here, from setting up your system to recording, and then editing (and more editing) to mixing. Now you're at the stage of creating a deliverable product—good job! Okay, break's over.

Before you can truly consider a project finished, there's usually some tweaking to be done. Then, when you're satisfied with the mix, it's time to mix it down to a file or pair of files that you can actually listen to on something other than your Pro Tools rig, like a CD player. And last but absolutely not least, there's the business of archiving your files. In this chapter, you'll learn how to:

- Tweak your mix automation in the Edit window
- Use a master fader
- Bounce to disk in a CD-ready format
- Back up your session efficiently

More Fun with Automation

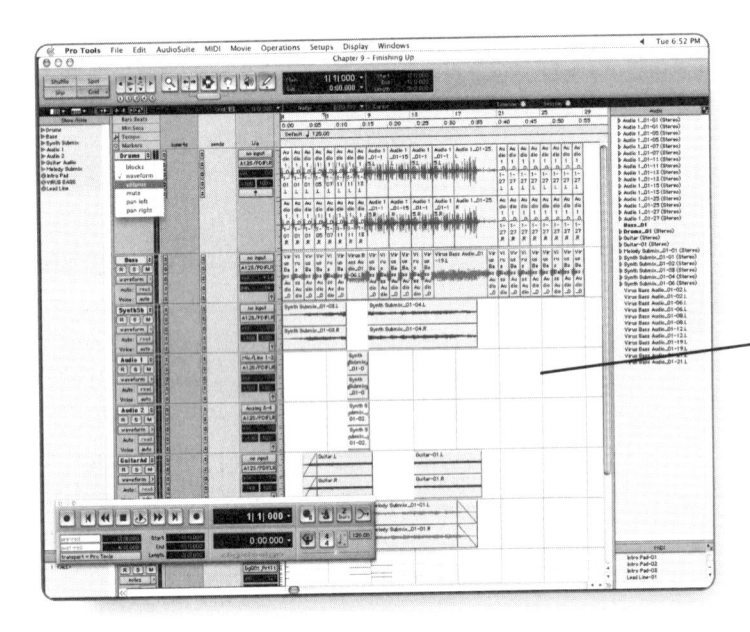

Creating mix automation by manipulating knobs, sliders, and faders with your mouse is a great feature, but it'll only take you so far. If you want to get really specific with your automation, sometimes the only place to do that is back in the Edit window.

1. If you're not already there, **go** to the **Edit window**. In this screen, you're looking at your regions, with waveform data inside. To edit your automation data, you have to see it first.

> **TIP**
>
> You can make a track a bit easier to view by increasing its height. To do this, click on the amplitude scale area (for audio tracks) or the keyboard area (for MIDI tracks) to the immediate left of the Track area. (You might remember that from way back in Chapter 2.)

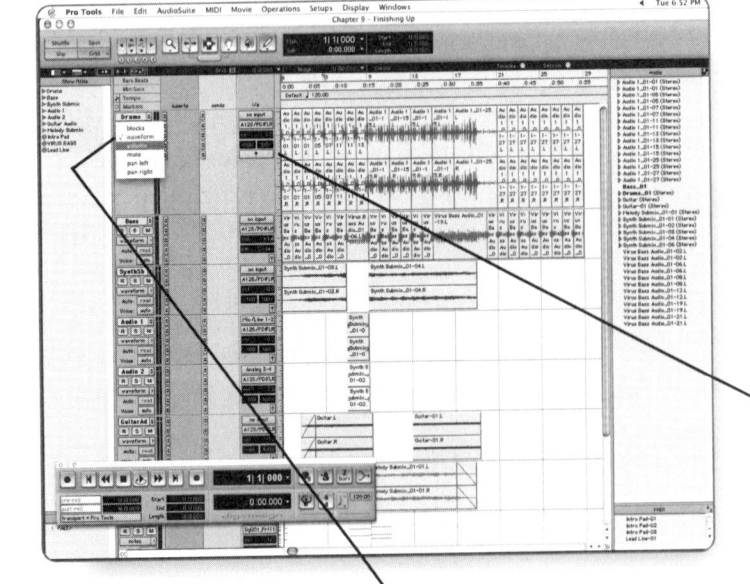

2. Click on the **track display format button**. A drop-down menu will appear, displaying available data that can be shown.

3. Click on the **data** you want to edit. (For this example, take a look at volume.) The volume data will appear.

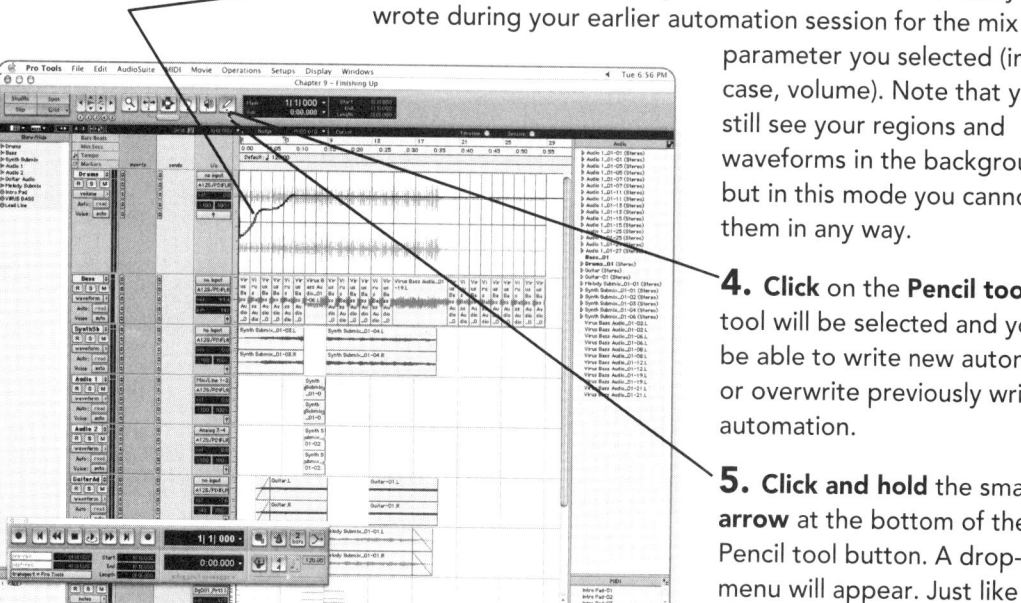

You can see a line that represents the movements that you wrote during your earlier automation session for the mix parameter you selected (in this case, volume). Note that you can still see your regions and waveforms in the background, but in this mode you cannot edit them in any way.

4. Click on the **Pencil tool**. The tool will be selected and you will be able to write new automation or overwrite previously written automation.

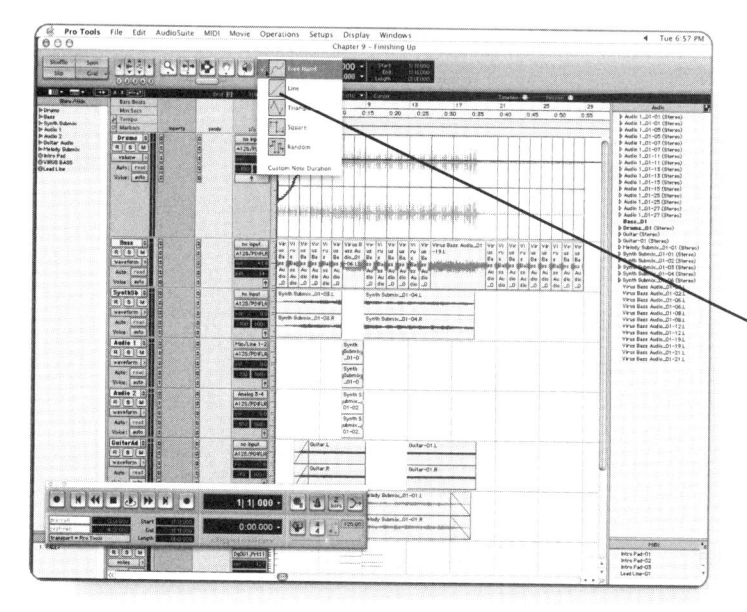

5. Click and hold the small **arrow** at the bottom of the Pencil tool button. A drop-down menu will appear. Just like the Trim and Grabber tools, the Pencil tool has some interesting options. For example, suppose you want to change this automation from the curve into a straight linear ramp (which, when you're looking at volume automation, would be a linear increase in volume). The best version of the Pencil tool to do this would be the Line option.

6. Click on the **option** you want to use. The option will be selected.

CHAPTER 9: FINISHING TOUCHES

7. Click and hold the **Pencil tool** at the point at which you want to begin writing new automation.

8. Drag the **mouse** to the right. The Pencil tool will progressively write new automation over what was previously written. In this case, a straight line will be drawn because the Line option for the Pencil tool was chosen.

9. Release the **mouse button**. Your new automation line will be written.

Of course, you can write more than just volume automation in a straight line. Go ahead and try some pan automation that ping-pongs from the left to the right side.

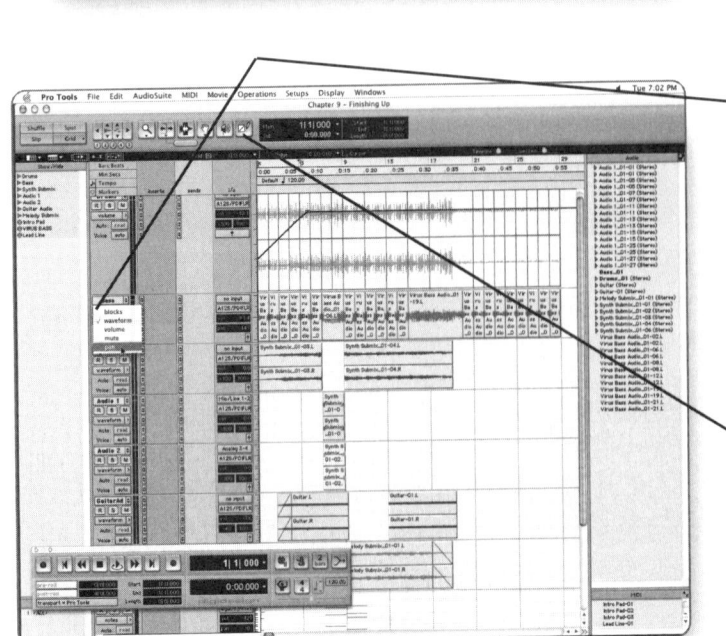

1. Click on the **track display format button** and **choose pan**. The pan data will appear as a line along your track, looking a lot like volume automation. With pan, though, you're not getting louder and softer as your curve moves higher and lower—you're panning from right to left.

2. Although you *could* draw a straight line from left to right over and over again, there's an easier way to do it. **Click and hold** the small **arrow** at the bottom of the Pencil tool button. A drop-down menu will appear.

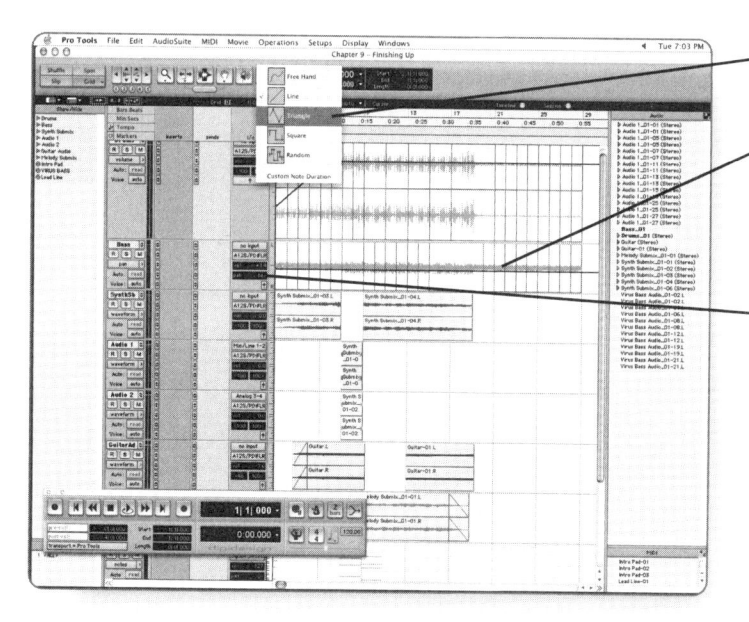

3. Click on the **Triangle option**. The option will be selected.

Note that the pan automation line is flat. This means that there is no panning change over time on this track.

Also notice that the line is a bit below the center of the track. With pan automation, that means that the pan position is a bit off center as well. If you look at the pan value display to the left of the track, you can see by how much the pan position is off center—14 (out of a possible 100) to the right.

4. When you're dealing with the Triangle, Square, or Random Pencil options, the grid setting will determine the frequency of the curve (even if you're not in Grid mode). In this case, you want to pan from side to side every measure, so **choose 1 bar** as your grid value.

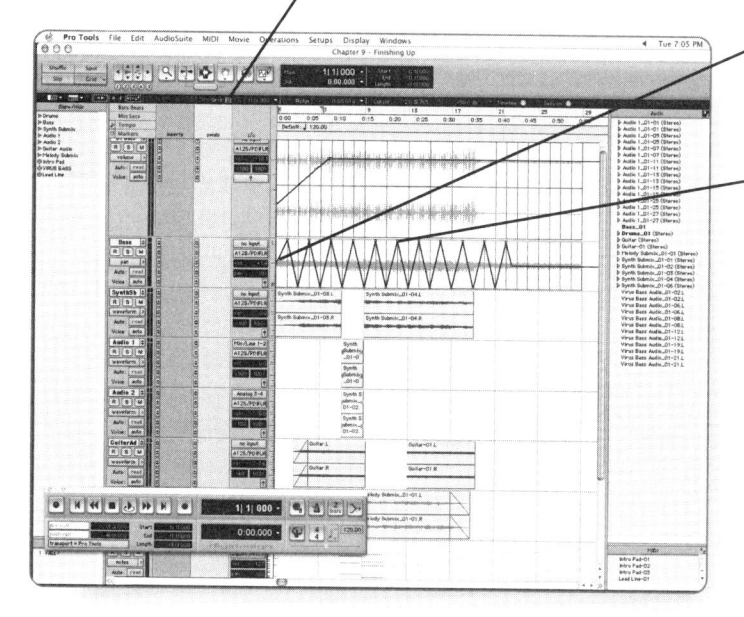

5. Click and hold the **Pencil tool** at the point at which you want to begin writing automation.

This time, as you drag to the right, a triangle wave will be drawn across the track. The frequency of your panning will be one measure, as set up in your grid value. The severity of the ping-pong is determined by your cursor's height in the track. In the case of pan automation, a higher and lower triangle wave will translate into a more extreme pan from left to right.

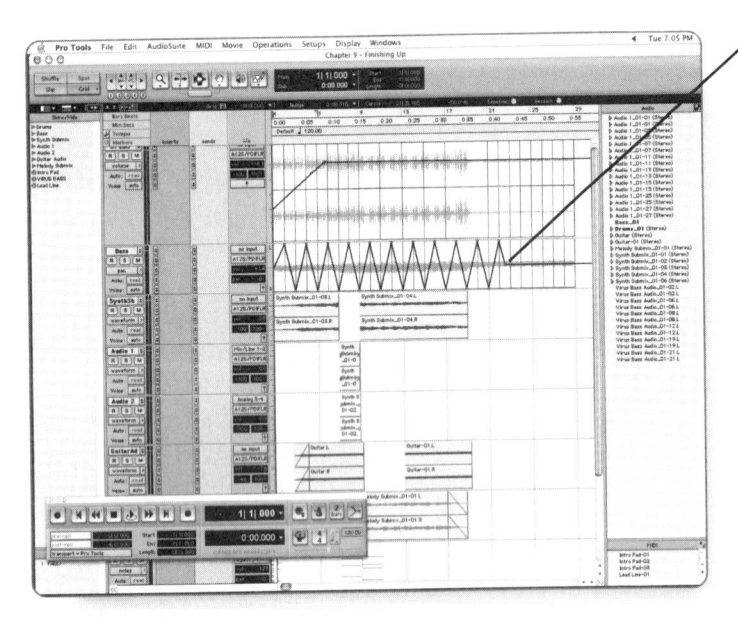

6. When you're finished, **release** the **mouse button**. The pan automation will be written to your track.

> **NOTE**
> Although the triangle wave will change based upon the grid value in any mode, if you want the apex of the triangle wave to fall on a grid line, you must be in Grid mode.

Copying and Pasting Automation

Once you've got a segment of automation that you like, you can cut and paste that automation from one location to another. It's easy!

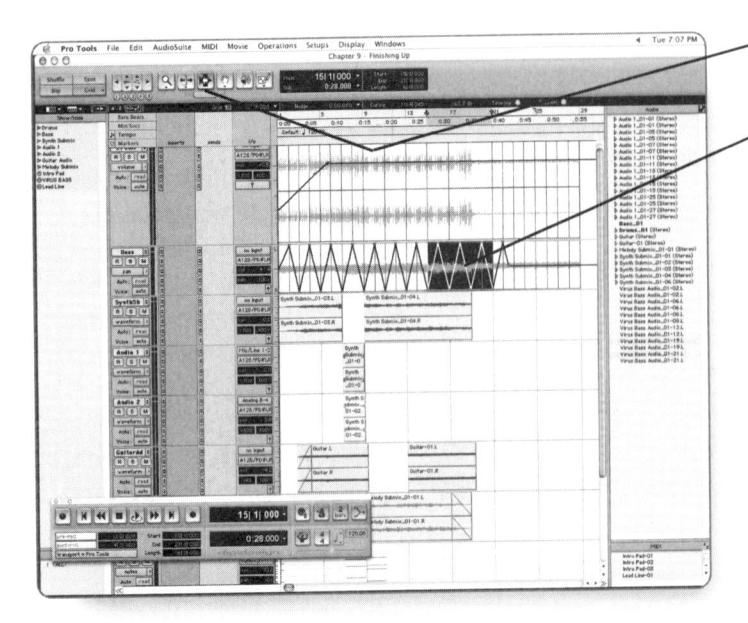

1. Click on the **Selector tool**. The tool will be selected.

2. Select the **area of automation** that you want to copy, just as if you were selecting a segment of audio. The area will be selected.

3. Click on the **Edit menu** and **choose** any of the **basic editing functions** (such as cut, copy, paste, or duplicate) you've used before.

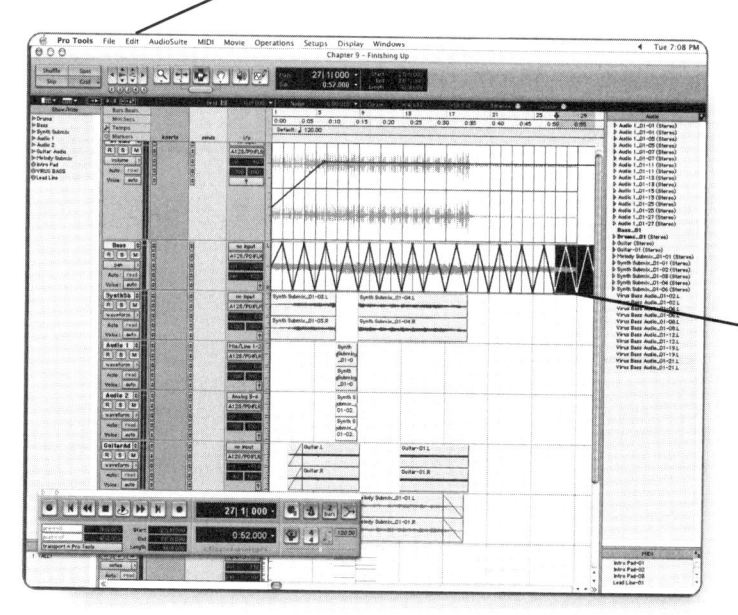

> **TIP**
> Remember, you can use the regular shortcut keys instead of clicking on the Edit menu.

After you perform the editing functions, you'll be able to see that the automation curve has been edited. One thing to keep in mind, though: Any edits you do for a specific automation parameter (pan, for example) will not affect any audio or any other automation parameters; they will only affect the parameter you're looking at right now.

> **NOTE**
> One thing to keep in mind when you work with moving regions: When you move (or copy) a region in the Edit window, all the automation associated with that region will also be moved (or copied), even though that automation is not visible at the time.

Using Master Faders

There's one kind of track I haven't touched on yet, called a *master fader*. Although it looks similar to an audio track, its function is substantially different than anything you've seen up to this point.

A master fader is a way to control output. This output can be the signal of a bus, in the case of complex mixing, but most commonly, a master fader is used to control the output of an interface. With this simple but powerful track, you can control the level of your session globally. The following sections will show you how a master fader works.

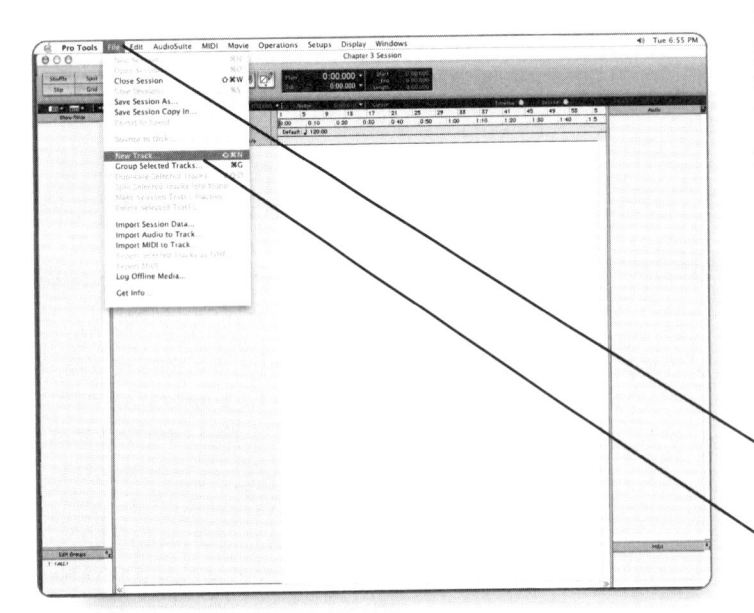

Creating a Master Fader

First things first . . . you need to create a master fader.

1. Click on **File**. The File menu will appear.

2. Click on **New Track**. The New Track dialog box will open.

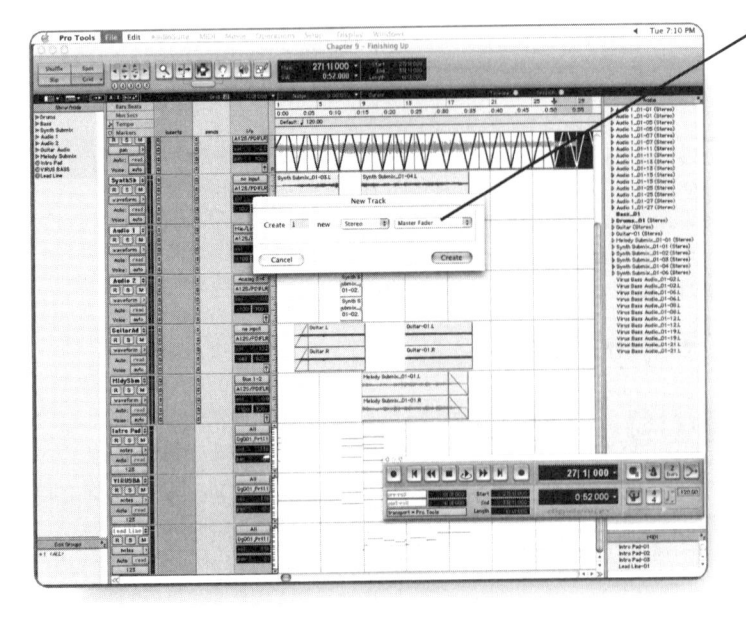

3. Create a **stereo master fader**. The new master fader will be created below the currently selected track. The master fader looks similar to any other track, but don't be fooled—it's significantly different!

USING MASTER FADERS 299

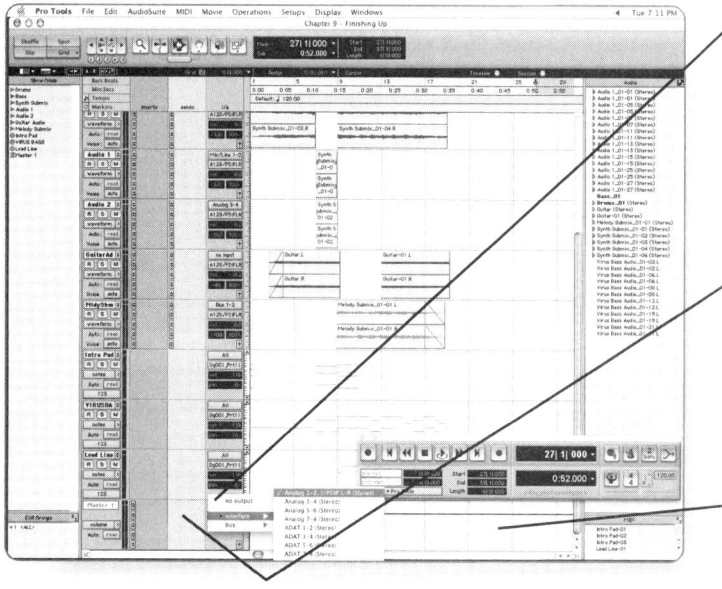

- You'll notice that the position on the track that would normally display an input button is conspicuously blank. That's because there is no input on a master fader; it is only a way to control an output.

- Notice also that there is no send on a master fader. That's because a master fader is a last step in the signal path, so there's nowhere to send a signal to.

- You cannot place regions on this track (similar to an aux track).

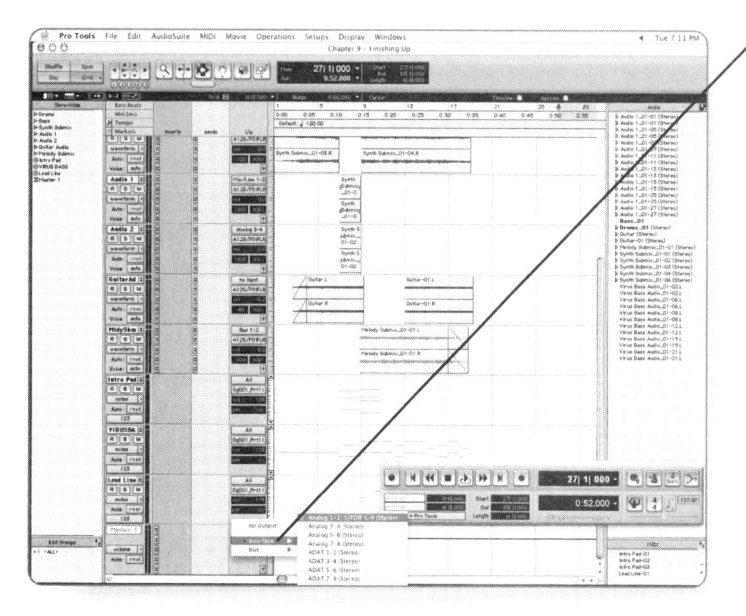

4. Click on the **output button** and **select** the **interface output** you are using to listen to your mix. The interface output will be selected.

Controlling Your Mix with a Master Fader

Now you can use your master fader to control your entire mix. For example, the following steps will show you how to create a fade-out for your entire mix in one easy process.

1. Select the **Pencil tool** and **choose** the **Line option** to create a straight fade-out. The option will be selected.

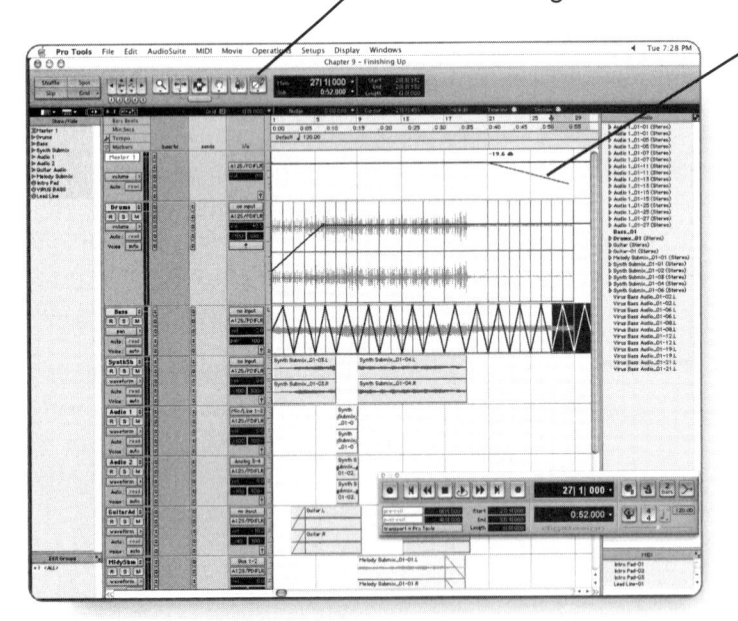

2. Write the **automation** on the track as if you were editing pre-written automation. You'll hear a linear change in the volume of your entire mix, starting at the point at which the master fader's automation begins.

> **NOTE**
>
> If you want to write automation onto your master fader in the Mix window, it's no problem. Simply write automation (in any of the automation modes) just as you would on any other type of a track!

Basic Mastering Techniques Using a Master Fader

Mastering is a post-mix process that further refines a mix to a professional quality. It is such an exclusive and important process that there is an entire segment of the professional audio community dedicated to the specific task of mastering others' mixes. That being said, the task of professionally mastering a mix is certainly not recommended for the non-specialist.

You might, however, want to try your hand at a little basic mastering to punch up your mix for your own enjoyment or to make an evaluation mix a little more palatable for your client. That's where master faders really shine. You see, there's another interesting difference between a master fader and any other track—one that might not be initially apparent. This difference is in the area of signal flow, making the track more functional as a mastering device. The inserts are *after* the fader in the signal chain. Read on. . . .

> **NOTE**
> The discussion in this section relates to mastering a mix in your own studio (as opposed to having your mix professionally mastered). If or when you decide to have your mix professionally mastered, the mastering engineer will want to do this job himself, usually with highly specialized (and costly) gear specific to the process of mastering. It's always a good idea to consult your mastering engineer before submitting your mix, so you can find out what they want from a mix.

Adjusting Dither

Dither is a common mastering tool used to offset some of the negative sonic qualities of digital audio. In simple terms, it is a very low-level noise that may be added to your digital audio to combat distortion introduced in the signal when the bit depth is reduced. For example, if you're working in a 24-bit session but you will be creating a 16-bit file for an audio CD, you can greatly improve the quality of your audio by applying a dither plug-in on a master fader.

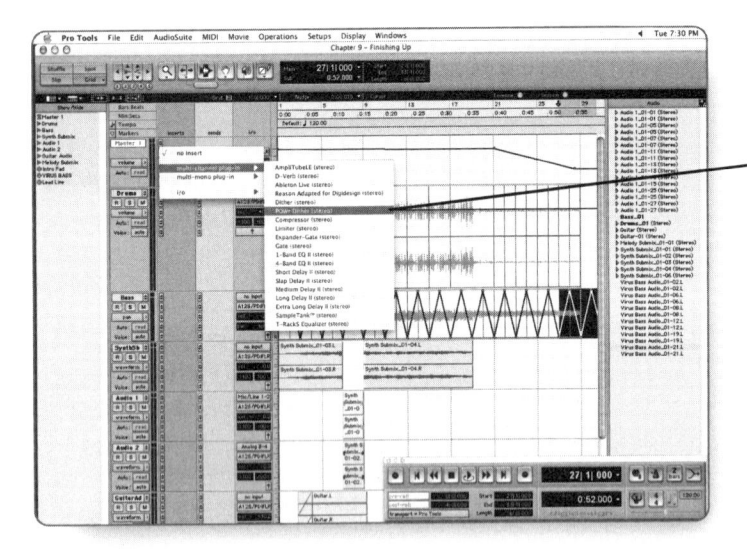

You can adjust the dither for your master fader by following these steps.

1. On the master fader's insert, **select** the **POWr Dither (stereo) option** from the multi-channel plug-in menu. The POWr Dither window will appear.

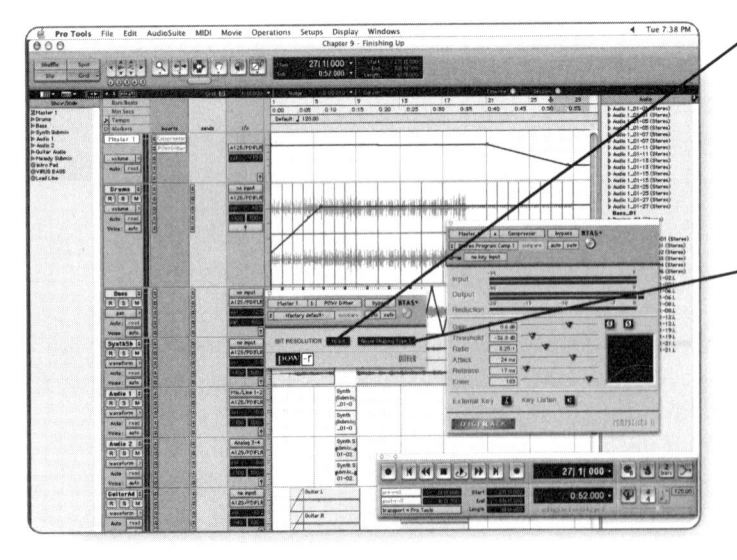

2. Click on the **Bit Resolution button** and **choose** the **final resolution** of your mix. For example, if you want to make an audio CD of the mix, you would choose the 16 bit option.

3. Noise shaping will help make the dither noise less audible. **Select** a **noise shaping option**. (For now, you can stick with the default shaping, but be sure to listen to different mixes with different noise shaping later.) The option will be selected.

Punching Up Your Mix with Compression

Another common process in mastering is compression. Applying compression to a mix is a tried-and-true method employed to narrow the music's dynamic range, thereby maximizing the overall power of the audio. Give it a try in the following steps.

1. On your master fader, **instantiate** a **compressor plug-in** on an insert before (above) the one you used for dither. The Compressor plug-in window will appear.

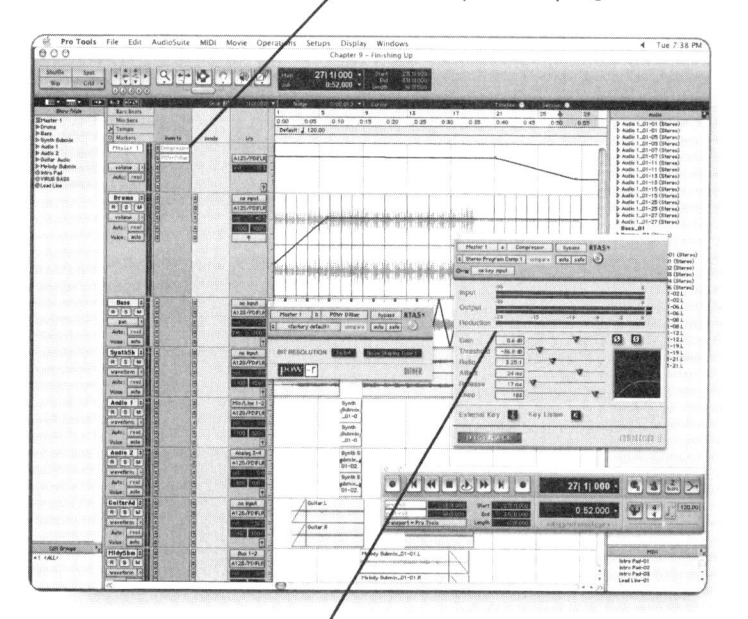

> **NOTE**
>
> If you're using dither *and* a compressor on a master fader, you'll want to arrange your inserts so that the dither is the last plug-in (on the lowest insert). Don't worry if your dither is on the top insert; you can just drag it down to a lower (and later in the insert's signal path) insert with your mouse and then create your compressor above it.

2. Adjust your compressor's **parameters** to punch up your mix to suit your taste. It'll take some experimentation to find your ideal settings, of course. You can start with a preset configuration specifically for mastering a mix, like the one shown in this example.

> **TIP**
>
> As mentioned on page 301, a defining characteristic of a master fader is that the inserts are post-fader. While this is great when applying dither to a mix, it is not always the best track to use for compression. For example, if you have a fade in or a fade out in your song, the compressor might behave inconsistently (any levels that are lower than your threshold won't be affected). The solution? Simply put the compressor on an aux input track and route your entire mix to it using a bus. Then assign the output of that aux track to another bus, and make that bus the input of the master fader (where the dither resides). Do your fade-ins/fade-outs on the master fader. That way, your mix will retain that compressed sound even when the overall volume levels are low!

Bouncing to Disk

When you're working in a Pro Tools session, you're in a multitrack environment. Even though you're listening through stereo monitor speakers, you're hearing many component tracks, artfully mixed together by Pro Tools' software mix engine. From a production standpoint, it's a pretty cool way to work, but if you ever want to hear your song outside of the Pro Tools environment, you'll have to somehow render the mix down to a format that is compatible with the outside world.

The Bounce to Disk function is the right tool for this job. It will mix down your session as it plays in real time and create a new audio file of your entire mix. It's a simple process, but one that demands attention to detail to be done just right, so I'll go over all the steps carefully. For example, here's how to go about bouncing to disk so you can burn an audio CD (red book format) of your entire mix.

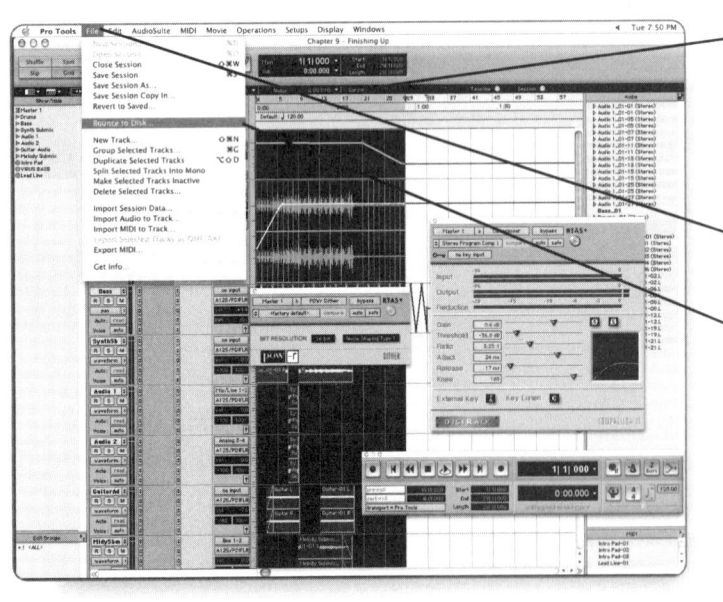

1. Using the Selector tool in the Rulers area, **select** the **area** of the session you want to bounce to disk. The area will be selected.

2. Click on **File**. The File menu will appear.

3. Click on **Bounce to Disk**. The Bounce dialog box will open.

BOUNCING TO DISK 305

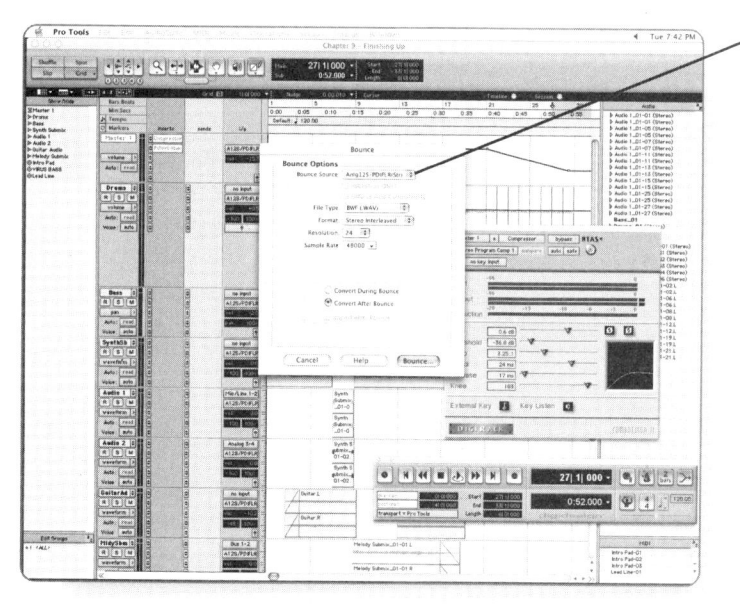

4. Select the **output** you are using to listen to this mix from the Bounce Source menu. This is perhaps the most important step in this process.

> **TIP**
>
> If you bounce to disk and then later find that your bounce is a silent audio file, you probably chose the wrong bounce source.

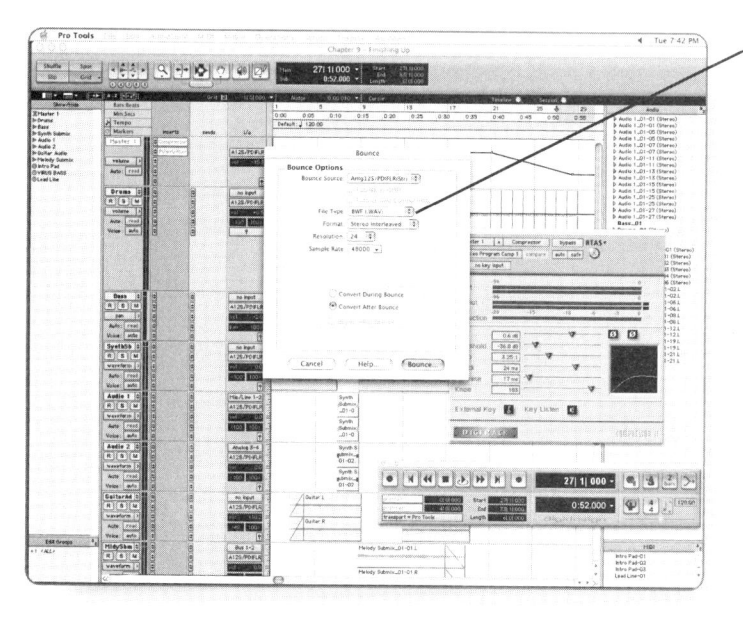

5. Click on the **File Type arrow**. The File Type menu will appear, displaying a list of available formats for your mixdown.

306 CHAPTER 9: FINISHING TOUCHES

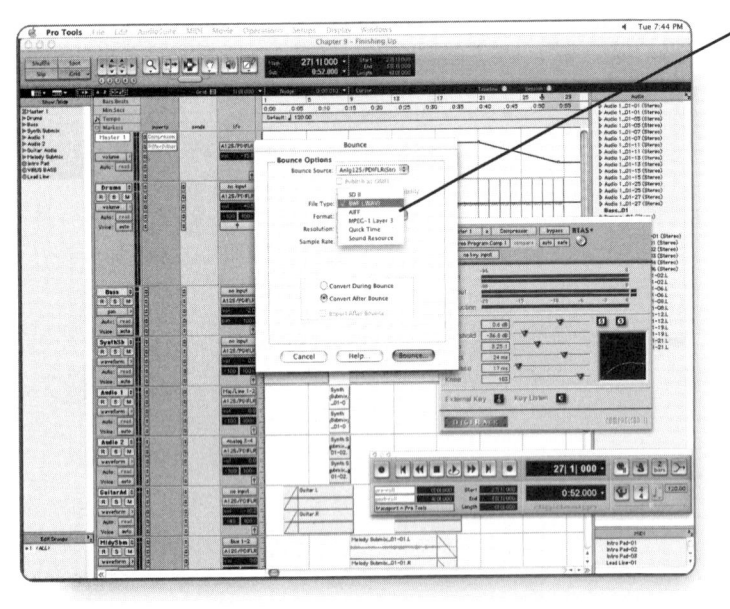

6. Choose the **file type** that suits your needs. The first three formats involve no data reduction, so they're well suited for tasks such as production or CD burning. The last three formats offer data reduction, which results in smaller file sizes.

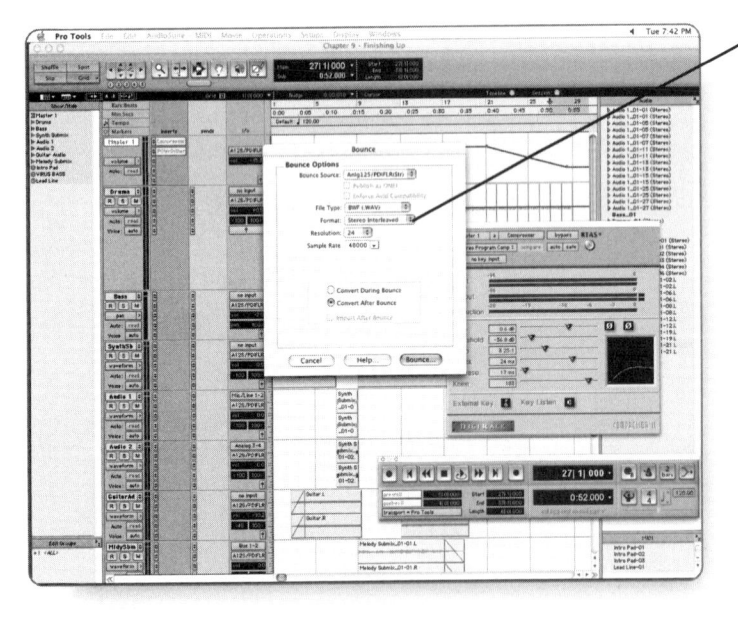

7. Click on the **Format arrow**. The Format menu will appear.

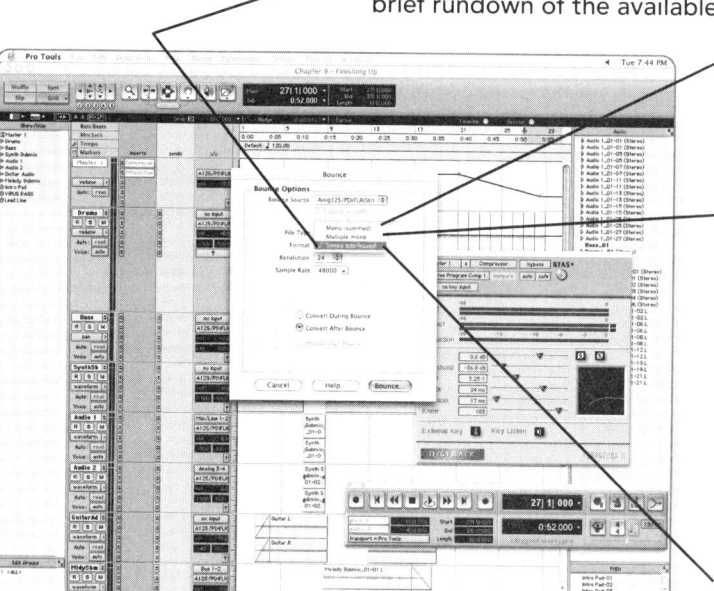

8. **Select** the **file format** that suits your purposes. Here's a brief rundown of the available formats:

- **Mono (summed).** With this option, your mix, even if it is stereo, will be mixed down to a single mono file.

- **Multiple mono.** With this option, your mix will be output to a pair of mono files—one for the left side (with an ".l" after the file name) and one for the right (with an ".r" after the file name). This is particularly useful for bounces that you intend to use in future Pro Tools sessions.

- **Stereo Interleaved.** Use this option for tracks destined for CD burning. Your mix will be rendered to a single stereo file.

9. Click on the **Resolution arrow**. The Resolution menu will appear, displaying the bit depths to which you can bounce.

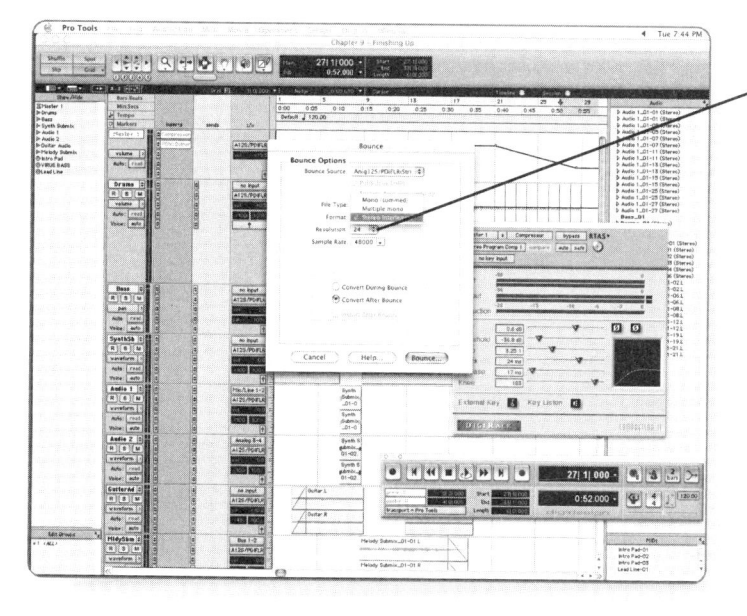

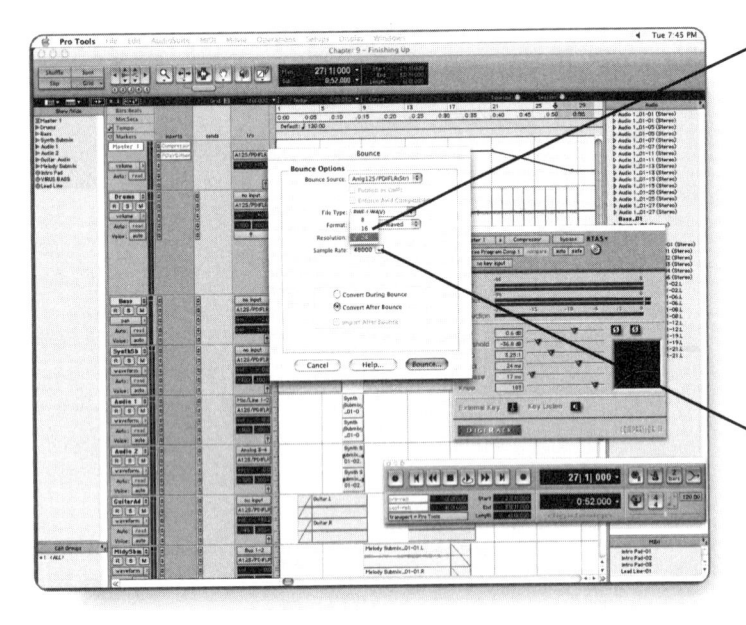

10. Select the **bit depth** you want your bounced file to be. The bit depth will be selected.

> **NOTE**
> For the purposes of CD burning, the bit depth must be 16.

11. Click on the **Sample Rate arrow**. The Sample Rate menu will appear, from which you can choose your bounce's sample rate.

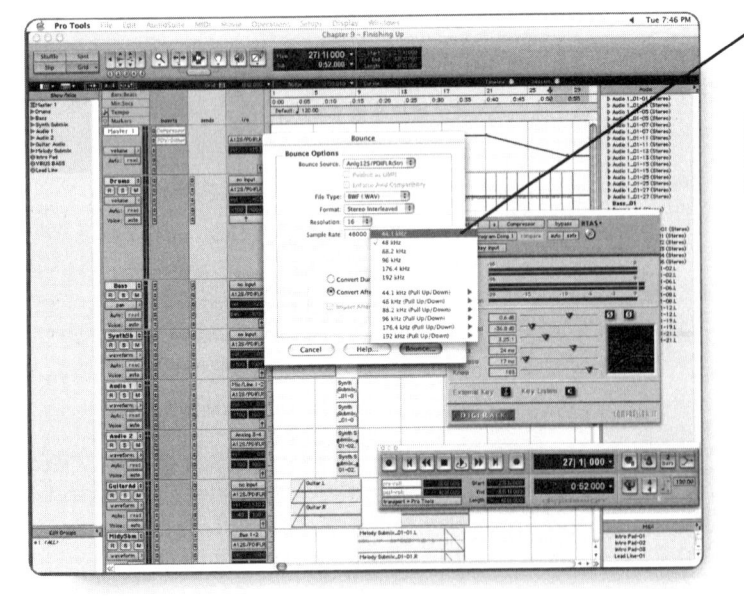

12. Click on the desired **sample rate** for your mix.

> **NOTE**
> For CD burning, the sample rate for your bounced file must be 44.1 kHz.

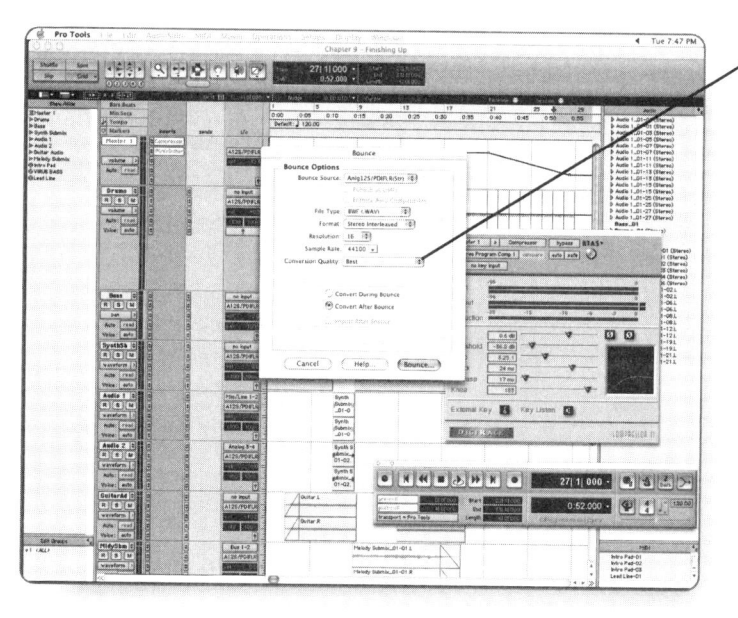

13. If the sample rate or bit depth you've chosen for your bounce file are different from those of your session, you will need to convert the bounce file. **Click** on the **Conversion Quality arrow**. The Conversion Quality menu will appear.

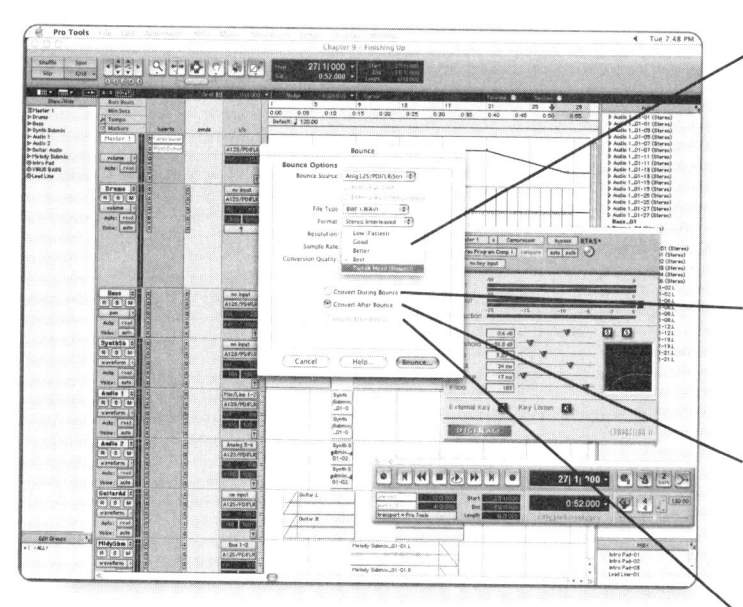

14. Choose a **conversion quality** (if conversion is necessary). The conversion quality will be selected.

15. If you need to convert, you have a few options:

- **Convert During Bounce.** This option allows you to convert during the bounce process (as your session plays).

- **Convert After Bounce.** This option allows you to convert after your bounce pass is completed.

- **Import After Bounce.** This option allows you to import your bounced file back into your session on an audio track.

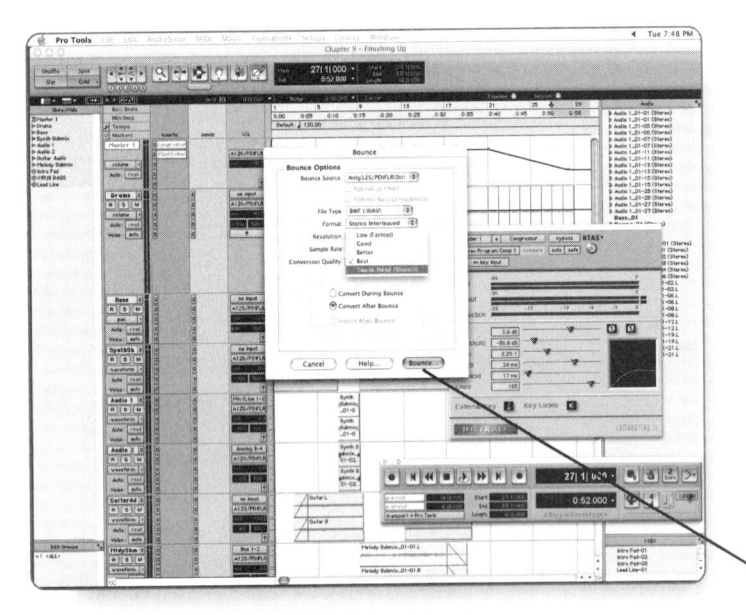

> **TIP**
>
> In some cases, the Convert During Bounce option can cause Pro Tools to not play back some types of automation (as a result of the extra burden of conversion while bouncing). For consistently good results, choose the Convert After Bounce option; it really won't take too long.

16. Click on **Bounce**. The Save dialog box will open.

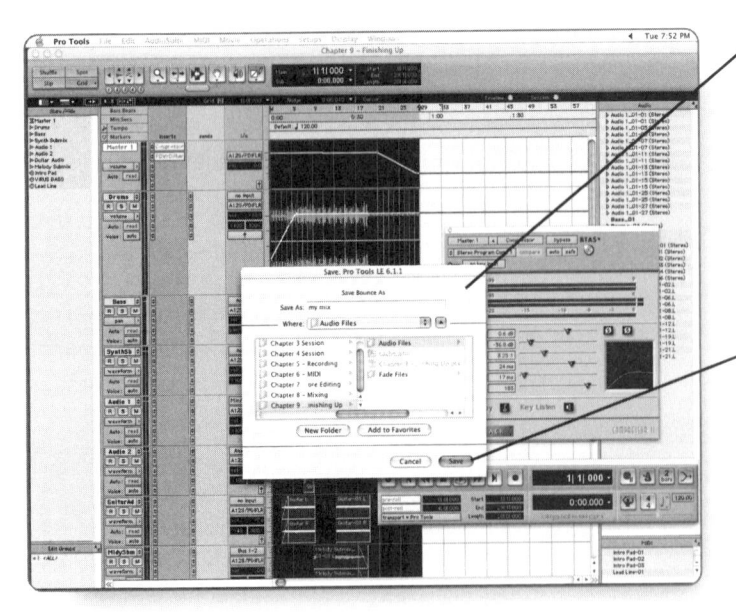

17. Save your **file** using the options in the Save dialog box. You can save your file under any name you want, in any drive and in any folder. For the purposes of illustration, I'll stick with the default location, which is within the session's Audio Files folder.

18. Click on **Save**. Your bounce will begin.

BOUNCING TO DISK 311

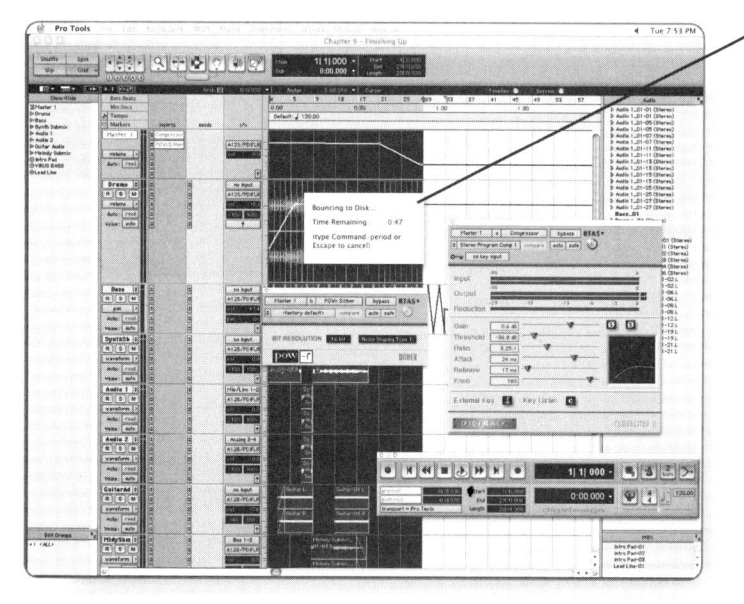

Your session will begin playing, and a small countdown window will indicate that bouncing is occurring.

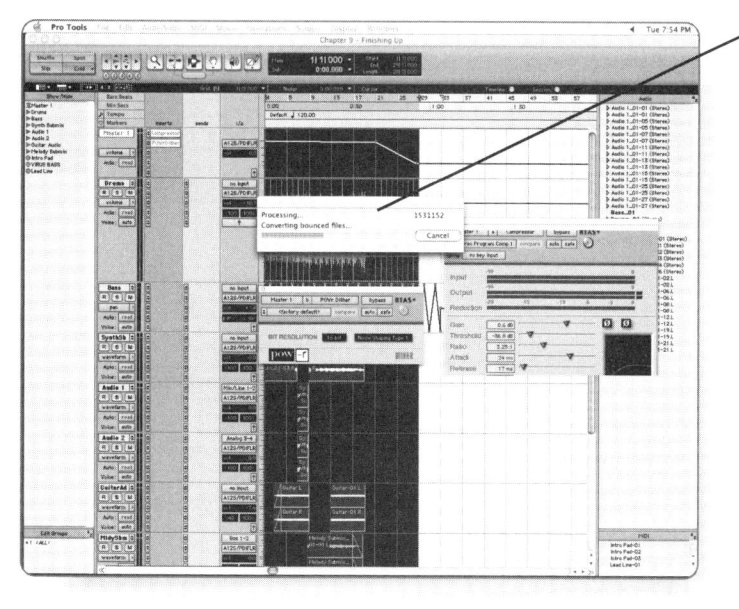

If conversion is necessary (and assuming you chose to convert *after* bounce), you'll see a quick conversion process after your session finishes the bounce.

Here's an example of what you'll end up with. It's important to know exactly where your files are created. If you followed the default location, your bounced file will be:

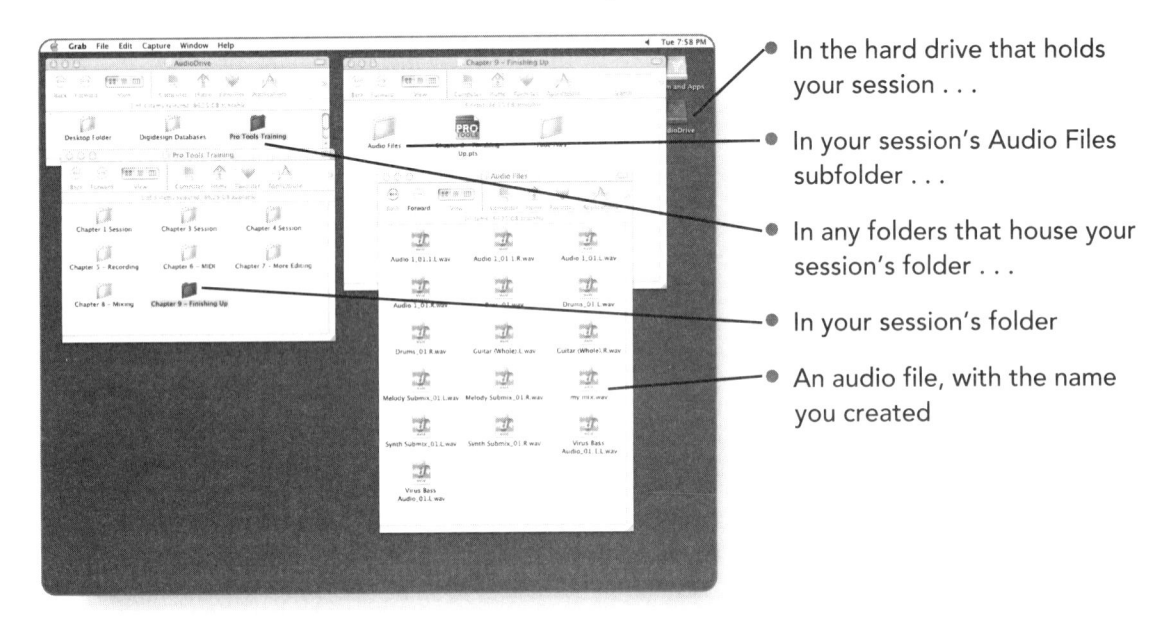

- In the hard drive that holds your session . . .
- In your session's Audio Files subfolder . . .
- In any folders that house your session's folder . . .
- In your session's folder
- An audio file, with the name you created

> **NOTE**
>
> As you can see, your bounced file can get hidden quite well beneath layers of folders on any number of drives. The point I want to emphasize is that it is extremely important to know exactly where and under what name your files are saved. (This goes for session files and other audio files as well.) You can save your bounced file anywhere you choose in your system, but with this great flexibility comes the added responsibility of using this power wisely.

Backing Up Your Files

Now that you've bounced your mix and your project is finished, you might want to start thinking about archiving your work. This means taking what you've learned so far about file management to the next level of organization and efficiency.

Clearing Unused Regions

In the course of production, it's pretty common to end up with regions that you aren't using on any of your tracks in your Audio Regions list. Although unused regions occupying space in the Audio Regions list doesn't adversely affect your session's performance, it can present organizational problems and take up space on your audio hard drive.

At the end of a project, when it's time to back up your session once and for all, it is a good idea to get rid of unused regions in your session. The following steps will show you how.

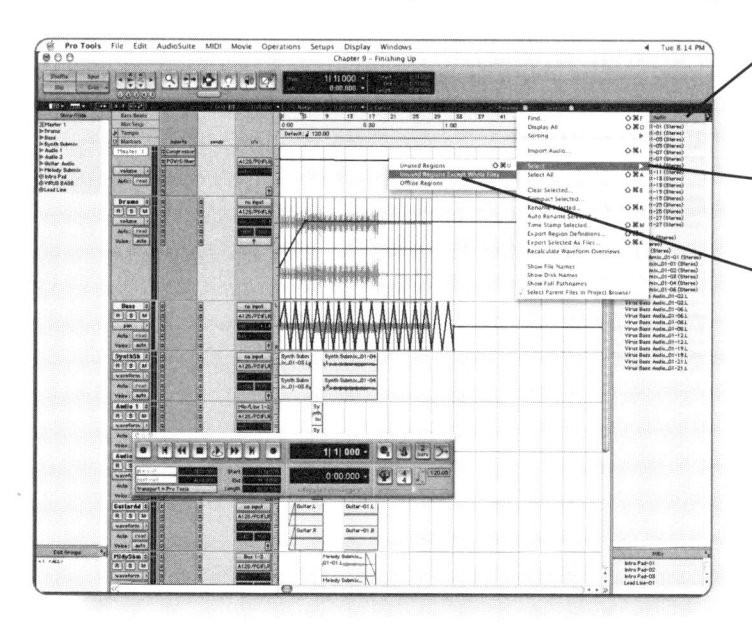

1. Click on the **Audio button** at the top of the Audio Regions list. The Audio menu will appear.

2. Click on **Select**. The Select submenu will appear.

3. Choose the kind of **regions** you will eventually clear out of your system. The option will be selected.

CAUTION

Be careful of the Unused Regions option. In this mode, if a whole file region is not being used, it will be selected and it might be deleted. If you delete an audio file from your hard drive and there are other Pro Tools sessions that refer to it, they will appear as empty offline regions, and they will make no sound. If you want to make sure you don't lose any valuable audio files, choose the Unused Regions Except Whole Files option.

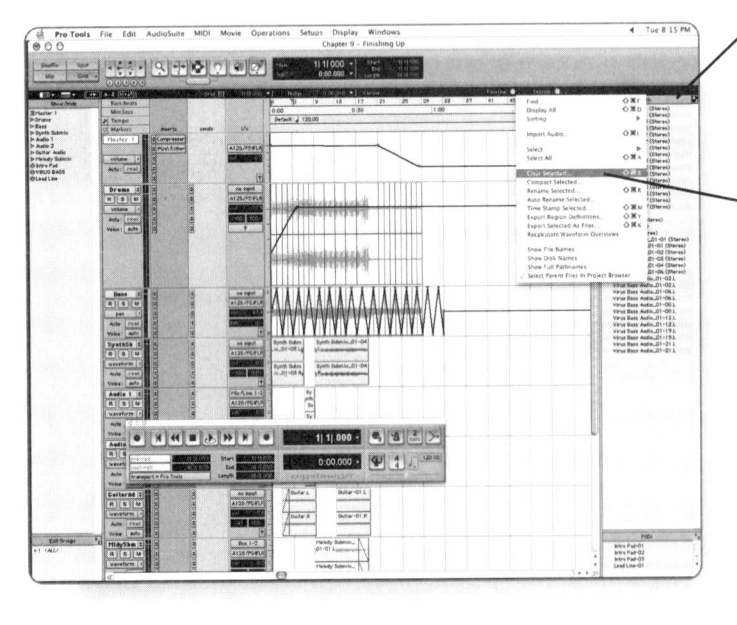

4. Click on the **Audio button** at the top of the Audio Regions list again. The Audio menu will appear.

5. Click on **Clear Selected**. The Clear Audio dialog box will open.

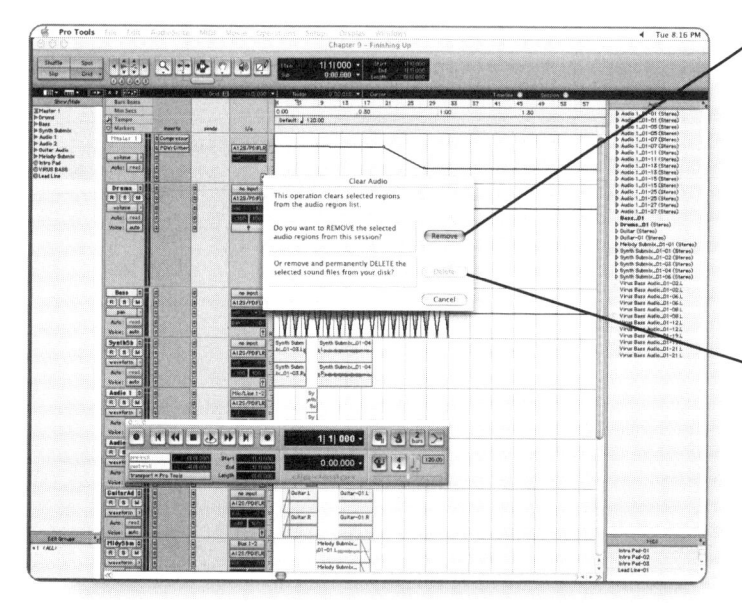

6a. Click on the **Remove button** to clear the regions from your Audio Regions list but leave any audio files on your hard drive. The regions will be removed from your Audio Regions list.

OR

6b. Click on the **Delete button** to clear regions from your session and remove selected audio files from your hard drive. This deletion is permanent and cannot be undone. This option is only available when whole file regions are selected to be cleared.

Compacting Your Session

Although clearing unused regions can certainly save space on your storage medium, there might still be unused sections within audio files used in your session. Compacting your session will minimize this wasted space.

CHAPTER 9: FINISHING TOUCHES

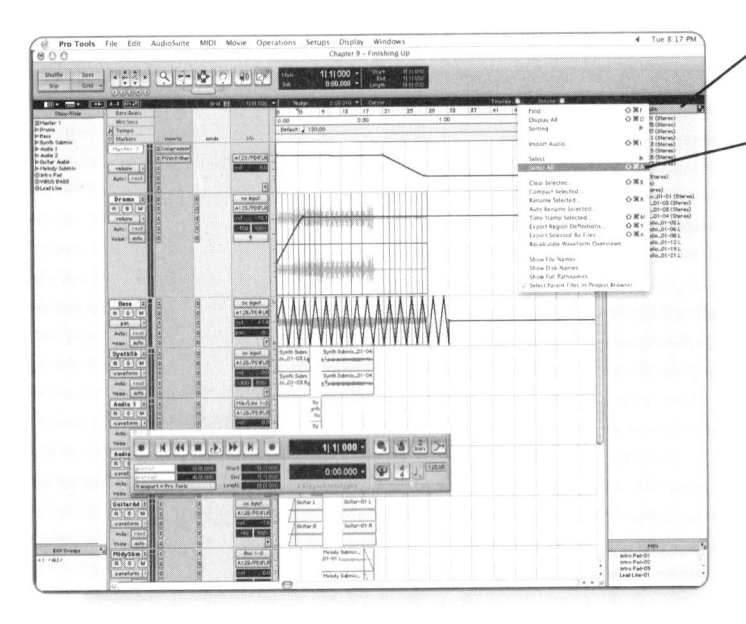

1. Click on the **Audio button**. The Audio menu will appear.

2. Click on **Select All**. All regions will be highlighted.

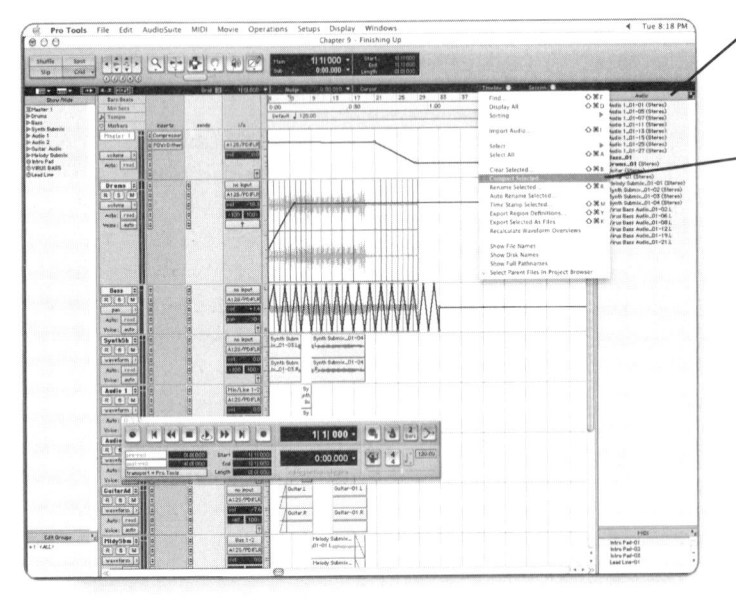

3. Click on the **Audio button** again. The Audio menu will appear.

4. Click on **Compact Selected**. The Compact dialog box will open.

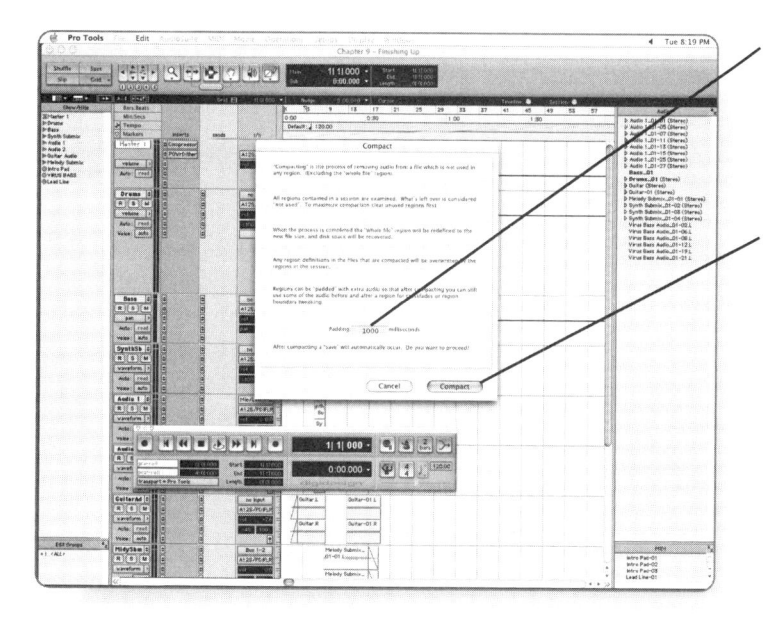

This dialog box is pretty descriptive. At this point, all you have to worry about is the amount of padding you want to use in the compaction process.

5. Click on **Compact**. Your session will be compacted.

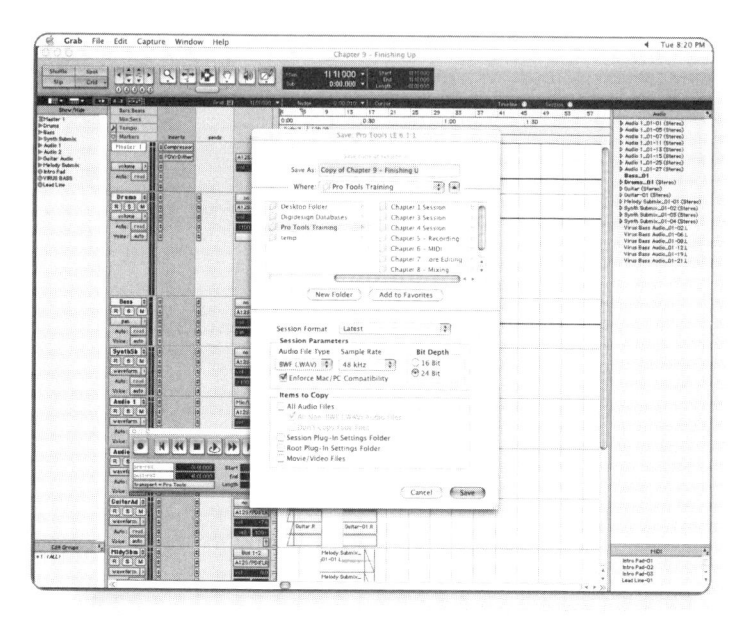

The last step in the process of good archiving practice is to use the Save Session Copy In function you learned about in Chapter 4. This will ensure that all the dependent elements of your session, regardless of where they might be hidden in your system, can be saved in one central session folder. Only one new thing to remember: Unless your bounced mix file is imported in your session, it won't be included in the Save Session Copy In process. (You'll have to save it manually.)

> **CAUTION**
>
> I know I said it before in this chapter, but it really bears mentioning one more time. The last two points I talked about, clearing and compacting, can be destructive processes, giving you the option of deleting audio files with the Unused Regions function and certainly deleting unused audio with the Compact Selected feature. Especially after you have put so much work into a session, you should take special consideration before you do anything that can't be undone.
>
> You might consider doing a Save Session Copy In before clearing and compacting your session. That way, you can do your clear and compact, and then play your session again to make sure you haven't deleted anything you need for your session to run. That way, even if you do happen to delete a necessary region, you can always go back to the original session file and start from scratch again. Once you've determined that everything works the way you want it to, you can then delete the original session and archive the copy you saved.
>
> Another consideration (and this is the way I prefer to work): Try not to permanently delete anything if you can help it. Of course it will consume extra space, but at least you'll be sure to have all of your session's elements intact. Also, you'll retain the option of importing any unused elements into other tracks. I try to live by Andy's Law (closely related to Murphy's Law): The moment you delete something, you'll need it!

That's it! Now, burn a data CD of your newly saved session, burn an audio CD of your mix, and enjoy—you've earned it!

10

Moving to the Next Level: Tips and Tricks

Pro Tools is a complex, professional application, and mastering it is a lifelong pursuit for industry professionals. This book is meant to provide you with a solid basic understanding of how to use this powerful product—a strong foundation upon which to build greater knowledge over time. The good news is that by mastering the previous chapters, you've attained that basic understanding.

Now, here's a laundry list of next-level functions, designed to allow you to be even more productive! In this chapter, you'll learn how to:

- Work more efficiently in the Edit and Mix windows
- Import and use movie files
- Boost your session's efficiency

Making the Most of Editing

The following sections detail processes that will make your editing even more efficient and fun!

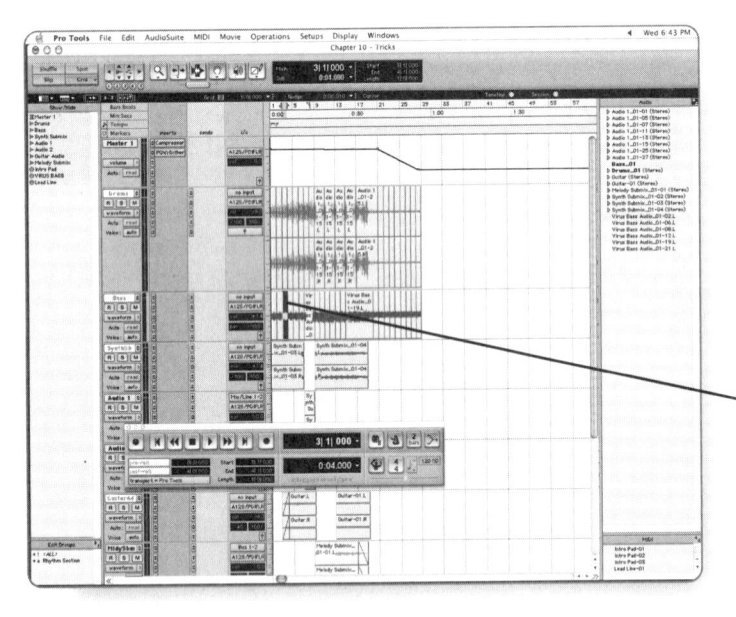

Zoom Toggle

Here's a cool little trick that will allow you to toggle between two zoom settings quickly. This is particularly useful when you're working with a specific selection, then zooming out to see your selection in the context of the rest of your session.

1. Make a **selection** in the Edit window.

2. Press Control+E (Mac) or ⊞+**E** (PC). Your selection will zoom in to fill the Edit window.

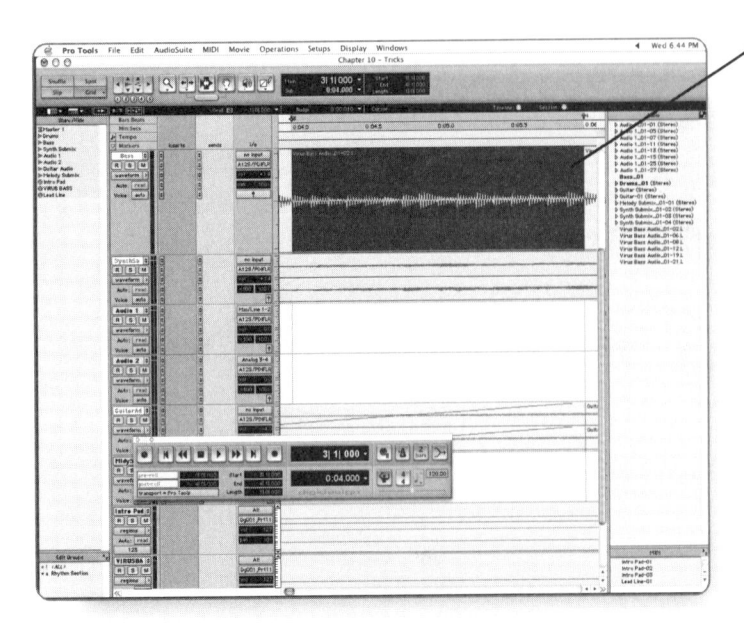

3. Press Control+E (Mac) or **Start+E** (PC). You will be toggled back to the previous zoom level.

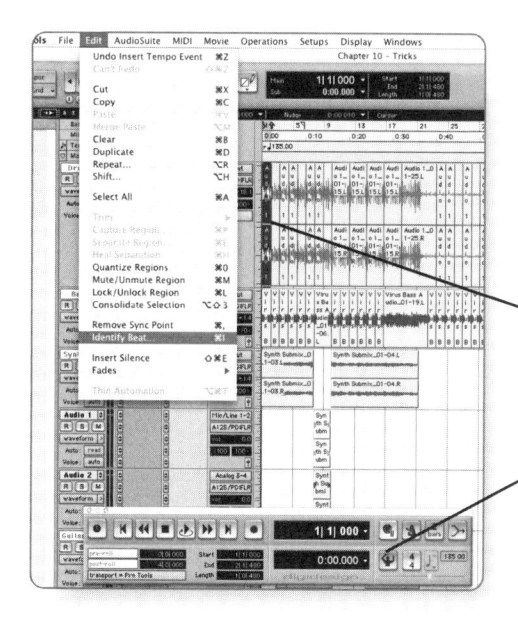

The Identify Beat Function

One of Pro Tools' greatest strengths is its ability to use MIDI and audio in the same environment. Before they'll work together, though, their tempos must agree. You can use the Identify Beat function to tell Pro Tools the tempo of your audio!

1. Make a **selection** of a specific musical length. (In this case, it's a measure that loops perfectly.) Use your ears to make this loopable selection—*not* your MIDI tempo or session grid.

2. Select the **Conductor icon** if it isn't already lit. The icon will be selected.

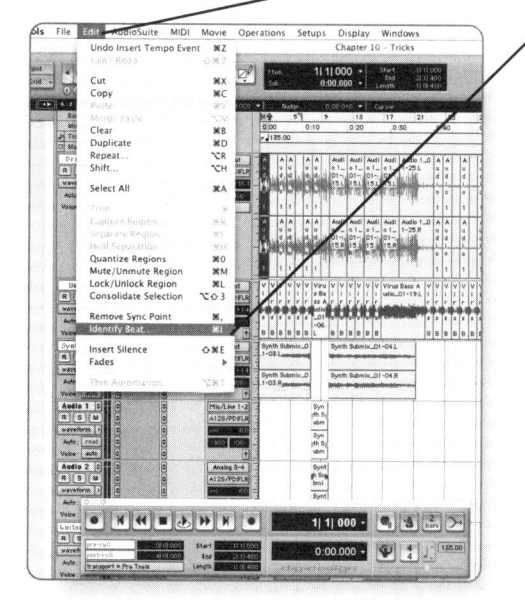

3. Click on **Edit**. The Edit menu will appear.

4. Click on **Identify Beat**. The Bar | Beat Markers dialog box will open.

CHAPTER 10: MOVING TO THE NEXT LEVEL: TIPS AND TRICKS

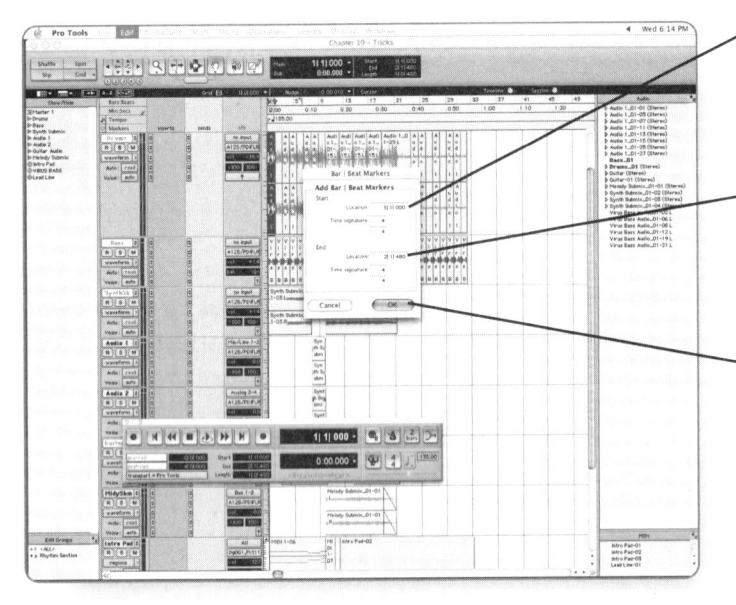

5. **Type** the **location** that your ears tell you is the beginning of the selection in the Location text box in the Start area.

6. **Type** the **location** that your ears tell you is the end of the selection in the Location text box in the End area.

7. **Click** on **OK**.

The Bar | Beat Markers dialog box will close and your tempo will change to match your audio.

> **TIP**
>
> You can use the Identify Beat function at any point in a session. For example, if you have a live drummer who gets a little faster during the chorus, just select the chorus and enter your loopable selection in the Bar | Beat Markers dialog box.

Relative Grid Mode

New with Pro Tools 6! In the normal Absolute Grid mode, you made regions snap to grid lines. If your grid resolution was set to 1 bar, for example, regions (and MIDI notes) snapped to the nearest bar. Relative Grid mode, on the other hand, will move the object not to the nearest grid, but by the selected grid resolution. For example, if you have a grid resolution of 1 bar, and a region is off the grid by, say, 10 milliseconds, the grid will always maintain its 10-millisecond distance from the nearest measure.

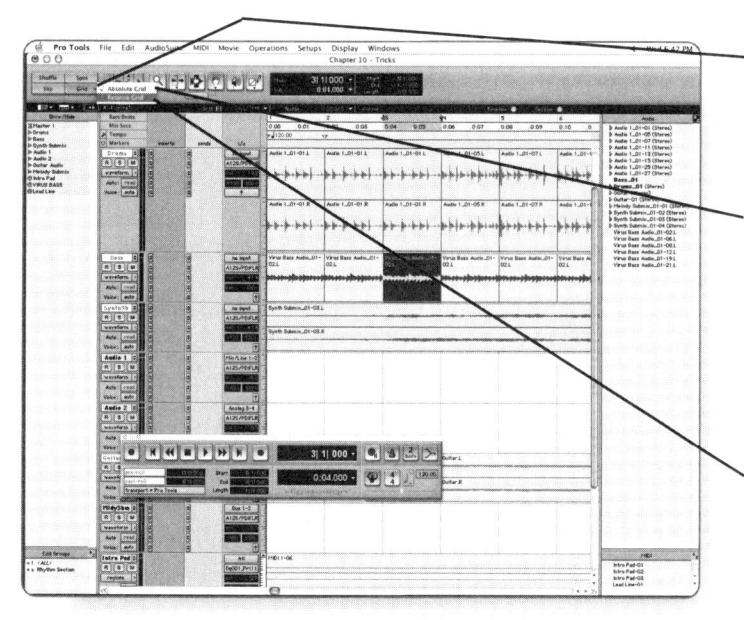

1. **Click** on the **arrow** in the lower-right corner of the Grid button. The following options will appear:

- **Absolute Grid.** This is Pro Tools' default mode. It is based on the absolute values that you set as your grid value. When you move regions or notes, they will snap to the grid lines.

- **Relative Grid.** In this variation of the Grid mode, regions and notes will move by grid *amounts* while maintaining a consistent distance from the closest grid line.

Tips for the TCE Trim Tool

The secret behind the TCE Trim tool is that it operates on the same software code as the AudioSuite Time Compress/Expand plug-in. Because of this, there are ways that you can customize its effectiveness. To do so, you first need to open the AudioSuite plug-in.

CHAPTER 10: MOVING TO THE NEXT LEVEL: TIPS AND TRICKS

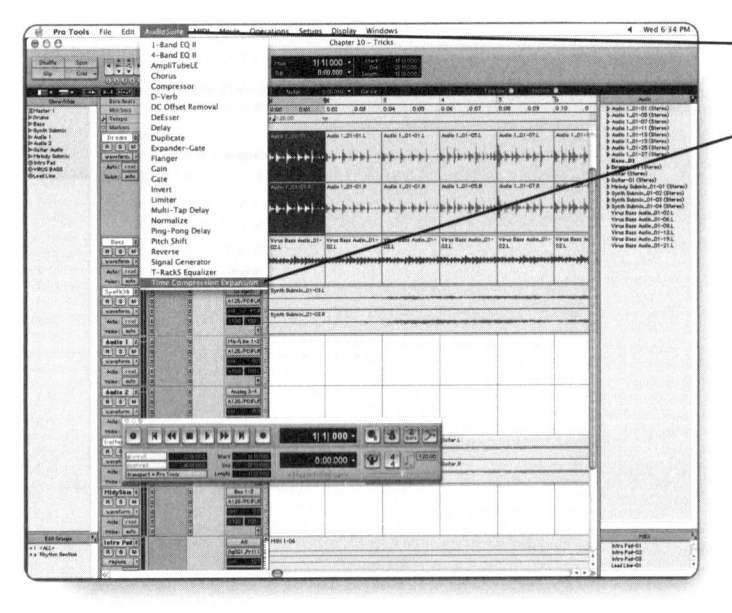

1. Click on **AudioSuite**. The AudioSuite menu will appear.

2. Click on **Time Compression Expansion**. The Time Compression/Expansion window will appear.

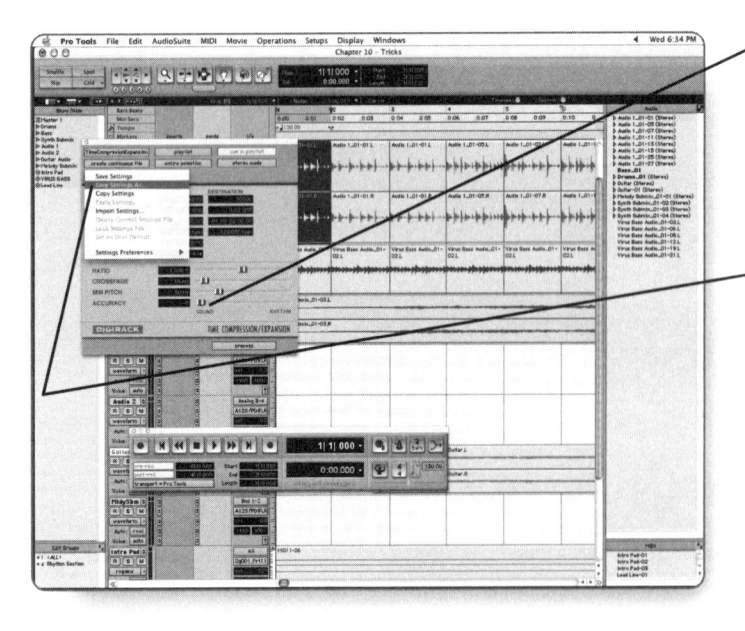

3. Set the plug-in's **parameters** to commonly used settings. For example, setting the Accuracy parameter to Sound is useful for minimizing phasing and other sonic artifacts.

4. Click on the **arrow button** to the left of the preset name and **choose Save Settings As**. The Save dialog box will open.

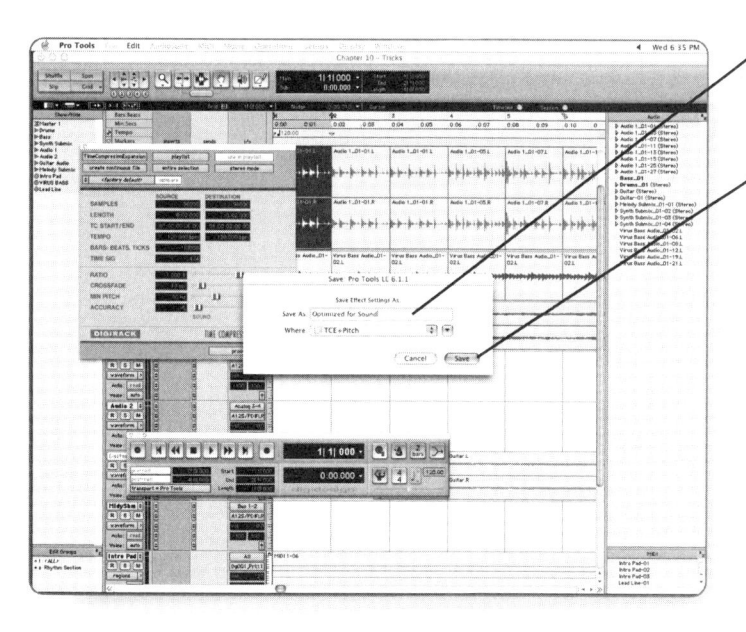

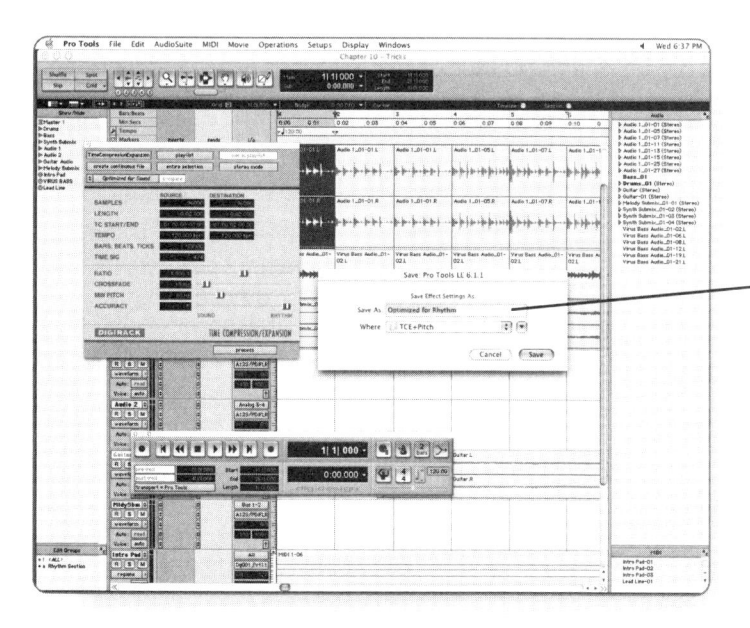

5. Type a descriptive **name** for this preset in the Save As text box.

6. Click on **Save**. The preset will be saved.

> **NOTE**
>
> Make sure you save your settings in the root settings folder. (Pro Tools defaults to this.) If you're not sure where you're saving your settings, click on the Settings menu (the arrow to the left of the setting's name in the plug-in window) and click on the Settings Preference option. From there, go to the Save Plug-in Settings To option and make sure Root Settings Folder is checked.

7. Just for example's sake, **create** another commonly used **preset**. In this example, I've set up a preset optimized for rhythmic accuracy. When you're finished adjusting the settings, save the preset.

CHAPTER 10: MOVING TO THE NEXT LEVEL: TIPS AND TRICKS

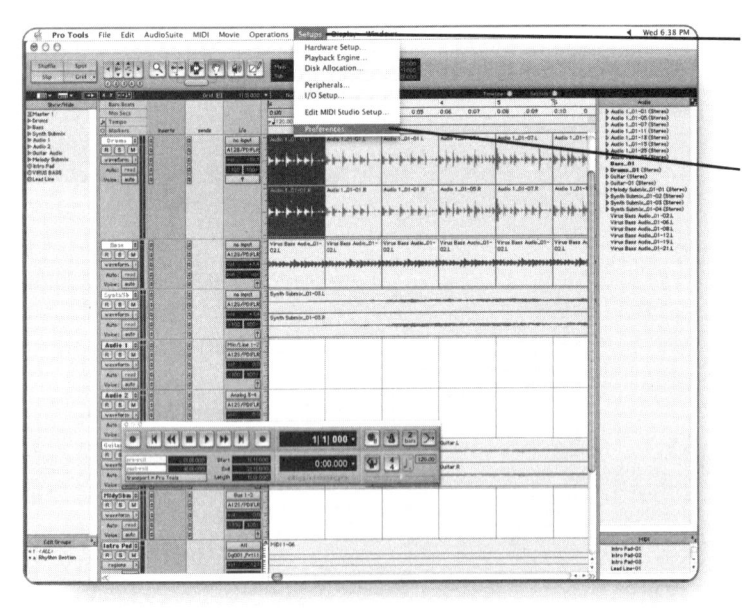

8. Now it's time to change the Trim tool. **Click** on **Setups**. The Setups menu will appear.

9. Click on **Preferences**. The Preferences dialog box will open.

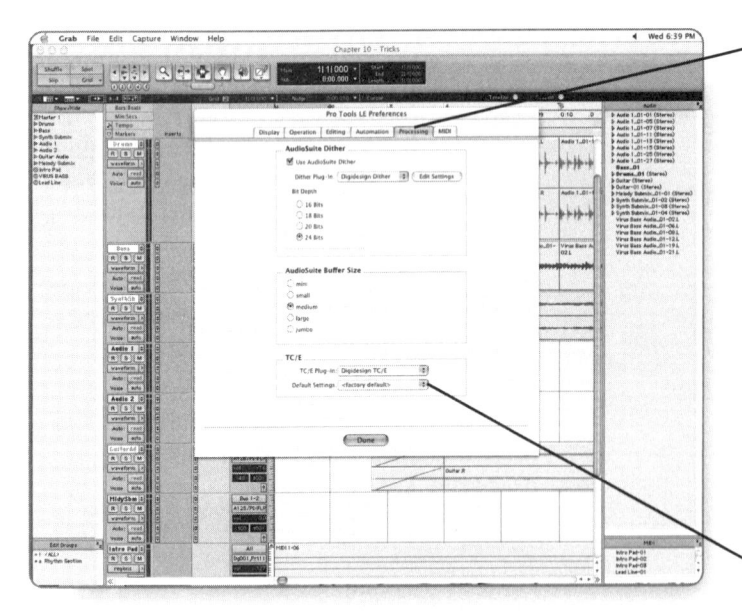

10. Click on the **Processing tab**. The tab will move to the front. The TC/E area will display the AudioSuite plug-in currently used for the TCE Trim tool. On a basic Pro Tools system, it should read Digidesign TC/E; however, if you install other third-party time compression/expansion plug-ins, you can change the software that the Trim tool will use by clicking on the arrow button and selecting the desired software.

11. Click on the **Default Settings arrow**. The Default Settings menu will appear.

MAKING THE MOST OF EDITING

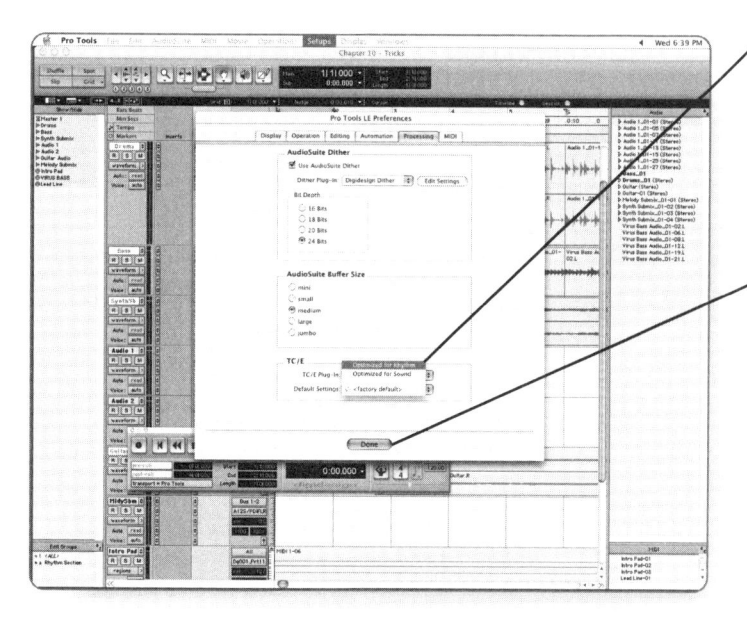

You'll see the presets you created in the AudioSuite Time Compression Expansion plug-in, available for you to choose as the TCE Trim tool's default settings.

12. Click on **Done**. The Preferences dialog box will close. From now on, until you change the default settings, the TCE Trim tool will have the chosen preset's parameter settings.

Using Strip Silence

Strip Silence is a nifty little editing tool that acts upon regions in a way similar to how a noise gate acts upon audio. Simply stated, when you use the Strip Silence feature, any audio below a specified volume threshold will be removed from your selection, leaving discrete regions that you can move and edit separately.

1. Click on **Windows**. The Windows menu will appear.

2. Click on **Show Strip Silence**. The Strip Silence window will appear.

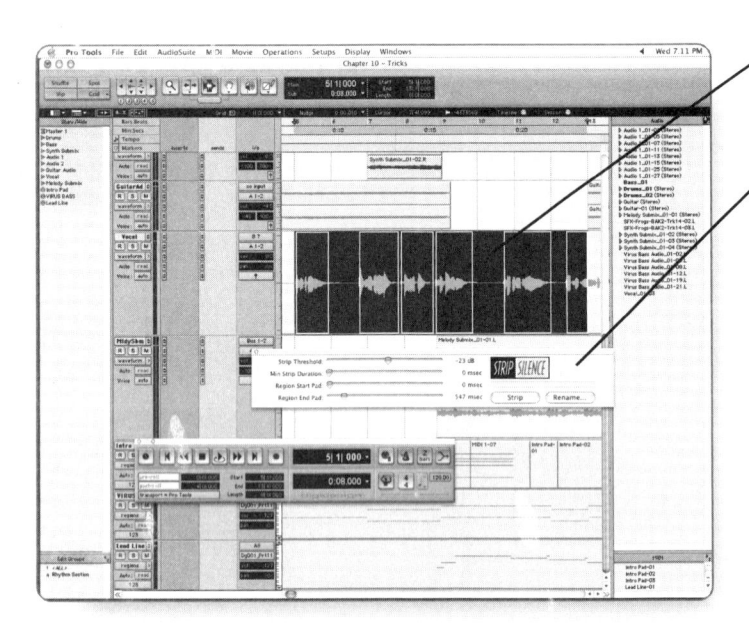

328   **CHAPTER 10: MOVING TO THE NEXT LEVEL: TIPS AND TRICKS**

3. Select the **area** in your session that you would like to strip. The area will be selected.

4. Adjust the **parameters** until you achieve the desired separation. (Before the regions are processed, you will see where new region boundaries will be created.)

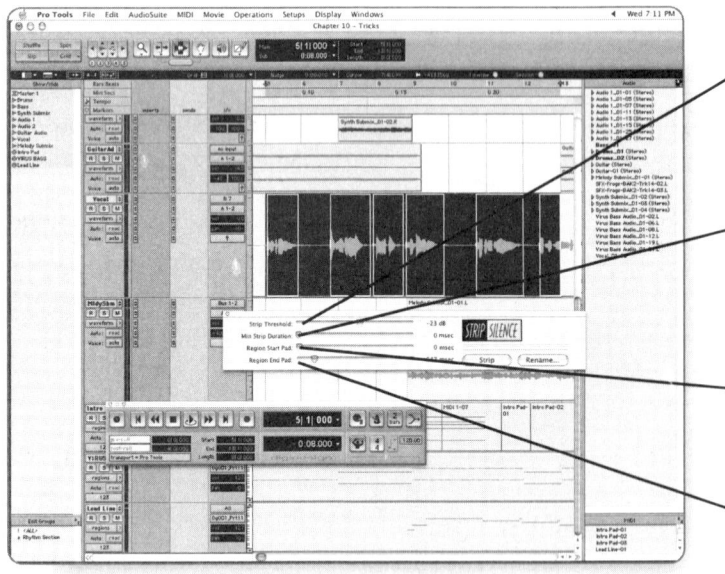

The available parameters include:

- **Strip Threshold.** Any volume level under the strip threshold will be removed from your selection.

- **Min Strip Duration.** This value determines the shortest region able to be created by strip silence.

- **Region Start Pad.** This slider will move the front region boundaries earlier in time.

- **Region End Pad.** This slider will move the back region boundaries later in time.

MAKING THE MOST OF EDITING 329

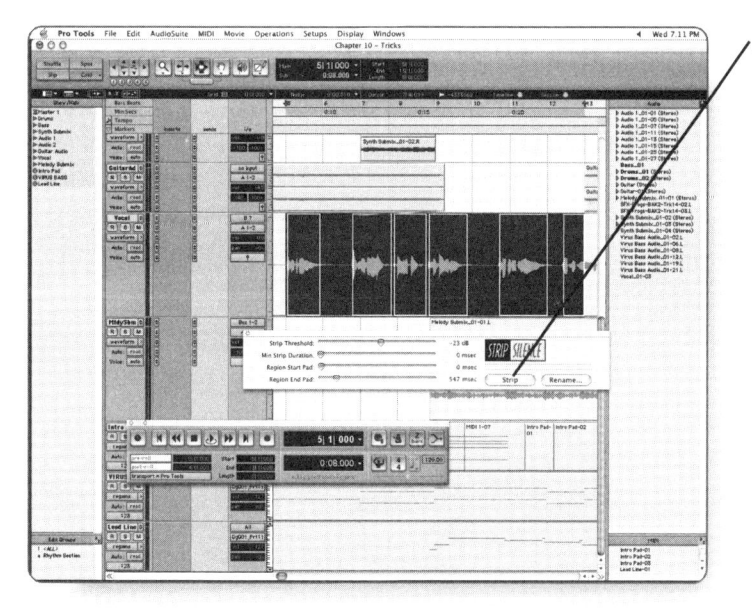

5. Click on **Strip**.

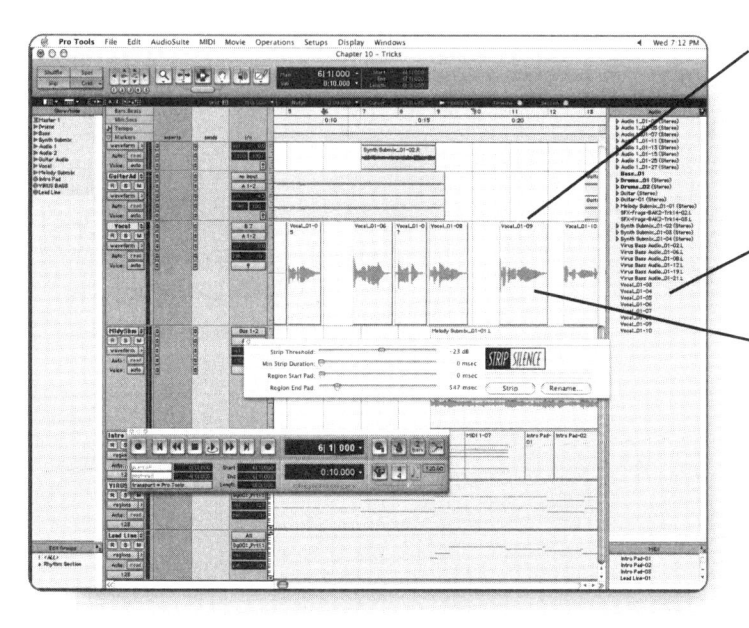

Your selection will be chopped into discrete regions, and the audio below your threshold value will be removed from the track altogether.

These new regions will be shown in the Audio Regions list.

Don't worry; you haven't deleted any audio. In fact, you can use the Trim tool and drag any region boundary out to recover the audio that has been stripped.

Edit Versus Timeline Selection

Throughout this book, whenever you have made a selection on a track, that selection has been reflected in the Rulers area (or the Timeline) and vice versa. Normally this is the way to work, but these two selections don't *need* to be linked.

1. Click on the **Link Edit and Timeline button** to deselect it. The button will be deselected.

2. Make a **selection** on any track.

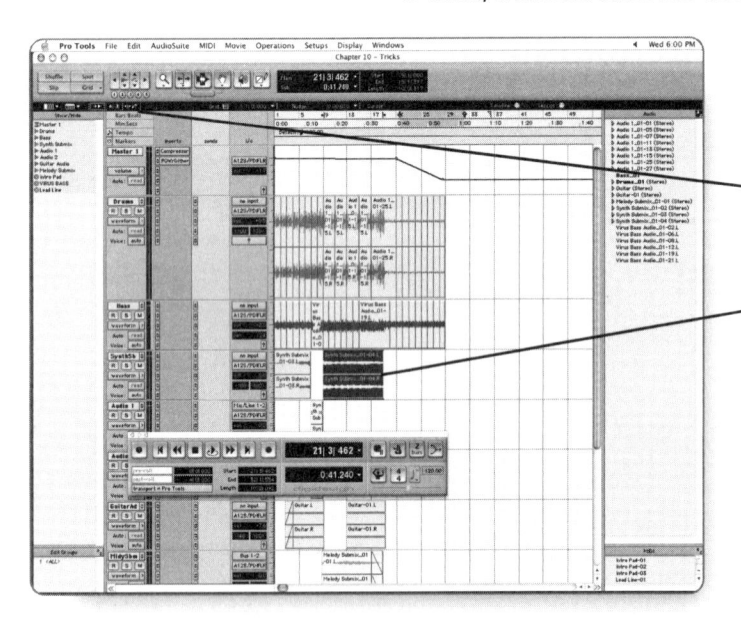

3. Make a different **selection** in the Rulers area. Note that the two areas do not reflect each other.

MAKING THE MOST OF EDITING 331

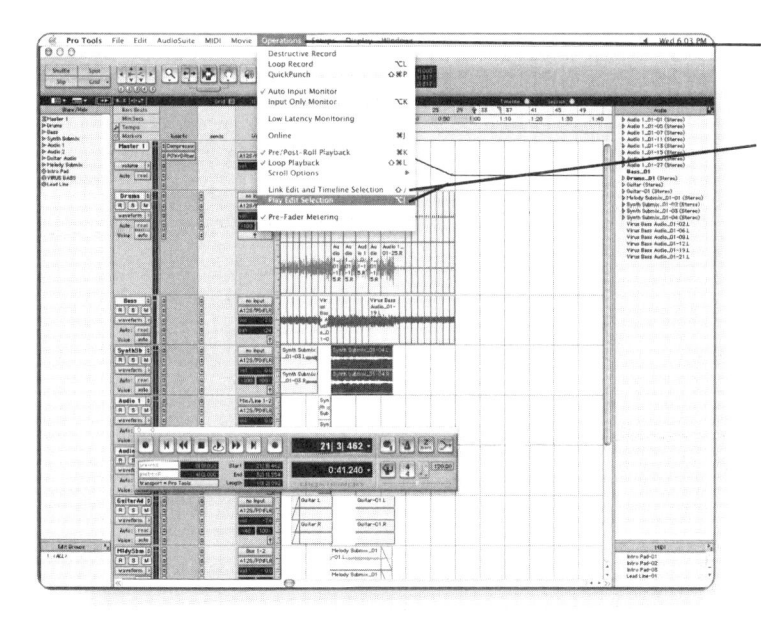

4. Click on **Operations**. The Operations menu will appear.

Note the playback options associated with this mode of operation.

5. Click on the **Link Edit and Timeline button** to re-enable it. The button will be enabled.

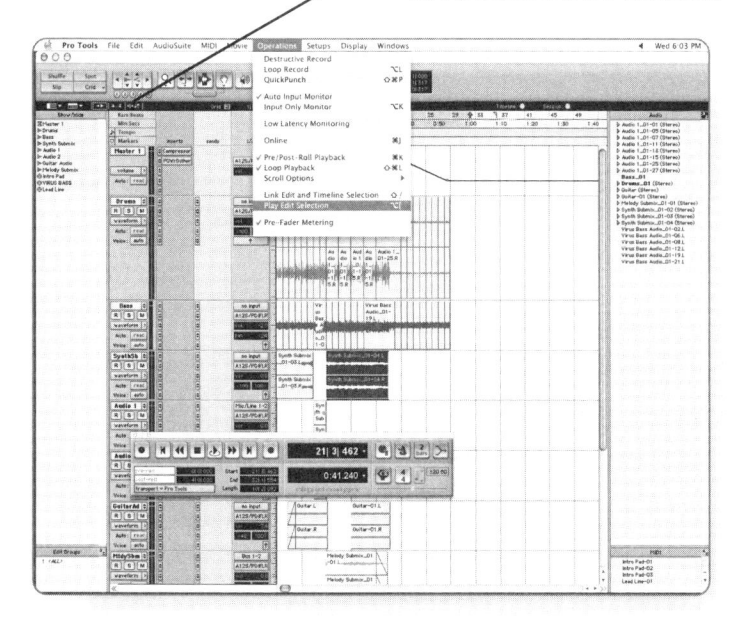

TIP

Before I close the discussion on editing, I want to show you a useful shortcut. On either a Mac or a PC, hold the Shift key and press the spacebar to play back your session at half of real-time speed. This feature comes in particularly handy when you're setting punch-in or punch-out points for a particularly tight spot. (Just make sure not to record that way, or your audio will be twice as high in pitch!)

Making the Most of Mixing

Here are a couple of tips to make your mixes rock!

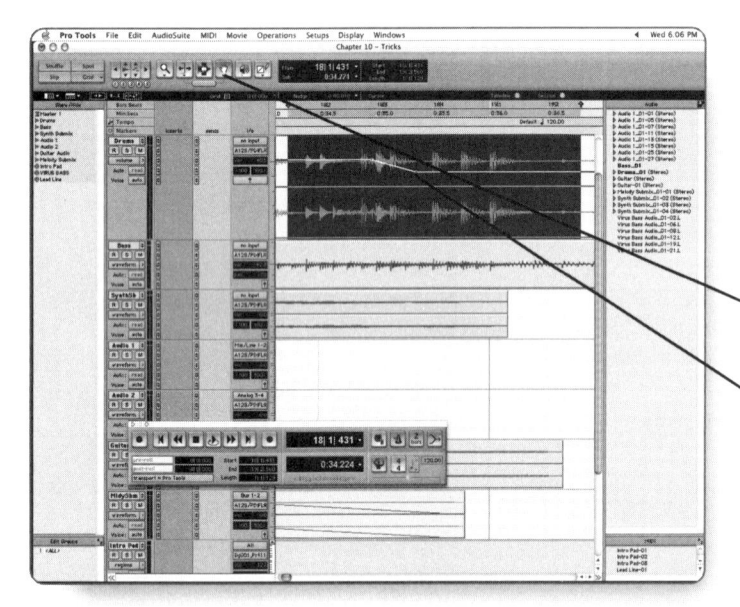

Using the Edit Tools

So far, you've only used the Pencil tool to edit your automation. This section will show you how to use a couple other tools.

1. Click on the **Grabber tool**. The tool will be selected.

2. Click on the **automation line**. A new breakpoint will be created. From that point, you can drag the breakpoint to the desired location.

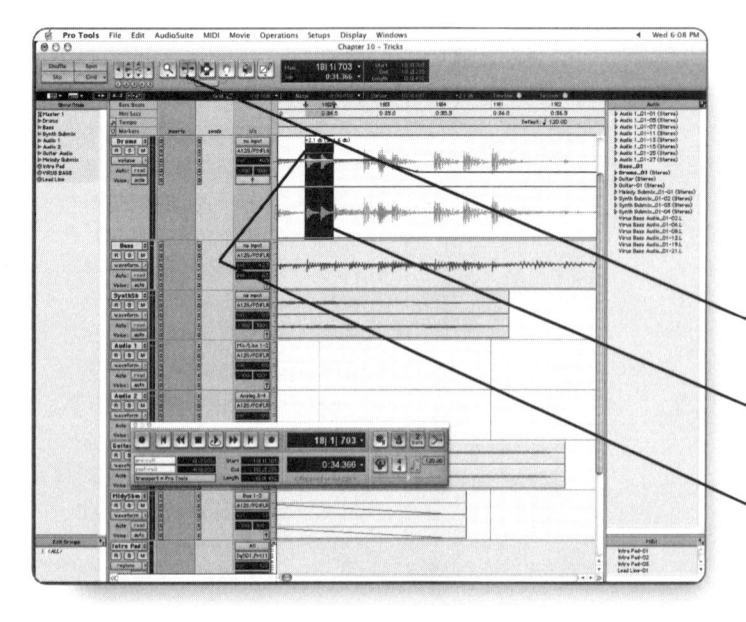

> **TIP**
>
> Hold the Option key (Mac) or the Alt key (PC) and click on a previously written breakpoint to remove it.

3. Click on the **Trim tool**. The tool will be selected.

4. Make a **selection** on a track you want to change.

5. Move the **Trim tool** into the selected area. The trim icon will appear on its side.

MAKING THE MOST OF MIXING 333

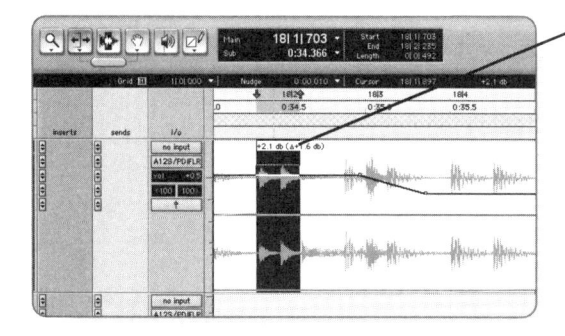

6. Click and drag your **mouse** up or down to change any prewritten automation proportionally. The amount of change effected upon your automation will be shown as a delta value.

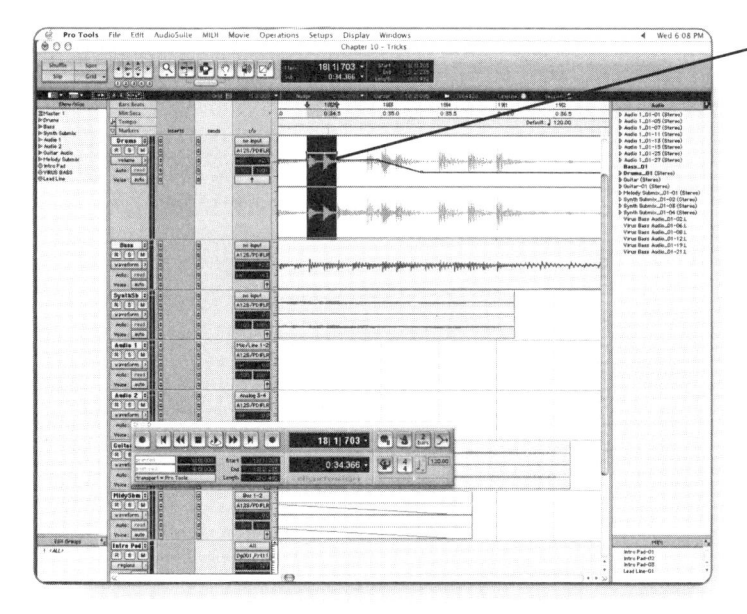

7. Release the **mouse button**. The automation will be proportionally changed in the selected area.

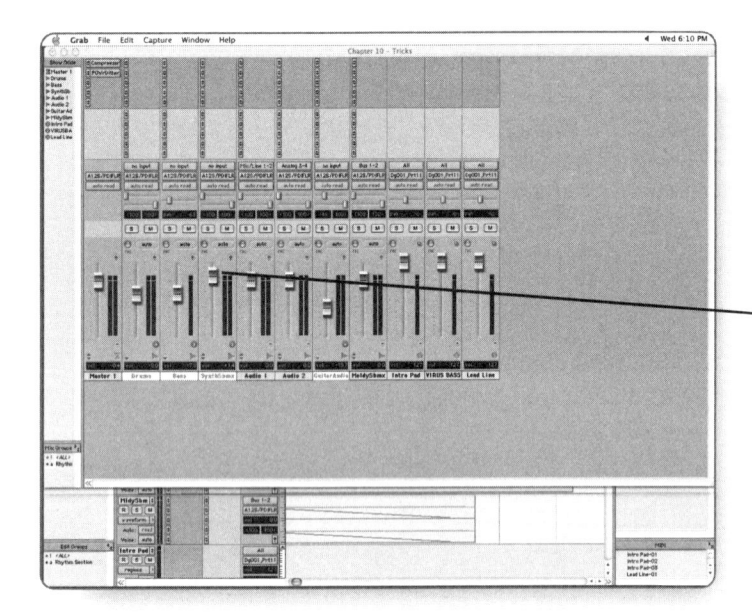

Toggling Groups

This section will show you how you can temporarily suspend active fader groups so you can quickly change the balance of the fader group.

1. Press and hold the **Control key** (Mac) or the **Start key**. You can change the volume of a track without affecting other tracks in the active group by clicking on a fader and moving it with your mouse.

2. Release the **key**. Groups will be re-enabled.

> **TIP**
>
> Before you leave the task of mixing, here's one more tip for your consideration. Remember when you used a send from a dry audio track to a wet aux track back in Chapter 8? Guess what? You can send from multiple tracks to a single aux. Just create identical sends on each track you want to route to a single aux, assigning each send to the same bus. This method is commonly used for assigning many tracks (such as drums, for example) to a single reverb. It's a simple and convenient way to work, and it conserves your CPU's resources as well!

ADVANCED RESOURCE MANAGEMENT

Advanced Resource Management

This section includes yet more ways to view and manage your data!

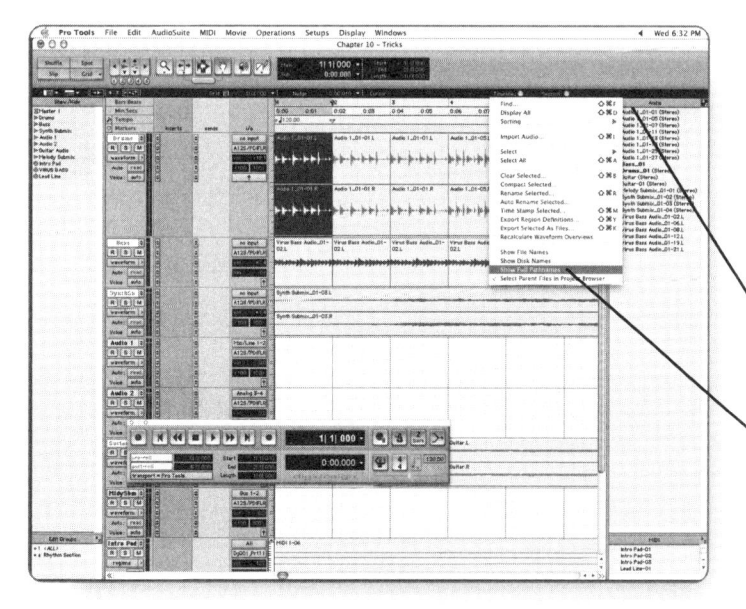

Showing Paths

Sometimes seeing only region names in the Audio Regions list isn't enough—you have to know the exact name and location of the files.

1. Click on the **Audio button** at the top of the Audio Regions list. The Audio menu will appear.

2. Click on **Show Full Pathnames**.

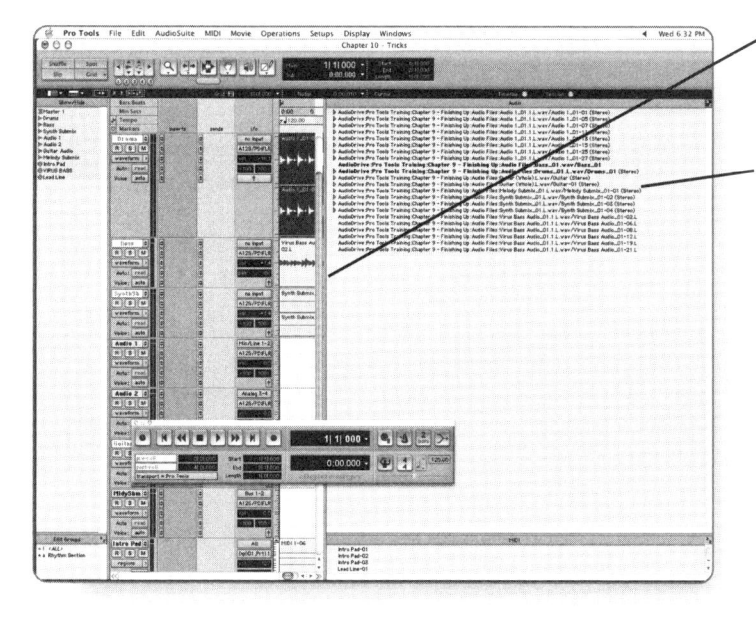

3. Click and drag the **edge** of the Audio Regions list to view all the new data at your disposal.

Note that each region is now represented by a complete path, pointing to its exact location on your computer.

Offline Regions and Inactive Elements

There's a difference between an element that's offline and one that's inactive in your session. An *offline region* occurs when source media is not found when you open a session. When that happens, the region will appear on a track, but the region will be empty. *Inactive elements* are deliberately disabled by the Pro Tools user. There are many good reasons to make a track or a plug-in inactive. Making tracks inactive allows you to create and work with tracks beyond the 32-track limitation of a Pro Tools LE system. An inactive plug-in will free up valuable CPU resources while maintaining automation and preset settings.

> **NOTE**
>
> When you open a session created or used on a TDM system, any tracks above 32 will open deactivated. You can still use them by deactivating any of the first 32 tracks to free up a voice, and then activating what you want to work on above 32.

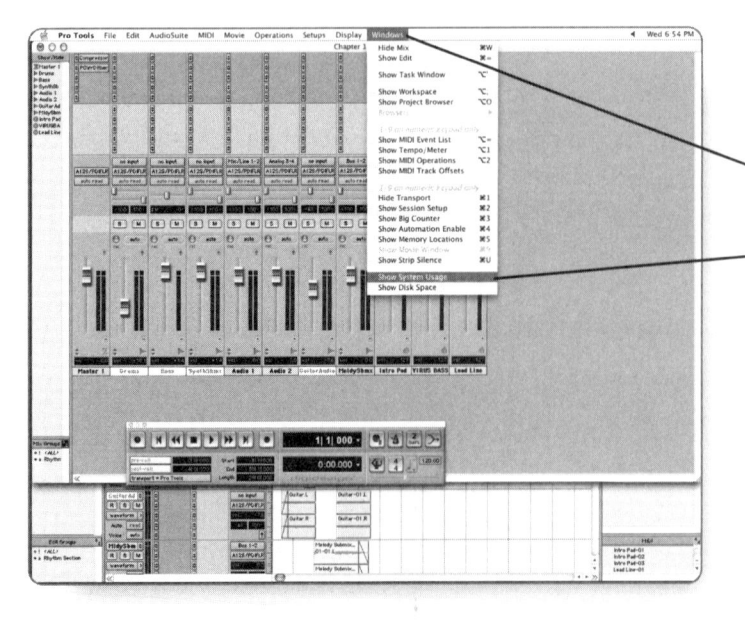

First take a look at a new window—the System Usage window:

1. Click on **Windows**. The Windows menu will appear.

2. Click on **Show System Usage**. The System Usage window will appear.

ADVANCED RESOURCE MANAGEMENT 337

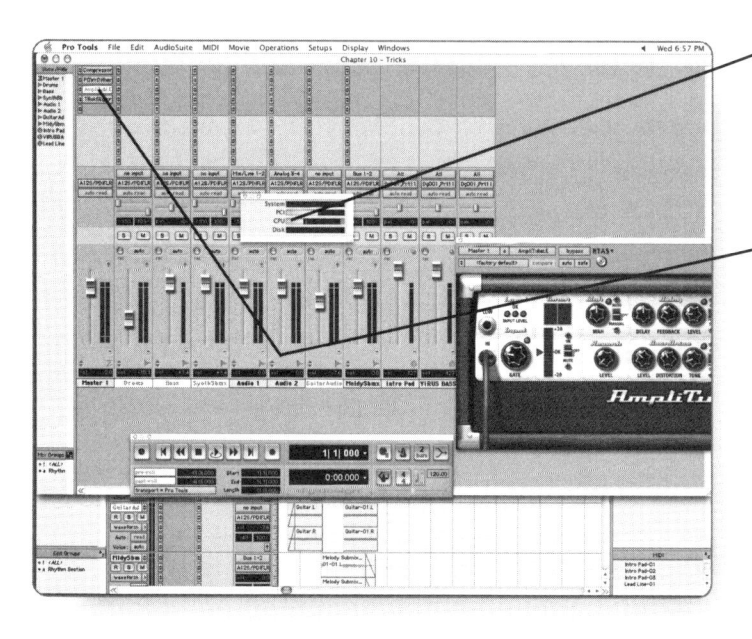

The most important graph in the System Usage window is the CPU graph because your computer's CPU is assigned the task of processing your plug-ins.

3. Press and hold the ⌘+**Control keys** (Mac) or the **Ctrl+**⊞ **keys** (PC) and **click** on the **effect** you want to disable.

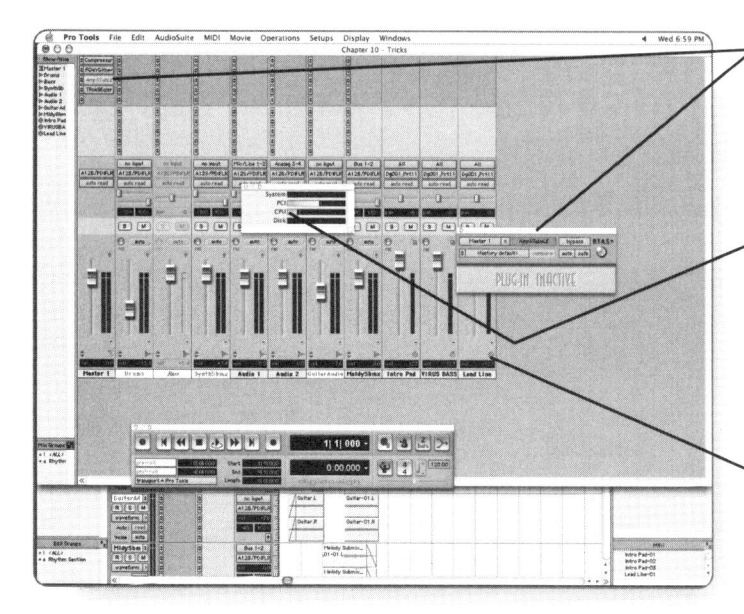

The label for the plug-in will switch to italic text, indicating that it is inactive. Also, the plug-in window will change to the Plug-In Inactive window.

For every effect you disable, your CPU gauge will decrease, leaving more processing room for new effects.

> **TIP**
>
> You can make an entire track (including all associated plug-ins) inactive by ⌘+Control clicking (Mac) or Ctrl+Start clicking (PC) on the small icon in the lower-right corner of the channel strip.

How to Consolidate (and Why)

One way to increase the efficiency of your system is to minimize its edit density. *Edit density* refers to the number of times your system must acquire data from your hard drive during playback. If you have many small regions (such as drum loops, for example), it can increase your edit density. In extreme cases, high edit density can cause playback errors.

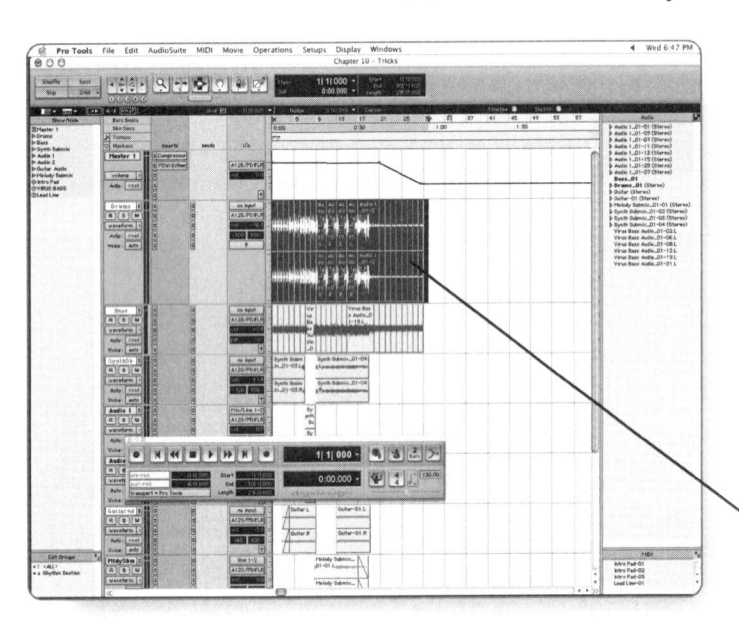

The trick is to decrease the number of regions without changing the sound of your session, and the consolidate function is the key . . .

1. Select a **section** of your session that is particularly dense with regions.

2. Click on **Edit**. The Edit menu will appear.

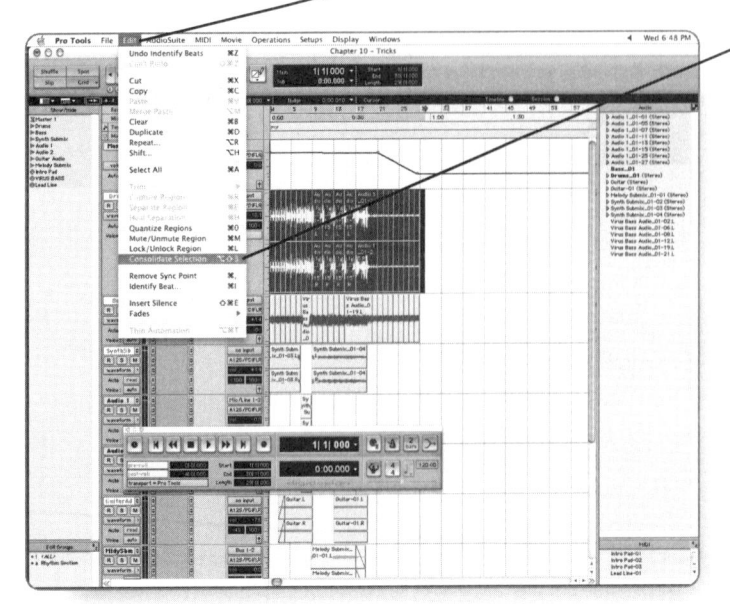

3. Click on **Consolidate Selection**. Your selection of multiple regions will be rendered into a single region.

ADVANCED RESOURCE MANAGEMENT 339

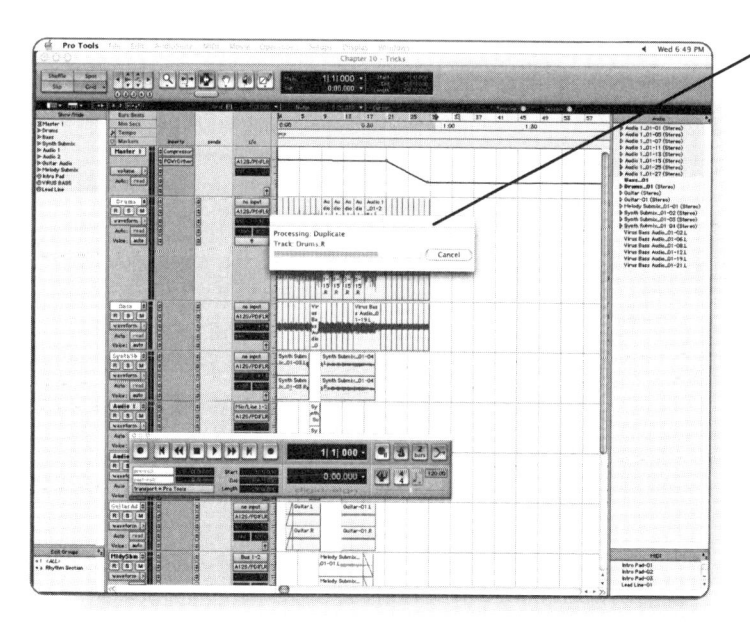

A window will display the progress of the rendering process.

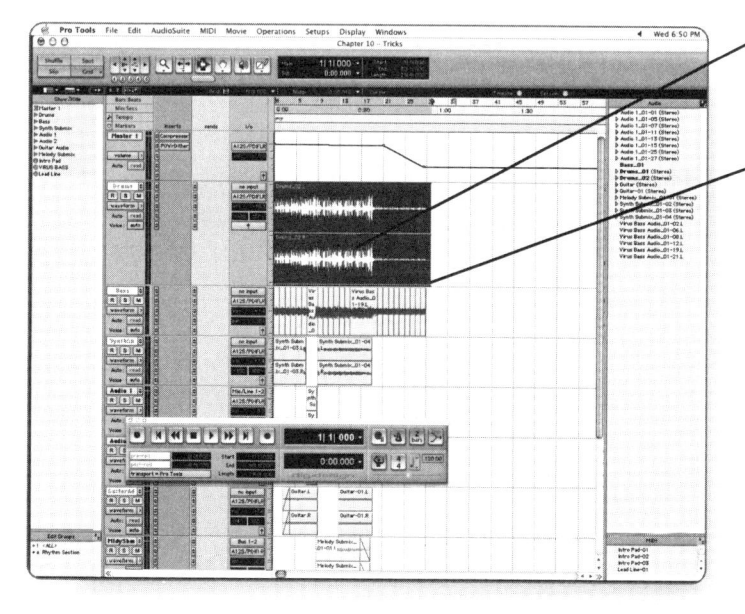

Your selection will be replaced with a single region that sounds identical to the original selection.

In this example, a small space was selected after the last region on the track. When you consolidate, that space will be rendered as silent audio as will any gaps in between regions in your selection.

Refer and Copy Files

Generally speaking, your session's dependent elements (such as audio files used in tracks) are stored in the appropriate subdirectory of your session folder (for example, Audio Files). However, in some cases you can refer to media outside your session folder. The most common instance of this occurs when you are importing tracks from another session.

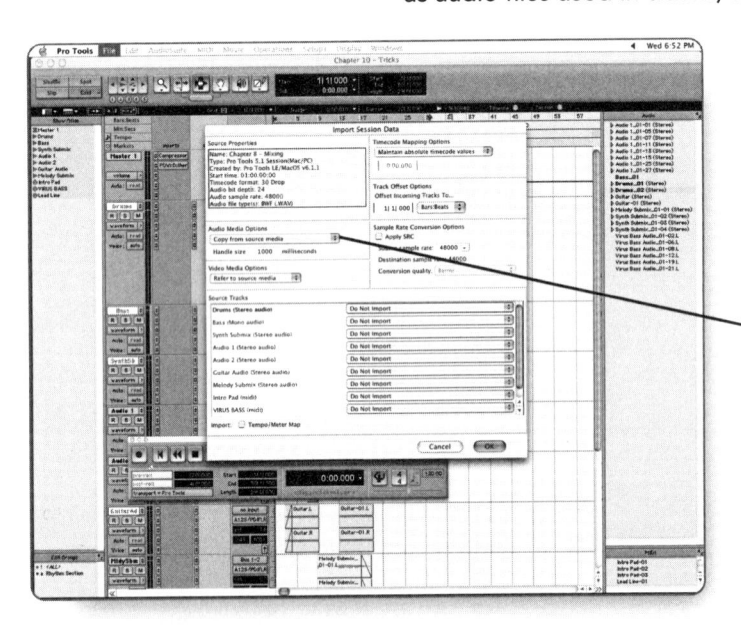

1. In the Import Session Data dialog box, **click** on the **Audio Media Options arrow**. The Audio Media Options menu will appear. The options include:

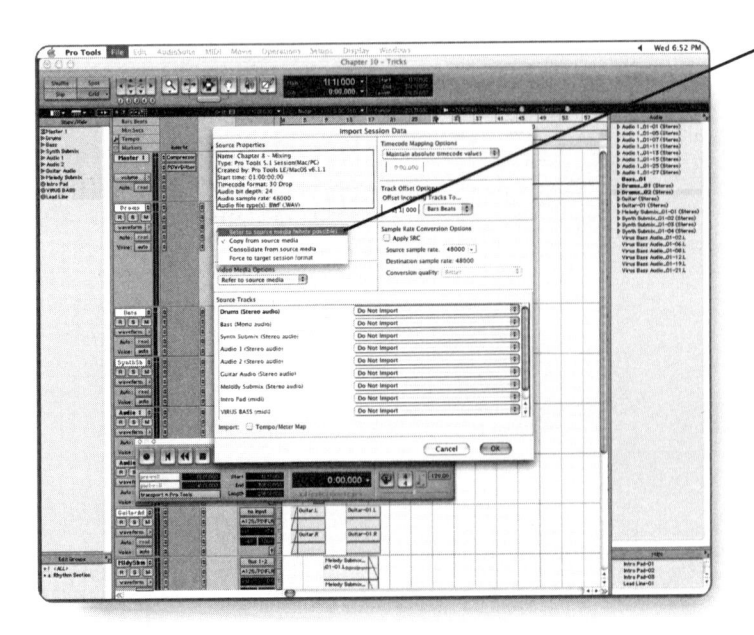

- **Refer to source media (where possible).** This option allows you to avoid copying audio files to your new session, which saves space on your hard drive. Instead, the audio files in the source session folder will be directly accessed by the destination session. This option is only available in situations where the source and destination sessions' sample rates and bit depths match.

ADVANCED RESOURCE MANAGEMENT 341

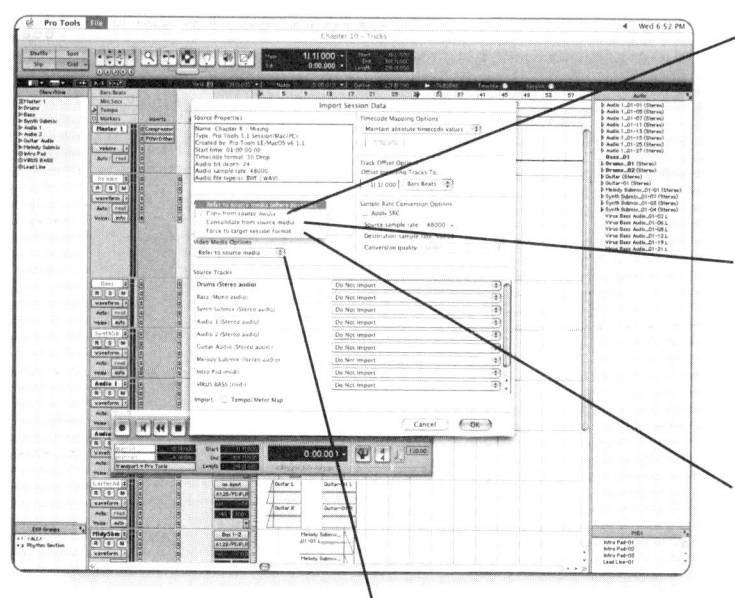

- **Copy from source media.** With this option, audio files used in the selected tracks will be copied from the source session to the destination session.

- **Consolidate from source media.** With this option, only used portions of the tracks' audio files will be copied from the source session to the destination.

- **Force to target session format.** This option allows you to manually select the format of the destination audio files.

2. You also have options for importing video files. **Click** on the **Video Media Options arrow**. The Video Media Options menu will appear. The options include:

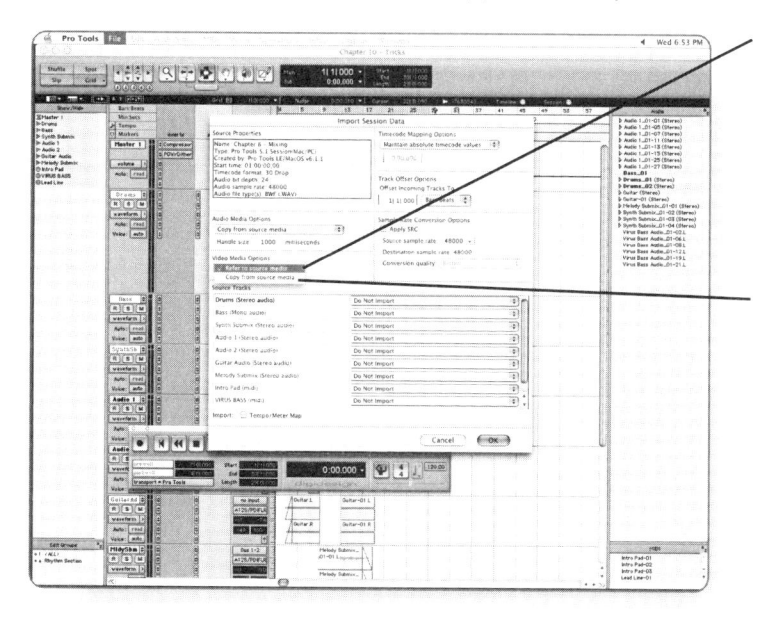

- **Refer to source media.** As with its audio counterpart, this option avoids making a copy of the video media. The destination session will refer to the video file in the source session's original location.

- **Copy from source media.** The video file will be copied into the destination session's folder.

CHAPTER 10: MOVING TO THE NEXT LEVEL: TIPS AND TRICKS

> **TIP**
> Referring to source media (audio and visual) instead of copying files is a very smart way to manage your hard drive's space. However, it is more important than ever to use the Save Session Copy In option when you archive your work. It is also crucial to select the appropriate files to be included in your save. Save Session Copy In will automatically gather your media together in one central location, regardless of its original location on your hard drive.

Working with Movies

Although Pro Tools is certainly an audio program, there is a degree of support for incorporating video into your session. Let's start with the process of importing audio, which couldn't be easier.

1. Click on **Movie**. The Movie menu will appear.

2. Click on **Import Movie**. The Open Movie dialog box will open.

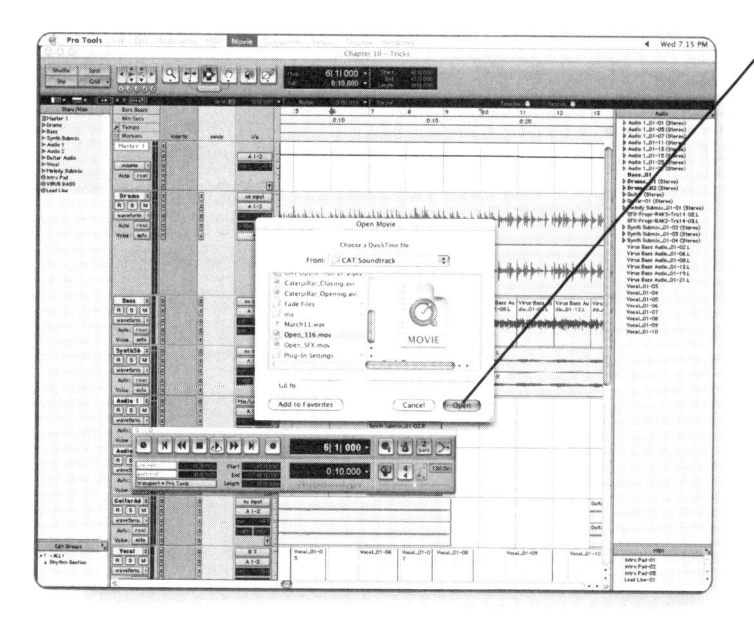

WORKING WITH MOVIES   343

3. **Navigate** to the **file** you want to use and **click** on **Open**. A new track will be created in your session. Although it's not an audio track, you'll see it displayed in your Edit window and the Track Show/Hide list. You can arrange the track in your session just as you would any other track. Additionally, a video window will appear.

4. **Click** on **Movie**. The Movie menu will appear.

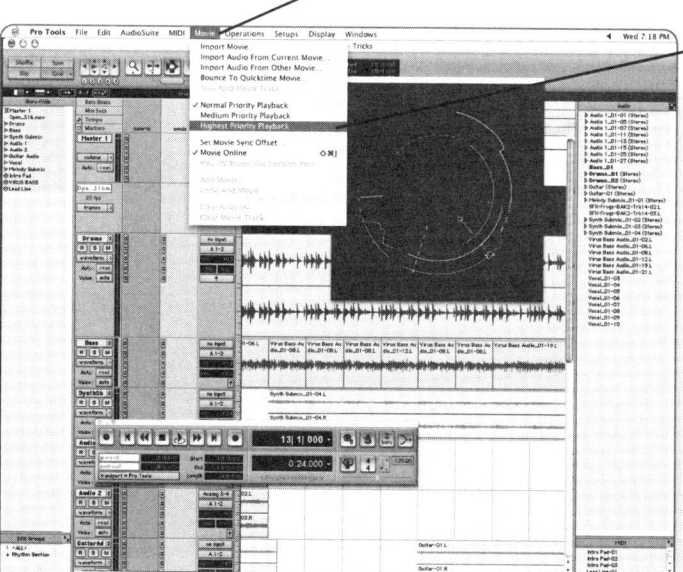

5. **Click** on a playback **priority**. The option will be selected. As you move to higher priorities, your video playback will get smoother, although this will take resources away from the rest of your Pro Tools window display.

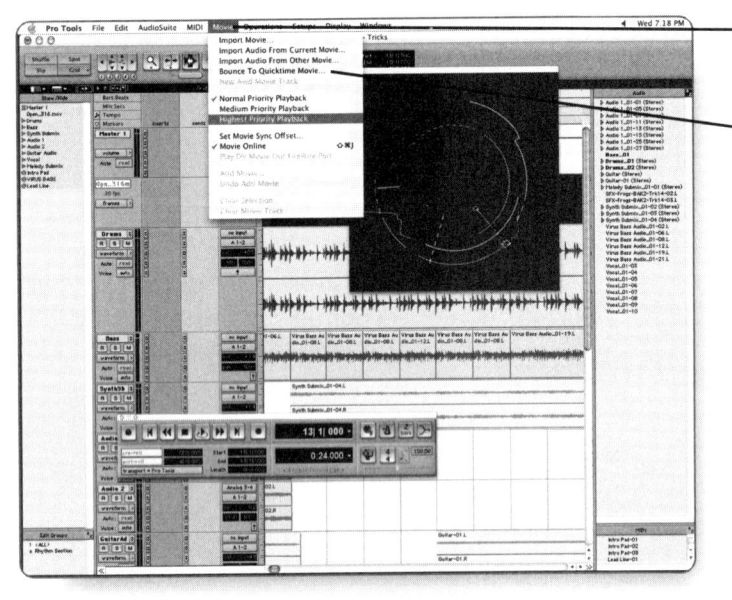

6. Click on **Movie** again. The Movie menu will appear.

7. Click on **Bounce to QuickTime Movie**. This option is similar to the Bounce to Disk function except it bounces the mixed audio into a QuickTime movie file.

Good Luck

Congratulations—you made it! You've gone through a comprehensive tour of Pro Tools' basic operations and features, and although this discussion of Pro Tools is certainly not a comprehensive listing of *everything* that Pro Tools can do, you can rest assured that your creative journey has started well. Over time, you'll not only learn more about Pro Tools, but undoubtedly you will find your own working style—a process that will be constantly refined as you gain experience and speed.

You've begun a great exploration and a worthwhile endeavor, in my humble opinion. I personally believe that artistic pursuits nourish not only the soul of the patron, but of the artist as well. It's my wish that this product and the technology to come serve to inspire you to push the limits of your creativity. Good luck!

A

Review Questions

Now it's time to put your money where your mouth is! Just kidding—there'll be no trick questions here, and it's not about passing or failing. I've just created a few questions based on each chapter so you can make sure you're getting the really important points. Good luck!

Questions

Chapter 1 Welcome to Pro Tools LE 6

1. Physical audio connections, which allow for audio to be recorded and played back, are connected to the _____.

2. Because a Pro Tools session refers to audio files that are stored elsewhere on your hard drive, Pro Tools is a _____- based application.

3. When audio files are recorded into your session, the files are stored in the _____ folder.

4. The two primary windows used in Pro Tools are the _____ and _____ windows.

5. The Open Session and Close Session commands are located in the _____ drop-down menu.

Chapter 2 Getting the Big Picture

6. The _____ list allows you to control what tracks in your session will be displayed.

7. The _____ list shows audio files and regions.

8. The _____ view will allow you to see more channels at one time in your Mix window.

9. What keyboard shortcut is used when you're changing the heights of all shown tracks at once?

10. When you create a session in Pro Tools, one group is created automatically and will be shown in the Group list. What is the name of that group?

Chapter 3 Getting Started with Audio

11. Can two active paths both use the same physical output?

12. Can two sub-paths use the same physical output?

13. What's the shortcut for creating a track?

14. True or False: Once tracks are created, they cannot be rearranged in the Edit window, so take special care in how you create them.

15. True or False: There's only one way to import audio into your session, and that's to the Audio Regions list.

Chapter 4 Basic Editing

16. How many edit modes are there, and what are their names?

17. Which edit tool do you use to adjust the beginning or end of a region?

18. Which edit tool do you use to move a region to another location?

19. What is the shortcut for duplicating a selected region?

20. True or False: The Save Session Copy In command can copy your entire session, including audio files, to another location.

Chapter 5 Recording Audio

21. What are the buttons in the I/O column of an audio track (medium track height), from top to bottom?

22. What kind of track should you use for the click plug-in?

23. What is the name of the mode in which you can create multiple punch-in and punch-out points for a single take?

24. True or False: Recording audio in Pro Tools is always non-destructive.

25. What will happen to your plug-ins when you go into Low Latency mode?

Chapter 6 Using MIDI

26. True or False: MIDI is not audible.
27. The Edit MIDI Studio Setup window can be opened from the _____ drop-down menu.
28. To listen to a MIDI instrument through Pro Tools, what kind of track do you use?
29. The _____ function can change the timing of your MIDI notes to snap to a grid.
30. The _____ tool is useful for editing MIDI notes because it takes on different functions depending on the position of the cursor.

Chapter 7 More Editing

31. How many zoom presets are there?
32. What's a transient in Pro Tools?
33. Which tool will allow you to change the tempo, but not the pitch, of an audio region?
34. The _____ tool will allow you to move a selected area of audio from within a region.
35. The _____ tool combines many of the most common editing functions (like trim, select, and grab) into one tool.

Chapter 8 Basic Mixing

36. You can create memory locations while Pro Tools is playing by pressing the _____ key.
37. What's the shortcut key combination for creating a group?
38. Of the two kinds of plug-in effects available on an LE system, which one is real-time?

39. Of the two kinds of plug-in effects available on an LE system, which one is not real-time?
40. What is the name of the component within Pro Tools that routes audio like a virtual cable?

Chapter 9 Finishing Touches

41. True or False: You can select a bus as an input on a master fader.
42. An insert on a master fader is a _____-fader.
43. True or False: Bouncing to disk happens in real time (for example, bouncing a three-minute song takes three minutes).
44. True or False: When you clear regions from your tracks, they will automatically be removed from your hard drive.
45. True or False: Audio can be deleted when you compact your session.

Chapter 10 Moving to the Next Level: Tips and Tricks

46. What is the shortcut key combination for toggling zoom levels?
47. The _____ feature allows Pro Tools, with your help, to compute the tempo of a selected area of audio.
48. What is the shortcut key combination for half-speed playback?
49. You can make an active plug-in inactive by holding which keys and clicking on the insert?
50. The option of bouncing to a QuickTime file is found in which drop-down menu?

Answers

1. Audio interface
2. Pointer
3. Audio files
4. Edit, Mix
5. File
6. Track Show/Hide
7. Audio Regions list
8. Narrow Mix window
9. Hold the Option key (Mac) or the Alt key (PC) while you change the height of any one track, and the heights of all shown tracks will change at once.
10. The All group
11. No
12. Yes
13. Shift+⌘+N (Mac) or Ctrl+Shift+N (PC)
14. False. You can drag a track up or down (in the Edit window) or left and right (in the Mix window) by clicking on the track name in the Track Show/Hide list or by clicking and dragging the track name in the track itself.
15. False. You can import to the Audio Regions list or straight to an audio file, or you can drag and drop from the workspace! No matter which method you use, though, the region will be added to the Audio Regions list.
16. There are four edit modes: Shuffle, Slip, Grid, and Spot.
17. The Trim tool
18. The Grabber tool
19. ⌘+D (Mac) or Ctrl+D (PC)
20. True
21. Input Selector, Output Selector, Volume, Pan, Tearaway Selector
22. An auxiliary input track
23. QuickPunch
24. False. Although most record modes will not overwrite audio files on your hard drive, Destructive Record mode can.
25. They will become inactive.
26. True
27. Setups
28. An aux input track
29. Quantize
30. Pencil
31. Five
32. A transient is the initial high-energy peak at the beginning of a waveform.
33. The Time Compress/Expansion (TCE) Trim tool
34. Separation Grabber
35. Smart
36. Enter
37. ⌘+G (Mac) or Ctrl+G (PC)
38. RTAS
39. AudioSuite
40. A bus
41. False. There are no inputs on a master fader.
42. Post
43. True
44. False. Audio files will not be automatically deleted when you clear them from your Audio Regions list, but it is an option when you choose the Clear Selected function (when your selected regions include whole files). Think twice before choosing to delete audio files—it can't be undone!
45. True, so be careful!
46. Control+E (Mac) or ⊞+E (PC)
47. Identify Beat
48. Shift+spacebar
49. ⌘+Control (Mac) or the Ctrl+⊞ key (PC)
50. Movie

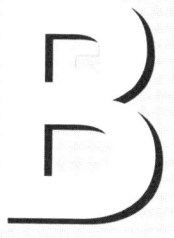

Sound, Digital Audio, and MIDI: A Primer

DAWs have revolutionized the audio profession. By applying the power of computers to the tasks required in the process of audio production, the industry has provided you with the power to change, edit, undo, and save your audio and MIDI data in a multitude of ways.

I like to think of DAWs' impact on the audio world as similar to the revolution that was brought to the literary world with the introduction of word processors. If you think about it, DAWs and word processors both bring a world of flexibility and power to their respective arenas, and both have boosted productivity and even creativity in the bargain. However, just as a basic understanding of language and vocabulary is fundamental to using a word processor, a basic understanding of the nature of audio and MIDI is essential to truly harnessing the power of a DAW such as Pro Tools.

A truly comprehensive study of analog and digital audio and MIDI can take a lifetime, with numerous books written on the subjects. You might want to check *MIDI Power!* by Robert Guérin (Muska & Lipman, 2002). For now, though, a relatively simple definition of basic concepts will suffice for your first steps into the world of DAW use.

Sound

Anything you hear as sound comes to your ears in the form of variations in air pressure as a result of a physical object's vibrations. These variations are called *compression* (higher air pressure) and *rarefaction* (lower air pressure). The speed of these compressions and rarefactions determines the *frequency* of the sound; the human ear can perceive between 20 and 20,000 compressions and rarefactions per second. Each compression and rarefaction per second is called a *Hertz* (Hz); this is the way you measure a sound's frequency. You can hear between 20 Hz and 20 kHz (kilohertz), with lower frequencies recognized as lower pitches and higher frequencies recognized as higher pitches.

The volume, or *amplitude*, of a sound refers to the intensity of the compressions and rarefactions. Subtle amounts of compression and rarefaction are heard as soft sounds, and greater intensities are perceived as louder sounds. The amplitude of a sound is measured in decibels of sound pressure level (dBSPL); the human range of hearing is from 0 dB (silence) to about 120 dB (the threshold of pain).

Digital Audio

Audible sound can be stored as digital information, which is called *digital audio*. Digital audio is a series of samples (momentary "snapshots" of sound) that, when played back in series, recreate the original sound (to varying degrees of quality). In a way, digital audio is similar in nature to film, which is a series of still pictures that recreate a sensation of motion when played back—digital audio also plays back still "images" (samples) at such a speed that you can recreate audio. When recording or creating these samples, you are making an analog to digital (A/D) conversion; when you play them back, the process is digital to analog (D/A) conversion.

The number of samples played per second is called the *sample rate*; it is an important parameter when you are discussing digital audio. There is a mathematical formula, called the Nyquist Theorem, which states that the sample rate must be twice as high as the highest frequency reproduced. For example, when you're talking about audio CDs, the sample rate is 44.1 kHz; therefore, an audio CD could accurately reproduce a maximum frequency of 22.05 kHz in a mathematically ideal system. (The realities of electronics make the maximum frequency just a little bit lower than that, but the concept is still sound.) This coincides nicely with the 20 kHz audible limit of the human ear. Reducing the sample rate below 44.1 kHz proportionally reduces the upper frequency limit accurate reproduction, often with audible results.

Each sample is composed of a number of bits (ones and zeros), which record the sample's amplitude. The number of bits per sample is known as the *bit depth* of the digital audio. Higher bit depths yield many advantages. First, they provide a greater dynamic range, with each bit adding 6 dB of dynamic range to the audio. Also, more bits mean greater resolution (or a more detailed "snapshot" of your digital audio), which greatly enhances the quality and accuracy of your recording. CD-quality audio, for example, has a bit depth of 16, which gives it a dynamic range of 96 dB (6×16) and a resolution of 65,536 discrete amplitude levels (2^{16}).

> **NOTE**
>
> As mentioned earlier in this appendix, CD-quality audio has a sample rate of 44.1 kHz and a bit depth of 16. These are good figures to commit to memory because you'll need to use these settings when you bounce your work to disk to make an audio CD.

> **TIP**
>
> When recording audio digitally, you'll want to use all the ones and zeros of your bit depth to their greatest advantage. To do this, you'll want to record as loud (or "hot") as possible without clipping. (Clipping will result in digital distortion, a very unpleasant sound!) Good, healthy recording levels will ensure that your audio is taking advantage of the resolution of your audio.

MIDI

The first obvious difference between MIDI and audio is the connections and cables used between devices. Instead of an audio cable, MIDI employs a five-pin DIN connector, which carries data on 16 channels per cable simultaneously. This transfer of data is one way, so a traditional connection between a MIDI device and a MIDI interface is to connect the MIDI out of the interface to the MIDI in of the device, and then connect the MIDI out of the device to the MIDI in of the interface. When this arrangement involves Pro Tools (among other products), MIDI data can be recorded, edited, and played back, a process called *sequencing*.

As I said before, MIDI isn't audio; rather, it is data that can control (among other things) a MIDI device that can make a sound, similar to the way an old-time piano roll can be used to control a player piano. To accomplish this task, MIDI employs many different kinds of messages transmitted along a MIDI channel. Among them are

- **Note Messages.** Each note letter and octave has its own number from 0 (C-1) to 127 (G9). Middle C's note number is 60.
- **Velocity.** This refers to how fast a key is pressed, with a range between 0 and 127.
- **Pitch Bend.** This controls the degree to which a note's pitch can be changed up or down. Because of the sensitivity of the human ear to changes in pitch, this parameter has a resolution of 16,384 (128×128).
- **Control.** These messages refer to other pedals, knobs, levers, and so on that can enhance a device's expressiveness. Popular among control messages are Bank Select (controller #0), Modulation Wheel (controller #1), Breath Controller (controller #2), Foot Controller (controller #3), Volume (controller #7), Pan (controller #10), and Sustain Pedal (controller #64).

Although this list is far from complete, these are some of the most commonly used messages. For more information, you can refer to the MIDI Manufacturer's Association Web site at http://www.midi.org.

C

Shortcuts

For increased operational speed and ease of use, there are many Pro Tools keyboard shortcuts to give you fast access to a wide variety of tasks. This appendix, reprinted courtesy of Digidesign, details the many keyboard shortcuts that are not shown within Pro Tools menus. The shortcuts are grouped by functional area for your added convenience and quick reference.

Mac OS Shortcuts

Function	Key Combination
Global Keyboard Commands	
Change all audio channel strips	Option + applicable function
Change audio channel strip and all selected audio channel strips	Option + Shift + applicable function
Toggle item and set all others to same new state	Option + click on applicable item
Toggle item and set all others to opposite state	⌘ + click on applicable item
Fine tune	⌘ + click on control slider/pot/breakpoints
Mix and Edit Groups	
Temporarily isolate channel strip from group operation	Hold down Control + any operation that affects groups
New group	⌘ + G (with two or more tracks selected)
Suspend/resume all groups	⌘ + Shift + G or ⌘ + click on Groups pop-up menu
Rename group	Double-click to far left of group name in the Groups list
Group enable/disable	Type ID letter on keyboard (To enable keyboard selection of groups, click box at top right of Groups list.)
Hide all tracks	Click on track symbol in Show/Hide menu
Show group members only	Control + click on group(s) in Groups list (Control + Shift + click for multiple groups)
Edit Selection Definition and Navigation	
Locate play/edit cursor to next region-boundary/sync point	Tab
Locate play/edit cursor to previous region-boundary/sync point	Option + Tab
Go to and select next region	Control + Tab
Go to and select previous region	Control + Option + Tab
Extend selection to next region-boundary	Shift + Tab
Extend selection to previous region-boundary	Option + Shift + Tab
Extend selection to include next region	Control + Shift + Tab
Extend selection to include previous region	Control + Option + Shift + Tab
Return to start of session	Return
Go to end of session	Option + Return
Extend selection to start of session	Shift + Return
Extend selection to end of session	Option + Shift + Return
Set selection start/end during playback	↓ / ↑
Set selection start/end to incoming time code while stopped	↓ / ↑
Select entire region in Edit window	Double-click with Selector
Select entire track in Edit window	Triple-click with Selector / ⌘ + A
Extend selection to a memory location	Shift + period key + mem loc number + period key (The first period key press is not required with "Classic" numeric keypad mode selected in Preferences.)

Function	Key Combination
Place play/edit cursor or create selection across all tracks	Option + click in Rulers
Extend play/edit cursor or selection across all tracks	Enable All edit group (! key) and Shift + click on any other track (To enable keyboard selection of Groups, click box at top right of Groups List.)

Record and Playback

Function	Key Combination
Open New Track dialog	⌘ + Shift + N
In New Track dialog cycle through track type	⌘ + < / >
Cycle up/down through New Track options	⌘ + ↑ / ↓
Start record	⌘ + spacebar/F12
Stop record	Spacebar
Stop record and discard take	⌘ + period key
Start/stop playback	Spacebar
Half-speed record	⌘ + Shift + spacebar
Half-speed playback	Shift + spacebar
Pause (pre-prime deck for instant playback)	Option + click on Transport play button
Pause (pre-prime deck for instant record)	Option + click on Transport play button during recording
Enable/disable online record	⌘ + Option + spacebar
Enable/disable online playback	⌘ + J / Option + spacebar
Toggle record modes (normal/Destructive/Loop/QuickPunch)	Control + click on Transport record button
Loop playback toggle	⌘ + Shift + L or Control + click on Transport play button
Record-safe track	⌘ + click on Record enable button
Solo-safe track	⌘ + click on Solo button
QuickPunch	⌘ + Shift + P
Enter/exit record during playback in QuickPunch	⌘ + spacebar/click Transport record button
Set and enable pre-/post-roll time	Option + click with selector before/after selection
Disable pre-/post-roll time	Option + click within selection closer to front/back
Scroll to selection start/end	← / → (when selection exceeds window view)
Toggle Transport Master (Pro Tools/Machine/MMC)	⌘ + \

Auditioning

When Transport = Pro Tools:

Function	Key Combination
Play by pre-roll value up to selection start/end	Option + ← / →
Play by post-roll value after selection start/end	⌘ + ← / →
Play by pre and post-roll value through selection start/end	⌘ + Option + ← / →
Play by pre-roll value to current location counter time	Option + ← / → (when no selection)
Play by post-roll value from current location counter time	⌘ + ← / → (when no selection)

When Transport = Machine/MMC:

Function	Key Combination
Cue transport to selection start/end	⌘ + ← / →
Cue transport with pre-/post-roll to selection start/end	Option + ← / →

Function	Key Combination
Scrub (Jog)/Shuttle	
Temporary scrub mode when using Selector	Control + click + drag
Extend selection while scrubbing	Shift + click + drag with Scrubber (also in temporary scrub mode)
Shuttle	Option + click + drag with Scrubber (also in temporary scrub mode)
Shuttle-lock	Control + number key (1–9, where 5 = real-time, 9 = max speed)
Change direction during Shuttle	+/− (e.g. shuttle backward = Control + number key + minus key)
Shuttle-lock stop	0 (press number key to resume shuttle)
Exit Shuttle-lock mode	Spacebar or ⌘ + period key
Editing, Nudging, and Trimming (+/− key usage is on numeric keypad only)	
Change grid value	Control + Option + +/−
Change nudge value	⌘ + Option + +/−
Nudge selection or region right/left by nudge value	+/−
Nudge data within current region to right/left by nudge value (keeps region start/end and moves underlying audio)	Control + +/−
Nudge left selection boundary right/left by nudge value	Option + Shift + +/−
Nudge right selection boundary right/left by nudge value	⌘ + Shift + +/−
Nudge back/forward by next nudge value	See Command Focus Mode section of this guide
Trim left edge of region to right/left by nudge value	Option + +/−
Trim right edge of region to right/left by nudge value	⌘ + +/−
Reverse Trimmer direction when trimming region	Option + Trimmer
Trim up to, but not over, adjacent regions	Hold down Control key while trimming
Duplicate region(s) in Edit window	Option + click selection and drag to destination
Delete selection in Edit window playlist	Delete
Constrain audio region to vertical movement	Control + move audio region with Grabber
Snap region start to stationary playhead or edit selection start	Control + click new region with Grabber
Snap region sync point to stationary playhead or edit selection start	Shift + Control + click new region with Grabber
Snap region end to stationary playhead or edit selection start	⌘ + Control + click new region with Grabber
Zoom	
Horizontal zoom in/out (audio and MIDI)	⌘ +] / [
Vertical zoom in/out (audio)	⌘ + Option +] / [
Vertical zoom in/out (MIDI)	⌘ + Shift +] / [
Fill window with selection	Option + click on Zoomer or Option + F
View entire session	Double-click on Zoomer or Option + A
Zoom vertical and horizontal axis	Hold down ⌘ key while using Zoomer
Zoom to previous horizontal zoom value	Option + click on display scale arrows

MAC OS SHORTCUTS

Function	Key Combination
Max zoom before waveform drawn from disk	⌘ + click on Zoomer (faster drawing from RAM)
Select five preset zoom levels	See Command Focus Mode section of this guide.

Memory Locations

Function	Key Combination
Create memory location	Enter
Reset a memory location	Control + click on memory location button
Delete memory location	Option + click on a memory location button
Recall a memory location	Period key + memory location number + period key (or click on memory location button) (The first period key press is not required with "Classic" numeric keypad mode selected in Preferences.)

Select Edit Tools/Modes

Function	Key Combination
Shuffle	F1 or Option + 1 on alpha keyboard
Slip	F2 or Option + 2 on alpha keyboard
Spot	F3 or Option + 3 on alpha keyboard
Grid	F4 or Option + 4 on alpha keyboard + repeated pressings toggle between relative and absolute Grid mode
Zoomer	F5 or ⌘ + 1 on alpha keyboard
Trimmer	F6 or ⌘ + 2 on alpha keyboard
Selector	F7 or ⌘ + 3 on alpha keyboard
Grabber	F8 or ⌘ + 4 on alpha keyboard
Scrubber	F9 or ⌘ + 5 on alpha keyboard
Pencil	F10 or ⌘ + 6 on alpha keyboard
SmartTool	(F6 and F7) or (F7 and F8) or ⌘ + 7 on alpha keyboard
Cycle through edit tools	Escape key
Cycle through edit modes	~ key

Commands Focus Mode

To use single keys on the commands below, click the A–Z button in the Edit window or use the Control key in combination with the single keys below.

Function	Key Combination
Zoom level 1–5	Alpha keys 1/2/3/4/5
Play to/from edit start by pre-/post-roll value	Alpha keys 6/7
Play to/from edit end by pre-/post-roll amount	Alpha keys 8/9
Copy edit selection to timeline selection	Alpha key 0
Copy timeline selection to edit selection	0
Track View toggle	– (minus key)
Capture timecode	= (on numeric pad)
Center timeline start	Q
Center timeline end	W
Zoom toggle	E
Zoom out horizontally	R
Zoom in horizontally	T
Snap start (of selected region) to timecode	Y (Not available in Pro Tools LE)
Snap sync point (of selected region) to timecode	U (Not available in Pro Tools LE)
Snap End (of selected region) to timecode	I (Not available in Pro Tools LE)
Snap Start (of selected region) to playhead	H

APPENDIX C: SHORTCUTS

Function	Key Combination
Snap Sync point (of selected region) to playhead	J (Not available in Pro Tools LE)
Snap End (of selected region) to playhead	K (Not available in Pro Tools LE)
Move Edit Selection up	P
Move Edit Selection down	; (semi colon)
Tab back	L
Tab forward	' (apostrophe)
Play timeline selection	]
Play edit selection	[
Trim start to insertion	A
Trim end to insertion	S
Fade to start (Available if no selection)	D
Fade (without showing Fades dialog)	F
Fade to end (Available if no selection)	G
Undo	Z
Cut	X
Copy	C
Paste	V
Separate	B
Timeline insertion follows playback (pref toggle)	N
Nudge back by next nudge value	M
Nudge back by nudge value	<
Nudge forward by nudge value	>
Nudge forward by next nudge value	/
Track View toggle	Minus Key (alpha only)
Zoom toggle	E
Zoom defaults	1 through 5

Fades

Function	Key Combination
Apply xfade to selection without accessing Fades window	⌘ + Control + F (uses default fade shape)
Edit fade-in only in Fades window	Option + click + drag fade-in curve (in None Link mode only)
Edit fade-out only in Fades window	⌘ + click + drag fade-out curve (in None Link mode only)
Audition start/stop in Fades window	Spacebar
Reset to default zoom in Fades window	Click on either zoom arrow
Reset standard or S-shape crossfades to default curves	Option + click in xfade window (in Equal Power/Gain modes)
Cycle up/down through Out Shape parameter options	Control + ↑ / ↓
Cycle up/down through In Shape parameter options	Option + ↑ / ↓
Cycle up/down through Link parameter options	↑ / ↓
Cycle up/down through preset Out Shape curves	Control + ← / →
Cycle up/down through preset In Shape curves	Option + ← / →

Regions List

Function	Key Combination
Select region by name	Type letter(s) A–Z (To enable keyboard selection of Regions, click box at top right of Regions list.)

Function	Key Combination
Clear selected region(s) from Regions list	Shift + ⌘ + B
Bypass dialog boxes during deletion of audio files	Option + click Delete/Yes button in respective dialog
Audition region in Regions list	Option + click and hold on region in Regions list
Rename region/file	Double-click region in Regions list or double-click with Grabber on region in playlist
Constrain region placement to start at play/edit cursor location or selection start	Control + click + drag region

Import Audio Dialog

Function	Key Combination
Remove item from list	⌘ + R
Remove all items from list	Shift + ⌘ + R
Add all	⌘ + Option + A
Random-access search through selected file	Move slider to desired location or click left/right side of slider
Import current selection	Enter
Import all	Shift + ⌘ + I
Convert and import current selection	⌘ + C
Convert and import all	Shift + ⌘ + C
Add currently selected region or audio file to list	Enter or Return
Audition currently selected audio file/region	⌘ + P or ⌘ + spacebar
Stop audition of selected file and retain selection	⌘ + P or ⌘ + S
Done	⌘ + W
Cancel	⌘ + period key

Mixing

Function	Key Combination
Make track active/inactive	Click on track symbol in Mix window while holding ⌘ and Control keys
Set all faders to their automation null points	Option + clicking on either automatch triangle
Reset a control to default value	Option + click on Control
Headroom/Track Level/Channel Delay indicator	⌘ + click on Track Level indicator
Clear peak/clip-hold from meter	Click on indicator
Peak counter reset in Headroom Indicator mode	Click on Headroom indicator
Bypass plug-in insert	⌘ + click on insert name in Inserts view
Send mute	⌘ + click on send name in Sends view
Toggle Send Display between All and Individual mode	⌘ + click on Send diamond, then select from pop-up

Automation

Function	Key Combination
Leave absolute minimum/maximum breakpoints while trimming	Hold down Shift key while trimming
Disable auto-creation of anchor breakpoints when trimming automation of a selection	Option + Trimmer
Access Plug-In Automation dialog	⌘ + Option + Control + click on parameters (in Plug-in window) or track display format selector (in Edit window)
Enable/disable plug-in automation	⌘ + Option + Control + click on parameters (in Plug-in window) or track display format selector (in Edit window)
Disable/enable automation playlist on selected track	⌘ + click on track display format selector

APPENDIX C: SHORTCUTS

Function	Key Combination
Disable/enable all automation playlists on selected track	⌘ + Shift + click on track display format selector
Vertically constrain automation movement	Shift + move automation with Grabber
Special paste of automation data between different controls	Control + ⌘ + V
Write automation to end of session/selection	Control + click on Transport End button
Write automation to start of session/selection	Control + click on Transport RTZ button
Write automation from start to end of session/selection	Control + Shift + click on Transport End/RTZ button
Copy to Send	⌘ + Option + H
Display automation playlist of automation-enabled control	⌘ + Control + click on control
Scroll to and display track in default view in Edit window	⌘ + Control + click on track name in Mix, or Insert window or Show/Hide Tracks list (Track defaults: disk=waveform; MIDI=regions; aux/master=volume)
Scroll to and select track in Mix/Edit window	Control + click on track name in Mix or Edit window or Show/Hide Tracks List

When all tracks in selection are displaying automation playlists, hold down Control key during the following operations to affect all playlists on every track in selection:

Delete	Delete
Cut	⌘ + X
Duplicate	⌘ + D
Copy	⌘ + C
Clear	⌘ + B
Insert silence	Shift + ⌘ + E

Numeric Entry

Function	Key Combination
Initiate time entry in Current Location and Big counters	= or * key on numeric keypad
Initiate time entry in Edit window Start/End/Length fields	/ on numeric keypad (Subsequent presses toggle through fields.)
Initiate time entry in Transport window fields	Option + / on numeric keypad (Subsequent presses toggle through fields.)
Capture incoming timecode in Session Setup window (with Start field selected), Spot dialog and Time Stamp Selected dialog	= (Hold down key for continued input.)
Move sub-unit selection to the right	Period key
Move sub-unit selection to the left/right	← / →
Calculator entry mode	+ or – keys followed by offset number
Increment/decrement the current sub-unit	↑ / ↓
Clear entered numeric value and stay in time entry mode	Clear
Apply entered numeric value	Return or Enter
Clear entered numeric value and exit time entry mode	Escape

Note: When Time Code is the selected time scale, initiating time entry highlights entire field, and numeric values are entered right to left.

MAC OS SHORTCUTS

Function	Key Combination
Text Entry	
Move down/up rows	Tab /Shift+Tab
Move to beginning/end of word	↑ / ↓
Move single letters at a time across a name label	← / →
Select entire word	Double-click on word
Peripherals Dialog	
Go to Synchronization window	⌘ + 1
Go to Machine Control window	⌘ + 2
Go to MIDI Controllers window	⌘ + 3
Go to Ethernet Controllers window	⌘ + 4
Go to Mic Preamps window	⌘ + 5
Preferences Dialog	
Go to Display window	⌘ + 1
Go to Operation window	⌘ + 2
Go to Editing window	⌘ + 3
Go to Automation window	⌘ + 4
Go to Processing window	⌘ + 5
Go to Compatibility window	⌘ + 6
Go to MIDI window	⌘ + 7
Plug-In Settings Librarian	
Save settings	⌘ + Shift + S
Copy settings	⌘ + Shift + C
Paste settings	⌘ + Shift + V
Keyboard Input for Plug-In Parameters	
Click mouse in text field	Type desired value
Move down/up parameter fields	Tab/ Shift + Tab
Increase/decrease slider value	↑ / ↓
Input value without leaving field	Enter
Enter value and exit keyboard entry mode	Return
For fields that support kilohertz	Type k after number multiplies by 1000
Numeric Keypad Modes	
Transport Mode	
MIDI metronome on/off	7
MIDI count on/off	8
Merge record on/off	9
Loop playback	4
Loop record	5
QuickPunch record	6
Rewind	1
Fast forward	2
Record	3

APPENDIX C: SHORTCUTS

Function	Key Combination
Play/stop	0
Shuttle mode (TDM systems only)	
1 X forward	6
1 X rewind	4
4 X forward	9
4 X rewind	7
1/4 X forward	3
1/4 X rewind	1
1/2 X forward	5–6
1/2 X rewind	5–4
2 X forward	8–9
2 X backward	8–7
1/16 X forward	2–3
1/16 X backward	2–1
Loop playback of edit selection	0

Note: Choose Classic, Transport, or Shuttle mode in Preferences>Operations menu.

Miscellaneous

Function	Key Combination
Display Takes pop-up list (appears only when selection start or flashing insertion point matches user time stamp of regions)	⌘ + click with Selector tool at selection start or current cursor location
Set all tracks to selected record drive in Disk Allocation dialog (for Pro Tools III—on same Disk I/O only)	Option + click on record drive
Access Playback Engine dialog during Pro Tools launch	Hold down N key while launching Pro Tools
Toggle between Hide All and Show All	Option + click in Show/Hide Tracks list
Bypass repeat dialogs when multiple items will be changed by single operation (e.g. Clear, Delete, Compact)	Option + click respective Proceed button in dialog
Wait for (MIDI note)	F11 (Preference option enabled)
Single key shortcut (with Commands Focus disabled)	Control + "single key"

MIDI Events List Entry
(All commands below are active only when the MIDI Event List window is open.)

Function	Key Combination
Enter start time field for editing	⌘ + Enter (numeric keypad)
Show Event Filter dialog	⌘ + F
Go to	⌘ + G
Scroll to edit selection	⌘ + H
Insert another	⌘ + M
Insert note	⌘ + N
Insert program change	⌘ + P
Insert controller	⌘ + L
Insert poly pressure	⌘ + O
Delete event in MIDI Events list	Option + click

Windows Shortcuts

Function	Key Combination
Global Keyboard Commands	
Change all audio channel strips	Alt + applicable function
Change audio channel strip and all selected audio channel strips	Alt + Shift + applicable function
Toggle item and set all others to same new state	Alt + click on applicable item
Toggle item and set all others to opposite state	Ctrl + click on applicable item
Fine tune	Ctrl + click on control slider/pot/breakpoints
Mix and Edit Groups	
Temporarily isolate channel strip from group operation	Hold down Start/right-click + any operation that affects groups
New group	Ctrl + G (with two or more tracks selected)
Suspend/resume all groups	Ctrl + Shift + G or Ctrl + click on Groups pop-up menu
Rename group	Double-click to far left of group name in the Groups list
Group enable/disable	Type ID letter on keyboard (To enable keyboard selection of groups, click box at top right of Groups list.)
Hide all tracks	Click on track symbol in Show/Hide menu
Show group members only	Right-click on group(s) in Groups list (Right-click + Shift + click for multiple groups)
Record and Playback	
Open New Track dialog	Ctrl + Shift + N
In New Track dialog cycle through track type	Ctrl + </>
Cycle up/down through New Track Options	Ctrl + ↑/↓
Start record	Ctrl + spacebar/F12
Stop record	Spacebar
Stop record and discard take	Esc or Ctrl + period key
Start/stop playback	Spacebar
Half-speed record	Ctrl + Shift + spacebar
Half-speed playback	Shift + spacebar
Pause (pre-prime deck for instant playback and record)	Start + spacebar or Alt + click on Transport play button
Enable/disable online record	Ctrl + Alt + spacebar
Enable/disable online playback	Ctrl + J / Alt + spacebar
Toggle record modes (normal/Destructive/Loop/QuickPunch)	Right-click on Transport record button
Loop Playback toggle	Start + click or right-click on Transport play button
Record-safe track	Ctrl + click on Record enable button
Solo-safe track	Ctrl + click on Solo button
QuickPunch	Ctrl + Shift + P
Enter/exit record during playback in QuickPunch	Ctrl + spacebar/click on Transport record button
Set and enable pre-/post-roll time	Alt + click with selector before/after selection
Disable pre-/post-roll time	Alt + click within selection closer to front/back

APPENDIX C: SHORTCUTS

Function	Key Combination
Scroll to selection start/end	← / → (when selection exceeds window view)
Toggle Transport Master (Pro Tools/Machine/MMC)	Ctrl + \

Auditioning

When Transport = Pro Tools:

Function	Key Combination
Play by pre-roll value up to selection start/end	Alt + ← / →
Play by post-roll value after selection start/end	Ctrl + ← / →
Play by pre- and post-roll value through selection start/end	Ctrl + Alt + ← / →
Play by pre-roll value to current location counter time	Alt + ← / → (when no selection)
Play by post-roll value from current location counter time	Ctrl + ← / → (when no selection)

When Transport = Machine/MMC:

Function	Key Combination
Cue transport to selection start/end	Ctrl + ← / →
Cue transport with pre-/post-roll to selection start/end	Alt + ← / →

Scrub (Jog)/Shuttle

Function	Key Combination
Temporary scrub mode when using Selector	Right-click + drag
Extend selection while scrubbing	Shift + click + drag Scrubber (also in temporary scrub mode)
Shuttle	Alt + click + drag Scrubber (also in temporary scrub mode)
Shuttle-lock	Start + number key (1–9, where 5 = real-time, 9 = max speed)
Change direction during Shuttle	+/– (e.g. shuttle backward = Start + number key + minus key)
Shuttle-lock stop	0 (press number key to resume shuttle)
Exit Shuttle-lock mode	Spacebar or Esc

Edit Selection Definition and Navigation

Function	Key Combination
Locate play/edit cursor to next region-boundary/sync point	Tab
Locate play/edit cursor to previous region-boundary/sync point	Ctrl + Tab
Go to and select next region	Start + Tab
Go to and select previous region	Start + Ctrl + Tab
Extend selection to next region-boundary	Shift + Tab
Extend selection to previous region-boundary	Ctrl + Shift + Tab
Extend selection to include next region	Start + Shift + Tab
Extend selection to include previous region	Start + Shift + Ctrl + Tab
Return to start of session	Enter
Go to end of session	Ctrl + Enter
Extend selection to start of session	Shift + Enter
Extend selection to end of session	Ctrl + Shift + Enter
Set selection start/end during playback	↓ / ↑

WINDOWS SHORTCUTS

Function	Key Combination
Set selection start/end to incoming time code while stopped	↓ / ↑
Select entire region in Edit window	Double-click with Selector
Select entire track in Edit window	Triple-click with Selector / Ctrl + A
Extend play/edit cursor across all tracks and create selection	Alt + click in Rulers
Extend play/edit cursor or selection across all tracks	Enable "All" Edit group (! key) and Shift + click on any other track (To enable keyboard selection of Groups, click box at top right of Groups List.)

Editing, Nudging, and Trimming (+/− key usage is on numeric keypad only)

Function	Key Combination
Change Grid value	Start + Alt + +/−
Change Nudge value	Ctrl + Alt + +/−
Nudge selection or region right/left by nudge value	+/−
Nudge data within current region to right/left by nudge value (keeps region start/end and moves underlying audio)	Start + +/−
Nudge left selection boundary right/left by nudge value	Alt + Shift + +/−
Nudge right selection boundary right/left by nudge value	Ctrl + Shift + +/−
Nudge back/forward by next nudge value	See Command Focus Mode section of this guide
Trim left edge of region to right/left by nudge value	Alt + +/−
Trim right edge of region to right/left by nudge value	Ctrl + +/−
Reverse Trimmer direction when trimming region	Alt + Trimmer
Trim up to, but not over, adjacent regions	Hold down Ctrl key while trimming
Duplicate region(s) in Edit window	Ctrl + click selection and drag to destination
Delete selection in playlist	Backspace
Constrain audio region to vertical movement	Right-click + move audio region with Grabber
Snap region start to stationary playhead or edit selection start	Start + click new region with Grabber
Snap region to stationary playhead or edit selection sync point	Alt + Start + click new region with Grabber
Snap region end to stationary playhead or edit selection start	Ctrl + Start + click new region with Grabber

Zoom

Function	Key Combination
Horizontal zoom in/out	Ctrl +] / [
Vertical zoom in/out (audio)	Ctrl + Alt+] / [
Vertical zoom in/out (MIDI)	Ctrl + Shift +] / [
Fill window with selection	Alt + click on Zoomer or Alt + F
View entire session	Double-click on Zoomer or Alt + A
Zoom vertical and horizontal axis	Hold down Ctrl key while using Zoomer
Zoom to previous orientation	Alt + click on display scale arrows
Max zoom before waveform drawn from disk	Ctrl+ click on Zoomer (faster drawing from RAM)
Select five preset zoom levels	See Command Focus Mode section of this guide

Function	Key Combination
Memory Locations	
Create memory location	Enter (on numeric keypad)
Reset a memory location	Start + click on memory location button
Delete memory location	Alt + click on a memory location button
Recall a memory location	Period key + memory location number + period key or click on memory location button (The first period key press is not required with "Classic" numeric keypad mode selected in Preferences.)
Select Edit Tools/Modes	
Shuffle	F1
Slip	F2
Spot	F3
Grid	F4
Zoomer	F5 or Ctrl + 1 on alpha keyboard
Trimmer	F6 or Ctrl + 2 on alpha keyboard
Selector	F7 or Ctrl + 3 on alpha keyboard
Grabber	F8 or Ctrl + 4 on alpha keyboard
Scrubber	F9 or Ctrl + 5 on alpha keyboard
Pencil	F10 or Ctrl + 6 on alpha keyboard
SmartTool	(F6 and F7) or (F7 and F8) or Ctrl + 7 on alpha keyboard
Cycle through edit tools	Center mouse click
Cycle through edit modes	~ key

Commands Focus Mode

To use single keys on the commands below, click the A–Z button in the Edit window or use the Start key in combination with the single keys below.

Zoom level 1–5	Alpha 1/2/3/4/5
Play to/from edit start by pre-/post-roll value	Alpha 6/7
Play to/from edit end by pre-/post-roll amount	Alpha 8/9
Copy edit selection to timeline selection	Alpha 0
Copy timeline selection to edit selection	0
Track View toggle	– (minus key)
Capture timecode	=
Center timeline start	Q
Center timeline end	W
Zoom toggle	E
Zoom out horizontally	R
Zoom in horizontally	T
Snap start (of selected region) to timecode	Y (Not available in Pro Tools LE)
Snap sync point (of selected region) to timecode	U (Not available in Pro Tools LE)
Snap end (of selected region) to timecode	I (Not available in Pro Tools LE)
Snap start (of selected region) to playhead	H
Snap sync point (of selected region) to playhead	J (Not available in Pro Tools LE)
Snap end (of selected region) to playhead	K (Not available in Pro Tools LE)

WINDOWS SHORTCUTS

Function	Key Combination
Move edit selection up	P (Not available in Pro Tools LE)
Move edit selection down	; (semi colon)
Tab back	L
Tab forward	' (apostrophe)
Play timeline selection	]
Play edit selection	[
Trim start to insertion	A
Trim end to insertion	S
Fade to start (Available if no selection)	D
Fade (without showing Fades dialog)	F
Fade to End (Available if no selection)	G
Undo	Z
Cut	X
Copy	C
Paste	V
Separate	B
Timeline insertion follows playback (pref toggle)	N
Nudge back by next nudge value	M
Nudge back by nudge value	<
Nudge forward by nudge value	>
Nudge forward by next nudge value	/
Track View toggle	Minus key (alpha only)
Zoom toggle	E
Zoom defaults	1 through 5

Fades

Function	Key Combination
Apply xfade to selection without accessing Fades window	Ctrl + Start + F (uses last selected fade shape)
Edit fade-in only in Fades window	Alt + click + drag fade-in curve (in "None" Link mode only)
Edit fade-out only in Fades window	Ctrl + click + drag fade-out curve (in "None" Link mode only)
Audition start/stop in Fades window	Spacebar
Reset to default zoom in Fades window	Ctrl + click on either zoom arrow
Reset standard or S-shape crossfades to default curves	Alt + click in xfade window (in Equal Power/Gain modes)
Cycle up/down through Out Shape parameter options	Start + ↑ / ↓
Cycle up/down through In Shape parameter options	Alt + ↑ / ↓
Cycle up/down through Link parameter options	↑ / ↓
Cycle up/down through preset Out Shape curves	Start + ← / →
Cycle up/down through preset In Shape curves	Alt + ← / →

Regions List

Function	Key Combination
Select region by name	Type letter(s) A–Z (To enable keyboard selection of Regions, click box at top right of Regions list.)

APPENDIX C: SHORTCUTS

Function	Key Combination
Clear selected region(s) from Regions list	Shift + Ctrl + B
Bypass dialog boxes during deletion of audio files	Alt + click Delete/Yes button in respective dialog
Audition region in Regions list	Alt + click and hold on region in Regions list
Rename region/file	Double-click region in Regions list or double-click with Grabber on region in playlist
Constrain region placement to start at play/edit cursor location or selection start	Right-click and drag region

Import Audio Dialog

Function	Key Combination
Add currently selected audio region/file to list	Alt + A
Convert and import currently selected audio region/file to list	Alt + O
Remove currently selected audio file/region	Alt + R
Remove all audio files/regions	Alt + M
Audition currently selected audio file/region	Spacebar
Stop audition of selected file and retain selection	Spacebar
Stop audition of selected file and go to top of scroll box	Home
Move between file windows	Tab
Done	Alt + E
Cancel	Esc or Alt + C
Random-access fwd/rew search through selected file	Drag slider to desired location or click left/right side of slider

Mixing

Function	Key Combination
Make track active/inactive	Click on track symbol in Mix window while holding Ctrl and Start keys
Set all faders to their automation null points	Alt + click on either automatch triangle
Reset a control to default value	Alt + click on control
Headroom/Track Level/Channel Level indicator	Ctrl + click on Track Level indicator
Clear peak/clip-hold from meter	Click on indicator
Peak counter reset in Headroom Indicator mode	Click on Headroom indicator
Bypass plug-in Insert	Ctrl + click on insert name in Inserts view
Send mute	Ctrl + click on send name in Sends view
Toggle Send display between All and Individual mode	Ctrl + click on Send pop-up

Automation

Function	Key Combination
Leave extremity breakpoints undisturbed while trimming	Hold down Shift key while trimming
Disable auto-creation of anchor breakpoints when trimming automation	Alt + Trimmer
Access Plug-In Automation dialog	Ctrl + Alt + Start + click on Parameters (in Plug-In window) track display format selector (in Edit window)
Enable/disable plug-in automation	Ctrl + Alt + Start + click on Parameters (in Plug-In window) track display format selector (in Edit window)

Function	Key Combination
Disable/enable automation playlist on selected track	Ctrl + click on track display format selector
Disable/enable ALL automation playlists on selected track	Ctrl + Shift + click on track display format selector
Vertically constrain automation movement	Shift + move automation with Trimmer
Special paste of automation data between different controls	Start + Ctrl + V
Write automation to end of session/selection	Start + click or right-click on Transport End button
Write automation to start of session/selection	Start + click or right-click on Transport RTZ button
Write automation from start to end of session/selection	Start + Shift + click or Shift + right-click on Transport End/RTZ button
Copy to send	Ctrl + Alt + H
Display automation playlist of automation-enabled control	Ctrl + right-click on control
Scroll to and display track in default view in Edit window	Ctrl + right-click on track name in Mix, Edit, Insert or Sends window or Show/Hide Tracks List (Track defaults: disk=waveform; MIDI=notes; aux/master=volume)
Scroll to and select track in Mix/Edit window	Right-click on track name in Mix, Edit, Insert or Sends window or Show/Hide Tracks list

When all tracks in selection are displaying automation playlists, hold down Start key during the following operations to affect all playlists on every track in selection:

Function	Key Combination
Delete	Ctrl + Backspace
Cut	Ctrl + X
Duplicate	Ctrl + D
Copy	Ctrl + C
Clear	Ctrl + B
Insert Silence	Ctrl + Shift + E

Numeric Entry

Function	Key Combination
Initiate time entry in Current Location and Big Counters	*
Initiate time entry in Edit window Start/End/Length fields	/ (Subsequent presses toggle through fields.)
Initiate time entry in Transport window fields	Alt + / numeric keypad (Subsequent presses toggle through fields.)
Capture incoming timecode in Session Setup window (with Start field selected), Spot dialog and Time Stamp Selected dialog	= (Hold down key for continued input.)
Move sub-unit selection to the right	Period key
Move sub-unit selection to the left/right	← / →
Calculator Entry mode	+ or − keys followed by offset number
Increment/decrement the current sub-unit	↑ / ↓
Clear entered numeric value and stay in time entry mode	Retype value
Apply entered numeric value	Enter
Clear entered numeric value and exit time entry mode	Esc

APPENDIX C: SHORTCUTS

Function	Key Combination
Text Entry	
Move down/up rows	Tab /Shift-Tab
Move to beginning/end of word	↑ / ↓
Move single letters at a time across a name label	← / →
Select entire word	Double-click on word
Peripherals Dialog	
Go to Synchronization window	Ctrl + 1
Go to Machine Control window	Ctrl + 2
Go to MIDI Controllers window	Ctrl + 3
Go to Ethernet Controllers window	Ctrl + 4
Go to Mic Preamps window	Ctrl + 5
Preferences Dialog	
Go to Display window	Ctrl + 1
Go to Operation window	Ctrl + 2
Go to Editing window	Ctrl + 3
Go to Automation window	Ctrl + 4
Go to Processing window	Ctrl + 5
Go to Compatibility window	Ctrl + 6
Go to MIDI window	Ctrl + 7
Plug-In Setting Librarian	
Save settings	Ctrl + Shift + S
Copy settings	Ctrl + Shift + C
Paste settings	Ctrl + Shift + V
Keyboard Input for Plug-In Parameters	
Click mouse in text field	Type desired value
Move down/up parameter fields	Tab / Shift + Tab
Increase/decrease slider value	↑ / ↓
Input value without leaving field	Enter (on numeric keypad)
Enter value and exit keyboard entry mode	Enter
For fields that support kilohertz	Type k after number multiplies by 1000
Numeric Keypad Modes	
Transport Modes	
MIDI metronome on/off	7
MIDI count on/off	8
Merge record on/off	9
Loop playback	4
Loop record	5
QuickPunch record	6
Rewind	1
Fast forward	2

WINDOWS SHORTCUTS 373

Function	Key Combination
Record	3
Play/stop	0

Shuttle Modes (TDM Systems Only)

Function	Key Combination
1 X forward	6
1 X rewind	4
4 X forward	9
4 X rewind	7
1/4 X forward	3
1/4 X rewind	1
1/2 X forward	5–6
1/2 X rewind	5–4
2 X forward	8–9
2 X backward	8–7
1/16 X forward	2–3
1/16 X backward	2–1
Loop playback of edit selection	0

Miscellaneous

Function	Key Combination
Display Takes pop-up list (appears only when selection start or flashing insertion point matches user time stamp of regions)	Ctrl + click with Selector tool at selection start or current cursor location
Set all tracks to selected record drive in Disk Allocation dialog	Alt + click on record drive
Access Playback Engine dialog during Pro Tools launch	Hold down N key while launching Pro Tools
Toggle between Hide All and Show All	Alt + click in Show/Hide Tracks list
Bypass repeat dialogs when multiple items will be changed by single operation (e.g. Clear, Delete, Compact)	Alt + click respective Proceed button in dialog

MIDI Events List Entry
(All commands below are active only when the MIDI Event List window is open.)

Function	Key Combination
Enter start time field for editing	Ctrl + Enter (numeric keypad)
Show Event Filter dialog	Ctrl + F
Go to	Ctrl + G
Scroll to edit selection	Ctrl + H
Insert another	Ctrl + M
Insert note	Ctrl + N
Insert program change	Ctrl + P
Insert controller	Ctrl + L
Insert poly pressure	Ctrl + O
Delete event in MIDI Events list	Alt + Click

Index

A

Absolute Grid mode. *See* Grid mode
ADAT lightpipe connection, 61
AIFF files, 20
All Notes Off command, MIDI, 210–211
Answerbase page, Digidesign Web site, 8
archiving files, 142
    bounced files, 313–318
arrow keys, selections with, 224
assembling tracks, 130–131
Audio File Type button, 20
Audio Files subfolder, 11
audio interface, 3–5
Audio Media Options menu, 340–342
Audio MIDI Setup dialog box, 178–179
Audio Regions list, 39
    for AudioSuite plug-ins, 269
    boundaries, adjusting, 44
    clearing unused regions, 313–315
    importing into, 81–85
    for loop recording, 168
    punch-in showing in, 163
    QuickPunch regions in, 165
    showing paths, 335
    triangle by name of region, 85
Audio Zoom Down button, 220
Audio Zoom Up button, 220
AudioSuite plug-ins, 268–272
    A/B comparisons, allowing, 271
    auditioning effects, 271
    entire selection option for, 270–271
    presets, choosing, 271–272
    processing options, 270
    TCE (Time Compress/Expand) Trim tool and, 323–327

auditioning
    AudioSuite plug-in effects, 271
    selections, 228–230
Auto Input Monitor option, 172
AutoFilter dialog box, 305
automation, 284–290
    copying, 296–297
    Edit window, working in, 292–296
    Grabber tool with, 332
    list of modes, 285
    into master fader, 300
    modes for, 284–288
    pasting, 296–297
    Pencil tool for working on, 293–294
    plug-in automation, 288–290
    Trim tool with, 332
Automation Enable window, 53
AutoName feature, enabling/disabling, 126
aux tracks
    click tracks as, 150–151
    creating, 76
    MIDI gear, monitoring, 190
    pre- and post-fader sends, 283
    voices and, 151

B

backing up files, 142, 313–318
Bar I Beat Markers dialog box, 321–322
bars for MIDI tracks, 204–206
Bass Cue Mix, 65
beat. *See* tempo
Big Counter window, 53
bit depths, 56
    for bounced file, 308–309

INDEX

for session, 21
single session, mixing and matching in, 83
Bounce to Disk function, 304–312
    bit depth, selecting, 308–309
    conversion quality, selecting, 309–310
    file formats, selecting, 307
    low latency monitoring and, 173
    sample rate, selecting, 308–309
    saving bounced files, 310, 312
Bounce to QuickTime Movie option, 344
buses
    names for, 68–69
    setting up, 68–69
BWF files, 20, 56

C

capturing selections, 123–125
CD burning, 304–312
Change Duration option, 202
Change Velocity option, 201
channel strips, 258. *See also* Mix window
    group icon, 263
    icons, meaning of, 261
    inserts, 259
    sections of, 259–261
    sends, 259
Chapter 1 session, downloading, 24
clearing unused regions, 313–315
Click/Countoff Options dialog box, 154–158
    for MIDI device click tracks, 192
click tracks
    accented beats, 153
    activating the click, 155
    as aux tracks, 150–151
    countoff, activating, 155
    defined, 150
    deleting, 175
    low latency monitoring and, 173–175
    meter, setting, 157
    to MIDI device, 192
    muting, 159, 175
    note value, setting, 157–158
    options, setting, 154–158
    plug-ins for, 151–153
    tempo, setting, 156–157
    tone, choosing, 153
    unaccented beats, 153
    volume of click, displaying, 156
clipping, volume controls and, 148
closing sessions, 23

columns
    Edit window columns, displaying, 46
    for memory locations, 257
    Mix window, selecting columns in, 50–51
    in Workspace window, 94
compacting sessions, 315–318
Compatibility page, Digidesign Web site, 8
compression, 303
computer requirements, 2
Conductor icon, 321
consolidating regions, 338–339
control surfaces with RTAS plug-ins, 276
conversion quality for bounced files, 309–310
Convert After Bounce option, 310–311
Convert During Bounce option, 310–311
Copy command, shortcut key for, 136
copying
    automation, 296–297
    outside folders, copying files to, 340–342
    regions, 135–136, 248
    session files, 13
CPU requirements, 2
create continuous files option for AudioSuite plug-ins, 270
create individual files option for AudioSuite plug-ins, 270
crossfades, creating, 242–244
crossover points for crossfades, 243
curves. *See* fades
Customer Service page, Digidesign Web site, 8
customizing
    Edit window, 41–48
    Mix window, 50–51
    sessions, 57–73
Cut command shortcut key, 137
cutting regions, 137

D

DAW (Digital Audio Workstation), 1
dedicated computers, 2
delay effects, 280
deleting
    click aux tracks, 175
    fader groups, tracks from, 266
    input paths, 59
    MIDI cables, 184
    multiple tracks, 138
    permanent deletes, avoiding, 318
    with Selector tool, 121
    tracks, 138–139
    unused regions, clearing, 315

destructive recording, 169–170
Digi 001 interface features, 4
Digi 002 interface features, 4–5
Digidesign Web site
    compatibility of hardware information on, 6
    for installation information, 8
    specifications for hardware on, 5
    support listing, 8
Disk Space window, 54
dithering
    adjusting dither, 301–302
    compressors with, 303
documentation, 17
downloading Chapter 1 session, 24
Drum Cue Mix, 65
drum tracks, Transpose option with, 203
dry mixing. *See* wet/dry mixing
duplicating regions, 131–132
dynamic-based effects, 280

E

echo effects, 280
edit density, 338
Edit Groups list. *See* Edit window
Edit menu, 29
Edit window, 28–30. *See also* Audio Regions list; editing; MIDI Regions list; Timeline; timeline insertion; Track Show/Hide list; tracks; zooming
    Audio button, 39
    Audio Regions button, 42
    automation, working with, 292–296
    boundaries of regions, adjusting, 44
    columns, displaying, 46
    customizing, 41–48
    Edit Groups list, 37–38
        boundaries, adjusting, 44
    Groups button, 43
    height of tracks, adjusting, 48
    hiding regions, 45
    location displays, 106
    Main location display, 107–109
    MIDI button, 39
    MIDI Regions button, 43
    Mix window, toggling between, 30
    moving tracks in, 80
    navigating in, 106–112
    regions in, 13–14
    ruler types in, 40
    shortcut keys in, 112
    size of regions, adjusting, 44

    Sub location display, 107–109
    Tab key in, 110–111
    Tab to Transient button, 111–112
    time scales
        displaying, 47
        for Sub time display, 107
    Tools area, 40–41
    tools in, 104–106
    Track area, 36
        columns, displaying, 46
        selections in, 109
    transients in, 111–112
    viewing menus in, 41–43
editing. *See also* MIDI menu; zooming; specific modes
    assembling tracks, 130–131
    capturing selections, 123–125
    copying regions, 135–136
    cutting regions, 137
    duplicating regions, 131–132
    MIDI Event List, non-note data on, 209–211
    MIDI tracks, 193–197
    modes for, 41
    non-destructive editing, 15–16
    pasting regions, 136–137
    repeating regions, 133–134
    separating regions, 125–128
    trimming regions, 128–129
effects. *See also* inserts; plug-ins
    dynamic-based effects, 280
    time-based effects, 281–284
e-mailing session files, 13
Enforce Mac/PC Compatibility check box, 22, 57
Enter key
    memory locations, creating, 255
    selections with, 224–226
exporting MIDI data, 213–214

F

Fade Files subfolder, 12
    fade file in, 239
fade-outs
    creating, 240–241
    with master fader, 300
fader groups, 263–267
    adding and removing tracks from, 266
    creating, 264–266
    names for, 265
    nested fader groups, 267
    selections in, 266–267
    toggling in, 334

INDEX

working with, 266–267
fades. *See also* master faders
    automation modes, 284–288
    creating, 236–248
    crossfades, creating, 242–244
    crossover points for crossfades, 243
    Fade Files subfolder, 12
    fade-ins, creating, 237–239
    for MIDI tracks, 189
    with Smart tool, 245–248
Fades dialog box
    for crossfades, 242–244
    for fade-ins, 237–239
    for fade-outs, 240–241
File menu, 16–17
files. *See also* specific types
    management of, 17
    names of, 11
    referring files, 340–342
    regions *vs.*, 13–14
filters, MIDI input, 206–208
FireWire connections, 5
Flatten Performance option, 200–201
folders. *See also* specific folders
    new folder for session, creating, 18–19
    referring files to outside folders, 340–342

G

Grabber tool, 105
    with automation, 332
    fades, adjusting, 248
    MIDI Event List, editing velocity data in, 210
    MIDI tracks, editing, 195–196
    for mixing, 332
    regions, moving, 248–249
    Separation Grabber tool, 232–234
    in Shuffle mode, 118
    working with, 122
Grid mode, 104
    Bars:Beats grid scale, 115
    changing grids, 134–135
    for punching in, 160
    Relative Grid mode, 323
    TCE (Time Compress/Expand) Trim tool in, 232
    trimming regions, 128–129
    working with, 114–117
Groove Quantize feature, 199–200
groups. *See* Edit window; fader groups
Groups list, 258
Guitar Cue Mix, 65

H

half-speed playbacks, 331
hard drives, 5–7
    partitioning hard drive, 7
    second hard drives, using, 6–7
    speed requirements, 5
height of tracks, adjusting, 48
help with installation, 8
hiding. *See* showing/hiding

I

I/O settings
    for new sessions, 144–145
    selecting, 22
    session, effects on, 96–98
I/O Setup dialog box, 57–73. *See also* buses; inputs; inserts; outputs
    Audition button, 70
    Default Output button, 71
    Default Output setting in, 96
    managing I/O settings, 70–73
    Meter setting, 71
    recovering settings, 73
    saving settings, 72
icons
    channel strip icons, 261
    Conductor icon, 321
    group icons, 263
    for TCE (Time Compress/Expand) Trim tool, 231
IDE/ATA connections, 5
Identify Beat function, 321–322
Import Audio dialog box, 81–83
Import Session Data dialog box, 89
    Source Properties section, 89–90
importing, 81–96. *See also* tracks
    into Audio Regions list, 81–85
    bounced files, 310
    I/O settings, 68–73
    locating files for, 81–84
    MIDI data, 211–213
    movies, 342–343
    storing converted files, selecting location for, 84–85
    in Workspace window, 91–96
inactive tracks, 336–337
input filter for MIDI tracks, 206–208
Input Only Monitor option, 172
Input Quantize option, 204

inputs, 3
    assigning paths, 62
    changing path input, 64
    customizing, 59–60
    for inserts, 66
    master faders and, 299
    MIDI inputs
        connecting, 184–185
        track input options, 186–187
    mono, configuring path as, 61
    names for, 60
    for recording, 146
    setting up, 57–58
    signal flow order for, 262
    stereo, configuring path as, 61
    sub-paths, setting up, 62–63
    for tracks, 146
inserts, 259. *See also* Mix window
    for click plug-in, 152
    with RTAS plug-ins, 273–274
    setting up, 66–68
    signal flow order for, 262
installing Pro Tools software, 7–8
instruments
    transients, 111
    virtual instruments, using, 277–279
Items to Copy section, Save Session Copy In
        command, 142

L

L (left) files, 83, 87
latency
    low latency monitoring, 173–175
    MIDI latency, eliminating, 215
LE systems, 2
Link Edit and Timeline button, 330–331
Loop Playback mode, 100
    Timeline Insertion Follows Playback preference,
        227–228
Loop Record mode, 166–168
low latency monitoring, 173–175
    with Mbox interface, 176

M

Main output, 65
manufacturer name for MIDI device, adding, 182
Marker time property, 253
master faders, 77, 297–303
    automation, writing, 300
    controlling mix with, 300

    creating, 298–299
    dither, adjusting, 301–302
    icon for, 261
    mastering techniques with, 300–303
mastering, 300–303
    compression, 303
    dither, adjusting, 301–302
Mbox interface
    features, 3
    low latency monitoring in, 176
memory locations, 252–257
    creating, 252–255
    recalling, 255
    settings, selecting, 254
    working with, 256–257
Merge feature for MIDI tracks, 193
meter
    click track meter, setting, 157
    for MIDI tracks, 204–206
MIDI channels
    input filter for, 206–208
    for multi-keyboard setup, 187
MIDI clock, 183
    virtual MIDI inputs, 187
MIDI Controller, 188
MIDI data
    editing, 193–197
    exporting, 213–214
    importing, 211–213
    in session files, 10
    system exclusive data, 207–208
    with virtual instruments, 279
MIDI devices. *See also* MIDI tracks
    aux tracks for monitoring, 190
    channels, choosing, 183
    click tracks, assigning, 192
    connecting, 184–185
    deleting cables, 284
    future of, 215
    manufacturer name, adding, 182
    new configuration, creating, 179–180
    patch list for, 191
    signal path, managing, 185–189
    studio, setting up, 178–185
MIDI Devices menu, 185
MIDI Event List
    All Notes Off command, 210–211
    viewing non-note data, 209–211
    window, 208–209
MIDI machine control option, 183

INDEX

MIDI menu, 197–204
    Change Duration option, 202
    Change Velocity option, 201
    Flatten Performance option, 200–201
    Groove Quantize feature, 199–200
    Input Quantize option, 204
    Quantize function, 198–199
    Restore Performance option, 200–201
    Select Notes/Split Notes option, 203
    tempo, setting up, 204–206
    Transpose option, 202
MIDI Regions list, 39
    boundaries, adjusting, 44
    importing data to, 213
    size, adjusting, 44
MIDI time code (MTC), 183
    virtual MIDI inputs, 187
MIDI time stamping, compatibility with, 215
MIDI tracks, 77. *See also* MIDI menu
    bars, setting up, 204–206
    faders for, 189
    Grabber tool, editing with, 195–196
    importing data to, 213
    input, 186–187
    input filter for, 206–208
    keyboard graphic, 195
    keyboard-like display, 48
    Merge feature, 193
    meter, setting up, 204–206
    naming, 186
    outputs for, 188–189
    pan value for, 189
    Patch Every *n* Sec check box, 191
    Pencil tool, editing with, 197
    Randomize feature, use of, 199
    recording, 191–193
    routing signal in, 218
    tempo, setting up, 204–206
    tools, editing with, 194–197
    Trim tool, editing with, 196
    virtual instruments, using, 277–279
    virtual MIDI inputs, 187
    volume, adjusting, 189
    zooming on, 221
MIDI Zoom Down button, 221
Mini track height, Smart tool and, 236
Mix window, 28–30, 257–262. *See also* tracks
    Channel Strips area, 49
    columns, selecting, 50–51
    customizing, 50–51
    Edit window, toggling between, 30

    inserts, 51
    layout of, 49–50
    Mix Groups area, 49
    moving tracks in, 80
    Narrow Mix Window mode, 257–258
    narrowing, 51
    overview of, 30
    sends, 51
    Show/Hide area, 49
    terminology, 258–261
mixing. *See also* automation; fader groups; wet/dry mixing
    Bounce to Disk function, 304–312
    Edit tools for, 332–333
    mastering, 300–303
    memory locations, 252–257
    signal flow, 261–262
    terminology, 258–261
    tips for, 279–284
monitoring
    low latency monitoring, 173–175
    modes, 172–175
mono, configuring path as, 61
mono (summed) file format, 307
movies, working with, 342–344
moving
    regions, 14, 248–250
    tracks, 79–80
multi-keyboard setup, MIDI channels for, 187
multi-mono plug-ins, 274–275
multiple mono file format, 307
muting tracks, 97–98
    click tracks, 159, 175

N

names. *See also* renaming
    for bounced files, 312
    of buses, 68–69
    for captured selection, 124–125
    for fader groups, 265
    of files, 11
    for folders, 19
    for I/O settings, 72
    for input paths, 60
    for memory locations, 253
    for MIDI configuration, 180
    for MIDI tracks, 186
    for separated regions, 126
    in session files, 10
    for sessions, 17–19, 102
    for tracks, 78, 171

INDEX

Narrow Mix Window mode, 257–258
navigating
    in Edit window, 106–112
    between folders, 18
    for movie file tracks, 343
    in selections, 228–230
    Workspace window, 93
nested fader groups, 267
New Group dialog box, 264–265
New Session dialog box, 56
    Last Used I/O settings default, 144
New Session shortcut key, 25
New Track dialog box
    aux tracks, creating, 76
    shortcut keys for opening, 73
noise shaping options, 302
non-destructive editing, 15–16
non-linear environment, 14
None link mode for crossfades, 244
None time property, 253
notes. *See also* MIDI menu
    click track note value, setting, 157–158
Nudge function, 249–250
nudging regions, 249–250

O

offline regions, 336–337
Open dialog box, 24–25
Open Session shortcut key, 25
opening
    I/O settings, 73
    non-launched Pro Tools, opening session where, 27–28
    pre-existing session, 24–26
Operations menu
    for Loop Record mode, 166–168
    low latency monitoring, 173
    playing selections with, 100
output volume
    for click tracks, 151
    for recording, 147
    track output volume, setting, 147
outputs, 3. *See also* master faders
    for inserts, 66
    MIDI outputs, connecting, 184–185
    for MIDI tracks, 188–189
    for recording, 146–147
    renaming output paths, 65
    setting up, 64–66
    signal flow order for, 262
    sub-paths, assigning outputs to, 63
    for tracks, 146–147
overwrite files option for AudioSuite plug-ins, 270

P

pan sliders
    signal flow order for, 262
    stereo/mono designation, 261
panning
    automation modes, 284–288
    Edit window, working in, 294–295
    for MIDI tracks, 189
    resetting, 149
    for tracks, 148
partitioning hard drive, 7
Paste command shortcut key, 137
pasting
    automation, 296–297
    regions, 136–137
Patch Every *n* Sec check box, 191
patch list for MIDI clock, 191
paths
    inputs, assigning, 59–60
    overlapping, 66
    selecting all paths, 67
    showing paths, 335
Pencil tool, 105
    automation, working on, 293–294
    MIDI tracks, editing, 197
playback. *See also* Loop Playback mode
    at half speed, 331
    for loop recording, 167
    muting tracks, 97–98
    in QuickPunch mode, 166
    selections, playing, 99–100
    soloing tracks, 97–98
    Timeline Insertion Follows Playback preference, 227–228
playlist for AudioSuite plug-ins, 269
Plug-in Settings subfolder, 13
plug-ins, 66, 267–279. *See also* RTAS plug-ins
    AudioSuite plug-ins, 268–272
    automation, 288–290
    click plug-in, using, 151–153
    compressor plug-ins, 303
    inactive plug-ins, 337
    multiple windows, opening, 276
    virtual instruments, using, 277–279
    wet/dry mixing and, 284

INDEX

pointer, defined, 9
pointer-based applications, 9–13
post-fader sends, 262, 283
post-roll option, 161–162
pre-existing session, opening, 24–26
pre-fader sends, 262, 283
pre-roll position, 162
    for destructive recording, 170
    for loop recording, 167
Preferences dialog box, fade settings in, 247
presets
    for AudioSuite plug-ins, 271–272
    memory locations, 252–257
    zooming presets, 221–223
Pro Tools
    LE systems, 2
    TDM systems, 2, 336
production phases, 103
pts file extension, 10
punching in/punching out, 160–163
    adjusting selection, 224
    monitor modes and, 172

Q

Quantize function, 198–199
QuickPunch recording, 164–166
QuickTime Movies, Bounce to, 344
quitting Pro Tools session, 33–34

R

R (right) files, 87
rackmount effects, 66
Random Pencil option for pan, 295
Randomize feature, 199
Reason Adapted software, 278
recording
    basic recording, 158–159
    destructive recording, 169–170
    I/O settings, changing, 144–145
    input, setting up, 146
    Loop Record mode, 166–168
    MIDI tracks, 191–193
    naming tracks before, 171
    output, setting up, 146–147
    output pan, setting, 148
    playing back, 159–160
    post-roll option, 161–162
    pre-roll option, 162
    punching in/punching out, 160–163

QuickPunch recording, 164–166
    segment of audio, replacing, 160–163
    stopping recording, 159
    tear-away strips, using, 148–149
recovering I/O settings, 73
referring files, 340–342
regions. *See also* Audio Regions list; Grid mode; MIDI Regions list; Shuffle mode; Spot mode
    for AudioSuite plug-ins, 269
    capturing selections, 123–125
    clearing unused regions, 313–315
    consolidating regions, 338–339
    copying, 135–136
    duplicating regions, 131–132
    Edit window for managing, 29
    fade region, 239
    files *vs.*, 13–14
    master faders and, 299
    moving, 14, 248–250
    non-destructive editing, 15–16
    nudging, 249–250
    offline regions, 336–337
    pasting regions, 136–137
    renaming new regions, 130
    repeating regions, 133–134
    separating regions, 125–128
    Separation Grabber tool for moving, 232–234
    Slip mode, working with, 113–114
    trimming regions, 128–129
    voices with, 151
    working with, 14
renaming
    output paths, 65
    regions, 130
repeating regions, 133–134
Restore Performance option, 200–201
Return key, selections with, 224–226
reverb effects, 280
    multiple tracks, sends from, 334
ReWire software, 278
RTAS plug-ins, 272–276
    instantiating, 276
    multi-mono plug-ins, 274–275
    on stereo tracks, 274–275
    Target button, 276
    virtual instruments, using, 277–279
    working with, 273–274
Ruler area
    Edit window, ruler types in, 40
    link areas in, 330–331
    Track area, 109

S

S curve for fade-ins, 238
S/PDIF connection, 61
sample-accurate sync, 248
Sample Rate button, 20
sample rates
    for bounced file, 308–309
    selecting, 20–21
single session, mixing and matching in, 83
Save As command, 101–102
Save As text box, 17
Save command, 101–102
Save Session As command, 101–102
Save Session Copy In option, 140–142
    for archiving, 142
    on clearing unused sessions, 318
    on compacting sessions, 318
    when referring to source media, 342
saving
    bounced file, 310, 312
    I/O settings, 72
    on quitting Pro Tools session, 33
    session files, 13
    sessions, 57
    TCE (Time Compress/Expand) Trim tool settings, 325
Scrub tool, 105
SCSI connections, 5
SD II files, 20
searching audio with Workspace window, 92–96
second hard drives, using, 6–7
Selection time property, 253
selections
    with arrow keys, 224
    auditioning, 228–230
    with Enter key, 224–226
    in fader groups, 266–267
    navigating in, 228–230
    with Return key, 224–226
    Separation Grabber tool for, 232–234
    with Tab to Transient function, 226–227
Select Notes/Split Notes option, 203
Selector tool, 105
    automation, copying and pasting, 296–297
    for bouncing to disk, 304
    copying regions with, 135
    for destructive recording, 169–170
    for fade-ins, 237
    for loop recording, 167
    for memory locations, 253

MIDI Event List, editing velocity data in, 210
    pasting regions with, 136–137
    for trimming region, 129
    working with, 106–109, 121–122
semitones, adjusting, 202–203
sends, 51, 259
    master faders and, 299
    from multiple tracks, 334
    signal flow order for, 262
separating regions, 125–128
Separation Grabber tool, 232–234
    Smart tool with, 235
session files, 10
    copying, 13
    saving, 13
session folders, 9–10
Session Format menu, Save Session Copy In command, 141
Session Parameters section, Save Session Copy In command, 141
Session Setup window, 52
sessions
    closing, 23
    compacting sessions, 315–318
    customizing, 57–73
    names for, 17–19, 102
    new sessions, creating, 16–22
    parameters, choosing, 19–23
    quitting Pro Tools session, 33–34
    sample rate for, 20–21
    Save As command for, 101–102
    Save Session Copy In command, 140–142
shortcut keys, 17
    for audio zooming, 220
    for Copy command, 136
    for Cut command, 137
    for Duplicate function, 132
    in Edit window, 112
    for half-speed playback, 331
    for MIDI height zooming, 221
    New Session shortcut key, 25
    for New Track dialog box, 73
    for nudging regions, 250
    Open Session shortcut key, 25
    for Paste command, 137
    paths, selecting all, 67
    for record/play, 159
    zoom presets, switching between, 223
Show/Hide Tracks area, 37
    boundaries, adjusting, 44
    drop-down menu, 42

INDEX

showing/hiding. *See also* Mix window
    Edit window regions, hiding, 45
    transport features, 32
Shuffle mode, 104
    assembling tracks in, 131
    Grabber tool in, 118
    working with, 117–118
Slip mode, 104
    for punching in, 160
    working with, 113–114
Smart tool, 234–236
    fades, creating, 245–248
snap to grid. *See* Grid mode
soloing
    repeated regions, 134
    tracks, 97–98
sorting memory locations, 256
source media, referring files to, 340–342
Split Notes option, 203
Spot mode, 104
    working with, 119
spotting, 119
Square Pencil option for pan, 295
stereo interleaved file format, 307
Stereo Mix setting, 57
stereo tracks. *See also* master faders
    configuring path as, 61
    RTAS plug-ins on, 274–275
Strip Silence
    parameters for, 328
    tips for, 327–329
subpaths
    overlapping, 66
    setting up, 62–63
synth to MIDI, adding, 181–183
system exclusive data for MIDI, 207–208
System Usage window, 54

T

Tab key in Edit window, 110–111
Tab to Transient function, 111–112
    selections with, 226–227
TCE (Time Compress/Expand) Trim tool, 230–232
    presets for, 325–327
    tips for, 323–327
TDM systems, 2
    inactive tracks, 336
tear-away strips, using, 148–149
Tech Support page, Digidesign Web site, 8

tempo
    click track tempo, setting, 156–157
    Identify Beat function, 321–322
    importing MIDI data, 212
    for MIDI tracks, 204–206
Tempo/Meter Change dialog box, 204–206
throughput, 5
time-based effects, 281–2824
time scales. *See* Edit window
Timeline, 40–41
    link areas in, 330–331
    playing selection shown in, 99
    zooming out and in on, 219
timeline insertion, 32, 108. *See also* memory locations
    post-roll option and, 162
    Tab key with, 110
    Timeline Insertion Follows Playback preference, 227–228
    zooming centering on, 112
Timeline Insertion Follows Playback preference, 227–228
tools, 120–122. *See also* specific tools
    MIDI data, editing, 194–197
Tools area, Edit window, 40–41
Track area. *See* Edit window
Track Height drop-down menu, 48
track heights, 48
    Smart tool and, 236
Track Show/Hide list, 258
    icons in, 261
    for movie tracks, 343
    moving tracks in, 80
tracks. *See also* aux tracks; click tracks; fader groups; master faders; MIDI tracks; recording
    assembling tracks, 130–131
    deleting tracks, 138–139
    importing audio
        directly to track, 86–88
        previous session's tracks, importing, 88–91
        source of audio, choosing, 86–87
        storing converted files, selecting location for, 87–88
    inactive tracks, 336–337
    increasing height of, 292
    input for, 146
    making tracks, 74–75
    moving, 79–80
    naming tracks, 78, 171
    output for, 146–147
    pan of track's output, setting, 148
    selecting tracks, 36

INDEX

tracks *(continued)*
    showing/hiding, 37
    tear-away strips, using, 148–149
    volume for output, setting, 147
transients. *See also* Tab to Transient function
    defined, 111
Transport window, 31–32
    basic controls in, 31
    Play button, 158
    Record button, 158
    showing/hiding features, 32
Transpose option, 202–203
Triangle Pencil option for pan, 295
Trim tool, 105
    with automation, 332
    MIDI Event List, editing velocity data in, 210
    MIDI tracks, editing, 196
    in QuickPunch mode, 166
    regions, trimming, 128–129
    TCE (Time Compress/Expand) Trim tool, 230–232
    working with, 120–121
trimming regions, 128–129

U

Undo function, 128
Unused Regions option, 313–315

V

velocity
    Change Velocity option for MIDI, 201
    MIDI Event List data on, 210
video, working with, 342–344
Video Files subfolder, 13
views and viewing
    Edit window menus, 41–43
    MIDI Event List, non-note data on, 209–211
virtual instruments, using, 277–279
voices, defined, 151

volume. *See also* master faders; output volume
    click volume, displaying, 156
    dynamic-based effects for, 280
    MIDI tracks, adjusting volume for, 189
    resetting, 149
    signal flow order for volume fader, 262
    stereo/mono designation for volume meters, 261
    Strip Silence for, 327–329
    time-based effects for, 281–284

W

WAV files, 20
waveforms for fade-ins, 238
Web sites. *See* Digidesign Web site
wet/dry mixing, 68, 281
    plug-ins and, 284
    pre- and post-fader sends, 283
windows, 28–30. *See also* specific windows
    Automation Enable window, 53
    Big Counter window, 53
    Disk Space window, 54
    for new sessions, 23
    Session Setup window, 52
    System Usage window, 54
Workspace window
    columns, arranging, 94
    importing audio in, 91–96
    navigating, 93
    searching for audio with, 92–96

Z

Zoom In button, 219
Zoom Out button, 219
zooming, 218–223
    MIDI data, 220–221
    presets, 221–223
    toggling between settings, 320
    tools for, 41, 105, 112–113

INTERACTIVE TRAINING
for serious musicians
Cool School Interactus™ CD-ROMs

If the "show me" style of learning is what you prefer,
check out the products available for:

Pro Tools | Cubase SX | Digital Performer | Logic Audio | SONAR | Audio Plug-ins

Find these CD-ROM tutorials and more at www.courseptr.com!

coolbreeze systems
A division of Course Technology

Call **1.800.842.3636** to order
Or order online at www.courseptr.com

THOMSON COURSE TECHNOLOGY

Professional ■ Trade ■ Reference

Are you ready to master Pro Tools®?

For interactive training, check out Cool School Interactus CD-ROMs. You'll get hardware/software configurations, software simulations, and movie tutorials.

CSi Vol. 2.1—Pro Tools Tips and Plug-Ins
ISBN: 1-59200-159-9

CSi Vol. 8—Pro Tools 6
ISBN: 1-59200-166-1

CSi Vol. 1.1—Pro Tools Basics
ISBN: 1-59200-158-0

CSi Vol. 5—Pro Tools 5
ISBN: 1-59200-162-9

CSi Starter—Pro Tools LE
ISBN: 1-59200-169-6

Looking for in-depth coverage of Pro Tools tasks? Our books give you the skills you need to complete a variety of Pro Tools projects.

Pro Tools Power!
ISBN: 1-929685-57-2

Advanced users will get production tips and shortcuts for using Pro Tools' digital audio workstations. Post, music or dance mixers can get right to work! Veteran Pro Tools operators will get the advanced tips they're looking for.

Pro Tools for Video, Film, and Multimedia
ISBN: 1-59200-069-X

Learn about the equipment you need to use Pro Tools with video, get tips for efficient trimming and timing of audio, and master processing outside the mixing environment. You'll also get in-depth coverage of film mixing file formats.

THOMSON COURSE TECHNOLOGY

Professional ■ Trade ■ Reference

Call **1.800.842.3636** to order
Order online at **www.CoursePTR.com**